014566513 Liverpool Univ

University of Liverpool

Withdrawn from stock

fifth edition

# economics
# for business

fifth edition

# economics
## for business

### David Begg
### and Damian Ward

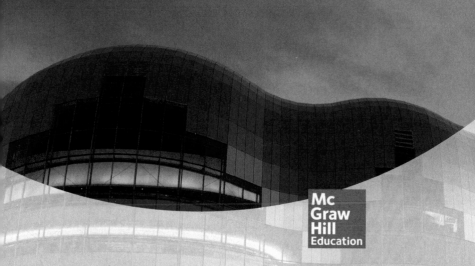

McGraw
Hill
Education

London   Boston   Burr Ridge, IL   Dubuque, IA   Madison, WI   New York
San Francisco   St. Louis   Bangkok   Bogotá   Caracas   Kuala Lumpur
Lisbon   Madrid   Mexico City   Milan   Montreal   New Delhi
Santiago   Seoul   Singapore   Sydney   Taipei   Toronto

*Economics for Business*
*Fifth Edition*
David Begg and Damian Ward
ISBN-13 9780077175283
ISBN-10 007717528x

Published by McGraw-Hill Education
Shoppenhangers Road
Maidenhead
Berkshire
SL6 2QL
Telephone: 44 (0) 1628 502 500
Fax: 44 (0) 1628 770 224

Website: www.mheducation.co.uk

**British Library Cataloguing in Publication Data**
A catalogue record for this book is available from the British Library

**Library of Congress Cataloguing in Publication Data**
The Library of Congress data for this book has been applied for from the Library of Congress

Content Acquisitions Manager: Emma Nugent
Product Developer: Laura Rountree
Content Product Manager: Ben Wilcox
Marketing Manager: Geeta Kumar

Text Design by Kamae Design, Oxford
Cover design by Scott Poulson
Printed and bound in Lebanon by Arab Printing Press, Beirut

Published by McGraw-Hill Education. Copyright © 2016 by McGraw-Hill Education. All rights reserved. No part of this publication may be reproduced or distributed in any form or by any means, or stored in a database or retrieval system, without the prior written consent of McGraw-Hill Education, including, but not limited to, in any network or other electronic storage or transmission, or broadcast for distance learning.

Fictitious names of companies, products, people, characters and/or data that may be used herein (in case studies or in examples) are not intended to represent any real individual, company, product or event.

ISBN-13 9780077175283
ISBN-10 007717528x
© 2016. Exclusive rights by McGraw-Hill Education for manufacture and export. This book cannot be re-exported from the country to which it is sold by McGraw-Hill Education.

# Dedication

For my mum – Margaret Ward

Damian Ward

For my beloved Jen

David Begg

# Brief Table of Contents

# Detailed Table of Contents

# Preface

This book is for students interested in business. It is not an economics book with some business applications. Instead, we highlight problems faced by real businesses and show how economics can help solve these decision problems.

## Our approach

This approach is new, and focuses on what as a business student you really need. It is issue driven, utilizing theories and evidence only after a problem has been identified. Business decisions are the focus on the screen, and economic reasoning is merely the help button to be accessed when necessary. Of course, good help buttons are invaluable.

## Our coverage

Our book offers a complete course for business students wanting to appreciate why economics is so often the back-up that you require. After a brief introduction, we help you to understand how markets function and how businesses compete, then we train you to evaluate problems posed by the wider economic environment, both nationally and globally.

As a business student, you do not need to know, nor should you want to master, the whole of economics. Your time is scarce and you need to learn how to manage it effectively. *Economics for Business* gets you off to a flying start by focusing only on the essentials.

## Cases and examples

Business does not stand still and neither should you. You need a course embracing topical examples from the real world as it evolves. Whether we are discussing the pricing of Madonna's concert tickets, the profitability of Apple Inc. or the Greek debt crisis, we aim to bring you the business issues of the day and challenge you to think about how you would respond to them.

## Strategic learning

Business students want an instant picture of where they are, what the problem is, and how an intelligent response might be devised. Each chapter begins with the executive summary 'at a glance' and concludes with a summary and learning checklist, providing an informative link in the flow of ideas.

You are thus encouraged to become a 'strategic learner', accessing resources that support your particular lifestyle and learning pattern. You can follow the order that we propose, but you can also browse and move from one topic to another, as you might on the Internet. Active learning both engages your interest and helps you remember things.

## Online of course

Our online supplements include access to Connect, McGraw-Hill's web-based assignment and assessment platform. Connect allows instructors to assign auto-graded quizzes and tests, view reports on students' results and get a clearer picture of student progress. For students, Connect provides access both to assignments from your lecturer and to resources for independent study. It provides immediate feedback on how well you know each topic from the book and gives you reading suggestions, MP3 revision notes, additional case studies, animations and practice tests to improve your understanding.

## Summing up

We were prompted to write this book because fewer and fewer students are studying economics for its own sake. More and more students are switching to courses that study business as a whole.

This creates a market.

David Begg
Damian Ward
August 2015

# About the Authors

David Begg is Professor of Economics at Imperial College Business School. He has been a Research Fellow of the Centre for Economic Policy Research since its inception in 1984 and an adviser to the Bank of England, the Treasury, the IMF, and the European Commission.

Damian Ward is Dean of the Business School at University of Hertfordshire. He has experience of teaching undergraduate and MBA students, including executive management programmes for leading global organizations. His research interests focus on the application of economic theory to the workings of the financial services industry. He regularly appears on TV and radio providing economic commentary and has acted as an adviser to the UK Financial Services Authority.

# Acknowledgements

Our thanks go to the following reviewers for their comments at various stages in the text's development:

Adelina Gschwandtner, University of Kent

Alexander Tziamalis, Sheffield Hallam University

Chiara Donegani, Birmingham City University

Chris Jones, Aston University

Dragana Radicic, Bournemouth University

Georgios Magkonis, University of Bradford

Gerald O'Nolan, University of Limerick

Gráinne Tuohy, University of Ulster

Jassodra Maharaj, University of East London

Mario Pezzino, University of Manchester

Michael Wood, London Business School

Neelu Seetaram, Bournemouth University

Pedro Martins, Queen Mary University of London

Sean Ryan, University of Limerick

Shumei Gao, Heriot-Watt University

Stefan Lutz, University of East London

Rebecca Purves, University of West of England

Rob Simmons, Lancaster University

Robert Gibbons Wood, Robert Gordon University

Roy Batchelor, City University London

We would also like to thank the following contributors for the material which they have provided for this textbook and it's accompanying digital resources:

Abhijit Sharma, University of Bradford

Chiara Donegani, Birmingham City University

Chris Jones, Aston University

Dragana Radicic, Bournemouth University

Gráinne Tuohy, University of Ulster

Hurol Ozcan, Leeds Trinity University

Mario Pezzino, University of Manchester

Nigel Grimwade, London South Bank University

Stefan Lutz, University of East London

Every effort has been made to trace and acknowledge ownership of copyright and to clear permission for material reproduced in this book. The publishers will be pleased to make suitable arrangements to clear permission with any copyright holders whom it has not been possible to contact.

# Guided Tour

Each chapter opens with a set of **Learning outcomes**, summarizing what you will take away from each chapter.

## Learning outcomes

By the end of this chapter you should be able to:

Economic theory

LO1 The cultural, political and economic drivers of globalization

LO2 Explain the concept of comparative advantage

LO3 Discuss the use of tariffs and quotas

Business application

LO6 Recognize impediments to an exploitation of comparative advantage

LO7 Identify the sources of

## At a glance   Market theory

### The issue

The price and the amount of goods and services traded change over time. But what causes these changes in particular product markets?

### The understanding

Price changes in all markets, whether it is the price of a coffee, entrance to a nightclub or the price of a DVD, stem from changes in supply and demand. Sometimes the price may change simply because demand or supply has changed. In more complex cases, demand and supply could change together. Understanding how and why supply and demand change and the implications for market prices are important business skills.

At the start of each chapter, the **'At a Glance'** Box provides a snapshot of the chapter and what's to come.

**Key Terms** are highlighted and defined in the margins near where they are first mentioned in the text to solidify your understanding of core concepts. They are also collected together in the **Glossary** at the back of the book and online.

there is no reason to suggest that they will be happy making TVs. So, in this makers do not find comparative advantage particularly attractive.

However, uncompetitive industries do not have to simply roll over a industry has political influence, perhaps stemming from the number they potentially employ, then the government can be asked to pro **protectionist measures**.

*Tariffs* are examples of trade protection. A tariff is a tax on imports a raises the price of imports.

For a more in-depth example of tariffs, we can examine Figure 16.3. Without in

> **Protectionist measures** seek to lower the competitiveness of international rivals.

**Table 16.5** Leading exporters and importers, 2015

| Rank | Country | Value (trillion) US$ | % Share of world exports | Rank | Country | Value (trillion) US$ | % Share of world imports |
|------|---------|------|------|------|---------|------|------|
| 1 | China | 2.248352598 | 10 | 1 | United States | 2.7625 | 12 |
| 2 | United States | 2.1942 | 10 | 2 | China | 2.016504 | 9 |
| 3 | Germany | 1.622616449 | 7 | 3 | Germany | 1.414795 | 6 |
| 4 | Japan | 0.874353952 | 4 | 4 | Japan | 0.992055 | 4 |
| 5 | United Kingdom | 0.790991836 | 3 | 5 | United Kingdom | 0.845441 | 4 |
| 6 | France | 0.754625245 | 3 | 6 | France | 0.80749 | 4 |
| 7 | Korea, Rep. | 0.688932622 | 3 | 7 | Korea, Rep. | 0.654764 | 3 |
| 8 | Netherlands | 0.675270873 | 3 | 8 | Netherlands | 0.600461 | 3 |
| 9 | Russia | 0.597056401 | 3 | 9 | Hong Kong | 0.589422 | 3 |
| 10 | Hong Kong | 0.592391187 | 3 | 10 | Canada | 0.583302 | 3 |

Source: World Bank.

Each chapter provides a number of **Figures** and **Tables**, which will help you to visualize key economic models, and illustrate and summarize important concepts.

Scattered throughout the book, contemporary **Business Applications** bring the economic theory to life by applying topics to real business situations.

 **16.1** Business problem: how do we take advantage of the global economy?

The world has changed. As little as 20 years ago, taking a holiday in Spain was common, but taking a holiday in the Caribbean, the Far East or even Australia was something very different. Now backpacking around the world by students, and the retired, is reasonably common. Perhaps part of the mystique associated with international travel was the

**Box 16.1**
**Alibaba can become bigger than Walmart, says founder**

The founder of Chinese internet giant Alibaba has said he hopes his company will be bigger than US retail conglomerate Walmart within ten years.

Jack Ma told the World Economic Forum that he believes Alibaba will serve some 2 billion customers over time, compared to the 300 million people it currently serves.

He also envisages an expansion of the business beyond China to become a truly dominant Internet business.

Mr Ma, said that he wants his business to become a platform for small businesses all around the world, rather than just in his home nation.

'My vision is, if we can help a small business in Norway sell things to Argentina, and Argentinean customers can buy things online from Switzerland we can build up an e-WTO (World Trade Organization),' he continued.

'The WTO is great but last century. Today, the Internet can help small business sell things across the oceans.'

From *The Telegraph*. 23 January 2015. 'Alibaba can become bigger than Walmart, says founder'. James Quinn © Telegraph Media Group Limited (2015)

Lively and engaging **Examples** from the world of business are provided throughout the text to demonstrate economic principles in a relevant context.

The **Chapter Summary** consolidates your learning by summarizing the main points discussed throughout each chapter.

## Summary

1. The reasons for increasing globalization are numerous but technological, economic and political.

2. Comparative advantage is an important economic reason t globalization. Comparative advantage states that countries goods and services which they are comparatively better at

## Learning checklist

You should now be able to:

- List and explain the main drivers of globalization
- Explain comparative advantage and identify potential sources of c advantage
- Explain the impact of tariffs and quotas on domestic prices, firms a

A **Learning Checklist** enables you to check your progress against the learning outcomes for each chapter.

**Review Questions** and **Exercises** at the end of each chapter test your understanding of the checklist topics, so that you can confidently progress to the next chapter or discover which topics you may need to revisit before moving on. They are split by difficulty to provide a wide range of questions.

## Questions

1. Identify the various factors that have promoted the globalization of b

2. How does comparative advantage explain international trade?

3. If the terms of trade improve for a country, then how has the price of changed relative to the price of imports?

4. Economies of scale and product differentiation are important for exp

# connect®

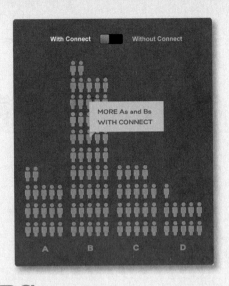

With Connect    Without Connect

MORE As and Bs
WITH CONNECT

A    B    C    D

McGraw-Hill Connect Economics is a learning and teaching environment that improves student performance and outcomes whilst promoting engagement and comprehension of content.

You can utilize publisher-provided materials, or add your own content to design a complete course to help your students achieve higher outcomes.

**PROVEN EFFECTIVE**

## INSTRUCTORS

With McGraw-Hill Connect Economics, instructors get:

- Simple **assignment management,** allowing you to spend more time teaching.
- **Auto-graded** assignments, quizzes and tests.
- **Detailed visual reporting** where students and section results can be viewed and analysed.
- Sophisticated **online testing** capability.
- A **filtering and reporting** function that allows you to easily assign and report on materials that are correlated to learning outcomes, topics, level of difficulty, and more. Reports can be accessed for individual students or the whole class, as well as offering the ability to drill into individual assignments, questions or categories.
- **Instructor materials** to help supplement your course.

# Get Connected. Get Results.

## INSTRUCTOR SUPPORT

Available online via Connect are a wealth of instructor support materials, including:

- Animated PowerPoint presentations to use during your lectures
- Case studies with questions to help supplement your teaching
- Technical worksheets and answers
- Guide answers to the end of chapter questions in the textbook
- Lecture outlines to help support your teaching preparation
- Image library of artwork from the book

## STUDENTS

With McGraw-Hill Connect Economics, students get:

Assigned content

- Easy **online access** to homework, tests and quizzes.
- **Immediate feedback** and 24-hour tech support.

With McGraw-Hill SmartBook, students can:

- Take control of your own learning with a personalized and adaptive reading experience.
- Understand what you know and don't know; SmartBook takes you through the stages of reading and practice, prompting you to recharge your knowledge throughout the course for maximum retention.
- It promotes the most efficient and productive study time you can achieve by adapting to what you do and don't know.
- It hones in on concepts you are most likely to forget to ensure knowledge of key concepts is learnt and retained.

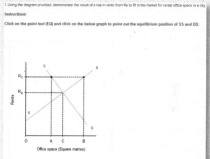

# RESOURCES

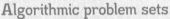

Is an online assignment and assessment solution that offers a number of powerful tools and features that make managing assignments easier, so faculty can spend more time teaching. With Connect Economics, students can engage with their coursework anytime and anywhere, making the learning process more accessible and efficient.

## Graphing Tools

Enable students to develop their graphical ability, calculating and plotting data as part of basic and complex questions. Auto-graded graphing questions are available throughout the assignable and student self-study content and can provide immediate feedback.

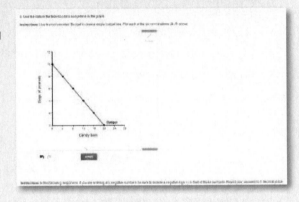

## Algorithmic problem sets

Provide repeated opportunities for students to practise and master concepts with multiple versions of each problem. Or use the algorithmic problems in class testing to provide each student with a different version than that seen by their peers.

## Calculation questions

Test students' mathematical understanding with auto-graded calculation questions.

## Short-answer questions

Ensure students develop strong writing skills with short-answer and essay questions. Each question provides a guide answer and allows you to review and mark student responses. These questions are clearly marked as being manually graded, so you can include or skip these as you see fit.

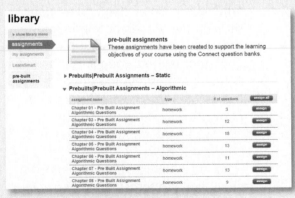

## Pre-built assignments

Assign all of the end of chapter or test bank material as a ready-made assignment with the simple click of a button.

## SmartBook™

Fuelled by **LearnSmart**—the most widely used and intelligent adaptive learning resource—**SmartBook** is the first and only adaptive reading experience available today. Distinguishing what a student knows from what they don't, and honing in on concepts they are most likely to forget, **SmartBook** personalizes content for each student in a continuously adapting reading experience. Valuable reports provide instructors with insight as to how students are progressing through textbook content, and are useful for shaping in-class time or assessment.

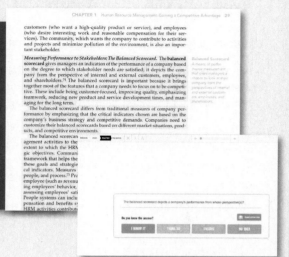

## LearnSmart™

McGraw-Hill **LearnSmart** is an adaptive learning program that identifies what an individual student knows and doesn't know. **LearnSmart's** adaptive learning path helps students learn faster, study more efficiently, and retain more knowledge. Now with integrated learning resources which present topics and concepts in different and engaging formats, increasing student engagement and promoting additional practice of key concepts. Reports available for both students and instructors indicate where students need to study more and assess their success rate in retaining knowledge.

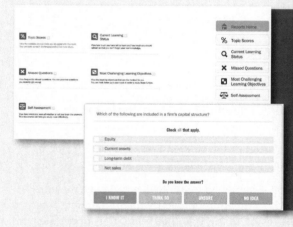

## Let us help make our content your solution

At McGraw-Hill Education our aim is to help lecturers to find the most suitable content for their needs delivered to their students in the most appropriate way. Our **custom publishing solutions** offer the ideal combination of content delivered in the way which best suits lecturer and students.

Our custom publishing programme offers lecturers the opportunity to select just the chapters or sections of material they wish to deliver to their students from a database called CREATE™ at

### create.mheducation.com/uk

CREATE™ contains over two million pages of content from:

- textbooks
- professional books
- case books – Harvard Articles, Insead, Ivey, Darden, Thunderbird and BusinessWeek
- Taking Sides – debate materials

Across the following imprints:

- McGraw-Hill Education
- Open University Press
- Harvard Business Publishing
- US and European material

There is also the option to include additional material authored by lecturers in the custom product – this does not necessarily have to be in English.

We will take care of everything from start to finish in the process of developing and delivering a custom product to ensure that lecturers and students receive exactly the material needed in the most suitable way.

With a **Custom Publishing Solution**, students enjoy the best selection of material deemed to be the most suitable for learning everything they need for their courses – something of real value to support their learning. Teachers are able to use exactly the material they want, in the way they want, to support their teaching on the course.

Please contact your local McGraw-Hill Education representative with any questions or alternatively contact Warren Eels e: warren.eels@mheducation.com

**Improve your grades!**

**20% off any Study Skills book!**

Our Study Skills books are packed with practical advice and tips that are easy to put into practice and will really improve the way you study.

Our books will help you:

- Improve your grades
- Avoid plagiarism
- Save time
- Develop new skills
- Write confidently
- Undertake research projects
- Sail through exams
- Find the perfect job

**Special offer!**

As a valued customer, buy online and receive 20% off any of our Study Skills books by entering the promo code **BRILLIANT!**

www.openup.co.uk/studyskills

Section

1

# Introduction

## Section contents

# Economics for business

## Chapter contents

## Learning outcomes

By the end of this chapter you should be able to:

**Economic theory**

LO1   Define economics as the study of how society resolves the problem of scarcity

LO2   Describe the concept of opportunity cost

LO3   State the difference between microeconomics and macroeconomics

LO4   State the difference between market and planned economies

**Business application**

LO5   Discuss how firms operate within microeconomic and macroeconomic environments

LO6   Identify the main economic resources within major economies

## At a glance   Economics for business

### The issue

What is economics and how does economics relate to business?

### The understanding

Economics seeks to understand the functioning of marketplaces. Microeconomics examines consumers, firms and workers within markets, seeking to understand why prices change for particular products, what influences the costs of firms and, in particular, what will influence a firm's level of profitability. Macroeconomics examines the whole economy as one very large market. Macroeconomics seeks to address how the government might manage the entire economy to deliver stable economic growth, including current topics of managing debt and implementing austerity packages. The basic economic concepts will be introduced to you through the development of the production possibility frontier and an initial discussion of markets.

### The usefulness

Firms operate within an economic environment. The revenue they receive from selling a product is determined within a market. Furthermore, the costs that the firm has to pay for its labour, raw materials and equipment are also priced within markets. Microeconomics addresses the various market influences that impact upon a firm's revenues and costs. Macroeconomics addresses the economy-level issues which similarly affect a firm's revenues and costs. Understanding, reacting to and possibly even controlling micro- and macroeconomic influences on the firm are crucial business skills.

## 1.1   What is economics?

Think about everything you would like to own, or consume. Table 1.1 contains a list of material items as examples, but it could equally contain items such as a healthy life and peace in the world.

Now list the resources that might contribute to paying for these desirable items; Table 1.2 shows ours.

You will be quick to note that the wish list is significantly longer than the resources list and there will be a significant gap between the expense required by the wish list and the likely yield of the resources list.

So, we have a problem: we have a wish list that is very long and a resources list that is very short. What will we spend our resources on and what will we decide to leave in the shops?

**Table 1.1**   Wish list

| | |
|---|---|
| Big house | Luxury restaurant meals |
| Luxury car | Designer clothes |
| Top of the range smartphone | Membership of a fitness club |
| Holiday in an exotic location | A case (or two) of fine wine |
| Designer shoes | Large flat-screen television |
| Carbon-frame cycle | Games console |
| Premiership season ticket | Tickets to the Monaco Grand Prix |

**Table 1.2**  Resources list

| Salary | Royalties from book |
|---|---|
| Consulting fees | Generous friends |

**Infinite wants** are the limitless desires to consume goods and services.

**Finite resources** are the limited amount of resources that enable the production and purchase of goods and services.

**Factors of production** are resources needed to make goods and services: land, labour, capital and enterprise.

This problem is economics, one which recognizes the difference between **infinite wants** and **finite resources**.

We as individuals would all like to consume more of everything; bigger houses, bigger cars, etc. But we only have finite resources with which to meet all our wants.[1] Firms also have infinite wants. They would like to be operating in more countries, selling larger product ranges. But firms are limited by their access to shareholders' funds and good labour. Governments too have infinite wants, providing more health care and better education, but are limited by their access to tax receipts.

## Factors of production

Economists start their analysis by focusing on the entire economy and noting that there are a variety of wants from individuals, firms and governments, and only a limited number of resources, or **factors of production**, which economists group into four categories: land, labour, capital and enterprise.

Land is where raw materials come from: oil, gas, base metals and other minerals. Some economies have enormous access to such resources and build entire economies around resource extraction. These would include Saudi Arabia and oil; Australia and iron, copper and coal; and Qatar and gas. Box 1.1 provides information about the discovery of new oil and gas reserves. Importantly, new discoveries of oil and gas have been declining. Similarly, the creation of new oil and gas wells—that is, the conversion of new finds into fully working oil and gas fields—is also declining.

Labour is the ability of individuals to work. Populous economies such as India and China have workforces that run into hundreds of millions. This provides these economies with the huge potential to generate enormous amounts of economic activity and wealth. In modern developed economies in Europe, labour forces are much smaller, but they are more highly educated and skilled. This enables many high-valued goods and services, such as aeronautics and banking, to be produced. Whereas India and China create value through the volume of workers, Europe achieves wealth creation through the quality of workers.

Capital is production machinery, computers, office space or retail shops. Again, in many modern economies access to productive capital is good. Many banking and retail companies have good access to information technology (IT) infrastructure. In economies like Dubai there has been a massive expansion of commercial and residential construction, providing much needed offices and homes. In China, the government is spending huge sums of money improving and expanding road, rail and energy infrastructure.

Enterprise is the final factor of production that brings land, labour and capital together and organizes them into business units that produce goods and services with the objective of making a profit. Shareholders are perhaps the simplest form of enterprise. Shareholders provide companies with financial backing that enables risk taking and the pursuit of profits.

In spotting new market opportunities entrepreneurs are often innovators and risk-takers, committing resources to commercial projects that may flourish or, alternatively, perish. There are a number of famous entrepreneurs and innovators who have created enormously successful companies:

- Richard Branson and Virgin
- Philip Green and the Arcadia Group (Top Shop)
- Steve Jobs and Apple
- Michael O'Leary and Ryanair.

---

[1]This is true at least at one point in time. In the future, capital could be expanded by firms investing in additional capital.

## Box 1.1
## Discoveries of new oil and gas reserves drop to 20-year low

Preliminary figures suggest the volume of oil and gas found last year, excluding shale and other reserves onshore in North America, was the lowest since at least 1995, according to previously unpublished data from IHS, the research company. Depending on later revisions, 2014 may turn out to have been the worst year for finding oil and gas since 1952.

The slowdown in discoveries has been particularly pronounced for oil, suggesting that production from shales in the US and elsewhere, and from Opec, will play an increasingly important role in meeting growing global demand in the next decade.

Because new oilfields generally take many years to develop, recent discoveries make no immediate difference to the crude market, but give an indication of supply potential in the 2020s. Peter Jackson of IHS said: 'The number of discoveries and the size of the discoveries has been declining at quite an alarming rate . . . you look at supply in 2020–25, it might make the outlook more challenging.' So far there has not been a single new 'giant' field—one with reserves of more than 500 million barrels of oil equivalent – reported to have been found last year, although subsequent revisions may change that.

Last year, the number of exploration and appraisal wells drilled worldwide was only 1 per cent lower than in 2013. This year, exploration budgets are being cut back across the industry and the number of wells drilled is likely to fall further.

New discoveries are not the only sources of future oil supply. Companies can also add to their production potential with extensions of existing fields, and there are large known reserves—both 'unconventional', including shale in North America and heavy oil in Canada and Venezuela, and 'conventional' in countries including Saudi Arabia, Iran, Iraq and the United Arab Emirates.

The weakness of new discoveries increases the need for production from those sources to rise if, as expected, global demand for oil continues to increase.

The shale boom has transformed the outlook for oil in the US, and played a critical role in creating the oversupply that led to the collapse in prices, but it is still relatively small on a global scale, Mr Jackson said, accounting for about 5 per cent of world oil production. There are also very large shale oil reserves in countries including Russia, China, Argentina and Libya, but the industries there are still in their infancy.

Shale is also a relatively high cost source of oil compared with reserves in the Middle East, and requires higher crude prices to be commercially viable. Mr Jackson said that with crude prices around their present levels, it would be 'very difficult' to start up new shale production projects.

From the *Financial Times*. 15 February 2015. 'Discoveries of new oil and gas reserves drop to 20-year low'. Ed Crooks. © The Financial Times Limited 2015. All Rights Reserved.

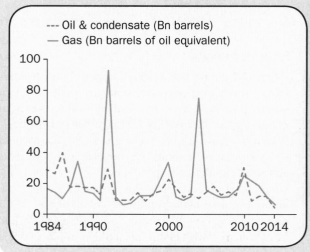

However, entrepreneurs are often in charge of small to medium sized companies while enterprising risk-takers look for adventure, a challenge and the chance of making a profit. See Box 1.2 for an example of two students starting their own business.

## Production possibility frontier

The **production possibility frontier** is an important illustrative tool because it can be used to highlight crucial economic concepts. These are:

- Finite resources
- Opportunity costs

> Production possibility frontier **shows the maximum number of products that can be produced by an economy with a given amount of resources.**

## Box 1.2
## Best mates set up cereal bar in Leeds

It's a well-known staple of the student diet—and now a pair of enterprising Leeds graduates have decided to turn their love of breakfast cereal into a business.

Best mates Jen Gibb and Zoe Blogg, both 23, who met on a marketing degree at Leeds Beckett University, are set to launch Moo'd Cereal House in the student heartland of Headingley next month. Serving 100 types of cereal from a bar-like set-up—complete with 'beer pumps' full of milk and 'guest cereals'—the venue is the first of its kind in Yorkshire. Jen said: 'We're very excited, but nervous. We've put some posters up and everyone seems positive about it. Because it's a whole new concept, they all seem quite excited to see what it's about.' The flatmates started planning the bar before they graduated last May, having grown frustrated at the lack of eateries to feed their love of cereal.

They now hope to mirror the success of London's Cereal Killer Cafe which opened to great fanfare as 'the UK's first cereal cafe' in December. Jen explained: 'We just always ate cereal. It was like a running joke at our house. We were sitting in Headingly in a cafe and said "wouldn't it be amazing if somewhere just served cereal".' We then looked it up and saw that one was opening in London—this was about six months before that opened—and thought it would be great if there was one in Yorkshire.'

Moo'd will serve cereal from £2 a bowl as well as offering children's portions and a Man Vs Food-style 'mega bowl'. It will also serve a range of milks—including chocolate, strawberry, almond and lactose-free—as well as tea, coffee and smoothies.

Adapted from an article in the
*Yorkshire Evening Post,* 30 January 2015.

- Macroeconomics and microeconomics
- Planned, market and mixed economies.

We will discuss each in turn.

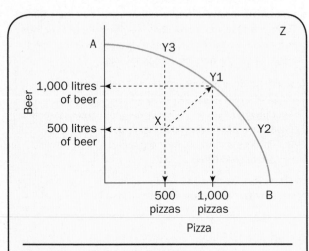

Figure 1.1　Production possibility frontier

The production possibility frontier shows the maximum amounts of beer and pizza that can be produced with a fixed amount of resources. At Y1, 1,000 litres of beer and 1,000 pizzas can be produced. At Y3, more beer can be produced but some pizza production has to be sacrificed, while at Y2, beer can be sacrificed in order to produce more pizzas. Z cannot be achieved with current resource levels and X represents unemployment, with production of beer and pizzas below the optimal levels attainable on the frontier, such as Y1, Y2 and Y3.

### Finite resources

Figure 1.1 shows the production possibility frontier for an imaginary economy that produces only two goods, pizza and beer, and highlights the constraint created by access to only a finite amount of resources. With a fixed quantity of resources an infinite amount of beer, or pizzas, cannot be produced. If all resources were allocated to the production of beer, then we would be at point A on the diagram, with a maximum amount of beer being produced and no pizzas. But if all resources were allocated to pizzas, then we would be at point B, with a maximum number of pizzas being produced and no beer. The curve between points A and B indicates all the maximum combinations of beer and pizza that can be produced. The frontier shows what it is possible to produce with a limited amount of resources.

Operating on the frontier is optimal; all finite resources are employed. Operating at a point such as Z is currently impossible. The economy does not have the resources to produce at Z. Operating at X is inefficient, because some resources must be unemployed. More output could be produced by employing all factors of production and moving towards the frontier.

## Box 1.3
## Maximizing gains

If the benefit of reading this book to you can be estimated at £1 per hour and the benefit of watching television can be estimated at £0.50 per hour, then the opportunity cost of reading this book, rather than watching television, is £0.50, the benefit you have given up. In contrast, if you watched television, then the opportunity cost would be £1—the benefit forgone from not reading this book. Given the ratio of these benefits, you can minimize your opportunity cost by reading this book. If we add in an option to reflect the true student lifestyle, a night out with your friends might be worth £5 per hour to you. Staying in and reading this book would then represent an opportunity cost of £5 per hour, while going out and not reading the book would only represent an opportunity cost of £1 per hour, the benefits forgone by not reading this book. In terms of opportunity cost, it is cheaper to go out with your friends than to stay in and read this book. If you fail this module, at least you can understand why.

### Opportunity costs

If pizza production is reduced in order to make more beer, then the **opportunity cost** consists of the benefits that could have been received from the pizzas that have not been made. Opportunity costs give the production possibility frontier a negative slope; simply, more pizzas must mean less beer. Reading this book now has an opportunity cost. You could be watching television. Recalling that the economic problem is one of infinite wants and finite resources, ideally you will try to make your opportunity cost as low as possible. With your limited resources you will try to maximize your gains from consumption. This way you are sacrificing the least amount of benefit.

> Opportunity costs are the benefits forgone from the next best alternative.
>
> Macroeconomics is the study of how the entire economy works.
>
> Microeconomics is the study of how individuals make economic decisions within an economy.

### Macroeconomics and microeconomics

By focusing on points X, Y and Z in Figure 1.1, we can draw your attention to two important distinctions in economics: (i) the study of **macroeconomics** and (ii) the study of **microeconomics**.

Points X and Z in Figure 1.1 represent mainly macroeconomic problems. At point X, the economy is not operating at its optimal level; we said point X was likely to be associated with unemployment. This occurs during a recession. Part of macroeconomics is understanding what creates a recession and how to remedy a recession. Governments and the central bank adjust interest rates, taxation and government spending to try to move the economy from point X towards point Y. Point Z is also a macroeconomic issue. The economy cannot achieve point Z now, but in the future the economy could grow and eventually attain point Z. How do we develop policies to move the economy over the long term to point Z? This question has been the recent focus of economic policy-makers, with the focus placed upon the issue of 'sustainable economic growth'.

Microeconomics places the focus of analysis on the behaviour of individuals, firms or consumers. Rather than looking at the economy as a whole, it attempts to understand why consumers prefer particular products. How will changes in income or prices influence consumption patterns? In relation to firms, microeconomists are interested in the motives for supplying products. Do firms wish to maximize sales, profits or market share? What factors influence costs and how can firms manage costs? What determines the level of competition in a market and how can firms compete against each other?

By focusing on individual consumers, firms and the interaction between the two, the economist is particularly interested in the functioning of markets. This particular aspect of economics can be highlighted by examining movements along the production possibility frontier. Point Y1 on the frontier has been described as being efficient. But points Y2 and Y3 are also on the frontier and are, therefore, equally efficient. At Y1, the economy produces a balanced mix of pizza and beer. At Y2, the economy specializes more in pizza and, at Y3, the economy specializes more in beer production. How will the economy decide among operating at Y1, Y2 and Y3? The answer lies in understanding resource allocation mechanisms.

### Planned, market and mixed economies

In a **planned economy**, the government plans whether the economy should operate at point Y1 or another point. Historically, these systems were common in the former Soviet Bloc and China, and are still in use in Cuba and North Korea.

In a planned economy, the government sets an economic plan, typically for the next five years. Within the economic plan are decisions about which industries to support and how much output each industry should produce. This could include a plan for car production, house building and the expansion of travel infrastructure, including rail, roads and air. The economic plan may also go so far as to set prices for goods, services and wages.

In planned economies, the government is the major owner of the factors of production, and in the case of Cuba around 76 per cent of the entire workforce is employed by the government.

In a **market economy**, private individuals own the majority of economic factors of production. Market economies have two important groups: consumers that buy products and firms that sell products. Consumers buy products because they seek the benefits associated with the consumption of the products. For example, you eat food because it stops you feeling hungry; you drive a car because it helps you to travel between various locations. Similarly, firms sell products in order to make a profit.

In the marketplace information is exchanged between consumers and firms. This information relates to the prices at which consumers are willing to buy products and, similarly, the prices at which firms are willing to sell. For any particular product you will have a maximum price at which you are willing to buy. The more desirable you find the product, the greater will be your maximum price. In contrast, firms will have a minimum price at which they are willing to sell. The easier, or cheaper, it is to make the good, the lower this minimum price will be. If the minimum price at which firms are willing to sell is less than consumers' maximum willingness to pay, then the potential for a market in the good exists. Firms can make the product in the clear expectation of making a profit.

Firms are likely to move their productive resources—land, labour, capital and enterprise – to the markets that present the greatest opportunities for profit. Given our discussion above, profits will vary with the willingness of consumers to pay and the costs incurred by firms. If consumers are willing to pay higher prices, or production costs fall, then profits will increase. Increasing profits will lead firms to move resources into the market. In contrast, as consumers reduce their willingness to buy a product, or if firms' costs increase, profits will fall and firms will look to reallocate their resources into more profitable markets.

> In a planned economy, the government decides how resources are allocated to the production of particular products.
>
> In a market economy, the government plays no role in allocating resources. Instead, markets allocate resources to the production of various products.

## Box 1.4
## Pizza and beer

In our pizza and beer example, let us consider the following: we are at point Y1 on Figure 1.1 and suddenly scientists show that beer is very good for your health. Following this news, we would expect consumers to buy more beer. As beer increases in popularity, beer producers are able to sell for a higher price and make greater profits. As consumers allocate more of their income to beer, pizza producers begin to lose sales and profits. Over time, pizza makers would recognize that consumers have reduced their consumption of pizzas. In response, pizza producers would begin to close down their operations and move their resources into the popular beer market. The economy moves from Y1 to Y3 in the figure.

## Comparing command and market economies

Market economies rely on a very quick and efficient communication of information that occurs through prices. Firms ordinarily set a price that indicates their willingness to sell. Consumers communicate their willingness to buy by purchasing the product at the given price. The problem of what should be produced and what should not be produced is solved by the price system.

The command (or planned) economy, in setting production levels for various goods and services, requires similar market-based information regarding the costs of production and the consumption requirements

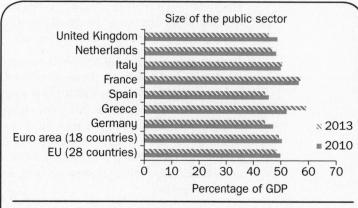

Figure 1.2   Government expenditure as a percentage of GDP

*Source:* Eurostat © European Communities.

of consumers. But how would you go about setting food, clothing, drink, transport and education output levels for an economy? You might conduct a questionnaire survey asking consumers to rank the different products by level of importance. However, this has a number of problems. It is costly, the respondents might not represent the views of all consumers and it might not be timely with the questionnaire only being carried out every couple of years. The collection of information required for effective planning is very complicated and costly within a command economy, especially when compared with the simple and efficient exchange of information in the market economy through the pricing system. It is of little surprise that, in recent years, planned economies have become less popular.

In reality, many economies function as an amalgam of planned and market economies—a **mixed economy**.

For example, within many modern economies the sale of groceries is a purely market solution, with private firms deciding what they will offer to consumers within their own supermarkets. The provision of public-health care is an example of the government deciding what health-care treatments will be offered to the population.

One means of measuring the planned side of the economy is to examine the size of government expenditure as a percentage of **gross domestic product (GDP)**. Government expenditure can include spending on infrastructure such as roads, health care, education, defence and social contributions such as unemployment benefits.

> In a mixed economy, the government and the private sector jointly solve economic problems.
>
> Gross domestic product (GDP) is a measure of overall economic activity within an economy. (See Chapters 9 and 10 for more details.)

Figure 1.2 illustrates the size of the planned or public sector for a number of European economies. For most economies, the size of the planned economy is large and for some economies, such as Greece, is more than 50 per cent of the economy.

In summary, economics studies how individuals, firms, governments and economies deal with the problem of infinite wants and finite resources. Microeconomics examines the economic issues faced by individuals and firms, while macroeconomics studies the workings and performance of the entire economy. We will now indicate why an understanding of economics can provide an essential understanding for business.

## (1.2) Why study economics for business?

Business and management draw upon a number of different disciplines, including, but not limited to, accounting and finance, human-resource management, operations management, marketing, law, statistics and economics. Each discipline has a particular focus and set of issues that it specializes in understanding.

The economist's analysis of business begins with a simple assumption: firms are in business to make profits for their owners. Moreover, firms are in business to maximize profits, or make the highest amount of profit possible.

The assumption that firms are profit-maximizers is clearly a simplification. Firms represent a collection of workers, managers, shareholders, consumers and perhaps individuals living within the locality of the firm's operations. Each of these groups may have a different interest within the firm. For example, shareholders may seek greater profit, but workers and managers may seek increased wages. These conflicts generate complexity within the organizational environment of firms. Economists try to simplify the complex nature of reality. Therefore, rather than attempt an understanding of all the complex interrelationships within a firm, economists simply assume that the firm is in business to maximize profits.

Economists are not arguing that the complex interrelationships between the various interest groups within a firm are not important. However, economists are assuming that, without profits, firms would find it difficult to survive financially. Therefore, while subjects such as human-resource management, organization theory and corporate social responsibility focus upon how the firm might manage the conflicting relationships between the competing interest groups of shareholders, workers and wider society, business economists have focused upon an understanding of firms' profits.

Firms, as profit-making organizations, can be viewed as a combination of revenue-based cash flows going in, and cost-based cash flows going out. Within this view of firms, economics for business can be simplified to an analysis of the economic influences that enhance revenues and reduce costs, thereby increasing firm-level financial performance or, more directly, profit.

In Figure 1.3, the firm is positioned between its revenue and its costs. In placing the firm in the middle of the diagram, it is also recognized that the firm operates within microeconomic and macroeconomic environments. The micro and macro environments are covered in detail by the various chapters within this book but, importantly, and perhaps simplistically, each chapter adds to an understanding of how the firm can improve its revenue and/or cost position. Broad areas of interest and importance are now discussed.

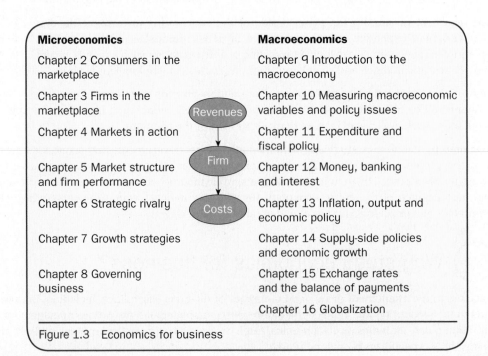

Figure 1.3   Economics for business

## Markets and competition

The particular focus of economics is on the functioning of markets. Markets are important for firms in a number of ways. First, a marketplace is where a firm will sell its product and, therefore, generate revenue. Second, a firm's inputs—land, labour, capital and enterprise—are all purchased through markets and, therefore, markets influence a firm's level of costs. The level of competition varies across markets: some are highly competitive; others are not. Throughout life, if you wish to be a winner, it is easier to achieve success when the competition is weak; and business is no different. In highly competitive business environments prices will fall, while in low competitive environments price competition will be less severe. If interested in enhancing revenues, it is important to understand how to recognize issues likely to promote competition and influences that will enable competition to be managed and controlled. It is also important to understand how a firm can change its mode of operations in order to improve its competitive advantage. Growth by acquisition of a rival clearly reduces competition, but growth by the purchase of a raw material supplier into the industry also places your rivals at a disadvantage, because you then own what your rivals need. Good business people understand how to manage and exploit competitive opportunities.

## Government intervention

Governments can also intervene in markets. Society, or government, does not view excessive pollution of the environment as desirable. Some pollution may be an unavoidable consequence of beneficial production. In order to manage pollution the government can attempt to influence the commercial activities of firms. This usually involves increased taxes for firms that pollute, and subsidies, or grants, for firms that attempt to operate in a more environmentally friendly manner. Therefore, the government can seek to influence firms' costs and revenues, boosting them when the firm operates in the interest of society, and reducing profits when the firm operates against the public interest. Firms need to be able to understand when their activities are likely to attract the attention of government, or pressure groups, and what policies could be imposed upon them.

## Globalization

Finally, firms do not operate within singular markets; rather, they function within massive macroeconomic systems. Traditionally, such systems have been the national economy but, more recently, firms have begun to operate within an increasingly global environment. Therefore, in order for firms to be successful, they need to understand how macroeconomic events and global change will impact on their current and future operations.

National economies have a tendency to move from economic booms into economic recessions. If a firm's sales, and therefore revenues, are determined by the state of the macroeconomy, then it is important for the firm to understand why an economy might move from a position of economic prosperity to one of economic recession. Similarly, during a recession firms struggle to sell all of their output. Price discounts can make products and inputs—such as labour, raw materials and capital equipment—cheaper, thereby reducing a firm's costs.

While understanding the state of the macroeconomy is important, it is also beneficial to have an understanding of how the government might try to manage the economy. How will changes in taxation affect consumers, firms and the health of the economy? How will interest rate changes influence inflation and the state of the economy? These are common governmental policy decisions with important implications for business.

Moreover, within the global economy matters of international trade, exchange rates, European monetary union and the increasing globalization of business all impact upon the operations and competitive position of business. Operating internationally may enable a firm to source cheaper production or access new markets and revenue streams. However, equally, international firms can access UK markets, leading to an increase in competition for UK domestic producers. Successful companies will not only recognize these issues but, more importantly, they will also understand how these issues relate to themselves and business generally. From this, strategies will be developed and firms will attempt to manage their competitive environment.

In order to develop your understanding of these issues, this book is separated into a number of parts that build on each other. In Section II you will be introduced to the workings of marketplaces. Section III will develop an understanding of competition in markets, followed by an overview of firm governance by shareholders and government. This will conclude the microeconomic section of the book. Macroeconomics is split into two obvious parts: macroeconomics in the domestic economy and macroeconomics in the global economy. At the domestic level, you will be introduced to how the macroeconomy works, the factors leading to the level of economic activity and the options available to a government trying to control the economy. At the global level, you will be provided with an understanding of international trade and the workings of exchange rates. This will lead to the important issue of European monetary union. Finally, an assessment of globalization and the implications for business will be provided.

In order to highlight the relevance of economics to business, each chapter begins with a business problem. Theory relevant to an understanding of the problem is then developed. Each chapter closes with two applications of the theory to further highlight the relevance of the theory to business and management. In this way, economic theory is clearly sandwiched between real-world business issues and practices, highlighting for you that economics, where appropriate, is a subject to be applied in the understanding of business problems.

##  1.3  Business data application: understanding the main economic resources within major economies

Economists love data. This love of data comes from the potential to illustrate trends and movements in important economic variables. Throughout this book, and at the end of every chapter, we will suggest to you where business people can find useful economic data and how these data can be interpreted using the economic frameworks developed in each chapter. The purpose of such an approach is to emphasize the applicability of economics to business problems and to help students solve business problems, once they graduate, by indicating where to find useful economic data. We begin in this chapter by highlighting some key trends in factor resources for a selection of important economic regions.

We have identified economic resources as land, labour, capital and enterprise. Such resources represent the economic fabric of a region and can help determine the attractiveness of a particular location to business. Therefore, understanding where to find data on the resources of an economy, and assessing the quantity and quality of those resources, can be an important business skill.

One provider of economic data, which covers resources, is the World Bank (www.worldbank .org). Identifying key measures of economic resources is not as easy as simply saying there is land, labour, capital and enterprise. These four headings are nothing more than broad categories. Under each category it is possible to list a number of important indicators of resource availability. For example, under land we might ask how much land in an economy is allocated to agricultural, urban and commercial purposes. Under labour, the size of the population and then the percentage of the population participating in employment may give an indication of the amount of labour resource, while statistics on the number of individuals gaining a university-level education may indicate the economy's access to skilled and productive labour. Under capital, there would be interest in commercial, public and household infrastructure. Asking how many individuals have access to the Internet, how much power consumption occurs in the economy, how many roads are paved and how many international flights the nation's airports support, are all ways of addressing the capital endowment of the economy. Finally, in assessing enterprise we can assess the extent to which well-functioning stock markets and banking sectors are developed, providing an indication of the economy's ability to provide financial support to business.

The list of measures can be extensive and in Figures 1.4a and 1.4b we present data on a selected number of resource measures for three major economic areas: North America, the European Union and China. Note that the World Bank has not tracked all of the measures for the same amount of time. Some resource measures have become more interesting to measure and easier to collate during recent times, therefore the time periods for each of the measures do not always coincide.

Looking at the percentage of land used for agriculture in the top left of Figure 1.4a, we can see modest declines for North America and the European Union. Agriculture is often viewed as a low value-adding activity within an economy and as such does not generate lots of economic wealth. As economies become more industrialized and perhaps even more knowledge based, then we expect to see a move away from land being used for agriculture. That said, the upward movement in land used for agriculture in China is likely to reflect the fast-growing population and the need to expand food production. The move towards more knowledge-based economies can be seen in the top right of Figure 1.4a, with an increase in research and development (R&D) expenditure for all three areas, most notably China, highlighting the importance of scientific knowledge as an economic resource.

In terms of labour, the bottom half of Figure 1.4a shows that China has the highest percentage of those in the working age group in employment, the so-called 'labour participation rate'. This pattern may reflect China's industrial reliance on labour to generate economic growth,

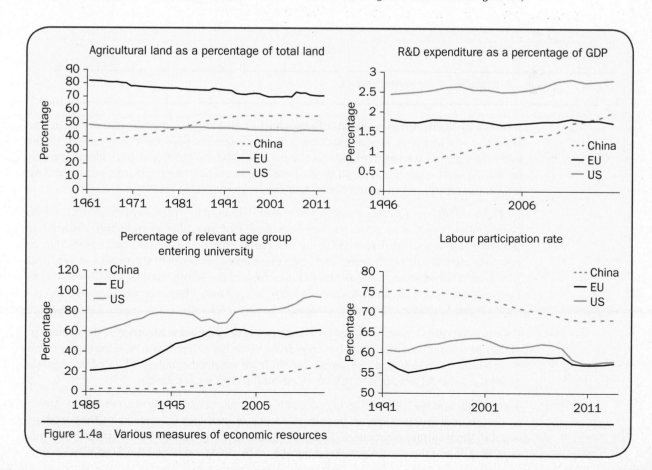

Figure 1.4a    Various measures of economic resources

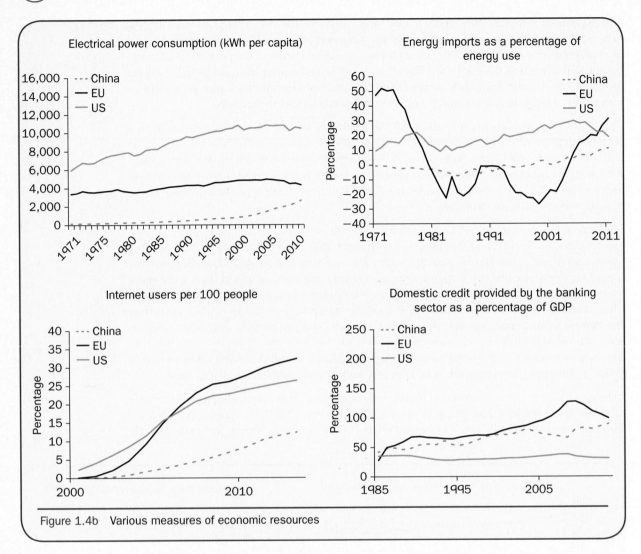

Figure 1.4b    Various measures of economic resources

whereas in North America and the European Union there is a greater use of non-labour resource—for example, capital machinery in the production process. The quality of labour in terms of advance cognitive skills can be measured by the number of individuals entering university level education. For all three areas, the trend has been upwards, but China lags behind the European Union and North America.

In Figure 1.4b we provide evidence on some additional resources. Electrical power consumption per capita provides some evidence of the power-producing capacity of the economy; it may also provide some indication of the assets and resources within an economy that are power hungry, including computers, server centres, retail centres, train travel, metal production, such as aluminium, and into the future, electrically powered cars. Power consumption in North America is huge. In contrast, China's power consumption per capita is much smaller.

Energy imports as a percentage of total energy use provide some measure of the economy's ability to meet internal energy demands from domestic oil, gas and coal reserves. North America is very reliant on energy resources from other economies, while China in some years has actually managed to export more energy than it uses itself.

Technology and the availability of information are important economic resources. Access to the Internet has become an important means of enabling consumers to find products and for firms to find consumers. The proportion of the population using the Internet has exploded during the last decade, most notably in North America and the European Union.

Finally, the provision of financial credit to enable firms to grow is important, and for our three areas we have witnessed a huge increase in the ability of the banking sector to provide financing. For all of the areas, domestic credit provided by banks is greater than the value of annual economic output, known as GDP. In the case of North America, the figure is double that of GDP. The extent to which bank credit can grow and facilitate economic growth will undoubtedly fall following the financial crises of recent years.

By examining a small number of resources we can draw useful, though admittedly broad, insights for business. In particular, China is still relatively committed to agriculture. It has an economy which is heavily dependent upon labour and at present it is not very energy intensive. In contrast, the European Union and to a greater degree North America are less dependent upon labour, but that labour is more educated. Science, in terms of research and development, is an important activity; the use of technology within the economy, as evidenced by Internet use, is strong; and power consumption is high. These factors would tend to suggest that China as an economic location currently facilitates economic activities which require lots of labour, such as assembly work. North America and the European Union are regions which provide more knowledge-intensive products and more energy-intensive production and consumption. Some of these ideas we will discuss in more detail in Chapter 16 when we explore the global nature of business.

We now encourage you to visit the statistical area of the World Bank website and explore other data measures for other economies. The web address is http://data.worldbank.org.

# 1.4 Appendix: the economist's approach

Economics as a subject has a number of characteristics associated with it and, to aid your learning, it is worth pointing them out to you.

## Language

The economist makes use of terms and phrases that are particular and peculiar to economics. For example, from the above discussion economics is the study of why you cannot have everything. But the economist talks about infinite wants, finite resources, opportunity costs and production possibility frontiers. Using the economic terminology will help you. Economists use particular terminology because it helps them to understand each other when communicating ideas. Succinct terms, such as opportunity cost, once understood, convey complex ideas quickly to anyone else who understands the phrase.

## Abstract models

Economists think about the world in terms of **models** or **theories**.

Economists recognize that the world is extremely complicated and, therefore, prefer to make models using simplifying assumptions. The complexity of the real world is stripped out in favour of a simple analysis of the central, or essential, issues. As an example, consider Box 1.5, where we discuss how an economist might approach how Christiano Ronaldo bends free kicks.

## Normative and positive economics

A **positive economics** question and a **normative economics** statement will help to clarify the differences:

Positive question:      What level of production will maximize the firm's profits?

Normative statement:    Firms should maximize profits.

> **Models** or **theories** are frameworks for organizing how we think about an economic problem.
>
> **Positive economics** studies objective or scientific explanations of how the economy works.
>
> **Normative economics** offers recommendations based on personal value judgements.

## Box 1.5
## Professor Ronaldo

In modelling Ronaldo's ability to bend free kicks, economists would strip out the complex issues, such as natural talent, good practice and high-pressure championship experience, and take the simplifying assumption that Ronaldo behaves like a professor of physics. Ronaldo must behave like a highly accomplished physicist because he can clearly calculate all the angles and force needed to bend a free kick and score a goal.

In reality, Ronaldo probably has no more understanding of physics than many of us. So, to say that Ronaldo behaves like a physicist seems peculiar. However, the important point is that the theory *predicts;* it need not *explain.* The theory does not *explain* why Ronaldo can bend free kicks and score goals with such accuracy. But it does *predict* that Ronaldo will score spectacular goals if he behaves like a world-class physicist. This is because a leading physicist, indeed any physicist, could use the Newtonian laws of motion to work out the perfect angle and trajectory for the football to travel in a spectacular arc into the back of the net. But why

should economists wish to develop strange abstract assumptions about reality, leading to theories that predict, as opposed to theories that can explain?

The answer to this question is that economists try to keep things simple and extract only the important points for analysis. The world is very complex, so what we try to do as economists is to simplify things to the important points. Ronaldo is probably a football player because of some natural talent, a good deal of practice, championship experience and perhaps some poorer opponents. All these would explain why Ronaldo can score great goals. But to keep things simple we will assume he behaves like a leading physicist. If theoretically true, then Ronaldo will also be an amazing free-kick specialist. Therefore, the predictive approach is a theoretical short-cut that enables economists to simplify the complex nature of reality. So, whenever you come across a theory in this book that is not a true reflection of reality, do not worry. We economists are happy in our little fantasy world where people like Ronaldo, David Beckham, Zico and Diego Maradonna all double up as Einstein.

The positive question seeks to address a technical point—can economics identify the output level where firms will make the largest profit? The normative statement, in contrast, seeks to assert the opinion that profit maximization is best—it is making a value judgement. In the case of the positive question, economists can make a response with theory consisting of a set of accepted rational arguments that provide a technical answer to the question. However, in respect of the normative statement, economists can only reply with similar, or alternative, value statements: for example, firms should not focus entirely on profit maximization; I believe they should also consider the needs of wider stakeholders such as workers, the environment, suppliers and customers.

This is an important distinction. Positive economics is the technical and objective pursuit of economic understanding. As a subject it seeks to provide answers to questions and propose solutions to problems. Normative economics is different in that it does not seek to answer questions; rather, it seeks to assert and represent particular beliefs—which are difficult, if not impossible, to provide positive answers to.

Economics is not peculiar in exhibiting a tension between objective and subjective approaches to reason. In art, the positive approach may centre on a technical understanding of various media. But the use of these media, the choice of images to create and how to interpret them are all normative, value laden and subjective.

## Diagrams

Quickly flick through all the pages of this book. How many diagrams did you see? Economists like diagrams. For the economist, diagrams are an effective way of communicating complex ideas. In order to develop your understanding of economics, you will need to develop your competence in this area, as it is almost impossible to manage without them—which is disappointing for any of you who detest them with a passion.

As a brief reminder, diagrams, at least as we will be using them, provide a visual indication of the relationship between two variables. For example, consider a fridge and an oven. Neither is currently switched on. When we do switch them on we are interested in seeing how the temperature inside the oven and the fridge changes the longer each appliance is on. This is not rocket science: the fridge will get colder and the oven hotter. A maths teacher would say that there is a **positive relationship** between time and temperature in the cooker.

In our example of the oven, as time increases—1 minute, 2 minutes, etc.—the temperature of the oven also increases. Our two variables, time and temperature, increase together.

In contrast, the maths teacher would say that there is a **negative relationship** between time and temperature in the fridge.

In our example of the fridge, as time increases, the temperature of the fridge decreases. Figure 1.5 is a diagram showing the positive relationship between time and temperature within the oven, while Figure 1.6 is a diagram of the negative relationship between time and the temperature inside the fridge.

We will be doing nothing more complicated than this. We might reasonably argue that, as prices increase, consumers will buy less; we therefore expect to see a negative relationship between the price of a product and the amount of the product purchased by consumers. Similarly, in the case of a positive relationship we might argue that consumer expenditure increases as income levels rise. Essentially the diagrams are a simple visual illustration of the relationship between two variables. The more you try to understand them and gain confidence in using them, the easier economics becomes.

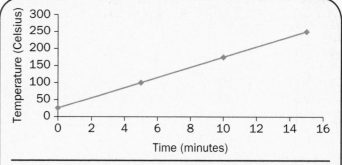

Figure 1.5 Positive relationship: oven temperature against time

Positive relationship: temperature increases the greater time oven is switched on.

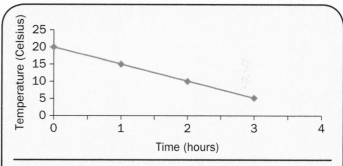

Figure 1.6 Negative relationship: fridge temperature against time

Negative relationship: temperature decreases the greater time fridge is switched on.

A positive relationship exists between two variables if the values for both variables increase and decrease together.

A negative relationship exists between two variables if the value for one variable increases (decreases) as the value of the other variable decreases (increases).

Equation of a straight line is $Y = a + bX$

## Equations of lines

We can also describe relationships between variables using equations. If there is a linear relationship between two variables, then we can use the general **equation of a straight line** to describe the relationship. The general linear relationship states that $Y = a + bX$, where a is the intercept and b is the gradient of the line. The intercept is the value of Y when X is zero. The gradient is the steepness of the line.

In Figure 1.7, the two axes are Y and X and the equation of the straight line describing the relationship between Y and X is $Y = 2 + 1X$; that is, $a = 2$ and $b = 1$. So, when X is zero, $Y = 2$; and for every one-unit increase in X, then Y also increases by 1. So if X is 4, Y must be $2 + 4 = 6$.

In Figure 1.8, we have altered the equation to make the gradient twice as steep. The relationship between Y and X is now $Y_2 = 2 + 2X$. So, when $X = 4$, then $Y = 2 + (2 \times 4) = 10$. If we changed the intercept to, say, 4, then the line for $Y_2$ would move up the Y axis and start from $Y = 4$, and not $Y = 2$.

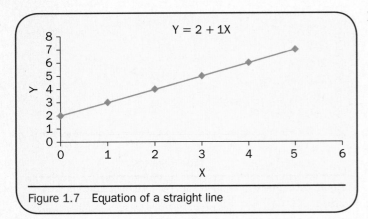

Figure 1.7    Equation of a straight line

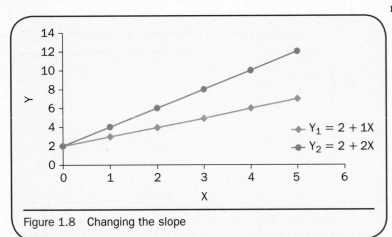

Figure 1.8    Changing the slope

A quadratic is generally specified as $Y = a + bX + cX^2$

The gradient is a measure of the slope of a line.

Differentiation is a means of understanding the gradient.

If we require a negative relationship, then we simply change the sign of the gradient to minus. So $Y = 10 - 2X$. This is illustrated in Figure 1.9. When $X = 0$, then $Y = 10$. When $X = 3$, then $Y = 10 - (3 \times 2) = 4$.

We may also need to consider a non-linear relationship, such as a **quadratic**. A quadratic is generally specified as $Y = a + bX + cX^2$. In Figure 1.10, we have plotted two quadratic relationships, one of the form $Y = 20 - 6X + X^2$, which creates a U-shaped relationship. Then, by simply changing the signs on b and c, we can create $Y = 25 + 6X - X^2$, which creates an n-shaped relationship. (We changed a, the intercept, to generate vertical distance between the two lines.)

## Gradients and turning points

The **gradient** measures the slope or steepness of a line. One method of measuring the gradient of a line is to calculate the ratio $\Delta Y / \Delta X$, where the symbol $\Delta$ means change. The values for $\Delta Y$ and $\Delta X$ can be calculated by drawing a triangle against the slope of a line. If we examine the slopes in Figure 1.8, for $Y_2$ over the range $X = 3$ to $X = 4$, then $\Delta X = 1$. At the same time, Y increases from 8 to 10, so $\Delta Y = 2$. So the gradient = $2/1 = 2$.

Recall that the general equation of a straight line is $Y = a + bX$, where b is the gradient. From $Y_2$, we can see that $b = 2$, which corresponds with our measure based on Figure 1.8.

There is also another means of gaining a measure of the gradient. This involves the use of a simple mathematical function called **differentiation**. Differentiation involves a very simple rule: the differential of $X^n$ is $nX^{n-1}$ (and all constants become zeros); so the differential of $X^3$ is $3X^2$.

Importantly, if you differentiate any mathematical equation, then you will always be left with the gradient. For example, consider the linear equation $Y_2 = 2 + 2X$, which is laid out in Table 1.3 and then differentiated.

So differentiating equation $Y_2$ results in the answer of 2, which we already know is the gradient.

**Table 1.3**    An example of differentiation

| Equation | Differentiate | Differential |
|---|---|---|
| $Y_2 =$ | | |
| 2 | is a constant and so becomes → | 0 |
| + | + | + |
| 2X | can be written $2X^1$. So this becomes $1*2X^0$ → | 2 |

Differentiation is an important tool because it enables us to work out the turning point for a given relationship. Recall the non-linear u- and n-shaped relationships in Figure 1.10. The turning point is where the relationship changes direction. For $Y_2$, we would call the turning point a maximum and, for $Y_1$, we would call the turning point a minimum.

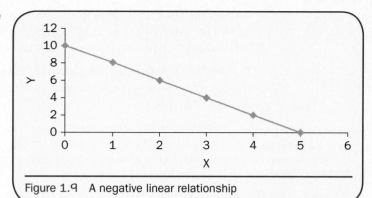

Figure 1.9    A negative linear relationship

If we want to know where a relationship is maximized (or minimized), we simply need to recognize that at the turning point the gradient is flat and therefore equal to zero. So if we have an expression for the gradient, then we have to equate it with zero and solve. Consider $Y_2 = 25 + 6X - X^2$, which is laid out in Table 1.4.

So the differential and therefore the gradient for $Y_2$ is $6 - 2X$. At the turning point, the gradient is equal to zero. So, at the turning point $0 = 6 - 2X$, therefore $X = 3$. Check this answer by looking back at Figure 1.10.

Figure 1.10    A non-linear quadratic relationship

Mathematical equations and differentiation can be powerful tools for economists and business analysts. If we wish to know the price that maximizes revenues, then we need to find a mathematical equation which describes the relationship between prices and revenues. We then simply differentiate, set to zero and solve to find the best price to maximize revenues. Equally, if we want to discover the level of production that leads to minimum costs per unit, then we need a mathematical equation which links production and costs, differentiate, set to zero and solve to find the ideal level of production.

## Economic data

Economists make use of data to examine relationships between variables. Data can be categorized into **time series data** and **cross-sectional data**.

For example, the price of a cinema ticket recorded for each year between 1990 and 2010 is an example of one variable measured at various points in time. The time period between each observation is usually fixed. So, in the case of cinema tickets,

Time series data are the measurements of one variable at different points in time.

Cross-sectional data are the measurements of one variable at the same point in time across different individuals.

| **Table 1.4** | Differentiating an equation | |
|---|---|---|
| Equation | Differentiate | Differential |
| $Y_2 =$ | | |
| 25 | is a constant and so becomes $\rightarrow$ | 0 |
| + | + | + |
| 6X | can be written $6X^1$. So this becomes $1*6X^0 \rightarrow$ | 6 |
| $-X^2$ | So this becomes $-2X^1 \rightarrow$ | $-2X$ |

the variable, price, is measured once every year. However, time series can be measured in a variety of periods—yearly, monthly, daily, hourly or by the minute. The price of shares on the London stock market is measured in all of these formats.

The profits of individual companies in the supermarket industry in 2010 would be an example of cross-sectional data, with profits of different companies being measured at the same point in time.

Rather than measure the profits of individual supermarkets in 2008, we could also measure individual companies' profits in 2009, 2010, 2011 and so on. This way, we are combining cross-sections and time, thus providing us with **panel data**.

**Panel data** combine cross-sectional and time series data.

**Percentage** measures the change in a variable as a fraction of 100.

**Index numbers** are used to transform a data series into a series with a base value of 100.

## Using data

In using data, economists employ a number of simple mathematical techniques, including calculations of percentages and the use of index numbers. Both are simple to understand, but a refresher may help your understanding.

In order to measure the change in a variable, we can use **percentages**. We can use Table 1.5 to understand how big a particular percentage change is.

Since a percentage measures the rate of change in a variable, we need both the variable's original and new value.

We calculate the percentage as the absolute change divided by the original number, then multiplied by 100:

$$\frac{(\text{New value} - \text{Original value})}{\text{Original value}} \times 100$$

For example, the share price of Company A was £2.00 in 2010 and £3.00 in 2011. The percentage change is therefore:

$$\frac{(£3.00 - £2.00)}{£2.00} \times 100 = 50\%$$

## Index numbers

As an example of the use of **index numbers**, take the data series in Table 1.6, which measures the price of a pint of beer.

The price of beer is in pounds sterling. To convert this data series into a unit-less series with a base value of 100, we first need to select the base year. In Table 1.6, we have selected 2009 as the base year. In order to generate the index, we simply take the price of beer in any year, divide by the base year value and times by 100. So, in 2009, we have (£2.40/£2.40 × 100 = 100. In 2010, we have (£2.60/£2.40) × 100 = 108.

**Table 1.5** Percentage changes

| Percentage | Size of change | |
|---|---|---|
| 10 | 10% = 10/100 = 1/10 | The variable has increased by one-tenth of its original value |
| 25 | 25% = 25/100 = 1/4 | The variable has increased by one-quarter of its original value |
| 50 | 50% = 50/100 = 1/2 | The variable has increased by one-half of its original value |
| 100 | 100% = 100/100 = 1 | The variable has increased by the same amount as its original value; it has doubled in size |
| 200 | 200% = 200/100 = 2 | The variable has increased by twice its original value; it has tripled in size |
| 500 | 500% = 500/100 = 5 | The variable has increased by five times its original size |

A sensible question to ask is why do we use index numbers? There are a number of reasons. The first is to recognize that, since we have a base value of 100, it is very easy to calculate the percentage change in the variable over time. From Table 1.6 we can readily see that between 2009 and 2012 beer increases in price by 25 per cent.

The second reason is that index numbers facilitate averaging. Assume we are interested in how prices across the economy are rising. If an index was created not only for beer prices but also for car prices, cigarettes and in fact all products that are commonly sold, then an average of all the indices would enable an assessment of average price rises in the UK.

The Retail Price Index does exactly this. It is an average of many individual product price indices. The average is weighted by the importance of the product within the average household's consumption. For example, since housing costs represent a major element of household consumption, the house price index receives a higher weight in the Retail Price Index than the price index for sweets and confectionery. The FTSE 100 is another example of an index and combines as an average the prices of all shares in the FTSE 100. The value of the index increases (decreases) if, on average, share prices in the FTSE 100 increase (decrease).

In summary, index numbers are used to create data series that are unit-less. They have a base year of 100 and can be used to calculate percentage changes from the base year with ease. By virtue of having a common base year value of 100, index numbers can also be used to create averages from many different indices, such as price level indices or stock market indices.

**Table 1.6**   Index numbers

| Year | Price of beer | Index |
|------|---------------|-------|
| 2009 | £2.40 | 100 |
| 2010 | £2.60 | 108 |
| 2011 | £2.90 | 121 |
| 2012 | £3.00 | 125 |

**Table 1.7**   Arithmetic and geometric means

| Observations | Arithmetic mean | Geometric mean |
|--------------|-----------------|----------------|
| 2, 2 | $(2 + 2)/2 = 2$ | $(2 \times 2)^{1/2} = 2$ |
| 2, 3, 4 | $(2 + 3 + 4)/3 = 3$ | $(2 \times 3 \times 4)^{1/3} = 2.88$ |

## Methods of averaging in economics

Economists tend to use two different types of averages: the arithmetic and geometric means. The arithmetic mean is the more familiar one and simply adds up all the observed values for a variable and then divides by n, the number of observations. The geometric average calculates the product of all the observations and then calculates the nth root. See Table 1.7 for examples.

In the first example, we have two observations, both of which are equal to two. So the arithmetic mean is 2. The geometric mean is also 2. We have used this simple example so that both means can be worked out easily and without the aid of a calculator. However, you should not be fooled into thinking that the two means will always be the same. In the second example, we use three observations, all of which are different. This time, the arithmetic mean is larger than the geometric mean.

An important question to ask is, why use two different ways to calculate the mean? The answer is because economists are often interested in rates of growth. How fast is the economy growing? How slowly have prices increased? What rate of return is an investment generating? When measuring growth, the use of arithmetic means would create a compounding problem. For example, if the value of a share was £100 and then increased by 5 per cent in year one and 15 per cent in year two, then the arithmetic average rate of return would be 10 per cent. This would suggest that the value of the share at the end of year two is £100 × 1.1 = £110; and then £110 × 1.1 = £1.21. But if we use the actual growth rates, 5 and 15 per cent, we get £100 × 1.05 = £105; and then £105 × 1.15 = £120.75. The arithmetic mean therefore generates an error. This is simple to understand because we are dealing in percentages. Five per cent of £100 and 15 per cent of £105 are not comparable, because the base values (£100 and £105) are not the same. The geometric mean solves this problem.

## Summary

1. Economics assumes that everybody would like to consume more of everything, but we only have a limited amount of resources with which to facilitate such consumption.

2. Economic factor resources are split into four categories: land, labour, capital and enterprise.

3. The production possibility frontier is used by economists to provide an illustration of finite resources. The production possibility frontier shows the maximum total output that can be produced using the limited amount of factor inputs. As more of one good is produced, less of the remaining good can be produced.

4. Opportunity cost is measured as the benefits forgone from the next best alternative.

5. Operating on the frontier represents full employment and is defined as productively efficient. Operating inside the frontier is inefficient as the output of both goods can be increased by making an efficient utilization of the underemployed factor resources. Operating outside the frontier is currently impossible. However, over time the economy may become more productively efficient, producing more output for a given level of input, or the economy may gain access to additional factor inputs, also enabling output to increase.

6. Macroeconomics is an examination of the economy as a whole and, therefore, considers issues such as the level of economic activity, the level of prices, unemployment, economic growth, and international trade and exchange rates.

7. Microeconomics focuses upon the economic decision making of individuals and firms. Microeconomics examines how individual markets function and how firms compete with one another.

8. Where on the frontier an economy operates, producing more beer than pizza, or vice versa, depends upon the resource allocation mechanism. In command economies, the government plans how much of each good to produce. In market economies, the interaction of consumers and firms through the pricing system of the market directs resources away from non-profitable markets and towards profitable ones.

9. Measures of various economic resources for different economies are available from a variety of sources. One global resource is the World Bank dataset.

10. Economics has a language and terminology; this aids communication of ideas and should be mastered.

11. Economics uses abstract models. In reality, the world is very complex. In economics, simplifying assumptions are deployed in order to make the world simple. As a consequence, an explanation of reality is often sacrificed for prediction.

12. Positive economics seeks to address objective questions with theory. Normative economics seeks to assert value judgements on what is preferable economic behaviour.

13. Economists place an emphasis on diagrams when explaining ideas and theories. A positive relationship exists between two variables if both variables increase together. A negative relationship between two variables exists when, as one variable increases, the other decreases.

14. Economic data can be time series, cross-sectional or a combination of the two (panel data). Time series data are the measurements of one variable at various points in time. Cross-sectional data are the measurements of one variable at the same point in time, but across a number of firms or individuals.

15. A percentage measures the change in a variable as a fraction of 100. You can calculate a percentage change as (New value - Original value)/Original value × 100.

16. An index converts a variable into a unitless data series with a base year of 100. This is achieved by dividing each value by the base year value and then multiplying by 100.

17. Index numbers can be combined to create averages. Common examples are the retail price index and the FTSE 100. Changes in the individual price indices then lead to changes in the average indices.

## Learning checklist

You should now be able to:

- Explain the economic problem of scarcity
- Understand the concept of opportunity cost
- Explain the difference between microeconomics and macroeconomics
- Highlight the differences between market and planned economies
- Explain why an understanding of economics is important for business
- Source data on different measures of economic resource for different economies.

## Questions                                                          connect

1. Explain the concept of opportunity cost.

2. List goods, or services, that compete for your income. Similarly, list activities that compete for your time. In deciding what you will spend your income on and how you will allocate your time, do you minimize your opportunity costs?

3. Consider whether it is ever possible to solve the problem of scarcity.

4. An economy produces two goods, Ferraris and Ray-Ban sunglasses. Using a production possibility frontier, assess what must happen to the production of Ferraris if the production of Ray-Ban sunglasses decreases.

5. The same Ferrari and Ray-Ban economy receives an influx of migrant workers. What do you think will happen to the production possibility frontier for this economy?

6. How does the production possibility frontier illustrate the concept of opportunity cost?

EASY

7. Why does the law of diminishing returns require the production possibility frontier to be curved rather than a straight line?

8. Explain the resource allocation mechanism within a market economy and also a planned economy.

9. Using examples, highlight why your own economy is probably best described as a mixed economy.

10. State whether the following relate to macroeconomics or to microeconomics.
(a) During the last 12 months average car prices have fallen; (b) inflation for the past 12 months has been 3.5 per cent; (c) strong sales in the housing market have prevented the Bank of England from reducing interest rates.

11. Is the labour market a microeconomic or macroeconomic topic?

12. Why does business need to understand the functioning of markets?

13. Why does business need to understand the functioning of the economy?

Questions 14 and 15 relate to material within section 1.4.

14. Which of the following is positive and which is normative? (a) It is in the long-term interest of the UK to be a member of the euro. (b) Will entry into the euro reduce UK inflation?

15. Using the data listed in Table 1.8, plot house prices on the Y axis and time on the X axis. Is there a positive or a negative relationship between time and house prices?

Convert the data series on house prices into an index using 2005 as the base year.

Calculate the percentage increase in house prices for each year.

**Table 1.8**

| Year | Average price of a house |
| --- | --- |
| 2005 | £100,000 |
| 2006 | £120,000 |
| 2007 | £155,000 |
| 2008 | £190,000 |
| 2009 | £170,000 |
| 2010 | £150,000 |

## Exercises

1. True or false?

   (a) Economics is about human behaviour and so cannot be a science.

   (b) An expansion of the economy's productive capacity would be reflected in an outward movement of the production possibility frontier.

   (c) China is an example of a command economy in which private markets play no part.

   (d) When you make a choice there will always be an opportunity cost.

   (e) 'Firms should operate in the interests of their wider stakeholders' is an example of a normative economic statement.

   (f) Economists assume that business operates in a purely economic environment.

2. In Figure 1.11:

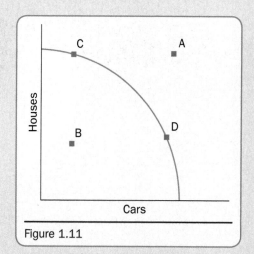

Figure 1.11

(a) Which combination of goods can be produced, with surplus resources being unemployed?

(b) Which combination of goods would represent full employment, with resources mainly allocated to the production of houses?

(c) Which combination of goods cannot currently be achieved?

(d) Which combination of goods represents full employment, with resources mainly allocated to the production of cars?

(e) How might the level of output identified in (c) be achieved in the future?

(f) Can you envisage circumstances under which the production possibility frontier could move to the left?

Section

2

# Understanding markets

## Section contents

# Consumers in the marketplace

## Chapter contents

## Learning outcomes

By the end of this chapter you should be able to:

**Economic theory**

LO1  Illustrate demand lines

LO2  Recognize the factors leading to a change in demand

LO3  Analyse the price elasticity of demand

LO4  Discuss the cross-price and income elasticity

**Business application**

LO5  Demonstrate how measures of elasticity can lead to improved management of total revenue

LO6  Debate how an appreciation of consumer surplus can lead to enhanced pricing strategies

LO7  Investigate how market research data can be understood using demand-based ideas

## At a glance    Demand theory

### The issue

Setting the price for a product is crucial for the product's and a company's success. But what is the best price for a particular product?

### The understanding

As a product becomes more expensive, consumers will begin to demand less. In some markets, consumers will be very sensitive to a change in price. In others they may not react at all. This reaction is measured using elasticity. An examination of demand theory and the concept of elasticity will develop these ideas more fully.

### The usefulness

If the price of the product can be made to rise at a quicker rate than the decline in demand, then total revenue will rise. Therefore, by understanding how consumers respond to price changes we can optimize the price charged.

## 2.1   Business problem: what is the best price?

What is the best price? The best price is determined by the firm's objectives. The following provides a common list of objectives for a firm:

1   To maximize the amount of profit made by the firm
2   To maximize the market share for the firm's product
3   To maximize the firm's total revenues.

These are all commercial objectives. Firms could also adopt non-commercial objectives, such as reducing environmental impact or being a socially responsible employer. But, for the purpose of this chapter, we will concentrate on the three objectives listed above. It is generally not possible for a firm to choose more than one of these objectives. For example, in order to maximize market share, a firm might reasonably be expected to reduce its prices in order to attract more customers. But, by dropping its prices, the firm could be sacrificing profit. Therefore, we will assume that a firm seeks to maximize one of our three objectives[1] and the best price can be defined as the one that enables the firm to meet its preferred objective.

How are prices set? Take the case of supermarkets. When walking around a supermarket have you, as a consumer, ever set the price for a product? The answer is probably no. Now, compare the case of supermarkets with buying a house, or a car. When we purchase a house or a car we might make an opening offer to the vendor as part of a negotiation over the price. At the supermarket, by contrast, we would never consider negotiating over a trolley full of shopping; nor would we negotiate in many other types of shop, such as a clothing retailer. Admittedly, we may have an indirect effect on prices by refusing to buy a product that we consider too expensive, but in the main it appears that supermarkets, retailers and perhaps even the producers of the products are controlling the prices that we have to pay.

For business students, it is important to recognize the position of product suppliers. This is because control is essential when seeking to set the best price and achieve the

---

[1] We will examine the objectives of a firm more fully in Chapters 5 and 7.

firm's objectives. But herein lies the business problem: what is the best price? To illustrate the problem, consider the following: very high sales can be generated with low prices, while very high prices will tend to generate low sales. But which option is preferable? As an example, we can show that these alternative scenarios can be similar. If a low price of £5 generates ten sales, then total revenue is £50; if a high price of £10 generates only five sales, then total revenue is also £50. Given that these options are identical, a businessperson would really like to know if there is a pricing option of around £8, selling to eight customers, making a total revenue of £64.

Whether £8 is the best price, or indeed whether £8.25 is even better, is a difficult question to address. When a national supermarket chain is selling beer, soap powder or even oven chips by the hundreds of thousands, a small change in the price can generate huge changes in total revenue. By the end of this chapter you will understand how you assist the supermarkets in finding the best price. Every time you pass through the till at the supermarket, scanner data are stored and matched with promotional offers such as 'buy one get one free'. This is then modelled and used to address strategic price changes.

It is clearly important to recognize that firms will price items relative to their cost structures. If a firm wishes to make a profit, then the price must be greater than costs. If the firm wishes to maximize market share, while not making a loss, then the price cannot fall below the cost of making the product. While recognizing the importance of costs, in this chapter we will simply focus on the interaction between pricing and consumers' willingness to buy a particular product. In Chapters 3, 4 and 5 we will develop a fuller understanding of pricing decisions by recognizing both firms' cost structures and consumers' willingness to purchase. In this chapter, we begin this analysis by developing a clear understanding of demand theory.

## 2.2 Introducing demand curves

In attempting to understand consumer behaviour, economists use a very simple construct known as the **demand curve**.

> The demand curve illustrates the relationship between price and quantity demanded of a particular product.

Figure 2.1 is an example of a demand curve, where the line $Q_D$ represents quantity demanded. The slope of the demand curve $Q_D$ is negative. This simply depicts the rather obvious argument that, as prices fall, more of a product will be demanded by consumers. Using our previous example, at a price of £10 the demand curve indicates that consumers across the market are willing to demand five units in total. But if the company dropped the price to £5, then it might expect to sell ten units.

The negative relationship between price and quantity demanded is often exploited by businesses. For example, Figure 2.1 could be an example of a 'buy one get one free' offer. Firms use such offers because they are sometimes reluctant to reduce the price of their product. This is because overt price reductions could lead to a retaliatory price war from rivals. Lower prices may also provide a signal to the market that the product is of an inferior quality. A 'buy one get one free' offer allows the published price to stay the same, but the effective price for consumers is halved. Under such an offer, consumers are more willing to demand the product and, not surprisingly, companies use such promotions to boost sales and gain market share.

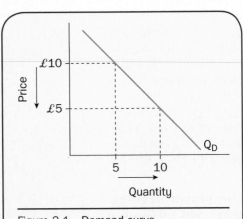

Figure 2.1    Demand curve

As the price falls, consumers are willing to demand greater amounts of the good.

Furthermore, we all like end-of-season sales at our favourite clothing retailers. But sales simply represent an attempt by the retailer to shift stock that we, as consumers, would not buy at the higher price and are, therefore, another example of the demand curve in action.

## Box 2.1
## GM cuts prices in China as foreign brand sales slow

General Motors Co. cut its prices in China after reporting a decline in deliveries there last month, joining Volkswagen AG in stepping up discounts as growth slows in their largest market. GM's joint venture with SAIC Motor Corp. announced price cuts of as much as 53,900 yuan ($8,700) on 40 models across its Buick, Chevrolet and Cadillac brands, according to a statement on its website. Chevrolet deliveries dropped 5.6 per cent last month, while Buick sales slumped 8.5 per cent, according to the company.

Foreign automakers have come under increasing pressure in China as economic growth slows in the world's largest auto market and local brands gain market share by offering cheaper sport utility vehicles. Passenger-vehicle sales rose at the slowest pace in

five months in April, with most of the expansion coming from local brands.

'In years to come we expect 2015 to be known as the start of China's "Great Moderation", as pricing and margins fall from levels far above global norms,' Robin Zhu, senior analyst at Sanford C. Bernstein Ltd., wrote in a report today. 'The ramifications of a drop in Chinese market profitability may be substantial.'

Besides discounts, foreign automakers are offering incentives such as subsidized insurance, zero down payment, interest-free financing, exemption of purchase tax and trade-in subsidies, according to Bernstein.

From Bloomberg. 12 May 2015. 'GM Cuts Prices in China as Foreign Brand Sales Slow'. Bloomberg News. ©2015 Bloomberg L.P. All Rights Reserved.

In Box 2.1 we have a business example of price cutting by car manufacturers in order to stop falling demand for cars in China.

## (2.3) Factors influencing demand

It is also possible to consider movements in the demand line itself. Assume that we have 100 customers and we ask them about their willingness to demand at various prices. We could use the data collected to draw a demand line. If we then had 200 customers and we surveyed them about their willingness to pay, where we would we be likely to draw the demand line? Equally, where would we draw the demand line if we only had 50 customers to survey? The answer to these questions is fairly easy. Because the x-axis is the quantity demanded, then an increase in the number of customers will lead to more demand at all prices and so the demand line moves to the right in the direction of the x-axis; see $Q_{D1}$ in Figure 2.2. Similarly, if we have fewer customers, then less will be demanded at each price and so the demand line will move to the left in the direction of the x-axis; see $Q_{D2}$ in Figure 2.2.

There are a number of other circumstances which will lead to an increase or decrease in the number of customers, or an increase or decrease in the amount of units demanded by customers. These circumstances are listed overleaf and each will be discussed in detail.

1 Price of substitutes and complements
2 Consumer income
3 Tastes and preferences
4 Price expectations.

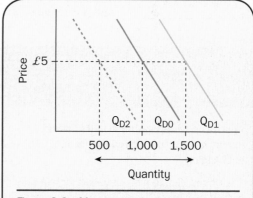

Figure 2.2   Movements in demand

Demand shifts to the left following: (i) a reduction/increase in the price of a substitute/complement product; (ii) a reduction/increase in income if the good is normal/inferior; or (iii) a fall in consumers' preferences for the product. Demand shifts to the right following: (i) an increase/reduction in the price of a substitute/complement product; (ii) an increase/reduction in income if the good is normal/inferior; or (iii) an improvement in consumers' preferences for the product.

## Price of substitutes and complements

> Substitutes are rival products; for example, a BMW car is a substitute for a Mercedes, or a bottle of wine from France is a substitute for a bottle from Australia.

**Substitutes** are competing products in the same marketplace, seeking to gain customers from their rivals. So, if French wine producers decided to reduce the price of their wine, they would hope to gain some of the Australian wine producers' customers. As a result, the Australians sell less wine for the same price. This is depicted in Figure 2.2, with the demand curve for Australian wine moving in to the left to $Q_{D2}$ and Australian wine consumption decreasing from 1,000 to 500 units at a constant price of £5 per bottle. Clearly, the opposite will also be true. If the French increased their prices, then they might expect to lose customers to the Australians. This would be depicted as a rightward shift in the demand curve, from $Q_{D0}$ to $Q_{D1}$.

Box 2.2 provides details on Australian wine exports to the UK. Twenty years ago Australian provided cheap wine to the UK, but with increased competition and more substitution at cheap price points, Australian producers have moved to higher-quality wines at higher prices where they hope to face fewer substitutes.

> Complements are products that are purchased jointly. Beer and kebabs would be a youthful and modern example; another would be cars and petrol.

**Complements** are products that are demanded together. For example, if you buy a car, then you will have to buy petrol. This, therefore, means that the demand for the two products is related. If cars become cheaper, then more cars will be demanded. As a consequence, more petrol will also be demanded. If Figure 2.2 represents demand for petrol, then a reduction in the price of cars will lead to increased demand for cars. This increased demand for cars will lead to a higher demand for petrol. The demand curve for petrol will shift to the right from $Q_{D0}$ to $Q_{D1}$, with more petrol being demanded at the existing price of £5 per gallon.

## Consumer income

> Normal goods are demanded more when consumer income increases and less when income falls.
>
> Inferior goods are demanded more when income levels fall and demanded less when income levels rise.

In understanding the effect of income on demand, we need to distinguish between **normal goods** and **inferior goods**.

If we consider Australian wine to be a normal good, as income increases we buy more. Then, in terms of Figure 2.2, when income increases, the demand curve for Australian wine shifts right to $Q_{D1}$ and more is demanded at every possible price. However, during a recession, when incomes are likely to fall, consumers will cut back on wine and the demand curve shifts left to $Q_{D2}$.

---

### Box 2.2
### Australian wine

**Australia's wine reputation in its largest export market, the United Kingdom, is changing**

The United Kingdom is Australia's largest wine export market by volume, worth $370 million a year. In the past, Australia has been a good source of cheap, everyday drinking wines for UK consumers.

In the last 20 years, at the start of that time period, Australia was thought of as a source of good value, inexpensive, juicy everyday wine. There's much more understanding now that it's a source of really serious wine, from lots of different microclimates. It still produces good everyday stuff, but we sell much more expensive and more serious Australian wine than we did 10 or 15 years ago in this country.

Wine Australia regional director Aaron Brasher says overall the United Kingdom wine market is in decline. 'Australia's exports decreased by a few percentages in value and volume terms.' Mr Brasher says one of the few wine exporters to grow in the UK market is Chile, filling out the bottom end of the market.

There's more good quality cheap wine for sale in the UK, making it important to compete at a higher price point. South America, Spain and even France are improving their simple everyday wines. It's important Australia demonstrates it can make serious wines at the other end of the scale.

29 September 2014. 'Australia's wine reputation in its largest export market, the United Kingdom, is changing'. Laura Poole. Reproduced by permission of the Australian Broadcasting Corporation—Library Sales © 2014 ABC

Inferior goods tend to be those characterized as cheaper brands—products that we stop purchasing once our income rises and we move to more normal types of goods. 'Inferior' does not necessarily mean that the product has a lower quality than a normal good. Rather, we consume less when incomes fall and vice versa.

Think about the things you buy at the supermarket as a poor indebted student and the things your parents buy as significant income earners. You will tend to be buying inferior types of goods, such as supermarkets' own-label items. Your parents will be buying normal types of goods, such as branded lines in bread, alcohol and frozen foods. In terms of Figure 2.2, as income rises, the demand curve for an inferior good would shift left to $Q_{D2}$. When income falls, the demand curve for an inferior good would shift right to $Q_{D1}$. In brief, the behaviour of the demand curve for normal goods is opposite to that of inferior goods.

## Tastes and preferences

Tastes and preferences reflect consumers' attitudes towards particular products. Over time, these tastes and preferences are likely to change. Fashion is an obvious example: what might be popular this year will be out of fashion next year. Technological development might be another. Companies supplying smartphones incorporate new technological capabilities into their phones to attract more customers. We can survive quite well without such technology but, through advertising, companies try to influence our tastes and preferences for such advanced capabilities.

In order to represent a positive improvement in tastes and preference for a product, in Figure 2.2 the demand curve would shift right to $Q_{D1}$, with more products being sold at any given price, while a reduction in consumer backing for a product would lead to a leftward shift in the demand curve, with less being sold at any given price. For example, in recent times flat-screen, high-definition televisions have begun to replace cathode-ray televisions, reflecting changed tastes and preferences for flat-screen technologies and, therefore, lower demand for cathode-ray televisions at all prices.

Box 2.3 provides evidence of the resurgence of car sales in the UK. The growth in car sales exhibits a number of economic ideas that we have highlighted above: reduction in prices, improved incomes and raised demand for a normal good, availability of debt which is a complement of car sales; and a change in taste and preferences towards electric sales (see below for more details on the role of tastes and preferences).

### The role of advertising

Advertising can play at least one of two roles in demand theory. First, it provides consumers with information about products. Advertising informs consumers that new products have arrived on the market, that a product has new features, or that a product is being offered at a lower price. In this way, advertising plays a very valuable informational role for firms and for consumers. Demand for products increases simply because consumers are informed about the nature and availability of the product. Therefore, when advertising plays an informational role, the demand curve for the product shift s out to $Q_{D1}$ as more consumers become informed about the existence of the product.

There is, however, another role for advertising. If adverts are simply about informing consumers about the existence of products, why are they played repeatedly over very long periods of time? Moreover, why do product suppliers hire well-known celebrities to appear in their adverts? How many adverts do you see on the television, or in the press, that provide information about the product's characteristics, price or availability? Advertising is also about trying to change consumers' tastes and preferences. We all know that mobile phones are capable of sending pictures and video, so why would we be interested in knowing that celebrities use such technology? We all know that a Swiss watch looks good and can keep reasonable time, so why would we be interested in knowing which celebrities wear such watches? One possible answer is that the product provider is not simply selling a product.

## Box 2.3
## UK new car registrations reach 10-year high in 2014

- 2,476,435 new cars registered in the UK in 2014—the most in a calendar year since 2004.
- Year was fourth-largest of all time; only 2002, 2003 and 2004 saw more cars registered.
- 2014 market grew 9.3 per cent over the previous year, ahead of the EU average of 5.7 per cent.
- UK remains second largest market in EU (behind Germany and ahead of France, Italy and Spain), and recorded second-largest growth of these top five EU markets.
- Every month in 2014 saw an increase, with December's 8.7 per cent rise the 34th consecutive month of growth.
- Huge growth for plug-in car market, which saw volumes quadruple from 3,586 in 2013 to 14,498 in 2014.

Mike Hawes, Society of Motor Manufacturers and Traders, SMMT Chief Executive, said, 'UK new car registrations returned to pre-recession levels in 2014, as pent-up demand from the recession years combined with confidence in the economy saw consumer demand for the latest models grow consistently and strongly.

'The year was particularly strong for alternatively fuelled vehicles as increased choice, coupled with a growing desire for reduced costs and greater efficiency, resulted in a quadrupling of plug-in car registrations over 2013. With a variety of new plug-in models expected in 2015, this area of the market will continue to grow significantly. For the market as a whole, we expect a more stable 2015 as demand levels off.'

From SMMT. 7 January 2015. 'UK new car registrations reach 10-year in 2014'. © SMMT 2015.

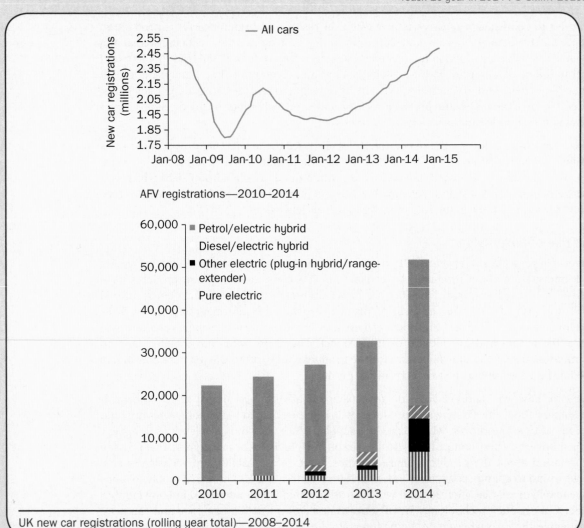

UK new car registrations (rolling year total)—2008–2014

Instead, they are selling you a desirable lifestyle. We do buy technologically advanced mobile phones because they are useful; but we also buy such phones because we believe that they say something positive about who we are. By emphasizing these less tangible aspects of a product, it is possible to build additional differentiation into the product. Two mobile phones might provide the same functions, but only one is used by a world-class footballer. Accordingly, advertising is not simply about informing consumers about what they *can* buy; it is also about informing them about what they *should* buy. Whether advertising is providing information, or developing consumers' tastes and preferences, the overriding aim is to shift the demand curve from $Q_{D0}$ to $Q_{D1}$, while at the same time shifting the competitors' demand curves from $Q_{D0}$ to $Q_{D2}$.

## Price expectations

If you expect prices to fall in the future, then it may be wise to wait and delay your purchase. For example, recently launched computers, televisions and smartphones are often sold in the market at premium prices. Within three to six months, newer models are brought out and the old versions are then sold at lower prices. If you do not have a taste or preference for cutting-edge technology, you can cut back on consumption today in the expectation that prices will fall in the future. In terms of our demand curves, if we expect prices to fall in the future, then demand today will be reduced, shifting back to $Q_{D2}$. But the demand curve for three to six months' time will shift right to $Q_{D1}$.

Opposite **price expectations** can also be true. It is possible to believe that in the future prices will rise. Property may be more expensive in the future, share prices might increase or oil will be more expensive in six months' time. Therefore, if you expect prices to rise in the future, you are likely to bring your consumption forward and purchase now. In terms of our demand curves, your demand for now shifts out to $Q_{D1}$, but your demand in the future shifts back to $Q_{D2}$.

We now understand that the demand for a product is influenced by (i) its own price, (ii) the price of substitutes and complements, (iii) the level of consumer income, (iv) consumers' tastes and preferences, and (v) price expectations. We are now in a position to introduce the **law of demand**, which states that, *ceteris paribus*, as the price of a product falls more will be demanded. The law is saying that if (i) through to (v) stay the same, i.e. '*ceteris paribus*', then price and demand are negatively related.

> Price expectations are beliefs about how prices in the future will differ from prices today: will they rise or fall?
>
> The law of demand states that, *ceteris paribus,* as the price of a product falls, more will be demanded.
>
> *Ceteris paribus* means all other things being equal.

### *Do higher prices attract higher demand?*

The negative relationship between price and quantity demanded can cause students and business managers problems. For example, designer clothes and perfumes would not be purchased if they were cheap. So, does a positive relationship exist between price and willingness to demand luxury items? While it remains an appealing idea, the answer to this question is still no, since all products have a negative demand curve. This is because even when you are very rich you still have a budget constraint.

Assume you are fortunate to have an annual expense account of £500,000. Your designer clothes cost £300,000 per year, champagne is another £100,000 and the private jet another £100,000. If your favourite designer suddenly increases their prices by £50,000, you are faced with a choice. If you continue to buy the same quantity of clothes, they will now cost £350,000, and you will have to cut back on the champagne and the jet. Alternatively, you could cut back on your clothes and maintain the same amount of champagne and the private jet. However, most probably you will reduce some of your demand for designer clothes, perhaps buying fewer clothes at the higher price of £325,000, as opposed to the £350,000 it would cost to buy the same quantity as last year. The extra £25,000 might come from reducing your flights and the amount of champagne that you drink.

It is important to understand, from the example above, that higher prices for one product limit how much money you can spend on *all* goods and services that you like to consume.

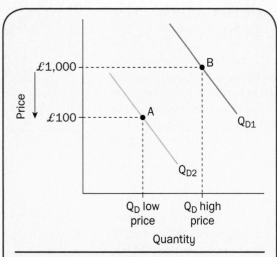

Figure 2.3   Demand for Louis Vuitton

$Q_{D1}$ and $Q_{D2}$ are the demand curves for Louis Vuitton bags. Under $Q_{D1}$, stores are not allowed to sell Louis Vuitton bags at discount prices, while under $Q_{D2}$ they are able to sell them at discounted prices. Consumers with a taste and preference for expensive and exclusive bags are willing to buy bags at £1,000. But once discounting by stores makes Louis Vuitton bags become cheap and not exclusive, consumers are less willing to buy bags. Demand shifts from $Q_{D1}$ to $Q_{D2}$ and fewer bags are purchased. The reason we sometimes think there is a positive relationship between price and willingness to demand is because we only focus on points A and B. If we joined up these two points, we would see a positive relationship between price and quantity demanded. But this is a mistake, as we really need to focus on the shifts in the demand curves reflecting a change in tastes and preferences.

The demand curve for designer clothes should have a negative slope, because you will decrease the quantity of clothes purchased in order to retain consumption of the champagne and jet travel.

Therefore, for luxury items, how do we explain the positive relationship between price and quantity demanded? Some consumers prefer products that have an element of exclusivity. A high price not only ensures exclusivity, but also signals that the product is special. A low price would not create the same image. Therefore, the high price attracts particular consumers into the market. This leads to the demand curve shifting out to the right in Figure 2.2 and means that the positive relationship between price and quantity is associated with a change in tastes and preferences. As such, the positive relationship of price and demand is best described as a shift of the demand curve, rather than a movement along the curve.

These points are picked up in Figure 2.3, with product providers such as Louis Vuitton keen to avoid their product being sold at discount prices. The high price of the product and the distribution of the product through licensed clothing retailers are deliberately managed in a way to promote the product's high-quality image. Consumers' tastes and preferences have been developed by Louis Vuitton to the extent that consumers expect Louis Vuitton bags to be expensive and more exclusive than cheaper alternatives. Louis Vuitton will be concerned to protect the high-price image of its product, fearful that a low price would have a detrimental effect on consumers' tastes and preferences. The demand curve for Louis Vuitton will shift to the left, reducing the number of bags sold.

In Figure 2.3, $Q_{D1}$ represents the demand for Louis Vuitton handbags among consumers who have a strong taste and preference for expensive and exclusive bags. At a price of £1,000, demand is $Q_D$. $Q_{D2}$ is the demand for Louis Vuitton among consumers who do not have a strong taste and preference for expensive and exclusive bags. We can see that, at a price of £1,000, none of these consumers will buy—the line from £1,000 does not touch $Q_{D2}$. However, at a discounted price of £100, consumers represented by $Q_{D2}$ are willing to buy Louis Vuitton. The demand curves $Q_{D1}$ and $Q_{D2}$ both have a negative slope. However, if we were to focus mistakenly on points A and B, and draw a line connecting the two points, then we might be led to believe that increases in price lead to increases in demand. This would be a mistake, because it is the differing tastes and preferences for cheap and exclusive brands that lead to the shift between the two points A and B.

##  Measuring the responsiveness of demand

You have been introduced to the demand curve and the factors that cause demand to shift. However, for the business person it is not enough to know that the demand for a product is determined by (i) its own price, (ii) the price of substitutes and complements, (iii) the level of consumer income, (iv) consumers' tastes and preferences, and (v) expectations regarding future prices. As a person in the marketplace making real pricing decisions, the business person needs to know the impact of price changes on the quantity demanded.

Figure 2.4 provides an illustration of **elasticity**. In Figure 2.4a, a small change in the price leads to a much bigger change in the quantity demanded. But in Figure 2.4b, a very large change in the price leads to a small change in the quantity demanded. So, we might say that in Figure 2.4a demand is responsive to a change in price, while in Figure 2.4b demand is not very responsive to a change in price.

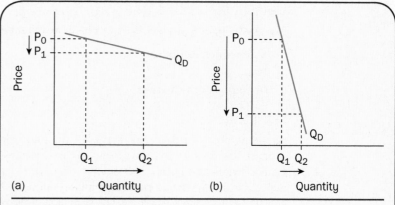

Figure 2.4    Price and quantity changes

(a) A small change in the price leads to a large change in demand
(b) A large change in the price leads to a small change in demand

Businesses use elasticity ideas to formulate competitive strategies, including pricing decisions, promotional decisions and product-placement decisions relative to rivals. Understanding what your consumers want and how sensitive to price your consumers are enables companies to develop innovative business models. Examine in Box 2.4 how Starbucks are taking a highly substitutable cup of coffee and making consumer demand price inelastic by adding into the experience the roasting and grinding of beans and the environment in which you drink the coffee. These additional features bring a niche element to the enjoyment of the coffee which is difficult to replicate, reduces consumer price sensitivity and enables Starbucks to contemplate charging $6 for a latte.

> **Elasticity** is a measure of the responsiveness of demand to a change in price.

## Box 2.4
## To compete with fancy brewers, Starbucks opens a shrine to coffee

These days, Starbucks stores function more like gas stations: they're everywhere, and frequented for fuel. If you're invested in the flavour, aroma, roast and the mouth feel of your brew these days you wouldn't walk into a Starbucks; you'd go to a joint like Stumptown, Blue Bottle or Intelligentsia, where baristas toil for several minutes to prepare your $6 cup of imported coffee.

Soon, if all goes to plan, those discerning drinkers might go to a Starbucks Reserve store. Over the next five years, the company will roll out more than 100 new stores dedicated to its line of Reserve coffees, which, as the name suggests, appear in limited editions and smaller batches than its other blends. To kick all this off, Starbucks this week opened the Reserve Roastery and Tasting Room in Seattle, just a few blocks from it's very first store, opened in 1971, at Pike Place Market.

The Roastery, which covers 15,000 square feet, is a coffee lab-meets-museum. 'We wanted to create this interactive space, but like a Willy Wonka factory,' says Liz Muller, who designed several of Starbucks's concept stores in recent years.

Customers can watch as employees schlep burlap sacks of green coffee beans from the trucks outside and begin the roasting process. At a bar, baristas prepare coffee using some popular, more handcrafted methods, like pour over, with a Chemex, or with a Clover. Because the latest specialty coffee is a scientific exercise—the precise brewing temperature and time required to brew the coffee as much as the bean—it's fitting that parts of the Reserve look like massive chemistry sets, encased behind glass walls.

Perhaps most importantly for the future of the standalone Reserve stores, the spaciousness of the Reserve means that Starbucks can double the size of its Reserve coffee programme. Buyers who previously might have struck upon an amazing new bean, but had nowhere for experimenting and roasting, can now do that in Seattle. And as beautiful as the Reserve may be, if Starbucks does win over coffee purists from Blue Bottle and the like, it's going to be strictly about what's in the cup.

December 15th 2014. 'To Compete With Fancy Brewers, Starbucks Opens a Shrine to Coffee'. Margaret Rhodes/Wired © Conde Nast

## Determinants of elasticity

The elasticity of a product is determined by a number of factors:

1 Number of substitutes
2 Time
3 Definition of the market.

### Substitutes

As the number of substitutes increases, the more elastic will be demand. For example, if a product has no substitutes and the supplier decides to increase its prices, then consumers cannot switch to a cheaper alternative. Therefore, when the price increases for this product, demand will only fall by a small amount. In contrast, when a product has a very large number of substitutes, its price elasticity will be very high. If the price of the product increases, consumers will very quickly switch to the cheaper alternatives. Cigarettes—and, more importantly, nicotine as an addictive drug—have few, if any, substitutes. Therefore, if the price of cigarettes increases, then few smokers will quit cigarettes. Alternatively, in the market for mobile telecommunications, with many competing suppliers, if one provider reduces its prices, then there will be a rapid change in demand, with consumers switching to the cheapest provider.

### Time

Time is also important, as it is likely to influence the development and introduction of substitutes. Initially, new products or markets will only have a small number of substitutes. Only if these products are successful will new entrants come into the market and begin to compete. Therefore, in the early periods of a new market, demand is likely to be inelastic, but in the long term, as more products enter the market, demand is likely to become more elastic. For example, the launch of alcoholic drinks for the youth market, mixing alcoholic drinks with soft drinks, started with a small number of product offerings. As sales in the market have grown, the number of competing products has also increased.

### Market definition

Market definitions are also important when measuring elasticity. The demand for beer is relatively unresponsive to a change in price. As the price of beer increases, consumers still continue to buy beer, because they perhaps view wine as a poor alternative. In contrast, the demand for a particular brand of beer is likely to be price responsive. This is because all the separate beer brands are competitive substitutes. So, if one brand becomes more expensive, it is likely that drinkers will switch to the cheaper alternatives.

Box 2.5 provides information of the changing market shares for supermarkets in the UK. The UK supermarket sector has a number of competing companies who provide very effective competition for each other. In the eyes of consumers, these competitors are good substitutes. Changes in the intensity of price competition, such as the launch of price wars, alter consumer demand and market share for each company. Growth in the number of stores over time by some of the companies also enables consumers to be more price sensitive and shop around.

## Measuring elasticity

Mathematically, economists can measure elasticity, or the responsiveness of demand to a change in price, using the following formulae.

### Formulae for elasticity

$$\varepsilon = \frac{\text{Percentage change in quantity demanded}}{\text{Percentage change in price}} \tag{2.1}$$

$$\frac{\text{Change in quantity demanded}}{\text{Change in price}} \times \frac{\text{Price}}{\text{Quantity demanded}} \tag{2.2}$$

## Box 2.5
## Big four supermarkets continue to find the market tough

Grocery share figures from Kantar Worldpanel, for the 12 weeks ending 4 January 2015, show sales at Sainsbury's fell by 0.7 per cent over the latest period, but in a tough market this was the best performance among the big four supermarkets.

Tesco's sales fell 1.2 per cent compared with last year, but this is their best performance since March 2014 and represents a notable improvement. Sales fell by 1.6 per cent at both Asda and Morrisons.

While the bigger supermarkets have continued to find the market tough, Aldi and Lidl have grown by 22.6 per cent and 15.1 per cent to finish the year with market shares of 4.8 per cent and 3.5 per cent respectively. More than half of all British households visited at least one of the two retailers over the past

12 weeks. Waitrose also maintained its strong run as sales rose 6.6 per cent to take its market share to 5.1 per cent.

Shoppers were the big winners at Christmas with cheaper grocery prices encouraging them to spend more at the tills. Like-for-like prices have fallen by 0.9 per cent due to lower commodity costs and an ongoing price war which has continued as the large retailers battle for market share.

Competition between the grocers has been fierce and there is now a gap of just 0.5 per cent sales growth separating the four largest retailers. Such a tightly fought race is unprecedented in records dating back to 1994.

Adapted from an article by Fraser McKevitt, 13 January 2015
Source: Kantar

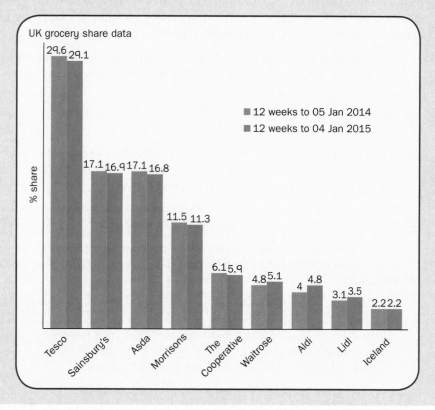

The value of $\varepsilon$ for elasticity will lie between zero and infinity $(0 < \varepsilon < \infty)$.[2] Since this is a very large number range, economists break the range down into regions that they can describe and utilize. Using the first formula, each of these regions is described in Table 2.1.

---

[2]You will shortly understand that elasticity must lie between zero and minus infinity. This is because, if we increase prices, then quantity demanded will decrease. So, a negative change in demand will be divided by a positive change in the price. So the elasticity measure will always be negative. Economists ignore the negative sign and simply look at the numerical value for elasticity.

**Table 2.1**   Important elasticity measures

| | Percentage change in price | Percentage change in demand | Numerical calculations | Elasticity value | Description |
|---|---|---|---|---|---|
| 1 | 10 | 0 | $\frac{0}{10} = 0$ | $\varepsilon = 0$ | Perfectly inelastic |
| 2 | 10 | 5 | $\frac{5}{10} = 1/2$ | $\varepsilon < 1$ | Inelastic demand |
| 3 | 10 | 10 | $\frac{10}{10} = 1$ | $\varepsilon = 1$ | Unit elasticity |
| 4 | 10 | 20 | $\frac{20}{10} = 2$ | $\varepsilon > 1$ | Elastic demand |
| 5 | 10 | Infinitely large | | $\varepsilon = \infty$ | Perfectly elastic |

We will begin with an easy example. If the price of cigarettes increased by 10 per cent, how many smokers would cut back on the number of cigarettes smoked? Many smokers would continue smoking. In an extreme situation, a 10 per cent change in the price of cigarettes could lead to no change in the quantity demanded. (In reality this would not happen, but the example provides a reasonable description of a theoretical extreme.)

In economic terms, demand is said to be perfectly **inelastic** when $\varepsilon = 0$; that is, demand does not respond to a change in price. This is detailed in the first row of Table 2.1.

Clearly, *perfectly inelastic demand* is an extreme situation. So, in the second row of Table 2.1, we consider the situation where a 10 per cent change in the price leads to a 5 per cent change in demand.

The demand for Coca-Cola may well be inelastic. If Coke increased its prices by 10 per cent we might expect it to lose a small, rather than large, number of customers. So, demand is not very responsive to a change in price.

In row 3, we have the situation where a 10 per cent change in the price leads to a 10 per cent change in the quantity demanded—**unit elasticity**.

In row 4, we consider the situation where a 10 per cent change in the price leads to a much bigger change in quantity demanded, in this case 20 per cent, resulting in **elastic demand**.

Consider the price of mobile phone contracts; nearly all competing networks offer very similar menus and prices. One of the reasons for this is that demand is reasonably elastic. If one company raised its prices, then over time many of its subscribers would switch to another network. Therefore, similar prices are offered because each network recognizes that demand is responsive to price differences.

> Inelastic demand is where elasticity $\varepsilon < 1$, or a change in the price will lead to a proportionately smaller change in the quantity demanded.
>
> Unit elasticity is when $\varepsilon = 1$, or demand is equally responsive to a change in price.
>
> Elastic demand is where $\varepsilon > 1$, or demand is responsive to a change in price.
>
> Perfectly elastic demand exists when $\varepsilon = \infty$. In other words, demand is very responsive to a change in price.

Finally, in row 5, we consider **perfectly elastic demand**. In this case, the change in price is 10 per cent and, in response, demand changes by a very large amount. The London financial markets come close to a situation of perfectly elastic demand. If the market price of shares in Shell is £10, then you can sell all of your holdings at £10. But if you offered to sell at £10.01, you would not sell a single share, as potential buyers would move to the many other sellers offering to sell at £10.

## Elasticity and the slope of the demand curve

We mentioned above that the slope of the demand curve is only an indication of how elastic demand is. In fact, we can now show that the elasticity of demand changes all the way along a particular demand curve. We will do this by using the second formula for elasticity (see Figure 2.5).

During a basic maths course you will have been told that, to measure the slope of a line, you need to draw a triangle next to the line. The slope, or gradient, of the line is then the change in the vertical distance divided by the change in the horizontal distance. In our case, the gradient is the change in price (the vertical) divided by the change in quantity demanded (the horizontal). For our second formula we need the 'inverse' of the slope: that is, we need the change in quantity demanded (horizontal) divided by the change in price (vertical). But what we can say is that the slope of the line is constant, so the inverse of the slope is also constant. We have measured the slope and the inverse in the middle of the line and it is equal to 10/10 = 1. In fact, in our example, because the slope is constant, it does not matter where we measure the slope—it is always 10/10 = 1. disruptive.

We can now calculate the elasticity of demand at two special points, A and B. At A, the demand line just touches the vertical axis. The price is so high that demand is zero. At B, the demand line just touches the horizontal axis. The price is zero and demand is very high. Using our second formula for elasticity, at A the elasticity is:

$$(10/10) \times (\text{price}/0) = \text{infinity} = \infty$$

Because at A the demand is zero, the elasticity of demand must be infinite. We know that this means that demand is perfectly elastic.

The elasticity at B is:

$$(10/10) \times (\text{quantity demanded}/0) = 0$$

Because at B the price is zero, the elasticity of demand must be zero. We know that this means that demand is perfectly inelastic.

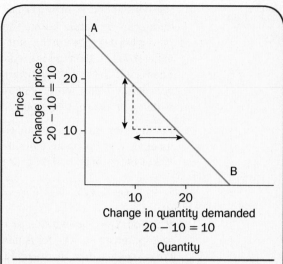

Figure 2.5  Elasticity changes along the demand curve

Elasticity = (Change in demand/Change in price) × (Price/Quantity)

The change in price equals 10 and the change in quantity demanded also equals 10 At A the price is so high, quantity demanded is zero, so:

elasticity at A = (10/10) × (P/0) = ∞

At B the price is 0, and the quantity demanded is very high, so:

elasticity at B = (10/10) × (0/Q) = 0

Therefore, all the way along the demand curve the elasticity changes from being perfectly elastic to perfectly inelastic, even though the slope has remained constant. This is because the elasticity of demand is influenced by the slope of the demand line *and* by the ratio of price and quantity demanded. When the price is very high, a small reduction in the price will generate a proportionately bigger change in demand. But when the price is very low, a small change will not generate a proportionately bigger change in demand.

In simple terms, consumers react to price reductions when a product is very expensive. But they are less motivated by price reductions when a product is already very cheap. Therefore, demand is more elastic at higher prices than at lower ones.

**Income elasticity** measures the responsiveness of demand to a change in income.

**Cross-price elasticity** measures the responsiveness of demand to a change in the price of a substitute or complement.

## 2.5 Income and cross-price elasticity

Before considering the application of this knowledge, it is also worth introducing you to two related measures: **income elasticity** and **cross-price elasticity**.

$$\text{Income elasticity} = Y_\varepsilon = \frac{\text{Percentage change in demand}}{\text{Percentage change in income}}$$

For normal goods, income elasticity is above zero because as consumers' income rises, say during an economic boom, more normal types of goods will be produced. If $Y_\varepsilon < 1$, the product is described as income inelastic, or demand will grow at a slower rate than income, while if $Y_\varepsilon > 1$, demand is income elastic, or demand will grow at a faster rate than income. The recent UK and US housing booms were a reflection of positive income elasticity, with consumers being more willing to spend money on property as their incomes increased within a prosperous economy.

For inferior goods, income elasticity lies between zero and minus infinity because, as incomes rise, consumers buy fewer inferior goods. This time demand is income inelastic if $Y_\varepsilon$ lies between zero and –1, or is income elastic if $Y_\varepsilon$ is smaller than –1, e.g. –5.

$$\text{Cross-price elasticity} = XY_\varepsilon = \frac{\text{Percentage change in demand of product X}}{\text{Percentage change in the price of product Y}}$$

If X and Y are substitutes or rivals, then, as the price of Y increases, the demand for X will increase, so $XY_\varepsilon$ for substitutes lies between zero and plus infinity. If X and Y are complements, then, as the price of Y becomes more expensive, less X will also be purchased; $XY_\varepsilon$ must lie between zero and minus infinity.

**Table 2.2**  Elasticity measures for bus travel

| | |
|---|---|
| Price elasticity | (–)0.1 |
| Cross-price elasticity (with cars) | +0.3 |
| Income elasticity | –2.4 |

In Table 2.2 we have examples of price, cross-price and income elasticity for bus travel. With a price elasticity of demand equal to 0.1, demand is price inelastic. A drop in prices would not generate many more bus travellers. A cross-price elasticity of +0.3 indicates that buses and cars are substitutes and, since the value is less than 1, the relationship is inelastic. Therefore, even if cars became more expensive, few drivers would opt for buses instead. The income elasticity of –2.4 suggests that bus travel is an inferior good and highly income elastic. Therefore, even a small rise in income will cause bus travellers to cut their demand for bus travel, and perhaps move to car travel.

##  2.6  Business application: pricing strategies i—exploiting elasticities

Finding the best price was this chapter's business problem. After introducing demand theory and the concept of elasticity, we are now able to return to this particular problem.

### Cost-plus pricing

A rather simple approach to pricing is to simply take the costs of producing the product and add a mark-up, such as 30 per cent. This might cover some stray, unaccounted-for costs and also the required profit margin. The benefit of this approach lies in its computational simplicity, only requiring a basic idea of costs and a grasp of a desirable profit margin. It may also appear to be fair. Who would begrudge a firm asking for a 30 per cent mark-up? After all, they are taking a risk and they should be able to generate a decent financial return.

Unfortunately, while it may seem appealing, cost-plus pricing neglects almost everything we have introduced you to in this chapter. That is, it fails to take account of consumers' willingness to demand. There is no guarantee that consumers will be willing to buy your product when the mark-up is 30 per cent. Alternatively, 30 per cent may not be a sufficiently high mark-up. Consumers may exhibit a very keen preference for your product and a low elasticity of demand. While 30 per cent appears fair, you might be able to gain good sales volumes with a mark-up of 50–100 per cent. It therefore appears that we need also to consider demand theory when setting prices.

## 'Buy one get one free'—discounting or price experiment?

**Table 2.3** Total revenue

| Price | Quantity | Total revenue |
|-------|----------|---------------|
| £5 | 10 | £50 |
| £8 | 8 | £64 |
| £8 | 6 | £48 |

In simple terms, the need to find the best price stems from a broader need to generate revenues. At the beginning of this chapter, in the business problem example, it was suggested that, at a price of £5, we might sell ten units, making £50 of revenue. But, at a price of £8, we might sell eight units, making a total revenue of £64. This looks like a better option. But how can we be sure that moving from £5 to £8 is a good idea? We might have ended up selling only six units, making a total revenue of only £48 (see Table 2.3).

Price elasticity measures the response of demand to a change in price. We face two outcomes when changing the price: demand falls to eight or six units. Falling from ten to eight units is a small response to a change in price or, in our new terminology, demand is inelastic. But when demand falls to six units, the response is much bigger and demand can be described as elastic. But what happens to total revenues? When demand is inelastic, total revenues have increased to £64. But when demand is price elastic, total revenues have fallen to £48. We can expand upon these simple ideas using Figure 2.6.

In Figure 2.6a, we have a price-elastic demand curve. So, at a price of $P_0$, we can expect to sell $Q_0$ units. Therefore, **total revenue** is represented by the rectangle defined by $P_0$ and $Q_0$.

> Total revenue is price multiplied by number of units sold.

If we drop the price to $P_1$, then sales increase to $Q_1$ and total revenue is now equal to the new rectangle defined by $P_1$ and $Q_1$. The impact of a price reduction on total revenue is the difference in size between the two rectangles. By selling at a lower price, we lose some total revenue. For example, if we were selling at £10 and now we are only asking for £8, we are losing £2 per unit. But by reducing the price we will also gain some total revenue by selling to more customers—in this example, $Q_1$ as opposed to $Q_0$ customers. Hence, when demand is price elastic, selling at a lower price will boost total revenues. In contrast, if we examine the case of inelastic demand in Figure 2.6b, we see that reducing the price leads to a drop in total revenues.

We now have economic guidance for business. If demand is elastic, then dropping prices raises total revenues; but if demand is inelastic, prices should be increased in order to increase total revenues.

If we return to our business problem, the best price occurs when price elasticity equals 1, which is exactly in between the elastic and inelastic region. With unit elasticity, a 10 per cent increase in the price leads to a 10 per cent change in quantity demanded. Total revenue does not change; the maximum has been found.

Admittedly, firms may not always target a price elasticity equal to 1. They may not have revenue maximization as their objective. They may wish to maximize market share or profits. Changing the price involves the development of new pricing plans and the communication of price changes to retailers of the product. As a result, change can be costly and not offset by improvements in

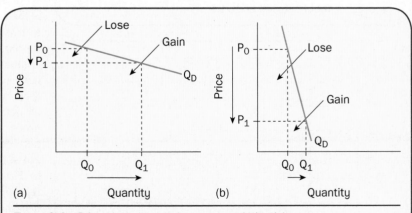

**Figure 2.6** Price changes, total revenue and elasticity

(a) Change in total revenue when demand is elastic
(b) Change in total revenue when demand is inelastic.

revenue. Change can also represent a risk. Competitors could react to your price changes. A reduction in your price could lead to a price war, which you may not find attractive. Furthermore, you may not fully understand the price elasticity of demand for your product. If you consider the demand for your product to be elastic, you should think about reducing your price. But if you have got it wrong and demand is inelastic, your revenues will fall, not rise. It is, therefore, important to understand how you might measure your elasticity of demand.

## Elastic or inelastic?

Cigarettes were used as an example of inelastic demand and mobile phone networks as an example of elastic demand. Cigarettes have few substitutes: if all cigarettes become expensive, smokers will not switch to another type of vice, as there are few sources of nicotine. If one telephone network increases its prices, however, mobile phone users can switch to the cheaper networks. It is the level of competition for a product that influences its elasticity.

The level of competition provides an indication of how elastic demand is. However, if we wish to target unit elasticity we will need a measure of how far our current pricing is from this best price. To find the best price we need to gather data that will enable the demand curve for our product to be plotted, or mathematically modelled.

Once we have a demand curve, we can see the relationship between price and quantity and measure the elasticity of demand at various prices. Unfortunately the data required for a demand curve are difficult to find. Ideally, an experiment should occur where the price of a product is changed and the effect on demand noted, but product suppliers are not keen to change the price of the product to see what happens to the demand. Indeed, if they raise the price they are likely to lose customers to a rival brand. Recognizing this problem, market researchers can make use of promotional exercises. For example, a 'buy one get one free' offer is basically a 50 per cent discount in the market. A 'buy two get the third free' offer is a 33 per cent discount. When you buy a product at the supermarket, so-called 'scanner data' are created. Therefore, for any given period of time the supermarket knows how much soap powder was sold and what discounts were on offer. Market research companies make it their business to buy scanner data from a large selection of supermarkets across the country. They then use this to advise companies on pricing, because by using the data on sales and promotional discounts they can begin to estimate the elasticity of demand. For each price at which the product is sold, the market researchers also note down how many units of the product are sold at the tills. They then plot this as in Figure 2.7. The plot shows a negative relationship between price and quantity demanded. To smooth out this relationship the researchers then use a computer to calculate the trend line, as in Figure 2.8. The trend line is in fact the demand curve that we have been using throughout this chapter.

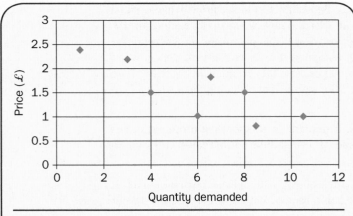

Figure 2.7    Plot of demand and price

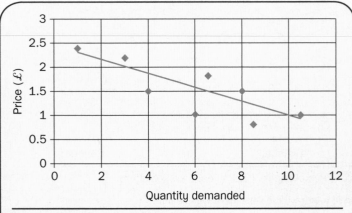

Figure 2.8    Adding in the trend line

By using mathematical techniques known as *econometrics*, the trend line can be analysed and manipulated to provide an estimate of the price elasticity of demand. Knowing that unit elasticity is optimal, product managers can then make an informed decision about whether to raise or lower prices. In your working life you are unlikely ever to calculate the elasticity of demand for a product, but being able to understand the concept will be very important.

Going one step further, competitors within a product category can use price promotion activities to analyse cross-price elasticity. It is then possible to understand the degree to which consumers are price sensitive between competing brands. If there is a high degree of cross-price elasticity, then price discounts may be effective in attracting new customers, whereas a low cross-price elasticity would suggest that price discounts are an ineffective and expensive means of attracting new customers. Take the data in Table 2.4 as an example. Brand A could be the leading brand in the biscuits, pizzas or soft drinks category. Brand B is a much weaker competitor. Brand B reduces its price by over a half for a period of one week. The price reduction for Brand B does cause some customers to switch over from Brand A. However the change in demand is not particularly large and in percentage terms is much less than the percentage change in B's price. The cross-price elasticity is therefore calculated at 0.33, which would suggest that Brands A and B are substitutes, but many customers of Brand A are not price sensitive. In commercial terms Brand B has to question whether a price promotion is profitable, unlikely, and perhaps more important, how Brand A has managed to lock in customers for what is likely to be a fairly generic product within the biscuits, pizza or soft drinks category.

## Big data

The increasingly digital and online world is generating greater amounts of data. Commercial use of these data is increasingly helping firms to understand who their customers are and what tastes and preferences they have. We are all familiar with products we have searched for appearing as adverts on the pages we view online. This is because cookies follow online shoppers and help advertisers target customers who are interested in their products.

Box 2.6 provides an insight into how the UK's leading radio station is using new forms of data to assess demand for music. Using this information enables the station to pick the songs to play which are most likely to appeal to their target listener. A decade ago these data would not have been available to the radio station; they would have relied on the Top 40 chart positions. These new data sources provide good indications of demand for music and more importantly the data are free!

## Product life cycle and pricing

The preceding discussion analysing elasticity and total revenue for the most part neglects the time-varying nature of competition and elasticity. When a new and innovative product emerges onto the market, it faces very few competitors. In the technology industry, BlackBerry was a leader in bringing email, Internet and telecommunications to the mobile market. But this lead was quickly chased down by Apple and its iPhone, which then faced

**Table 2.4** Cross-price elasticity example

| | Original demand for A | Demand for A when B reduces its price | Change in demand | Percentage change in demand | Cross-price elasticity |
|---|---|---|---|---|---|
| Brand A | 256956 | 211572 | −45384 | −0.18 | 0.33 |
| | Original price for B | Discount price for B | Change in price | Percentage change in price | |
| Brand B | £1.28 | £0.60 | −0.68 | −0.53 | |

## Box 2.6
## Demand for music

### How does Radio 1 decide which songs to get behind?

A strong wind sweeps through Portland Place in central London. Behind various locked doors and black-suited security guards, 12 people are meeting to decide the future of British music. This is the Radio 1 playlist committee, a meeting so covert that it took several hundred emails for me to be allowed to sit in on it. I'm here to find out how and why artists make the cut.

At the head of the meeting table sits George Ergatoudis. He's funny, he's smart, and—as Radio 1's head of music—he's the most powerful man in the music industry. Ergatoudis decides whether your band gets daytime airplay on the biggest radio station in the country (Radio 1 reaches 12 million listeners a week, including 42 per cent of all 15- to 24-year-olds, and its Facebook community numbers 15 million). Ergatoudis, therefore, decides whether you're going to make it commercially or be exiled to the darkest corners of the musical underground.

The playlist committee's job is to choose around 40 records each week for repeated daytime play (A-list records get 25 plays a week, B-list 15, and C-list eight to 10).

After deciding whether to keep current playlisted tracks, the discussion moves on to new additions. A snatch of each song blares through speakers before Ergatoudis lists the artist's YouTube views, Soundcloud hits, Shazam ratings, Twitter followers and Facebook likes.

'[Indie foursome] Wolf Alice's Moaning Lisa Smile video has had 15,000 views on YouTube and they've got 11,000 followers on Twitter,' Ergatoudis tells the room. 'James, you want to go first?' 'We really love them on the show,' James, who is Fearne Cotton's producer, says. 'It's something we can play, which is a first for them.'

They move on to Victory Line by Cambridge rock band Lonely the Brave. 'So far no official video on YouTube,' says Ergatoudis. 'Twitter followers 12,000 [quite low].' Natasha points out that Lonely the Brave have been nominated for a Kerrang award, 'so they have people backing them.' 'It sounds like Feeder to me,' offers Matt, Nick Grimshaw's producer. 'It's a bit dirgy. I'd take Wolf Alice over it, there's a bigger audience demand for them online.'

From *The Guardian*. 25 May 2014. Radio 1's playlist secrets uncovered: the battle of the "brands". Nadia Khomami.
© Guardian News & Media Ltd 2015

competition from Google Android phones. In the automobile industry, Renault was the first to convert a Mégane into a Scénic and create the MPV segment of the market, but Citroën soon followed with a Picasso, Ford has a C Max and Toyota has its Verso range. Successful innovation spawns imitation and aggressive competition as the market grows.

Eventually consumers will become tired of old designs and concepts. Newer models and ideas will emerge and sales will track the latest fashion. Demand for iPhone-type products and MPVs will fall, competitors will leave the market and competition will become less severe. These arguments are captured in the concept of a product life cycle, which is illustrated in Figure 2.9.

Successful products go through four phases of the product life cycle: introduction, growth, maturity and decline. (Unsuccessful products never pass introduction.) At each stage of the product life cycle the number of competitors is different. This leads to differing substitutability and differing elasticities of demand for the products.

### Pricing at launch

In the introduction stage, an innovative product is likely to be unique and face few, if any, competitors. For early adopters who wish to be seen with the latest technology, demand will be price inelastic. Firms could, therefore, seek to price high in order to capture the high demand from this set of consumers.

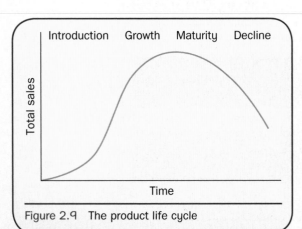

Figure 2.9    The product life cycle

### Pricing during growth

In the growth phase, companies who have witnessed the success of the innovative product also join the market. This increases competition and substitutability and increases the elasticity of demand. Recognizing the inverse relationship between price and consumers' willingness to demand, firms can seek to gain a dominant position by cutting prices in the hope of gaining market share. Under this strategy firms are trading a revenue-maximizing strategy for a sales-maximizing strategy. This could be temporary: maximizing sales and market coverage in the short run and winning the hearts and minds of customers, only to then exploit this commercial position in the long run with a strategy which maximizes revenues.

### Pricing during maturity

The ferocity of competition is most acute during the mature phase of the cycle, sales are at a peak and the market can be supplied by the largest number of competitors. The potential for a high degree of price elasticity in the mature phase of the cycle provides a basic rationale for the sales-maximization strategy during the growth phase—gain market share, cut out competition or face the consequences of merciless price competition in the mature phase of the cycle. High price elasticity means little control over pricing, as competitive pressures force the price down to the lowest possible level.

### Pricing during decline

In the decline phase of the market, consumers will begin to leave the market. In response, some firms will also exit, seeking better commercial opportunities elsewhere. Competition will fall and the degree of price sensitivity among consumers will diminish. Firms remaining in the market will see the elasticity of demand begin to become more inelastic, and an element of price stability and, hopefully, price rises, might occur. Therefore, throughout the product life cycle the pricing strategy has to be reactive to the changing competitive nature of the market.

## 2.7 Business application: pricing strategies ii—extracting consumer surplus

### Consumer surplus—the island of lost profits

Here is a true but curious thought: when you buy a product you are nearly always willing to pay *more* for it. This is the concept of **consumer surplus**.

> Consumer surplus is the difference between the price you are charged for a product and the maximum price that you would have been willing to pay.

For example, you may have been willing to pay £750 for a flight to Australia, but you manage to find a flight for £500. Your consumer surplus is £250.

Figure 2.10 illustrates the idea of consumer surplus using the demand curve. You are charged £500, but you are willing to pay £750. Indeed, in the market there may be some consumers who would be willing to pay even more than you. The entire amount of consumer surplus in the market is the area under the demand line down to the price charged of £500. This area represents the amount each consumer would be willing to pay in excess of the price charged.

Consumer surplus represents a benefit for consumers, but clearly for a firm it represents missed profits, because you were willing to pay £750 and were only charged £500. This is not good. So, as a business person, how do you discover a consumer's true willingness to pay and charge them accordingly?

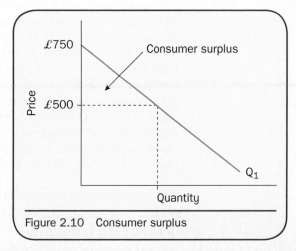

Figure 2.10    Consumer surplus

## Price discrimination

> **Price discrimination** is the act of charging different prices to different consumers for an identical good or service.

In order for a firm to extract consumer surplus, it needs to undertake **price discrimination**—the act of charging different consumers different prices for the same good. For price discrimination to be successful, three conditions must exist. First, the firm must have some control over its prices: it therefore cannot face a perfectly elastic demand line. Economists refer to this as having some degree of market power in setting prices. Second, the firm must be capable of identifying different groups of consumers who are willing to pay different prices. Third, resale of the good or service must be prohibited. If it isn't, a consumer who buys at a low price can then sell to a consumer who is willing to buy at a high price. The profits from price discrimination then flow to the consumer, rather than the firm. Economists identify first-, second- and third-degree price discrimination.

### First-degree price discrimination

Under first-degree price discrimination, each consumer is charged exactly what they are willing to pay for the good or service. This is unlikely to work in practice because it would involve each customer freely admitting to the top price that they would be willing to pay. For example, an airline might line up all of its passengers and ask them to write on a large card the price they would be willing to pay to fly on the aircraft. The passengers would then be admitted onto the aircraft in price order. Highest first, lowest last. Those who bid too low may not fly if the aircraft is full. However, passengers might not write a truthful price and why should they? In addition, the entire process is very costly in terms of time and administration to carry out.

First-degree price discrimination is therefore seen to be difficult to carry out in practice. Instead, a seller looks for cues or signals of a consumer's willingness to pay. For example, a builder, plumber or electrician might charge for work based on the type of car parked on the drive. Car sales people are trained to look at items worn by a potential buyer, such as the watch, coat, clothes and even areas where they live. These all provide reasonable, but imperfect, signals of someone's ability to pay and perhaps willingness to pay. Finally, there is the use of auctions, where each potential buyer is forced to bid for an item. In bidding, each buyer is communicating their willingness to pay. The highest bidder wins when the price is above every other bidder's willingness to pay—that is, every other bidder has no consumer surplus. However, auctions are costly to organize, only one sale at a time occurs and there is no guarantee that bidders will attend.

### Second-degree price discrimination

Under second-degree price discrimination, consumers are charged according to the number of units they buy. For example, gas, electricity and telephones tend to be offered under two-part tariffs. The first part is a fixed element to cover the cost of the infrastructure. The second part covers the cost of using additional units of electricity, gas, etc. If the fixed element is £10 per month and each unit costs £0.1, then a user of 100 units a month is charged £10 + (100 × £0.1) = £20. Taking account of the fixed element, the cost per unit is £20/100 = £0.2. Now consider someone who uses 200 units: their monthly bill is £10 + (200 × £0.1) = £30, which equates to a cost per unit of £30/200 = £0.15. The higher user gains a discount of 25 per cent. But how does this extract the consumer surplus? The listed unit cost of £0.1 per unit is the price charged to all consumers. The fixed price element is set to extract the consumer surplus. Because the consumer surplus is not constant across all consumers, the fixed element can also be varied across consumers through the provision of pricing menus. High users with a presumably high willingness to pay are offered a high fixed access price, but a low cost per unit. Low users with a presumably low willingness to pay select a low fixed access price but a high cost per unit. These pricing strategies are also used beyond the utility industry—for example, membership of gyms and golf clubs often includes a fixed and variable element.

### Third-degree price discrimination

Finally, we have third-degree price discrimination where each consumer group is charged a different price. This tends to occur where firms can identify different market segments for a similar product or service. In the case of airlines, young students are fairly flexible when it comes to flying around the world. If the plane is full on Monday, they can fly on Tuesday. In fact, demand by young travellers is elastic, as different days of travel provide substitutes. A business traveller is more likely to have very specific needs. The overseas meeting will take place on a specific date and they will need to be back in the UK very quickly to attend more meetings. These travellers are less sensitive to price and so exhibit price-inelastic demand.

Therefore, rather than offering each traveller the same product at the same price, you can segment the market. Offer two different products at different prices: cheap economy tickets with no frills to the student; and expensive business-class tickets to the business person, with comfortable seats, good food and access to airport lounges.

Premium television channels use the same idea. Instead of paying one fee for all digital channels, consumers are offered a menu. The base price includes the standard assortment of channels. The sport and movie channels are additional extras. Consumers that value sport highly will pay the higher price.

This is known as de-bundling the product. If the product is composed of many different parts, in our case various television channels, the offering is not sold as one bundle; rather, it is sold as a number of separate bundles, each with an individual price.

This stripping-out of valued products from the standard range enables companies to deal with the problem of consumer surplus by targeting customers with the combination of products that they value the most.

Similar tactics are arguably employed by Apple when marketing iPhones and iPads. Apple sells iPhones and iPads with different screen sizes and different amounts of memory. Rather than sell one version of the iPhone or iPad to all customers at one price, Apple instead sells a range of devices at different prices. This is an attempt by Apple to extract some of the available consumer surplus. Customers who are willing to pay a high price are those who are most likely to place the highest value on screen size and storage space. To access these features, such customers have to buy the most expensive iPhone or iPad. By meeting a variety of demand needs at various prices, Apple has become a profitable company. More important, by targeting a variety of segments, Apple has achieved revenue growth through the extraction of consumer surplus. The alternative route to revenue growth involves cutting prices and driving volumes. This approach can be self-defeating, requiring ever cheaper versions of the product to continually drive volume growth. By pricing high and meeting consumer needs across many segments, Apple has successfully managed a premium price strategy. Of course, this may fail if a recession cuts demand for premium goods, such as Apple's.

A summary of price discrimination is provided in Table 2.5.

**Table 2.5** Key features of each type of price discrimination

| Price discrimination | Key features |
| --- | --- |
| First degree | Each consumer is charged their maximum willingness to pay. All consumer surplus is reduced to zero. An auction would be an example. Very costly to implement in markets where there are many buyers. |
| Second degree | Customers pay a fixed amount and a unit amount. Often seen in utility markets such as gas and electricity. The combination of fixed and unit prices results in a price which varies across consumers according to usage. Easy to implement and enables some extraction of the consumer surplus. |
| Third degree | Products are differentiated according to features which are valuable to the consumer. Easy to implement if the product has multiple features and providers are skilled at product differentiation. Some consumer surplus can be extracted. |

## Box 2.7
## The Glazers continue to thrive while Manchester United flounder

Amid the reams of corporate boasting in the Glazer family's pitch to make $200 million from selling a small slice of Manchester United plc shares, a section trumpets to likely investors United's concerted raising of Old Trafford ticket prices since the Americans bought the club in 2005 and loaded it with their own £525 million debt.

Supporters are confronted with the legacy of £700 million drained out in interest, fees and bank charges by the Glazers' takeover, botched planning and underinvestment, which can be traced back to 2009. Then United reached the Champions League final, where they lost to Barcelona, then sold Cristiano Ronaldo to Real Madrid for £80 million, a windfall that was not reinvested in recruiting new players.

Edward Woodward was in 2005 a banker at JP Morgan and a senior architect of the Glazers' debt-loading takeover, including the high-interest £265 million 'payments in kind' loaned by hedge funds, which has cost United so far that scarcely believable £700 million. Woodward is now reinvented, installed by the Glazers as the club's vice-chairman, charged with actually running the famous club.

On 30 July, with the season about to start and player reinforcements clearly needed, the Glazers released their 167-page prospectus, to sell 12 million shares at $17 each in Manchester United plc—registered by them in the Cayman Islands tax haven and floated on the New York stock exchange. The document extols with familiar breathlessness the money made,

the 659 million global 'followers' for United and listing 29 of the club's 'global and regional' sponsors, from Chevrolet on the shirts, Japanese instant noodles company Nissin, to Cho-a Pharm, United's 'official pharmaceuticals partner in Korea and Vietnam'.

At Old Trafford, the Glazers' prospectus explains they have increased matchday income 'by restructuring the composition of our stadium'. A section has been corralled for some fans who still like to sing in the way they grew into as kids, when entry was cheap, but the prospectus does not mention that. Instead, it stresses modern Premier League reality: 'A particular emphasis on developing premium seating and hospitality facilities to enhance our overall matchday profitability.' The Glazers have also 'changed the composition of our general admission seats,' creating many different 'options' for buying a ticket and introducing, like most Premier League clubs, 'a categorized approach'.

This, the Glazers assure investors, means fans are now paying significantly more. 'Between the 2005–06 season [the first after their takeover] and the 2013–14 season,' the prospectus says, 'the weighted average general admission ticket prices for our Premier League matches played at Old Trafford increased at a compound annual growth rate of 4.4 per cent.' Or 41 per cent per year more following nine years of ownership by the Glazers.

From *The Guardian*. 20 August 2014. 'The Glazers continue to thrive while Manchester United flounder'. David Conn. © Guardian News & Media Ltd 2015

Box 2.7 highlights the importance of price discrimination in raising additional revenues for companies. When the Glazers purchased Manchester United using high levels of debt, they need cash flows to finance the interest payments. Identifying which fans would pay more for a ticket and developing new ticket options has enabled the club to raise revenues by more than 40 per cent over nine years.

## 2.8 Business data applications

Companies generally turn to market research companies when seeking data on how a market is growing, developing and changing. There are many market research companies in the world and some of the leading and popular sources of market research data are listed in Table 2.6. Your university may have online access to reports published by one of these companies.

When reviewing a market, sector or product category, a market research company is likely to use many of the frameworks developed in this chapter—for example revenues, output, the changing nature of substitutes and developing needs or tastes and preferences among consumers.

**Table 2.6** Market research companies

| | |
|---|---|
| AC Nielsen | http://www.acnielsen.com/ |
| Datamonitor | http://www.datamonitor.com/ |
| Euromonitor | http://www.euromonitor.com/ |
| Ipsos-Mori | http://www.ipsos-mori.com/ |
| Kantar | http://www.kantar.com/ |
| Mintel | http://www.mintel.com/ |

Mintel provides data on the UK soft drinks industry. The data in Figure 2.11 show that sales of carbonated soft drinks have increased over the period 2009–14 to £7.2 billion and are forecast to reach £8.4 billion by 2019.

The fall in sales in 2012 reflected a particularly cold and wet summer, which reflects a seasonal change in taste and preferences for cold drinks. The modest growth in sales through to 2014 reflects growing concern amongst health practitioners and consumers about sugar consumption, which can be particularly high in carbonated drinks. Appealing to these tastes and preferences for healthier drinks, the forecast growth in sales out towards 2019 is based on the presumption that innovations in sugar substitutes, e.g. stevia leaf extract used in Coca-Cola Life, will help to boost the attractiveness of carbonated drinks.

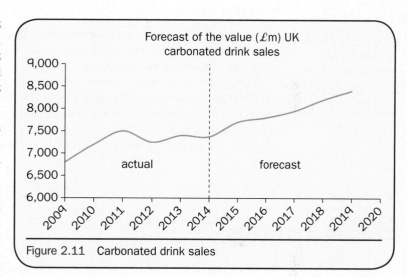

Figure 2.11    Carbonated drink sales

The data in Figure 2.12 show that both Coca-Cola and Diet Coke hold strong market shares. This information might lead to some belief that these two products have relatively inelastic demand. Consumers find these two products attractive and may not reduce their demand if price changed. This argument would need to be tested, but we might be more confident of price inelastic demand for Coca-Cola and Diet Coke than, say, for Own Label.

At the level of the market, elasticity and substitutes are a complex issue when considering carbonated drinks and depend very much on a concept we introduced earlier in this chapter: what is the definition of the market? We could consider substitutes only within the cola market. We could

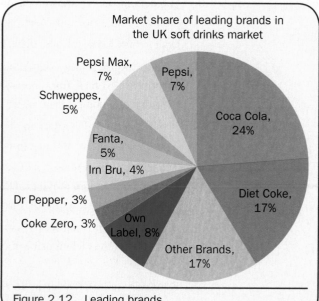

Figure 2.12    Leading brands

consider substitutes within the carbonated drinks market. We could go wider and consider substitutes within the soft drinks categories, which include tea, coffee, bottled water, sports drinks and juices. Broader still and we begin to include alcoholic beverages.

Relevance is important: which of these market definitions is most relevant to an understanding of which substitutes are attracting consumer demand? Growing tastes and preferences for healthy lifestyles, nutritious diets, international fruit flavours and natural ingredients are driving demand away from carbonated and particularly sugary drinks. Fresh juices, smoothies and botanical-flavoured drinks are all growing in importance at the expense of carbonated drinks and might help to explain the lack of growth in the mature carbonated drinks sector.

> Market penetration is the percentage of total consumers who purchase the product. A market penetration of 10 per cent would be low. Only 1 in 10 consumers buy the product.

In terms of income, the UK does not offer much scope for future growth. Income levels are already well developed and consumers can easily afford to purchase soft drinks, and price wars amongst supermarkets support lower affordability for the consumer. These arguments reflect a **market penetration** of 84 per cent. That is to say 84 per cent of all consumers are already consuming soft drinks on a regular basis.

One benefit of an economic understanding is that a business manager has a defined set of issues to consider when seeking to understand demand. What is currently happening to sales, revenues and prices, and what impact will substitutes, complements, income and taste and preferences have on future demand? Understanding price elasticity is also likely to be important. The difficult part then becomes finding and understanding the data. But with an economic framework you know what questions to ask and what data to find. You have a process which has a relatively sound academic basis behind it and you should then be capable of being an effective business decision maker.

## Summary

1.  A key characteristic of modern economic life is that companies set prices. With companies in such a powerful position, what is the optimal price to set for a product?

2.  The demand curve shows consumers' willingness to demand a product at various prices. As the price increases, consumers are less willing to demand the product.

3.  Demand is also seen to be influenced by the price of substitutes and complements.

4.  Substitutes are rivals; complements are products that are purchased together. As a substitute becomes more expensive, demand for the rival product will increase. As the price of a complement rises, demand for the remaining product will fall.

5.  Rising income will lead to an increase in demand for normal goods. But it will lead to a fall in demand for inferior goods.

6.  The tastes and preferences of consumers change over time. As goods become popular, consumers move into the market. As products become unfashionable, consumers leave the market and demand falls.

7.  Price elasticity, income elasticity and cross-price elasticity measure how much demand changes when price, income or the price of a substitute or complement changes.

8.  If the percentage change in demand is greater than the percentage change in price, then demand is said to be elastic. If the percentage change in demand is less than the percentage change in price, demand is said to be inelastic.

9. Companies use the concept of elasticity when setting prices. If demand is elastic, reducing prices will lead to a rise in total revenue. When demand is inelastic, raising prices will lead to an increase in total revenue.

10. Companies measure the elasticity of demand by analysing mathematically what happens to sales when they offer promotional discounts in the market.

11. Consumer surplus is the difference between the price charged and how much a consumer would have been willing to pay. This difference represents lost profit.

12. It is possible to capture some consumer surplus by de-bundling product offerings. Consumers can be offered a base package but extras are offered at much higher prices.

## Learning checklist

You should now be able to:

- Draw a demand curve for a good or service
- Understand how changes in income, the price of substitutes and complements, tastes and price expectations shift the demand curve left or right
- Explain the concept of price elasticity of demand and understand the distinction between elastic and inelastic demand
- Understand and use income and cross-price elasticity to develop pricing strategies in relation to consumer income, substitutes and complements
- Explain how total revenue can be improved by understanding how elastic demand is for a good or service
- Explain how firms can develop strategies to access consumer surplus
- Understand where to gain market data and use economic ideas to understand the important trends within the data.

## Questions                                                    connect

1. Draw a demand line which illustrates the effect of a price reduction on consumers' willingness to demand.

2. Identify the main factors which can lead to a shift in demand.

3. If a consumer's willingness to demand a product is sensitive to a change in the price, then is their elasticity of demand elastic, or inelastic?

4. The price of pasta at the supermarket falls. What do you think will happen to the demand for rice?

5. Explain the difference between an inferior and a normal good.

6. How would you expect your consumption of normal and inferior goods to change over your lifetime?

7. Provide examples of your own consumption activities where your consumer surplus is high and also where it is small.

8. A successful advertising campaign has a slogan which is adopted by teenagers across your economy. Illustrate what will happen to the demand line for the product being advertised.

EASY

9. How does consumer surplus vary with elasticity? How might firms use this to their advantage?

EASY

10. Products that have low price elasticity have low prices and high volumes. Products that have high elasticity have smaller volumes and higher profit margins. Do you consider these statements to be true?

11. Assess how easy it is for firms to measure the elasticity of demand for a given good or service.

INTERMEDIATE

12. List five products that you think are price elastic. List five products that you think are price inelastic.

13. Is consumer surplus greater under elastic or inelastic demand?

14. How would you advise a company to go about changing the elasticity of demand for one of its products?

DIFFICULT

15. Using ideas relating to income elasticity, how would you build a portfolio or collection of products that would perform well when the economy was growing during a boom and contracting during a recession?

16. The diagram provided shows an inelastic demand curve (D). What will happen to revenue when price decreases from £10 to £4?

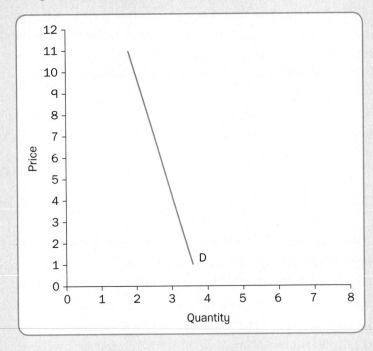

## Exercises

EASY

1. True or false?

    (a) An increase in income will cause an increase in demand for all goods.

    (b) Two goods are complements if an increase in the price of X results in an increase in demand for Y.

    (c) Price elasticity measures the responsiveness of the quantity demanded to the change in the price.

(d) The price elasticity is constant along the length of a demand line.

(e) If a car costs £15,000 and a consumer is willing to pay up to £18,000, then the consumer surplus is £3,000.

(f) If a product is price inelastic, revenues will rise following an increase in the price.

2. (a) Plot the demand curve and associated total revenue curve for Table 2.8.

- Calculate the elasticity at each price.

- What is the change in total revenue if the firm moves from a price of £8 to £4?

- Which price maximizes total revenue?

- What is the elasticity when revenue is maximized?

(b) As a result of rising income, demand increases at all prices by five units. Explain whether this good is normal or inferior.

(c) Is the new demand line more or less elastic than the original? Why do you think this should be the case?

**Table 2.7**

| Price (£) | 10 | 8 | 6 | 4 | 2 |
|---|---|---|---|---|---|
| Demand | 1 | 2 | 3 | 4 | 5 |
| Total revenue | | | | | |
| Elasticity | | | | | |

3. You have been hired by Louis Vuitton to advise the firm on its pricing strategy. Your brief is to cover each of the following:

(a) The benefit of raising its existing prices.

(b) The potential of broadening the brand's appeal through a gradual reduction in prices.

(c) The potential benefits of launching a new brand called 'Louis'. Who should this product be sold to and at what price level?

4. Using data from a market research company, produce a short report for a product category which identifies current demand patterns. In addition, identify the impact that substitutes, complements, income and taste and preferences will have on future demand patterns.

# Firms in the marketplace

## Chapter contents

## Learning outcomes

By the end of this chapter you should be able to:

| Economic theory | | Business applications | |
|---|---|---|---|
| LO1 | State the difference between the short and the long runs | LO7 | Demonstrate why low pricing and high-volume sales strategies, deployed by budget airlines, reflect high fixed costs |
| LO2 | Arrange costs into variable, fixed and total costs | LO8 | Discuss why qualification for the Champions League by leading football clubs is a strategy for dealing with the high cost of owning and employing footballers |
| LO3 | Define the concepts of marginal product and marginal costs | | |
| LO4 | Explain the law of diminishing returns | | |
| LO5 | Identify economies of scale | LO9 | Identify when a firm should close down |
| LO6 | Explain the concept of minimum efficient scale | LO10 | Conduct research on labour costs and productivity |

## At a glance    Cost theory

### The issue

All companies need to manage their costs as an important step towards making a profit. A company's costs are related to the purchase of economic resources which we discussed in Chapter 1. Costs are therefore linked to the purchase of raw materials, labour, capital and the cost of financial support from entrepreneurs (company owners). Some economic resources can be extremely expensive, and having a clear business model for managing the level of costs and ensuring a commercial return are essential. For example, world-class footballers cost in excess of £50 million, and the Superjumbo A380 costs $264 million. Neither are cheap. So how does a business make money when using such expensive assets?

### The understanding

Such assets represent costs that do not vary with the level of output. The way to exploit such assets is to make them productive. The more games Ronaldo plays for Real Madrid, the cheaper per game he becomes. The more flights a plane flies, the cheaper per flight the plane becomes. Unfortunately, over short periods of time, volume may come up against a problem known as the 'law of diminishing returns', while in the long run firms can encounter an additional problem known as 'diseconomies of scale'. By the end of this chapter you will understand each of these problems and how costs can be managed in the short and the long runs.

### The usefulness

This chapter will enable you to understand why successful airlines sell their seats at low prices, why teams such as Manchester United are desperate to stay in the Champions League and why research and development (R&D)-intensive technology products need to conquer world markets.

## ( 3.1 )  Business problem: managing fixed and variable costs

### Economists categorize costs as being fixed or variable

Supermarket stores represent **fixed costs**. If the store attracts one shopper or 1,000 shoppers per day, the cost of developing and maintaining the store is fixed. However, the number of checkout staff does change with the number of shoppers and, therefore, represents a **variable cost**. The cost of developing Apple's iPhone was a fixed cost. Development costs do not increase if more iPhones are sold. Rather, the cost of producing more iPhones increases. Universities are a vast collection of fixed costs. The cost of lecture theatres, lecturers, library resources, central administration units and computer facilities is not hugely influenced by the number of recruited students. For example, the cost of lecturing to 50 students is the same as lecturing to 250 students.

> Fixed costs **are** constant. They remain the same whatever the level of output.
>
> Variable costs **change** or vary with the amount of production.

The nature of fixed and variable costs has enormous implications for business. As an example, consider the contrasting differences between employing workers in a fast-food restaurant and professional footballers.

Workers at fast-food restaurants are perhaps paid no more than £7 per hour. The majority of employed hours are on weekends, evenings or lunch times, periods when consumer demand is highest. This is because the employment of workers at a fast-food restaurant is linked to the demand for burgers. More workers are employed at lunch times and weekends when demand, and therefore the production of burgers, is highest. As a result, the cost of employing fast-food workers is a predominantly variable one. The wages paid rise and fall with the level of output. Ultimately, if demand for burgers drops dramatically, restaurants can generally terminate

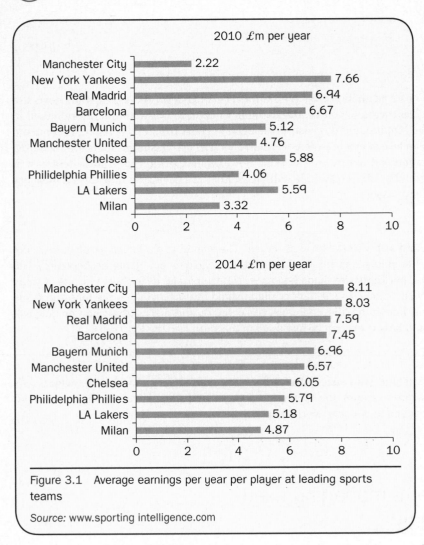

**2010 £m per year**

|  |  |
|------|-------|
| Manchester City | 2.22 |
| New York Yankees | 7.66 |
| Real Madrid | 6.94 |
| Barcelona | 6.67 |
| Bayern Munich | 5.12 |
| Manchester United | 4.76 |
| Chelsea | 5.88 |
| Philidelphia Phillies | 4.06 |
| LA Lakers | 5.59 |
| Milan | 3.32 |

**2014 £m per year**

|  |  |
|------|-------|
| Manchester City | 8.11 |
| New York Yankees | 8.03 |
| Real Madrid | 7.59 |
| Barcelona | 7.45 |
| Bayern Munich | 6.96 |
| Manchester United | 6.57 |
| Chelsea | 6.05 |
| Philidelphia Phillies | 5.79 |
| LA Lakers | 5.18 |
| Milan | 4.87 |

Figure 3.1    Average earnings per year per player at leading sports teams

*Source:* www.sporting intelligence.com

the employment of their workers by giving one month's notice.

The data in Figure 3.1 show that professional footballers in Europe are the highest-paid team players in the world. The highest paid in 2014 were professional footballers at Manchester City who were paid on average £8.1 million per year, or £156,000 per week. Notably, Manchester City has increased its wage bill by a factor of four since 2010; a massive increase in labour costs.

The wages of footballers may fall by a fraction if they are on the substitutes' bench or when they are injured. Similarly, their wage may increase with bonuses if goals are scored or after a specified number of first-team appearances. It is important to note that the bulk of a professional footballer's wages is not linked directly to the creation of output: namely, football games. Playing games or sitting on the subs' bench only leads to relatively small changes up or down in the wages paid to the player. The cost of employing professional footballers is, therefore, a predominantly fixed cost. A club's wages bill is changed very little by the number of games played. Furthermore, because footballers' contracts are fixed for anything up to five years, if the club wishes to terminate the employment of the player two years into the contract, it would have to pay three years' worth of compensation. These employment differences between footballers and fast-food workers are crucial.

The business problem associated with employing footballers, or fixed costs, is *not* that they cost huge sums of money, but that the *nature* of the cost *does not change* with *output* and *revenues*.

If the revenues received from fans and television rights drop, clubs still have to honour their contractual obligations with their players. In contrast, fast-food restaurants can change the number of workers when demand falls. The transfer of football players between clubs is the transfer of both an asset and a liability. The buying club gains what it believes is a good player, but at the same time it also commits itself to an increase in its fixed costs.

It is important for businesses to recognize the various components of their cost structures and to differentiate between fixed and variable costs. By doing so, they can then develop business models that accommodate the financial commitment associated with fixed costs. Box 3.1 highlights how shipping companies are turning to larger and larger ships. Such assets are enormous fixed costs, as is the fuel used to move them around the world. The CSCL Globe cost $175 million to build. By carrying more cargo on each journey the cost per unit falls and the ship becomes more competitive and potentially more profitable. When first designed, the CSCL could carry 18,400 containers but, during construction, design engineers

## Box 3.1
## A quarter of a mile long and heading for the UK—the world's largest ship

**CSCL Globe, the new holder of the title of the world's biggest container ship, is steaming towards Britain**

She's a quarter of a mile long, weighs 186,000 tonnes and is the biggest cargo ship on the seas. The CSCL Globe, the new holder of the contentious title of world's largest ship, set out on her maiden voyage from Shanghai on Monday and is scheduled to call at the port of Felixstowe early next month.

Owned by China Shipping Container Lines, the Globe measures 1,312ft from stem to stern—longer than four football pitches—and has a beam of 192ft—wider than each of the runways at Heathrow. But her crowning glory is the fact she can accommodate 19,100 standard 20ft shipping containers, known in the industry as 'TEU', short for Twenty Foot Equivalent Units.

The Globe is the same length and slightly narrower than the world's previous record-holder, Maersk's Triple-E class of ships. What gives the Globe the edge is that she sits 53ft deep in the water. This means her TEU capacity is higher than the Triple-E's 18,270 TEU.

If all the 20ft containers that the Globe can carry were stacked end to end on top of each other, they would reach 382,000ft into the sky—more than 13 times the height of Mount Everest.

CSCL said that the Globe is also capable of carrying 300 million tablet computers in a single load.

The Globe is the first of five ships ordered in a $700 million contract by the Chinese company from South Korean shipbuilder Hyundai Heavy Industries.

When cargo containers first become widespread in the 1950s, most ships could carry fewer than 1,000. However, they soon started growing. Panamax ships—so named because they were the largest that could fit through the Panama Canal—carry almost 5,000 TEU and were common by the 1980s.

The size of vessels is only really held back by the ability of ports to handle such massive vessels. When Maersk's Triple-E class came into service last year, there were only 16 ports in the world certified to handle them because the ships stood 20 storeys tall.

Trevor Blakeley, chief executive of the Royal Institution of Naval Architects, said: 'Ship owners will want them as big as they can be and as long as there is a dock big enough to build them in and enough steel there's no theoretical limit on the size they can become.'

But despite ships growing ever bigger, they are also slowing down.

Marc Pauchet, a senior analyst at Braemar ACM Shipbroking, said: 'They are not being built to go as fast now. They used to go much faster to deliver their cargos faster. Since the financial crisis they have slowed down—slow steaming means they burn less oil and save money.'

From *The Telegraph*. 9 December 2014. 'A quarter of a mile long and heading for the UK - the world's largest ship'. Alan Tovey. © Telegraph Media Group Limited (2014)

figured out how to increase the capacity to 19,000 containers. A 3 per cent improvement in carrying capacity may not sound like a lot, but everything helps when trying to transport more containers to recover a $175 million build cost. Once you own a large ship you need a route which can provide lots of cargo. A standard journey for the ship is from China, to Felixstowe (UK), then Rotterdam (Holland), then Hamburg (Germany), then Zeebrugge (Belgium) then back to Rotterdam (Holland) to refill, then back to China.

By the end of this chapter you will understand how to manage high fixed-cost structures highlighted by our initial discussion. But in order to achieve this, you need to develop a broader understanding of cost theory.

## 3.2  The short and long runs

We will begin by considering a firm that employs two factors of production: labour in the form of workers and capital in the form of computers and office space.

If a firm needs to increase its level of output in the **short run**, it is fairly easy to employ more workers. Agencies specializing in temporary employment are able to offer

> **Short run** is a period of time where one factor of production is fixed. We tend to assume that capital is fixed and labour is variable.

> **Long run** is a period of time when all factors of production are variable.
>
> **Total product** is the total output produced by a firm's workers.
>
> **Marginal product** is the addition to total product after employing one more unit of factor input. In economics, marginal always means 'one more'.
>
> **Task specialization** occurs where the various activities of a production process are broken down into their separate components. Each worker then specializes in one particular task, becoming an expert in the task and raising overall productivity.

suitable candidates within a day, or even an hour. In contrast, it is not as easy to expand the amount of office space. It takes time to find additional buildings, arrange the finance to purchase the buildings, and then fit out the buildings with suitable furniture and equipment. The problem also exists when trying to downsize. It is fairly easy to lay off workers, but it takes time to decommission a building and sell it to some other user. Therefore, only in the **long run** are all factors of production seen to be variable.

Given our business problem, we should not confine our thinking to capital as the only fixed factor of production. Clearly, the nature of employment can make labour fixed. Contracts signed by footballers, company chief executives and many academics are for a fixed period of time. Contracts for fast-food workers and many other types of work are open-ended, with the employer and employee given the right to terminate the relationship with, typically, one month's notice. In the latter case, the employment of labour is reasonably variable, whereas for footballers labour is fixed.

A reasonable question is, how long is the long run? The answer is, it depends. For some companies it can be very long. Airlines place orders with aircraft suppliers up to five years in advance, while an Internet company might be able to buy an additional Internet server system within a week and double its output capacity.

However, an important issue is to understand how costs behave in the short and long runs. In the next two sections we will see how in the short run costs are determined by the fixed amount of capital being exploited by more workers, while in the long run costs are influenced by varying the amount of capital.

##  The nature of productivity and costs in the short run

### Productivity in the short run

If we are interested in knowing how the level of costs changes with the level of output, then we need to consider more than just the cost of employing labour and capital. We are also interested in understanding how the productivity of labour and capital changes. If labour becomes more productive, then output increases for any given amount of cost.

In assessing productivity, we need to distinguish between **total product** and **marginal product**.

Consider the following. An online supplier of electrical goods has two vans for deliveries, the fixed factor of production. The firm can also employ up to 10 workers, the variable component. The total product and marginal product at each level of employment are detailed in Table 3.1. When the firm employs one worker, total product is 40 delivered items per day. This worker has to collate the orders, pick the items from the warehouse, package them for delivery, print off invoices, load the van, deliver the items and then deal with any enquiries and returned items. When the firm employs a second worker, total output increases. This second worker can utilize the additional van and may specialize in dealing with enquiries and returns. When the third worker is employed, they do not have access to a van, but they could help by specializing in collating orders, picking and packing. This again would help to raise output. The fourth worker might load vans and print invoices. The fifth worker might then help the third by specializing in picking orders from the warehouse, and so on and so on. The important point is that task specialization helps to raise productivity, as evidenced by the increasing marginal product for workers two, three and four, but thereafter diminishes. There is only so much **task specialization** that can occur without leaving a worker without a full day's work. Workers five, six and seven, and onwards, will be filling the remainder of their working day by answering emails, checking their text messages, making coffee and collecting sandwiches for lunch—activities which do not raise the total product of the firm.

**Table 3.1** Total and marginal product of labour with a fixed amount of capital

| Labour input (workers) | Total product (number of deliveries) | Marginal product of labour (number of deliveries) |
|:---:|:---:|:---:|
| 1 | 40 | 40 |
| 2 | 90 | 50 |
| 3 | 145 | 55 |
| 4 | 205 | 60 |
| 5 | 255 | 50 |
| 6 | 295 | 40 |
| 7 | 325 | 30 |
| 8 | 345 | 20 |
| 9 | 355 | 10 |
| 10 | 360 | 5 |

The productivity of all the workers in our example is constrained by the number of vans the firm uses. With only two vans, there is an upper limit to how many orders can be met per day, no matter how much task specialization occurs at the warehouse.

Most working environments are characterized by a mixture of workers and capital, in various forms: lecturers and lecture theatres, office staff and computers, fast-food workers and burger grills. The relationship depicted in Figures 3.2 and 3.3 is therefore very important and economists know it as the **law of diminishing returns**.

The law of diminishing returns is highlighted by the marginal product of labour (see Figure 3.3). When we have a fixed factor of production, such as capital, and we add workers to the production process, these workers can exploit an underutilized resource. So, the marginal product rises. When we begin to over-resource the

> The law of diminishing returns states that, as more of a variable factor of production, usually labour, is added to a fixed factor of production, usually capital, then at some point the returns to the variable factor will diminish.

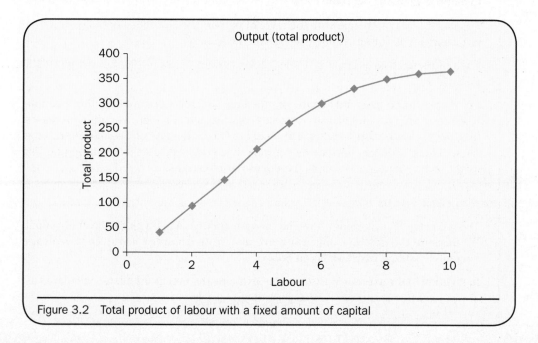

Figure 3.2  Total product of labour with a fixed amount of capital

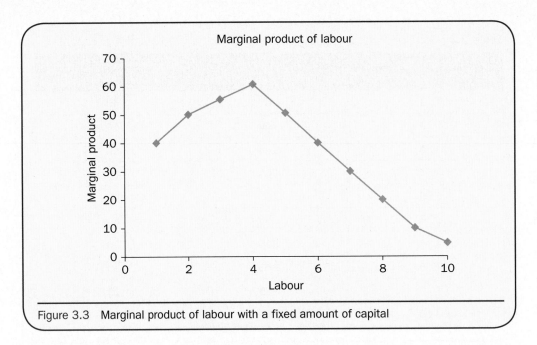

Figure 3.3 Marginal product of labour with a fixed amount of capital

production process with too much labour, there is no more capital to utilize. As a result, the marginal product begins to fall. This is the point at which the law of diminishing returns occurs. In our particular example, additional workers are able to exploit the vans and become more productive. But once we begin to employ more workers, and there are not enough vans, the productivity of labour must begin to fall.

## Costs in the short run

Now that we have an understanding of how productivity changes, we need to begin to think about how costs behave. In the short run, we have three types of cost: variable, fixed and **total costs**.

Variable costs change with the level of output. This was picked up when we discussed the fast-food workers. The higher the level of output, the more labour we employ and the higher the amount of variable cost.

Fixed costs do not change with the level of output. If we produce nothing, or a very large amount of output, fixed costs remain the same.

Each of these costs is listed in Table 3.2 for various levels of output, and plotted in Figure 3.4.

Fixed costs are represented as the orange line, which is horizontal. In this example, fixed costs are constant at £30. Variable costs rise, slowly; then, as output increases, they begin to rise more quickly. This simply reflects the law of diminishing returns. As additional workers become less productive, costs rise quicker than output. The total cost line in purple is simply fixed plus variable costs.

## Average costs

The next step is to consider how the cost per unit changes with the level of output. We measure the cost per unit using average costs (**average total cost, average variable cost** and **average fixed cost**).

In addition to the average costs, we also examine the **marginal costs**, calculated as:

$$\frac{\text{Change in total cost}}{\text{Change in output}}$$

**Total costs** are simply fixed costs plus variable costs.

**Average total cost** is calculated as total cost divided by the number of units produced.

**Average variable cost** is calculated as total variable cost divided by the number of units produced.

**Average fixed cost** is calculated as total fixed costs divided by the number of units produced.

**Marginal cost** is the cost of creating one more unit.

**Table 3.2** Short-run costs

| Output | SFC (short-run fixed costs) | SVC (short-run variable costs) | STC (short-run total costs) |
|---|---|---|---|
| 0 | 30 | 0 | 30 |
| 40 | 30 | 22 | 52 |
| 90 | 30 | 38 | 68 |
| 140 | 30 | 48 | 78 |
| 180 | 30 | 61 | 91 |
| 210 | 30 | 79 | 109 |
| 235 | 30 | 102 | 132 |
| 255 | 30 | 131 | 161 |
| 270 | 30 | 166 | 196 |
| 280 | 30 | 207 | 237 |

(Since the marginal cost is the cost of producing one more unit, the change in output should be 1.)

However, firms rarely increase output by one unit and in our example output initially increases from 0 to 40 units of output: therefore, by dividing the change in total cost by the change in output of 40, we can approximate the marginal cost, or the cost of making one more unit:

$$\text{Marginal cost} = (52 - 30)/(40 - 0) = 0.55$$

The calculations for average and marginal costs are listed in Table 3.3, and plotted in Figure 3.5.

The average variable and average total cost curves are both U-shaped. This simply reflects the law of diminishing returns. Towards the left of the figure, the output is low. At this low level of output, we have a small number of workers using the fixed capital. As we employ more workers, productivity increases and costs per unit fall. As the number of workers continues to increase, however, the law of diminishing returns predicts that productivity will fall. As a consequence, the cost per unit will increase. This point is also picked up in the marginal cost curve, which is the cost of producing one more unit. As labour becomes less productive, then costs of producing additional units must rise.

### Relationship between the average and the marginal

It should also be noted that the marginal cost curve cuts through the minimum points of the average total and average variable cost curves. This is because of a simple mathematical

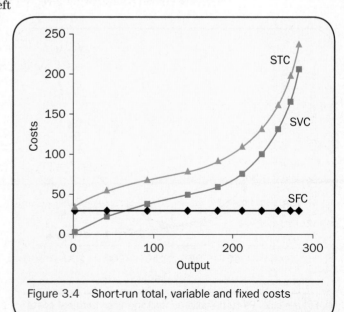

Figure 3.4   Short-run total, variable and fixed costs

**Table 3.3**　Short-run average and marginal costs

| Output | SAFC (short-run average fixed costs) | SAVC (short-run average variable cost | SATC (short-run average total costs) | SMC (short-run marginal costs) |
|---|---|---|---|---|
| 0 | | | | |
| 40 | 0.75 | 0.55 | 1.30 | 0.55 |
| 90 | 0.33 | 0.42 | 0.76 | 0.32 |
| 140 | 0.21 | 0.34 | 0.56 | 0.20 |
| 180 | 0.17 | 0.34 | 0.51 | 0.33 |
| 210 | 0.14 | 0.38 | 0.52 | 0.60 |
| 235 | 0.13 | 0.43 | 0.56 | 0.92 |
| 255 | 0.12 | 0.51 | 0.63 | 1.45 |
| 270 | 0.11 | 0.61 | 0.73 | 2.33 |
| 280 | 0.11 | 0.74 | 0.85 | 4.10 |

relationship between the marginal and the average. Assume your average examination score is 50. Your next exam is your marginal exam. If you gain a score of 70, then your average will increase. But if you gain a score of 20, your average will come down. Therefore, whenever the marginal is lower than the average, the average will move down; and whenever the marginal is higher than the average, the average will rise. Therefore, the marginal cost curve has to cut through the average cost curves at their minimum point.

### Average fixed costs

The average fixed cost curve is different. It is always falling as output increases. This reflects simple mathematics. If fixed costs are £100 and we produce 10 units, the average fixed costs are £100/10 = £10. But if we increase output to 100 units, then average fixed costs become £100/100 = £1. Accountants refer to this as 'spreading the overhead'. As fixed costs are spread over a larger level of output, the fixed costs per unit will fall.

This relationship has important implications for managers. Consider the case of the Super Jumbo Airbus A380. Development costs are thought to have been around €12 billion. If we assume Airbus found two customers to buy the A380, the average fixed cost would be €12/2 billion = €6 billion. Therefore, in order for Airbus to break even, it will require its two customers to pay at least €6 billion; and then there are the variable costs of making the aircraft! Airbus has orders for 236 A380s, up from 100 in 2008, which helps to reduce the fixed cost per unit. But at a list price of €250 million, Airbus will have to sell many more A380s in order to recoup its variable costs of manufacturing and its fixed costs of development.

The existence of large fixed costs also presents buyers with a negotiating opportunity. Firms with large fixed costs need volume. If you as a

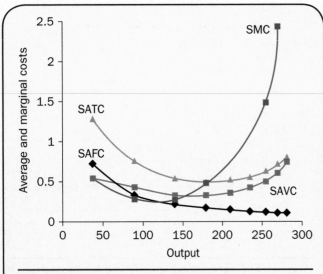

Figure 3.5　Plotted short-run average and marginal costs

buyer can provide large volumes of sales, then you are more valuable and should use this to negotiate a larger discount. Figure 3.6 presents order data for the A380. The first A380 was delivered in 2008 and, by 2014, 152 had been delivered. But look at the order data in 2007, the year before the first A380 was delivered. In 2007 Airbus had orders for 189 A380s. Thirteen were made in the first year and even after six years of production Airbus have still not delivered all the A380s that were ordered before the first was ever made. In the run up to 2008 airline companies placed bulk orders for the A380 and negotiated large discounts for providing volume to the A380 project. Emirates airlines is by far the biggest buyer of A380s, placing orders over many years which total around 140, often gaining

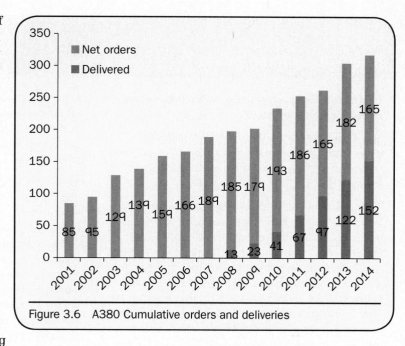

Figure 3.6    A380 Cumulative orders and deliveries

discounts which are rumoured to be close to 50 per cent off list price! China Southern has ordered 5, and will have gained a discount, but nothing like the 50 per cent Emirates managed.

## 3.4 Output decisions in the short run

Now that we have an understanding of how costs behave in the short run, we can begin to examine the firm's output decisions. In Chapter 5 we will see how we can find the level of output that will maximize the firm's profits. However, at this point we merely wish to show you when the firm will produce and when it will close down.

If the output is being sold at the same price to all consumers for £1.50, then the average revenue is also £1.50. If we now re-examine the short-run average total costs, SATC, in Table 3.3 and plotted in Figure 3.5, we can see that the maximum value for SATC is £1.30 at an output level of 40 units. As output grows, SATC drops to a minimum of £0.51. Clearly, therefore, at the current price of £1.50 the firm can make a profit at any output level.

Now consider two much lower prices, £0.45 and £0.30. At both prices the firm will make a loss as its minimum SATC is only £0.51, so its revenues will never be greater than its costs at either of these prices. But there is an important difference between the two scenarios. In the short run, the firm will operate and make a loss at prices of £0.45, but it will shut down and cease operating at prices of £0.30.

The understanding rests on whether or not the firm can make a positive contribution to its fixed costs. If the firm produces nothing, its fixed costs are £30 and its losses will also be £30. However, if the price is £0.45 there are output levels where the firm's average variable costs, SAVC, are less than £0.45. For example, at an output of 180 units, SAVC = £0.34. So, if the firm operates at 180 units of output, it can cover its variable cost per unit of £0.34 and have £0.45 − £0.34 = £0.11 per unit left over. Selling 180 units represents 180 × 0.11 = £19.80. The £19.80 can be used to make a contribution towards the fixed costs. So, by producing 180, the loss drops to £30 − £19.80 = £11.20, as opposed to a loss of £30 (the fixed costs) if it produced nothing.

However, when the price drops to £0.30 the firm cannot cover any of its variable costs. Therefore, if it did decide to operate, then, not being able to cover its entire wage bill, it would be adding to the losses generated by its fixed costs. Hence, the best the firm can do is to shut down and incur only the fixed-cost losses of £30.

## Box 3.2
## Recovering fixed costs

### Is Airbus's A380 a 'superjumbo' with a future or an aerospace white elephant?

Airbus executives knew they faced big questions about their biggest jet as they sat down to an annual showdown with the media at the plane maker's Toulouse base.

A late surge in orders meant Airbus could claim victory in the yearly sales battle with Boeing, landing 1,456 orders last year compared with its US rival's 1,432. But there was a specific matter that the press wanted to talk about: the growth, or lack thereof, in orders for the A380—Airbus's double-decker 'superjumbo'. The failure in 2014 to secure significant new orders for the giant four-engine airliner had fuelled rumours that the programme was in trouble because airlines preferred lower-cost, twin-engine jets.

The speculation intensified in December after an investor conference in London when Harald Wilhelm, chief financial officer at Airbus, raised the prospect of 'discontinuing' the A380—news that hit the company's shares. His words also earned Airbus a sharp rebuke from the A380's biggest customer, the airline Emirates. Sir Tim Clark, chief executive of the Gulf-based carrier, which has 140 of the jets in service or on order, warned that Emirates was 'on the hook' for the aircraft, 'with so much at stake'. The A380 makes up almost a quarter of the 200-plus jets in the airline's fleet.

Airbus is not concerned about the current size of the A380 market. 'We never said it was going to be a gigantic market,' Mr Leahy told reporters. 'But we absolutely dominate it. Some say, who cares about dominating a small market? We do, because it is a very good market and it is one that is going to grow.'

Airbus's forecast predicts a demand for 1,230 very large aircraft between now and 2033. However, others are not so sure of the A380's future. Saj Ahmad, chief analyst at StrategicAero Research, described Airbus's goal of breaking even on the jet this year as a 'red herring'.

'While Airbus may produce A380s this year which cost the same to sell them, the programme sports the worst financial balance in aviation history. Airbus has been selling this thing since 2000 to customers with delirious discounts to secure orders,' he said. 'That sort of discipline is never going to make the A380 break even on a total programme cost basis, let alone ever be profitable.' Others say that the A380 programme might break even once Airbus has sold round 450 jets. But Mr Ahmad says that may never happen: 'It's already looking technologically obsolete versus Boeing's 787 and 777X jets and even Airbus's own A350XWB. Mr Bregier had no choice but to speak up for the A380—not doing so would spook investors and airlines even more.'

Aviation analyst Howard Wheeldon added that Boeing's 747, which made its runway debut in the 1960s, had its best year of sales 25 years later and he had no doubt that the A380's future is assured, predicting its best year for sales will come in 2020, as passenger numbers continue to grow.

If forecasts about demand for air travel doubling every 15 years are right, Airbus could have made the right decision to 'go large' with the A380. Many passengers have already been won over by Airbus's superjumbo. Now the company just needs to find a way to convince more airline bosses.

From *The Telegraph*. 18 January 2015. 'Is Airbus's A380 a 'superjumbo' with a future or an aerospace white elephant?'. Alan Tovey. © Telegraph Media Group Limited (2015)

We can now go one step further. The marginal cost is the cost of producing one more unit. If the firm can receive a price that is equal to or greater than the marginal cost, then it can break even or earn a profit on the last unit. If the firm maximizes profits, clearly it will supply an additional unit of output when the price is equal to or greater than marginal cost. If we couple this argument with the previous point, that firms will not operate below short-run average variable cost, we can show, as in Figure 3.7, that the firm's supply curve is in fact the firm's short-run marginal cost curve above short-run average variable costs.

In Figure 3.8, we have a **supply curve** for firms A and B and the industry. Unlike the demand curve, the supply curve has a positive slope.

At each price, firm B is willing to supply more output than firm A. This is because the marginal cost at each output level is lower for firm B. At a price of £5, B is willing to supply 1,500 units; A is only willing to supply 1,000 units. Therefore, at all prices B is

> The supply curve depicts a positive relationship between the price of a product and firms' willingness to supply the product.

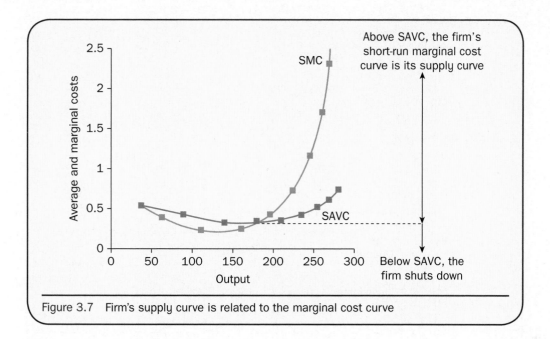

Figure 3.7  Firm's supply curve is related to the marginal cost curve

more willing to supply than A. The industry's willingness to supply is equal to the sum of A and B's willingness to supply.

Therefore, at a price of £5, the industry willingness to supply is 1,000 + 1,500 = 2,500.

The industry supply curve in Figure 3.8 is the sum of each firm's willingness to supply at each possible price.

Just as we discussed with the demand curve, we also need to think about the factors that will lead to a shift in supply:

- If more firms enter the market, then supply must shift out to the right with more industry output being offered for sale at any given price. Conversely, if firms close down and exit the market, then the supply curve must shift in to the left, with less industry output being sold at any given price.

- If the costs of labour, or other inputs, increase, profits must fall. As the potential to make profits decreases, firms will be less willing to supply and so the supply curve will move in to the left. Conversely, if input prices fall, the ability to make a profit increases and supply will shift out to the right.

## Box 3.3
## Theme parks

Theme parks offering thrilling rollercoaster rides often close down during the winter. We can now offer an economic explanation for why they close. The rides are capital and represent fixed costs. The staff who operate the rides and keep the theme park clean are the variable costs. During the summer months many people are willing to go to a theme park and pay the entrance fee. The revenues generated cover the theme park's fixed and variable costs. However, in the winter, when it is cold and wet, very few people are willing to go to the theme park.

The revenues generated by the theme park would be unlikely to cover the wages it would have to pay to its staff to open the park. It is, therefore, best for the theme park to close and incur no variable costs during the winter; and simply incur its fixed costs. If the theme park decided to stay open during the winter, its losses would rise since the wage bill would not be covered by the small number of paying visitors to the park. Firms, therefore, are only willing to supply output if revenues are greater than variable costs.

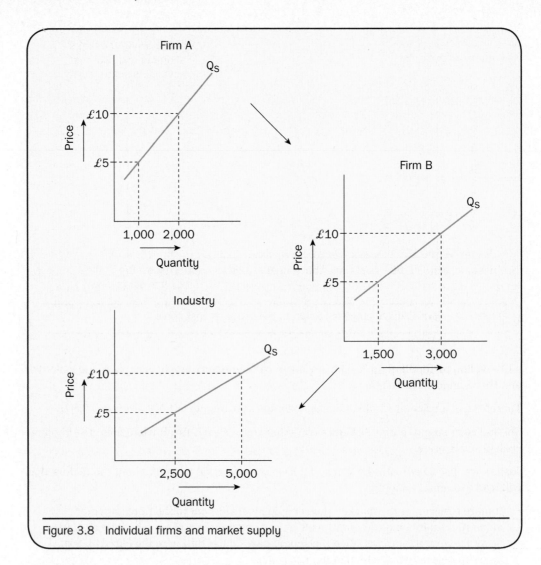

Figure 3.8　Individual firms and market supply

- If a new technology is invented that enables firms to be more productive, then their costs will fall. This makes profits increase and firms are willing to supply more. The supply curve will then move out to the right.

For firms A and B, as the price increases, willingness to supply also increases. At each price, firm B is more willing to supply than firm A. For example, at £5 A is willing to supply 1,000 units and B is willing to supply 1,500. The industry supply is simply the sum of A and B. So, at £5 the industry's willingness to supply is 1,000 + 1,500 = 2,500. Clearly, as more firms enter the industry, the industry's willingness to supply will increase and the industry supply curve will shift to the right. Similarly, as firms leave the industry, the willingness to supply will reduce and the industry supply curve will shift to the right.

## Elasticity of supply

The **elasticity of supply** is a measure of how responsive firms' output is to a change in the price and is measured as the percentage change in supply divided by the percentage change in the price. The elasticity of supply will always be positive because of the positive relationship between price and supply. Like the price elasticity of demand, values greater than 1 are defined as elastic and values between 0 and 1 are described as inelastic. A value of 0 would be perfectly inelastic and a value of infinity would be perfectly elastic.

Elasticity of supply is a measure of how responsive supply is to a change in price.

We can see from Figure 3.8 that firm B's willingness to supply is more price elastic than firm A. When the price rises from £5 to £10, B is willing to supply an extra 1,500 units; A is only willing to supply an extra 1,000 units.

The degree of supply elasticity is determined by the ability of firms to react to price changes. If firms are operating at full capacity, an increase in the price is unlikely to draw forward increased supply as firms simply cannot expand output. In contrast, if an industry has spare capacity, factories running below maximum capacity and access to additional sources of labour is relatively easy, then supply is likely to be more elastic, or responsive to an increase in the price. We will return to the importance of supply elasticity in Chapter 4 when discussing markets in more detail.

#  Cost inefficiency

Our discussion so far has assumed that firms are operating on the cost curve. This is troublesome, since some firms are more cost-effective than their rivals; and in addition some firms are better at raising productivity over time. In Box 3.4 the cost advantage of Ocado through its use of technology to improve the picking of groceries for customers is highlighted. Ocado has and continues to invest in innovative technology to boost its productivity. Notably in the online grocery market it is the only operator believed to be making a profit. Most of the traditional supermarkets who offer an online service report that this service operates at a loss.

## Box 3.4
### Ocado develops new robot system to pick and pack groceries

**Online supermarket files patent in US which cuts out need for warehouse aisles or the staff driving around them**

The online retailer Ocado is developing robots that could reduce its reliance on people to pick and pack groceries for shoppers.

In plans filed in an application to the US Patent and Trademark Office, Ocado describes a system that operates by using two types of robot mounted on a frame above the stacks of merchandise, removing the need for aisles to let people and machines travel around a warehouse. Taking out the aisles would mean Ocado, which delivers Morrisons and Waitrose groceries, could fit more goods into a smaller space, potentially improving efficiency and reducing costs.

It would also reduce the need for people to operate vehicles that move products around.

The company said: 'Ocado is always looking for ways to enhance its customer proposition through the development of industry-leading and proprietary technology. As a result, we file a number of patents each year but we may not choose to utilize everything that we patent. As the business grows in scale, we will continue to grow our workforce with a focus on providing the best and most efficient service to our customers.'

Automated warehouses have been in use for decades and Ocado already uses a variety of robots in its operations. Even the movement of the people working in its warehouses is guided by technology to ensure they work efficiently.

But existing systems based on removing containers from closely aligned stacks require mechanisms so expensive that they are rarely used, according to Ocado's patent application. It says its new system uses two independently operating robots to 'remove a target container quickly and with minimum use of resources'.

Ocado is investing heavily in technology as it tries to improve the efficiency of its operations. The company, founded by three former Goldman Sachs bankers in 2000, delivered its first profit in February after 15 years of investment in technology and warehouse systems.

The move into the black came after it signed a deal to deliver groceries for Morrisons. The company now wants to license and sell the technology it employs in its warehouses and distribution network to other retailers overseas.

From *The Guardian*. 7 May 2015. 'Ocado develops new robot system to pick and pack groceries'. Sarah Butler.
© Guardian News & Media Ltd 2015

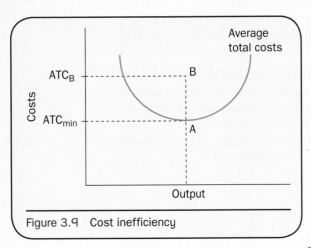

Figure 3.9   Cost inefficiency

If firms have the same productive technology, they have the same knowledge and manufacturing know-how. As such, they are assumed to share the same cost curves. However, if one firm pays more for its workers, or uses them less effectively, then this firm will operate off its cost curve, as illustrated in Figure 3.9.

Firms A and B are both operating at the output level which is associated with the lowest short-run average total cost. However, only A is operating on the curve and achieving minimum average total cost $ATC_{min}$. B has much higher costs and this reflects a significant degree of cost inefficiency and, as such, A has a cost advantage over its rival. The reasons why this can occur are numerous, and in the case of online groceries, Ocado achieves a point closer to A by investing in innovative, productivity-enhancing technology.

## 3.6  The nature of productivity and costs in the long run

> Returns to scale simply measure the change in output for a given change in the inputs.

In the long run, both capital and labour are variable. Firms can change the number of machines or the amount of office space that they use. Therefore, the law of diminishing returns does not determine the productivity of a firm in the long run. This is simply because there is no fixed capital in the long run to constrain productivity growth. So, in the long run, productivity and costs must be driven by something else. This something else is termed **returns to scale**.

Increasing returns to scale exist when output grows at a faster rate than inputs. Decreasing returns exist when inputs grow at a faster rate than outputs. Constant returns to scale exist when inputs and outputs grow at the same rate.

This is not complicated. Look at Figure 3.10: in quadrant 1, we have the short-run average total cost curve, SATC, with which we are familiar. Now consider adding more capital and labour to the production process.

When a firm changes its level of capital, e.g. machines, number offices or shops, it moves to a new short-run cost curve. If the investment in capital makes firm more efficient, then cost curve will move down to the right, as in quadrant 2. If investment in capital leaves productivity unchanged, as in quadrant 3, then there is no change in average costs. If capital investment makes the firm less productive, then average costs will increase, as in quadrant 4.

In so doing we have changed the scale of operation and we now have a new cost curve. In quadrant 2, we have the situation where the new cost curve $SATC_2$ moves down and to the right. The company can now produce the same level of output $Q_1$ for the lower average cost of $AC_2$. This is increasing returns to scale. As we increase inputs, outputs grow faster, so the cost per unit must fall. In quadrant 3, increasing the scale moves the cost curve $SATC_2$ to the right and leaves average costs constant, a case of constant returns to scale. In quadrant 4, increasing scale leads to the new cost curve $SATC_2$ shifting upwards and to the right, leading to an increase in costs, a case of decreasing returns to scale.

What economists tend to find in practice is that firms experience increasing, then constant and finally decreasing returns to scale: that is, firms move through quadrants 2, 3 and 4 in order. Therefore, the family of short-run cost curves can be put together and the long-run cost curve can be derived, as in Figure 3.11.

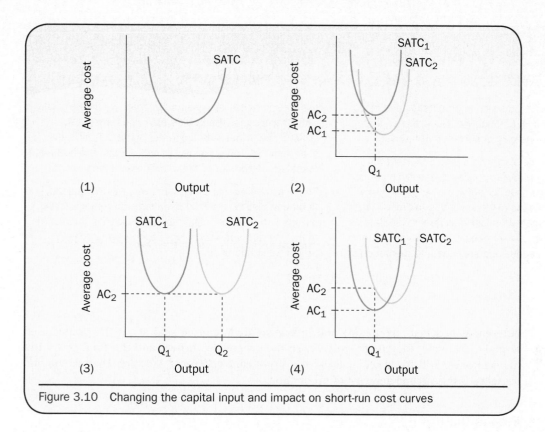

Figure 3.10  Changing the capital input and impact on short-run cost curves

The long-run average cost curve is simply a collection of short-run average cost curves, illustrating how costs change as fixed inputs.

The long-run average total cost curve, LATC, is a frontier curve. It shows all the lowest long-run average costs at any given level of output and is really nothing more than a collection of short-run cost curves. What we can clearly see, however, is that as we increase the scale of operation, the long-run average cost initially falls and then begins to increase. So, the long-run cost curve is also U-shaped. However, the reason for the U-shape is not the law of diminishing returns; rather, in the long run economies of scale are the important issue.

> Economies of scale cause long-run average costs to fall as output increases.

## Economies of scale: production techniques

**Economies of scale** exist for a number of reasons. Consider the production process associated with making Fords and Ferraris. At a Ford production facility, workers might be capable of making 1,000 cars in a 24-hour shift. Ferrari workers may only make 1,000 cars in a year. At massive levels of scale, Ford employs mass-production techniques: one person is responsible for fixing tyres, another for exhausts. This task specialization aids productivity and cuts costs. At Ferrari it is not possible to use mass-production techniques. The scale of operation is much lower. Therefore, as firms change their level of scale, they also change their production process and long-run costs fall.

Champagne can be ridiculously expensive, whilst prosecco can be much more affordable. Box 3.5 contains the writings of a sommelier (wine expert) about the key

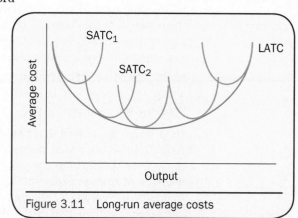

Figure 3.11  Long-run average costs

## Box 3.5
## Prosecco versus Champagne—what is the difference?

As a sparkling wine prosecco is both Italian and often cheaper than French Champagne. But are price and country of origin the only important differences?

Economies of scale also have a very important role to play. A sparkling wine can only be called Champagne if it comes from a specific region of France, contains specific grapes and is made according to the Champagne method. This last requirement creates a huge cost. Grapes are fermented in large vats, then bottled, sugar is added and secondary fermentation in the bottle creates the gas and bubbles we all associate with Champagne. The bottles are hand turned, the yeast sinks towards the cork, the bottle is frozen, the cork removed, the yeast is cleaned out and the bottle is resealed. Millions of bottles, millions of euros of cost.

Prosecco can be made the same way as Champagne, but it can also be made in large tanks and then carbon dioxide can be added. Then the producer fills thousands of bottles with sparkling wine. Economies of scale, good wine, good price.

differences between champagne and prosecco. Much can be said about the grapes used to make the wine, the land/terroir where the grapes are grown and the final taste. But the economist will focus on cost and the significant difference between champagne and prosecco is the method and cost of production.

## Indivisibilities

In order to operate as a commercial airline you have to buy a jumbo jet. Assume the jumbo has 400 seats and you plan to fly between Manchester and Dubai, but only manage to find 300 passengers a day. You cannot chop off the back of the plane to cut your costs! But if you increase your scale and buy a second plane and use this to fly between Dubai and Hong Kong, you might find another 100 passengers who wish to fly Manchester to Hong Kong, via Dubai. In essence, this is nothing more than spreading fixed costs. The same arguments can be made regarding professional corporate staff. A company may only need one accountant, one lawyer and one marketing executive. In a small company there are not many accounts to manage, many contracts to negotiate and sign, or many marketing campaigns to organize. However, as the scale of the company grows, the utilization of these expensive professional staff improves. The accountant manages more accounts and the lawyer oversees more contracts and, as a result, the cost per unit of output falls.

Box 3.6 highlights the construction of the world's tallest building, Burj Khalifa, Dubai. The indivisibility is land space. Once this has been purchased it can be increasingly exploited by building more floors. Air space is free, land space is not. Therefore, while often being monuments to engineering ingenuity and visually appealing, skyscrapers rest on the economic foundations of economies of scale. This is very true in areas of high population density and where land prices are high: New York, Shanghai, Taipei and Dubai—all places where skyscrapers are popular.

## Geometric relationships

Have you ever noticed that bubbles are always round? Engineers and business managers have. Bubbles are round because they provide the biggest volume for the smallest surface area. More specifically, volume grows at a faster rate than the surface area. Volume is a measure of storage capacity. So, if we need to create a tank to brew beer, and we decide to double the volume of the tank, the material needed to cover the surface area, the sides and bottom, will not double in size. Instead, it will grow at a slower rate. Hence, it becomes

## Box 3.6
## The world's tallest building: the Burj Khalifa, Dubai

**Burj Khalifa construction timeline**

| | |
|---|---|
| January 2004 | Excavation started |
| February 2004 | Piling started |
| March 2005 | Superstructure started |
| June 2006 | Level 50 reached |
| January 2007 | Level 100 reached |
| March 2007 | Level 110 reached |
| April 2007 | Level 120 reached |
| May 2007 | Level 130 reached |
| July 2007 | Level 141 reached—world's tallest building |
| September 2007 | Level 150 reached—world's tallest free-standing structure |
| April 2008 | Level 160 reached—world's tallest man-made structure |
| January 2009 | Completion of spire—Burj Khalifa tops out |
| September 2009 | Exterior cladding competed |
| January 2010 | Official launch ceremony |

**Construction highlights**

Over 45,000 m³ (58,900 cubic yards) of concrete, weighing more than 110,000 tonnes were used to construct the concrete and steel foundation, which features 192 piles buried more than 50 metres (164 feet) deep. Burj Khalifa's construction will have used 330,000 m³ (431,600 cubic yards) of concrete and 39,000 tonnes (43,000 ST; 38,000 LT) of steel rebar, and construction will have taken 22 million man-hours.

Exterior cladding of Burj Khalifa began in May 2007 and was completed in September 2009. The vast project involved more than 380 skilled engineers and on-site technicians. At the initial stage of installation, the team progressed at the rate of about 20 to 30 panels per day and eventually achieved as many as 175 panels per day.

The tower accomplished a world record for the highest installation of an aluminium and glass façade, at a height of 512 metres. The total weight of aluminium used on Burj Khalifa is equivalent to that of five A380 aircraft and the total length of stainless steel bull nose fins is 293 times the height of the Eiffel Tower in Paris.

In November 2007, the highest reinforced concrete core walls were pumped using 80 MPa concrete from ground level; a vertical height of 601 metres, smashing the previous pumping record on a building of 470 metres on the Taipei 101, the world's second tallest tower, and the previous world record for vertical pumping of 532 metres for an extension to the Riva del Garda Hydroelectric Power Plant in 1994. The concrete pressure during pumping to this level was nearly 200 bars.

The amount of rebar used for the tower is 31,400 tonnes—laid end to end this would extend over a quarter of the way around the world.

---

proportionately cheaper to build larger tanks than it does to build smaller tanks. Look around your lecture theatre—we expect it will be big.

## Diseconomies of scale

Long-run average costs will eventually begin to rise. The most obvious reason is that, as companies increase in size, they become more difficult to control and co-ordinate. More managerial input is required to run the business, and managers themselves require additional management. So, as the scale of the company increases, the average cost also increases. Excessive bureaucracy now offsets any productivity gains.

## Competitive issues

Firms within a market are often of different sizes. Within the grocery industry there are some very large supermarkets and some much smaller convenience stores. Within education, there are very large universities and some smaller schools and colleges; and within fast food there are huge global chains and small local operators. An important question is how big do you have to be in order to be competitive on cost? To answer this question economists have

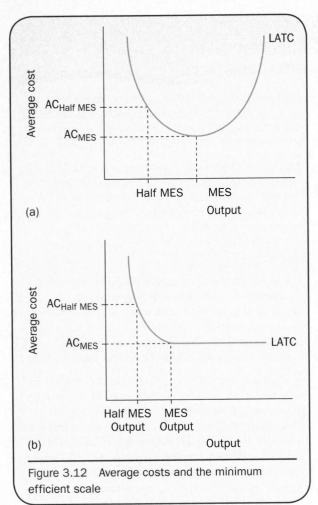

Figure 3.12   Average costs and the minimum efficient scale

developed the concept of **minimum efficient scale**, which is the minimum size a firm must be in order to achieve the lowest average total costs. This concept is illustrated in Figure 3.12.

The minimum efficient scale (MES) is the size of operation with the lowest average cost. Operating with a company size only half of the MES results in higher average costs. In Figure 3.12(a) the long-run average total cost is U-shaped and has a region of economies of scale and diseconomies of scale, with constant economies of scale at the minimum point. In Figure 3.12(b) the long-run average total cost curve has economies of scale and then constant economies; that is, as a firm increases its level of output, then average costs remain constant.

In either of the cases illustrated in Figure 3.12, if a company operates at a level of scale significantly below the minimum efficient scale, then it is likely to be competing against its larger rivals at a cost disadvantage. The size of this cost disadvantage varies. In some industries, economies of scale are small and the long-run average cost curve is fairly flat across all output ranges. In other industries, economies of scale are significant. As a general rule, industries that are capital and/or brand intensive generate higher fixed costs and lead to higher minimum efficient scale. Supermarkets, universities, fast food, plus banking and car manufacturing all require large capital and/or brand investment and therefore exhibit high minimum efficient scale.

Firms that are operate at, or in the case of Figure 3.12(b), beyond the minimum efficient scale can be described as following a **cost leadership strategy**. Such a firm leads the industry on cost and this is its main competitive strength. If a firm is small and does not have a cost advantage then it may undertake a number of alternative strategies. First, it might merge with another company in the same line of business. Clearly, the new company will be bigger than the two separate parts and economies of scale can be realized. Alternatively the company can pursue a **product differentiation strategy**. Under such a strategy the company seeks to make its products different from those of the cost leader. When competing products become different, then consumers view them less as substitutes. A product with fewer perfect substitutes faces less price-elastic consumers and the firm can charge a higher price and recover its higher costs.

Minimum efficient scale (MES) is the output level at which long-run costs are at a minimum.

Under a cost leadership strategy, a firm will seek competitive advantage by reducing average costs and pursuing economies of scale.

Under a product differentiation strategy, a firm will seek a competitive advantage by making its products less substitutable.

 **3.7** Business application: linking pricing with cost structures

Fixed costs have been a dominant feature of this chapter. Professional footballers were shown in the business problem to be fixed costs, as were larger container ships. The development of the Airbus A380 was seen as a fixed cost; and the indivisibility of a skyscraper was also seen as a fixed cost.

In every example, the fixed cost is a major component of total costs. Because an Airbus A380 without fuel weighs around 280 tons, the cost of moving the plane between two airports massively outweighs the cost of moving you and your suitcase. In fact, most airlines would let you fly between London and Sydney for as little as £30—the same amount as many cheap flights from the UK to some European destinations. This trivial amount is again the variable cost and this time is associated with the cost of issuing tickets, handling your luggage and feeding you en route. This is nothing more than the marginal cost of carrying you between two cities. Prices above £30 are a bonus to the airline. Using this cost-based knowledge, we can now explore the commercial decisions faced by the airlines that have ordered A380s.

More than any other commercial aircraft the A380 is a fixed cost for its operators, and moving the huge airframe between airports represents the bulk of the operators' costs. Interestingly, the aircraft is certified to carry 853 passengers, yet airlines appear to be ordering seating configurations between 480 and 580, presumably filling the free space with extra leg room, bars, gyms and other in-flight leisure facilities. However, we know that volume is crucial when fixed costs are high, because additional volume helps to spread the fixed cost over additional units of output. This lowers cost per unit sold, which ultimately lowers prices. With a simple piece of economic knowledge, it is easy to envisage airlines very quickly moving towards 850 seats on A380s in the pursuit of a cost advantage over their rivals. History also provides a precedent. When the Boeing 747 was first launched, no one knew what to place inside the front end 'bubble'. Ideas of gyms and bars were discussed, before operators decided on extra seating.

Discount airlines, while not yet flying A380s, gain competitive advantage by being cost-efficient. They know how to keep variable costs down through no-frills service and they are extremely effective in dealing with their fixed costs. Load factor is reported by all discount carriers such as Ryanair and easyJet on a monthly basis. Load factor measures how good the airline is at selling all its available seats, and discount carriers can often achieve a load factor of 85 per cent, beating their scheduled rivals (see Figure 3.13). As suggested earlier, the aircraft is a fixed cost of many millions of pounds. But also, as a scheduled airline, the company has committed to fly between two cities on any given day. So, if it flies with no passengers, or a full plane, the airline will still incur fuel costs, staff costs and airport fees. In a sense these costs are also fixed, as they do not vary with the level of output, in this case the number of passengers carried. In the case of no-frills easyJet, the variable costs are exceptionally low as no meals are offered and all tickets are electronic. Therefore, with such high fixed costs, airlines need to utilize their assets. They have to push volume through the aircraft and fill as many seats as possible. Each passenger makes a contribution to paying the huge fixed costs. The more passengers you carry, the more likely it is that you will be able to pay all of your fixed costs. Once this is achieved, you start to make profits.

How do you drive volume through an aircraft? The simple answer is volume itself. For example, if it costs £10,000 to fly a jet between Manchester and Amsterdam and the plane carries 50 passengers, then the average fixed cost per passenger is £10,000/50 = £200. Then the company needs to charge at least £200 per passenger and this is only for a one-way ticket! But if the plane carries 150 passengers, then the average fixed cost is £10,000/150 = £67.

From demand theory we know that we can generate higher demand at lower prices. So, we can drive volume by dropping the price. In part, easyJet tries to achieve this with a twist.

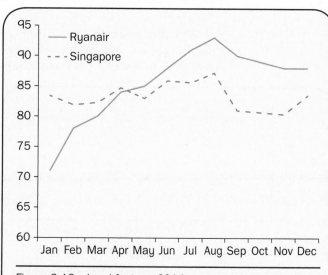

Figure 3.13   Load factors, 2014

*Source:* Airline websites.

If you want to book a flight three months in advance the price will be very cheap. This is because easyJet has lots of seats available and it has a higher need to drive volume. Once momentum picks up in the market and the flight date approaches, it raises the price and begins to extract profits from late bookers. But, crucially, what can be observed from a business perspective is that easyJet is using a fine-tuned pricing strategy to deal with a cost-based problem.

However, we should not be fooled into thinking that in ordering A380s with only 480 seats the likes of Singapore Airlines have got it all wrong. This is because Singapore Airlines' seats are worth more money; easyJet succeeds in driving the load factor forward by sacrificing revenue. Its heavy discounts in the marketplace are used to drive sales volumes. But driving volumes through price reduction damages revenue yields, and easyJet counters this revenue strategy by also minimizing its costs. It is a no-frills airline.

So, no meals, no reissue of the ticket if you miss the flight, plus the use of unpopular airports where the landing fees are lower. In contrast, Singapore Airlines uses popular airports. It undertakes extensive brand development. It provides meals and drinks onboard. It will assist passengers who have missed their flight. In summary, Singapore Airlines provides more than simply a means of transport between two points. It also provides extras such as late checking, drinks and meals during the flight and re-routing if you miss your flight. In addition, some of the earlier adopters of the A380 such as Singapore Airlines have an ability to offer a unique travel experience and can charge a premium price. With few other operators owning an A380, at least in the early years after launch, the demand for a flight on an A380 will be price inelastic. The added extras of gyms and bars are designed to exploit this demand. However, in 10 years' time, when the world is awash with A380s, 850 seats is likely to be common; and do not be surprised if easyJet or Ryanair owns one, or two, for short hops into Europe.

## 3.8  Business application: footballers as sweaty assets

A common business term for making your fixed inputs work harder is 'to sweat the assets' and this is exactly what easyJet is trying to do by making its planes operate at maximum capacity. But how are Premiership football teams utilizing their very expensive football stars?

Few football clubs are looking at the huge expense of footballers as a problem that requires a pricing solution. Admittedly, pricing may play a role. Football fans are willing to pay a higher price to watch a top Premiership side than, say, a Championship one. But the real and most obvious solution for Premiership sides is to increase the volume of games played.

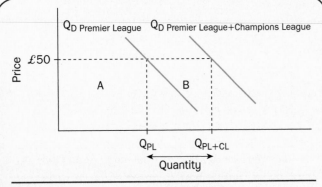

Figure 3.14    Demand for Premiership games and the Champions League

In Figure 3.14, we have the demand for tickets at football games. Assuming the ticket price is £50, the demand curve for Premiership games indicates how many fans will buy at £50. Total revenue from Premiership games is illustrated by rectangle A. If the team qualifies for the Champions League, then more games are played and ticket demand rises. Assuming a similar ticket price of £50, rectangle B defines the additional total revenue. In the recent past, Manchester United have been very successful in using this strategy. By focusing on qualifying for the Champions League and progressing within the competition they can literally sweat their assets, namely, the players. (Admittedly, making sports stars work harder may diminish their average performance and make them injury prone, so there could also be a variable cost to playing more games.)

Higher output resulting from more football games played yields more total revenue. This can go to paying the large fixed costs associated with employing top-class footballers.

However, by selling television rights to their games, replica team kits and other merchandising products, Manchester United do not rely only on the revenue streams from the turnstiles. However, once they fail to progress within the Champions League, then a financial hole appears in their business model. Players are utilized less, resulting in lower television revenue and gate receipts. Moreover, the value of the brand and the worth of merchandise decreases. Exposure and utilization of the players is a critical success factor for the business model underpinning the club.

Whether the problem is easyJet's or Manchester United's, it is the same problem: one of exploiting fixed costs. Economics provides you with an ability to identify this type of problem and suggests some possible solutions. Implementing and managing the strategic solution is perhaps a more challenging problem.

## (3.9) Business data application: wages and productivity

Finding data on firm-level costs is often very difficult. This is for a variety of reasons, including the fact that firms often view cost data as confidential. Notwithstanding this problem, economists do try to model cost curves for an industry and measure the size of any economies of scale effects. However, economists often only work with broad-level cost data made available within publically available documents, such as company's financial accounts. For example, total wages paid are often published, but this figure is a combination of workers', managers' and senior managers' earnings. The earnings of workers will vary with output. Higher output will be linked to increased overtime payments and greater use of temporary staff. Senior management pay is more likely to stay constant. Hence, the pay for one part of the labour force is variable and for another it is fixed. This inability to separate costs into fixed and variable makes much of the costs analysis within this chapter difficult to implement. In addition, any modelling of the long-run cost curve requires the use of advanced statistical techniques. Such techniques are beyond the scope of this textbook, but they do bring further complexity and problems to any attempt to understand costs within a firm, or industry. Therefore, with such a number of problems, what data are both easily available and of use to business managers?

A message from this chapter is that, when seeking to understand costs, it is not just wages that are of interest; the productivity of labour is also important. In the short run the law of diminishing returns highlights how labour productivity can change with output, while in the long run, economies of scale can result from higher labour productivity—for example, where a firm employs mass production techniques.

Reflecting the commercial and economic importance of wages and productivity is the good availability of data on these variables. Data relating to labour costs and labour productivity are often available at a national level and are useful to firms which are seeking to understand where to gain a competitive cost base in the global marketplace. Sources of national and international data on labour costs and productivity are generally available from government statistical agencies. A number of useful sources are listed in Table 3.4.

The US Bureau of Labor Statistics provides a reasonably rich source of employment, earnings and labour productivity data across a number of economies, enabling a comparison of key trends to be assessed over many decades.

**Table 3.4** Data sources for labour productivity and costs

| Data source | Link |
| --- | --- |
| US Bureau of Labor Statistics | http://www.bls.gov |
| Eurostat | http://epp.eurostat.ec.europa.eu |
| France, National Institute for Statistics and Economic Studies | www.insee.fr/en |
| Germany, Federal Statistical Office | http://www.destatis.de/en |
| UK, Office for National Statistics | http://www.statistics.gov.uk |

Figure 3.15 illustrates the trends in labour productivity, measured by output per hour within the US, UK and German manufacturing sectors between 1990 and 2011. Over that period of time, productivity has risen fastest in the US with an average annualized growth rate of around 5 per cent, compared with approximately 3 per cent for Germany and the UK. The same pattern emerges when we use output per employee to measure productivity (see Figure 3.16).

The rise in wages, as measured by hourly compensation, has increased the most in the UK over the period (see Figure 3.17), but the difference between the three economies is much less than the different growth rates in labour productivity.

Finally, if we bring together costs per hour and output per hour, then we have a measure of unit labour costs, i.e. the cost per unit of output (see Figure 3.18). Over the period 1990 to

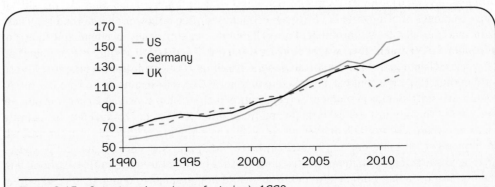

Figure 3.15　Output per hour (manufacturing), 1990–

Index, 2002 = 100

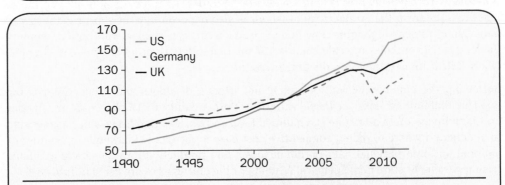

Figure 3.16　Output per employed person (manufacturing), 1990–

Index, 2002 = 100

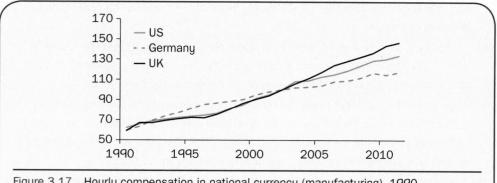

Figure 3.17  Hourly compensation in national currency (manufacturing), 1990–

Index, 2002 = 100

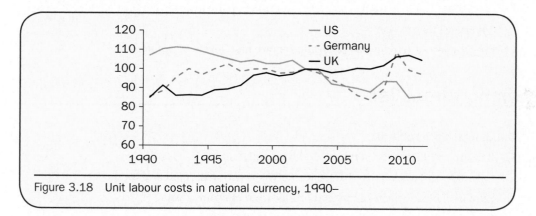

Figure 3.18  Unit labour costs in national currency, 1990–

2011 the US has exhibited an almost continuous decline in average unit labour costs, whereas in the UK and Germany unit labour costs have been increasing. Therefore, we can conclude that between 1990 and 2011 the US manufacturing sector improved its unit labour costs by boosting productivity and keeping wage growth in line with that of the UK and Germany.

A business manager seeking to understand where to locate a manufacturing facility would be interested in such figures in order to understand which locations/economies might be best from a unit labour cost perspective. Clearly, data for more countries would be useful, particularly for economies in Eastern Europe, China and South-East Asia, some of which are provided by the US Bureau of Labor Statistics. In addition, our discussion within the chapter would indicate that the manager, while interested in labour costs, would also be interested in the costs and productivity of capital, the mix of capital and labour within the factory and the potential to commission a large factory and gain significant economies of scale.

## Summary

1. In the short run one factor of production, usually capital, is assumed to be fixed.

2. Adding more variable factors of production, such as labour, to a fixed amount of capital will eventually lead to diminishing returns.

3. The impact of diminishing returns is a gradual decline in the productivity of labour. This lower productivity leads to a rise in average costs per unit.

4. The U-shaped nature of the average total and average variable cost curves is related to the change in productivity brought about by the diminishing returns.

5. Average fixed costs are always declining, as the fixed costs are divided by higher levels of outputs.

6. Marginal cost is the cost of producing one more unit. The marginal cost curve is, in effect, a reflection of the marginal product curve for labour. As marginal product declines due to the law of diminishing returns, the marginal cost increases.

7. Supply is linked to firms' marginal cost curves at prices above average variable costs. Entry of more firms increases supply. A reduction in costs would also increase firms' willingness to supply, by boosting potential profits. The price elasticity of supply measures how responsive firms' output is to a change in the price.

8. In the long run all factors of production are variable. Costs are no longer determined by the law of diminishing returns. Instead, they are related to economies of scale.

9. Initially, as companies grow in size, they benefit from economies of scale and unit costs fall. But eventually they will grow too big and diseconomies of scale will cause average costs to rise.

10. High levels of fixed costs generally require high levels of volume.

## Learning checklist

You should now be able to:

- Explain the difference between the short and long runs
- Calculate and explain the difference between variable, fixed and total costs
- Explain the concepts of marginal product and marginal costs
- Explain and provide examples of the law of diminishing returns
- Understand a firm's decision to operate or shut down and develop this understanding to explain how supply is linked to marginal cost at prices above average variable cost
- Understand the factors that will cause supply to increase
- Explain the concept of price elasticity of supply and understand how the degree of elasticity is linked to firms' abilities to respond to price increases
- Understand the concept of economies of scale and explain why economies of scale may exist
- Explain the concept of minimum efficient scale and understand the importance of operating at the minimum efficient scale
- Explain, using reference to fixed costs, why budget airlines sell at low prices
- Provide economic reasons relating to costs as to why Premiership clubs wish to be in the Champions League
- Understand where data covering labour costs and productivity can be found and how such data can be used to develop an understanding unit labour costs.

## Questions                                                                    connect

1. Explain the difference between the short and the long runs.

2. Is it sensible to consider capital, rather than labour, as a fixed factor of production?

3. How does the law of diminishing returns explain the short-run productivity of a firm?

4. What is the difference between total fixed costs, total variable costs and total costs?

5. In the short run, why do average total costs initially fall and then increase?

6. Explain why average fixed costs are always declining. What commercial strategies can be supported by falling average fixed costs?

7. What are marginal product and marginal costs?

8. Marginal costs must go through the minimum point of which other cost curves: average total costs, average variable costs or average fixed costs?

9. When should a firm shut down? Is it when prices go below average total costs, or average variable costs? Explain.

10. It is reported in the news that two firms have agreed to merge in the belief that they can generate cost savings. Which economic idea would support this belief?

11. Explain why airlines suspend some of their routes during the winter.

12. What are economies of scale and what are considered to be the main sources of economies of scale?

13. From a cost perspective, why do you think ice cream is on special offer in November, but not in July?

14. Is it ever sensible to operate at prices below average variable costs?

15. Do economies of scale offer a competitive advantage?

16. Contemporary aircraft design makes extensive use of aluminium alloys, particularly alloys making use of zinc as the main alloying element. Such alloys often have strength comparable to steel as well as good fatigue resistance. The diagram provided shows a hypothetical cost position of two aluminium extraction companies, Aluminium Mining Incorporated (AMI) and Aluminium Bergbau GmbH (ABG).

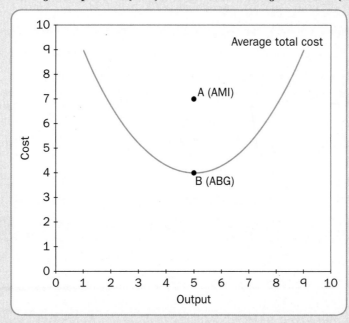

Assume that both AMI and ABG have identical average total cost curves. However AMI operates at point A, while ABG operates at point B. What can you conclude about cost efficiency of these two companies, given the cost information in the diagram?

17. A firm produces a widget using a special machine (M) in a factory in combination with inputs of labour. You are given information on the number of workers employed (N) and output per worker (Q).

EASY

INTERMEDIATE

DIFFICULT

a) Complete the table by filling in the missing values for total product (TP) and marginal product of labour (MPL).

DIFFICULT

| Number of machines (M) | Number of workers (N) | Output per worker (Q) | Total product (TP) | Marginal product of labour (MPL) |
|---|---|---|---|---|
| 1 | 1 | 5 | | |
| 1 | 2 | 6 | | |
| 1 | 3 | 7 | | |
| 1 | 4 | 8 | | |
| 1 | 5 | 9 | | |
| 1 | 6 | 10 | | |
| 1 | 7 | 11 | | |
| 1 | 8 | 10 | | |
| 1 | 9 | 9 | | |
| 1 | 10 | 8 | | |

b) How does the behaviour of MPL change as the number of workers employed increases?

## Exercises

EASY

1. True or false?
   (a) Specialization can lead to economies of scale.
   (b) Holding labour constant while increasing capital will lead to diminishing returns.
   (c) The long-run cost curve meets the bottom of each short-run cost curve.
   (d) Pursuit of minimum efficient scale can be a reason for merger.
   (e) A rising marginal cost is a result of diminishing returns.
   (f) Investing in brands represents a fixed cost.

2. A firm faces fixed costs of £45 and short-run variable costs (SAVC) as shown in Table 3.5.

INTERMEDIATE

| Table 3.5 Short-run costs of production |
|---|

| Output | SAVC | SAFC | SATC | STC | SMC |
|---|---|---|---|---|---|
| 1 | 17 | | | | |
| 2 | 15 | | | | |
| 3 | 14 | | | | |
| 4 | 15 | | | | |
| 5 | 19 | | | | |
| 6 | 29 | | | | |

(a) Fill in the remainder of the table, where SAFC is the short-run average fixed cost; SATC is the short-run average total cost; STC is the short-run total cost; and SMC is the short-run marginal cost.

(b) Plot SAVC, SAFC, SATC and SMC, checking that SMC goes through the minimum points of SAVC and SATC.

(c) The firm finds that it is always receiving orders for six units per week. Advise the firm on how to minimize its costs in the long run. Now consider Table 3.6.

**Table 3.6**  Short and long-run decisions

| Price | Short-run decision | | | Long-run decision | | |
|---|---|---|---|---|---|---|
| | Produce at a profit | Produce at a loss | Close down | Produce at a profit | Produce at a loss | Close down |
| 18.00 | | | | | | |
| 5.00 | | | | | | |
| 7.00 | | | | | | |
| 13.00 | | | | | | |
| 11.50 | | | | | | |

Cost conditions are such that LAC is £12; SATC is £17 (made up of SAVC £11 and SAFC £6). In Table 3.6, tick the appropriate short- and long-run decisions at each price.

3. Your company is considering where to locate a new manufacturing facility. The options include Japan, Singapore and Taiwan. Using data on productivity and wages, present a report which highlights the main trends in unit labour costs for each of these economies and also highlights any other cost concepts which you think your senior management team need to be aware of before taking a final decision on the location of the new facility.

**DIFFICULT**

4. Using data from one of the sources listed in Table 3.4, compare labour costs and productivity growth for three different EU economies.

# Markets in action

## Chapter contents

## Learning outcomes

By the end of this chapter you should be able to:

**Economic theory**

LO1    Describe the concept of market equilibrium

LO2    Illustrate how changes in demand and supply lead to changes in the market equilibrium

LO3    Analyse how price elasticity influences the size of changes in market price and output

LO4    Identify market shortages and surpluses as instances of market disequilibria

LO5    Differentiate between pooling and separating disequilibria

**Business application**

LO6    Construct a market shortage to boost sales and product—or brand—awareness

LO7    Analyse starting salaries for graduates

LO8    Debate the role of supply and demand in the car market

　Market theory

## The issue

The price and the amount of goods and services traded change over time. But what causes these changes in particular product markets?

## The understanding

Price changes in all markets, whether it is the price of a coffee, entrance to a nightclub or the price of a DVD, stem from changes in supply and demand. Sometimes the price may change simply because demand or supply has changed. In more complex cases, demand and supply could change together. Understanding how and why supply and demand change and the implications for market prices are important business skills.

## The usefulness

Markets with upward price expectations will look more attractive than markets with downward price projections. If businesses can appreciate how competing factors will influence the price for their products or of key inputs, they can begin to develop successful strategies for the firm.

 ## Business problem: picking a winner

How does a firm, or business person, know which product to promote and sell, and which to leave alone? Take Box 4.1 which contains an article on Samsung. Consumer electronics companies like Samsung are interesting examples when considering markets that might turn out to be gold mines. The variety of markets in consumer electronics is large, giving lots of opportunities. The skill that will determine Samsung's future success is the ability to choose markets where prices and volumes of sales will grow and remain strong.

In the past, Samsung invested in batteries, flash memory, flat screens and smartphones, all of which turned out to be highly profitable. Samsung's managers have previously demonstrated an ability to understand markets and spot the important characteristics that will create a market that has high volumes and good profit margins. Equally, they have been good at understanding when volumes are likely to fall, margins erode and it is time to exit.

It is clear from the article that Samsung is finding it more challenging to make profits from its smartphone business. There is more money to be made in supplying components to competitors. To support this view Samsung has invested $15 billion in a new chip fabrication factory, which is one big bet on the way the markets are shifting.

The importance of understanding future prices and volumes is not just limited to business. Consider your own futures. Some of you may wish to supply yourselves as marketing executives, others as accountants and perhaps some as business economists. The wage or price at which you will be hired will depend upon how many other workers wish to supply themselves to your chosen occupation; and how many firms demand such types of workers. Greater supply will increase competition and the price or wage rate will fall, while higher demand by firms will lead to higher wages. You, therefore, have to decide if the supply of workers into your chosen profession will rise or fall, and whether or not demand will rise or fall. Predicting correctly can potentially lead to higher income levels in the future.

The discussion in this chapter will offer you an economist's understanding of the marketplace, explicitly highlighting the link between demand and supply in marketplaces and illustrating how changes in demand and supply lead to changes in the market price of a product. By the end of the chapter you will have an understanding of how markets work and, more important, how business managers might try to make markets work for them.

## Box 4.1
## Samsung Electronics confident of reversing smartphone slump

A day after Apple announced record profits underpinned by booming iPhone sales in China, rival Samsung Electronics furnished new evidence of its struggles in that market—while voicing confidence that the worst of its smartphone slump is behind it.

Samsung's mobile phone division's operating profit of Won2.74 trillion ($2.6 billion) was 40 per cent higher than the previous three months, as Samsung cut costs by focusing on a smaller range of low- and mid-range phones as part of a turnround plan. It expected a further boost from strong demand for its new Galaxy S6 flagship phone, which went on sale this month.

Analysts had been awaiting the detailed report for signs of progress in Samsung's efforts to reverse the contraction in its smartphone business. The company was criticised last year for complacency in the face of competition from Chinese rivals such as Xiaomi, which are able to sell phones with similar technical specifications at a lower price.

Samsung did not reveal unit sales number but Strategy Analytics, a research group, estimates that the company sold 83.2 million smartphones in the period—down 7 per cent from a year before, but 12 per cent up from the prior quarter. This would mean it moved ahead of Apple to regain top spot as the global smartphone leader by market share.

The market performance of the Galaxy S6, which went on sale on April 10, will give a crucial indication of Samsung's prospects. The company said that early sales had comfortably exceeded those of last year's

Galaxy S5, prompting problems with its supply chain as it has struggled to meet demand.

The new phone's design, which includes a metal casing, and the curved screen in one version, have also pushed up production costs, according to IHS, the research group. It estimated this month that the curved screen Galaxy S6 Edge—which analysts expect to account for as much as 40 per cent of overall S6 sales—costs about $290 to produce. That compares with $240 for Apple's iPhone 6, which commands a US retail price $50 higher than the Samsung device.

Amid the uncertainty over its smartphone business, Samsung's performance has been bolstered by its semiconductor division, which remained the company's biggest earnings contributor for the third consecutive quarter, with operating profit rising 50 per cent from a year before to Won2.93 trillion.

Samsung has won a technological lead over rivals in the memory chip industry, accentuating the benefits from strong prices after consolidation in the sector. Its mobile processor business, which suffered losses last year, was boosted by Samsung's decision to use its own processors in the Galaxy S6, and will start producing chips for Apple later this year.

'The more important long-term story is components,' said one analyst.

From the *Financial Times*. 29 April 2015. 'Samsung Electronics confident of reversing smartphone slump'. Simon Mundy. © The Financial Times Limited 2015. All Rights Reserved.

## 4.2 Bringing demand and supply together

In Chapter 2, where we examined the price set in the market, we cheated by simply focusing on the willingness to demand. In Chapter 3, when examining the short-run costs of firms, we argued that the firm's supply curve is its marginal cost curve at prices above short-run average variable cost. We are now at a point where we can bring demand and supply together.

### Market equilibrium

> **Market equilibrium** occurs at the price where consumers' willingness to demand is exactly equal to firms' willingness to supply.

In order to understand the marketplace we bring consumers and firms together. In Figure 4.1, we have the supply and demand curve together. Where demand and supply meet is known as the **market equilibrium**.

As a more realistic example, consider buying a second-hand car. Assume the seller (supplier) offers to sell the car for £5,000. You examine the car and make an offer to buy at £4,000. This is not equilibrium as you and the seller are willing to buy and sell at different prices. A trade will not occur because you cannot agree on the price. But assume the seller is now willing to reduce the asking price to £4,500 and you accept. This is the equilibrium—you have both agreed a price at which you are willing to buy and the owner is willing to sell. As such, a trade will occur.

Before moving on, it is worth making a few comments about the equilibrium. First, we assume that the equilibrium is unique. The demand and supply curve only intersect at one point. Given the condition of *ceteris paribus,* all other things being equal, the equilibrium is a stable position as there are no forces acting to move the price away from the equilibrium. In the case of our car, both the seller and the buyer are happy to trade at the agreed price of £4,500. Second, any other combinations of price and quantity that are not the equilibrium values are described as market **disequilibria**.

Third, if the market is in disequilibrium, then, as with the case of our car traders, negotiations and resulting price changes will push the market towards its equilibrium position. We will explain these points as we develop your understanding of the market.

For those readers who are mathematically inclined, it is possible to think of the market equilibrium as the solution to a simultaneous equation problem. See Box 4.2 for further details.

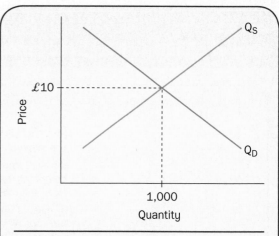

**Figure 4.1   Market equilibrium**

Market equilibrium occurs at the price where the willingness to demand by consumers meets the willingness to supply by firms. In this case, at a price of £10 consumers are willing to purchase 1,000 units and firms are willing to sell 1,000 units.

In situations of **disequilibria**, at the current price the willingness to demand will differ from the willingness to supply.

 ## Changes in supply and demand

The business problem concerned how market prices are likely to develop in the future. Now that we have a model of the market, we can use our understanding of the factors that shift demand and supply to examine how the market reacts to these changes. We will begin by considering changes in demand.

Demand shifts to the right:

- for a normal good when income increases, or for an inferior good when income falls
- following an increase in the price of the substitute
- following a reduction in the price of a complement
- when tastes and preferences for this good improve.

Figure 4.4 illustrates a shift in demand to the right. At the initial equilibrium point, 1,000 units are traded at a price of £10. But as demand shifts out to the right, a new equilibrium is achieved and now 2,000 units are sold at a higher price of £20.

This can be used to explain property prices when the price of loans is cheap and income is growing steadily. Loans are a complement when buying a home. If you buy a house, you buy a loan. So, cheaper loans increase both the demand for loans and the demand for houses. As income increases, then as a normal good, demand increases for homes. So, for these two reasons the demand line shifts to the right and the equilibrium price and quantity increase.

We can also bring price expectations into the analysis. If you think prices are going to rise in the future, then you will bring forward your consumption. The demand curve for consumption now, as opposed to consumption in the future, shifts to the right.

## Box 4.2
## Market equilibrium as simultaneous equations

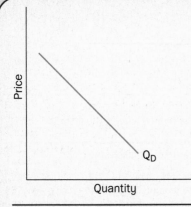

$$Q_D = a_d - b_d P$$

The slope of the demand line $= -b_d$

If $b_d = 0$, then the demand line would be horizontal/flat. So the bigger the number for $b_d$ the steeper the line.

$a_d$ tells us where the demand line touches the Price axis. $a_d$ tells us where the price is so high that demand $= 0$.

Figure 4.2    Demand line

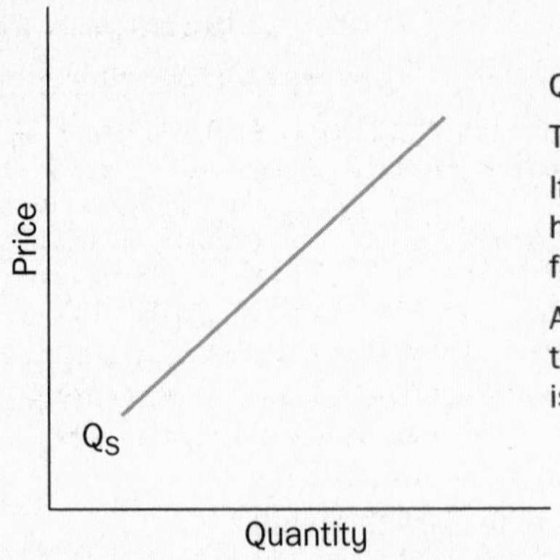

Since the demand and supply lines in Figure 4.1 are linear, they can be expressed using the equation of a straight line.

$$Q_D = a_d - b_d P$$

where $a_D$ is the intercept and $-b_D$ is the (negative) slope of the demand line.

$$Q_S = a_s + b_s P$$

where $a_s$ is the intercept and $b_s$ is the (positive) slope of the supply line.

In equilibrium demand equals supply, so $Q_D = Q_S$; we can therefore solve the two equations above for P.

So,

$$a_d - b_d P = a_s + b_s P$$

$$b_s P + b_d P = a_d - a_s$$

$$P = (a_d - a_s)/(b_d + b_s)$$

$$Q_S = a_s + b_s P$$

The slope of the supply line $= b_s$

If $b_S = 0$, then the supply line would be horizontal/flat. So the bigger the number for $b_S$ the steeper the line.

$A_S$ tells us where the supply line touches the Price axis. $a_S$ tells us where the price is so low that supply $= 0$.

Figure 4.3    Supply line

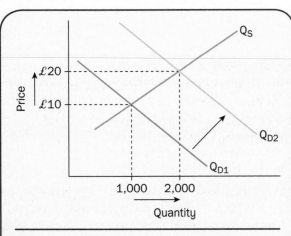

Figure 4.4    Shift in demand to the right

We can now explore what happens when demand shifts to the left, as in Figure 4.5. Demand shifts to the left:

- for a normal good when income falls, or for an inferior good when income rises
- following a decrease in the price of the substitute
- following an increase in the price of a complement
- when tastes and preferences for this good deteriorate.

This time we have simply changed the diagram around. We start at an equilibrium price of £20 selling 2,000 units and then demand shifts to the left. The equilibrium price falls to £10 selling only 1,000 units. Fewer companies are exporting goods around the world, so there is less demand for ships. The demand line shifts to the left and the equilibrium price and quantity fall.

Now let us consider supply. Supply shifts to the right:

- if more firms enter the market
- if the cost of inputs, such as labour, becomes cheaper
- if technological developments bring about productivity gains.

In Figure 4.6, supply has shifted to the right. The equilibrium moves from a price of £20 selling 1,000 units to £10 selling 2,000 units. If we assume that the supply has moved to the right because more firms are competing in the market, then this outcome appears sensible.

Increased competition should lead to a drop in prices and more consumers taking up the product. The Internet is a significant technological development and it effectively cuts the costs of being a product provider. For example, rather than having to buy or lease many high-street shops, a new retailer can deal with its customers over the Internet. This significantly reduces its costs. Hence, the market price, in major Internet areas such as travel, should fall. Lower prices mean lower profits and therefore economists predicted the dot.com crash with ease. We will return to Internet-based business in the business applications at the end of the chapter.

Let us now examine a shift in supply to the left. Supply shifts to the left:

- if firms exit the market
- if the cost of inputs, such as labour, becomes too great.

If supply shifts to the left, as in Figure 4.7, then the equilibrium price moves from £10 selling 2,000 units to £20 selling 1,000 units. This might occur if one firm exited the market or took steps to reduce its capacity. Airlines sometime use this strategy. They take aircraft off unpopular routes, or swap large jumbos for smaller ones. Both tactics reduce capacity/supply on particular routes. As this happens, the cost of running the airline drops and the market price for tickets increases. The airline is then more likely to make a profit.

In Box 4.3 the large drop in oil prices is explained by considering demand and supply in the global market for oil. Continuing weakness in many economies means that the demand for oil also remains weak, which in our framework could mean a move to the left for demand (see Figure 4.5).

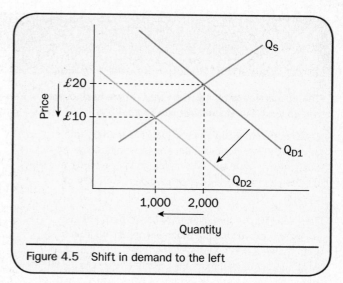

Figure 4.5 Shift in demand to the left

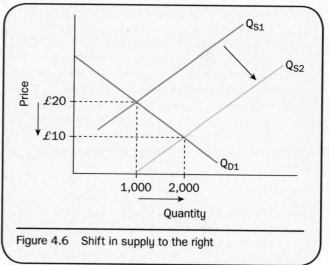

Figure 4.6 Shift in supply to the right

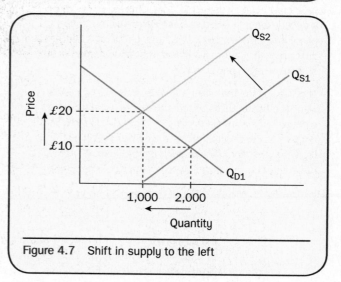

Figure 4.7 Shift in supply to the left

The supply side of the oil market is more complicated to understand. New technology has enabled US oil producers to expand the shale oil market. Low interest rates have fuelled

## Box 4.3
## The new economics of oil: sheikhs v shale

**The economics of oil have changed. Some businesses will go bust, but the market will be healthier**

OPEC states that the group's goal is 'the stabilisation of prices in international oil markets'. It has not been doing a very good job. In June the price of a barrel of oil, then almost $115, began to slide; it now stands close to $70.

This near-40 per cent plunge is thanks partly to the sluggish world economy, which is consuming less oil than markets had anticipated, and partly to OPEC itself, which has produced more than markets expected. But the main culprits are the oilmen of North Dakota and Texas. Over the past four years, as the price hovered around $110 a barrel, they have set about extracting oil from shale formations previously considered unviable. Their manic drilling—they have completed perhaps 20,000 new wells since 2010, more than ten times Saudi Arabia's tally—has boosted America's oil production by a third, to nearly 9 million barrels a day (b/d). That is just 1 million b/d short of Saudi Arabia's output. The contest between the shalemen and the sheikhs has tipped the world from a shortage of oil to a surplus.

**Fuel injection**

Several members of OPEC want it to cut output, in the hope of pushing the price of oil back up again. But Saudi Arabia, in particular, seems mindful of the experience of the 1970s, when a big leap in the price prompted huge investments in new fields, leading to a decade-long glut. Instead, the Saudis seem to be pushing a different tactic: let the price fall and put high-cost producers out of business. That should soon crimp supply, causing prices to rise.

There are signs that such a shake-out is already under way. The share prices of firms that specialise in shale oil have been swooning. Many of them are up to their derricks in debt. With their revenues now dropping fast, they will find themselves overstretched. A rash of bankruptcies is likely. That, in turn, would bespatter shale oil's reputation among investors. Even survivors may find the markets closed for some time, forcing them to rein in their expenditure to match the cash they generate from selling oil. Since shale-oil wells are short-lived (output can fall by 60–70 per cent in the first year), any slowdown in investment will quickly translate into falling production.

This shake-out will be painful. But in the long run the shale industry's future seems assured. Fracking, in which a mixture of water, sand and chemicals is injected into shale formations to release oil, is a relatively young technology, and it is still making big gains in efficiency. IHS, a research firm, reckons the cost of a typical project has fallen from $70 per barrel produced to $57 in the past year, as oilmen have learned how to drill wells faster and to extract more oil from each one.

The firms that weather the current storm will have masses more shale to exploit. Drilling is just beginning (and may now be cut back) in the Niobrara formation in Colorado, for example, and the Mississippian Lime along the border between Oklahoma and Kansas. Nor need shale oil be a uniquely American phenomenon: there is similar geology all around the world, from China to the Czech Republic.

Most important of all, investments in shale oil come in conveniently small increments. The big conventional oilfields that have not yet been tapped tend to be in inaccessible spots, deep below the ocean, high in the Arctic, or both. America's Exxon Mobil and Russia's Rosneft recently spent two months and $700 million drilling a single well in the Kara Sea, north of Siberia. By contrast, a shale-oil well can be drilled in as little as a week, at a cost of $1.5 million. The shale firms know where the shale deposits are and it is pretty easy to hire new rigs; the only question is how many wells to drill. The whole business becomes a bit more like manufacturing drinks: whenever the world is thirsty, you crank up the bottling plant.

From *The Economist*. Sheikhs v shale.
© The Economist Newspaper Limited, London (6 December 2014)

cheap financing, enabling US shale producers to borrow money to fund further growth in shale oil production. This expansion of shale oil has moved the supply of oil to the right (see Figure 4.6). So weak demand and strong growth in supply has pushed down the price of oil. But in the long term, weak oil prices might lead to the collapse of many shale oil companies who are unable to pay their debts. Exit from the oil market would be a reduction in supply and an increase in price (see Figure 4.7). Read on in Box 4.3 for more information.

## Elasticity and changes in the equilibrium

It is also worth noting that the elasticity of supply and demand will influence how the equilibrium changes. In Figure 4.8, we have an inelastic and an elastic supply curve and we can observe what happens to the equilibrium when we shift demand to the right.

Under inelastic supply we should expect that supply will not react strongly to a change in the price, and this is what we observe. The price rises from £10 to £30, but output only increases from 100 to 200 units. In the case of elastic supply, the increase in demand brings about a large change in output, 100 to 500 units, but only a small rise in the price, from £10 to £13.

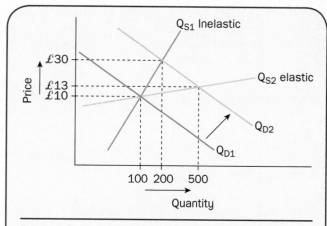

Figure 4.8   Impact of demand changes when supply is elastic or inelastic

Following a change in demand, price changes are greater if supply is inelastic, while output changes are greater if supply is elastic.

### Why might supply be inelastic?

The elasticity of supply reflects the ability of the supply side of the market to react to price changes. So, if prices increase, will suppliers be willing to supply more? If supply is inelastic, then the answer to this question will be no. Inelastic supply can result from an inability to react to prices, or indeed a desire to control supply.

If the ability to supply is determined by access to fixed assets, such as office, retail or manufacturing space, then even with higher demand, it takes time for increased capacity to be built and for supply to increase. However, if during a recession, demand is low and firms are not utilizing all of their capacity, then any increase in prices is likely to result in a rapid increase in supply. Therefore, excess capacity can lead to elastic supply.

Firms, industries and professions may also actively seek to control, or at least influence, supply. Lawyers and accountants restrict supply into their professions through the need to pass professional examinations in order to act as a lawyer or an accountant. Some people comment that lawyers and accountants have a licence to print money and, in part, you now know why.

Sport is also a successful industry. Formula 1 (F1) motor racing strictly controls the number of teams in the sport and the number of races in a season. It also controls television rights for the F1 season and it can thereby limit the means by which the races are supplied to the viewing public. This is all done with the objective of running a commercially profitable sporting event. The success of Premiership football and other leagues across Europe is similarly linked to the control of supply. Television access to games is strictly controlled by governing bodies, which sell television rights en bloc to television networks. The alternative would be for each club to sell its games on an individual basis. For example, one week Manchester United might sell their game with Liverpool to one broadcaster, while the week after they could sell their game with Chelsea to another channel. Instead, the supply of games is managed. Out of a possible 400 games a season, around 60 are shown per year by a small number of television networks. By making the product scarce, or by engineering inelastic supply, the price in the television market for football games will rise.

In Figure 4.9, we consider how a change in supply affects the equilibrium when demand is elastic or inelastic. When demand is elastic, the increase in supply brings about a small change in the price, dropping from £30 to £22, with output increasing from 100 to 500 units. In the case of inelastic demand, the increase in supply generates a large drop in the price from £30 to £10, but only a small change in output from 100 to 200 units.

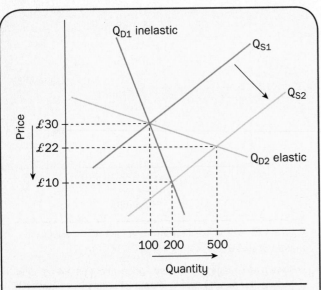

**Figure 4.9** Supply changes under elastic and inelastic demand

Following a change in supply, the price change is greater if demand is inelastic. But the output change is greater if demand is elastic.

The clear lesson from this example is that, if faced with inelastic demand for your product, do not increase your production capacity and thereby increase supply, because the price will drop quicker than output increases and your total revenues will fall. However, if you are faced with elastic demand, do consider increasing your capacity and supplying more to the market, as output grows at a faster rate than the declining price and so total revenues will rise.

## 4.4 Disequilibrium analysis

So far we have only considered the market to be in equilibrium, where demand equals supply. In reality, markets may never be in equilibrium; they may instead always be moving between equilibrium positions. First, let us consider a situation in which the price is higher than the equilibrium.

In Figure 4.10, the current market price of £10 is higher than the equilibrium price of £8. At a price of £10 consumers are willing to demand 1,000 units, but firms are willing to supply 2,000 units. This is clearly not an equilibrium position. With supply exceeding demand by 2,000 − 1,000 = 1,000 units, the market is said to be running a surplus. In effect, firms will be left with excess stock in their warehouses. We suggested earlier that natural forces would push the market towards the equilibrium, so how might this happen?

If the firm has too much stock, then, in accounting terms, its working capital is tied up. The firm has spent money making the product and it now needs to sell the product in order to free its cash for future production. The only way to sell the excess stock is to begin discounting the price until everything is sold. The more excess stock a firm has, the bigger the discount it has to offer. You will have noticed the trick used by clothing retailers: '50% off' is written large but 'on selected ranges' is written much smaller. The goods that are discounted by 50 per cent will almost certainly be those that few, if any, people wanted at the original price. The biggest discounts are generally offered on the products where the retailer has observed the biggest difference between its willingness to supply and consumers' willingness to demand. Therefore, the biggest discounts are offered on the products where the retailer has the biggest level of unwanted stock.

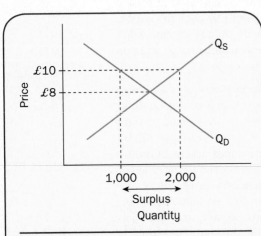

**Figure 4.10** A market surplus

When the price is set above the equilibrium, firms are very willing to supply but consumers are not willing to demand. As a consequence, more is supplied than demanded. Firms are left with excess stock. In this case, at a market price of £10, firms supply 2,000 units but consumers only demand 1,000 units, leaving a surplus of 1,000 units.

Figure 4.11 illustrates the opposite situation, a market shortage. This time we have the market price of £8, which is below the market equilibrium price of £10. At £8, we can see that consumers are willing to demand 2,000 units, but firms are only willing to supply 1,000 units. We now have a shortage of 2,000 − 1,000 = 1,000 units. Consumers would like to buy twice as much of the product as firms are willing to provide. Two responses are likely. Firms may recognize the high demand for their products and raise the price. Or consumers may begin to bid up the price in order to gain access to the product. If you really want to see the market in action, then watch the Internet auction sites for the most popular Christmas presents, such as game consoles, the latest mobile phones or recent film releases on Blu-ray or DVD.

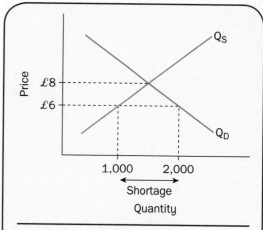

Figure 4.11   A market shortage

When the price is set below the equilibrium, firms are less willing to supply but consumers are very willing to demand. As a consequence, more is demanded than supplied. In this case, at a market price of £8, firms supply 1,000 units but consumers demand 2,000 units, leaving a shortage of 1,000 units.

## 4.5 Price floors and ceilings

Governments are sometimes interested in preventing prices from going too high or too low. For example, enormous capacity and economies of scale in the brewing and alcoholic drinks sector, plus strong competition among retailers and supermarkets have forced down the price of drinks, fuelling increased consumption of alcohol. To address the excess consumption of alcohol, the government may consider imposing a **minimum price**. The minimum price then acts as a floor below which it is illegal to set a price. To be effective in reducing consumption, the minimum price must be higher than the market equilibrium price.

Figure 4.12 illustrates the impact of a minimum price. In Figure 4.12 a proposed minimum price of £2 for a bottle of wine is above the market price. A minimum price above the market equilibrium results in supply exceeding demand and a surplus of output on the market. Where might that surplus (wine) go? Firms may seek to sell the wine illegally below the minimum price. Some wine may be re-exported to other countries, which would boost supply in that country, reduce the price and fuel binge drinking in another economy. Perhaps not very good for international relations.

> A **minimum price/** price floor prevents prices from falling below a set level.
>
> A **maximum price/** price ceiling prevents prices from rising above a set level.

Some readers may consider a cheap bottle of wine to be one that costs less than £2. Others might be happy to pay £4 to £5 for what they consider to be a cheap wine. A minimum price of £2 is therefore unlikely to be above the equilibrium price for wine and would have no effect on consumption. If consumers are willing to pay £4, then the only way to reduce consumption is to make the minimum price higher, say £4.50.

A government may also be concerned when prices, especially for important items, such as fuel and energy can become too high. In such circumstances, the government may impose **maximum prices**. A maximum price acts as a price ceiling above which it is illegal to set prices. Figure 4.13 illustrates the impact of a maximum price on the demand and supply for fuel. If the government sets a maximum price of £1 per litre of fuel, then with an equilibrium price of around £1.40, the market is likely to be in disequilibrium and be characterized by a significant shortage of supply. While households may find the fuel price attractive, the inability to find fuel, coupled with the likelihood of having fuel stolen/siphoned from your car will be extremely annoying.

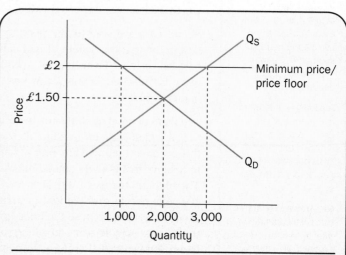

Figure 4.12   Impact of a minimum price/price floor on demand and supply

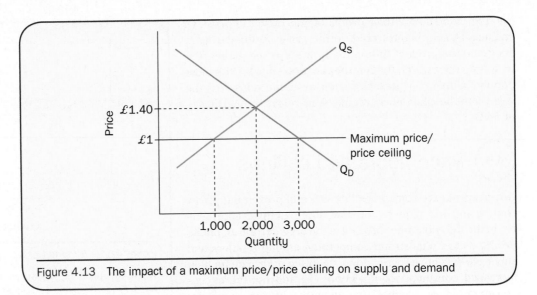

Figure 4.13 The impact of a maximum price/price ceiling on supply and demand

## 4.6 Pooling and separating equilibria

Consider the second-hand car market and assume good-quality cars cost £5,000 and bad-quality cars cost £2,500. Sellers of good and bad cars specialize in each type of car. So, if you want a good car, you go to a good car seller. Under these arrangements you would be willing to pay £5,000 if you wanted a good car, or £2,500 if you wanted a bad car. This is a **separating equilibrium**, as each type of product is sold in a separate market.

Now consider a more realistic situation where good and bad cars are sold together. This is a **pooling equilibrium**, where the consumer finds it difficult to differentiate between good and bad products. So, unlike the separating equilibrium, both types of car are sold in the same market.

When you arrive at the dealership you are offered the following option. In a cloth bag are a number of car keys: 50 per cent open up good cars, 50 per cent open up bad cars. How much would you be willing to pay to put your hand in the bag and drive away with a car?

The statistical approach is to work out the expected value of the car. You have a 0.5 chance of gaining a good car worth £5,000 and a 0.5 chance of ending up with a bad car worth £2,500. The expected value is therefore $0.5 \times £5,000 + 0.5 \times £2,500 = £3,750$.

So, all cars are sold at the pooling equilibrium price of £3,750. If this permeates across the market, sellers of bad cars gain an extra £1,250, while suppliers of good cars lose £1,250. Over time more bad cars will come to the market and good cars will leave the market. This is known as **Gresham's Law**, where bad products drive out good products.

Suppliers of good-quality cars under a pooling equilibrium are disadvantaged because they are unable to differentiate their products from the bad offerings. In order to solve this problem they need to find a way of creating a separating equilibrium. The way to achieve this is to do something that the bad suppliers would be unwilling to copy. Therefore, in the used car markets we can observe car dealerships offering cars with 100-point checks and 12-month warranties. Offering a 12-month warranty is cheap for good-car sellers because the likeli-hood of the car breaking down is low. In contrast, the bad-car suppliers are unwilling to offer warranties because the bad cars are likely to break down and, therefore, the cost of honouring the warranties would be very high.

In terms of a further example, consider the purchase of car insurance. The insurance company asks for many details before quoting you a price for car insurance. How old

**A separating equilibrium** is where a market splits into two clearly identifiable submarkets with separate supply and demand.

**A pooling equilibrium** is a market where demand and supply for good and poor products pool into one demand and one supply.

**Gresham's Law** states that an increasing supply of bad products will drive out good products from the market.

are you? How many years no claims bonus do you have? Where do you live? What type of car do you drive? The insurer is trying to separate the market by assessing whether you are a good or bad risk. If it did not do this, then clearly the market for insurance risks would move towards a pooling equilibrium. Every driver would be charged the same price for car insurance. However, in such a market bad drivers, with high accident or theft rates, pay less than they should, while good drivers, with low accident and theft rates, pay more than they should. Therefore, by separating the market the insurance company is able to charge the right insurance premiums for good and bad drivers.

## (4.7) Business application: marketing pop concerts—a case of avoiding the equilibrium price

The preceding discussion argued that markets will always find the equilibrium. So-called 'market forces' push the market to a state where demand equals supply. This seems fairly reasonable, but how might a firm manage its market for strategic benefit? Or, can a firm control market forces? A successful business person would more than likely answer this last question with a yes.

Take, for example, the task of managing a pop star. Whether or not you like Madonna, the Rolling Stones, or One Direction, they are undoubtedly megastars. Some of their status stems from talent, but some also stems from commercial management. By way of an example, assume you are a concert promoter and have to oversee the pricing of concert tickets for one of these music acts.

A typical music arena might hold 20,000 people. The supply of seats at this venue is fixed at 20,000, so supply is perfectly inelastic. If we plot demand and supply, then the result may look like Figure 4.14.

In equilibrium, demand equals supply. The task is to sell 20,000 tickets, so your business problem becomes one of finding the price that will generate a demand of 20,000. In this example, we have assumed that £100 is the price that will ensure a demand of exactly 20,000.

Unfortunately, £100 as an equilibrium price is not a good outcome for your global music star. Selling all of the 20,000 tickets for £100 is a huge success but, since £100 is the equilibrium price, the concert is only just a sell-out. Your music megastar, along with the media and press, expect the concert to sell out in a matter of minutes. A price of £100 will *only just* ensure that the concert sells out just before the show begins.

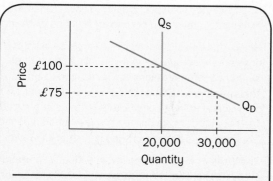

Figure 4.14   Managing the market

The equilibrium price of £100 clears the market with supply equalling demand. But at a discounted price of £75, a market shortage of tickets can be engineered, with demand outstripping supply. This helps to ensure an instant sell-out success for the concert.

However, if we set a ticket price of £75 we can engineer a ticket shortage in the market. At £75, 30,000 fans are willing to buy a ticket. With only 20,000 seats the concert will be a sell-out, with an additional 10,000 fans still trying to find a ticket on the black market. The importance of a sell-out concert will be evidenced by the positive media attention—column inches in the celebrity pages of the press confirming your act's global popstar status. In this way, music management companies sacrifice ticket revenue, but gain free advertisements in the press.

However, because the market values these concert tickets at £100 each, there is a chance to make £25 profit per ticket, or £0.5 million if you can buy all the tickets and sell them on. That is a huge financial incentive to build a computer robot that buys tickets. Read on in Box 4.4.

## Box 4.4
## Are 'bots' the reason you can never get tickets for popular concerts and matches? How software helps touts grab hundreds of tickets the second they go on sale

It's a disappointment thousands of music and sporting fans will have faced: you're ready with credit card in hand the minute tickets go on sale for a gig or match, but no sooner do they go on sale than they sell out. Then minutes later you spot tickets on reselling websites.

Today experts revealed the new hidden threat that is snatching tickets from under the noses of genuine fans: ticketing bots.

Ticketing bots are software that buy up huge numbers of tickets for events as soon as they go on sale. Buyers then use secondary ticketing websites to sell them on.

Reg Walker, Britain's leading ticket-fraud expert, explains that 'botnets' are computer programmes pre-loaded with different names, addresses and credit card details, which are used to target ticketing agents. 'They then harvest tickets at high speed and that effectively blocks out genuine fans from being able to purchase tickets at face value,' he claims. 'These tickets are then immediately resold on secondary ticketing platforms.'

He adds: 'I've seen one case where three pairs of tickets were bought in the same minute from three different addresses using the same credit card details. This was at a time when there were 80,000 people on the website trying to buy tickets for the same event.' The bots are for sale online for a few hundred pounds. 'You just buy a bot and off you go,' says Mr Walker.

Reg Walker, who has been investigating ticket fraud for 16 years, said he investigated 120,000 ticket sales for high-demand events this year. Of these, he claims more than 30 per cent went to touts who are selling them on secondary sites.

Ticketing websites say they are doing everything they can to beat the scourge of ticketing bots. A spokesperson for Ticketmaster says it invests

significantly in its technology to differentiate the real fans from the bots.

'The work that we do is successful as we continue to fend off millions of bot attacks each year. We have a series of automatic checks that are in place, including Captcha and IP address monitoring, as well as a team who manually checks all orders for any suspicious activity.' It adds that all websites have to fight bots 'from Google to Twitter and Facebook to much smaller ecommerce sites'.

So why haven't they been stopped?

Sharon Hodgson believes the use of ticketing bots is so lucrative that it's almost impossible to stop. 'It's turned into an arms race,' she says. 'You can introduce new security protocols, but it won't be long until someone will have found a way around it.' She claims that while touts are able to make thousands of pounds buying and selling tickets for profit, they will find a way to do it.

Some believe secondary ticketing sites could also be doing more to crack down on ticketing bots and touts. They claim that while it is still possible for touts to sell on tickets to secondary sites, they will find a way to do it. Reg Walker claims that it is not in the interests of secondary ticketing websites to crack down on touts – after all they benefit from the resale of tickets.

'The secondary websites know exactly who has huge numbers of tickets, but apparently refuse to ask questions about their provenance,' a parliamentary source adds. 'They are in effect aiding and abetting people who use bots. They could be doing a lot more.'

However secondary ticketing sites claim that it is up to ticket sellers to regulate whom they sell their tickets to, not up to secondary sites.

Adapted from an article by Rachel Rickard Straus, 11 December 2014 from *This is Money* (www.thisismoney.co.uk).

##  Business application: labour markets

### Input markets

> **Input markets** are where factor inputs, such as land, labour, capital or enterprise, are traded.

Firms not only sell into markets, they also buy inputs, such as labour and raw materials, from markets. It is therefore important to understand how these **input markets** will develop as rises in input prices will lead to increases in firms' costs.

For example, consider the market for professional staff, bankers, lawyers and accountants. In recent years the wages offered to these individuals were very high.

These high wages reflected a booming economy, where the demand for services offered by professionals in lending, property transactions and financial management were high. The demand shifted to the right, as in Figure 4.15, and wage rates increased.

Two further influences then occurred. First, the high wage rates being paid to professional staff attracted workers into the banking, legal and accounting industries, graduates entered the sector and new student recruitment at university level moved towards professional services courses. The supply of capable workers shifted to the right and wage rates softened. Then the credit crunch recession led to many firms going bust and massive cutbacks in employment.

So, when thinking now about your future employment plans, it is essential to have a view on the future path of demand and supply in your chosen career area. See Table 4.1 for details on earnings and employment for graduates by industry. High wages in some sectors are likely to attract increased supply. By the time graduates leave university, the extra supply, in the absence of additional demand, will lead to falling wages. So what might appear to be an attractive career today may not be that attractive once you enter the labour market.

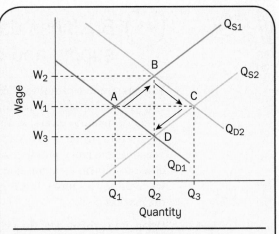

Figure 4.15    Input price changes over time

Beginning at A: demand for professional workers shifts to the right following a rise in demand for their services in a booming economy. The equilibrium moves to B and wage rates rise to $W_2$. Higher wages attract new additional workers into the market and supply shifts from $Q_{S1}$ to $Q_{S2}$. The equilibrium is now at C and wages fall to $W_1$. Following the credit crunch recession, demand for professional staff shifts back to the left from $Q_{D2}$ to $Q_{D1}$. The equilibrium is now at D and wages have fallen to $W_3$.

**Table 4.1**   Graduate recruitment and starting salaries, 2015

| | Recruitment target | % change from 2014 | Median starting salary £s | % change from 2014 |
|---|---|---|---|---|
| Accounting | 4624 | 10.8 | 30,000 | 1.7 |
| Armed forces | 1246 | 13.9 | 30,300 | 1 |
| Banking and finance | 1319 | 20.8 | 36,500 | 9 |
| Consulting | 610 | −2.4 | 31,500 | 0 |
| Consumer goods | 396 | 10.3 | 29,000 | 0 |
| Engineering and industrial | 1708 | 5 | 27,500 | 3.8 |
| Investment banking | 1820 | 2.3 | 45,000 | 0 |
| IT and telecommunications | 845 | 0 | 30,000 | 2.4 |
| Law | 780 | 10.6 | 40,000 | 1.3 |
| Media | 661 | 14.5 | 30,000 | 0 |
| Oil and energy | 394 | −11.7 | 32,500 | 0 |
| Public sector | 3771 | 13.7 | 20,000 | −9.1 |
| Retailing | 1314 | 13.9 | 26,000 | 0 |

*Source:* www.highfliers.co.uk

## (4.9) Business data application: understanding supply and demand in the car market

The car market provides a useful environment in which to apply and explore our new concepts of supply and demand. Car production is undertaken by a relatively small group of major manufacturers, so the units of production, supply, can be measured by surveys. In addition, when a new car is sold, that car has to be registered, so there is data on demand/consumer purchases. The data are not perfect, because there is not sufficient detail to inform us about consumers' willingness to demand at different prices, or firms' willingness to supply, but it does provide us with a general indication of movements in the market.

Using data provided by the UK Society of Motor Manufacturers, new car registrations grew 9.3 per cent in 2014 to 2.5 million units. This rise in overall demand for cars in the UK was matched by a massive increase in demand of plug-in cars, with new registrations rising from 3,586 in 2013 to 14,498 in 2014.

In terms of supply, the data available from the Society of Motor Manufacturers show that car production rose 1.2 per cent in 2014 to 1.5 million units of which 1.2 million units were exported, representing a decrease of 0.5 per cent on the number exported the year previously.

What do these data on purchases and production tell us about the market for cars? Are prices likely to rise or fall, what other information would we need and how might we worry about near-term equilibrium between supply and demand, and long-term trends towards greater demand for alternative fuel vehicles?

Using the frameworks developed in this chapter we might at first sight worry that supply is outstripping demand and prices could fall, but if we dig into the numbers a little, we can see that domestic production accounts for very little of UK car supply. In 2014 2.5 million cars were purchased in the UK but only 0.3 million of cars produced in the UK were for domestic consumption. Of the cars made in the UK, 1.2 million are being supplied somewhere else, and 2.2 million cars purchased in the UK are being made somewhere else. Given it is costly to transport cars, then the most likely source is Europe.

Data from the European Automobile Manufacturers Association show that new car registrations have changed dramatically across different countries. In Figure 4.16 we can see strong demand growth in the UK, Portugal and Poland. This growth is offset by plummeting demand in the Netherlands, Italy, Czech Republic and Finland. Interestingly, these patterns were reversed three years ago: i.e. the strongest growth markets back then are some of the weakest now. Fortunately, the entire European market grew by 1.6 per cent in 2014, giving UK motor manufacturers some chance of selling their increased output.

What these patterns would tend to suggest is that managers in the automotive sector have to be good at

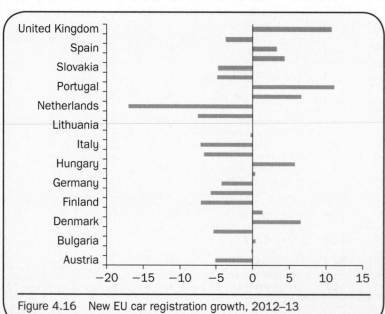

Figure 4.16 New EU car registration growth, 2012–13

spotting long-term emerging trends and also quickly rebalancing supply capacity to demand conditions across many different markets. For example, over time manufacturers will need to react to the growing demand for alternative fuel vehicles and protect themselves from the falling demand for petrol-powered vehicles. Following these long-term trends requires investment, vision and commitment to technology and particular customer groups.

In contrast, balancing existing supply and demand on an annual, perhaps even quarter by quarter, basis requires car manufacturers to know what their supply capacity is and where demand is growing and slowing across Europe. Matching supply and demand by diverting stock and output from declining markets to growing markets will require stockholding facilities and responsive logistic and transport systems. But when £20,000 or more is locked within a motor vehicle, there is a strong incentive to know your market and know where you can find an equilibrium sale.

## Summary

1. The supply curve shows a positive relationship between the market price and the willingness to supply.

2. The industry supply curve is the sum of all the individual firms' supply curves.

3. The market equilibrium occurs where the willingness to supply equals the willingness to demand.

4. The equilibrium is changed whenever demand or supply changes. If demand increases, the price will rise and more will be traded. But if supply increases, the price will drop while more will be traded. A reduction in demand leads to a reduction in prices and the amount traded, while a reduction in supply leads to higher prices and less being traded.

5. If the current price is above the equilibrium, supply will exceed demand and the market will show a surplus. Suppliers are likely to discount the price to shift excess stock and eventually return to the equilibrium price.

6. When the current price is below the equilibrium, demand will exceed supply and the market will show a shortage. The price will rise in the market as consumers seek out scarce supply and eventually the market will return to its equilibrium.

7. If consumers cannot differentiate between quality differences among competing products, the market is said to exhibit a pooling equilibrium. Providers of good-quality products will strive to create a separating equilibrium by undertaking behaviour that poor-quality providers are unwilling to match.

8. Good businesses can attempt to control or influence the market. Setting a price below the market equilibrium can help to launch a product and gain valuable market share.

9. Understanding how the market will develop in the future requires an understanding of supply and demand. Such an understanding can be used to forecast changes in product prices and input prices, all of which are essential for strategic planning.

# Learning checklist

You should now be able to:

- Explain the concept of market equilibrium and use a demand and supply diagram to show the equilibrium
- Use demand and supply diagrams to analyse changes to price and quantity following changes in demand and supply
- Explain how changes in the equilibrium price and quantity are influenced by the elasticity of demand and supply
- Explain the difference between a shortage and a surplus
- Explain the difference between a pooling and a separating equilibrium
- Explain how firms can benefit from pricing below the equilibrium price
- Explain how an understanding of future trends in demand, supply and prices is of use to business

# Questions

connect

1. At a price of £10, consumers are willing to demand 20,000 units and firms are willing to supply 20,000 units. Is this market in equilibrium?

2. Following an economic crisis, a number of banks collapse. What do you think happens to the supply of banking services and the price of banking services in general?

3. If income levels fall in an economy, what do you think will happen to the price of inferior goods and services?

4. As incomes in China rise, the global price of chicken and pork increases. Why?

5. An expansion of the world's shipping fleet threatens to depress the daily charter rates for oceangoing freighters. What must happen to demand in order to keep charter rates relatively constant?

6. Draw a diagram to illustrate a market surplus and a market shortage.

7. If there is a surplus amount of rental office space in a city, what do you expect to happen to rents? Use a diagram to explain your answer.

8. The elasticity of demand for electricity is relatively price inelastic. Will a change in supply have a large or a small impact on the equilibrium price and quantity?

9. What is the difference between a pooling and a separating equilibrium?

10. List three markets where pooling equilibria are a problem.

11. Why is the market for new staff characterized by the problem of adverse selection?

12. Celebrity status brings riches, but will the increase in the number of boy bands, docusoaps and reality television programmes, such as *Big Brother*, change the market price of celebrities?

13. If incomes were falling in an economy would you wish to invest in a house-building company?

14. Is studying for a degree a strategy for creating a separating equilibrium in the labour market?

15. Health care in the UK is free. Draw a diagram illustrating how waiting lists for hospital treatment in the UK reflect a market shortage at zero price.

EASY

INTERMEDIATE

DIFFICULT

# Exercises

1. True or false?

   (a) An increase in demand for coffee will lead to a higher price at Starbucks.

   (b) The merger of two firms can lead to higher prices.

   (c) The equilibrium price is always optimal for a firm.

   (d) Demand and supply are said to move separately under a separating equilibrium.

   (e) The adoption of a brand of phone by celebrities will raise the equilibrium price of that brand's phones.

   (f) Prices above the equilibrium will create a shortage.

2. Suppose that the data in Table 4.2 represent the market demand and supply for baked beans over a range of prices.

INTERMEDIATE

**Table 4.2** Demand and supply

| Price | Quantity demanded (million tins per year) | Quantity supplied (million tins per year) |
|---|---|---|
| 8 | 70 | 10 |
| 16 | 60 | 30 |
| 24 | 50 | 50 |
| 32 | 40 | 70 |
| 40 | 30 | 90 |

   (a) Plot on a single diagram the demand and supply curve, remembering to label the axes appropriately.

   (b) What would be the excess demand or supply if the price was set at 8p?

   (c) What would be the excess demand or supply if the price was 32p?

   (d) Find the equilibrium price and quantity.

   (e) Suppose that, following an increase in consumers' incomes, demand for baked beans rises by 15 million tins per year at all prices. Find the new equilibrium price and quantity.

3. Consider Box 4.4:

   (a) Explain the difference between a market surplus and a market shortage.

   (b) Draw a demand and supply diagram which illustrates a surplus for the Rolling Stones' live performances.

   (c) Is the practice of minimizing the supply of concerts by leading artists one of risk minimization or sales maximization?

4. Consider Box 4.3, which examines the price of oil.

   (a) Find data on the price of oil for the last year.

   (b) Graph your data so that trends in the price of oil over the last year can be seen.

   (c) By reading through news articles can you discover how changes in supply and demand for oil explain the changes in the price of oil?

Section

3

# Competition and profitability

## Section contents

# Market structure and firm performance

## Chapter contents

## Learning outcomes

By the end of this chapter you should be able to:

**Economic theory**

LO1 Explain why firms maximize profits by producing an output where marginal cost equals marginal revenue

LO2 Discuss the model of perfect competition

LO3 Compare normal and supernormal profits

LO4 Demonstrate how profit and losses lead to entry and exit

LO5 Explain the model of monopoly

LO6 Discuss how barriers to entry protect supernormal profits

LO7 Compare profit, output and prices between perfect competition and monopoly

**Business application**

LO8 Debate how a monopoly may end up competing with itself

LO9 Review the extent to which a firm can change its competitive environment

LO10 Apply data and Porter's five forces model to assess the strength of competition in an industry

## At a glance   Perfect competition and monopoly

### The issue

An essential business skill is being able to understand why different market structures create differing levels of competition and, therefore, business performance, particularly in terms of profit. On this matter, economics offers some interesting insights.

### The understanding

The understanding rests on how firms compete with each other. Firms can find themselves with any number of competitors. But instead of modelling every possible scenario, economists have concentrated on three: perfect competition, where there are many competitors; monopoly, where there are no competitors; and oligopoly, where there is only a very small number of competitors.

### The usefulness

This chapter will provide you with an understanding of the important industrial characteristics which in part influence the level of competition and profitability that your business will generate.

##  5.1  Business problem: where can you make profits?

The simple answer is that you can make profits in any market where consumers are willing to pay a price that exceeds your costs. But an economist and a successful business person have a more valuable insight into this problem. They can identify markets that are more likely to make profits. They can do this because they understand the factors that determine whether the market price will be in excess of the firm's costs.

However, before we begin the theory, we will take a semi-empirical approach to this problem. Think about a business that you are familiar with and consider how profitable it is. We will take some common examples. Consider the pizza and kebab shops located near your university or accommodation. Are they profitable? We suspect that they make money. But you rarely see a local outlet growing and operating more than one or two outlets. The interiors of the shops are often basic and the decorations tend to be worn. Refurbishments occur only occasionally. So, given that the owners do not grow the business, or invest in new fixtures and fittings, it might be argued that profits are limited.

Now consider Apple, the most valuable company in the world. Apple received more than $180 billion in revenues in 2015, leading to a profit of almost $44 billion. The stock market values Apple at $700 billion, making it the most expensive company in the world, and beating even the historic long-term mega-corporations of the world such as the oil company Exxon. While Apple faces competition, its rivals such as Samsung and HTC are struggling to match the profitability of Apple. See Box 5.1.

So why is it that Apple is so successful and kebab shops are not? It can be argued that Apple has been successful in managing its market and principally its competition. By managing competition effectively, Apple has grown into a successful company. In contrast, there are many kebab and pizza shops around your university. They are all competing with each other. Demand is elastic: if one shop drops its prices, students will flock to this shop. So price competition, or the threat of price competition, keeps prices low. Apple currently faces

## Box 5.1
## How the iPhone makes more money than all other smartphones combined

**Apple's iPhones account for around 90 per cent of profit made within the mobile industry, with Samsung taking the majority of the rest, a report claims**

Apple makes 90 per cent of all profit within the mobile industry, with Korean rival Samsung mopping up the rest, according to a new report. The Californian company's commitment to producing high-end handsets with unashamedly high price tags has translated into utter dominance of the industry's profits.

Apple and Samsung handsets account for more than one in three smartphone sales, and by far the majority of industry profits. In recent years HTC, LG and Sony's smartphone sales have slumped, and Samsung's have also suffered under increasing pressure from native brands in China and India at the cheaper end of the market, where Xiaomi and Micromax are hugely popular.

In July Samsung reported an 8 per cent drop in net profit over the course of a year, its seventh consecutive quarter of loss in profits. Taiwanese manufacturer HTC announced operating losses of NT$4.94bn (£100m) for the three months ended September 30, in the wake of announcing plans to slash its workforce by up to 15 per cent.

Sony's chief executive Kazuo Hirai announced this week the company would 'continue with the [mobile] business as long as we are on track with the scenario of breaking even next year onwards... Otherwise we haven't

eliminated the consideration of alternative options'. The company currently holds less than 1 per cent of the North American smartphone market. LG's earnings almost halved during the second financial quarter, with overall net profit falling 45 per cent compared to the year before.

Similarly, Microsoft's chief executive Satya Nadella explained away the company's decision to write off $7.6bn related to its $9.5bn acquisition of Nokia's mobile division in 2013 and cut 7,800 jobs as 'a change to our operating approach'. 'I'm not going to launch a phone a day,' he said. 'I'm going to focus on a few phones that actually grab share that, in fact, showcase our uniqueness.'

All of these brands offer a mix of handsets within their product lines, from the highly-specced to a variety of mid-range and modestly priced entry level models.

The opposite approach seems to have yielded the best results for Apple. The arrival of the iPhone 6s and 6s Plus models last month triggered the removal of the plastic iPhone 5c, the closest thing the company has ever had to a lower-tier priced phone. Apple's latest set of financial results reported a quarterly net profit of $10.7bn and record sales figures for its latest iPhones, which sold more than 13m units within three days.

From *The Telegraph*. 9 October 2015. 'How the iPhone makes more money than all other smartphones combined'. Rhiannon Williams. © Telegraph Media Group Limited (2015)

less competition, its products are distinctive and consumers value the brand. With limited substitutes, Apple faces relatively inelastic demand.

In this chapter we will present the assumption that firms are in business to maximize profits. After explaining how firms should maximize profits, we will examine how the different market structures of perfect competition and monopoly influence the amount of profits earned by a firm in each type of market structure.

 ## Profit maximization

Economists assume that firms are in business to maximize profits. This seems reasonable. As an investor, you take a risk when investing in a company and so you expect a financial return. In Chapter 7, we will challenge the assumption of profit maximization, but for now it will suffice as a reasonable assumption for the firm.

> **Marginal revenue** is the change in revenue from selling one more unit.
>
> **Average revenue** is the average price charged by the firm and is equal to total revenue/quantity demanded: (PQ)/Q.

The profits of a company are determined by the degree to which revenues are greater than costs. Therefore, in order to understand both (1) the output level at which profits are maximized and (2) the amount of profit generated at the maximum, we need to understand average and marginal revenue, plus average and marginal costs. We discussed average and marginal costs in detail during Chapter 3, but we need to develop your understanding of **marginal** and **average revenues**.

## Average and marginal revenues

Consider the demand data in Table 5.1. In the first two columns we have data from a demand curve; as the price increases in column 1, the quantity demanded, listed in column 2, decreases. Total revenue = price × quantity: for example, at a price of £7 demand is six units, therefore total revenue = £7 × 6 = £42. The remaining total revenue values are provided in column 3.

Average revenue = (price × quantity)/quantity. Therefore, at a price of £7 we have (£7 × 6)/6 = £7. The average revenue is the same as the price. You can see this clearly by noting that the column for price and the column for average revenue in Table 5.2 are identical. If you were asked to plot the demand curve (price against quantity demanded) and then also asked to plot the average revenue line (average revenue against quantity) on the same piece of graph paper, the two lines would lie on top of each other. If you are not convinced, take the data from Table 5.1 and use a spreadsheet package such as MS Excel to create an XY scatter plot of the demand and average revenue. You will only see one line on the screen, not two.

The demand line and the average revenue line are therefore the same thing.

In the final column, we have the values for marginal revenue. Marginal revenue is the revenue received by selling one more unit and is often expressed as $(\Delta PQ)/\Delta P$), or the change in

**Table 5.1** Demand and total, average and marginal revenue

| Price (£) | Quantity demanded | Total revenue (PQ) | Average revenue (PQ/Q) | Marginal revenue ($\Delta PQ)/\Delta P$) |
|---|---|---|---|---|
| 12 | 1 | 12 | 12 | |
| 11 | 2 | 22 | 11 | 10 |
| 10 | 3 | 30 | 10 | 8 |
| 9 | 4 | 36 | 9 | 6 |
| 8 | 5 | 40 | 8 | 4 |
| 7 | 6 | 42 | 7 | 2 |
| 6 | 7 | 42 | 6 | 0 |
| 5 | 8 | 40 | 5 | −2 |
| 4 | 9 | 36 | 4 | −4 |
| 3 | 10 | 30 | 3 | −6 |
| 2 | 11 | 22 | 2 | −8 |
| 1 | 12 | 12 | 1 | −10 |

**Table 5.2** Monopolistic average and total revenues

| Price | Quantity | Total revenue (PQ) | Average revenue (PQ/Q) | Marginal revenue ($\Delta PQ)/\Delta P$) |
|---|---|---|---|---|
| 12 | 4 | 48 | 12 | |
| 11 | 5 | 55 | 11 | 7 |
| 10 | 6 | 60 | 10 | 5 |

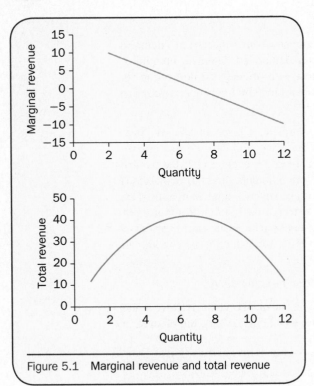

Figure 5.1   Marginal revenue and total revenue

revenue divided by the change in price. Therefore, in moving from one unit to two units (selling one more unit), our revenues have increased from 12 to 22. Marginal revenue is therefore 22 − 12 = 10. All the values for marginal revenue are plotted in Figure 5.1.

The marginal revenue line slopes down, reflecting an increase in output which requires a reduction in the price and the impact of the price reduction on previous units. Total revenue is greatest when marginal revenue is zero; this is because selling one more unit neither adds to nor subtracts from the total revenue.

The marginal revenue line slopes down. This is the result of of two factors. First, marginal revenue is related to the demand curve. In order to sell one more unit, we know from Chapter 2 that we have to reduce the price of the product. Second, in reducing the price we are also reducing the price of all the previous units. Consider the following. We can sell seven units at a price of 6, or reduce the price to 5 and sell eight units. In comparing the two situations, we gain one more unit at a price of 5, but we are reducing the price from 6 to 5 on the other seven units. Therefore, the marginal revenue associated with selling one more unit is $+ 5 - (7 \times 1) = - 2$. We can see that in order to sell one more unit we also have to accept a reduction in marginal revenue and not just the price.

Finally, in the bottom half of Figure 5.1, we have the plot of total revenue. You can see that maximum revenue occurs where marginal revenue equals zero in the top diagram. This is because a marginal revenue of 0 lies between positive and negative marginal revenue. When marginal revenue is positive, each unit adds a positive amount to total revenue. Once marginal revenue becomes negative, each additional unit reduces total revenue.

## Profit maximization

We can now combine our understanding of revenue and costs to understand how firms maximize profits. Firms will maximize profits or, in other words, make the most amount of profit, when the marginal cost of the last unit of output equals the marginal revenue, or MC = MR.

It is important to note that MC = MR and profit maximization are not policy prescriptions for firms. Economists are not saying firms must behave in this way. Rather, economists have said profit maximization is a reasonable assumption to hold about the behaviour of firms; and if we do model firms as profit-maximizers, then output must be at the point where MC = MR. In Chapter 8 we will revisit the assumption of profit maximization and consider other assumptions, including growth maximization and revenue maximization.

In understanding how the economist arrives at the **profit maximization** rule of MC = MR, we need to make some assumptions. The firm does not decide to produce 10 or 20 units of output; rather, it decides if it wants to produce one unit of output. Then it decides if it wants to produce the second unit. At some point it will decide not to produce any more. So the economist is assuming that the firm is making stepped decisions.

In Table 5.3, we have added marginal cost data to the marginal revenue data discussed above. In the fourth column we have marginal revenue minus marginal cost.

The firm maximizes profits when marginal cost equals marginal revenue, i.e. MC = MR. If MC = MR, then MR − MC = 0. The firm maximizes profits when the **marginal profit** = 0.

Profit maximization is the output level at which the firm generates the highest profit.

Marginal profit is the profit made on the last unit and is equal to the marginal revenue minus the marginal cost.

**Table 5.3** Marginal revenue and marginal cost

| Quantity | MR | MC | MR–MC | Output decision | Profit |
|---|---|---|---|---|---|
| 1 | 1 | 15 | 6 | Raise | 6 |
| 2 | 19 | 11 | 8 | Raise | 14 |
| 3 | 17 | 8 | 9 | Raise | 23 |
| 4 | 15 | 7 | 8 | Raise | 31 |
| 5 | 13 | 8 | 5 | Raise | 36 |
| 6 | 11 | 10 | 1 | | 37 |
| 7 | 9 | 12 | −3 | Lower | 34 |
| 8 | 7 | 14 | −7 | Lower | 27 |
| 9 | 5 | 16 | −11 | Lower | 16 |
| 10 | 3 | 18 | −15 | Lower | 1 |

This is similar to revenue maximization in Figure 5.1. When MR > MC, the firm is making a marginal profit—each additional unit generates a positive profit and adds to overall profits. However, once MR < MC the firm is making a marginal loss—each additional unit generates a loss and therefore diminishes total profits. We can, therefore, argue that the firm will increase production if marginal revenue is greater than marginal cost, i.e. MR > MC. But the firm will reduce output if it is incurring a marginal loss, i.e. MR < MC.

Using these insights we can take our stepped approach to discover the profit-maximizing output. Let's assume the company makes celebration cakes for birthdays, etc. From Table 5.3, if the firm produced one unit of output, one cake, then the marginal profit would be 21, the marginal cost would be 15 and the profit would be 6. Since this is positive, the firm will make one unit. The cake company now decides whether or not to make the second cake. The additional or marginal profit associated with making the second cake is 8. Again, since this is positive the firm will make the second cake. Likewise, the firm will decide to make cakes three, four, five and six, as the marginal profits are all positive. The firm will not produce beyond the sixth cake because the marginal profits are negative. For example, a loss of 3 is associated with making the seventh cake. Profits are, therefore, maximized at 6 units of output, or six cakes per day. This can be seen in the final column of Table 5.3, with profits peaking at 37 with an output of 6.

In the cake-making business, if you wish to sell more cakes, then the price has to come down. You may find one person per day who is willing to pay £21 per cake, but to generate demand for 6 cakes you need to drop the price to £11 per cake. As you make more cakes, then the cost of making the next cake may increase. For example, you may be able to have one person mixing and baking cakes. To make more cakes, they only need a bigger mixing bowl and more ingredients, not much of an increase in costs. However, decorating a cake with icing might be more involved and so for more cakes you need more staff and so the marginal cost increases.

Admittedly, we stated that the firm will maximize profits when MC = MR and in our example profits appear to peak at six units of output, where marginal revenue is one unit greater than marginal cost. From an examination of the data, we might argue that MC = MR somewhere between six and seven units, let us say 6.5. Some products are easy to divide into smaller units of output, for example oil, beer and milk. A firm could decide to produce 6.5 litres of milk. But it would not be sensible to produce 6.5 cars. We can, therefore, say that MC = MR is strictly and mathematically correct, but it is not always the most practical output level for a firm to maximize profits at. If the firm produces whole units, it will stop at the highest level of output

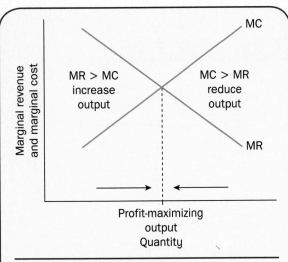

Figure 5.2   Marginal revenue, marginal cost and profit maximization

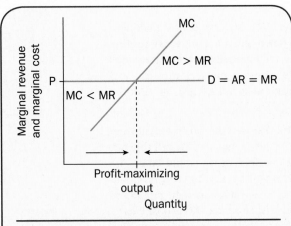

Figure 5.3   Profit maximization under perfectly elastic demand

with a positive marginal profit. This way, the firm chooses a level of output that is nearest to its profit-maximizing level of output.

Figure 5.2 provides a diagrammatic illustration of profit maximization where marginal cost equals marginal revenue. Firms will increase output if marginal revenue is greater than marginal cost; and they will reduce output if marginal cost is greater than marginal revenue.

The firm maximizes profits where MC = MR. Alternatively, the firm will produce an additional unit of output if the MR is greater than the MC, because it then makes additional profit. But it will not produce any more output if the marginal revenue is less than the marginal cost, because this will generate a loss on the last unit produced, leading to a reduction in overall profits.

In Box 5.2 we provide evidence of output decisions by two of the world's largest suppliers of iron ore. At a marginal revenue of $70 per tonne and costs of $40 ($20 for mining and $20 for shipping), they are both inclined to expand output to increase profits.

## Profit maximization and differences in demand

In Chapter 3, when considering costs, we saw that marginal cost always has a positive slope – that is, all firms face diminishing returns in the short run. However, firms in different markets face different demand conditions and this leads to different average revenue and therefore different marginal revenue lines. However, under the assumption of profit maximization the optimal output will still occur where MC = MR.

In Figure 5.3, we consider an important and special case where demand is perfectly elastic. We explained

## Box 5.2
## Rio sitting prettier than BHP as commodities slide

This week's production updates from BHP Billiton and Rio Tinto were broadly surprise-free zones. Until now, iron ore has dominated the picture and underpinned dividend payout at both as they boosted output to meet robust demand from China—even as the steelmaking commodity's price halved over the past year to trade below $70 a tonne.

Mad though their increased ore output looks to outsiders, it's a no brainer for Rio, the lowest cost producer, and BHP. To recap, BHP's iron ore output in its second-quarter to end-December rose by 16 per cent from a year ago to 56.5mt (metric tonnes), setting yet

another record for the 2014 calendar year—and driving down its marginal cost of production.

For its part, Rio's fourth-quarter iron ore production was 12 per cent higher at 79.1mt, and its shipments—to you-know-where (China)—rose by 13 per cent to 82.2mt, as it drew on stockpiles to meet Chinese demand.

Rio is sitting pretty. Its marginal cash cost of production is about $20/t. Add $20/t more to land it in China—probably less with the lower oil price—and it still has ample room for manoeuvre at current levels.

From the *Financial Times*. 21 January 2015. 'Rio sitting prettier than BHP as commodities slide'.
© The Financial Times Limited 2015. All Rights Reserved.

in Chapter 2 that a perfectly elastic demand line is horizontal. Firms can sell *any* amount of output at the current price, but if they price above the market price they sell nothing, because customers are extremely price sensitive.

The consequences of a perfectly elastic demand line are that average revenue and marginal revenue are also horizontal lines. Each unit of output is sold for the same price, so the average revenue is constant (and equal to the price); and the revenue from the last unit is equal to the revenue from the previous unit. Therefore, marginal revenue is also constant and equal to the price.

Figure 5.3 follows a similar reasoning to Figure 5.2. When marginal cost is below marginal revenue, the firm can expand output and raise profits. However, once marginal cost is greater than marginal revenue, the firm should reduce output and profits will rise. The important difference between Figures 5.2 and 5.3 is the relationship between marginal cost and price. In Figure 5.3, under profit maximization $MC = MR = AR = P$, or in shorthand $MC = P$. However, in Figure 5.2, $MC = MR$, but $MR \neq AR$ (also see the columns in Table 5.1 and Figure 5.1 to remind yourself of this fact). Therefore, $MC \neq P$. As we explore perfect competition and monopoly later in this chapter, the importance of this distinction will become clearer.

## Changes in costs and revenues

In Figures 5.4 and 5.5 we examine what happens if either marginal revenue or marginal cost changes. If demand increases for a product, then the marginal revenue curve will similarly shift to the right. This is because when the market price increases at all output levels, the firm will receive a higher price for each additional unit of output. In Figure 5.4, we illustrate this idea and see that marginal revenue now meets marginal cost at a much higher level of output. In response, the firm can maximize profits at a much higher level of output. Therefore, firms do not increase output because prices rise; rather, they increase output because the marginal revenue has risen above marginal cost. The motive for increasing output is, therefore, one of increased profits, not increased prices. In contrast, if demand for the product fell, then the marginal revenue curve would shift to the left. With lower marginal revenues, the profit-maximizing output would be reduced.

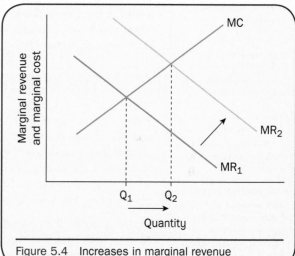

Figure 5.4   Increases in marginal revenue

If demand increases for the firm's product, then the marginal revenue curve will also move out to the right. Marginal revenue now equals marginal cost at a much higher level of output and the firm will therefore produce more output in order to maximize profits. We can now view increased output as a reflection of increasing profits rather than simply increasing prices.

If a firm experiences productivity growth, then its marginal costs may fall. With lower marginal costs at all levels of output, the firm will be more able to maximize profits at a higher level of output. We can now view increased output as a reflection of increasing profits rather than simply decreasing costs.

In Figure 5.5, we illustrate a reduction in marginal cost. We saw in Chapter 3 that marginal cost is influenced

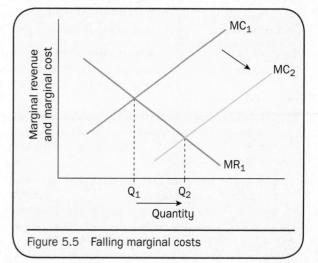

Figure 5.5   Falling marginal costs

by the price of factor inputs such as labour and factor productivity. If labour became more productive it could produce more output and the marginal cost would fall. We see from Figure 5.5 that, if this did occur, then the marginal cost would fall below marginal revenue and the firm would increase output in order to maximize profits. Similarly, marginal cost could increase because labour wage rates increase. The marginal cost curve would then shift to the left. With higher marginal costs at all levels of output the profit-maximizing level of output would be reduced.

We have now brought together the understandings of demand and prices from Chapter 2 and cost theory from Chapter 3. Combining the two enables an understanding of how the firm will maximize its profits. Unlike in Chapter 2, where we discussed a firm's response to changes in the price of the final good or service, and in Chapter 3, where we analysed a firm's responses to cost changes, we can now see how the firm changes its output level based on an interaction of revenue and costs. In the economic sense, the firm is not concerned with prices or costs per se, but rather profit, which is a combination of the two.

Having highlighted profit as the major incentive for firms, we now need to consider how market structure will impact upon the marginal revenue and perhaps even marginal cost of a firm. By examining perfect competition and monopoly, we will see how the level of profits at the profit-maximizing output level is likely to be lower under perfect competition than under monopoly. However, before we embark upon the theory, it is fairly straightforward to understand that profits will be lower in perfect competition. This can be seen from our definition that perfect competition is the market environment with the greatest amount of competition. With lots of competitors all chasing the same customers, profits have to be small. Now let us provide the theoretical, rather than common sense, framework.

## (5.3) The spectrum of market structures

We can see in Figure 5.6 that **perfect competition** and **monopoly** are extreme and opposite forms of market structure. In reality, it is difficult to find true perfectly competitive markets or even monopolies. Financial markets trading shares in companies are highly competitive, as are commodity markets trading such goods as oil, copper and gold. But, as we will see below, while such markets are *highly* competitive, they are not necessarily *perfectly* competitive.

Perfectly competitive signifies that competition in the market is the greatest possible. No alternative market structure can be more competitive. Similarly, Microsoft is not a perfect example of a monopoly, as its products compete with a number of smaller suppliers, such as Linux. Likewise, Angelina Jolie and Brad Pitt have a monopoly on their lifestyle, image and personalities but, in the celebrity market, they still face competition from a range of married celebrity couples.

Other types of market structure are **imperfect competition** and **oligopoly**. Imperfect competition is very competitive, but differs from perfect competition by the recognition of product differentiation. Small service-sector industries tend to have the characteristics of imperfect competition. The supermarket industry and the banking industry are oligopolistic. These are clearly more common modes of **market structure** and we will analyse imperfect competition and oligopoly in more detail in Chapter 6.

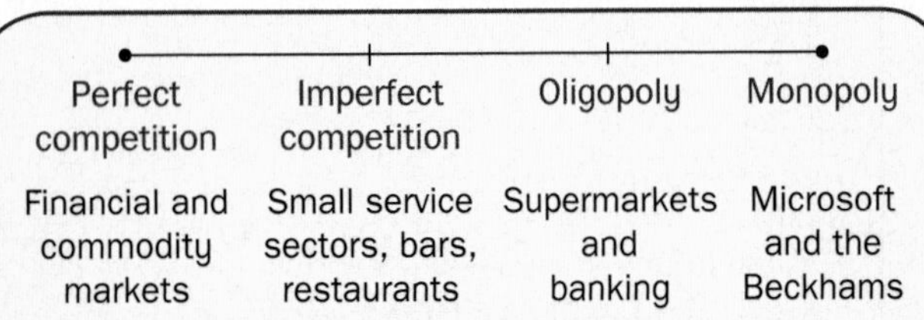

We will see when we examine the alternative market structures of perfect competition and monopoly that important competitive structures are: (1) the number of competitors; (2) the number

**Perfect competition** is a highly competitive marketplace.

**Monopoly** is a marketplace supplied by only one competitor, so no competition exists.

**Imperfect competition** is a highly competitive market where firms may use product differentiation.

**Oligopoly** is a market that consists of a small number of large players, such as banking, supermarkets and the media.

**Market structure** is the economist's general title for the major competitive structures of a particular marketplace.

| Perfect competition | Imperfect competition | Oligopoly | Monopoly |
|---|---|---|---|
| Financial and commodity markets | Small service sectors, bars, restaurants | Supermarkets and banking | Microsoft and the Beckhams |

Figure 5.6    Range of possible market structures

of buyers; (3) the degree of product differentiation; and (4) the level of entry and exit barriers. Further explanation of these concepts will be provided when we discuss perfect competition in detail, where we will see very clearly how the structure, or characteristics, of a market determines the level of competition and, ultimately, profitability.

 ## 5.4 Perfect competition

Perfect competition is the most competitive type of market structure. Economists assume that perfect competition is characterized by the following structure:

- Many buyers and sellers
- Firms have no market power
- Homogeneous products
- No barriers to exit or entry
- Perfect information.

These elements are explored below:

- **Buyers, sellers and market values**—the first two assumptions are related. The market has many different buyers and sellers. Because of this, no firm, or indeed buyer, has any market power. Market power is the ability to set prices. By many buyers and sellers we do not mean 10, 50 or 100—we mean *many*! Each buyer and seller is a very small part of the market. For example, the market for shares in any FTSE-100 company might be in excess of 10 million traded shares per day. But an individual shareholder may only hold 1,000 shares, which is clearly small when compared to the entire market. The individual shareholder, therefore, has little power over the market price; they simply accept the current price on the stock exchange screens.
- **Homogeneous products**—if all products are homogeneous, all firms provide identical products. Milk is an example; milk from one supermarket is the same as milk from another. Cars are heterogeneous or differentiated.
- **No barriers to exit or entry**—in order to operate a 4G telecommunications network you require a licence from the government and a very large amount of investment. Both restrict entry into the market and, therefore, act as an **entry barrier**. Similarly, if a firm decides to leave the 4G market, then the cost associated with selling the accumulated assets, whether technical network infrastructure or brand-name capital, will be costly and act as a restraint on exit. Alternatively, if you wished to start selling flowers from your garden, then you only need some seeds, sunshine and water. The entry barriers into the flower market are limited. Similarly, if you decided to stop producing flowers in your garden, then you would face little if any **exit barriers** or costs. You simply pull up the flowers and lay some additional turf.
- No barriers to exit or entry means that a business person can move economic resources into a market in the pursuit of profit and can also move them out. This transfer of resources is assumed to be effortless and relatively inexpensive, if not free.
- **Perfect information**—if you have a secret ingredient for your kebabs, then any competitor will be able to discover what the ingredient is. They can send in a customer and then arrange for the kebab to be analysed by a scientist or master kebab chef. So any informational advantage will be short-lived. Similarly, if a firm decided to sell at a higher price than its competitors, everyone in the marketplace would know that the price was expensive. In the stock market, all offers to sell and buy are published on the brokers' screens, hence there is **perfect information** regarding prices.

Barriers to entry make entry into a market by new competitors difficult.

Exit barriers make exit from a market by existing competitors difficult.

Perfect information assumes that every buyer and every seller knows everything.

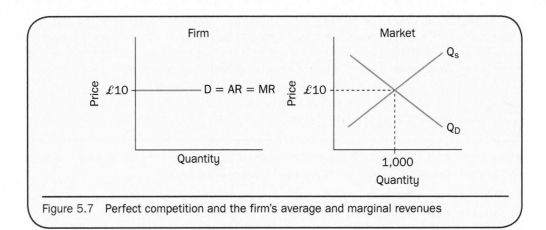

Figure 5.7  Perfect competition and the firm's average and marginal revenues

## Perfect competition and the firm's demand curve

We will now see how the assumptions of perfect competition drive the outcomes of a perfectly competitive market. For example, the assumption regarding a lack of market power is illustrated in Figure 5.7.

Buyers and sellers in the marketplace set the price of £10. Each firm, as a price taker, then accepts the market price and can sell any amount of output at the market price. Therefore, the firm's average revenue (AR) is £10, and so is marginal revenue.

In the marketplace many buyers and sellers come together and the market price of £10 is set. This is illustrated in the right-hand side of Figure 5.7. As the firm has no market power it simply accepts the market price.

> A **price taker** is a firm that accepts the market price.

As a **price taker**, the demand curve for a perfectly competitive firm is perfectly elastic. The firm can sell whatever quantity it likes at £10. This is illustrated on the left-hand side of Figure 5.7. While a perfectly competitive firm can sell whatever quantity it likes at the market price, this does not mean that the firm produces everything the market can bear. Rather, all firms can reasonably expect to sell their profit-maximizing level of output at the market price.

Since the firm faces many competitors, its market share will be extremely small. When this competition is coupled with perfect information, if the firm raised its prices above the equilibrium level it would sell nothing, with customers quickly swapping to the cheaper suppliers. In contrast, because the firm can sell all that it likes at the current market price, there is no reason to sell below the market price. Taking these points together, the firm faces a perfectly elastic demand curve, because demand reacts instantly, fully and perfectly to an increase or decrease in the firm's price.

## Average and marginal revenue

Marginal revenue is the revenue received by selling one more unit. In perfect competition, the firm faces a perfectly elastic, or horizontal, demand line. If it decides to sell one more unit, then it does not have to reduce its price. Therefore, if the market price is £10, the firm can sell one more unit and receive an additional £10. Unlike in our discussion of Table 5.1 and Figure 5.2, the perfectly competitive firm does not have to suffer a reduction in revenue on its previous units. Therefore, the marginal revenue line is also horizontal and equal to the average revenue line, but only in the special case of perfect competition.

## Adding in costs

We can now take Figure 5.7 and add in the short-run average cost curves developed in Chapter 3 to produce Figure 5.8. In so doing, we will have average revenue and costs on

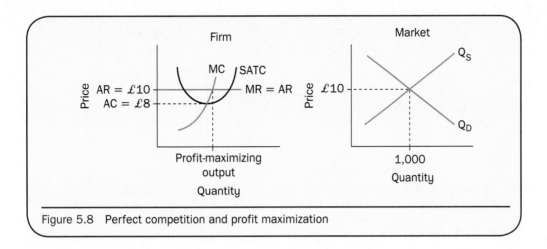

Figure 5.8    Perfect competition and profit maximization

the same figure as well as marginal revenue and marginal cost. We can then examine the profitability of the firm.

Introducing costs into the analysis enables an examination of the firm's profits. The firm produces at the profit-maximizing output, where MC = P. The average cost of this output is AC = £8, while the average revenue is AR = £10. Total profit is (£10 − £8) × output.

The diagram is fairly straightforward. Remember, we are assuming the firm is a profit-maximizer and we would simply like to know how much profit the firm would make. So:

- **Step 1:** The firm maximizes profits by producing the profit-maximizing level of output associated with MC = MR.
- **Step 2:** What does it cost to produce the profit-maximizing output? Simply draw the line up from the profit-maximizing output until it touches the short-run average total cost curve, SATC. So, in this case, £8 per unit.
- **Step 3:** What revenue will the firm earn by selling the profit-maximizing output? Simply draw the line up from the profit-maximizing output until it touches the average revenue line, AR. So, in this case, £10.
- **Step 4:** Profit per unit is AR minus AC, so £10 − £8 or £2 per unit.
- **Step 5:** Total profit is profit per unit times the number of units produced. Or, in our figure, the rectangle defined by AR − AC and the profit-maximizing output.

So, we can see that this particular firm is making a profit. In economic terms, it is making a 'supernormal profit'. See the next section on normal and supernormal profits.

We can also consider the situation where a firm is making a loss, and this is depicted in Figure 5.9. In comparison to Figure 5.7, we have simply reduced the market price from £10 to £7, and therefore the AR and MR to £7. At this market price, the firm's average revenue is below even the lowest point on the firm's average cost curve, so the firm cannot make a profit at any output level. The firm will now seek to minimize its losses rather than maximize its profits. It will achieve this in the same way as it maximizes its profits—that is, by selecting the output level where MR = MC. The loss generated by the firm will be equal to (AR − AC) × loss-minimizing output.

With the average revenue of £7 less than the average cost of £8, the firm will seek to minimize its losses. It will do this by selecting the output level where MC = MR. The overall loss will therefore be (AR − AC) × loss-minimizing output, or (7 − 8) × loss-minimizing output.

## Normal and supernormal profits

Importantly, economists and accountants differ in their definition of profits. In Figure 5.10, we illustrate each of these views. An accountant calculates profits by taking total costs

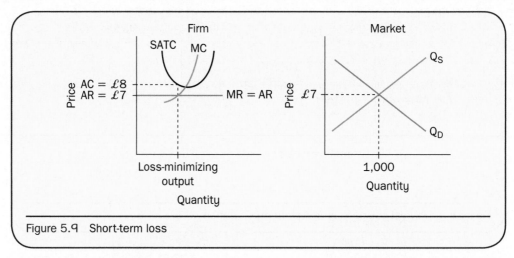

Figure 5.9   Short-term loss

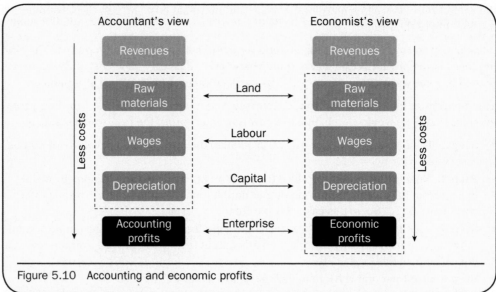

Figure 5.10   Accounting and economic profits

away from total revenues. The accountant would generally categorize raw materials, labour and depreciation as costs. Taking these costs from revenue leaves **accounting profits**.

The accountant calculates profits as revenues less the costs of land, labour and capital. The economist calculates profits as revenues less the costs of land, labour, capital and enterprise.

Accounting profits are revenues less raw material costs, wages and depreciation.

Economic profits are revenues less the costs of all factors of production.

Normal economic profits are equal to the average rate of return which can be gained in the economy.

The economist also takes costs away from revenues. By contrast, the economist thinks about the costs of using economic factors of production. These, from Chapter 1, are land, labour, capital and enterprise. The first three in this list map directly onto the accountant's cost categories. For example, the cost of labour is wages. But what is the cost of our fourth factor of production, namely that of enterprise? Recall that enterprise is individuals who are risk-takers and provide financial capital for companies. Entrepreneurs receive the benefits of taking financial risks. They receive profits. Therefore the economist views profits as a cost of using enterprise and we call these **economic profits**.

Economists further divide economic profits into two categories, *normal* and *supernormal*. **Normal economic profits** are the minimum rate of return required for an entrepreneur to retain their investment in a company. If the entrepreneur can gain 5 per cent by placing their money in a bank account, then this may act as a benchmark rate of normal return. We would then adjust this figure upwards for the degree of risk offered by the company. If the company was very risky, then we might say the normal rate of return for the company is 10 per cent. If the company was less risky, we might expect an entrepreneur to be seeking 7 per cent from their investment.

Anything above the normal rate of return is called **supernormal profits**; and anything less than normal profits is called a *supernormal loss*.

> Supernormal profits are financial returns greater than normal profits.

## Long-run equilibrium

Having seen supernormal profits and losses in the short run, it is now time to recall the remaining assumptions regarding perfect competition. Perfect information implies that all business people outside the industry are aware of the profits to be made inside this industry. No barriers to entry imply that entry into this market is easy. Therefore, businesses know about the profitable opportunities in this market and can enter the market with ease. The consequences of increased market entry for profits are illustrated in Figure 5.11.

At a price of £15, firms are making supernormal profits, with average revenues greater than average costs. These high profits attract new entrants into the market and the supply curve moves from $QS_1$ to $QS_2$. The price falls until it reaches £10. At this price the average revenue and average costs are equal, the firm earns normal profits, and firms are no longer attracted into the market. At a price of £5, firms are making losses, with average revenue below average costs. These losses force some firms out of the industry. Supply moves from $QS_3$ to $QS_2$. The price rises to £10 and firms earn normal profits.

If we begin in market equilibrium at $QS_1$ and QD, the market price is £15. This sets an average revenue $AR_1$, which is higher than firms' short-run average costs, SATC. Firms are making supernormal profits and this attracts new entrants into the industry. The supply curve moves to $QS_2$, the market price falls to £10 and firms are making normal profits. There is no longer any reason to enter the market, as similar risk-adjusted profits can be earned by putting money in the bank. We can also consider the situation where firms are making a loss. When market supply is at $QS_3$, the market price is £5 and this sets average revenue $AR_3$ less than short-run average cost, SATC. Firms are making losses and some exit the market. This leads to $QS_3$ moving towards $QS_2$. Once the market price returns to £10, the remaining firms in the industry are making normal profits and exit stops.

Box 5.3 examines the market for Whole Foods. Profit margins have been very high, but the product is relatively homogenous, entry barriers are low, there are many buyers and sellers and information on pricing and products is good. Profits as predicted by perfect competition are falling.

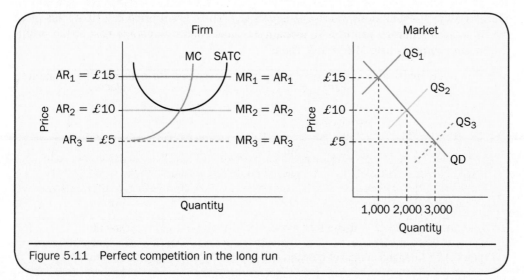

Figure 5.11   Perfect competition in the long run

## Box 5.3
## Whole Foods Market—victim of success

The colourful chalkboards and baskets of fruit that greet customers at the entrances of Whole Foods Market's shops paint a rosy picture. Yet shares in Whole Foods Market's, the American seller of organic and natural food, have fallen by more than 40 per cent since hitting a peak last October. It is not that the retailer is in immediate crisis: its latest quarterly figures, on July 30, showed sales and profits both up a bit. And it is not that people are going off the idea of paying more for food produced without chemical fertilisers, pesticides or additives. Market research predicts that the American market for such foods—the world's largest—may grow by 14 per cent by 2018.

The problem is that at Whole Foods, shoppers have been paying way over the cost of regular produce, and its success in getting them to do so has now attracted a lot of competitors, from rival organics chains like Sprouts and Trader Joe's to mass-market retailers like Walmart and Costco. As a result, the price premium for organic produce is crashing down. On a recent shopping trip, a pound of organic apples cost $2.99 at Whole Foods but just $1.99 at Sprouts and even less at Costco.

The firm has been trimming costs to keep its margins up, but the slump in its share price reflects investors'

expectation that this cannot continue, that profits will suffer and that Whole Foods' dominance of the market is coming to an end.

Organic foods' claim to superiority is questionable anyway. Both Britain's Food Standards Agency and the *Annals of Internal Medicine,* a journal, concluded after reviewing the extensive studies on the issue that there is no substantial difference in the nutritiousness of organics and non-organics. As for 'natural' foods, there is no official definition of this, in America at least; so the label, which Whole Foods also applies to many products, is close to meaningless. Alan McHughen, a botanist at the University of California, Riverside, argues that the whole industry is '99% marketing and public perception,' reeling people in through a fabricated concept of a time when food, and life in general, was simple and wholesome.

If true, the trick has worked nicely for Whole Foods. But its success has attracted so many imitators that it is losing its uniqueness. Even recent speculation about a takeover bid has failed to lift its shares. It may insist its food is sustainable. But it seems its prices are not.

From *The Economist*. 'Whole Foods Market - Victim of success'. © The Economist Newspaper Limited, London (2 August 2014)

Clearly, entry and exit are not the only factors that will influence the market equilibrium. We can envisage a number of short-term scenarios leading to a long equilibrium. In scenario 1, the good is a normal good. Income increases and, therefore, the market demand shifts to the right. The market price increases and the firm's marginal revenue and average revenue rise relative to costs. Increased profits then attract new entry into the market. The market supply curve shifts to the right and the market equilibrium price drops until average revenues equal average costs and only normal profits are earned. These points are highlighted in Figure 5.12.

The market is in equilibrium where $Q_{D1}$ equals $Q_{S1}$. The market price is £10. At this price the firm earns a normal profit, with average revenue equal to average cost at the profit-maximizing output, where $MR_1 = MC$. Then:

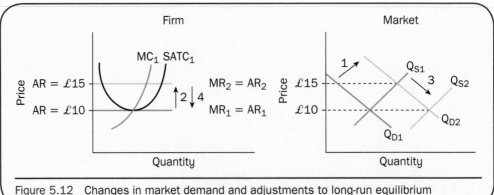

Figure 5.12   Changes in market demand and adjustments to long-run equilibrium

1. Income levels in the economy increase. The good is income normal and therefore the demand curve shifts to the right to $QD_2$ (consumers use the increased income to buy more of the good). The equilibrium price rises to £15.
2. The average revenue for the firm rises to £15, reflecting the increased market price. The marginal revenue also increases to £15 and the profit-maximizing output increases. Since average revenues exceed average cost, the firm is making a supernormal profit.
3. The supernormal profits attract new entrants into the market and supply shifts from $Q_{S1}$ to $Q_{S2}$ and the market equilibrium price falls to £10.
4. The average and marginal revenues fall to £10. The profit-maximizing output returns to its original level and the firm generates normal profits.

In scenario 2, following wage negotiations the cost of labour increases. The firms' marginal cost curves shift to the left and average costs rise upwards. Firms' profits decrease. Exit occurs and the market supply curve shifts to the left. As a result, the market equilibrium price increases until the average revenues earned by the firms match the higher cost level brought about by increased labour costs. Normal profits are earned and exit stops. These points are illustrated in Figure 5.13.

The market is in equilibrium where $Q_D$ equals $Q_{S1}$. The market price is £10. At this price the firm earns a normal profit, with average revenue equal to average cost at the profit-maximizing output. Then:

1. Negotiations lead to a rise in the wages paid to the firms' labour forces. This leads to an increase in the individual firm's costs. The average and marginal costs rise to $SATC_2$ and $MC_2$.
2. The firms' costs are now greater than the average revenue of £10, leading to losses. Some firms exit the industry and the industry supply curve shifts to the left, to $Q_{S2}$.
3. The equilibrium market price rises to £20, also raising average revenue to £20. This is just enough to cover the increase in the firms' costs. Firms again generate normal profits at the profit-maximizing output.

The review questions contain an additional scenario to test your understanding and use of the diagrams.

It is important to remember that, whether we begin with a supernormal profit or a supernormal loss, firms in perfect competition will always end up earning only normal profits in the long run. That is, firms in a perfectly competitive long-run equilibrium will be indifferent between being in business and placing their money in the bank.

In the long-run equilibrium, the perfectly competitive firm is operating at the minimum point of the average cost curve. This means that the firm is **productively efficient** as it is producing at least cost.

> Productive efficiency means that the firm is operating at the minimum point on its long-run average cost curve. Moreover, in long-run equilibrium the firm is charging a price that is equal to the marginal cost. This means that the firm is also allocatively efficient. We highlighted this outcome in section 5.2 and Figure 5.3.

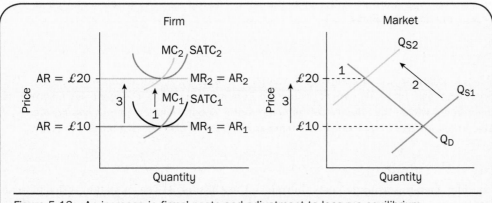

Figure 5.13   An increase in firms' costs and adjustment to long-run equilibrium

Recall that the cost of using scarce factor resources to produce one more unit of output is the marginal cost; and the price paid by consumers reflects the value placed on the final good. If the marginal cost of making a laptop computer is £300 and consumers are willing to pay no more than £250, then there is an inefficient use of society's scarce resources. The £300 of resources, including labour, capital and raw materials, which went into the laptop are not worth £300 to consumers. If the same resources could have been used to produce the latest high-tech mobile phones and consumers were willing to pay £300 per phone, then society's scarce resources would have been allocated efficiently. The value of the phones produced is exactly equal to the value of the resources used. In summary, **allocative efficiency** occurs when price = marginal cost. We will return to these points when we compare perfect competition with monopoly.

> Allocative efficiency occurs when price equals marginal cost, or $P = MC$.

## A quick consideration of kebab shops

Now let us consider the kebab shop sector and in particular assess the kebab market against the assumptions of perfect competition. There are many (buyers) students and there are many (sellers) kebab shops. A kebab is a fairly homogeneous product—kebabs from different shops are fairly similar. Prices are listed on boards inside the shop and are usually visible from the street, so information regarding prices is near perfect. Barriers to entry are fairly limited. You need a shop, a food licence, some pitta bread and some cheap meat. All are easily available. The kebab market is not perfectly competitive, but the characteristics of the market are close to perfectly competitive. Profits are likely to be low in the kebab market and so it is likely to be an unattractive business proposition. Let us now see if monopoly is better.

##  Monopoly

In a strict sense, a monopoly is said to exist when only one firm supplies the market. In practice, the UK competition authorities define a monopoly to exist if one firm controls more than 25 per cent of the market. So, clearly, a monopoly exists if there is a dominant firm in the market with few rivals.

Monopolies tend to exist because of barriers to entry, where barriers to entry restrict the ability of potential rivals to enter the market.

Let us begin with some easy examples.

### Licences

The National Lottery is a monopoly. Only one firm, currently Camelot, is licensed by the government to operate a national lottery in the UK. Licences also act as a barrier to entry on the railways. Until recently, only Eurostar was allowed to operate high-speed trains between London and Paris.

### Patents

When a pharmaceutical company develops a new drug, it can apply for a patent. This provides it with up to 20 years of protection from its rivals. While everyone can discover the ingredients within the cholesterol-reducing statin Zocor, only the patent owner, Merck, is able to exploit this knowledge in the market. So, patents also act as a barrier to entry.

### Natural monopoly

Consider long-run average costs, introduced in Chapter 3. The minimum efficient scale (MES) is the size the firm has to attain in order to operate with minimum costs. If the MES is a plant capable of producing 1 million units per year and consumers demand around 10 million units per year, then the market can support about ten firms. However, if the MES is a plant producing around 10 million units, then the market can only support one firm—creating a **natural monopoly**.

> Natural monopoly exists if scale economies lead to only one firm in the market.

Natural monopolies were thought to exist in the utility markets, such as water, gas and telecommunications, where the infrastructure required to operate in these markets was so large that it restricted entry. For example, the scale needed to operate an effective telecommunications network in the UK was thought to be so large, because of all the cables, switches and exchanges that were required, that only one firm was capable of investing and generating a return. Two firms would double the amount of investment, but at best share the market and, therefore, the financial returns. However, when telecommunications began to move from copper wire to mobile communications, other firms could build networks much more cheaply. The barriers to entry fell and more firms now operate in the telecommunications market.

## Ownership of a key resource or skill

If a company owns a key resource, then it prevents competitors from accessing that resource and entering the market. For example, universities usually occupy central locations within cities. It positions the universities on important city and national travel networks which are essential for moving high volumes of students and staff around. Once a university has established itself within a city, then, unless that city is large and has more city centre land resource, the entry of new competitors is limited. Consider Manchester and Leeds. Both are large cities and both have multiple universities. Now consider Derby or Wolverhampton. These are much smaller cities with less space for an additional university and fewer students to share amongst multiple universities.

Other examples include take-off and landing slots at airports. British Airways dominates slots at Heathrow airport, which restricts the entry of new competitors to Heathrow.

Beer-brewing companies once owned large numbers of pubs and bars, which severely limited access to the key distribution channel to drinkers for new beer-brewing companies.

Finally, in terms of skills Oxford University has close to 225 world-leading active research staff members in biological sciences. How does any other university in the world, never mind the UK, enter this market for scientific expertise when so much capacity is already employed by Oxford?

What does one firm and significant entry barriers mean for firm-level profitability?

In Box 5.4 we highlight the arrival of apps for taxis, of which Uber is one of the most well-known. Taxis are licensed in most cities in the world and these licences are enormously expensive. In Hong Kong for example, a taxi plate can sell for more than $1 million, whereas in London, Black Cab drivers have to study for many years to show they have 'The Knowledge' to drive customers around London. The Knowledge and a taxi licence are significant entry barriers, but GPS-based apps like Uber's are a competitive threat.

## Revenues and costs in monopoly

Just like perfect competition, we need to think about the revenues and costs generated by a monopoly. In perfect competition, MR and AR are the same. As a price-taker, the firm does not cause the market price to fall if it sells more output, so its MR and AR stay constant. In a monopoly, the situation is different. As the only supplier in the market, the monopoly faces the downward-sloping market demand curve. Therefore, if it sells more output, the price must fall. This has implications for the monopoly's AR and MR.

## Box 5.4
## Uber's blitz on London leads to drop in black-cab recruits

London's famous black cabs, which have ferried city-goers around the capital for more than a century, are in danger of being run out of town by upstart US taxi app Uber Technologies Inc.

Data obtained by Bloomberg from Transport for London, the transit authority, show black-taxi licence applications, which include new licences and renewals, are down 20 per cent so far this year from the same period a year earlier. The industry is laying the blame squarely at Uber's door. At the same time, the number of budding cabbies looking to take 'The Knowledge'—the notoriously difficult test that all black-taxi drivers must pass—has fallen more than two-thirds at one of the main examination centers.

'I've never seen declines like this and I've been driving a taxi for 30 years,' said Steve McNamara, head of the Licensed Taxi Drivers Association, who estimates 1,200 new Uber drivers are starting up in London every month. The company itself declines to give a figure.

The Knowledge, which can mean four years of study and requires the memorizing of 25,000 streets and 20,000 landmarks, isn't needed at Uber, whose drivers rely on GPS technology to navigate town.

In London, while the service is loathed by traditional cabbies, it's popular with city-dwellers. Unlike many black cabs, Uber drivers take credit cards, cars can be ordered to your door and they offer cheap fares.

For Ricky Neighbour, a 36-year-old who's been getting up at 5 a.m. every day for 18 months to pursue The Knowledge, the thought of taking Uber's easy route has zero appeal. 'With The Knowledge I'm training to be the best in the world and I want to be part of something special,' he said. 'Having that taxi badge, that means something.'

From Bloomberg. 14 May 2015. 'Uber's blitz on London leads to drop in black-cab recruits'. Kristen Schweizer and Amy Thomson. Used with permission of Bloomberg L.P. Copyright © 2015. All rights reserved.

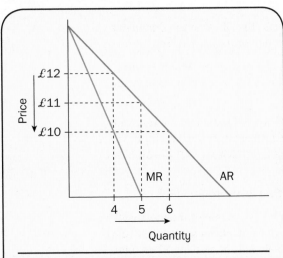

Figure 5.14   Monopoly's marginal and average revenue

Consider Figure 5.14. The average revenue line, AR, is downward sloping and this follows from above. If the firm sells more output, then, under the law of demand, consumers will only demand more output at lower prices. So, as the price drops, the average price per unit must drop.

When the price falls from £12 to £11, average revenue falls. But marginal revenue falls by more. One more unit is sold for £11, but the previous four units sold at £12 are now selling for £11, resulting in lost revenue of £4. Marginal revenue is therefore + £11 − £4 = £7.

Marginal revenue is more difficult to understand. Again, consider Figure 5.14 and Table 5.2. Initially, we are selling four units at £12. Total revenue is £48 and average revenue is the price, £12. To sell one more unit, we need to drop the price to £11. This generates total revenue of £11 × 5 = £55, and the average revenue is now £11. But what has happened to marginal revenue? Two things have occurred. First, we are selling one more unit for £11 but, second, we are losing £1 per unit on the previous four units. So marginal revenue = £11 − (4 × £1) = £7. So, MR = £7, while AR = £11. Now let us drop the price to sell one more unit. Selling six units at £10 generates a total revenue of £10 × 6 = £60. The marginal revenue from selling the sixth unit is £60 − £55. So, MR = £5, while AR = £10. Going from the fifth to sixth unit changed the price from £11 to £10; in effect, we reduced the average revenue by £1. However, the marginal revenue changed from £7 to £5, a change of £2. We can therefore see that, in selling more units, we have to accept a bigger reduction in marginal revenue than in average revenue. Reflecting this point, in monopoly, the marginal revenue line will always be steeper and below the average revenue line.

As with perfect competition, we now need to add in the firm's cost curves (see Figure 5.15).

The monopoly's profits are maximized at Q, where MC = MR. The average cost of producing Q is £10; the average revenue from selling Q is £20. Total profit = (£20 − £10) × Q. Unlike perfect competition, the price of £20 charged by the monopoly is greater than the marginal cost of £8. This difference between the price and the cost of making the last unit is an indication of market power.

The monopoly will also maximize profits where MC = MR. This point defines the profit-maximizing output. If we then draw the line up from Q until it touches the short-run average total cost curve (SATC), then we see that the average cost equals £10. Drawing the line further until it touches the average revenue line, we see that the output can be sold for £20 per unit,

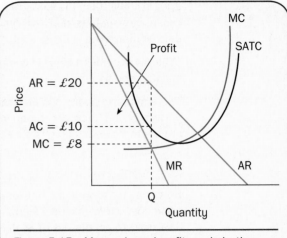

Figure 5.15   Monopoly and profit maximization

making a profit per unit of £20 − £10 = £10. Total profit is £10 per unit multiplied by the profit-maximizing output Q. This is the short-term, profit-maximizing position and, because of significant entry barriers, this profit will not be competed away in the long run. So, unlike perfect competition, monopolies can expect to earn supernormal profits in both the short and long runs.

## Perfect competition and monopoly compared

The long-term profit position of monopoly is not the only difference and so it is worth comparing perfect competition and monopoly in more detail. In order to do this, we will assume that we have a perfectly competitive industry, with 1,000 firms supplying the market. Overnight, a business person buys out all the firms and begins to act as a monopoly.

As a consequence of this transfer of ownership from 1,000 people to one person, the cost structure will not change; the monopoly will simply have a cost curve that is the sum of all the 1,000 individual cost curves under perfect competition. The same will apply to the marginal cost curve, and this is illustrated in Figure 5.16. The customers in the market have not changed, so the demand curves or AR lines faced by the perfectly competitive industry and the monopoly are identical. The marginal revenue lines are different. Remember, in perfect competition, marginal and average revenue are the same, but in monopoly they are different. We can now use Figure 5.16 to assess the differences between perfect competition and monopoly.

To maximize profits, the perfectly competitive firm sets $MC_{pc} = MR_{pc}$, while the monopoly sets $MC_{mp} = MR_{mp}$. When compared with monopoly, perfect competition provides more output at lower prices.

In order to maximize profit, the perfectly competitive industry will set $MC_{pc} = MR_{pc}$. Its profit-maximizing output is $Q_{pc}$ and the price it sells for is PC. The monopoly sets $MC_{mp} = MR_{mp}$ and its profit-maximizing output is $Q_{mp}$ and the price it sells this output for is MP. It is now clear to see that, in moving from perfect competition to monopoly, the industry output drops and the price increases. Furthermore, in perfect competition the price equals the industry's marginal cost, but in monopoly the

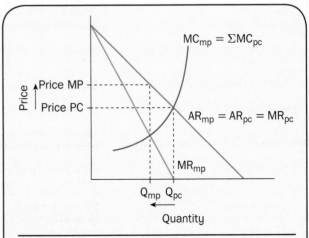

Figure 5.16   Comparing perfect competition and monopoly

price is higher than the industry's marginal cost. This difference between price and marginal cost in monopoly is known as 'market power', which is the ability to price above the cost of the last unit made.

Table 5.4 provides a concise comparison of the key differences between perfect competition and monopoly.

The summary points within Table 5.4 are generally accepted key differences between perfect competition and monopoly. Below we discuss some important challenges to the argument that monopoly is always bad for society and the consumer.

## Monopoly and economies of scale

However, the arguments put forward are weak. The idea that a monopoly would have the same cost curves as a perfectly competitive industry neglects the points made in Chapter 3 relating to economies of scale. A monopoly may be capable of reducing costs. A single company is unlikely to operate 1,000 separate plants. Instead, it is more likely to rationalize the 1,000 plants into a smaller number of very large plants, which can exploit economies of scale. If this is true, then the cost reduction would lead to the monopoly's marginal cost curve moving out to the right. This is shown in Figure 5.17, with the marginal cost for the monopoly shifting to the right. At all output levels, the marginal cost of the monopoly is now lower than the marginal cost of the perfectly competitive industry. The monopoly is now more cost-efficient than perfect competition. The profit-maximizing output for the monopoly

**Table 5.4**  Key comparisons of perfect competition and monopoly

|  | Perfect competition | Monopoly |
|---|---|---|
| *Assumptions:* | | |
| Number of buyers | Many | Many |
| Number of suppliers | Many | One |
| Barriers to entry and exit | None | High |
| Product | Homogeneous | Not considered |
| Information | Perfect | Not considered |
| *Outcomes:* | | |
| Costs | Productive efficiency—average total costs minimized | Productive inefficiency—average total costs not minimized |
| Average revenue and marginal revenue | Average revenue = marginal revenue | Average revenue > marginal revenue |
| Short-run losses and profits | Supernormal | Supernormal |
| Long-run profits | Normal | Supernormal |
| Price | Allocative efficiency: price = marginal cost | Allocative inefficiency: price > marginal cost |
| Market power | No market power, price = marginal cost | Market power, price > marginal cost |
| Level of prices | Monopoly price is higher than in perfect competition unless monopoly benefits from economies of scale | |
| Level of output | Monopoly output is lower than in perfect competition unless monopoly benefits from economies of scale | |

now occurs where marginal revenue intersects the new marginal cost curve under economies of scale. Output is higher than in perfect competition and the market price is lower than in perfect competition.

By exploiting economies of scale, the monopoly's marginal cost curve shifts to the right. Therefore, at all output levels the marginal cost of the monopoly is lower than the marginal cost of the perfectly competitive industry, illustrating the improved cost efficiencies of the monopoly. The profit-maximizing output for the monopoly is now greater than the output of the perfectly competitive industry and the monopoly price is also lower.

Of course, it also needs to be recognized that a monopoly has no incentive to improve efficiency, as it has no competition. So why should it try to exploit economies of scale? Moreover, it is also possible that the monopoly may be too large and displays diseconomies of scale. Its costs would then be greater than the perfectly competitive industry, with the marginal cost curve shifting to the left. This would lead to even higher prices and a greater reduction in output under monopoly.

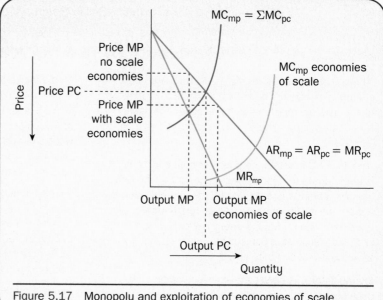

Figure 5.17   Monopoly and exploitation of economies of scale

## Creative destruction

An alternative argument in favour of monopoly is that of **creative destruction**. Under this approach, monopolies are generally accepted as raising prices, restricting output and earning supernormal profits, which are potentially all bad. However, what should also be recognized is the benefits which stem from the supernormal profits, especially when they act as an incentive to innovate. Firms which are not monopolies can be motivated to be innovative and creative, developing new products for the market or new production techniques which provide them with a competitive advantage and destroy the entry barriers of the incumbent firms or monopoly. The innovating firm, through creative destruction, then becomes a monopoly. The firm benefits from higher profits; and society benefits from the supply of new innovative goods and services. One potential drawback with this approach is that firms have to undertake expensive **rent-seeking behaviour** and they may not always be successful. Some inventions work, others do not. So, for every monopoly brought about by innovation, there can be many failures which have used the scarce resources of the economy.

Creative destruction occurs when a new entrant outcompetes incumbent companies by virtue of being innovative.

Rent-seeking behaviour is the pursuit of supernormal profits. An economic rent is a payment in excess of the minimum price at which a good or service will be supplied.

The power of creative destruction is to be found in the continued competition brought about by innovation. For example, Microsoft was once one of, if not the most, dominant player in the personal computer software market with its Windows operating system and Office group of programs. However, as computing moved to the Internet, Microsoft's position has come under threat from companies that have pioneered new technologies—for example, Google search—and from companies that have pioneered the use of new technologies, such as YouTube, Facebook and LinkedIn.

In Box 5.5 the new home-battery storage system offered by Tesla is discussed. The system can take solar-generated energy from panels on your roof and store it for use later at night. The battery is very expensive, but if the cost comes down and consumers buy it, then it will have the potential to destroy traditional power station energy generation.

## Box 5.5
## Will Tesla's home battery really transform our energy infrastructure?

'The goal is complete transformation of the entire energy infrastructure of the world,' Tesla founder Elon Musk told reporters as he launched the electric car company's new home power storage battery on Thursday.

'This is actually within the power of humanity to do. It is not impossible. Electricity storage is the "missing link" in weaning the economy off fossil fuels,' said the entrepreneur with characteristic understatement. But the ticket price for Musk's energy revolution is $3,000 (£1,981). So even if homeowners want to sign on and save the world, can they afford it?

Energy storage is seen as a vital piece of the decarbonization puzzle, and this is perhaps why the Tesla announcement has been greeted with wide media coverage and excitement from the tech sector. The past few years have seen incredible upheavals in energy markets driven by the rise and rise (or more appropriately fall and fall) of solar power. The costs of photovoltaic panels has dropped so much in recent years that in 2016 solar power will reach grid parity in 36 US states in 2016. In the Australian state of Queensland rooftop solar has become such a force that fossil fuel burners have had to pay others to pick up their extra generation during times of traditionally high demand.

These incredible steps forward have been tempered by solar's major limitation—it doesn't work when the sun isn't shining. Hence, the need for an affordable way to store the power until the night-time demand spike. The world's largest private bank UBS told its investors last year that storage was the key to a future in which large carbon-spewing power stations were redundant.

To meet this demand, battery prices have been steadily dropping. Tesla's Powerwall represents a further improvement, said Dr Jonathan Radcliffe, an energy storage expert at Birmingham University, but for anyone watching their bills, the technology remains economically unsupportable.

'It's a good development to see the costs coming down for this sort of battery and I think the idea of having distributed energy storage could be quite important in some markets and really contribute to deploying small-scale renewables,' said Radcliffe. But he said the reality for consumers trying to balance bills was that the Tesla battery was still not worth the up front cost. 'The battery they promote for daily cycling is 7kWh. Electricity costs in the UK are about 15p per kWh, so you're holding about £1 of value in this £2,000 wallet.'

From *The Guardian*. 1 May 2015. 'Will Tesla's home battery really transform our energy infrastructure'. Karl Mathiesen.
© Guardian News & Media Ltd 2015

## ( 5.6 ) When is a monopoly not a monopoly?

Licensing and patents are means of creating entry barriers and establishing a monopoly. Companies and individuals use licensing, patents and copyright to protect their intellectual capital, innovations and creative outputs, but to what extent do they create a monopoly?

At a simplistic level, a film studio which copyrights its latest release creates a monopoly for that one film. No one can legally copy the film and distribute it for sale, except for the studio and those companies to which it licenses the film. However, the market for films is well served with many competing films; and so, while a studio maybe a monopoly provider of its own film, it is not a monopoly provider of all films and, therefore, the value of the film monopoly is perhaps not that great to the studio.

A durable good is one in which consumption is ongoing, for example, a DVD.

A perishable good is one which either decays: for example, fruit and vegetables, or is consumed quickly: for example, wine, Coca-Cola.

Next consider an extremely successful and popular film, perhaps a film which wins a number of awards, such as an Oscar. The value of the film, its copyright and its monopoly is now greater and of considerable interest to the film studio. However, films have an inherent commercial flaw which damages their monopoly value. This flaw is most apparent in the DVD/Blu-Ray market for films. When a consumer buys a film on DVD or Blu-Ray, they receive a **durable good**. A durable good, in contrast to a **perishable good**, is one which lasts over time and does not degrade despite repeat usage. Wine is not durable, you drink it and then it is finished. Cars are not durable, you drive them and they need maintaining and repairing. Movies on a disc are durable. You watch them and can then watch them again and again and again. Durable goods create a problem for monopoly providers.

Consider the film studio; it launches the DVD and Blu-Ray versions of its latest blockbuster and it sets a price which maximizes its profits. Let us assume that at the profit-maximizing price half of the studio's consumers are willing to buy the film; the remaining consumers think the film is too expensive.

Importantly, because the DVD or Blu-Ray disc is a durable good, once the studio has sold the film, then it does not generate any repeat business. The only customers available to the studio are those that found the launch price too expensive. So, in order to generate further sales, the studio must attract new customers by reducing the price of the DVD and Blu-Ray discs.

Price reduction of films is often observed in practice. The film is initially released on disc at a high price and then over time the price is reduced and customers know this happens. This practice creates an acute problem for studios: if they price too high at launch, then more customers will wait for the price to fall and buy later. To protect revenues, it may therefore be better to price lower during the launch period and then not have to discount to many more customers in later periods.

The heart of the problem is that the studio as a provider of a durable good is in competition with itself over time and is therefore not a monopoly. It then becomes interesting to ask, apart from reducing prices at launch, what other tactics might be used by the studio to raise profits? There are a number of tactics used, including adding in additional bonus material. But an interesting approach and one with applicability to other products is to ensure that the good or service being provided is not durable. In the case of DVDs and Blu-Rays this does not mean making discs that fall apart, break and stop working. Instead, renting the disc, rather than selling it converts the transaction from one of a durable good, to that of a perishable service. At the end of the rental term, the disc must be returned and cannot be shared around friends or watched again without an additional rental.

Some e-books are now being rented, particularly e-textbooks for periods of up to two years; and photocopying machines are often rented as a means of generating ongoing revenues, rather than one-off payments from buyers. Firms are clearly very adaptive and create business models to deal with many types of problems. Our task is to understand what problems exist and how economics can be used to understand why a particular tactic is being used. The problem just discussed is known within economics as the *Coase conjecture* and is something we will return to in Chapter 8 when we discuss carbon trading.

##  Business application: 'Oops, we're in the wrong box'—the case of the airline industry

Financial performance is essential, or, in other words, profits count. The firm's revenues and costs determine profits. If we look closely at revenues and costs, we find they are both influenced by prices. A firm's revenues are determined by the price it sells its output for, and a firm's costs are determined by the price it has to pay for its labour, capital and raw materials. Price is determined by market structure—it is higher in monopoly and lower in perfect competition. We can use this to think about business structures that are optimal for business by considering the input–output matrix in Figure 5.18.

Output markets are where firms sell products. Input markets are where firms buy their labour, raw materials and capital inputs. When selling output, the firm desires a high price, so monopoly is best. But when buying inputs, the firm likes to keep its costs down, so perfectly competitive markets are preferable. Therefore, from a firm's perspective the best combination is associated with box B.

|  | Output market | |
|---|---|---|
|  | Perfect competition | Monopoly |
| **Perfect competition** | A<br>Low revenues<br>Low costs | B<br>High revenues<br>Low costs |
| **Monopoly** | C<br>Low revenues<br>High costs | D<br>High revenues<br>High costs |

(rows labelled down the side under "Input market")

Figure 5.18  Optimal mix input and output markets

Across the top, we have the market structure of the firm's output market, where it sells its product. Down the side, we have the market structure for the firm's input markets, where the firm purchases its labour, capital and raw materials. Box C could be the worst box to be in. The input markets are characterized by monopoly supply, so cost will be high, and the output markets are perfectly competitive, so revenues will be low. Box B is the best box for business. Inputs come from a perfectly competitive market, so costs are low, while output is sold in a monopoly market, so revenues will be high. Box B is where there is the greatest chance to make a profit. Box A is probably preferable to box D. In A, both markets are perfectly competitive so supernormal profits are unlikely. But how do you think box D compares with box C? In C and D, both firms face a monopoly input supplier. But firms in C have a perfectly competitive output market. This could actually make it more attractive than D. With a perfectly competitive output market the firm will make only normal profits, so the monopoly input supplier cannot afford to squeeze the perfectly competitive firms. In fact, there are no profits to squeeze; but in D, the monopoly output will create profits that the monopoly supplier can try to expropriate for itself by charging higher input prices. So D may be less attractive than C.

Rarely will a firm find itself comfortably inside box B, but it might be expected to try to move towards box B over time. For example, in box D the obvious solution is to purchase the monopoly input supplier and make it part of your company. This is known as *vertical integration*, and it will be discussed at length in Chapter 7. In box A, you would try to buy up your competitors or force them out of the market. This way, competition is reduced and the market moves towards monopoly.

However, for a more illuminating example, let us look at the airline industry. First, examine its key inputs: aircraft, landing rights at international airports, and pilots. There are only two major aircraft manufacturers in the world, Airbus and Boeing. The market is not perfectly competitive. Most major cities have one airport, a monopoly. Pilots are expensive and unionized. Unions are effectively a monopoly supplier of labour. So, on the input side, airlines are not in a good position. In terms of output, tickets for airlines are sold via travel agents or via the Internet. Most travellers say, 'I would like to go on this date between these two cities: who is offering the cheapest fare?' Ten options appear upon the screen and the cheapest option is generally selected. This would suggest that the market is highly competitive. This is clearly not good for the airline industry.

## Solutions

With monopoly suppliers and competitive output markets, airlines are firmly located in box C. How can they deal with this situation? Airline alliances are a likely solution. In such alliances, airlines come together and in the first instance they agree to share passengers—so-called

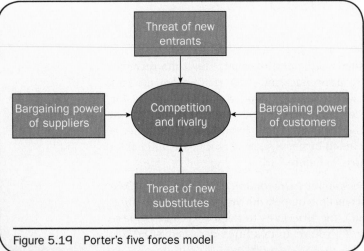

Figure 5.19  Porter's five forces model

'code sharing'. This reduces competition in the output market and moves airlines towards box B. In addition, airlines may also swap landing rights at various airports and share the training of pilots. On the aircraft front, they can place joint orders for aircraft and, as with many products, a bulk order usually generates a substantial discount. This provides some control over input prices and again moves airlines towards box B.

A more intriguing idea is the exploitation of natural monopolies. As discussed earlier, a natural monopoly exists where scale economies lead to one supplier in the market. Often these are associated with industries which require enormous levels of infrastructure such as utilities—gas, water and electricity—but they are equally applicable in much smaller markets. Consider the level of demand for flights between two regional airports, say, Leeds in the UK and Nice in France. It is a two-hour flight and around 80 people a day wish to fly direct between the two airports. A small commercial jet might carry 120 passengers, so this route will only be supplied by one airline—a monopoly.

Now consider flying from Leeds to Singapore. Here are a couple of suggested routings: Leeds, Heathrow, and then either direct to Singapore or via Dubai, Bangkok or Kuala Lumpur; or Leeds, Amsterdam and then either direct, or via Dubai, Bangkok or Kuala Lumpur. There are many other options. Therefore, because international airlines utilize hub-and-spoke operations, the market for flights from Leeds to Singapore is a combination of many sub-markets. There is no natural monopoly on these routes. Airlines can fill planes with passengers who are travelling to multiple destinations.

What can we learn from this? Discount airlines tend to fly point-to-point between small regional airports. International carriers operate hub-and-spoke operations. Discount airlines make huge profits; international airlines do not. So are discount airlines natural monopolies? If they are, the very intriguing thought is that they could charge a lot less than they currently do.

#  5.8 Business data application: understanding the forces of competition

Understanding the strength of competition is one of the most important aspects of being a business manager. Markets closer in character to perfect competition will normally generate weaker levels of profit. Harvard Business School professor Michael Porter, drawing on the key characteristics of perfect competition, developed an often used tool within business, Porter's five forces model of competition (see Figure 5.19). Using data to measure and quantify the level of each force of competition enables a business manager to form a view about the sources of competition, the degree of competition and ultimately the likely impact on profitability.

Porter's five forces model identifies the five key drivers of competition in an industry.

Around the outside of Figure 5.19 are four drivers of competition: the threat of entry, the threat from substitutes and the buying power of buyers and suppliers. These characterize an industry's initial competitive environment. The firms within the industry then have to decide how to react. The level of competition and rivalry could be high, or they may decide to collude with each other and lower competition. The intensity of each of these five competitive forces determines the overall level of competition within the industry.

Porter's five forces model is closely related to the assumptions of perfect competition. Many buyers and many sellers relates to the bargaining power of buyers and sellers. The threat of new entrants is linked to the assumption of no entry barriers. The threat from substitutes links to the assumption of homogeneous products, where the threat of substitutes is very high under perfect competition. In essence, Porter has taken the abstract assumptions of perfect competition and turned them into tangible concepts that business managers can understand and use to assess the degree of competition in their industry.

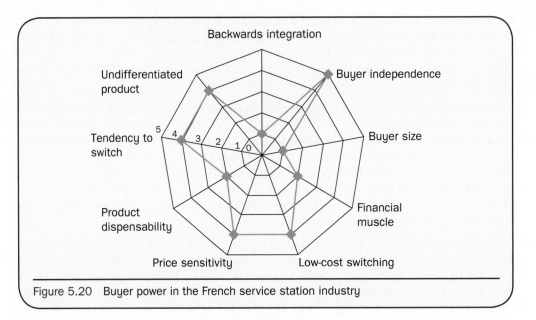

Figure 5.20   Buyer power in the French service station industry

Porter's approach is very useful in enabling managers to scan and audit their business environment. The approach directs managers to assess sensible and measurable drivers of competition. Many industry reports often include a section covering competition and Porter's five forces approach is nearly always applied. We consider the market for service stations, fuel, etc. in France (Figures 5.20–5.24).

Buyers in this industry are drivers of cars and commercial vehicles. A number of possible aspects of buying power are listed around the outside of the diagram and are then rated on a scale of 0 to 5, where 5 denotes that the buying power is very strong. There is mixed evidence in support of strong buying power. Buyers are small in size, they lack financial muscle and their demand for fuel is very price inelastic. However, there are many substitutes in the market, differentiation is low and the cost of switching to alternative suppliers of fuel is low. Hence, buying power is judged as being moderately strong overall.

Major oil companies are the major suppliers to service stations. Fuel is not very differentiated and independent service stations and large supermarket chains can to some degree dispense with one fuel supplier and begin trading with another with improved financial terms.

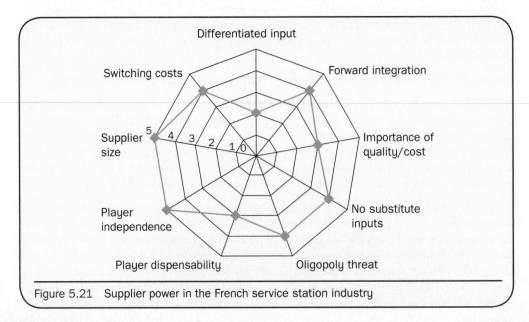

Figure 5.21   Supplier power in the French service station industry

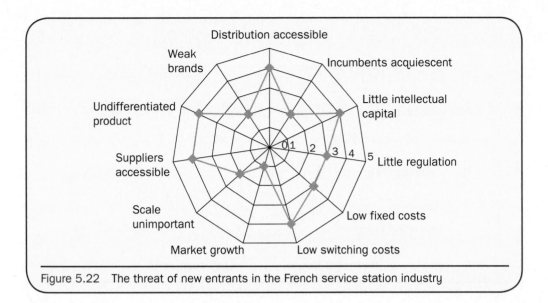

Figure 5.22  The threat of new entrants in the French service station industry

However, it needs to be noted that oil companies also own service stations and so have a route to market without having to sell to supermarkets and independent retailers. Oil companies have few competitors, enormous size and financial resource and therefore have strength as suppliers.

Entry into the service station market is relatively easy. There is limited need for specialist knowledge and/or intellectual capital. Fixed costs and regulation are low. Access to supply is easy and the need for a differentiated product is low. However, the market is unlikely to accommodate a new entrant, growth is low and strong incumbents are likely to resist entry. The threat of entry is therefore moderate.

Cheap alternative fuels are available, such as bio-fuels. However, the cost to switch to these alternatives is generally high for consumers and availability is low. Therefore, the threat of substitutes is low.

Rivalry in the industry is characterized by an undifferentiated product, low switching costs, large dominant supermarket chains and limited growth to expand the market. Rivalry is therefore judged as very high.

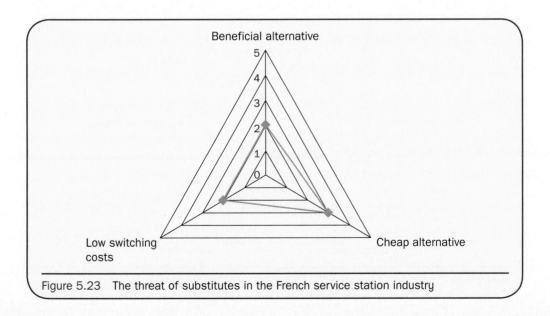

Figure 5.23  The threat of substitutes in the French service station industry

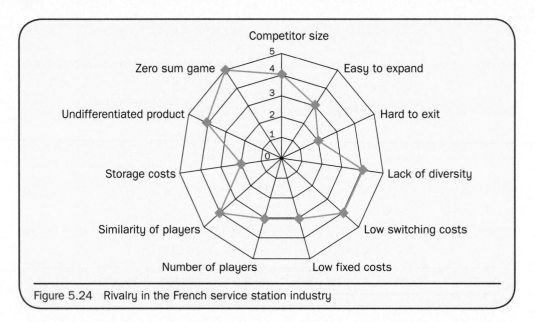

Figure 5.24   Rivalry in the French service station industry

We can then combine these assessments into one diagram (Figure 5.25) and summarize the strength of competition in each area.

Rivalry and supplier power are reasonably strong in the industry, which will constrain the ability of firms to generate profits. However, lack of new entry, few substitutes and lack of buyer power help to strengthen profitability. The task of a manager in this sector is to understand these competitive forces, avoid rivalry and gain some control over supply. It should therefore be of no surprise that supermarkets as large retailers of fuel have been most successful in this industry. By their size they gain some negotiating power over the major fuel suppliers and equally smaller independent chains are unwilling to engage with them in direct competition.

The strength of Porter's five forces approach is in its simplicity. Important aspects of competition can be categorized around five key themes and then assessed with a reasonable degree of accuracy. The importance of economics is that, through the models of perfect competition and monopoly, it highlights to businesses the consequences for profit. If a company has a weak understanding, or lack of control over its competitive forces, then profits will plummet. In contrast, if the firm can understand and manage the forces of competition that it faces, then it has a better chance of becoming a monopoly.

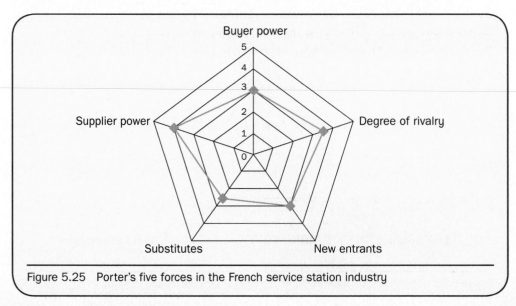

Figure 5.25   Porter's five forces in the French service station industry

## Summary

1. The profitability of a market is determined by the competitive structure of the market.
2. Perfect competition is highly competitive. It has no entry barriers, perfect information, homogeneous products and buyers and sellers.
3. In the short run, firms in perfect competition can earn supernormal profits. But in the long run, rivals will enter the market and compete away any excess profits.
4. Monopoly is a market supplied by only one firm.
5. Entry barriers such as licences, patents, economies of scale or switching costs make it difficult for competitors to enter the market.
6. Supernormal profits can exist in the short run and, because of high entry barriers, can also persist into the long run.
7. In monopoly, output is lower and prices are higher than in perfect competition.
8. Monopolies are seen as desirable by business but usually undesirable by government.
9. Many successful business ventures occur because managers are capable of steering a strategic path from competitive environments to low competitive environments.

## Learning checklist

You should now be able to:
- Explain why firms maximize profits when marginal cost equals marginal revenue
- Recall the main assumptions behind perfect competition
- Explain why the demand curve faced by a perfectly competitive firm is perfectly elastic
- Explain the level of profits in the short and long run in a perfectly competitive industry
- List the potential barriers to entry used by a monopoly
- Explain why the marginal revenue line is steeper than the average revenue line in monopoly
- Draw a diagram to illustrate the amount of profit earned by a monopoly
- Explain the key differences between perfect competition and monopoly
- Explain when perfect competition and monopoly are good for a firm
- Provide examples of how firms have created monopolies
- Use Porter's five forces to assess the strength of competition in an industry.

## Questions                                                     connect

1. If a firm is a profit-maximizer, then marginal cost and marginal revenue must be ____ (Fill in the blank)
2. A firm discovers that its marginal cost is less than its marginal revenue. Should it increase or decrease output?
3. Describe the key assumptions that characterize a perfectly competitive market.
4. In the short run, a firm in perfect competition finds that average revenues exceed average costs. Is this firm making a normal profit, a supernormal profit, a normal loss or a supernormal loss?

EASY

**EASY**

5. Taking the scenario described in question 4, what do you think will happen to supply in the long run?

6. How would you establish a benchmark for normal profits in your own economy?

7. What barriers to entry are associated with monopolies?

8. Is equilibrium in monopoly associated with allocative efficiency?

9. List markets that you think are (a) perfectly competitive and (b) monopolies.

10. Does the concept of creative destruction paint monopolies as good or bad for an economy?

**INTERMEDIATE**

11. Explain the difference between accounting profits and economic profits.

12. Draw a diagram for a perfectly competitive industry with firms earning normal profits. All firms in the industry use oil as a key input. Using your diagram, illustrate a reduction in the price of oil. Will firm-level profits increase or decrease and will market supply increase or decrease?

13. Identify the key differences between perfect competition and monopoly.

14. Assess whether Porter's five forces model of competition has greater value for business managers than the models of perfect competition and monopoly.

15. Would the lack of competition in monopoly result in the company making losses?

16. Minnie's Bowtique is a perfectly competitive firm operating in Mouseland which is world famous for its fabulous collection of bows and bowties. Unfortunately it faces an increasingly competitive market and has to rethink its business strategy. The diagram provided shows the demand curve (D) that Minnie's Bowtique faces and her marginal cost curve (MC). What would happen to Minnie's profits if she increases her output from 4 to 7?

**DIFFICULT**

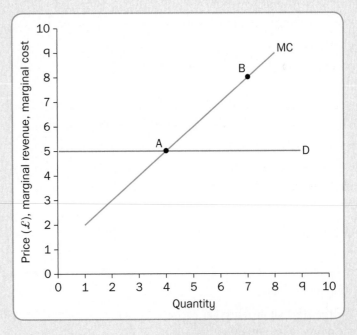

17. You are provided information on quantity produced by the firm or output (Q), the firm's marginal costs (MC) and marginal revenue (MR).

    (a) Complete the table by filling in the missing values for MR-MC and determine the output decision made by the firm at various levels of output.

| Quantity produced (Q) | Marginal revenue (MR) | Marginal cost (MC) | MR-MC | Output decision |
|---|---|---|---|---|
| 1 | 26 | 18 | | |
| 2 | 24 | 14 | | |
| 3 | 22 | 11 | | |
| 4 | 20 | 10 | | |
| 5 | 18 | 11 | | |
| 6 | 16 | 12 | | |
| 7 | 14 | 14 | | |
| 8 | 12 | 17 | | |
| 9 | 10 | 19 | | |
| 10 | 8 | 21 | | |

DIFFICULT

(b)  In order to maximizse profits, which of the following relationships must hold true?

(c)  At what level of output will the firm's profit be maximized?

## Exercises

1.  True or false?

EASY

(a)  Price is equal to marginal revenue for a firm under perfect competition.

(b)  A firm making normal profits is said by an accountant to be breaking even.

(c)  A monopoly makes supernormal profits because it is more efficient than a perfectly competitive firm.

(d)  A perfectly competitive firm will sell at a price equal to marginal cost. A monopoly may sell at a price above marginal cost.

(e)  A patent protects a monopoly by not enabling perfect information.

(f)In perfect competition, if price is above short-run average cost, firms will exit the market.

2.  Figure 5.26 shows the short-run cost curves for a perfectly competitive firm.

INTERMEDIATE

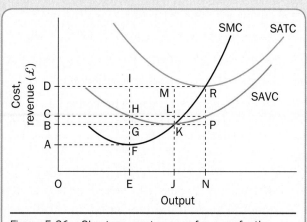

Figure 5.26  Short-run cost curves for a perfectly competitive firm

(a) What is the shutdown price for the firm?

(b) At what price would the firm just make normal profits?

(c) What area would represent total fixed cost at this price?

(d) Within what range of prices would the firm choose to operate at a loss in the short run?

(e) Identify the firm's short-run supply curve.

(f) Within what range of prices would the firm be able to make short-run supernormal profits?

A perfectly competitive industry is taken over by a monopolist who intends to run it as a multi-plant concern. Consequently, the long-run supply curve of the competitive industry (LRSS) becomes the monopolist's long-run marginal cost curve ($\text{LMC}_m$); in the short run, the SRSS curve becomes the monopolist's $\text{SMC}_m$. The position is shown in Figure 5.27.

(g) What was the equilibrium price and industry output under perfect competition?

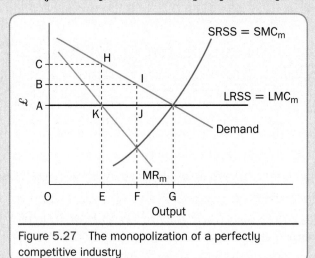

Figure 5.27   The monopolization of a perfectly competitive industry

(h) At what price and output would the monopolist choose to operate in the short run?

(i) At what price and output would the monopolist maximize profits in the long run?

(j) What would be the size of these long-run profits?

3. (a) List the key characteristics of a perfectly competitive market.

DIFFICULT

(b) Which of the characteristics do not apply to Google and why?

(c) Do you think Google has undertaken any rent-seeking behaviour?

(d) Do you think Google will suffer creative destruction?

4. Using Porter's five forces framework presented in section 5.19 examine the strength of competition in either the supermarket industry in your country, or the market for coffee drinks.

# Strategic rivalry

## Chapter contents

## Learning outcomes

By the end of this chapter you should be able to:

Economic theory

LO1 Define monopolistic competition

LO2 Identify natural and strategic entry barriers

LO3 Identify oligopolies and underline the importance of strategic interdependence

LO4 Explain the kinked demand curve model

LO5 Use game theory to assess strategic behaviour

Business application

LO6 Debate why it may be better for leading technology firms to co-operate on standards, rather than compete

LO7 Discuss why supermarkets use blind auctions to prevent co-operation between suppliers

LO8 Assess how an understanding of oligopolies can be used to assess competition within the market for cinema.

## At a glance | Strategic rivalry

### The issue

Firms in perfect competition earn normal economic profits. But can firms avoid direct price competition, say by product differentiation, and, if so, what are the consequences for pricing and profits? In addition, in markets where there are only a small number of large players, should firms compete or try to co-operate with each other? Co-operation leads to increased profits; competition does not.

### The understanding

Many firms in highly competitive markets, such as bars, restaurants and hairdressing, differentiate themselves by location, style and range of products or services. Prices then often vary across differentiated providers, but this may not necessarily lead to supernormal profits. We will address these issues using the model of monopolistic competition.

In terms of co-operation, or competition, we will examine the concept of strategic interdependence. For example, while co-operation is likely to lead to increased profits, it is not necessarily the correct option. If you decide to be friendly and your rival is aggressive, then they will win. So, given that your rival is aggressive, it is best if you are also aggressive. This is an essential part of the understanding; optimal strategies are developed from an understanding of what your rival is going to do, not from what you would like to do. This is known as strategic interdependence. The strategy of one firm is dependent upon the likely strategy of its rivals. We will explore these ideas more fully by examining game theory.

### The usefulness

An understanding of monopolistic competition provides insights into the consequences for prices and profits resulting from product positioning and differentiation, especially in service sector markets characterized by numerous small-scale providers.

An understanding of strategic interaction from the perspective of game theory is extremely powerful. Government uses game theory when designing auctions for telecommunications licences. Sporting associations and team owners use game theory and auctions when selling television rights. Car dealerships use game theory when selling second-hand cars, and so should you. Finally, supermarkets use it to reduce the price that they have to pay for own-label products by applying game theory to auctions.

## ( 6.1 ) Business problem: will rivals always compete?

A good competitor can control its rivals. In sport, Formula 1 drivers try to achieve this from pole position and, in war, armed forces try to gain control through air supremacy. In fact, any successful competitor, whether it be in sport, war, politics or business, will ordinarily have a good strategy.

An important recognition is that competition is expensive. War is hugely expensive, particularly in terms of lost lives. Ferrari's F1 annual racing budget exceeds €400 million. Competition in business is also expensive. In monopoly, with no competition, profits are higher and more sustainable than in the highly competitive environment of perfect competition.

So, if competition is expensive, should rivals always compete? The answer depends on the expected response of your rival. Consider this old, but illuminating, true story. When the Spanish arrived in Central America in the seventeenth century they were greeted by fearsome-looking locals, sporting war paint and shaking menacing spears in the air—a clear declaration that they were willing to compete with the Spanish invaders. In response, most of us would sensibly pull up the anchor and sail away. The Spanish burnt their boats and walked onto the beach. If a fight between the Spanish and the Incas started, the Spanish had to fight or die: no boats, no escape plan. The local Incas quickly understood the Spanish soldiers' need and desire to win and retreated inland. So, by committing to a fight, the Spanish influenced the behaviour of their rivals. This is a significant point for business.

In perfect competition, the behaviour of one firm will not influence its rivals. Each firm is a price taker and it can sell any amount of output at the market price. If the market price is £10, there is no point starting a price war and selling at £5 because you can sell everything at £10. There is said to be no **strategic interdependence**. We will also assume that there is no strategic interdependence when we discuss monopolistic competition. However, under *oligopoly*, if one firm begins a competitive move, such as starting a price war, then this will have immediate implications for its rivals. The actions of one firm are linked to the actions of its rivals. Strategic interdependence exists.

> Strategic interdependence exists when the actions of one firm will have implications for its rivals.

In developing your understanding we will begin by introducing the model of monopolistic competition. While not directly addressing the issue of strategic interdependence, it does examine the profitability of many small firms under product differentiation. As such, it provides an insight into how firms in near-perfect competition try to deal with competitive rivalry. We then develop the analysis through an examination of the characteristics of an oligopolistic market. In discussing why oligopolies exist, we will consider both natural and strategic entry barriers. Finally, we will turn our discussion to strategic responses and in so doing develop your understanding of game theory. We will then utilize the insights from game theory to understand the operation and optimal design of auctions.

## 6.2  Monopolistic competition

We begin with an examination of **monopolistic competition**, which for the most part is an industry much like perfect competition except for the existence of product differentiation. So, we are still assuming a large number of competitors, freedom of entry and exit, but not homogeneous products. Rather, firms produce similar goods or services which are differentiated in some way.

> Monopolistic competition is a highly competitive market where firms may use product differentiation.

There are many examples of monopolistic competition and they all must relate to differentiation in some form or other. Bars can be differentiated by location, the beers or other drinks offered for sale, type of food served, or theme, such as a cocktail or sports bar. Shops can be differentiated by distance. Local shops sell newspapers and many people will not walk more than 300 yards for a paper. They will, however, drive a number of miles to access a supermarket. Even bread, a fairly standard product, is differentiated: brown, white, soft, with seeds, with fruit, and different varieties from around the world. Even your classes are differentiated by day of the week and time of day.

Importantly, because each supplier offers a similar but not identical product, each supplier does not face a perfectly elastic (horizontal) demand line, as they would in perfect competition. Instead, the element of differentiation lowers the degree of substitutability between rival offerings—and results in each firm facing a downward-sloping demand line.

The result of this differentiation is for each small firm to have a monopoly over the differentiated version of the product or service that it provides. We, therefore, have lots of small firms offering similar but slightly different competitive offerings to consumers with varied tastes and preferences. This combination of competition and monopoly gives rise to the term 'monopolistic competition'. In Box 6.1 the story of McDonald's collapse in

## Box 6.1
## Shake Shack rocks McDonald's to its foundations—but which is better?

It started life as a single hot dog stand in Manhattan's Madison Square Park. Little more than a decade later, Shake Shack has expanded to 63 outlets in nine countries and is preparing for an initial public offering (IPO) that will value the company at $568m (£374m).

Shake Shack is one of a string of hipster-ish fast food chains, including Five Guys, Chipotle and Smashburger, which are eating into McDonald's profits. On Friday, McDonald's reported a 15% plunge in global annual profits, making 2014 one of its worst financial years.

Don Thompson, McDonald's president and chief executive, conceded that the upstart chains had contributed to a 'challenging year' and warned investors that the home of the Big Mac 'continues to face meaningful headwinds'.

McDonald's, which has also been hit by food safety scandals and widespread protests from workers over low pay, is cutting down its menu in order to concentrate on the quality of its core products. 'We know that when our customers feel good about us and about eating at McDonald's they visit us more often,' Thompson said

The average transaction in McDonald's rings up at about $5, while the lowest-priced Shackburger comes in at $5.19 – add in fries and a shake and the average spend is about $13. It may sound like an unusual name for a burger joint, but it's catchier than the other options founder Danny Meyer was tossing around when he first set up shop in 2001. 'We entertained a bunch of names for the kiosk (most of them pretty bad – like Custard's First Stand, Dog Run and Madison Mixer) and ultimately settled on Shake Shack,' he said in a letter to prospective shareholders.

From *The Guardian*. 24 January 2015. 'Shake Shack rocks McDonald's to its foundations'. Rupert Neale.
© Guardian News & Media Ltd 2015

sales is discussed. McDonald's faces strong competition from a large number of fast-food retailers ranging from Burger King, and Starbucks to new entrants like Shake Shack. Each competitor adapts its menu to appeal to a wider market of customers and take business away from its rivals in the market for quick food.

Each monopolistic firm can influence its market share to some extent by changing its price relative to its rivals. By lowering drink prices a bar may attract some customers from its rivals, but it will not attract all the rivals' customers. Differentiation will lock in some customers to the more expensive provider; for example, if one bar provides beers while another specializes in fruit and alcoholic cocktails. Cheap prices in the beer bar will not attract drinkers who have a strong taste and preference for cocktails.

Monopolistic competition also requires an absence of economies of scale. Without the ability, or need, to exploit size and scale, a monopolistic industry will be characterized by a large number of small firms. We will see that, when we discuss oligopoly in the next section, the existence of economies of scale can lead to a small number of large players.

The demand curve for the firm depends upon the industry demand curve, the number of firms and the prices charged by these firms. A bigger industry demand, with a fixed number of firms, will result in a higher demand for each firm. An increase in the number of firms will lead to a reduced share of the market for each firm. The price of a firm, relative to its rivals, will also determine its level of demand.

In Figure 6.1, we have drawn a diagram depicting a firm's supply decision under monopolistic competition. Initially, the firm faces an average revenue line of $AR_1$ and marginal revenue line MR of $MR_1$. Under profit maximization, the firm will produce $Q_1$ units and sell at a price of $P_1$. With an average cost per unit of $AC_1$, the firm will make $(P_1 - AC_1) \times Q_1$ profit. These supernormal profits will attract entry into the market. As more firms enter this market, the firm will lose market share and the demand curve for the firm will move back towards the origin. Entry stops when each firm is breaking even. This is when the new demand line, $AR_2$, just touches the average cost line at a tangent. The firm now makes $Q_2$ units at a price of $P_2$. Economic profits are now zero since $P_2 - AC_2 = 0$, and therefore entry into the industry stops.

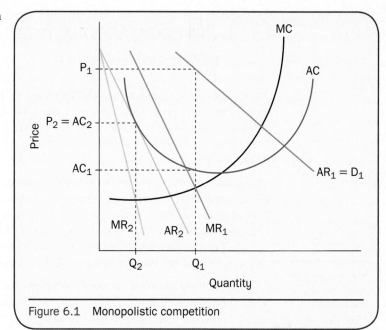

Figure 6.1   Monopolistic competition

## Excess capacity

The monopolistic long-run equilibrium has some important features. First, the **tangency equilibrium** results in average costs being above minimum average costs. In comparison with perfect competition, long-run equilibrium in monopolistic competition does not result in firms operating at minimum average total costs. Therefore, monopolistic competition is not productively efficient. In fact, firms in monopolistic competition operate with excess capacity. They could increase output and reduce costs.

> Tangency equilibrium occurs when the firm's average revenue line just touches the firm's average total cost line.

This productive inefficiency might suggest that the excess capacity in monopolistic competition is bad for society. It may be, but it is also important to recognize that monopolistic competition delivers greater choice for consumers that have varied tastes and preferences. So, in assessing whether monopolistic competition is good or bad for society, it is necessary to consider the gains from increased choice against the costs of excess capacity and inefficient production.

## Market power

In long-run equilibrium, firms in monopolistic competition have some monopoly power because price exceeds marginal cost. In perfect competition, freedom of entry and exit ensures that in long-run equilibrium price, average cost and marginal cost are equal. There is no market power in perfect competition. Firms in perfect competition are indifferent between serving a new customer and turning them away. This is because the revenue from one extra sale is equal to the cost of the sale (P = MC). In monopolistic competition, the revenue from one more sale is always higher than the costs (P > MC). Firms in monopolistic competition will always be willing to sell to one more customer. This in part may explain why firms in monopolistic competition, such as food outlets, bars and hairdressers, are willing to engage in promotional activities such as advertising as a means of drawing in extra customers.

The characteristics of monopolistic competition—product differentiation, few opportunities for economies of scale, zero economic profits, but some power over pricing—are those we often associate with service sector businesses, such as bars, restaurants, local grocery stores, hairdressers, estate agents and fast-food outlets. As such, the model of monopolistic competition has some merit in being able to explain the characteristics of many service sector industries. However, apart from a simple consideration of product differentiation, the model does not provide much of an insight into strategic interdependence. This is principally because monopolistic competition still assumes a large number of small players. Each firm is small relative to the market, and its competitive actions have only limited consequences for all of its rivals. This negligible impact results in strategic interdependence being almost entirely ignored. We will address this concern by considering oligopolies and, in particular, game theory.

## 6.3 Oligopoly theory: natural and strategic entry barriers

An oligopoly is a market with a small number of large players. Unlike in perfect competition, each firm has a significant share of the total market and therefore faces a downward-sloping demand curve for its product. Firms in oligopolies are price setters as opposed to price takers. Obvious examples of oligopolies include supermarkets, banks and the soft drinks market.

Oligopolies are often referred to as highly concentrated industries, implying that competition is concentrated in a small number of competitors. A simple measure of concentration is the **N-firm concentration ratio**, which is a measure of the total market share attributed to the N largest firms. Table 6.1 presents the market shares for the leading five UK supermarkets. The five-firm concentration ratio is 83 per cent. Table 6.2 lists the most and least concentrated industries for the UK economy.

A natural question to ask is why are some industries, such as soft drinks, highly concentrated and others, such as furniture, not? The key to the answer lies in recognizing the importance of entry barriers.

Entry barriers can exist for natural or strategic reasons.

### Natural entry barriers

The costs for a firm can be exogenously or endogenously determined. Our natural entry barriers are concerned with **exogenous costs**, so let us concentrate on them first.

> **N-firm concentration ratio, CR,** is a measure of the industry output controlled by the industry's N largest firms.
>
> **Exogenous costs** of the firm are outside its control.

The fact that exogenous costs are outside the firm's control does not mean that these costs are uncontrollable; rather, the firm does not influence the price of labour, machines, raw materials and the production technology used. For example, the price of labour is a market price determined outside the firm's control. The level of costs associated with a particular industry, as we saw with monopolies, can create an entry barrier.

In Figure 6.2, we have the long-run average cost curve LRAC and the minimum efficient scale. (We considered these in Chapter 3.) At the minimum efficient scale, MES, the average cost is £10. But with a much smaller plant, $Q_1$, the cost per unit rises to £20. In order to enter and compete in the industry it is essential to build a plant that is at least as big as the MES. In oligopolies, the MES is large when compared to the overall market. For example, if we have 50 million customers and the MES is 10 million units per year, then we might reasonably expect 50m/10m = 5 firms in the market.

If we consider supermarkets, it is easy to see why natural barriers to entry may exist. In the case of supermarkets, the big players have in excess of 500 stores each. So the MES must be around 500 stores. This level of scale is probably essential when trying to negotiate discounts from

**Table 6.1** Supermarket market shares

| Supermarket | Percentage market share |
| --- | --- |
| Tesco | 28 |
| Asda | 17 |
| Sainsbury's | 16 |
| Morrisons | 11 |
| Co-operative | 7 |

*Source:* Kanter (2015) at www.kanterworldpanel.com

**Table 6.2** Most and least concentrated UK industries

| Most concentrated industries (5-firm CR > 80%) | Least concentrated industries (5-firm CR < 10%) |
| --- | --- |
| Sugar | Metal forging |
| Tobacco | Plastic pressing |
| Gas distribution | Furniture |
| Banking | Construction |
| Soft drinks | Structural metal products |

*Source:* ONS

product suppliers, optimizing marketing spend and building efficient distribution systems to move stock from suppliers to the stores. Given that the UK is a small island with around 60 million inhabitants, it is sensible that we should only see a small number of large supermarket chains. Four large players operating at 500-plus stores is all that the UK market is capable of supporting. So, it is the natural, or exogenous, cost characteristics, coupled with the market size that leads to a natural entry barrier and the creation of an oligopoly.

## Strategic entry barriers

What happens if the MES is not very big when compared with the market size? Entry is easier and aids competition. Consider the case of soft drink manufacturers. If you wish to enter the soft drinks market, then you need to buy a bottling plant and a big steel factory to house it in and a warehouse; and a couple of trucks for deliveries will also help. The cost will not exceed £5 million. (It is amazing what you can learn when taking summer jobs as a student.) For many businesses £5 million is not a huge sum of money. The MES is not big and, therefore, the entry barrier into the market is limited. So, as a firm inside the market, how do you prevent entry? Easy—you change the cost characteristics of the industry and make the MES bigger, or, as the economist would say, you **endogenize** the cost function.

Coca-Cola and Pepsi are clear examples of how to achieve this strategy. The core assets for these companies are not production facilities; rather, they are brand names. A successful brand may cost £100 million or more to buy, or develop through advertising. Therefore, the entry barrier is not a £5 million factory, it is instead a £100 million brand.

Figure 6.3 illustrates these points. $LRAC_{Production}$ is the cost curve that relates to production only. $LRAC_{Production + Advertising}$ is the cost curve when we consider production and advertising together. The MES for production is much smaller than the MES for production and advertising. Therefore, by strategically changing the cost nature of the soft drinks industry, from production based to managing brands, the dominant players can try to prevent entry.

Perhaps more important, the £100-million brand development fee is a **sunk cost**. This means that if the entrant decided to exit the market after spending £100 million on brand development, it would be unlikely to sell the asset on. The asset has no value to any other business and so the cost is sunk. In contrast, the production facility could be sold on. A soft drinks manufacturer may not buy the plant, but some other food processing company could be interested in the facility. This asset can be sold on, so its costs are not sunk. As a consequence, the need for a

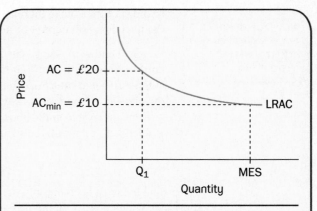

**Figure 6.2**  Economies of scale and natural entry barriers

The minimum efficient scale (MES) is the minimum scale of operation, or size of factory, that is needed in order to operate at lowest cost. If, however, the firm chooses a lower level of operation, then average costs will be higher. If the MES is very high, it can act as a barrier to entry.

> If costs are endogenized, the firms inside the industry have strategically influenced the level and nature of costs.
>
> A sunk cost is an expenditure that cannot be regained when exiting the market.

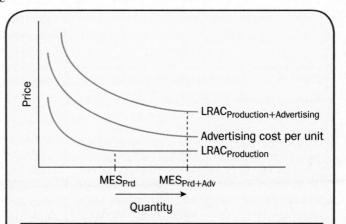

**Figure 6.3**  Strategic entry barriers

When the MES is naturally low, entry can be easy. Incumbents can change this by altering the cost characteristics of the industry. One suggestion is to move away from production and build in large investments in intangible assets such as brand names. This can substantially increase the MES and reduce entry.

> A contestable market is one where firms can enter and exit a market freely.

brand simultaneously increases the size of entry into the market and it makes it more risky as the asset cannot be sold on. The investment is lost.

The existence of sunk costs is important because without them markets are **contestable**. With freedom to enter and exit, contestable markets proxy perfectly competitive markets. So, even if the market has only a small number of large players, the absence of sunk costs enables potential rivals to threaten future entry. The only way to prevent entry is to make it look unattractive, with low levels of profit. So, contestable markets, even with oligopolistic structures, only produce normal economic profits.

## Examples of contestable markets

The airline industry is commonly used as an example of contestability. An aircraft does not represent a sunk cost. A jumbo jet can be used on a route between Heathrow and New York. It can equally be used on a route between Heathrow and Hong Kong. There are no costs in moving the asset (aircraft) between the two routes, or any other route. Therefore, the airline can quickly and easily move the aircraft to the most profitable route. This ability should keep profits low on all possible routes, as the threat of entry by rivals is very real, with no entry barriers.

For decades supermarkets have been seen as a market with very high entry barriers. The cost of building one store can run into millions. The cost of building and maintaining a network of 500 or more stores is a huge entry barrier and hence the market is less contestable. But what if supermarkets promoted online shopping to gain greater market share? What if shoppers became less reliant on visiting stores to shop for groceries? What if there are other online retailers who could easily move into the grocery market? When you think of Amazon you do not think books, which is where Amazon started. So Amazon delivering your groceries is not an impossible idea.

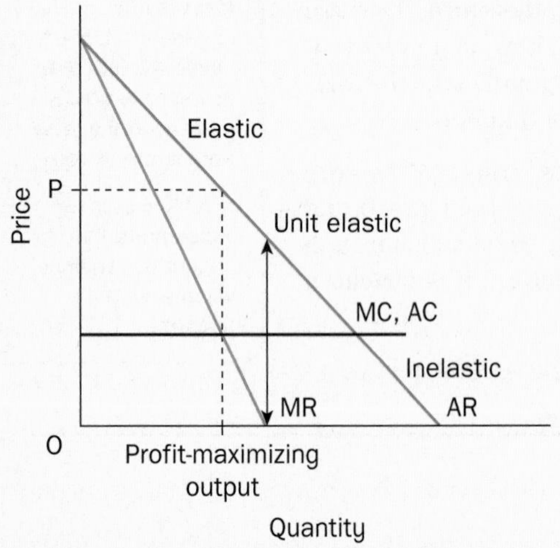

Figure 6.4 Collusion versus competition

Marginal cost has to be positive. It is not possible to produce one more unit of output for a negative amount of money. Resources such as labour will have to be paid for. Under profit maximization MR = MC, therefore if MC has to be positive, MR also has to be positive in order for the two to be equal. From the above, positive marginal revenue is only associated with output levels where demand is price elastic. With price-elastic demand, reducing the price and expanding output will lead to higher total revenues. Since costs are constant, revenues will grow more quickly than costs and profits will increase for the individual firm. With constant cost levels, the individual firm can expand output, raise revenues and therefore boost profits.

## 6.4 Oligopoly theory: competition among the big ones

Now that we have an understanding of why oligopolies exist, it is important to understand how competition occurs between rival firms within an oligopoly. A simple fact is that firms in an oligopoly are torn between a desire to compete and the benefits of colluding. The following discussion illustrates this point.

Optimally, all firms in an oligopoly should agree to co-operate and act as one monopolist, as this generates the highest level of profits. This is known as a *cartel* and is illustrated in Figure 6.4. For simplicity, assume all firms face identical constant marginal and average costs. These are shown as a horizontal line in Figure 6.4. The profit-maximizing output occurs where MR = MC. This output maximizes the joint profits of all the firms in the cartel, acting as a monopoly. However, each firm will quickly recognize that it can undercut the market price and raise its own profits at the expense of its rivals. Why?

The answer rests in an understanding that a profit-maximizing monopoly will only operate in the price-elastic region of its demand curve. Marginal cost has to be positive,

## Box 6.2
## The future of the grocery sector in the UK

The UK's grocery sector is one of the most competitive and cut-throat in retail. It also risks being one of the unhealthiest, with demand flat lining and overcapacity eroding the big players' profitability. Against this backdrop of multi-million-pound price wars and investor concern, the KPMG/Ipsos Retail Think Tank (the RTT) met in April to discuss what may play out in the future.

### What impact are the discounters really having on the UK's grocery sector?

The rise of the discount grocers has been heavily analysed, with some commentators portraying them as playing a leading role in reshaping the grocery sector, tempting cash-conscious consumers away from the established brands of the British market. However, while there is no doubt these discount brands have eroded the edges of the big four's market share and continue to do so, the RTT questioned how significant their effect has really been. Despite recessionary-induced changes in shopping behaviour, the RTT believes it is difficult to see the big four's hold on the main grocery market being seriously challenged, simply because of their commanding (75 per cent+) store network market penetration—a market share which has existed for almost ten years.

### What's next for the sector?

The modern consumer wants a cheap, ideally free, online shopping service, with long sell-by dates and no substitutions. This is the golden chalice of grocery, but the cost of delivery is a major barrier to grocers and consumers. Whether grocers with significant property estates will ever strive to provide this level of service is debatable. However, the RTT believes consumers may embrace 'drive through' shopping, where consumers can quickly pick up their preordered shopping at a location convenient to them.

However, the economic reality is that it's not in the interests of the big four to move quicker towards online sales and home delivery, irrespective of whether the demand is there. The costs of the online sales and homes delivery model remain fiercely prohibitive.

### The arrival of the online rival

The RTT believes that price alone or a competitive environment will not reshape the grocery sector whilst all the players keep using similar formats. Instead, a new entrant could change the balance. This could take the form of a new online only retailer like Amazon entering the fray, or price comparison websites playing a greater role in the market. It is inevitable that this change will be greatly accelerated if a big grocer fails. This would leave room for new market entrants to come in and offer consumers something different.

Tim Denison of Ipsos said: 'The competitive advantage Amazon has is that they know a lot more about their customers than the traditional grocers. If they can find the right local partner and target just the top 5 per cent of customers in the UK who could deliver the majority of their sales, then this could be a game changer. Despite the widespread use of patronage and loyalty cards by consumers, supermarkets have failed to reap the benefits of the data and insight these offer to them.'

### Conclusion

New market entrants and changing consumer buying habits have left the UK grocery market in a state of flux, and the RTT warns that the majority need to reconsider their long-term strategy and assess if it is still fit for purpose.

The discounters aren't the slayer of the big four, but they have piqued the interest of a UK consumer bored with the middle-ground brands and keen to make their money go further, whilst buying food and products they can enjoy.

However, the current status quo would only be at risk if one of the big four were to disappear: in order to gain significant market share the discounters will require a stratospheric store opening programme or the failure of a competitor. The RTT believes the answer to securing sales doesn't lie on a price tag, but in strong product ranges tailored to the local market's tastes alongside delivery options, charges and times to suit the consumer. If a grocer can work out how to offer free home delivery, with no substitutions, products with a long shelf life and exact delivery times then they will pull ahead of the pack.

If a well-financed player can find the right supply-chain model and partner in the UK to deliver its online grocery model service then this could be a pivotal moment in the history of UK grocery, and completely change the face of UK retail.

Either way, the old blueprint for a UK grocer is out of date and radical investment in store infrastructure, online delivery and click and collect is urgently needed if the grocery sector is to deliver the service the modern consumer demands.

From The KPMG/Ipsos Retail Think Tank. 19 June 2014.
'The future of the grocery sector in the UK'.
© 2015 KPMG/Ipsos Retail Think Tank

because it is impossible to produce an additional unit of output without incurring additional costs. Therefore, if profits are maximized when MC = MR, then, because MC is positive, MR must also be positive. If marginal revenue is positive, reducing the price to sell one more unit has made a positive contribution to total revenue. We saw in Chapter 2 that cutting prices and raising total revenue only occurs when demand is price elastic.

Therefore, a single firm within the cartel illustrated in Figure 6.4 can see that its marginal and average costs are constant. However, reducing prices will generate greater revenues because demand is price elastic. The individual firm can, therefore, earn more profit by cheating on its cartel colleagues and expanding output. Unfortunately, any member of the cartel could recognize that, being on the elastic part of the demand curve, it could also drop its own prices and raise revenues. Therefore, all rivals would respond by dropping their prices, leaving the cartel and in effect competing with each other. This is strategic interdependence in action. Should firms in oligopoly co-operate with each other and act as a monopoly, or compete with each other and start a price war?

## When a cartel might work

Some basic points at this stage help in understanding when a cartel can work and when competition will prevail. Collusion is likely to fail when there is:

- a large number of firms
- product differentiation
- instability in demand and costs.

Collusion is much harder when there are many firms in the industry: co-ordination and enforcement are too complex and it is easy for firms to blame each other for cheating. If the product is not standardized, perhaps differentiated in some way, then collusion is unlikely to work. Differentiation is a means of reducing substitutability. Why agree on price fixing when your products are not near-substitutes? Finally, collusion benefits from stability in demand and costs. If the equilibrium is changing frequently, then the cartel has frequently to adjust its agreed prices. It is costly to co-ordinate and the variation in market conditions provides firms with the cover needed to cheat and not get caught.

Examples of price fixing include the Organization of Petroleum Exporting Countries (OPEC), which meets on a frequent basis to agree oil-production levels for all member countries. By managing oil production, OPEC is seeking to influence oil supply in the world and ultimately set the world price for oil. Since this is an agreement between countries, it is not illegal, although perhaps it is not desirable.

Recent commercial examples include the agreement between British Airways and Virgin to fix fuel surcharges on transatlantic flights. Sony and Hitachi were suspected of agreeing to fix the price for LCD screens used by Nintendo; and in Europe both Unilever and Proctor and Gamble have been fined for fixing the price of detergents. The level of fines has increased across the globe and the use of prison sentences for senior executives is becoming more common. In Box 6.3 some further examples are given. In most cases the number of large competitors is small, the product displays little differentiation and costs are relatively stable, all of which provide a possible mechanism for co-ordinating price increases. Table 6.3 presents further examples ranked by the size of the fine imposed by the European Union (EU) Competition Commission. Again, a quick consideration of each case would suggest fairly homogeneous products and large economies of scale, leading to a small number of firms and relatively stable costs and demand.

Price fixing can have economy-wide implications and in many countries and economic regions cartels are considered an illegal activity. Within the EU, suspected cartels are investigated by the European Competition Commission, which under antitrust legislation has the power to seek penalties in the courts for up to 10 per cent of a company's global turnover. In practice, big headline cases are most likely to suffer the 10 per cent penalties,

## Box 6.3
## Global fines for price-fixing hit $5.3bn record high

Fines meted out to companies for price-fixing reached a record high in 2014, as antitrust authorities cracked down on cartels that rigged the markets for products ranging from auto parts to sausages.

France and Germany both imposed their highest fines, with French authorities levying a $1.2 billion penalty on a single cartel, and Germany fining three cartels nearly $1 billion in total.

Hotels and bistros were revealed as the preferred venue for price-fixing deals. Investigators found that the price of wurst was being rigged by a cartel that included leading makers Herta, Böklunder, and Wiesenhof, which met at the Atlantic hotel in Hamburg. Similarly, French authorities raided a Parisian restaurant as part of a probe into the price fixing of household and personal-care products, involving such companies as L'Oréal and Unilever.

Brazil emerged as one of the toughest enforcers of competition law, imposing fines of $1.6 billion over the year, including its highest ever single fine of $1.4 billion, levied on a cement cartel. A Brazilian court also imposed the longest jail sentence for price-fixing last year, ordering a Brazilian executive found guilty of bid rigging between two airlines to spend more than 10 years in prison and pay a $156 million fine.

'Individual accountability is slowly becoming a mantra of more and more authorities globally, with antitrust offenders now facing prison time on multiple continents,' said John Terzaken, an antitrust partner at A&O. 'This is a particularly sobering reality for senior executives responsible for global business lines, who risk severe sanctions for their own conduct as well as for wilfully ignoring violations of their subordinates.'

From the *Financial Times*. 6 January 2015. 'Global fines for price-fixing hit $5.3bn record high. Caroline Binham. © The Financial Times Limited 2015. All Rights Reserved.

while the vast majority of cases pay fines which equal less than 1 per cent of their global turnover. Any company involved in a cartel can seek immunity from prosecution under the Commission's leniency policy. The leniency policy provides protection to companies that inform on other members of the cartel and/or assist in the investigation and prosecution of a cartel. In order to gain immunity under the leniency policy, a company must be the first to inform the Commission about the cartel. If a company is not the first to inform the Commission, then a reduction in penalties can be achieved if that company provides the Commission with evidence which reinforces its ability to prove the existence of the cartel.

**Table 6.3** Ten highest EU cartel fines per case since 1969

| Year | Case name | Amount in € million |
|------|-----------|---------------------|
| 2012 | TV and computer monitor tubes | 1,470 |
| 2008 | Car glass | 1,384 |
| 2009 | Gas | 1,106 |
| 2013 | Euro interest derivatives | 1,042 |
| 2014 | Automotive bearings | 953 |
| 2007 | Elevators and escalators | 832 |
| 2010 | Airfreight | 799 |
| 2001 | Vitamins | 791 |
| 2008 | Candle waxes | 676 |
| 2010 | LCD | 648 |

*Source:* European Competition Commission Cartel Statistics.

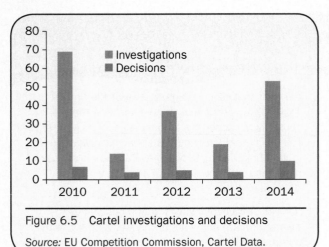

Figure 6.5   Cartel investigations and decisions

*Source:* EU Competition Commission, Cartel Data.

Again the first company to provide evidence gains most, with a possible penalty reduction of 30–50 per cent, the second company can gain a reduction of 20–30 per cent and subsequent companies up to 20 per cent. In addition to placing large fines on the companies involved in cartels, a number of countries have begun to make company directors face criminal prosecution and, where guilty, serve prison sentences.

Figure 6.5 provides data on the number of suspected cartels investigated between 2010 and 2014 by the EU Competition Commission and the number of decisions where the case was proven. While the number of investigations has varied over the years, the number of decisions has remained fairly constant.

## 6.5  Competition among rivals

We now understand that oligopolies are industries characterized by a small number of large firms and that entry barriers are a likely cause of them. We now need to develop a framework which will enable an understanding of how firms within an oligopoly will decide to compete or co-operate.

> A kinked demand curve shows that price rises will not be matched by rivals, but price reductions will be.

Economists' earliest attempts to model oligopolies involved the **kinked demand curve**, shown in Figure 6.6. The idea behind the kinked demand curve is that price rises will not be matched by rivals, but price reductions will be matched. The kinked demand curve is therefore often used to explain the pricing behaviour of competing petrol stations. Since car drivers can always drive on to the next filling station, each petrol station has a number of nearby competitors. If one station increases prices, then all others will hold prices and attract additional traffic. If a station cuts prices, then more traffic will flow to that station and competing outlets will counter the move by matching the price cut. It is only when the price of oil changes that all petrol stations move prices together.

At the price of £10, there is no point in a firm changing its prices. If it increases prices, all rivals will hold their prices; but if the firm drops prices, all rivals will also reduce their prices. Therefore, above the price of £10 demand is price elastic and below demand is inelastic, thus leading to the kinked demand curve.

The marginal revenue line is vertical at the profit-maximizing output. This is because the demand curve changes slope at this output level. The difference between the elastic and inelastic demand curves leads to a stepped change in the marginal revenue.

As a result, the demand curve has a different shape above and below the current market price:

1.  If the firm raises its price, rivals will keep their prices constant. The firm will, therefore, lose customers when it raises prices. As a result, demand above the current market price is elastic.

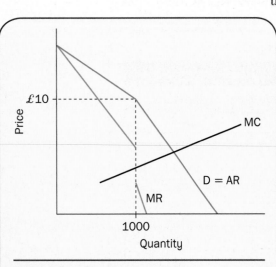

Figure 6.6   Kinked demand curves

Above the equilibrium price, demand is price elastic; competitors do not follow price increases. Below the equilibrium price, demand is inelastic; competitors match price cuts.

2. In contrast, if the firm reduces its prices, all rivals will match the price reduction. The firm will not gain more demand by reducing prices. Demand below the current market price is therefore inelastic.

We will see below that economists question the theoretical merits of the kinked demand curve, but it provides a reasonable starting point for understanding some real-world examples. The pricing of petrol, or at least the reduction in petrol prices, can be explained using the kinked demand curve. Once one petrol supplier announces a price reduction, all other petrol suppliers respond with similar price reductions in order to protect their market share. We might therefore argue that demand is inelastic for price reductions. Similarly, no firm would increase prices without full knowledge that other firms would follow. This occurs in the petrol market because of the cost of oil. So, price rises only occur when all firms face increased input costs and are therefore willing to increase prices together. But no firm would make a decision to be more expensive than its rivals. Furthermore, because of the vertical portion of the marginal revenue line, the change in the marginal cost of oil has to be quite large in order to deliver a change in the equilibrium price of petrol. Therefore, because of the kinked demand line, modest daily changes in oil prices are unlikely to feed into erratic daily price changes at the petrol pumps.

In Box 6.4 the mortgage price war is discussed. Mortgages are relatively homogenous products being a loan of money over a long-term period. Because mortgage repayments can be a substantial amount of monthly household expenditure, borrowers hunt for good deals. Since a mortgage is homogenous, borrowers have lots of substitutes to choose from and so

## Box 6.4
## Mortgage price war reaches new intensity as banks launch record-low fixed-rate deals

Low inflation and expected delays in lifting interest rates have raised the prospect of a fresh mortgage price war after HSBC and First Direct launched cheap fixed-rate deals.

The new mortgages prompted one leading broker to say the pricing of fixed-rate home loans had reached 'new record lows' as lenders continue to battle for custom despite new lending curbs and signs that a recent boom in the housing market is coming off the boil.

HSBC's new deals include what may be the lowest ever two-year fixed-rate home loan, priced at 1.29 per cent. This deal is restricted to customers with a 40 per cent deposit and it includes a fee of £1,499, but it trumps the bank's previous offering priced at 1.49 per cent.

HSBC's subsidiary First Direct has also launched cheap fixed-rate mortgages, including a loan fixed at 2.39 per cent for five years. This is understood to be the lowest ever five-year fix, cheaper than a 2.44 per cent deal offered by Yorkshire building society last year.

First Direct has also launched a three-year fixed-rate mortgage at 1.99 per cent, which is well below what many other lenders are charging, and has become the latest bank to move into offering 10-year, fixed-rate deals. Banks and building societies have been rushing out decade-long, fixed-rate mortgages, with experts attributing this to plunging inflation and a growing expectation that interest rates will stay low for longer.

The moves by HSBC and First Direct come as competition in the mortgage market has pushed many rates to the lowest on record. The price cuts have tended to centre on fixed rates, which have been hugely popular with borrowers lately because of the certainty they provide. At some points in recent months about 9 in 10 of new mortgages have been taken out on a fixed basis.

'Some of the rates on offer are very attractive,' said David Hollingworth of mortgage broker London & Country. Adding that fixed rate mortgages have reached new record lows, he said: 'I think it indicates a continuation of the trend that fixed rates are falling. There are a lot of very attractive deals out there, and lenders are competing hard.'

From *The Guardian*. 2 January 2015. 'Mortgage price war reaches new intensity as banks launch record-low fixed-rate deals'. Rupert Jones and Angela Monaghan.
© Guardian News & Media Ltd 2015

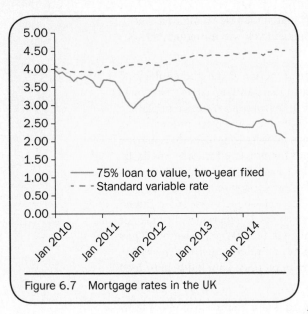

Figure 6.7    Mortgage rates in the UK

their demand is price elastic. If one lender reduces its price/interest rate, other lenders will follow in order to protect their market share.

In Figure 6.7 interest rates on popular two-year fixed rates are compared to standard variable rates. Whilst standard variable rates climbed in the period 2010 to 2014, the price war on popular two-year fixed deals has almost continuously pushed prices down.

## Problems with the kinked demand curve

The kinked demand model has a number of positive features. First, the demand curves for the firm are based on potential or expected responses from the firm's rivals. Hence, strategic interdependence is a feature of the model. Second, the model predicts stability in pricing. This occurs because of strategic interdependence: rivals will react to price changes in a way that makes them ineffective. Also, price stability occurs because, even when the firm's costs increase, as a result of the vertical portion of the firm's MR line the profit-maximizing output and price are unlikely to change. Only when costs change by a large amount will the intersection of marginal cost and marginal revenue move from the vertical portion of the marginal revenue line.

The major drawback associated with the kinked demand curve is that it does not explain how the stable price is arrived at in the first place. There must be a prior process that determines the price. The kinked demand curve merely explains the stability once the price is set. We therefore need an approach that understands strategic interdependence more fully.

## (6.6) Game theory

Game theory seeks to understand whether strategic interaction will lead to competition or co-operation between rivals.

In response to this challenge, economists have now turned to **game theory** as a means of understanding strategic interdependence. In economic jargon, a game has players who have different pay-offs associated with different strategic options. In the business sense, we could have two firms (players): they could start a price war and compete against each other or they could try to co-operate with each other (strategic options). Each combination has different profit outcomes (pay-offs) for the two firms.

The original version of game theory is known as the *prisoners' dilemma*, where two criminals have to decide to co-operate or compete with each other in order to win their freedom. The prisoners' dilemma is similar in style to the end game in the television show *Golden Balls*, where opposing players have to decide to steal or share, in order to win the cash prize.

## The prisoners' dilemma

Two criminals, Robin Banks and Nick Scars, are arrested by the police. There is little evidence against the criminals and they face a short spell in prison if convicted. The police decide to offer each prisoner a deal. If they provide evidence against their fellow criminal, then they will go free. The dilemma facing the prisoners is illustrated in Figure 6.8.

|  |  | **Robin Banks** | |
|---|---|---|---|
|  |  | Stays silent | Betrays |
| **Nick Scar** | Stays silent | Nick Scar: short sentence<br><br>Robin Banks: short sentence | Nick Scar: long sentence<br><br>Robin Banks: goes free |
|  | Betrays | Nick Scar: goes free<br><br>Robin Banks: long sentence | Nick Scar: medium sentence<br><br>Robin Banks: medium sentence |

Figure 6.8    The prisoners' dilemma

The matrix of sentences represents the possible pay-offs to each prisoner. If they both stay silent, then they will receive a short sentence. If Nick Scars stays silent and Robin Banks provides evidence, then Nick Scars receives a long sentence and Robin Banks goes free. Sitting in separate cells, with no ability to communicate, both prisoners are most likely to provide evidence and receive medium sentences. They will cheat, or compete with each other, when it would have been in their interests to co-operate and stay silent. Just as with the game *Golden Balls*, sharing is attractive, but it is possibly outweighed by the gains of stealing—but only if the other player does not steal as well.

To understand why competing, rather than co-operating, with a rival is preferable, we need to understand the importance of the Nash equilibrium.

The Nobel Laureate John Nash proved that the optimal solution for any game must result in each player making an optimal decision given the potential response of its rival. This is now known as the **Nash equilibrium**. The important point to note from the Nash equilibrium is that each firm considers what its rivals can do before deciding on its own strategy. A player does not simply decide what it wants to do. For example, Liverpool or Barcelona do not decide to run on the pitch and kick the ball in the back of the opposition's net. Clearly, this is what they want to do. Instead, they think about what their rivals will do, how they play, what formation they might use and who their opponent's key players are. Liverpool or Barcelona can then develop a football strategy based on what their rivals are going to do. The Nash equilibrium is just formalizing this obvious decision-making process by saying, 'Consider your rival's likely behaviour before you decide what you are going to do'.

> Nash equilibrium occurs when each player does what is best for themselves, given what their rivals may do in response.
>
> Dominant strategy is a player's best response, whatever its rival decides.
>
> In a single-period game, the game is only played once. In a repeated game, the game is played a number of rounds.

Now let us examine a price war game in Figure 6.9, using Nash's argument. Firm A looks at firm B and sees that B can do one of two things: co-operate or start a price war. We can begin by examining what happens if B decides to co-operate. If A then also co-operates, it will earn £50 million, but if A begins a price war, then it will earn £60 million. Firm A now thinks about B's other option, which is to start a price war. If A tries to co-operate, it will only earn £20 million, but if A also takes up the option of a price war, then it will earn £30 million. Firm A now knows that, whatever B does, it is always optimal for A to start a price war. Firm B will go through a similar decision-making process and come to the same conclusion—that whatever A does, B will start a price war. The Nash equilibrium has both firms embarking on a price war earning £30 million each.

In this example, each firm's optimal decision is independent of its rival's decision. A's optimal decision is to cheat, regardless of whether B cheats or co-operates. A is known as having a **dominant strategy** and, given that our example has symmetric pay-offs for B, then B also has a dominant strategy.

When each player has a dominant strategy, the Nash equilibrium will be unique—only one cell in the pay-off matrix will provide an equilibrium solution. However, this unique equilibrium is not necessarily optimal. In the case of the prisoners' dilemma, both players would be better off if they co-operated.

## Repeated games

Starting a price war or displaying 'non-cooperative' behaviour is a general response in a **single-period game**. Therefore, as a rule, whenever you play a game once, as our rivals did in Figure 6.8,

|  | | Firm A | |
|---|---|---|---|
|  | | Co-operate | Price war |
| **Firm B** | Co-operate | 50:50 | 20:60 |
|  | Price war | 60:20 | 30:30 |

Figure 6.9 Game theory, pay-off-matrix

The numbers in each box are the pay-offs to each firm (firm B is always on the left and firm A right). The Nash equilibrium is where both firms choose to start a price war, earning £30 million each. This is because when choosing its strategy A examines B's options: if B tries to co-operate, A's best response is to start a price war; and if B starts a price war, A's best response is again to start a price war. B will come to the same conclusion when examining its response to A.

or strategically interact with someone once, then cheat. For example, consider buying a second-hand car from the classified ads. You see a car and go to meet the owner. You will say the car is not perfect and the owner will tell you that the car is fantastic. It does not matter whether the car is good or not; you are both displaying non-cooperative behaviour. You both do this because you do not expect to meet again to buy or sell cars in the future. It is a one-period game, so you both cheat. You would like the price to fall; they would like the price to rise.

The way to move from a non-cooperative Nash equilibrium to a co-operative Nash equilibrium is to play the game repeatedly and use a strategy known as 'tit-for-tat'. Under tit-for-tat, you will co-operate with your rival in the next round if they co-operated with you in the last round. If they cheated on you in the last round, you will never co-operate with them again.

In the game above, if A and B co-operate they both receive £50 million. If, in the next round, A decides to cheat and start a price war, it will earn £60 million, or £10 million more than from co-operation. But in the next rounds B will always commit to a price war, so the most A can earn is £30 million. Firm A has the choice of gaining £10 million in the next round and then losing £50 million – £30 million = £20 million for every round afterwards. Therefore, short-term gains from cheating are outweighed by the long-term losses of a repeated game.

However, in order for tit-for-tat to work, the threat to always display non-co-operative behaviour, if your rival cheated in the last round, has to be a **credible commitment**.

> A credible commitment or threat has to be one that is optimal to carry out.

Recall the Spanish invaders who burnt their boats—their threat to fight the local Incas, rather than sail off to a safer shore, was very credible when they no longer had any boats!

For a business illustration, let us go back to the car example. This time consider buying a car from a dealer of one of the major manufacturers. With a second-hand car they usually provide a warranty. They do this because they value your repeat business. The dealer does not want to sell you a bad car. Instead, they would like you to feel secure in the fact that the car is good and they will fix any problems. They are not cheating; they are trying to co-operate. In fact, by offering warranties they are making a credible commitment to provide you with a trouble-free car. They are willing to do this because the potential revenue streams from your repeat business outweigh any gains from selling you a bad car at an expensive price.

Finally, we can consider the market for love. Marriage is a repeated game. If one partner cheats by seeing someone else, then divorce is a fairly robust method of never agreeing to co-operate with the cheating partner again. In the singles market, in contrast, seeking co-operation for fun with someone you find attractive could be a one-period game if you only expect to see them once. If they ask what you do, it is better to cheat. Claiming to be a catwalk model or a professional footballer are better options than admitting to being an indebted student.

In summary, strategic decisions require an understanding of the potential responses. If a firm, or individual, plays a game once, they should cheat. If they play repeatedly, then they should try to co-operate for as long as their rivals co-operate.

## (6.7) Game theory extension: reaction functions

The prisoners' dilemma is a simplification, and the existence of joint dominating strategies is not always assured. A further complication is that players may not make decisions simultaneously; instead players may make decisions sequentially. For example, eBay made the decision to become an online auction provider and Gumtree then followed. Starbucks decided to be a global provider of coffee shops and many other national companies then decided to enter the market.

When one firm is able to make a decision before its (future potential) rivals, then it might be able to achieve a **first-mover advantage**.

Let us assume that firm A is the leader and firm B is the follower. Firm A and B sell coffee. Firm A is thinking of opening a coffee shop in a small town which currently does not have a coffee shop. Market research informs firm A that the market in the new town will provide sales of 60 coffees per hour and each coffee drinker takes 30 minutes to drink their coffee. Firm A therefore needs 30 chairs and tables for its new shop.

> First-mover advantage ensures that the firm which makes its strategic decision first gains a profitable advantage over its rivals.

Firm A opens its shop with 30 chairs and trades successfully for six months. Firm B now needs to make a decision: should it open a shop in the town? Knowing that firm A has a shop which can serve the entire market, the opportunity for firm B looks unattractive. If it decided to open a 30-seat shop, it would have to fight out a price war with firm A to attract enough business to fill the shop. Therefore, seeing that firm A has already successfully entered, firm B's best decision is to stay away from the market or enter with a much smaller shop.

In contrast, if both firms had made simultaneous decisions to enter, then we might expect them to have both opened shops with 15 seats—that is, they would have tried to share the market. By being able to go first, firm A choose a size of entry that raised its profits and reduced the size of the opportunity for firm B.

Of course first-mover advantage is not always a guarantee of assured future success. The first-mover has to take a market position that its rivals fear they cannot match or beat. Look for example at the ability of Apple to follow and out-perform its rivals in the smartphone market in Box 6.5

## Box 6.5
## Asian tech groups fail to exploit early advantage against Apple

Soon after Apple launched its larger-screen iPhones last week, rivals in Asia sent out mocking messages on Twitter, taunting the US company for being slow to catch up with the industry trend. 'No one is going to buy a big phone,' Samsung Electronics teased, quoting a 2010 remark by Apple's late co-founder Steve Jobs: 'Guess who surprised themselves and changed their minds?'

The light-hearted tone of the messages concealed a serious headache for Apple's Asian competitors. While they have often moved into new product areas such as large-screen phones, smartwatches and payment technology before the US tech group, they have consistently been unable to match the excitement generated by Apple product launches—or its success in monetizing and globalizing their usage.

Apple's two new iPhones have larger screens than their predecessors, taking the company into 'phablet' territory pioneered by Samsung, which launched the fourth version of its Galaxy Note at the beginning of September.

'When the Note was announced, I couldn't understand it,' said Ben Wood at the research group CCS Insight, referring to the 2011 launch of Samsung's first phablet. 'It looked ridiculous. And now it's become a legitimate category.' Samsung declined to reveal how many Notes it has sold since the new launch, but said it shipped 10 million units of the previous model in the first two months after its launch last year.

Still, analysts believe that Apple's lead in the brand stakes—in spite of Samsung's huge outlays on marketing, on which it spent $14 billionn last year—will eat into the Korean group's first-mover advantage. 'Consumers have an incredible emotional engagement with the Apple brand,' said Mr Wood. 'Samsung hasn't achieved that.' If Samsung's advertising campaigns have at least helped it narrow the popularity gap with Apple, Taiwan's HTC shows the challenges facing smaller Asian smartphone producers seeking to compete at the high end of the market.

While its One series of phones have been praised by some reviewers as the most attractively designed smartphone to date, the lack of marketing clout to support it has left the company floundering commercially. HTC has predicted a 12th consecutive quarter of declining revenues in the third quarter of this year.

From the *Financial Times*. 16 September 2014. 'Asian tech groups fail to exploit early advantage against Apple'. Simon Mundy in Seoul and Kana Inagaki in Tokyo.
© The Financial Times Limited 2014. All Rights Reserved.

## 6.8 Business application: compete, co-operate or gain a first-mover advantage?

If we return to our game theory illustration in Figure 6.9, the most desirable box for firm A is top right, where it earns 60. However, from our discussion we know that A will never find itself in this box. In a one-period game its rival will also compete and the two firms will earn 30 each, while in a repeated game both firms will try to co-operate and earn 50 each. Earning 60 in the top right is a situation where firm A competes and B decides to be friendly. A, therefore, dominates its rival B and in so doing controls the market. So, how do you convince your rival not to compete? We now know that the answer to this question rests on gaining a first-mover advantage.

This is a problem which taxed Sony and Toshiba, who battled for supremacy in the high-definition DVD market. Sony developed and launched Blu-ray, while Toshiba led the HD DVD project. The competing approaches used different recording formats and were incompatible with each other.

The race to win market share can be viewed as a game. If Toshiba and Sony had agreed to co-operate and develop the same format, then movie-makers and consumers would have been very happy. Movie-makers would have felt assured that they could sell high-definition DVDs of their films, and consumers would have been happy to purchase a high-definition DVD player and television to view the films. The market would have grown and Sony and Toshiba would have shared a higher level of overall profits. This would be the top-left box of Figure 6.9.

In contrast, if Sony and Toshiba continued competing, movie-makers did not know which format to support and consumers ran the risk of buying a machine that could only play one format of discs. The market was slow to grow, and both firms earned reduced profits. This would be the bottom-right box of Figure 6.9.

Alternatively, if one company had won enough support that it became commercially unattractive for the remaining competitor to continue, then the winning firm would have been a monopoly and earned huge profits. Depending upon which firm won, this would be the top-right or bottom-left box of Figure 6.9.

In order to try to win, Sony and Toshiba sought out and gained the support of leading film studios. At times, some film studios changed sides and the balance of power between Blu-ray and HD DVD was finely balanced. Fortunately for Sony, it possessed a strategic option which offered the chance of first-mover advantage—PlayStation 3 (PS3). By building Blu-ray into the PS3, Sony accelerated the adoption of its technology into many households around the world. In contrast, Toshiba's hopes of being adopted rested on the family decision to upgrade the trusted and reliable DVD player. By going first, or quickest, into households Sony gained a commanding lead in the market. Film studios realized and switched allegiance from Toshiba to Sony. Blu-ray is now the dominant format for high-definition films.

## 6.9 Business application: managing supply costs—anonymous auctions for supermarket contracts

We have seen that, in repeated games, firms are likely to behave co-operatively. This presents a substantial risk to supermarkets who repeatedly run auctions to provide them with products. In particular, because supermarkets are retailers, they do not ordinarily manufacture their 'own-labelled' products. Instead, they ask competing manufacturers to bid for contracts. Today, it might be next month's lemonade contract; tomorrow, it might be fish fingers or soap powder. The firm that can produce the product most cheaply wins the contract. With supermarkets coming to the market repeatedly, it is in the interest of competing manufacturers to co-operate with each other. For example, rival manufacturers of fish fingers could agree to split the market. When bidding for supermarket X's contract, company A would never undercut company B. In return, when bidding for supermarket Y's contract, B would never undercut A.

For a supermarket, this is a serious problem. The way to stop it is to prevent co-operation. Supermarkets try to achieve this by organizing blind auctions over the Internet. The fish finger contract opens for bidding at 2.00 p.m. on Wednesday and companies make bids. The web page shows the amount of it, but it does not say who made it. The bidders now find it difficult to co-operate. In fact, it is now very easy to cheat, because only the supermarket knows who you are. In this example, supermarkets can see the problem of co-operation and take steps to prevent its occurrence.

There is, however, a problem with the supermarket's strategy. In generating competition among its suppliers, it runs the risk of pushing some of them out of business. Therefore, in the long run the supermarkets could end up with monopoly suppliers in their key product markets rather than competitive industries, and we saw in Chapter 5 that such a situation could be dangerous.

## 6.10 Business data application: competition in the cinema market

In 2013 the UK Competition and Markets Authority reported on the proposed merger of two cinema chains, Cineworld and Picturehouse. The market-share data in Table 6.4 taken from the investigation report clearly show that the cinema market in the UK is oligopolistic. The 3-firm concentration ratios exceeds 65 per cent, with Odeon, Cineworld and Vue all taking over 20 per cent of the market each.

The merger of Cineworld with Picturehouse hardly looks problematic at first sight. Picturehouse has 1.7 per cent of the UK market. The merger with Cineworld is hardly going to alter the balance of competition in the overall UK market.

**Table 6.4**   Market shares for various UK cinema companies

|  | Market share % | Sites (as at Jan 2013) | Screens (as at Jan 2013) |
|---|---|---|---|
| Odeon | 24.9 | 114 | 799 |
| Cineworld | 24.7 | 102 | 859 |
| Vue | 21.5 | 79 | 746 |
| Showcase Cinemas | 6.1 | 20 | 264 |
| Empire Cinemas Limited | 3.8 | 16 | 150 |
| Picturehouse | 1.7 | 21 | 59 |
| Apollo Cinemas Limited | 1.4 | N/A | N/A |
| Others | 15.9 | 417 | 921 |
| Total | 100 | 769 | 3,798 |

However, consumption of cinemas occurs at a local, not a national level. The data in Figure 6.5 show that most people who go to the cinema travel from home, 88–89 per cent for both cinema chains. Most travel by car (62 per cent); and the vast majority travel no more than 20 minutes.

The crucial part of the analysis for the Competition and Markets Authority is not whether the market is an oligopoly at a national level, but whether there is restricted competition at a local (city) level. Moreover, will the merger between Cineworld and Picturehouse lessen competition in any one particular city?

By drawing 20-minute drive-time boundaries around each cinema, it was possible to identify three cities where competition would be reduced because of the merger. These were Aberdeen, Bury St Edmunds and Cambridge. As a result, it was proposed that the Picturehouse cinemas in each of these cities would be sold to a third operator to increase competition.

Some of the analysis and thinking undertaken by the Competition and Markets Authority is quite complicated: take a look at their reports on their website. However, at the core of their approach are some simple economic ideas which you now understand.

**Table 6.5**  Travel data for people using UK cinemas

|  | Cineworld | Picturehouse | All London cinemas | All non-London cinemas |
|---|---|---|---|---|
| Travelled from home | 88 | 89 | 89 | 90 |
| Travelled from work | 10 | 9 | 12 | 9 |
| Other/don't know | 2 | 2 | 2 | 1 |
| Walked | 16 | 32 | 25 | 26 |
| Travelled by rail/London underground | 9 | 8 | 23 | 2 |
| Travelled by car | 62 | 36 | 31 | 53 |
| Travelled by bus | 10 | 16 | 17 | 12 |
| Cycled | 2 | 7 | 2 | 7 |
| Travelled 0–10 minutes | 22 | 20 | 24 | 20 |
| Travelled 10–20 minutes | 39 | 37 | 37 | 38 |
| Travelled 20–30 minutes | 23 | 25 | 22 | 25 |
| Travelled more than 30 minutes | 16 | 18 | 16 | 17 |

*Source:* Competition and Markets Authority, all figures in per cent.

## Summary

1. Under monopolistic competition, there are a large number of small firms, freedom of entry and exit, few opportunities for economies of scale, and the use of product differentiation.

2. Long-run equilibrium in monopolistic competition is a tangency equilibrium, which results in zero economic profits, excess capacity, above-minimum average costs and price in excess of marginal costs.

3. Oligopolies are marketplaces with a small number of large firms, typically four or five. UK banking, supermarkets and even the media industry are good examples.

4. An important feature of oligopolistic markets is strategic interaction. If one firm makes a strategic change, all other firms react. When one UK supermarket decided to open on Sundays, all other supermarkets followed.

5. Two interesting questions occur when examining oligopolies: (i) Why do oligopolies exist? (ii) How will firms compete with each other?

6. Oligopolies can exist because of exogenous economies of scale. The natural cost structure of the industry results in only a small number of large firms meeting the minimum efficient scale.

7. Alternatively, natural scale economies might be limited and so, in order to create entry barriers, existing firms might manipulate the cost characteristics of the industry by perhaps making advertising a large component of operating costs. This creates high levels of endogenous costs and reduces entry.

8. Sunk costs cannot be recovered when exiting a market. If large costs are associated with brand development, then these will be sunk. This increases the risk of entry and so can also lead to the creation of entry barriers.

9. Without sunk costs, markets are contestable. Potential rivals can threaten to enter a market. In order to limit entry, firms within the market will reduce prices and profits to make entry less attractive. As a result, even with a small number of large firms, contestable markets will approximate to perfect competition.

10. Game theory can be used to understand strategic interaction. Games consist of players, pay-offs and decision rules.

11. A Nash equilibrium is where players make an optimal decision based on what their rivals might do. In single-period games, the Nash equilibrium requires each player to cheat or display non-cooperative behaviour. In a multi-period game with no known end, the optimal strategy is tit-for-tat, where if you co-operated in the last round, your rival should co-operate with you in the next round. If not, you should never co-operate with them again.

12. When players make sequential decisions it is possible for the lead firm to gain a first-mover advantage, capture more profits and reduce the commercial opportunities available to rivals who may follow.

13. In the repeated environment of firms bidding for supermarkets' own-label contracts, it is likely that co-operation will occur, where rivals agree not to undercut each other on price. In order to prevent this and generate competition in the auction, supermarkets run blind auctions, where it becomes difficult for rivals to co-ordinate their bids. It even enables rivals to cheat on each other behind a cloak of secrecy.

## Learning checklist

You should now be able to:

- Explain monopolistic competition
- Provide examples of oligopolies
- Explain the concept of strategic interdependence
- Identify natural and strategic entry barriers
- Understand the kinked demand curve model of oligopoly and provide a critical review
- Explain game theory, the concept of a Nash equilibrium and optimal strategies in single-period and repeated games
- Understand first-mover advantage
- Examine and review Competition Commission reports on the degree of competition using economic concepts.

## Questions connect

**EASY**

1. How do the assumptions of perfect competition and monopolistic competition differ?
2. List five industries which are likely examples of monopolistic competition.
3. How do the equilibrium conditions differ between perfect competition and monopolistic competition?
4. What are the main types of entry barrier that are likely to be associated with oligopoly?
5. Under a kinked demand line, is demand more or less elastic above and below the equilibrium price?
6. When is collusion likely to fail?
7. What is a Nash equilibrium?
8. In the single-period prisoners' dilemma, both prisoners confess. Is this optimal?
9. How might two strategically interdependent players be encouraged to co-operate with each other?
10. Is it possible and sensible to gain a first-mover advantage?

**INTERMEDIATE**

11. Monopolistic competition is sometimes criticized for displaying excess capacity. Explain why excess capacity exists in equilibrium and evaluate whether it is bad for society.
12. Do you consider it fair that whistle-blowers, who are the first to admit to being in a cartel, are immune from prosecution?
13. Assume your company is operating in a cartel, agreeing to raise prices and reduce output. If the cartel is ongoing, then the game is in effect repeated. Under what circumstances would your company cheat?

14. Electrical retailers promise to match each other's prices. Is this co-operation or competition?

15. A firm is considering whether it should be first to invest in a new market. Provide the company with your best economic advice.

16. Using the diagram provided for a kinked demand curve for an oligopoly situation (e.g. UK supermarkets), answer the following:

   (a) Identify the equilibrium quantity and demand.

   (b) What will happen to prices charged by other firms if one firm raises its price from £6 to £8? D denotes the demand curve, MC shows marginal cost and MR shows marginal revenue schedules.

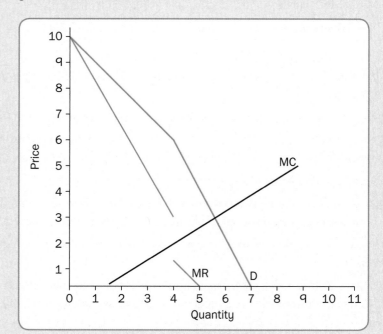

DIFFICULT

## Exercises

1. True or false?

   (a) A key aspect of an oligopolistic market is that firms cannot operate independently of each other.

   (b) Cartels may be workable if members enter into binding pre-commitments.

   (c) Under a kinked demand curve, demand is assumed to be price inelastic under a rise in prices.

   (d) In a one-period game, the strategy of tit-for-tat is optimal.

   (e) In a repeated game with no known end, it is always optimal to cheat.

   (f) With private values, an English auction format will raise the highest revenue for an item.

EASY

INTERMEDIATE

2. Suppose that there are two firms (X and Y) operating in a market, each of which can choose to produce either 'high' or 'low' output. Table 6.6 summarizes the range of possible outcomes of the firms' decisions in a single time period. Imagine that you are taking the decisions for firm X.

**Table 6.6** Firms' decisions

| | | Firm Y | | | |
|---|---|---|---|---|---|
| | | Low output profits | | High output profits | |
| | Profits: | X | Y | X | Y |
| Firm X | Low output profits | 15 | 15 | 2 | 20 |
| | High output profits | 20 | 2 | 8 | 8 |

(a) If firm Y produces 'low', what level of output would maximize your profit in this time period?

(b) If you (X) produce 'high', what level of output would maximize profits for firm Y?

(c) If firm Y produces 'high', what level of output would maximize your profit in this time period?

(d) Under what circumstances would you decide to produce 'low'?

(e) Suppose you enter into an agreement with firm Y that you both will produce 'low': what measures could you adopt to ensure that Y keeps to the agreement?

(f) What measures could you adopt to convince Y that you will keep to the agreement?

DIFFICULT

3. Supermarket sectors in many countries are often oligopolies, a small number of large players. Why do we often see strong competition amongst supermarkets, rather than collusion?

4. Source recent data on the 5-firm concentration ratio for supermarkets in a country of your choice. Evaluate whether your measures of concentration provides a good insight into the strength of competition.

# Growth strategies

## Chapter contents

## Learning outcomes

By the end of this chapter you should be able to:

### Economic theory

LO1 Identify horizontal, vertical and diversified growth

LO2 Explain learning curves

LO3 Categorize transaction costs

LO4 Explain the hold-up problem

LO5 Discuss economies of scope

### Business applications

LO6 Analyse why a small company within an oligopoly wished to merge with a rival

LO7 Debate why major recording artists are leaving record labels.

LO8 Assess why Google is branching out beyond search technology

LO9 Recognize and understand recent patterns in merger and acquisition activity

## At a glance    Growth strategies

### The issue

If firms are profit-maximizers, then it seems reasonable to assume that, in the longer term, increasing profits will be associated with increased size. Admittedly, in the near term some profits may have to be sacrificed in order to grow the business. Managerial time might be diverted to finding and selecting growth opportunities, rather than concentrating on generating profits from the current operations. It therefore becomes important to understand how a firm can grow, benefit from and manage the problems associated with different modes of growth.

### The understanding

A firm can grow in three main ways. First it can 'do more of the same'. A car-maker might decide to make more cars. Second, a firm might reduce its trading relationships by providing its own inputs, or by organizing its own distribution and retailing. Third, a firm might begin to operate in a completely different market. These three options are, respectively, known as *horizontal, vertical* and *diversified* growth. The reasons behind each type of growth are varied, but essentially they relate to the ability to increase revenues and reduce costs. This chapter will provide an understanding of these issues.

### The usefulness

An understanding of growth options is essential for understanding how a business can exploit profitable opportunities. Moreover, an understanding of growth options provides an insight into strategic behaviour and, therefore, how the firm can gain greater control over its markets and its competitors.

## ( 7.1 ) Business problem: how should companies grow?

> Organic growth is an increase in sales from the same or comparable retail space.
>
> Horizontal growth occurs when a company develops or grows activities at the same stage of the production process.
>
> Diversification is the growth of the business in a related or unrelated market.

Box 7.1 highlights the growth achieved by French supermarket Carrefour by investing in emerging markets. This type of growth would be classed as **organic growth**. A key question for business managers is: how fast and how sustainable is organic growth?

In a market with rapidly expanding demand, organic growth can be very sustainable. In mature markets, such as the European supermarket sector, organic growth can be slow and limited to the rate of growth of consumer spending on food and other grocery items. Also, organic growth can be reduced by competition. Strong competition can cut prices and volumes. Prices across all supermarkets fall and customers may move to the cheapest competitor. So organic growth can be good, but it also has its problems.

Not all growth has to be organic. Companies can expand their existing capacity by acquiring or combining their current assets with those of another company and/or competitor. In Box 7.1 two of the largest taxi-hailing app companies have agreed a merger.

Merging two similar companies is referred to as **horizontal growth** because the company is growing its current operations. While such growth brings in more sales, it may also enable a company to achieve economies of scale and bring down operating costs.

Growth is not always horizontal. It can be seen from Box 7.1 that Alibaba and Tencent have a number of different commercial interests. Expansion into multiple areas of business is classified as diversification by an economist. **Diversification** is not a particularly easy category to define because it can include related and unrelated diversification. For example,

## Box 7.1
## Alibaba and Tencent taxi-hailing apps to merge

Chinese Internet groups Alibaba and Tencent have put aside fierce rivalry to merge their popular taxi-hailing applications. The combined company would be worth about $6 billion, local media calculate based on recent fundraisings. Last month, Kuaidi Dache raised $600 million from Japanese telecoms group SoftBank and existing shareholders while Didi Dache raised $700 million in December.

The two firms are neck-and-neck in China's competitive market, with the potential for expanding mobile payment systems the prize for their backers. Kuaidi Dache (Speedy taxi') had 54.4 per cent market share in China as of the third quarter, while Didi Dache ('Honk Honk Taxi') had 44.9 per cent market, according to Analysys International, a research group.

The two gave no detail on how they are defining a merger that entails few obvious synergies and a high degree of de facto independence. 'The combined company expects to conduct the businesses of Kuaidi and Didi

independently under separate brands. The co-CEOs are especially grateful to the company's shareholders for their support of the company's independent operations,' the two companies said in a statement.

The duo use two incompatible payment systems: Kuaidi Dache has Alibaba's Alipay, and Didi Dache uses Tencent's mobile payment system. Their announcement did not say which system they would adopt, or whether they would in future accept both systems.

Taxi-hailing apps are extremely popular in China's largest cities, where rush-hour taxis are so hard to find that unlicensed cabs run a thriving business. Regulators have cracked down on private cars using apps in a bid to protect state-regulated taxi companies whose fares are capped. Many of China's largest taxi companies are ultimately owned by municipal government entities.

From the *Financial Times*. 17 February 2015. 'Alibaba and Tencent taxi-hailing apps to merge'. Lucy Hornby.
© The Financial Times Limited 2015. All Rights Reserved.

an online company operating auction sites, social media and taxi-hailing apps could be viewed as having unrelated diversification, but they could equally be seen as different aspects of the use of personal data in online retail.

A company may grow in a diversified way to offset risk. Auction site sales may grow more slowly than online advertising fees, or commissions from taxi companies.

There is also a third means of growth and this is known as *vertical growth*. Online retail activities are a collection of separate and sequential operations. Sourcing, producing, retailing and distributing goods and services constitute what economists refer to as separate aspects of the **vertical chain of production**. For example, Alibaba owns a taxi-hailing app, but it does not (currently) own a taxi company. Therefore, Alibaba could grow its vertical presence and become a player in the transportation market by also owning a taxi company.

One reason for integrating all stages of production, is to seek greater control over the value chain and is described by economists as **vertical integration**. By owning all parts of the value chain, Alibaba or Tencent can achieve greater control over the service provided to customers. For example, by only owning the taxi-hailing app, neither company has control over the quality of the taxis or the taxi drivers that collect their app users.

In order to understand why a company might wish to grow horizontally, vertically or in a diversified manner, we need to understand the benefits and problems associated with horizontal, vertical and diversified expansion.

> Vertical chain of production encapsulates the various stages of production from the extraction of a raw material input, through the production of the product or service, to the final retailing of the product.
>
> A company is said to be vertically integrated if it owns consecutive stages of the vertical chain.

## 7.2 Reasons for growth

If we begin by accepting the general proposition that firms are in business to maximize profits, then it seems reason able to suggest that firms grow in order to improve profitability.

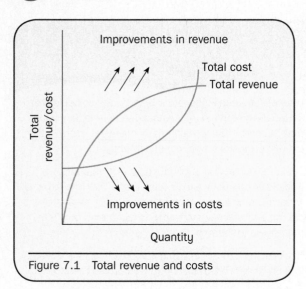

Figure 7.1　Total revenue and costs

If this is true, then, as we examine Figure 7.1, a firm seeking horizontal, vertical or diversified growth must be expecting to gain from increases in total revenues and/or decreases in total costs. In this way, the two curves in Figure 7.1 will move further apart from each other. As the curves move apart, both the profit-maximizing level of output and the amount of profit-maximizing profit will increase.

We will examine horizontal, vertical and diversified growth in turn.

If a firm is a profit-maximizer, then the pursuit of growth opportunities is arguably linked to either revenue or cost improvements. As revenue increases and costs are reduced, the profitability at each level of output is improved.

## 7.3　Horizontal growth

Horizontal growth, or expansion at a singular point on the vertical chain, can occur in a number of ways.

Organic growth is associated with firms growing through internal expansion. For example, a manufacturer might build additional production facilities, such as assembly lines, or a new factory. A retailer, such as a supermarket, might build more outlets. An airline might buy more aircraft. Crucially, the firm is growing by investing in new assets, which add to its current stock of capital. As an alternative, a firm might consider growth by **acquisition** and **merger**.

**Acquisition** involves one firm purchasing another firm. This might occur by mutual consent or, in the case of a hostile takeover, the managers of the acquired firm might try to resist the takeover.

**Merger** generally involves two companies agreeing by mutual consent to merge their existing operations.

In either case, the company grows by merging its activities with those of an existing operator. By going back through the theory established in previous chapters, we can now begin to analyse the benefits of horizontal growth.

### Horizontal growth and revenue

In Chapter 2 we examined the elasticity, or responsiveness, of demand to a change in price. The greater the number of substitutes, or rival products, the greater the price elasticity of demand. If demand is elastic, then a small change in the price results in a huge change in the quantity demanded. Therefore, in price-elastic markets, with lots of substitute products, we argued that there is a clear incentive for firms to engage in a price war. If one firm reduces its prices, it quickly attracts market share from its rivals. However, in response, rivals may also drop their prices and each firm will retain the same market share but be selling at a lower price. If demand is price inelastic, or not responsive to a change in price, then a price reduction will not have a significant impact on demand. Moreover, total revenues will decline.

Therefore, the optimal response underprice-inelastic demand is to raise prices in order to boost total revenues.

### Reducing competition

If we now think about merger and acquisition, by definition the number of competitors in the market is reduced by one. Therefore, because merger and acquisition lead to a reduction in the number of substitutes, it is likely that the elasticity of demand is reduced. When competition is reduced, price wars are less likely and firms have more scope for increasing, rather than decreasing, prices.

London's Heathrow airport is one of the world's busiest. It only has two runways and take-off and landing slots owned by different airlines are sold at very high prices. SAS sold different pair slots for £22 million and £60 million.

IAG, which owns British Airways and Iberia, wishes to buy the Irish carrier Aer Lingus. One reason is that Aer Lingus owns 23 take-off and landing slots at Heathrow. If IAG can acquire those slots, it will have a great control of the Heathrow market (see Box 7.2). By gaining control of 23 pair slots IAG can stop other competitors from strengthening their position on routes into Heathrow.

If we also think about perfect competition, oligopoly and monopoly, as discussed in Chapters 5 and 6, we can reinforce the arguments made above. Under perfect competition with a large number of competitors, prices and profits are lowest. Under monopoly, prices and profits will be highest. In the case of oligopoly, consolidation in the industry can lead to greater co-operation as opposed to increased competition. As discussed in Chapter 6, it is optimal for a cartel to act as a monopoly supplier and reduce output to the market. However, it is in each firm's interest to cheat and increase output. It is easier to monitor and enforce the tacit or explicit agreement made among the members of a small cartel than of a large one. In a small cartel you only need to gain agreement among, say, two or three companies. In a large cartel you need to gain agreement among a much larger number of companies, which is difficult. Therefore, mergers and acquisitions can lead to increased co-operation and the success of cartels.

## Exploiting market growth

Aside from any changes in the price elasticity of demand, horizontal growth may be undertaken in order to exploit revenue growth. Growing demand could stimulate organic growth. As more customers move into a market, the firm can exploit increased revenue opportunities by investing in more productive assets. As more passengers have been willing to fly with low-cost airlines, easyJet and Ryanair have purchased more aircraft. In recent

---

### Box 7.2
### SAS nets $22 million from Heathrow slot sale—deal underscores value of Aer Lingus rights at the airport

Scandinavian airline SAS has sold further rights at Heathrow Airport in a deal that will net it $22 million and which follows an earlier sale for $60 million. The two transactions underscore the value the landing and take-off slots at the hub owned by Aer Lingus and which are a flashpoint in the debate over whether it should be sold to rival International Consolidated Airlines' Group (IAG).

SAS said on Friday that it is selling one slot pair to Turkish airlines that will net $22 million for the Scandinavian carrier during the second quarter of the year. The slots are for the winter season, which begins on 25 October, and are for afternoon flights.

Earlier this month, SAS sold a summer-schedule slot pair to an unknown buyer, possibly a US or Middle Eastern carrier, for $60 million. That deal implied a

value of more than €1 billion on Aer Lingus's 23 pairs at Heathrow. However, the value of individual slot pairs varies considerably.

IAG's chief executive, Willie Walsh, has told the Government and Oireachtas that the group is prepared to guarantee that Aer Lingus's slots will only be used to service Irish routes for five years after any take-over.

The Government wants this to be extended before agreeing to sell the State's 25.1 per cent stake in the airline, although Mr Walsh has said that he would be 'crazy' to offer any longer.

From *The Irish Times*. 27 February 2015. 'SAS nets $22 million from Heathrow slot sale'. Barry O'Halloran.
© 2015 The Irish Times

years, coffee bars have suddenly appeared on many high streets, seeking to meet and exploit the rapid increase in customers.

In summary, the rewards from revenue and horizontal growth are: first, a reduction in the number of competitors and, therefore, a fall in the price elasticity of demand, making price rises easier and price wars less likely; and second, to be able to take advantage of customer growth opportunities in the market.

## Horizontal growth and costs

The obvious reason for horizontal growth relates to costs. In Chapter 3 we discussed economies of scale at length. However, in summary, as a firm increases its scale of operation, by increasing its capital input it generally experiences a reduction in long-run average costs. Therefore, we can argue that a firm will try to grow in order to exploit economies of scale. This is often used as a rationale for merger. When bringing two companies together, managers often talk up the potential for cost reductions by reducing and sharing managerial functions. Two companies need two chief executives; one company needs only one chief executive. Two companies need two finance, legal, marketing and human resource management (HRM) departments; one company needs only one of each. These single departments will generally be capable of operating at a size which is less than the sum of the two separate departments, achieving this through greater staff utilization. This is often referred to as **rationalization**.

> Rationalization is associated with cutbacks in excess resources in the pursuit of increased operational efficiencies.
>
> The learning curve suggests that, as cumulative output increases, average costs fall.

However, it is also possible that a firm can become too big. We saw in Chapter 3 that a very large firm can experience diseconomies of scale, where problems of control and co-ordination make the productivity of a large firm decrease, leading to a rise in long-run average costs. Therefore, it is sometimes the case that large firms decrease the scale of their operations in order to bring about cost improvements.

An alternative cost reason for horizontal expansion is the benefit to be had from the **learning curve**.

This is depicted in Figure 7.2 and shows that, as the firm produces successive units, or adds to its cumulative output, average costs fall. Importantly, the firm is considered to be in long-run equilibrium. The fall in average costs is not driven by the law of diminishing returns. Instead, as a firm produces additional output, it learns how to improve productivity. The classic example is the production of a jumbo jet. This is a massive project and requires careful planning and learning. In what order should the plane be assembled? When are the wings attached, when is the wiring completed, when can the seats be added? If wings are added too early, there is the risk of having to remove them at a later date in order to finish another task, such as adding the fuel tanks. However, once the mistake is made and learnt, it will not be made again. So, when the next plane is built, fewer assembly mistakes will occur. The plane will be built more quickly and at a lower cost. As more planes are built, the assembly teams will learn how to carry out each assembly task more quickly and develop new operating techniques. Eventually, at high levels of cumulative output, all learning opportunities are exploited and the reduction in costs diminishes to zero. At this point the learning curve becomes flat.

As the firm produces additional output, its cumulative output increases. By learning how to make the product more efficiently, the cost per unit falls. This is the so-called 'learning effect'.

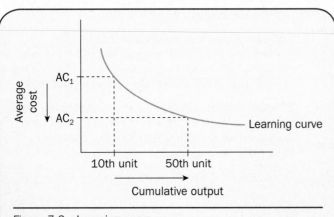

Figure 7.2   Learning curve

A firm producing 100 units a day learns faster than a firm producing ten units a day. In recognizing this point, a firm could grow organically in order to be in a position to exploit the learning effect sooner than its rivals. Alternatively, a competitor may have already produced many units and acquired the relevant cumulative experience through learning. An attractive strategy is to merge with or acquire the existing firm, in an attempt to gain the acquired experience. However, it is debatable how easy it is to transfer experience between organizations. The experience of one company is likely to be related to the systems, producers and cultures of that company. The learning effect stems from the experiences of a group of individuals with shared memories, values and understanding. Transferring such intangible understandings and benefits effectively to another organization is likely to be problematic.

 ## 7.4 Vertical growth

## Cost reasons

When a firm grows vertically, either moving up or down its vertical chain, it is attempting to integrate additional value-adding activities into its existing activities. There can be a number of reasons for doing this, which include location, economies of scale and transaction costs.

### Location benefits

Integrating consecutive activities from the vertical chain can reduce production costs. For example, steel-smelting plants are often located next to steel-rolling plants. This reduces transport and heating costs. Extremely high temperatures are needed to produce steel. Similarly, in order to roll the steel into usable sheets, the steel has to be hot. With the plants co-owned and located next to each other, the hot steel can be transferred easily to the rolling plant. If the two activities were separate, the new hot steel would have to be cooled, transferred by road to the rolling plant, re-heated and then rolled—resulting in much higher production costs.

The importance of co-location is also relevant in understanding **industrial clusters**. In particular locations similar industries cluster together in order to gain advantages, either in terms of cost, or in accessing supporting technologies and expertise. In Figure 7.3 we can see that financial services clusters are located in particular countries and indeed cities: UK (London), France (Paris), Germany (Frankfurt) and Switzerland (Zurich). Banks, insurance companies, investment companies, lawyers and accountants co-locate, providing a concentrated pool of expertise which facilitates the growth of the cluster.

> Industrial clusters occur when related industries co-locate in a region. Examples include Silicon Valley and electronics, Germany and automotives, London and finance.

In the automotive sector the strongest clusters are in Germany, Czech Republic and Sweden, where there is design expertise, supply lines and assembly activities.

### Economies of scale

In contrast, when economies of scale are important, vertical disintegration may also result in cost benefits. For example, the manufacture of a product may require a particular raw-material input. If the manufacturer developed its own raw-material division, then, without supplying other companies, the division would be likely to be operating at a very small scale. However, if a raw-material supplier is able to operate independently and supply many manufacturers, it is possible that it can exploit economies of scale. If economies of scale are important in a value-adding activity, it could be better for the manufacturer to abandon its raw-material division and instead buy from a larger independent company.

## Problems from monopoly

While economies of scale might be important cost considerations, it is also possible that raw materials might be supplied by a monopoly, in which case the price of the raw material

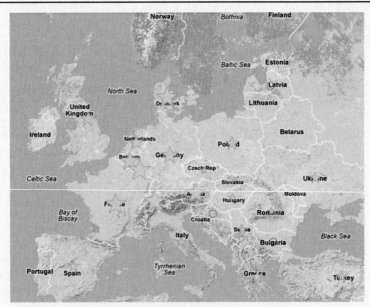

Cluster star rating for financial services

Cluster star rating for the automotive industry

Figure 7.3 Industrial clusters

*Source:* The European Cluster Observatory, www.clusterobservatory.eu.

could be higher than under a competitive market. A simple solution to this problem is to purchase the monopoly supplier and transfer the raw material between divisions of the same company. But what price will the production division pay the raw-material division? The optimal price for transferring the raw material to the production division is the marginal cost of production in the raw-material division. Under such a price, allocative efficiency would hold with the price being equal to marginal cost. As an explanation, the price paid and, therefore, the value of the last unit will be exactly equal to the cost of producing the last unit. This enables the combined profits of the raw- material division and the production division to be maximized. More important, if we return to an argument made in Chapter 5, the monopoly price is always greater than the marginal cost. Therefore, buying the raw-material supplier and charging an internal price equal to the marginal cost has to be cheaper than the price charged by a monopoly supplier.

## Transaction costs

In order to fully develop your understanding of the various cost reasons for vertical growth, we need to introduce a new cost concept. In Chapter 3, when examining costs, we only focused on production costs. These are the costs of the factor resources—land, labour, capital and enterprise—used by the firm in the production of the good or service. In addition to production costs, we also need to consider what are known as **transaction costs**.

> **Transaction costs** are the costs associated with organizing the transaction of goods or services.
>
> Under a complete contract all aspects of the contractual arrangement are fully specified.

When goods or services are traded, the costs of organizing the transaction can range from low to very high. At the most simplistic level, if a contract or agreement is entered into for the supply of goods or services, the time of managers negotiating the contract and the cost of lawyers hired to write the contract both represent transaction costs. Economists highlight a number of factors that are likely to lead to higher transaction costs. These factors are all related to the degree to which the contract or agreement can be declared '**complete**'.

For example, the nature of the product, including its characteristics, the materials used to make it and its size, will all be described within the contract terms. The price and time of delivery will also be covered by the contract. Finally, the contract will also set out how the performance of the product supplier will be measured and how the contract will be enforced through the legal system, should the terms of the contract be breached.

Clearly, given the conditions detailed above, no contract is ever complete. However, for some products it is much easier to write a nearly complete contract, while for others it is almost impossible. As examples, it is much easier to write a complete contract for a bag of sand than it is for lecturing services. Sand comes in standard bag sizes, a limited number of ranges, such as river sand or building sand, and if a company agreed to deliver a bag you would be able to verify its arrival. Now consider writing a contract for lecturing services. For a complete contract it would be necessary to define many things, including: during which hours the lectures would be given; what textbooks should be used; what topics should be covered each week; how the module should be examined; what topics and questions should be used during the tutorials; how difficult the examination should be; how marks should be awarded; how many students are expected to pass; how tutorial staff should be managed; and much more. It is clearly very difficult to define in full all the actions a lecturer should take during the running of a module. As a consequence, universities, like many employers, use incomplete contracts. Instead of defining all possible actions, contracts resort to simple statements such as 'a lecturer will be expected to communicate and expand knowledge'.

Rather than being complete, the contract is extremely vague. A sensible interpretation of the statement is that a lecturer is expected to communicate knowledge through teaching and expand knowledge through research. But of course there are many other interpretations. For example, answering the telephone and handling student enquiries is communicating and expanding knowledge. If the university expected the lecturer to teach and research, but the lecturer decided to simply answer telephone enquiries, then the university would experience substantial transaction costs. This is because the lecturer is choosing to undertake activities that the university did not intend. Aside from the ability to reinterpret the meaning of the contract, it is also very difficult for the university to measure the lecturer's performance. For example, let us assume many students fail the module. There could be many explanations, but let us concentrate on two. First, the lecturer did not perform well and the students did not benefit from the lectures. Second, even if this is true, the lecturer could blame the poor performance on the students' lack of effort during tutorials and revision. Because the effort of the lecturer and the students is not monitored by anyone from the university, it is difficult to support either argument. This therefore creates an environment within which the lecturer could act less than professionally. Lower performance by the lecturer represents a transaction cost.

We will shortly see how firms, and in our case universities, try to deal with these problems. But, first, it is useful to provide an understanding of the general factors which lead to greater transaction costs.

### Complexity

Complexity is an obvious factor. Sand is an uncomplicated product; lecturing is a very complicated product. As the product or service becomes more complex (simple), the more incomplete (complete) the contract becomes. As the contract becomes more incomplete (complete), the higher (lower) are the costs of transacting.

### Uncertainty

Uncertainty also affects the ability to write a complete contract. In the case of a bag of sand, uncertainty is less of an issue. You are not going to request a different bag of sand depending upon the nature of the weather. By contrast, in the case of lecturing services a university will expect the lecturer to be adaptable in the face of future changes. New theories may enter the subject, new ways of teaching might emerge, or the quality of the students each year could change. The university cannot write a contract detailing how the lecturer should deal with these changes, but a good lecturer will be expected to deal with these problems and opportunities using their professional discretion.

So, as uncertainty increases, the ability to write a complete contract diminishes and the cost of transacting increases.

### Monitoring

While complexity and uncertainty are problems associated with writing a contract, monitoring and enforcement are problems associated with managing a contractual arrangement. The more simple and certain the environment, the easier it is to monitor a contract. Again, let us compare a bag of sand with the lecturer. It is very easy to monitor whether or not a bag of sand is delivered. You can see it, you can feel it and you can weigh it. But how do you know if a lecturer has communicated and expanded knowledge? How do you measure effective communication, or teaching? A high pass rate for the module could indicate good teaching. But it could equally indicate good students, or an easy examination.

In general when the good or service is more complex and the environment is more uncertain, the ability to monitor the incomplete contract is more difficult and costly.

### Enforcement

When the contract is incomplete, the enforcement of the contract, by use of the legal process, is much more difficult.

If a company does not deliver your sand, it is fairly easy to prove breach of contract and ask a court to enforce delivery. However, if you cannot effectively define or measure the activities of a lecturer, then it is almost impossible to prove breach of contract. For example, if the university says that the lecturer has not communicated knowledge effectively, it will have to find a way of measuring the lecturer's level of effective communication. Since measuring communication is very difficult, it will be almost impossible to ask a judge to enforce the contract on a lecturer. The legal system cannot be used to enforce the contract. In knowledge of the fact that a university will find it difficult to measure and enforce performance, the lecturer can use the discretion provided within the contract to teach what they like, in a fashion that they prefer and examine the topics that they would like. Some do it well, others less well. The difference is transaction costs.

## Make or buy?

In the case of production costs, we argued that firms are cost-efficient when they operate with minimum average costs at the lowest point on the average cost curve. It therefore also seems sensible to argue that firms will try to minimize transaction costs. In fact, the reduction or control of transaction costs is of fundamental importance for economists, because transaction costs are the very driving force behind firms. Without transaction costs, firms would not exist.

Transaction costs can be managed through competing systems. These are the market and the hierarchy, or managerial structure, of a firm. Theoretically, the system with the lowest transaction cost will be chosen.

The hierarchy, or managerial structure, of a firm is composed of the various managerial layers, beginning with directors, then moving down to senior managers, and eventually ordinary workers.

## Transaction costs and markets

For market-based transactions to have a low transaction cost, the contract has to be as complete as possible. This requires low complexity and low uncertainty. In addition, monitoring must be easy and enforcement feasible. In such situations the ability to write a contract is easy and, therefore, low cost. Furthermore, the scope of the provider to perform below expectation in the delivery of the good or service is constrained by the easy monitoring and legal enforcement of the contract. The transaction costs of operating through the market are low.

In contrast, when the product is complex and uncertainty is high, it becomes more difficult and, therefore, more costly to write a contract. In addition, as the contract becomes more incomplete, greater discretion is handed to the provider of the good or service. Monitoring of the output becomes difficult, as the output is not clearly defined by the contract. As a result, enforcement becomes impossible. Recall the lecturer communicating and expanding knowledge. The output of the lecturer is not defined. It is left to the lecturer to use their discretion when designing the syllabus and delivery of the module. The potential for very high transaction costs by operating through the market becomes very high.

## Transaction costs and hierarchies

The alternative is to organize the transaction within the firm and use the hierarchy or managerial structure to organize the transaction. The problem with incomplete contractual relationships is that they provide the producer of the good or service with too much discretion. To economize on writing a complete contract the university uses the phrase 'communicate and expand knowledge'. But by using the managerial structure of the university, it is possible to minimize the resulting transaction costs. For example, when a lecturer begins employment, they will ordinarily be placed on probation for perhaps three years. Removal from probation and the confirmation of employment will only follow a set of successful lectures. Before a module begins the lecturer will not generally be allowed to choose any set of topics. Rather, they will be required to work to a module descriptor, which details the topics to be taught, the nature of the assessment and the key learning outcomes of the module for the students.

At the end of the module, students are asked to evaluate the module on various criteria. This is monitoring, and over a number of years and across a range of taught modules the university can develop an understanding of how well the lecturer performs. Through annual appraisals, annual training programmes and departmental discussions, the lecturer can begin to understand peer expectations regarding the acceptable level of lecturing performance and the nature of acceptable teaching styles. Management and colleagues have the potential to condition the lecturer's discretion, by advising on what is acceptable behaviour at work. Finally, with a shared understanding of acceptable performance the university can attempt to enforce acceptable delivery of lecturing services through pay awards and promotions. Lecturers who continually provide superior services, develop new teaching methods and lead research will generally be promoted. In contrast, over time, management will also be able to see who is not performing optimally and their cases for promotion might be declined.

Essentially, in the marketplace the legal process and competition among the various suppliers are used to enforce contractual commitments and keep transaction costs low. Within firms, contractual commitments are enforced through long-term monitoring by the managerial hierarchy and the periodic pay awards and promotion associated with good performance. In this way, transaction costs are reduced.

> **Nexus of contracts** is a collection of interrelated contractual relationships, where the firm represents a nexus or central point, at which all these interrelated contractual relationships are managed in the pursuit of profit.

Firms therefore exist in order to reduce transaction costs. In fact, economists often refer to firms as a **nexus of contracts**. Box 7.3 contains information about the way in which smartphone technology is reducing transaction costs associated with employment and enabling an on-demand workforce.

## Transaction costs and vertical growth

How can we use these insights in order to understand how and when a firm will grow or shrink along its vertical axis?

If we consider the vertical chain, the answer is simple. The firm as a nexus of contracts will grow up or down its vertical chain when it needs to reduce its transaction costs by making use of its hierarchy or managerial structure to control its transactions. Similarly, a firm will shrink, or reduce in size as a nexus of contracts, when it believes it is possible to use the market to control its transactions. Consider the following examples.

Hospitals produce health care, but we need to recognize that health care is a combination of various value-adding activities: medical treatment from doctors and nurses, plus catering and cleaning services. Traditionally, all three services were performed by employees of the hospital. More recently, catering and cleaning services have been subcontracted to independent private companies. In doing so, the hospital has not grown vertically; rather, it has reduced its vertical boundaries. This is illustrated in Figure 7.4. The dotted lines represent the boundaries of the hospital's activities. In the left half of Figure 7.4, cleaning, catering and medical treatment are all inside the dotted lines. This is how hospitals traditionally organized themselves. Staff of the hospital carried out all three activities. In the right half of

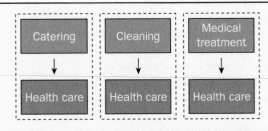 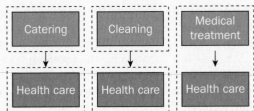

Traditional health-care integration The dotted lines represent the boundary of the firm's or hospital's activities. Traditionally, catering, cleaning and medical services were all carried out by hospital employees. Therefore, the scope of the hospital's activities covered all three areas. The modern structure, opposite, has seen significant changes.

Modern health-care integration Hospitals have begun to recognize that it is more expensive to have catering and cleaning done by in-house departments. The cheaper option is to have such services provided by private companies. The vertical boundary of the hospital, or the scope of its activities, is now concentrated on medical treatment.

Figure 7.4   Vertical integration

## Box 7.3
## There's an app for that

**Freelance workers available at a moment's notice will reshape the nature of companies and the structure of careers**

Handy is creating a big business out of small jobs. The company finds its customers self-employed home-helps available in the right place and at the right time. All the householder needs is a credit card and a phone equipped with Handy's app, and everything from spring cleaning to flat-pack-furniture assembly gets taken care of by 'service pros' who earn an average of $18 an hour. The company, which provides its service in 29 of the biggest cities in the United States, as well as Toronto, Vancouver and six British cities, now has 5,000 workers on its books; it says most choose to work between five hours and 35 hours a week, and that the 20 per cent doing most earn $2,500 a month. The company has 200 full-time employees. Founded in 2011, it has raised $40 million in venture capital.

Handy is one of a large number of startups built around systems which match jobs with independent contractors on the fly, and thus supply labour and services on demand. In San Francisco—which is, with New York, Handy's hometown, ground zero for this on-demand economy—young professionals who work for Google and Facebook can use the apps on their phones to get their apartments cleaned by Handy or Homejoy; their groceries bought and delivered by Instacart; their clothes washed by Washio and their flowers delivered by BloomThat. Fancy Hands will provide them with personal assistants who can book trips or negotiate with the cable company. TaskRabbit will send somebody out to pick up a last-minute gift and Shyp will gift-wrap and deliver it. SpoonRocket will deliver a restaurant-quality meal to the door within ten minutes.

On-demand labour is a far cry from the traditional idea of having a good job means being an employee of a particular company. The huge companies created by the Industrial Revolution brought armies of workers together, often under a single roof. These companies introduced a new stability into work, a structure which differentiated jobs from one another more clearly than before, thus providing defined roles and new paths of career progress.

**Coase and effect**

The way economists understand firms is largely based on an insight of the late Ronald Coase. Firms make sense when the cost of organising things internally through hierarchies is less than the cost of buying things from the market; they are a way of dealing with the high transaction costs faced when you need to do something moderately complicated. Now that most people carry computers in their pockets which can keep them connected with each other, know where they are, understand their social network and so on, the transaction costs involved in finding people to do things can be pushed a long way down.

The on-demand economy is unlikely to be a happy experience for people who value stability more than flexibility: middle-aged professionals with children to educate and mortgages to pay. On the other hand it is likely to benefit people who value flexibility more than security: students who want to supplement their incomes; bohemians who can afford to dip in and out of the labour market; young mothers who want to combine bringing up children with part-time jobs; the semi-retired, whether voluntarily so or not.

From *The Economist*. 'There's an app for that'. © The Economist Newspaper Limited, London (3 January 2015)

Figure 7.4, we see that only medical treatment is within the dotted lines of the overall health care provided by a hospital. Catering and cleaning are within their own dotted lines. This signifies that private companies provide catering and cleaning. Cleaning and catering are now being provided, or transacted, through the market. Periodically, the hospital will hold a tendering process, where it in effect holds an auction for its catering or cleaning contracts. The firm willing to offer its services at the lowest cost may win the contract.

Why have cleaning and catering been moved into the market, while medical treatment has been retained inside the hospital? The answer is that, from a transactional perspective, it is cheaper to buy catering and cleaning services from the market, but it is cheaper to provide medical treatment in-house. Consider trying to write a contract for cleaning services. It is reasonably easy to write a near-complete contract: each hospital ward must be cleaned twice a day, each waiting room once, and operating theatres after each operation. Now consider trying to write a complete contract for a heart surgeon. For each possible heart problem the contract would have to stipulate how the surgeon would treat the patient. This is very complex and, therefore, just as in the case of the university lecturer, it is better to leave treatment to the surgeon's discretion using an incomplete contract, where the contract might simply state that the 'surgeon will provide medical expertise in the cardiovascular department'. The hospital needs to measure the surgeon's performance against the contract. However, the performance of the surgeon can only be monitored over time by the hospital's management team. Good surgeons are promoted; poor ones are advised to move on. This long-term monitoring is best done inside the hospital's management systems, where other medical consultants can periodically provide a review of the surgeon's efforts and expertise. Such a process is very difficult if the hospital decided to contract surgeons on a short-term basis through the market.

## Vertical growth: strategic considerations

An important transactional problem, not discussed above, is associated with asset specificity and the **hold-up problem**.

**Hold-up problem** is the renegotiation of contracts, and is linked to asset specificity.

A specific asset has a specific use; a general asset has many uses.

An aircraft can be used on a number of routes. Its use is more general than specific. A production line designed to make bumpers for a Ford Focus is a very **specific asset**, as it is very difficult to use the production line to make bumpers for any other car.

Consider the vertical chain for airlines. A new aircraft is purchased and used to fly between cities A and B. Additional value-adding inputs are landing slots at each city's airport. If the route between A and B is highly profitable, one of the airports, say B, might try to gain some of the airline's profit by increasing its landing charges. However, since the aircraft is a general asset, the airline has the option of moving the aircraft to a route between A and C (assuming this route is also profitable). The airline can use the general nature of aircraft to discipline airport B and prevent an increase in landing charges.

Now consider the producer of bumpers for a particular car. Each car model is unique and the shape of the car's bumper will be very specific. The production plant will be dedicated to producing bumpers for this one type of car. The car manufacturer could approach the bumper manufacturer and ask for a new production facility to be built for its bumpers. In return, the car manufacturer agrees a price for each bumper. We might assume that the agreed price is £100 per bumper. This price per bumper will make the investment in the new plant profitable for the bumper manufacturer. However, once the plant is up and running, the car manufacturer has a substantial incentive to renegotiate a discount price for the bumpers. Why? Because, unlike the airline company, the bumper manufacturer has a specific asset; it only makes one type of bumper. The plant cannot be used to produce bumpers for another car manufacturer, so it is dependent upon the one car maker. This is the hold-up problem.

The car manufacturer can take advantage of the bumper producer's investment in a specific asset. In fact, so obvious is this type of hold-up problem that the bumper producer would not invest in the production facility. The car producer, therefore, has to build its own bumper-producing plant. The car manufacturer grows vertically and begins to produce one of its key inputs. For many car parts, this approach is very common. Take a look at a car and find the most obvious component on the car that has not been made by the car-maker itself. It will probably be the tyres. This is because tyres are round and will fit on many different types of car. Tyres, or more correctly the plant making tyres, is a general asset. The production of tyres for Ford can easily be switched to the production of tyres for Toyota. A producer of tyres, therefore, does not face a hold-up problem, because it is not dependent upon one buying relationship. A bumper manufacturer would be.

The hold-up problem can also represent a strategic opportunity when one firm is able to gain a monopoly position in the vertical chain. Consider Figure 7.5. For simplicity, assume an industry has three firms, all manufacturing a similar product, beer. In the left half of Figure 7.5, each firm is a producer of beer, buying hops from farmers and selling the beer on

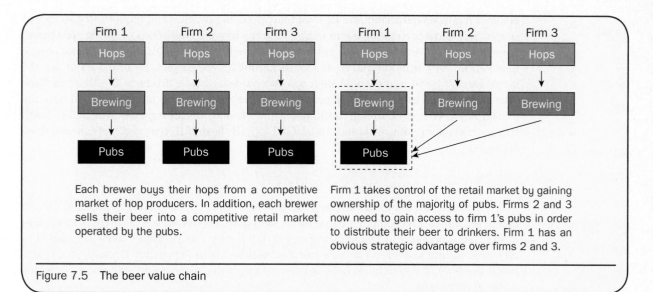

Each brewer buys their hops from a competitive market of hop producers. In addition, each brewer sells their beer into a competitive retail market operated by the pubs.

Firm 1 takes control of the retail market by gaining ownership of the majority of pubs. Firms 2 and 3 now need to gain access to firm 1's pubs in order to distribute their beer to drinkers. Firm 1 has an obvious strategic advantage over firms 2 and 3.

Figure 7.5   The beer value chain

to independent pubs. In the right half of Figure 7.5, firm 1 has gained ownership of the pubs. As a monopoly supplier of beer retailing, firm 1 can promote its own brands and negotiate cheap beer supplies from the remaining brewers. An equally effective growth strategy would have been to gain control of the hop supply and gain a monopoly position at the top of the vertical chain. It could then sell hops to itself cheaply, but charge brewing rivals a very high price.

In summary, firms will grow vertically up or down the vertical chain if the transaction costs of operating through the market are too high. By internalizing transactions, or making the value-adding product or service inside the company, the firm will attempt to control its transaction costs more effectively. Similarly, when the transaction costs of the market are very low, a firm will seek to reduce its vertical integration and begin to seek subcontractors for some of its inputs. Buying in, rather than making the product or service, has lower transaction costs. In addition to the costs of organizing the transaction, we also need to consider the transaction costs generated by the hold-up problem. The firm will grow vertically along the vertical chain whenever it can gain strategic advantage over its rivals and whenever the market refuses to supply products for fear of the hold-up problem.

 ## Diversified growth

Diversification involves a company expanding its operations into related or unrelated markets. This can occur for a variety of reasons, but a strong cost reason centres on the concept of **economies of scope**.

> Economies of scope are said to exist if the cost of producing two or more outputs jointly is less than the cost of producing the outputs separately.

If two products, A and B, are being produced, then economies of scope are sometimes expressed as:

$$\text{Cost (A)} + \text{Cost (B)} > \text{Cost (A + B)}$$

This suggests that the cost of producing A on its own, Cost (A), plus the cost of making B on its own, Cost (B), is greater than making A and B together, Cost (A + B).

An obvious example can be found in the news-gathering services of the BBC. News on politics, business, world affairs and crime can be collected centrally. This is then drawn on by BBC News 24, BBC Evening News, Radio 1, 2, etc., and by BBC News Online. If each division operated separately, then the news would be collected many times. By centralizing news gathering, the BBC cuts down on duplication and exploits economies of scope. An alternative example can be found in the business activities of Virgin. The brand name of Virgin is very important, but just like the news gathering of the BBC, it can reduce duplication. As Virgin initially invested many millions developing its brand name for the music industry, the brand could then also be used to launch products in other markets. This has included airlines, mobile phones, financial services and much more. Admittedly, money has to be spent building the Virgin airlines brand, but the expense is arguably much less than starting with no brand and launching all these different commercial activities separately.

## Diversification and risk reduction

Diversification can reduce a company's exposure to risk. Consider a company operating in only one market. The company could be making good profits. However, there is a risk that in the future profits will change. Profits will fall if new competition enters the market, a recession occurs and sales fall, or a raw material becomes expensive. Equally, profits will rise if the level of competition falls, sales increase during a recession, or the cost of a raw material decreases.

Profits can, therefore, go up or down. But they can go up or down for any firm, or industry. More important, profits at any particular point in time might go up for one firm or industry, but come down for another. It is, therefore, possible to have multiple operations and reduce the variability in overall profits. By operating in more than one market, or industry, falling profits in one operation can hopefully be offset by rising profits in another part of the business.

Tesco, the leading UK supermarket chain, is a reasonable example. Operating across grocery, non-food items such as CDs, magazines and home electricals, and financial services, including insurance and banking, enables Tesco to reduce its operating risks. If grocery and non-food profits fall, it is possible that financial services profits could rise. In order for this to be true the various operations must form a **diversified portfolio** of business activities.

> Diversified portfolio of activities contains a mix of uncorrelated business operations.

If two business activities are correlated, then the profit levels of each activity will move together. As such, the combined profits will still show large swings over time. For a diversified portfolio, business activities must be uncorrelated. This means the level of profits from one business activity is not related to the level of profits from another activity. The combined profits from diversified activities will now be less variable; as one operation incurs losses, another is likely to rise into profitability.

While diversification can reduce the financial risks of a company, it does not add value to the company. The problem lies in the fact that variability in profits is the risk of shareholders. If an individual shareholder wishes to diversify their risks, then they can do so at low cost. They achieve this by simply buying small amounts of shares in various different uncorrelated companies. If a Tesco shareholder is worried about future losses in the grocery business, they can buy shares in any high street bank. They do not need Tesco to create its own bank. Furthermore, the investor may already have shares in a bank. As a result of Tesco moving into the personal financial services sector, the investor's risk or exposure to the financial services sector has increased, not diminished. Therefore, diversification by a company does not add value for shareholders. So, why do companies diversify?

As we will see in Chapter 8, we need to make a distinction between shareholders and managers. On a day-to-day basis it is managers who run and control companies. Managers have a great deal of assets tied up in the company they work for. The company pays their salary and funds their pension. If the company closed, due to substantial losses, how likely is it that the manager would gain employment elsewhere? Managers, therefore, face substantial non-diversified risk from employment. Diversification is arguably more in the interests of managers than shareholders.

# 7.6 Evidence on mergers

In examining how mergers of all types improve firm-level performance, economists have used a variety of techniques. These techniques have included stock market studies, financial ratio analysis and case studies.

Stock market studies investigate whether shareholders from the buying firm or the acquired target firm gain most. Evidence tends to suggest that most of the stock market gains from merger accrue to shareholders of target firms. The price of target firms rises rapidly prior to merger and the stock price for the buying firm stagnates or even falls post-merger.

Financial and accounting studies examine merger activity within similar industries; banking, brewing and automobiles would be examples. Using statistical techniques, economists look for increases in revenues, reductions in costs, increased market share and improvements in operating efficiencies. The evidence is at best mixed; some firms and some industries have a greater tendency to deliver post-merger benefits. But this is not a common pattern and many firms manage to destroy value post-merger.

Case studies examine specific mergers and look for firm-specific examples of merger benefits. Again, these studies confirm the message from the stock market and financial accounting-based studies: mergers are not always a good idea.

So, if mergers are at best risky strategies—some work, some do not—then why do firms continue to engage in merger activity? A possible answer is that mergers are very much in the interests of managers. The pay of managers tends to increase more with firm size than with financial performance of the firm. Merger increases firm size and therefore can boost managers' pay. Faced with such incentives, managers may seek to convince shareholders that a merger is a good idea, but shareholders and regulators are becoming increasingly sceptical and the number of failed proposals to merge is rising (see Box 7.4).

## Box 7.4
## When giant deals fail, life rarely goes back to normal

Queen Victoria sniffed that, 'We are not interested in the possibilities of defeat.' For empire-builders in the corporate world, failure is all too common. On 5 August the octogenarian Antipodean Rupert Murdoch withdrew 21st Century Fox's unrequited pursuit of Time Warner. The deal would have been worth at least $70 billion and would have created a media monolith. Hours later Softbank, a Japanese conglomerate which owns Sprint, an American telecoms firm, abandoned its effort to buy control of T-Mobile US, another operator in America, with an enterprise value of more than $30 billion.

In 2014 there have already been two other big deal-making snafus—Pfizer's abortive bid for a fellow drugmaker, AstraZeneca, worth $125 billion, and the union of Publicis and Omnicom. The two advertising firms were supposedly engaged in a logical impossibility: an amicable Franco–American merger of equals. In fact their executives were fighting like rats in a sack.

In all, bids worth $390 billion have been terminated or withdrawn so far in 2014. That is huge in absolute terms,

though it mirrors the surge in mergers and acquisitions (M&A) this year. Typically 10–20 per cent of proposed deals end in tears, and this year has been no exception.

Companies usually overstretch in two ways. They propose combinations that annoy regulators. Or they propose deals that test the limits of their balance sheets and the patience of their investors. Mr Murdoch was offering a takeover premium of about $20 billion, more than the capitalized value of the cost savings that could have been achieved, suggesting the deal would have destroyed value for his shareholders. Reflecting this, his own share price had steadily fallen, reducing the value of the stock being offered to Time Warner.

By tradition, when deals flop, everyone pretends nothing has really changed. Thus Mr Murdoch declared that '21st Century Fox's future has never been brighter', while Mr Son said, 'Our focus moving forward will be on making Sprint the most successful carrier.'

In fact, failed transactions often have lasting consequences. Target firms that cook up ambitious forecasts as part of their defence face the hard task of meeting them. Astra said it expected sales almost to double by 2023 despite their being stagnant today. But usually a failed giant deal damages the credibility of the acquirer's managers and the coherence of its strategy. On 6 August Sprint said it would remove its chief executive, Daniel Hesse. Botched takeovers have tarnished other careers. Jack Welch, of General Electric, sullied his reputation by failing to buy Honeywell as a last hurrah before he retired in 2001. European regulators blocked the deal. Marius Kloppers, a young star who became chief executive of the world's biggest mining company, BHP Billiton, in 2007, lost his way after trying to buy its arch-rival, Rio Tinto, for $115 billion in 2008 and then, in 2010, the obscure Potash Corp of Saskatchewan for a very unobscure $43 billion. By 2013 he had left BHP.

For failed predators and escaped prey alike the key to re-establishing momentum is to demonstrate strong operating performance. If earnings are rising, investors, staff and clients will forgive almost anything. In 2010 Prudential PLC, a British insurer active in Asia, suffered a humiliating defeat when its own shareholders rebelled against its $36 billion takeover bid for AIA, a Hong Kong-based rival. Since then Prudential's boss, Tidjane Thiam, has rebuilt his reputation in spectacular style by doubling operating profits.

For chief executives, the slog of day-to-day operations is miserable compared with the glamour and gratification of the world of M&A. But they can be assured that if they fail both at dealmaking and the mundane task of boosting earnings, their shareholders, like Queen Victoria, will not be amused.

From *The Economist*. 'When giant deals fail, life rarely goes back to normal'.
© The Economist Newspaper Limited, London (6 December 2014)

## 7.7 Business application: horizontal growth by merger

Economic boom or bust, the attractions of horizontal merger always seem attractive to business. When the economy is growing rapidly, firms see the option to merge as a means of exploiting growth while achieving economies of scale. During a recession, in contrast, merger and economies of scale offer valuable cost-efficiencies.

The occurrence of mergers in both good and bad economic times possibly underlines the importance of economies of scale in providing firms with a competitive advantage. Size matters, costs matter. Achieving significant scale economies often costs huge sums of money and, once you merge with a rival, then that lowers the opportunities for other competitors to follow suit and achieve similar economies of scale. So, by merging, firms can achieve a competitive advantage which other competitors may find difficult to replicate. Economies of scale provide cost savings and provide the firm with the potential to dominate.

A merger also presents the opportunity to gain access to new markets through the channels of the combined company. Where one company has excellent brands and another company has good distribution networks in different global regions, combining the companies through a merger enables more brands to be pushed down more channels, to more customers.

In Box 7.5 a review of proposed merger activity in the beer industry is presented. Brewing beer benefits from enormous economies of scale. These scale economies stem from lower production costs, improved returns on marketing expenditure and improved distribution

### Box 7.5
### Billion dollar beer war is brewing

**SABMiller's rejected bid for Heineken shows takeovers and mergers are still sought after**

Charlene de Carvalho-Heineken and her husband Michel de Carvalho head one of the richest families in Britain, with a combined fortune estimated at more than £6 billion. Despite their significant influence, the pair prefer to lead a private life in London. Since inheriting control of the famous Heineken brewing concern more than a decade ago, Charlene de Carvalho-Heineken has made very few public appearances. However, in the coming months, the couple may find themselves reluctantly thrust into the spotlight as the unwitting kingmakers in a fierce race for dominance among the beer industry's titans.

A week ago the Heineken family received a surprise proposal from one of its biggest rivals, SABMiller. The Anglo-South African beer giant, which makes Peroni and is the second-largest brewer in the world, tabled a takeover bid for its Dutch counterpart, the world's number three player. The family controls just over 50 per cent of the brewer.

The response, however, was swift and unequivocal. In a statement the family said it rejected the approach and intended to 'preserve the heritage and identity of Heineken as an independent company'.

But sources believe the aborted approach could trigger a round of consolidation that could envelop every major name in brewing and lead to the industry map being completely redrawn. The question is: were that to happen, how would that map eventually look?

Ask seasoned beer-drinkers to guess what the best-selling brand in the world is and most would probably say Budweiser or, maybe, Heineken. They would be wrong. The number one selling beer on the planet is a pale, frothy variety that most in the West have never even heard of and connoisseurs say has an unremarkable taste: Snow Beer, a brand sold almost exclusively in China.

Created just two decades ago by SAB, Snow is the country's most popular beer by a long distance and 80 breweries are needed just to quench demand for Snow. As consumption across Europe and in the US falls, demand for beer in less developed countries in Latin America, Asia and Africa is rising quickly and the industry's giants are desperate to crack these markets quickly.

Deals have long helped to shape the brewing landscape but one buccaneering company has led the way when it comes to large-scale expansion: Anheuser-Busch InBev. Now known simply as ABI, it started just 25 years ago when a group of former bankers bought a tired Brazilian brewery for $50 million (£30 million). Under Carlos Brito, the 54-year-old deal junkie at the helm, it has become the largest brewer in the world. Brito has overseen nearly £100 billion of acquisitions, earning the nickname 'La Maquina'—Portuguese for 'the machine'—because of a reputation for ruthless

cost-cutting at the companies swallowed by his bulging empire.

The first big move came in 2004 when the company, then called Ambev, agreed a tie-up with Interbrew, a Belgian brewer whose roots went back to the 14th century. Four years later came the real game-changer—an audacious $52 billion hostile takeover of Anheuser-Busch in the US.

Brito had created the first brewing behemoth, with more than 200 brands—including famous names Budweiser, Beck's and Stella Artois—across five continents under one roof. Annual revenue leapt more than fivefold in one giant swoop.

SAB itself is no stranger to growth through takeovers. Over the past 20 years, it has gone from being primarily a South African brewer—where it was founded largely to supply ale to thirsty gold miners in the 19th century—to the world's No. 2 via acquisitions of Miller in the US, Colombia's Bavaria and Australia's Foster's. Combined, ABI and SAB would be colossal, with a stockmarket value of around $250 billion, and operations stretching into every corner of the globe. But SAB wants to forge its own path rather than become the latest target to be eaten up by the ABI machine. It is this fear of a looming approach from its bigger rival that many believe prompted SAB's surprise move on Heineken.

By moving first, SAB is now seen as having put itself in play and, in what would be the cruellest of twists, some senior City sources are speculating that Heineken could turn the tables completely and team up with ABI to bid for SAB. By carving up their Anglo-South African rival between them, it would mean competition concerns that would arise from a sole ABI bid could be quickly surmounted.

Wyn Ellis, analyst at Numis Securities, said: 'A combination of SAB and ABI could make life very difficult for the other major players. If it is looking like a real possibility, Heineken and Carlsberg might decide they would be better off joining forces with someone else to make a clear and very strong number two.'

Although no one quite knows what the next move will be, the beer industry looks to be on the verge of its biggest-ever arms race—and a somewhat secretive family that rarely speaks out could end up having the final say.

From *The Telegraph*. 20 September 2014. 'Billion dollar beer war is brewing'. Ben Marlow and Nathalie Thomas. © Telegraph Media Group Limited (2014)

and logistics. Moreover, as growth in beer consumption moves from Europe and the US to China, Africa and South America, then access to new growth markets supports merger activity.

**7.8** Business application: vertical growth—moving with the value

A common feature of many business environments is *change*. Technology changes, the product on offer changes and even the tastes and preferences of consumers change. The consequence of these changes is that the value added in each stage of the vertical chain of production also changes. As costs fall, or revenues rise, then one part of the chain becomes more valuable. Similarly, as costs rise or revenues fall, then another part of the chain becomes less valuable. Predicting and understanding these trends can help enormously in developing strategies for change and ensuring greater longevity of profits.

You may, or may not, like Madonna's music. But unquestionably she is an artistic and commercial success. U2 are also a long established successful band with a world-wide following. Madonna, U2 and even Mick Jagger from the Rolling Stones are known for their ability to understand how to make music into a huge commercial success, even when the market for pop music has changed enormously.

Until recently, the keys to the valuable parts of the pop music value chain were a competent music artist and access to music lovers through music publishing and distribution. Publishing and distribution were commonly achieved through the creation of CDs, which were then sold in music stores. Record companies were able to insist that buyers purchase all songs on an album. As such, the publishing and distribution stages of the vertical chain were extremely valuable.

As the distribution technology moved towards electronic storage and online delivery, the value of music publishing and delivery declined. Consumers were able to download music (illegally) for free, and online retailers of music began to offer downloads of tracks from albums, rather than the entire album. Such moves have led to a reduction in profits for record companies and for artists such as Madonna and U2.

When Madonna broke her relationship with music producer Warner's and signed with tour promoter Live Nation in 2007, she was also indicating where the profits lay. So were U2 when they joined Live Nation in 2008 on a 12-year contract. We can use our understanding of competition to understand the commercial attractions of concerts. If you wish to see Madonna or U2 in concert in your nearest capital city, then the event exists once. It happens, it is over, it is gone. You cannot experience a concert as a download. You cannot download parts of the concert and you cannot access the concert for free. Madonna or U2, in conjunction with Live Nation, are monopoly providers of Madonna and U2 concerts.

The value chain in music has changed. Previously, record companies owned recording artists through recording contracts. Now tour promotors own artists through tour contracts. The value chain into which the artist sells their talent has changed.

 **7.9** Business application: economies of scope

Google is everywhere and offering everything. Why? The range of services now offered by Google simply reflects economies of scope—the ability to provide services jointly at a lower cost than offering each separately. But where do these economies of scope stem from?

At the core of Google's success is a search engine which is arguably unsurpassed by any competitor. The technology advantage rests on clever computer programming and a vast bank of computers—some estimate as much as a 100,000-machine server farm. Such an asset base means it becomes technically feasible and economically cheap to launch related services, such as Gmail and Android. The more Google can exploit its massive technical advantage across products, the greater the economies of scope it can realize. As revenues and, ultimately, profits grow from its scope advantages, Google has more finance to pour back in to boost its technological advantage and remain dominant.

The growth of Amazon is also related to economies of scope. Amazon began by offering books for sale online. This was quickly expanded into music and movies. Currently, Amazon also sells toys, electronics, health and beauty and jewellery items. This all represents economies of scope. When Amazon built an Internet infrastructure to sell books and acquired a warehouse and distribution system for stocking and delivery, it made strong commercial sense to put more product ranges through the same pipe.

The examples of Amazon and Google illustrate what is perhaps related diversification. However, the economies of scope argument can also be used to explain some examples of unrelated diversification. Tesco, a UK supermarket chain, developed its business from grocery into non-food electricals, restaurants, film, TV, media content streaming, and prior to this into financial services. It simply capitalized on its huge existing customer base. With details about its customers gained from loyalty cards and online shopping, Tesco can use this marketing research data to sell not only groceries but also other products such as financial services, including personal loans and insurance. Therefore, by operating as a supermarket and as a personal financial services company, Tesco is able to reduce its costs by exploiting the customer-information base across multiple activities.

While grocery and financial services are very different activities, one of the core underlying assets that ensures success in both markets is an informative customer database. This database includes information on customers' ages, marital status, income levels, home address and products generally purchased within the Tesco stores. These data can be analysed and used to target particular customer groups with specific products.

## Economies of scope and control

An important issue when considering economies of scope is *control*. If we extend the economies of scope condition to Tesco, then we would have:

Cost (Grocery) + Cost (Financial Services) > Cost (Grocery + Financial Services)

An obvious reason for these economies of scope is lower production costs associated with the joint use of the Tesco customer base. But, in addition, we also need to consider transaction costs. Tesco does not have to enter the financial services market in order to exploit its customer base. Rather, it could sell its customer information to a number of third parties, including existing financial services companies. The obvious problem with such an approach is that valuable information could then find its way into the hands of Tesco's rivals in the supermarket sector. Lowering the transaction costs associated with the information's additional use, therefore, protects the value of the customer base. Tesco cannot risk selling the information in the marketplace; instead, in order to exploit the asset beyond grocery, it has to enter into the financial services sector.

We can also use the case of Tesco to address the issue of managerial motives for merger, as discussed in section 7.5. Managers may pursue diversification to protect their own employment, as opposed to adding value for shareholders. We even argued that, if a shareholder of Tesco was concerned about risks in the supermarket sector, they could easily diversify this risk by buying shares in a financial services company. However, we can now see that diversification will add value for shareholders if the control of the economies of scope reduces transaction costs. Tesco is a clear example of this. So too is the Google brand. Google has been able to take its expertise in online search to mapping, advertising, translation, glasses and much more.

## 7.10    Business data application: trends in mergers and acquisitions

Data on mergers and acquisitions provide an insight into the number of deals being undertaken, the amount of money being spent, the type of financing being used and geographic concentration of target and acquiring firms. Such data provide an indication of firms' appetite for growth, their ability to finance growth and where they see growth opportunities around the world.

Figure 7.6 illustrates the number of mergers and acquisitions undertaken on an annual basis in the UK. During the period 2001 to 2007 the number of deals exceeding £1 million rose from 500 to 875 per year. Following the financial crisis the number of deals fell to 320 per year. As an economy falters, then growth opportunities recede and firms become less willing to expand.

In addition, the financial crisis had an impact on the ability of firms to finance deals. Following the crisis, we can see in Figure 7.7 a huge switch in the use of share-based equity financing for mergers and a fall-off in the use of cash. The pattern reflected the inability of companies to access loans from the banking system. So in order to fund mergers and acquisitions companies turned to shareholder finance.

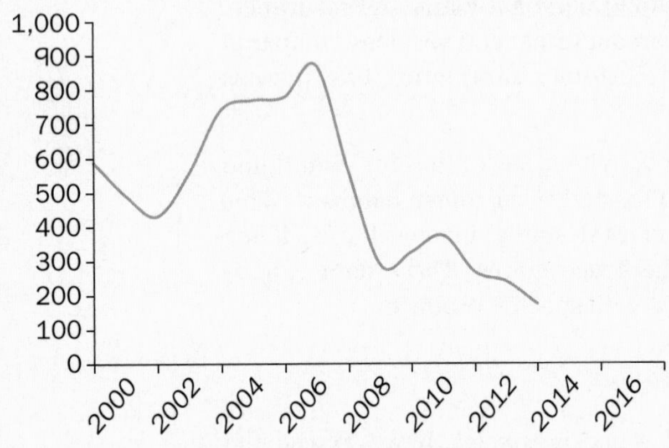

While the use of cash (sometimes borrowed from banks) has returned as a popular means of financing mergers and acquisitions, this pattern needs to be seen against the backdrop of falling deal numbers and lower valuations. Looking at Figure 7.8 we can see that the value of deals has fallen from a peak of £65 billion to a level of £4 billion in 2014. This low value may indicate an unwillingness of companies to do deals, an inability to access finance, or a combination of the two.

Figure 7.6    Number of UK mergers and acquisitions

*Source:* Office for National Statistics.

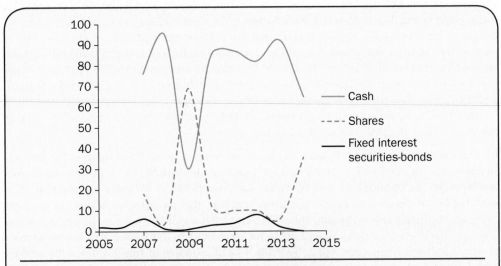

Figure 7.7    Percentage use of alternative financing methods

*Source:* Office for National Statistics.

Finally, it is worth exploring where firms undertake mergers and acquisitions, because such patterns should provide an indication of where firms see growth opportunities. Figure 7.9 illustrates key trends in the geographic pattern of mergers and acquisitions by UK firms.

Both before and after the financial crisis Europe and the USA have attracted most UK overseas merge and acquisition activity. Asia and Africa have been less important. However, while the number of deals for all regions has fallen, the impact on Europe and the USA has been greatest, with the number of deals in 2012 falling significantly below 2006 levels. The activity in Asia and Africa has also reduced and shows little evidence of being strong areas of merger and acquisition activity for UK firms.

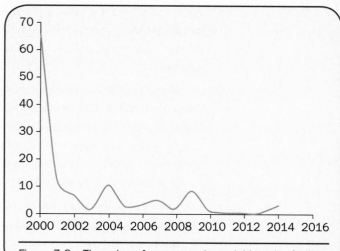

Figure 7.8    The value of merger and acquisitions in £ billion

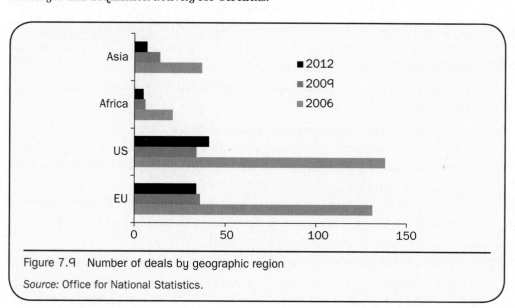

Figure 7.9    Number of deals by geographic region

*Source:* Office for National Statistics.

## Summary

1. Horizontal growth is the expansion of a firm's activities at the same stage of the production process.

2. Vertical growth is expansion of the firm up or down the value chain, incorporating more than one stage of production.

3. Diversified growth is an expansion of the firm's activities into related and unrelated markets.

4. Growth in its various forms can be organic, where the firm grows internally by developing ties to existing operations; alternatively, growth can occur externally, where the firm either acquires, or agrees to merge with, another firm.

5. Firms can grow for a variety of reasons, but if we accept that a firm is a profit-maximizer, then growth must be linked to long-term, profit-maximizing objectives. Growth opportunities must, therefore, offer revenue enhancements or potential cost savings.

6. Horizontal growth can promote revenue enhancements by exploiting growth in the market. As the market size grows, the firm can seek to expand its operations. Moreover, the firm can seek to grow its share of the market. Greater control of the market improves the potential to set prices. If greater market share stems from merger, or acquisition of a rival, then the elasticity of demand must fall and the potential to raise prices increases.

7. Economies of scale are important motives for horizontal growth. As a company increases its scale of operation, its average costs fall. In addition, the positive effects of learning can motivate horizontal growth. As cumulative production increases, the firm begins to learn how to produce the product more efficiently. The firm learns how to reduce its costs. However, if the size of the firm is bigger, the potential to erase cumulative output more quickly also exists.

8. Vertical growth can also be motivated by considerations of production costs. Consecutive stages of the value chain could be merged if production and transaction costs have the potential to be reduced.

9. In addition to production costs, transaction costs are also a potential reason for vertical growth.

10. Transaction costs are associated with organizing the transaction of goods and services. These include the costs associated with writing, monitoring and enforcing contractual relationships. Transactions are seen to increase when complexity and uncertainty are greater, monitoring is difficult and enforcement limited. If the transaction costs associated with buying the good or service through the market increase, then a firm will attempt to minimize its transaction costs by vertically integrating and making the good or service within the firm.

11. A specific asset is designed for one use only. Without the flexibility to deploy the asset to an alternative use, a firm can be subject to the hold-up problem. Contract prices can be renegotiated and the financial value of the specific asset can fall. In order to avoid such problems, firms will tend to vertically integrate and thereby avoid market negotiations.

12. Economies of scope exist if the production of two goods jointly is less expensive than producing the two goods separately. Diversification can sometimes be understood as a process of exploiting economies of scope, i.e. where a firm uses an asset that it has developed in its current operations to exploit opportunities in another market.

13. If diversification is pursued in an attempt to create a portfolio of activities, then the firm's overall financial risk might be reduced. However, it is questionable whether such strategies add value for shareholders who may already hold a diversified portfolio of shares in many different companies. Diversification is more likely to reduce the non-diversified employment risks faced by managers.

14. Data on mergers and acquisitions provides an insight into the willingness of firms to grow, their ability to finance growth and where they prefer to grow, and where they might be considering growth opportunities around the world.

## Learning checklist

You should now be able to:

- Explain the difference between horizontal, vertical and diversified growth
- Provide arguments for why firms may grow in a horizontal, vertical or diversified manner
- Explain how the learning curve links cumulative output with falling unit costs
- Understand and explain transaction costs
- Recognize the hold-up problem and explain why firms try to avoid this problem
- Explain economies of scope, provide examples and argue why firms might exploit scope economies
- Demonstrate an awareness of key patterns in recent merger and acquisition activity.

## Questions                                                    connect

1.  Is a merger between rivals horizontal, vertical or conglomerate growth?

2.  Horizontal growth can occur for cost and revenue reasons. Explain both of these justifications for horizontal growth.

3.  Formula 1 teams are banned from in-season tests to reduce costs. The learning curve says this is a bad idea. Why?

4.  What is the value chain?

5.  What are transaction costs and should firms be concerned about them?

6.  Your university decides to use an external catering company for the main university food outlets. What economic justifications can you provide for this decision?

7.  What is the hold-up problem and how might a firm deal with this particular type of issue?

8.  Explain why a range of activities can reduce risk. In order for diversification to be effective, has the correlation between activities to be high or low?

9.  Why are the benefits of diversification low for shareholders?

10. What is an economy of scope and how might it lead a firm to diversify?

11. If cost advantages from cumulative production were low, would the learning curve be steep or shallow?

12. Why are horizontal mergers sometimes blocked by governments?

13. Should governments also block vertical mergers?

14. Pubs in the UK are being encouraged to take on other activities, such as those of the Post Office. On economic grounds, how would you justify such initiatives?

15. How can a firm use horizontal, vertical or diversified growth to gain a strategic advantage over its rivals?

16. (a) Please show whether or not economies of scope exist for the five individual combinations highlighted in the table.

    (b) The cost of producing two goods K and L individually are denoted by C(K) and C(L), respectively. The cost of producing them jointly is denoted by C(K+L). When do economies of scope exist in this case?

| Cost of making good X | Cost of making good Y | Cost of making X and Y jointly | Existence of economies of scope |
|---|---|---|---|
| 20 | 30 | 55 | |
| 13 | 5 | 16 | |
| 44 | 54 | 100 | |
| 10 | 12 | 20 | |
| 100 | 55 | 140 | |

# Exercises

1. True or false?

   (a) Following a merger the price elasticity of demand should fall.

   (b) Economies of scale can be a rationale for merger.

   (c) Late delivery of supplies due to heavy traffic is an example of the hold-up problem.

   (d) An organization's total costs are production costs plus transaction costs.

   (e) Diversification reduces a firm's level of risk.

   (f) Free cash flow is cash in excess of funds required to invest in all projects with a positive net present value.

2. (a) Draw a long-run average cost curve and use it to explain the gains in scale achieved by two small firms merging.

   (b) Diversification is not about moving the firm's total cost and total revenue lines further apart; it is more concerned with reducing the volatility of earnings. Discuss.

3. Consider the following questions by referring to Box 7.5:

   (a) Explain what is meant by the term horizontal integration.

   (b) Evaluate the benefits of merger in the beer industry.

4. Find statistical evidence on the merger and acquisition activity of Chinese firms both inside and outside China. Is merger activity for Chinese firms growing?

# Governing business

## Chapter contents

## Learning outcomes

By the end of this chapter you should be able to:

**Economic theory**

LO1 Define principal–agent problems

LO2 Discuss the problem of separation of ownership from control

LO3 Compare alternative theories of the firm

LO4 Describe the concept of positive and negative externalities

LO5 Explain the notion of market failures

LO6 Analyse the use of tax and subsidies to correct market failures

LO7 Appraise the regulation of monopoly

**Business application**

LO8 Discuss why companies use stock options to reward chief executives

LO9 Defend why governments have introduced trading in carbon

LO10 Evaluate the costs and benefits associated with smart metering of energy

## At a glance    Governing business

### The issue

Actions taken by managers and workers are often not in the interests of their shareholders. Similarly, actions taken by firms, such as polluting the atmosphere, are often not in the interests of other stakeholders, such as wider society. Can these conflicts be resolved?

### The understanding

Conflicts exist because of a misalignment of interests. Without government control, firms can pollute the environment without cost to themselves. The cost of pollution is instead picked up by society. By making the firm bear the responsibility and costs of pollution, both the firm's and society's interests are aligned. The way to achieve this is to tax the firm if it pollutes; and perhaps even provide it with subsidies if it tries to operate without pollution. More generally, one solution to the misalignment of interests is the use of financial incentives to change the behaviour of one of the parties.

### The usefulness

Why do company executives receive huge bonuses via stock options? The answer is because stock options provide financial incentives for managers to act in the interests of shareholders. Can the government reduce carbon emissions by creating a market for pollution permits? We will now explore each of these issues.

## 8.1    Business problem: managing managers

Within all of us there is an element of Homer Simpson. The similarities at work are particularly acute, where we often have a willingness to do little but appear to be doing a great deal. Colleagues and perhaps even ourselves display a need to frequent the coffee room, the toilets or even the local pub during work hours. Such behaviour is a deviation from what our employers might consider best practice. They might consider we are employed to sit at our desks and pursue profit maximization. When such behaviour occurs, we might label it 'lazy', 'cheeky' or 'taking the Michael'. You will not be surprised to learn that economists prefer the more technical label, 'the **principal–agent problem**'.

> The principal–agent problem refers to the difficulties of a principal or owner in monitoring an agent to whom decisions have been delegated.

Principals can suffer two confounding problems when hiring agents to work for them. First, the interests of the agent and the principal may differ. For example, the principal may value hard work, while the agent may dislike hard work. Second, principals can often find it difficult to monitor the work and effort of their agents. Given the potential difference in interests and the difficulty associated with monitoring the agent, there is little reason why the agent should expend effort on the principal's behalf.

We can compare examples of a taxi driver and a manager to illuminate these arguments. In the case of the taxi driver, you may wish to be driven between two points using the shortest route. In contrast, the taxi driver may wish to take you via a much longer route, hoping to generate a higher fare. Hence, there is a difference in interest between you, as the principal, and the taxi driver, as the agent. However, since you are sitting in the taxi, you can monitor with ease the route taken by the driver. Therefore, if you know the area, and are not a tourist in a foreign land, the taxi driver will generally take you by the shortest route.

A manager of a company, the agent, may be tasked with improving the profitability of a company by the shareholders of that company, the principals. However, if the shareholders are buying and selling shares in many companies on the London stock market, they will find it difficult to monitor the manager on a daily basis. Unlike the passenger in a taxi, the shareholders cannot directly observe the behaviour of their manager. The manager could decide to sit in the office surfing the Internet, or practising their golf putting. When the profits of the company fail to increase, the shareholders will not be aware that the agent has been lazy. In fact, because of the lack of monitoring, the manager could blame the poor performance on external factors such as a lazy workforce, a bad sales manager or a fall in demand for the product.

Economists describe the manager as displaying **moral hazard** type behaviour.

The manager offers to increase the profits of the company but, once hired by the shareholders, exploits the monitoring problems of shareholders and behaves in their own best interests. In contrast, the taxi driver, actively monitored by the hiring passenger, does not display moral hazard-type behaviour, because the passenger will contest the higher fare.

Box 8.1 details how moral hazard-type behaviour by bankers might only come to light 7–10 years after they have been paid bonuses.

The costs of moral hazard-type behaviour, such as inferior performance by the agent, coupled with monitoring costs, result in what are more generally termed **agency costs**.

In the case of the taxi driver, agency costs are very low. Monitoring is easy and, therefore, moral hazard-type behaviour is unlikely. In the case of the manager, agency costs are very high, because monitoring is difficult and costly, and therefore this behaviour is likely.

A natural question arises as to how principals might seek to reduce agency costs. In particular, how can shareholders motivate managers to provide higher levels of output or, as the economist would say, how can we align the interests of firms and managers so that managers act in the interests of shareholders?

The answer will be developed throughout the first part of this chapter. In the case of managers, however, modes of corporate governance are placed on the firm that provide incentives for managers to work in the interests of shareholders. At a very simple level, managers can be turned into shareholders by providing them with shares in the company. As shareholders, managers then have an interest in working hard in order to improve

> **Moral hazard** occurs when someone agrees to undertake a certain set of actions but then, once a contractual arrangement has been agreed, behaves in a different manner.
>
> **Agency costs** reflect reductions in value to principals from using agents to undertake work on their behalf.

## Box 8.1
## Top City bankers must wait 10 years for guaranteed bonuses, watchdogs rule

The most senior bankers in the City may have to wait 10 years before they can be sure that their bonuses will not be clawed back.

From next year, any firm subject to an investigation into wrongdoing must put the bonuses of their top bosses at risk of being clawed back for 10 years. The timescale was suggested by the parliamentary commission on banking standards following the Libor-rigging scandal in 2012. Less senior bankers are subject to a seven-year clawback period, already in place. Non-executive directors will not be able to receive bonuses.

The 10-year period for top bankers will only kick in if their firm comes under a regulatory investigation. Martin Wheatley, head of the FCA, said: 'Our rules will now mean that senior managers face clawback of bonuses for up to 10 years, if misconduct comes to light. This is a crucial step to rebuild public trust in financial services, and allows firms and regulators to build long term decision making and effective risk management into people's pay packets.'

Oliver Parry, senior corporate governance adviser at the Institute of Directors, said: 'Today marks a significant milestone in overhauling pay practices in the City following the crisis of 2008. The era of rewards for failure along the lines of [former Royal Bank of Scotland boss] Fred Goodwin must be buried once and for all.'

From *The Guardian*. 23 June 2015. 'Top City bankers must wait 10 years for guaranteed bonuses, watchdogs rule'. Jill Treanor. © Guardian News & Media Ltd 2015

the performance of the company. In order to consider these ideas further, we will extend our analysis of how firms are owned and managed and examine why managers may not wish to follow the interests of shareholders. Only then can we return to the issue of how shareholders can try to motivate managers to act in their interests.

## 8.2  Profit maximization and the separation of ownership from control

Throughout this book we have assumed that firms are profit-maximizers. In fact, when we first introduced the idea in Chapter 5, we suggested that this was a sensible argument. We would now like to question this assumption.

In order to maximize profits, firms are required to set marginal cost, MC, equal to marginal revenue, MR. Even though professional accountants are also schooled in this central idea, many are incapable of calculating MC or MR from a company's cost and revenue data. Accountants are not fools, it is just that the task of measuring and collating data on MR and MC is extremely complex, especially when the firm makes and sells multiple products. Furthermore, the firm's costs and revenues may not be very stable. Changes in raw material prices or output prices will lead to repeated changes in MC and MR. Therefore, if anything, firms can at best only approximate profit maximization. They may seek to maximize profits, but they will never be sure what the optimal level of output and profits is.

Aside from these practical problems of trying to equate MC and MR, there are strong reasons why a firm might pursue objectives other than profit maximization. Crucially, it is often the case that the individuals who manage a firm are different from the individuals who own a firm. Table 8.1 provides data on the size of shareholdings within the telecommunications company BT. With 934,000 shareholders, it is reasonable to say that many people and investment companies own BT. BT employed just in excess of 100,000 individuals in 2014. Therefore, with 934,000 shareholders and only 100,000 workers, it is clear that shareholders and the people who work for BT are, in the main, different individuals. Among the largest shareholders, 198 holdings are greater than 5 million shares and represent 0.02 per cent of shareholders. We can see, therefore, that the vast majority of shareholders, small and large, are not the same people who manage BT. While BT is a popular share among many individuals in the UK, the pattern of dispersed shareholdings is common among large companies and is known as the separation of ownership from control.

**Table 8.1**  Analysis of BT shareholdings, 2014

| Range | Number of holdings | Percentage of total | Number of shares held (millions) | Percentage of total |
|---|---|---|---|---|
| 1–399 | 369,166 | 39.52 | 77 | 0.95 |
| 400–799 | 248,750 | 26.63 | 138 | 1.69 |
| 800–1,599 | 180,148 | 19.29 | 201 | 2.47 |
| 1,600–9,999 | 130,026 | 13.92 | 396 | 4.86 |
| 10,000–99,999 | 4,833 | 0.52 | 90 | 1.10 |
| 100,000–999,999 | 642 | 0.07 | 240 | 2.99 |
| 1,000 000–4,999,999 | 300 | 0.03 | 685 | 8.40 |
| 5,000,000 and above | 198 | 0.02 | 6320 | 77.54 |
| Total | 934,063 | 100.00 | 8151 | 100.00 |

The **separation of ownership from control** becomes more acute when shareholders become more disperse. With 934,000 shareholders, it is difficult for all BT shareholders to co-ordinate themselves and try to remove a poorly performing management team. Moreover, in the UK it is common for the largest shareholder to own less than 3 per cent of a company's shares. This is important because, if the largest shareholder wanted to remove a team of underperforming managers, then they would bear the full cost of this activity. This might include meetings with the managers, other large shareholders and legal advisers, and recruitment of a new management team. While bearing all these costs, the benefits of better company performance would be shared among all shareholders. Therefore, if the major shareholder has only 3 per cent, then it will only gain a 3 per cent share of the benefits of employing a new management team. All other shareholders are **free riders** on the back of the dominant shareholder.

> Separation of ownership from control exists where the shareholders, who own the company, are a different set of individuals from the managers that control the business on a day-to-day basis.
>
> Free riders are individuals, or firms, who can benefit from the actions of others without contributing to the effort made by others. They gain benefits from the actions of others for free.

Given the unattractive financial terms brought about by free riding and small shareholdings, even the dominant shareholder is unlikely to act against the incumbent management team.

Dispersed shareholdings, therefore, leave management teams, even bad ones, in a position where they do not have to react to shareholders' interests. So, while it might be reasonable to argue that shareholders are profit-maximizers, managers have the scope to pursue their own objectives. But what might these objectives be?

## Managerial objectives

Economists have proposed a number of alternative theories relating to the objectives that managers might pursue. The first relates to what is known as 'expense preference behaviour'. If shareholders are interested in maximizing profits, then managers are interested in maximizing their own satisfaction.

### Consumption of perquisites

So, rather than work hard for the company's owners, managers would rather indulge themselves in the purchase of expensive cars, jets, lavish expense accounts that can be used to dine clients (and friends) at the most fashionable restaurants and, of course, lots of personal assistants. A clear reason for doing this is a positive recognition provided by society for success, dominance and status. In trying to meet these requirements, managers use the company's funds to finance a prestigious image makeover and lifestyle.

Managers may even spend the company's money on business projects that have little value to the shareholder but have personal value to the company's managers. Diversification, as discussed in Chapter 7, is a case in point. Companies that specialize in one product line are vulnerable to competition, or a downturn in demand. In order to protect themselves, managers may diversify and use the company's money to buy unrelated businesses. Statements of strategic change along the lines of 'yes, I know we are in waste handling, but I think we should move into leisure and purchase a cruise ship' are extreme, but sadly evident among some senior managers. However, the essential problem is that managers are using the company's and, therefore shareholders', money to diversify a risk that only managers face. If shareholders are concerned about risk in one market, they can buy shares in other companies. Hence, diversification within firms does not protect shareholders; rather, it protects managers.

### Sales maximization

An alternative hypothesis recognizes that the measurement of profits can be subjective. How much will the firm decide to depreciate its assets and what provision for bad debts will it charge to the profit and loss statement this year? Given these problems, managers may prefer to maximize a more tangible measure of performance, such as sales. A common misunderstanding follows the reasoning that, if sales are increasing, then so are profits. But, as we have seen, this is not true—the law of diminishing returns and diseconomies of scale point to increases in costs as output increases. Sales maximization may, therefore, indicate that sales managers are doing a good job but, without an additional consideration of costs and ultimately profits, sales growth may not be a good indicator of overall performance.

### Growth maximization

The final hypothesis is that managers will seek to maximize growth, rather than profits. It is no surprise that the pay of top directors is linked to the size of the company. The bigger the company, the greater the responsibility. What is surprising is that chief executive (the leading director of a company) pay is linked more closely to company size than it is to financial performance, such as profitability. This suggests that managers have a financial, or salary, incentive to pursue growth maximization over profit maximization. However, while seeing this rather obvious argument, there are some subtleties. If a company grows at a faster rate now, will it be in a stronger position to outperform its rivals in the future? Economies of scale can be attained more quickly, leading to a reduction in costs. In addition, as we saw in Chapters 5 and 7, increased market share brings increased power over pricing. If this is true, growth maximization now is simply a strategy for profit maximization over the long term.

## Behavioural theories

Behavioural theories of the firm are based on how individuals actually behave inside firms. This is in contrast to theories such as profit maximization, which predict how individuals should behave. Important behavioural points are what goals will be set for the organization and how the targets will be set.

### Goal setting

Cyert and March[1] recognized that organizations are complex environments represented by a mixture of interest groups, including shareholders, managers, workers, consumers and trade unions. Even within managers there are various subgroups, including marketing, accounting and production. The goals of the organization, or firm, are more a reflection of these competing interests than a theoretical prediction such as profit maximization. If a marketing manager rises to the top of the organization, it is likely that marketing issues will rise to the top of the managerial decision-making agenda. Resources may flow into the marketing department and the goals of the organization may reflect marketing issues, such as the most recognized global brand or growing customer reach and market share. In contrast, if an accountant led the organization, then goals relating to sales growth, cost reduction and profitability might be set. Decision making, the development of targets and the focus of the organization are, therefore, a reflection of the coalition of interests within the organization. Whichever group has greater power, or enhanced negotiation skills, will have a greater say over the targets of the organization.

### Target setting

> Satisficing is the attainment of acceptable levels of performance.

Regardless of which goals or objectives predominate, the complexity of the environment will mean that measures and targets are difficult to set. Should sales growth be 10 per cent or 20 per cent? How do managers accommodate failure in meeting the target? In recognizing these points, Herbert Simon[2] developed the concept of **satisficing**.

---

[1] R.M. Cyert and J.G. March, *A Behavioral Theory of the Firm*, 2nd edn., Englewood Cliffs, NJ: Prentice Hall, 1963.

[2] H.A. Simon, *Models of Man: Social and Rational*. New York: Wiley, 1957.

For example, 20 per cent annual growth in sales could be the maximum possible. But a 10 per cent growth in sales would be acceptable, especially if other firms or organizations were achieving similar results; 10 per cent represents a satisfactory level of performance. If managers negotiate a 10 per cent target growth rate, rather than a 20 per cent target, they are displaying satisficing rather than **maximizing** behaviour. Why might they do this? First, the maximum growth rate is unknown; it could be 15, 20, 25 or even 50 per cent. Second, failure to meet a target creates tension between the group setting the target and the individuals pursuing the target. Therefore, in order to avoid failure in a complex world, where the maximum is unknown, it is perhaps better to set a realistic and satisfactory target. Behavioural considerations, therefore, lead to firms and organizations setting minimum levels of performance, rather than maximum ones.

> Maximizing is the attainment of maximum levels of performance.

Boxes 8.2 and 8.3 provide two discussions about satisficing behaviour. The first discussion, from the *Financial Times*, highlights the variety of economic behaviours that can be viewed as satisficing, as opposed to maximizing. The second discussion extends the concept of satisficing into managing Barcelona FC.

We do not have to decide which of the above alternative hypotheses is correct. Instead, we simply have to recognize that the separation of ownership from control provides managers with the incentive to pursue any of the above objectives. The problem for shareholders is the absence of direct control over managers: how might they motivate managers to behave in the interests of shareholders? The straightforward answer is to make managers shareholders. But the complex answer is to understand how difficult this might be. To understand the problem more fully, we will examine principal–agent theory.

## Box 8.2
## Push to beat rivals overtakes need to replace bad economic theory

We all have a competitive instinct. Humans' natural urge is to compete. Rather than do the best for ourselves that we possibly can, many of us instead aim just to do better than the other guy. A new book by George Cooper, *Money, Blood and Revolution,* examines such behaviour.

The basic notion that we are competitors above all can be illustrated from everyday life; people tend to want to keep up with the Joneses. We do not necessarily need a BMW, until next door has one. Then, for many, it becomes an imperative.

Or take sport. Cooper uses the example of the great Jamaican sprinter Usain Bolt. He famously does not maximize his performance (or finish in the fastest time possible). Rather, when the race is assured he tends to slow down and once, famously, beat his chest. In the office, people do not necessarily need to maximize their pay—but grow furious if they find they are paid less than a colleague.

It is an axiom of classical economics that people maximize utility, rather than competing with others. It

is not new to question this assumption. Behavioural economists have for years been substituting the findings from experimental psychology for traditional economic assumptions of rationality. The theory of the firm includes a healthy literature on 'satisficing,' in which companies try to make sure that their outcomes are satisfactory, rather than going all out to maximize their gains. But the relevance of these ideas to finance is obvious. Fund managers do not try to maximize their returns. They try to do better than their peers. And that is no surprise, as that is what they are paid to do. Fund flows, and management fees, go to those who have beaten their peers. As for big institutions such as pension funds, they tend to satisfice rather than going all-out for maximized growth.

Under these circumstances, funds tend to pour into the same things, bubbles grow and anomalies go unchecked. Contrary to the economic axiom, they do not tend towards equilibrium or fair value.

From the *Financial Times*. 13 April 2014. 'Push to beat rivals overtakes need to replace bad economic theory'. John Authers. © The Financial Times Limited 2014. All Rights Reserved.

## Box 8.3
## Could Mascherano be Barcelona's best option as captain?

Carles Puyol broke the news of his decision to end his playing career at Barcelona in March of 2014. Eyes had barely begun to dry before questions about who would fill his role emerged. The role in question was not his position as a central defender—Barcelona had been in need of one (more than one, in all honesty) since 2010. The issue on the table was regarding who would fill the void in leadership left by the legendary captain, a problem that increased in severity when the decision of Victor Valdes to not renew his contract and the almost imminent departure of Xavi Hernandez were factored in. Of the four club captains that began the 2013–14 campaign, only one of them, Andres Iniesta, will remain for the upcoming season.

The image of the ethereal Iniesta donning the captain's armband for the 2014–15 season is not one that will significantly trouble followers of the club. He is experienced, homegrown and a magnificent player. However, there have been whispers, which have been growing in volume, about the possibility of Javier Mascherano stepping into the role of captain instead.

Rewind a couple of years, Barcelona were the example of the apparent 'ideal' club, praised for their commitment to bringing players up through the ranks of their youth system, and it would have seemed fitting that their captain also come from within.

However, the image of Barcelona is not what it used to be. This is in large part due to the actions of the current board, who have treated the club more like a business than before, engaging in satisficing behaviour rather than sustainable development. While a shiny new signing has been delivered season after season, they have allowed huge talents, most notably Thiago Alcantara, to be sold for profit. Javier Espinosa, another youth team midfielder brimming with potential, has signed for Villarreal, yet one more example of the board letting young talent slip through their fingers. Cesc Fabregas, after failing to reach the lofty expectations of many, has been sold to Chelsea. Where there was once a genuine possibility of a competitive starting XI consisting purely of players who had, at one point or another, plied their trade in La Masia, now, one would be hard-pressed to construct one.

From *Inside Spanish Football*. 15 July 2014. 'Could Mascherano be Barcelona's best option as captain?'. Sheena Sidhu. © 2011–2015 Inside Spanish Football

##  Principal–agent theory

### Agency costs between managers and shareholders

When a business is small, the owner is also likely to be the manager. In this case, there is no agency relationship, because the owner and the manager are the same person. Therefore, there can be no misalignment of interests. The owner-manager is likely to work very hard to ensure the success of the business. Furthermore, even if the owner-manager decides to pursue expense-preference behaviour and spend the company's money on a top-of-the-range BMW, they are only robbing themselves as the shareholder. An important consideration is that the value of the company to the owner does not change with the behaviour of the manager; simply, the financial benefits are being paid to the same person in different ways. For example, if the company generated £100,000 in profits, but the owner-manager decided to use £30,000 to buy the BMW and only receive a dividend of (£100,000 – £30,000) = £70,000, then the owner-manager has still received £100,000 from the company.

We can now consider what happens when the company grows and the owner wishes to sell half their stake in the company. The original owner will still manage the company, but the new shareholder will just be an owner, not a manager. Before buying the stake, any potential buyer will attempt to value the company. Crucially, the value of the company now depends upon the expense preference behaviour of the owner-manager. When the owner-manager buys a BMW with the company's money, the other shareholder is paying for half of the car, but gaining no benefit. For example, if the company again generates £100,000 in profits, then each shareholder should receive £50,000. But if the shareholder who also manages the company uses £30,000 of the profits to buy the BMW, then the remaining profits are only £70,000. Split two ways, each shareholder receives £35,000. The owner-manager has received a £30,000 car plus £35,000 in dividends = £65,000. The shareholder who does not run the company has received only £35,000 in dividends. Therefore, the value of a share in the company is not £50,000, but rather £35,000. Indeed, the more a manager displays expense-preference behaviour, the lower the potential buyer will value the company.

This reduction in company value from employing an **agent** to manage the company is an example of an agency cost. Agency costs are not the wages associated with employing an agent; rather, they reflect reductions in value to **principals** from using agents to undertake work on their behalf.

> Agents run companies on behalf of shareholders (principals).
>
> Piece rates occur when a worker is paid according to the output produced. Under hourly wage rates, workers are paid for time at work.

The agency cost in our example is £50,000 − £35,000 = £15,000. It arises because the interests of the owner-manager are different from those of the other shareholder; and because the owner-manager is not monitored on a daily basis. It is, therefore, possible to use the company's money to fund benefits for the owner-manager at the expense of the remaining owner.

## Agency costs between workers and managers

Agency costs occur not just between owners and managers of companies. They can also occur when managers employ workers to do work for them. For example, let us consider two employment relationships. First, a supermarket employs a shelf stacker on **piece rates**. For each tray of tinned food put on the shelf, the shelf stacker receives £0.20. Second, a supermarket employs a shelf stacker on an hourly rate of £5.

If agency problems exist because principals find it difficult to monitor the effort of their agents, then piece rates will reduce agency costs. With an hourly wage rate of £5, the shelf stacker will earn £5 for one hour's work if they fill the shelf or if they sit in the staff restaurant drinking coffee and reading the paper. However, under piece rates the worker has to provide sufficient effort to place 25 trays of tinned food on the shelf in order to earn the same £5. Under piece rates, the employer does not have to continually monitor the effort of the agent; instead, they can merely add up all the output at the end of the shift. If the agent works hard, then greater output will lead to greater pay. If they are lazy and read the newspaper, then their pay will decrease. By linking pay more directly to the effort provided, the agency costs are reduced.

We tend to see piece rates used when the output is easy to verify. For example, car salespersons are paid a commission for selling cars. It is fairly easy to verify that a car has been sold. Packers are often paid by the number of boxes that have been filled; and bricklayers are paid by the square metre of laid bricks and not by the hour.

However, when it comes to managers and many other occupations, output is more difficult to verify. How do you measure if a manager has managed? The many activities undertaken by managers, including monitoring workers, communicating and implementing business plans, reviewing operations and making investment decisions, make it difficult to measure the total output of the manager. The outputs are numerous, varied and difficult to quantify. For example, how do you measure effective communication? However, given that we have shown that company value is reduced by increased agency costs, we need to develop a means of aligning managers' interests with those of shareholders, thereby reducing agency costs and boosting company value. How might this be achieved? We need an alternative way of reducing agency costs. In the following business application, stock options will highlight how agency costs associated with employing managers might be reduced.

## Business application: stock options and the reduction of agency costs

> Stock options provide individuals with the *option* to buy shares in the future at a price agreed in the past.

In order to reduce agency costs, principals have to develop contracts that align agents' interests with their own. Piece rates lower agency costs by forcing the agent to work hard to receive greater pay. A more complicated example is the use of **stock options** in the financial packages offered to senior managers of leading companies.

For example, assume the share price today for company X is £10. A manager at X may be offered the option to purchase 1 million shares at £10 in three years' time. Assume the manager works hard, the company makes profits and over the three years the shares rise to £12. The stock option has moved into the money. The manager can take up the option and buy at £10 and then sell instantly for £12, making £2 million profit. Stock options, therefore, link managers' and shareholders' interests via the share price. But how effective are stock options as a solution to agency problems?

An examination of the key points associated with stock options will help:

1.  Stock options transfer an element of shareholder risk to the manager. Under a fixed salary contract a manager will earn perhaps £30,000 per annum. The manager will earn this salary if the company performs well or not. Under a stock option, part of the fixed contract is swapped for the stock options. The manager may now be offered a basic salary of £20,000, plus stock options. When the company performs well, the manager's stock options move into the money. The manager's pay increases whenever the stock option moves into the money and the manager executes the option—that is, uses the option to buy the shares cheaply and make a profit. But when the company underperforms, the share price drops and the stock options are worthless. Therefore, performance contracts, such as stock options, swap part of the certain salary for a chance of earning a higher overall amount. This increase in risk may not be attractive to the manager and they could decide to reject the contract or work somewhere else.

2.  Stock options make a manager's pay contingent upon the share price. The share price is being used as a measure of the manager's hard work. The harder the manager works, the higher the share price climbs. But what if the share price is influenced by industry factors, such as the degree of competition, or by domestic government policy on interest rates? A manager may work very hard but, due to government policy, the share price may fall. This increases the risk being transferred to the manager. For this reason, the measure of performance should be linked closely to managerial, or worker, effort. In some cases, the measures can be very specific. Workers in telephone sales are paid a commission every time they secure a sale, while car salespersons are paid every time they sell a car. In contrast, the output measures for managers tend to be very general, based on overall profitability, or simply linked to the share price.

3.  The stronger the link between worker effort and the performance measure, the stronger the incentive. This merely reflects risk again. If you work hard, but the output measure does not reflect high effort, then you receive no pay. Managers are measured by share prices and car salespersons by number of sales. We might argue that there is a stronger link between worker effort and car sales than between worker effort and share price. At a simple level, if a salesperson works hard to sell a car, then a sale may materialize. But if a manager works hard, other managers may not and, therefore, due to a lack of teamwork, the share price is unaffected. As a reflection of these arguments, what tends to be observed is that, as a percentage of their overall pay, car salespersons receive a low fixed salary component and a high performance bonus. In contrast, managers tend to receive a high fixed salary component and a lower performance bonus. Therefore, as in the case of car salespersons, when the performance measure

is a more accurate measure of worker effort, the more likely it is that pay will move to performance-based, rather than fixed, salary.

4.  Incentive contracts can promote a single type of behaviour. Managers with stock options face incentives to raise the company's share price. But what if shareholders are interested in more than this? Box 8.4 provides Vodafone's strategic statement.

5.  Finally, a manager's behaviour and effort must be verifiable. It should not be possible for the worker or manager to influence the performance measure inappropriately. This was clearly not the case with Enron and Worldcom. With Enron, managers were able to keep liabilities off the company's balance sheet, thereby inflating its share price. Even though the company was performing badly, the managers were able to make it appear highly successful. The share price rose and stock options were cashed in. In the case of Worldcom, expenses on stationery were capitalized and moved to the balance sheet as an asset, rather than sent to the profit and loss statement as an expense. This is common practice for substantial assets such as buildings and cars, but not for stationery, which you may no longer own as you have sent it out in letters! But, again, profits were seen to rise, assets increased and the share price rose. Once again, managers cashed in on stock options.

Therefore, performance contracts can help to resolve the principal–agent problem. But only if:

*   workers accept the contracts, receiving greater rewards for higher risks
*   there is a link between worker effort and the performance measure
*   the performance can be co-ordinated across a number of objectives
*   workers cannot unduly influence the measure.

We can use these points to understand some of the concerns relating to the excessive rewards provided to managers through stock options. One of the potential reasons why executive compensation has increased so markedly is to do with risk. A guaranteed payment of £100 is better than a 50:50 chance of receiving £100 or £0. But how much money would you require in order to accept the 50:50 gamble and give up the guaranteed £100? Would you require £200, £300 or perhaps even £1,000? If you asked for £1,000, then you would be described as not liking risk, or as being **risk averse**, and, therefore, requiring a large reward for accepting the risk of the 50:50 gamble.

> **Risk averse** means disliking or avoiding risk, an alternative to being risk neutral or risk seeking.

Assume an executive is equally risk averse. For every £100 that is taken from their guaranteed salary, a potential reward of £1,000 has to be offered through the stock

---

## Box 8.4
## Vodafone's strategic direction

Vodafone is uniquely positioned to succeed through our scale and scope and the customer focus of all our employees. To achieve this success, we are focused on the execution of the six strategic goals that we outlined last year: delighting our customers, leveraging our scale and scope, expanding market boundaries, building the best global team, being a responsible business, and providing superior shareholder returns.

Vodafone's strategic vision is based on six approaches, of which one is shareholder returns. While each of the six approaches may seem sensible, it is difficult to envisage a performance contract which is able to reward managers for such a complexity of targets. Recently, companies have recognized this and some have moved to multiple measures of performance, splitting performance bonus between the short term and the long term. Performance is not necessarily measured by reference to the share price—it might include sales growth compared with the firm's three leading competitors, or profit growth compared to the top 25 per cent of the FTSE 100, or profitability compared with other leading global players in the sector.

*Source: Vodafone website, www.vodafone.com.*

option. So, executives can receive large financial rewards, but they receive such rewards for (it is hoped) improving shareholder value and taking personal financial risk. We can even suggest where the executive's risk stems from. Linking a large amount of executive wealth to one company's share price does not provide the executive with a diversified portfolio of investments. The bulk of the executive's wealth is linked to one asset. We saw in Chapter 7 that diversification reduces risk. Therefore, reduced diversification must increase risk and, in order to accept greater risk, executives require a higher potential reward. As a consequence, the size of executive stock options and executive remuneration contracts increases.

The alternative view of managers using stock options to camouflage large financial rewards also has some merit. Raising the executive's salary by 100 per cent is likely to attract the wrong type of attention from shareholders and the media. By contrast, raising total financial remuneration through stock market performance provides a tangible link between pay and performance that is more palatable to the public.

However, all of our discussion has been linked to shareholders offering managers contracts that are designed to align the interests of shareholders and managers. In reality, managers propose contracts to shareholders. It is then shareholders who reject or accept the proposed financial terms for the executive(s). This is generally discussed at the company's annual general meeting. Why is this a problem?

First, managers are defining pay and performance. Admittedly, this is achieved through the company's remuneration committee that supposedly consists of independent remuneration experts and non-executive directors of the company.

Non-executive directors are directors from other companies who provide independent advice to the boards on which they are non-executives. For example, Mr X may be an executive director of company Y, his main employer. But Mr X may also be a non-executive director of company Z, providing independent advice to the board.

From our discussion of behavioural theories of the firm, we might suspect that the targets set by remuneration committees will be satisficing, not maximizing, targets. From the behavioural perspective, there is a fear that executives can negotiate the proposed financial rewards, arguing with the members of the remuneration committee what reasonable targets and performance rewards are, given what is occurring in other companies. Second, due to the separation of ownership from control, once the executive(s) package is proposed, the dispersed nature of the shareholdings may lead to free riding among the shareholders, making a majority vote against the executive(s) financial terms difficult.

## Performance pay and the public sector

A current trend is to introduce performance pay within the public sector. Primary-care doctors in the UK are paid a fixed salary plus a performance element which is linked to certain health-care indices. These include reductions in blood pressure and cholesterol for patients at high risk of heart disease. Teachers are eligible for performance-related pay linked to pupil progression, and dental professionals are paid according to the number of units of dental treatment provided to patients.

The key, as with performance contracts in the private sector, is to ensure that workers can respond to the incentives and do not divert the effort of employees away from other important value-adding activities. For example, in the dental profession, the extraction of a tooth attracts the same reward as extensive root-canal work. The latter is more beneficial for the patient, but the former is quicker to deliver by the dentist. In the case of teaching, excellent teachers are increasingly allocated to teach marginal students where there is the greatest scope to improve pupil progression. Improving highly capable pupils is difficult and offers fewer financial rewards for good teachers.

## Box 8.5
## Barclays boss defends bonus as forex rigging fines weigh on bank results

The boss of Barclays has been forced to defend his £5.5 million pay packet as the bank set aside £1.25 billion in preparation for a wave of fines and penalties for rigging foreign exchange markets. Antony Jenkins—who is in the midst of cutting 19,000 jobs and scaling back the once-dominant investment bank—said he would take his first annual bonus of £1.1 million since taking the helm in the wake of the 2012 Libor-fixing scandal.

'I completely understand that I am very well remunerated for what I do. But ... I think it is appropriate that I accept my bonus,' said Jenkins, who revealed he was taxed on his worldwide income both in the UK and, as a green card holder, in the US. The bank provided a comparative figure of £1.6 million for his pay in 2013.

Frances O'Grady, general secretary of the TUC, said his £5.5 million pay would take someone working full time on the minimum wage 465 years to earn. A spokesman for the Robin Hood tax campaign said: 'Bonus season has again been dominated by pay controversies, scandals and fines—underlining that too little reform has taken place in the sector.'

However, the Institute of Directors, which was very critical of the bank a year ago for increasing bonuses as profits tumbled, felt placated by the fall in the bonus pool to £1.9 billion, 22 per cent down on a year ago.

Profits were knocked 21 per cent lower to £2.3 billion by a string of legal and regulatory issues, including £1.1 billion for compensating people mis-sold payment protection insurance. A £935 million hit for the way loans for education, social housing and local authorities are valued also ate into the bottom line, although the bank preferred to focus on adjusted profits, which increased by 12 per cent to £5.5 billion.

The bank acknowledged that part of the fall in the bonus pool was the result of separate allowances being handed out, alongside salaries and bonuses, to sidestep the EU bonus cap. The cap limits bonuses to one times salary or twice if shareholders approve.

With these allowances stripped out, the bonus pool was down 11 per cent. The bank said 359 people earned more than £1 million, compared with 481 the year before. Three received more than £5 million, including one who received around £10 million.

The investment bank, which grew rapidly under Jenkins' predecessor Bob Diamond, reported a 32 per cent fall in profits to £1.3bn and an increase in its cost–income ratio—a measure of efficiency—to 82 per cent from 77 per cent. Bonuses in the division were down by 24 per cent, on one measure, although the bank insisted payouts to staff had fallen in line with profits.

Simon Walker, the IoD director general, said: 'The group as a whole appears to be taking significant steps to change its structure and improve its internal culture.'

From *The Guardian*. 3 March 2015. 'Barclays boss defends bonus as forex rigging fines weigh on bank results'. Jill Trenor.
© Guardian News & Media Ltd 2015

The concern about performance-related pay is often levelled at those who receive enormous financial gain. In Box 8.5 we provide an example of banking and bonuses. Despite Barclays having what appears to be a bad year and a number of on-going investigations into market fixing, Barclays' CEO still pocketed £5.5 million payout. The article in Box 8.6 sheds light on what is arguably a far more concerning aspect of bonus pay. Amongst the New York legal firms bonus pay is rising rapidly. However, basic pay is not growing. Firms can use incentive pay as a means of shifting business risks from the firm to the employees.

# 8.5 Regulation of business

We have examined the governance of managers by shareholders. We would now like to examine the governance of firms within their marketplaces. We have already seen, in Chapter 5, that monopolies are an example of marketplaces that are not in consumers' interests, with higher prices and lower output than under perfect competition. We will now also show that, in other ways, markets can act against the interest of consumers, or even the public more generally. In representing the interests of society, governments can intervene in such markets in an attempt to improve the benefits society receives from the market. We will begin by providing an overview of the issues and some further examples.

## Box 8.6
## Bonus babies

**Why big end-of-year payouts for junior attorneys are a double-edged sword**

Nearly eight years have passed since young lawyers at large American firms last got significant pay rises. With law-school graduates plentiful and demand for corporate legal work tepid, the standard starting salary has been stuck at $160,000 a year since 2007. Heartbreaking, isn't it? But in the past month an unexpected financial arms race has erupted over year-end bonuses.

Unlike on Wall Street, legal bonuses have not generated much drama in recent years. What usually happens is that in early December Cravath, a big New York outfit, announces its payouts, then every firm that considers itself a peer matches them. However, on 21 November Simpson Thacher, which in 2007 had been the first firm to offer $160,000 starting salaries, jumped the gun. After a banner year in which it represented Alibaba, a Chinese e-commerce giant, in the largest stockmarket flotation yet seen, Simpson declared the biggest bonuses since the financial crisis. Associates in their first year will get $15,000 (50 per cent more than in 2013). Ones with seven years' experience will get a whopping $100,000, double last year's sum.

Most of Simpson's competitors promptly matched its scale. But four days later Davis Polk—a genteel firm hitherto averse to bidding wars—raised the ante with an extra $5,000–$10,000 for mid-tier associates. That forced Cravath and the rest to follow suit.

The bonuses reflect improving fundamentals: there has been a surge in mergers and acquisitions, a big source of legal work. And rising stockmarkets have encouraged hedge funds and private-equity outfits to compete with law firms for experienced legal talent.

But the form these payouts have taken also reflects the precariousness of the industry's recovery. Elite firms may be minting money now, but they face a highly uncertain future. Even after this year's boost, bonuses for first-years are just a third of what they got in 2007. That reflects their declining value: clients who once subsidized junior associates' on-the-job training now refuse to pay up for rote work that can be automated or outsourced.

Moreover, big clients that typically used to be loyal to one firm now force lawyers to bid against each other for work. A senior partner at one firm that reluctantly matched Davis Polk's bonuses, cutting its profits by 4 per cent, says furious clients have been inquiring why their exorbitant fees are funding associates' Christmas shopping sprees—a thinly veiled threat to take their business elsewhere.

As a result, though firms are happy to dispense beefy bonuses, they still refuse to raise base salaries, which would be harder to cut in a downturn. By embracing variable compensation, they are emulating many of their clients on Wall Street. But junior bankers do not have to attend costly graduate school, like legal associates, who thus need steady incomes to service their debt. When the bonuses arrive, young lawyers may be too busy popping champagne corks to realize it, but their bosses are shifting onto them a greater share of the risk in an industry on the brink of disruption.

From *The Economist*. 'Bonus babies'.
© The Economist Newspaper Limited, London
(20 December 2014)

How many times have you sat at a set of traffic lights having to listen to the loud bass tunes from the car drawn up next to you? The person playing the loud music obviously likes the artist. The unfortunate problem is that everyone within earshot of the car also has to listen. The driver sets the volume of the car stereo without considering the interests of the people they may be driving past. Effectively, the interests of the driver and those of a wider group of individuals are not aligned.

Not surprisingly, the private interests of firms and wider society also differ. Polluting the environment, rather than cleaning factory emissions, is a cheap alternative for a profit-maximizing firm. Unfortunately, society as a whole has to bear the costs of a polluted environment. This is again because the interests of society and the private firm are not aligned. The firm will choose to produce more pollutants than society finds desirable.

An important but underlying issue within this book, and many other texts on economics, is that markets are an optimal means of allocating society's scarce resources. That is why we have spent so much time looking at supply, demand, perfect competition and monopoly. How do markets work and how do firms operate within markets?

At the heart of most economists' understanding is that an economy characterized by perfectly competitive markets is **Pareto efficient**. In perfect competition firms operate at the minimum point on their long-run cost curves. Hence, they are productively efficient. Firms make the highest level of output for the lowest amount of cost. Also in perfect competition, price equals marginal cost. So, the price paid by consumers for the last unit also equals the cost of the resources used in making the last unit. Therefore, input resources are also allocated efficiently. Thus, in perfect competition the goods that consumers desire are the ones that are made and, moreover, they are made at lowest cost. Intuitively we can accept this as a good outcome, and economists go one step further and prove that it is Pareto efficient.

However, perfect competition is rarely achieved in reality and in some cases monopoly might exist. Under monopoly, products are not necessarily produced at lowest cost and they are not priced at marginal cost. So, Pareto efficiency will not hold.

Monopoly is an example of a **market failure**, with perfect competition providing a more efficient market equilibrium. But there can be other reasons for market failure. As we will discuss in detail below, socalled externalities can lead to a difference between the interests of private individuals and society and an inefficient production or consumption of goods and services from the perspective of society. For example, the production and consumption of loud music by our car driver is not an efficient (desirable) allocation of resources from the perspective of society (passers-by). We will now discuss externalities, monopoly and the problems relating to market failure. Following this, we can begin to assess various government intervention strategies for making markets potentially more Pareto efficient—that is, strategies that make people better off without making others worse off, thereby improving the well-being of society.

## 8.6 Externalities

**Externalities** occur when the production, or consumption, of a good or service results in costs, or benefits, being passed on to individuals not involved in the production, or consumption. **Negative externalities** occur when costs are passed on to society, or benefits are reduced. **Positive externalities** occur when costs to society are reduced or benefits are enhanced.

A number of examples will help to explain the concepts of positive and negative externalities.

The cost to the private firm of producing a particular output is the **marginal private cost** (MPC). We have previously referred to this as the *marginal cost*. The MPC measures the costs to the firm of producing one more unit and includes those of raw materials, labour and machinery. We now wish to also include in the analysis the **marginal social cost** (MSC). This is the cost to society of producing one more unit. As the private firm or individual is a member of society, then the MSC must include the MPC. However, in addition it will also include the costs associated with using or exploiting public assets, such as the environment. So, the MSC could include costs of pollution. In such cases, the costs to society will always be bigger than the costs to the private firm. These points are summarized in Table 8.2.

> **Pareto efficient** means that no one within an economy can be made better off without making some other people worse off. Therefore, the well-being of society is at a maximum.
>
> **Market failure** is a term used by economists to cover all circumstances in which the market equilibrium is not efficient.
>
> **Externalities** are the effects of consumption, or production, on third parties.
>
> **Negative externality** occurs if production, or consumption, by one group reduces the well-being of third parties.
>
> **Positive externality** occurs if production, or consumption, by one group improves the well-being of third parties.
>
> **Marginal private cost** is the cost to the individual of producing one more unit of output.
>
> **Marginal social cost** is the cost to society of producing one or more unit of output.

**Table 8.2** Marginal private and social costs

| Marginal private cost | Marginal social cost |
| --- | --- |
| Raw materials | Raw materials |
| Labour costs | Labour costs |
| Machinery | Machinery + Environmental costs of production |

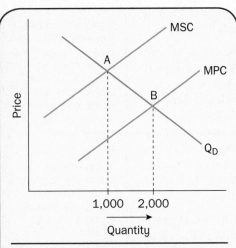

**Figure 8.1    Negative cost externalities**

The marginal private cost (MPC) is much lower than the marginal social cost (MSC). As a result, when choosing the optimal level of output, the private individual will choose a level of output that is higher than the socially optimal level of output. Pollution is a good example.

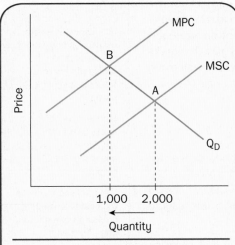

**Figure 8.2    Positive cost externality**

Marginal private benefit is the benefit to the individual from consuming one more unit of output.

Marginal social benefit is the benefit to society from the consumption of one more unit of output.

## MSC is greater than MPC

The consequences of this can be seen in Figure 8.1. The optimal level of output for society and the private firm will occur where marginal revenue equals marginal cost. If the firm is a price taker, then equilibrium for the private firm occurs at point B, where MPC equals demand and, therefore, marginal revenue. The output level is 2,000 units. However, for society, MSC equals demand and, therefore, marginal revenue at point A, with an output of 1,000 units. Therefore, when the private firm creates negative cost externalities for the rest of society, the private firm will choose a level of output that is greater than that deemed desirable by society. In its simplest terms, the firm does not recognize the costs of pollution; society does. Therefore, society has a desire to reduce output and pollution; the firm does not.

## MSC is less than MPC

If we reversed the arguments and the marginal social cost was lower than the marginal private cost, then society would find it desirable to produce more output than the private firm or individual deems optimal. The marginal social cost in Figure 8.2 is lower than the marginal private cost. The social equilibrium occurs at A with 2,000 units produced and consumed, whereas the private solution occurs at B with only 1,000 units produced and consumed. As an example, society might decide that it is optimal for all individuals to gain a degree. But this requires your input in terms of time, effort and tuition fees. The costs to you are greater than to society. Hence, when deciding whether to go to university, you did not take into account society's views.

## MPB is greater than MSB

The excessive car music example is a clear case of negative consumption externalities. The driver receives **marginal private benefit** (MPB) from consuming loud music. While the marginal private cost is linked to marginal cost, the marginal private benefit is linked to demand. If a consumer can place a financial value on the marginal benefit from consuming one more unit, then this value must equal the consumer's maximum willingness to pay.

The benefits for surrounding individuals are captured by the **marginal social benefit** (MSB). For simplicity, we will assume that the marginal social costs and the marginal private costs are equal. Figure 8.3 captures these points.

The optimal output of loud music for society occurs where MSC equals MSB at A, with 1,000 units of output. The optimal amount of output for private individuals is where MPB equals MPC at B, with 2,000 units of output. Therefore, we have 1,000 too many drivers playing their music too loud. This figure would also capture the negative externalities associated with passive smoking. Private smokers gain a higher satisfaction from smoking than do non-smokers. As a result, if society is dominated by non-smokers, then smokers exhale pollutants at a level beyond what society deems desirable.

What are the business implications? If you consider advertising, the private benefits for firms are (they hope) increased sales. The benefits for consumers in society are improved information about what products are available, where they can be sourced and at what prices. If firms value higher sales more than consumers value information, firms will advertise at levels that are greater than that deemed desirable by society. If you have ever hated the adverts appearing on television, become irritated by pop-up adverts on the Internet, or been plagued by junk (e)mail, then you now understand why you were angry.

## MSB is greater than MPB

If the marginal social benefits are greater than the marginal private benefits, then society gains more than a private individual from consumption. In Figure 8.4 the marginal social benefit line crosses the marginal social cost line at A and the market delivers 2,000 units. But the marginal private benefit line intersects the marginal private cost line at B and the market delivers just 1,000 units. Society in this case would prefer the higher output at A. Examples can include vaccinations and education. An individual gains health benefits from being vaccinated against a disease. However, society gains more, because the individual is both likely to be more healthy and less likely to pass on the disease to other individuals. In terms of education, a university graduate may gain employment benefits from their advanced education. Society gains from the taxes paid by this educated person, as well as the advanced skills and innovative thinking that can be used within firms to generate profit, wealth, new business and new jobs.

## 8.7 Dealing with externalities

Clearly, if the private actions of individuals, or firms, are at variance with those of wider society, there is a case for at least asking whether anything can be done to solve the problem. We will see that some solutions are fairly straightforward to describe, but they may be difficult to implement.

## Taxation and subsidy

The central problem with an externality is that the pricing mechanism does not impose the costs, or benefits, on the correct individuals. If a person smokes, or a firm pollutes the river, society bears the cost of living with a polluted environment. Therefore, a means has to be found whereby the private firm or individual internalizes, or pays all costs associated with, their behaviour. In Figure 8.5, we revisit the situation where the marginal social cost is greater than the marginal private cost, the case of river pollution by a firm. Society views 1,000 units of output as efficient; the firm would rather produce 2,000 units of output. The problem is that marginal private costs, MPC, are different from marginal social costs, MSC. So, the obvious solution is to make MPC and MSC equal. This is achieved by taxing the firm for polluting the river, or environment. This adds to the firm's costs and, optimally, the tax will be equal to the difference between the MPC and the MSC. The imposition of the pollution tax provides firms with an incentive to cut output and move from point B to point A, thus lowering output to the socially optimum level.

Road tax for cars across a number of economies is linked to the pollution output of the car. Heavy polluters pay more road tax. This provides drivers with a clear incentive to buy

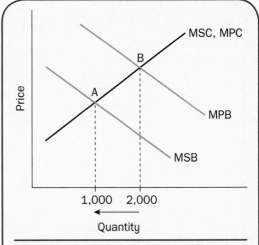

Figure 8.3   Negative benefit externalities

The marginal private benefit (MPB) is much higher than the marginal social benefit (MSB). Therefore, when choosing the optimal level of output, private individuals will consume a higher level of output than that deemed optimal by society. Loud music is an example.

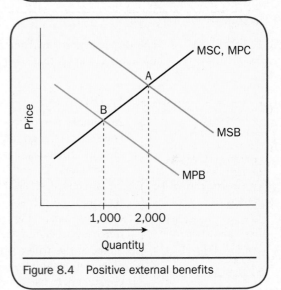

Figure 8.4   Positive external benefits

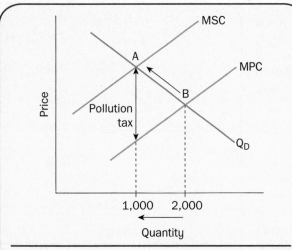

Figure 8.5   Dealing with externalities through taxation

The MPC is lower than the MSC, leading to over-production of the good from society's point of view. In order to encourage firms to produce less, the government can impose a tax. If the tax is set correctly, the MPC will become equal to the MSC, and result in private individuals choosing the same level of output as society.

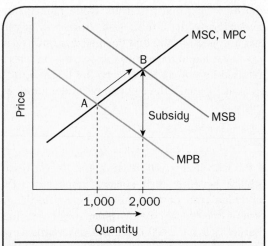

Figure 8.6   Dealing with externalities through subsidies

The MPB is lower than the MSB. As a result, private individuals under-consume the product. In order to increase the level of consumption, subsidies are offered to private individuals. This lowers the cost of consumption and individuals should consume more.

cars that are more environmentally friendly, and we saw in Chapter 4 when looking at the automotive market that strong growth had been seen in the alternative fuel market.

## Subsidies

A subsidy is a payment made to producers by government, which leads to a reduction in the market price of the product.

A merit good provides consumers with more benefits than they expect.

An alternative to taxation is **subsidy**. Subsidies make consumption, or production, cheaper for the private individual. For example, home improvements which enhance energy efficiency, such as loft and wall cavity insulation, are often subsidized by government. Clearly, with a subsidy more energy-efficient home improvements will be purchased, since they are cheaper. So, subsidies will be used when governments fear that the private level of output will be less than the socially optimal level of output. Consider Figure 8.6. The marginal private benefit, MPB, of an energy-efficient home is associated with lower electricity bills. The marginal social benefit, MSB, also includes the wider social benefits of a cleaner environment resulting from lower electricity generation. Hence, the MSB is greater than the MPB. In order to persuade consumers to use energy-efficient home improvements at the socially optimal level, a subsidy that is equal to the difference between MPB and MSB must be offered. This effectively reduces the price of energy-efficient home improvements and consumers buy in greater quantities.

Setting subsidies at the correct level can be difficult. Too little and consumers are unlikely to be incentivized. Too much and the cost becomes too large. The incentives also have to be aligned with the availability of complementary products and services. Box 8.7 highlights the importance of subsidizing electric cars in China, but the policy is constrained by the lack of charging points.

##  Merit, demerit and public goods

Economists categorize goods and services into particular groupings, including merit, demerit, public and private goods. **Merit goods** are seen by governments as providing

## Box 8.7
## China offers billions to subsidize electric cars on gas

China's ambitious plan to lower pollution by adopting five million electric cars is running into a problem—a lack of charging stations.

Eddy Wu, a Shanghai resident, bought a plug-in hybrid because the car was eco-friendly, subsidized by the government and exempt from licence-plate fees. Now he runs it mostly on gasoline, the electric capabilities largely wasted.

His apartment complex and office won't let him charge the BYD Co. vehicle in their parking lots, saying it poses a fire risk. Using the nearest public charging station means driving 5 kilometres (3 miles) and paying cash. With gas prices expected to tumble with the almost 40 per cent plunge in crude oil since June, there will even less incentive to charge his Qin sedan.

While a dearth of charging stations is holding back adoption of electric vehicles worldwide, the problem is particularly acute in China because the country has pledged to slash greenhouse emissions and cut a reliance on imported oil, while keeping domestic carmakers competitive amid an industry shift away from conventional gasoline-powered vehicles.

Demand for alternative-energy vehicles in China has been slow despite government subsidies that can reduce the cost of the cars by about 60,000 yuan ($9,750). As of September, the nation had achieved only 12 per cent of its target for alternative-energy vehicles to be introduced by 2015, according to government figures released last month. By 2020, the goal is to have 5 million of these autos on China's roads.

The vehicles also qualify for an exemption from a 10 per cent purchase tax, as well as free licence plates issued in cities including Shanghai, where plates for a conventional gasoline-powered auto can cost about $12,000.

The EU in October said it will cut emissions by 40 per cent in the four decades through 2030. Chinese President Xi Jinping pledged in November that his country's emissions will peak around 2030, as it boosts its use of renewable and nuclear energy. His announcement was made jointly with a pledge by US. President Barack Obama to slash emissions by 26 per cent to 28 per cent in the 20 years through 2025.

Dong Yang, secretary-general of the China Association of Automobile Manufacturers, urged the city of Beijing to speed up construction of charging stations in a blog post on Nov. 24.

'When plug-in hybrid owners decide whether to use electricity or gasoline, the determining factor is charging facilities,' Dong wrote. 'With the increase of charging facilities, the effects of reduced gas emissions from plug-in hybrid vehicles will become more apparent.'

The central government is considering spending as much as 100 billion yuan to build charging facilities and spur demand for new-energy vehicles, two people familiar with the matter said in August.

In Shanghai, the city's government plans to build 6,000 charging points by 2015, while it has a target of 13,000 alternative-energy vehicles on its roads during the same time frame. It's also working with companies including Bayerische Motoren Werke AG to build charging facilities.

When hybrid owners like Wu don't plug in their cars, their vehicles actually wind up using more gasoline than conventional cars, according to Hubertus Troska, Daimler's chief executive officer for the greater China region.

'You're carrying 150 kilos of electric components with you that add to the fuel consumption,' Troska told reporters in the city of Guangzhou last month. 'The effective reduction of emissions will only come if customers actually charge their plug-ins every day.'

From Bloomberg. 10 December 2014. 'China offers billions to subsidize electric cars on gas'. Alexandra Ho. Used with permission of Bloomberg L.P. Copyright © 2015. All rights reserved

greater benefits to consumers than consumers may recognize. Examples include education and health care and can often lead to positive externalities. Governments may support and promote the consumption of merit goods through subsidies, grants or cheap loans for university education, or communication policies promoting healthy eating or lifestyle choices. **Demerit goods** provide less benefit than consumers may recognize. Examples include smoking and drinking; and governments can seek to reduce consumption through higher taxes and restrictions on the advertising of such products.

> A demerit good provides consumers with fewer benefits than they expect.

Merit and demerit goods highlight a problem of **imperfect information**. For simple products, consumers are often capable of possessing complete (perfect) information about the product's important features. For example, if you buy fruit at the supermarket you can see if the fruit is ripe, fresh and undamaged. In contrast, if you are buying a mortgage or taking out a pension, then such products can be very complex, with different features, fees, options and penalties. When consumers do not understand all the features, or underestimate some of the risks associated with the product, then they have imperfect information and may make inappropriate consumption choices. Governments can address this problem by insisting that suppliers provide consumers with additional information. In the case of mortgages, borrowers are given key feature documents; and for alcohol and cigarettes health warnings are printed on packaging.

> Imperfect information exists when a consumer does not have all the facts relating to the key features of a product.
>
> A public good is a good that is both non-rivalrous and non-excludable.
>
> A good is non-rivalrous, if the consumption of the good does not prevent consumption by other consumers.
>
> A good is non-excludable, if suppliers cannot restrict supply to those consumers who have paid for the good.

**Public goods** display two important characteristics. Such goods are non-rivalrous and non-excludable. A good or service is **non-rivalrous** if the consumption of the good or service does not reduce the amount of consumption available to all other consumers. For example, if you listen to the radio, then you do not prevent anyone else from listening, but if you consume a soft drink, then no one else can consume the drink. A good or service is **non-excludable** if the supplier cannot restrict supply to those consumers who have paid. A car company can exclude you from car ownership if you do not pay the required price for the car. A radio company cannot exclude you from listening once it sends out a radio signal. Non-rivalrous and non-excludable make the free consumption of public goods very easy for consumers, but entirely unprofitable for suppliers. Hence, companies can decide not to supply and the market may fail.

In the past, common examples of public goods have included television and radio. Supply has been by public broadcasters who have financed themselves from a government subsidy or a licence fee levied on all households. Private-sector broadcasters financed themselves by showing adverts, rather than charging viewers. Now satellite and cable providers use encryption technologies to exclude viewers who have not paid for the service.

A more contemporary example of a public good is music and film. The availability of pirated music files and film for download from the Internet is both non-rivalrous and non-excludable. Without the prosecution of illegal downloaders for breaches of copyright and the closing of illegal download sites, suppliers would make less revenue, be less inclined to supply and the market could fail.

 ## Price volatility

The equilibrium prices for goods and services are not always stable. When demand and supply change, the equilibrium price of a good or service also changes. The more frequent the change in demand or supply, and the larger the change in demand or supply, the more unstable or volatile market equilibrium prices will be. These frequent and possibly large changes in equilibrium prices can make budgetary planning for households and firms very difficult; and perhaps more importantly, when prices are increasing household and firm budgets can come under pressure, leading to financial distress and hardship. In recent times we have seen large changes in fuel and food prices, as well as large increases in the price of important raw materials, such as copper, aluminium and rare earths used in smartphones.

In order to understand these prices changes it is necessary to utilize our understanding of markets developed in Chapter 4. The important factors which determine the scale of change in an equilibrium price are the amount of change in demand and supply and the price elasticity of demand and supply. Big drivers of demand changes have been the rising incomes of the emerging economies around the globe, such as China, India, Russia and Brazil. As incomes in these economies grow, there is an increase in demand for additional food stocks, increased demand for fuel and increased demand for raw materials, such as metals to enable the manufacture of cars, electronic consumables, property, roads, hospitals and factories. Developments in supply may not keep up with demand, leading to higher prices; and, where supply does grow, it is often high technology and/or high risk. For example, the world's insatiable demand for fuel supports high-risk exploration for oil, such as the Deepwater Horizon rig in the Gulf of Mexico. This rig, used by BP, caught fire, sank, leaked huge amounts of oil and reduced the supply of oil to the market. The global supply of commodities can also be constrained by the desire to secure national supply. When the wheat harvest in Russia failed in 2010, the Russian government cancelled all contracts to supply wheat outside Russia, ensuring domestic supply was protected. Such action resulted in a reduction of global supply and an increase in wheat prices, which impacted the price of bread, beer and other food items across Europe.

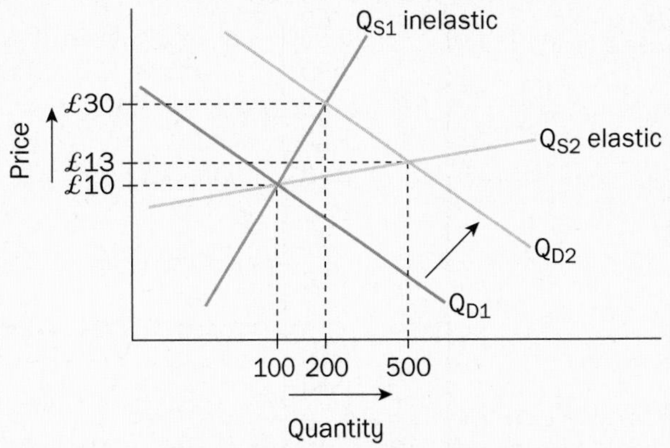

Inelastic demand or supply will only exacerbate any changes in demand and supply. In Figure 8.7 when supply is inelastic an increase in demand drives prices higher than when supply is elastic. Supply is likely to be inelastic when firms are unable to build additional supply, even when prices increase. New mines, new oil wells, new space for agriculture all require massive investment, which limits the development of supply.

In Figure 8.8 changes in supply move prices more when demand is inelastic. In the case of demand for stable food resources, energy and essential metals, demand is likely to be inelastic due to the lack of substitutes, hence greater changes in prices.

**Price volatility** is the variation in prices overtime. A price which changes by 5 per cent per month is not especially volatile when compared with a price which changes by 5 per cent, then 2 per cent, then 18 per cent, then 8 per cent. Measures of price volatility are, therefore, often achieved by measuring the **standard deviation** of prices over time.

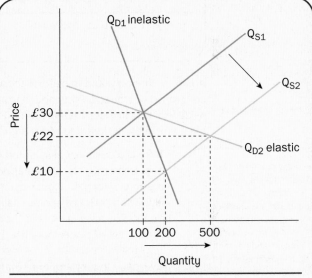

Figure 8.7    Impact of demand changes when supply is elastic or inelastic

Figure 8.8    Supply changes under elastic and inelastic demand

Figure 8.9 presents data on price changes at different stages of the value chain for food (see Chapter 7). We have farm gate, or agricultural commodity, prices; producer or factory prices; and consumer or retail prices. Price changes for agricultural commodity prices show the greatest variation, while consumer prices show the least amount of variation. This difference can, in part, be explained by changes in demand and supply and price elasticities. At the commodity level, changes in demand and supply of wheat are likely to be much bigger than the changes in final demand or supply for bread. Growing incomes around the world impact the demand for wheat, while bad harvests impact the supply. At the level of bread or beer, where wheat is an ingredient, there are not huge global forces influencing demand and supply. In addition, the demand elasticity for wheat is likely to be fairly inelastic as there are few substitutes for wheat, whereas consumers can, to some degree, substitute bread as a carbohydrate for potatoes and rice.

Other forces also impact price volatility at different stages in the value chain. Producers turn wheat into bread and thereby through the baking process add value. Retailers distribute

Price volatility measures how prices vary over time.

Standard deviation is a measure of how much a variable differs from its average value over time.

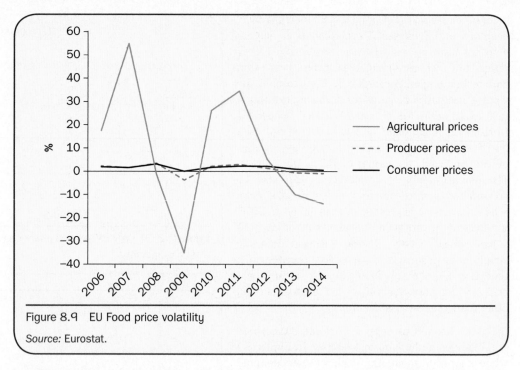

Figure 8.9    EU Food price volatility

*Source:* Eurostat.

bread to shoppers and therefore add value by making access to bread easy. Since bread is comprised of wheat, baking and distribution, the price component of wheat is less important as different value elements are added in. Hence, changes in wheat prices do not generate as big a variation in the price of bread.

> Menu costs are the costs associated with changing prices, which can include updating computer systems, printing new price lists, changing shelf price information.

There is also a cost associated with changing prices. Economists refer to these costs as **menu costs**. The more expensive the menu costs, the less likely a firm is to change its prices. Any gain from raising prices, for example, could be wiped out by the menu cost. There are few menu costs for wheat: buyers and sellers trade in a recognized commodity market in, say, London or Moscow, and they agree a price rather than follow a set of prices on a list. Bread, on the other hand, is sold by supermarkets and the price information is stored in computers, is listed on the shelf and maybe even advertised in newspapers. Changing the price is expensive.

Governments can try to bring some stability to the price of important staple items. Fuel has been targeted by the UK government through the fair fuel stabilizer. When crude oil rises above a certain price, then tax on the retail price of petrol and diesel will fall; and when the crude oil price falls below a certain price, then tax on the retail prices of petrol and diesel will increase. The reason why this policy may bring some stability in prices is that tax is a large part of the retail price of fuel and, in addition, petrol retailers are geared to, in fact experts at, changing prices quickly. You only have to see the large signs outside all petrol stations, which display the price, to see that the menu costs of changing prices are fairly simple. In contrast, while the price of the weekly shopping has also increased, the government has not sought to manage prices. There is little or no tax on most grocery items and much of the value added comes from manufacturing and retailing, not agriculture, so there is little or no scope to manage price changes in these markets.

## (8.10) Market power and competition policy

In Chapter 5 we compared perfect competition with monopoly and argued that under monopoly the price is higher and output is lower than under perfect competition. With the introduction of Pareto efficiency, we can now move on to show how monopoly, from the perspective of society, is not necessarily a desirable form of market structure.

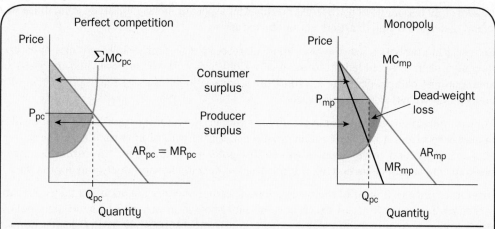

Figure 8.10   Welfare costs of monopoly

- The consumer surplus under perfect competition is greater than under monopoly simply because the price is lower under perfect competition.
- The producer surplus is greater under monopoly than under perfect competition simply because the price is higher under monopoly.
- However, the total of consumer and producer surplus is higher under perfect competition than under monopoly. This difference is known as the dead-weight loss of monopoly and represents a reduction in welfare to society. Since everyone can be made better off by moving to perfect competition, monopoly is not Pareto efficient.

In the left-hand side of Figure 8.10, we have perfect competition. The profit-maximizing level of output, $Q_{pc}$, is sold at a price of $P_{pc}$. *Consumer surplus* is the difference between the price a consumer is willing to pay and the price charged. In this case, the consumer surplus is the light-blue shaded area above the market price and below the demand curve. Consumer surplus is an important measure of welfare or well-being. If you are willing to pay £50 for a product and you can buy it for £30, then you are £20 better off.

Producers also have a surplus. **Producer surplus** is the difference between the price they would be willing to sell at and the price that they do sell at. Recall Chapter 5 and the discussion of profit maximization. Under the assumption of profit maximization, a firm is willing to supply one more unit of output if the price offered is greater than or equal to marginal cost. In this way, the firm at worst breaks even on the last unit supplied. So, given our definition of producer surplus and the concept of profit maximization, the firm is willing to sell at any price which is greater than marginal cost; we now only need the price that the firm sells at in order to measure producer surplus. In Figure 8.10, producer surplus is the darker blue area below the market price and above the marginal cost curve for the industry.

The case of monopoly is shown in the right-hand side of Figure 8.10. Under monopoly, the price increases and the output shrinks. Therefore, the consumer surplus must reduce. In contrast, because the monopoly sells at a higher price, producer surplus must increase. In essence, part of the consumer surplus is being transferred to the monopoly. However, and this is the important part, if we compare the total of consumer and producer surplus under perfect competition and monopoly, we can see that the total surplus is lower under monopoly. This difference is known as the **dead-weight loss** of monopoly. It is a loss of welfare to society. Under Pareto efficiency no one can be made better off without making someone else worse off. Monopoly is clearly not Pareto efficient because, if we change the market into a perfectly competitive one, then the deadweight loss will vanish. People can be made better off without making anyone else worse off. Essentially, more products are sold and sold at a lower price.

Producer surplus is the difference between the price that a firm is willing to sell at and the price it does sell at.

Dead-weight loss of monopoly is the loss of welfare to society resulting from the existence of the monopoly.

Dead-weight loss may not be the only detrimental aspect of monopoly. Many companies will spend resources trying to attain monopoly status.

Rent-seeking activities are the allocation of resources to non-socially optimal ends and they also need to be added on to the deadweight losses. However, following the ideas of an economist called Schumpeter, monopolies have enjoyed the academic protection of a concept known as 'creative destruction'.

For example, Microsoft is a global monopoly supplier of operating systems. If one innovator manages to invent a new and commercially successful way of operating computers, then Microsoft's position could be under threat. The potential to take over Microsoft's dominant position acts as a huge incentive for innovators to develop new products and approaches.

In terms of prices, output and deadweight losses, monopolies are not good, but they do create incentives for other firms to try to become monopolies. In order to become monopolies, firms invest in research and development. Innovation brings about the destruction of existing monopolies. So, rent-seeking behaviour, or the pursuit of monopoly, may actually create innovation, new products, new production processes and, hence, better economic efficiency. While these debates can be left to the academic economist, it is reasonably clear that monopolies can be suspected of being detrimental to economic performance, and it is with this view in mind that governments have developed competition policy.

## Competition policy

In the UK and the EU competition policy is focused on delivering fair competition and markets that function in the interest of consumers. Under UK and EU systems, the competition bodies are interested in removing cartels, preventing the abuse of dominant market positions by large companies and overseeing the merger and acquisition of companies which may lead to dominant positions. The EU also concerns itself with the competitive impact of state aid to national industries.

Within the EU, the home country normally takes the lead on competition policy, but will pass matters of concern to the EU Competition Commission if there is a significant EU element to the case: for example, if a cartel includes companies from a number of EU states, or a merger will create a dominant firm within the EU market.

> The Competition and Markets Authority investigates whether a monopoly, or a potential monopoly, significantly affects competition.

In the case of the UK, the Director General of Fair Trading supervises company behaviour and, when necessary, will refer individual companies to the UK **Competition and Markets Authority** for investigation. Companies can be referred if they are suspected of being involved in a cartel, are abusing a dominant position – for example, by using predatory pricing or, in the case of a merger, if the new combined firm will own more than 25 per cent of the market and/or the firm being acquired has turnover in excess of £70 million.

The focus of a UK Competition and Markets Authority inquiry is to establish whether there is a serious threat to competition. Should the Competition Commission establish that competition is under threat, then it has wide powers to make and enforce remedies.

If a UK merger or breach of competition has a European dimension, it can be examined by the European Commission for Competition. If the merged companies have a global turnover which exceeds €5 billion and turnover within the EU exceeds €250 million, then the EU Commission will investigate the merger. This investigation will occur even if the merging companies are not headquartered within the EU. The EU also evaluates mergers in terms of whether they will reduce competition. The EU has taken a fairly robust approach to situations which have reduced or threaten to reduce competition. Under the law, a company can be fined up to 10 per cent of its global turnover. In the case of Microsoft, which refused to follow EU restrictions imposed on its software, a fine of €899 million was imposed. In the case of Intel, which was accused of abusing a dominant position, a fine of €1.06 billion was imposed.

# Assessing government interventions

Government interventions to correct market failures can be costly and may not always be effective. In this section we examine how to evaluate government intervention and how to recognize some of the factors which are important in determining the effectiveness of policy interventions.

Government interventions are generally evaluated by a process known as **impact analysis** which seeks to understand the impact of a policy change by undertaking **cost–benefit analysis**. Under cost–benefit analysis all of the costs associated with an intervention are subtracted from all of the benefits. Different interventions, including no intervention, can then be compared by reference to the net monetary benefit of each intervention. Cost–benefit analysis is a very complicated process, since it is not easy to identify all costs and benefits, measuring all costs and benefits in monetary amounts may not be accurate, and even identifying who bears a cost and who gains a benefit may be debatable. Moreover, if time is also important—say the intervention lasts over many years—then it is also necessary to estimate how costs and benefits will develop over time and then apply an appropriate **discount factor or rate** (see Chapter 12, section 12.7). Choosing an appropriate discount factor can be very difficult when interventions are long lived.

As an example of some of the difficulties, consider subsidies for the development of nuclear power stations. Who benefits from lower carbon emissions into the environment, what are the benefits of lower carbon emissions and can these benefits be measured in monetary amounts? When considering the costs, decommissioning a nuclear plant and managing the waste become important. Since nuclear waste remains a problem for hundreds if not thousands of years, then at what rate do you discount the costs of dealing with the waste at say 100 years, 200 years and so on? It is fairly easy to discount a five-year project by simply taking the expected interest rate for the economy. But the interest rate might apply over an extremely long time horizon, such as 100 years.

In order for government policy to be effective, governments require a clear understanding of the problem. But just as consumers can suffer from imperfect information, so can governments. An example would be cost–benefit analysis. Since much of a cost–benefit analysis is an estimate, a government may choose a solution which looks good on paper, but in reality the costs may dramatically outweigh the benefits. To some extent, this can tackled by conducting cost–benefit analysis before and after implementation of the policy. Government agencies can also suffer from **regulatory capture**. A monopoly or group of dominant firms may be supervised by a regulator to ensure that prices are set at fair competitive levels rather than monopoly levels. The regulator will often need data from the regulated firms in order to set prices for the industry. The regulator is therefore reliant on those firms that it seeks to control. The regulated firms can then seek to influence (capture) the regulator and provide limited costing data and exaggerated investment demands in order to convince the regulator that prices need to rise higher for the firms to remain financially viable.

Finally, it is important to recognize the implications of second-best solutions. Under a **first-best solution** all market failures across the economy are removed and society's welfare is maximized. A first-best solution would see all industries as perfectly competitive and maximizing economic efficiency. A **second-best solution** is the best outcome that can be achieved when at least one market failure somewhere in the economy cannot be corrected. For example, it may be infeasible to convert a monopoly into a perfectly competitive industry. The second-best solution for the economy is not necessarily to leave all the other industries as perfectly competitive. The second-best solution for the economy often requires other distortions or market failures to be introduced into the economy by the government.

Impact analysis is a means of understanding the impact of a policy change on individuals and/or an economy.

Cost–benefit analysis provides a monetary evaluation of a government intervention.

Discount factor (or rate) provides a measure of the time value of money. If £100 saved for one year earns 2 per cent interest, at the end of year you will have £102. Equally, a cost of £102 in a year's time is worth £100 today.

Regulatory capture occurs when the regulated firms have some control or influence over the regulator.

In a first-best solution the economy has no market failures.

A second-best solution is the best outcome for an economy when at least one market failure cannot be corrected.

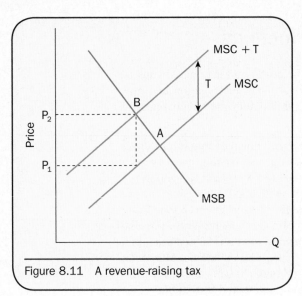

Figure 8.11 A revenue-raising tax

For example, if it is necessary to tax luxury cars to provide monetary support for the poor, then the tax will drive a wedge between the equilibrium marginal social cost and marginal social benefit for luxury cars. This is illustrated in Figure 8.11. Without the tax the marginal social benefit (MSB) and the marginal social cost (MSC) are in equilibrium at A. Adding a tax T, raises society's supply line to MSC + T and the equilibrium now occurs at B. Under the imposition of a tax, the marginal social benefit of luxury cars ($P_2$) exceeds the marginal social cost ($P_1$) and as such represents a market failure. If financial support for the poor is essential and the tax cannot be removed, then a second-best solution for the economy may require additional market failures by the imposition of taxes in other markets. As such, government policy in one area can have additional knock-on effects in order to achieve the second-best outcome.

## 8.12 Business application: carbon trading

Carbon dioxide, a greenhouse gas, is a by-product of burning fossil fuels such as oil and coal. Modern industrial economies consume vast amounts of energy on a daily basis and that energy is provided by burning fossil fuels. Oil and coal are used to generate electricity and are used to propel cars, lorries and aircraft. As a greenhouse gas, carbon dioxide is a pollutant. Unfortunately, the creation of carbon dioxide is an example of a negative externality. The marginal private cost of producing electricity does not reflect the full marginal social cost, which also includes the effects of pollution on the environment.

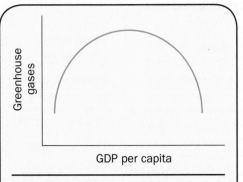

Figure 8.12 Environmental Kuznets curve

As GDP per capita increases, the production of greenhouse gases initially rises. When wealth and technical expertise reach a certain point, an economy's ability to develop alternative and environmentally friendly energy resources increases and the production of greenhouse gases falls.

Environmental and growth economists examine the rising production of greenhouse gases using an environmentally adapted Kuznets curve.[3] The environmental Kuznets curve shows an n-shaped relationship between the production of greenhouse gases and GDP per capita. This relationship is depicted in Figure 8.12. As an economy grows and GDP per capita rises, then a greater use of fossil fuel production results in the rising production of detrimental greenhouse gases. Once an economy reaches a certain size and affluence, then there is likely to be sufficient wealth and technical expertise to address the use of fossil fuels and the generation of greenhouse gases. Financial resource and engineering expertise can be allocated to the production of hybrid-fuel cars and wind-turbine generation of electricity. Therefore, in advanced high GDP per capita economies the production of greenhouse gases begins to decline.

The environmental Kuznets curve provides a useful framework for examining the rise in pollution around the world. Fast-growing economies, such as China and India, have rapidly increased GDP per capita and, as a consequence, have significantly added to the

---

[3]Kuznets's original analysis showed an n-shaped relationship between income inequality and GDP per capita. In the early stages of economic development, income growth is seen to flow to those individuals who own capital (and so are already affluent). In later stages of development, the provision of education to everyone enables non-capital owners to share in economic growth and so income inequalities fall.

global production of greenhouse gases. It is arguably unreasonable to ask these economies to avoid the use of fossil fuels and make greater use of environmentally friendly energy production. In particular, the developed economies of the world made ample use of fossil fuel technology throughout their own development, so why should China and India be expected to take a more expensive route to full economic development?

However, the Kuznets curve indicates that some of the additional greenhouse gases from developing economies can be balanced by a reduction in pollution from highly developed economies. Unfortunately, the statistical evidence relating to the environmental Kuznets curve suggests that even the USA, the world's largest economy, has not yet reached its peak.

In order to address the rise in greenhouse gases around the world, various governments have implemented schemes which aim to reduce carbon dioxide emissions. Two broad schemes are available. The first is the sale of licences to pollute; the second is permits to emit pollutants. In the former case, firms pay a fee for the right to pollute. If the fee is high enough, some firms may decide it is cheaper not to pollute. In the second system, governments issue permits which enable a given amount of pollution. This quantity-based system guarantees a direct impact on the amount of pollution, but the cost to polluters is unknown and determined by the market price for permits. Within Europe a cap-and-trade system has been adopted. This is a market for permits to emit and is a quantity-based system. The purpose of the scheme is two-fold. First, the scheme provides governments with a credible commitment to limit the number of permits. Second, the scheme provides benefits to firms that cut emissions and a penalty to those that do not. In understanding the need to credibly commit to a fixed number of permits, we will examine the **Coase conjecture**. We then move on to an examination of how the traded permit scheme provides financial incentives to limit pollution.

> The Coase conjecture argues that a monopoly provider of a durable good will sell at the perfectly competitive price.

Ronald Coase put forward the argument that a monopoly supplier of a durable good would have no monopoly pricing power and would sell all units of output at the perfectly competitive price. Consider a monopoly that can set prices for its durable good in two periods. In the first period, it will set a high price and sell to consumers who are desperate for the product today. In the second period, the monopoly has to set a price for all customers who decided to wait in period one. The monopoly clearly has an incentive to expand output and sell for a lower price in period two. If consumers correctly anticipate the monopoly's incentive to cut prices in period two and the good is durable, then more consumers will wait for period two. This then provides a greater incentive for the monopoly to mop up the residual demand in period two with yet more output and lower prices. In fact, it will be optimal for a monopoly to sell at the perfectly competitive price in all periods.

If a government was to sell licences to pollute, then it could be considered a monopoly provider of a durable good. The government could sell licences in period one and claim that, in order to reduce pollution, the number of licences in period two will be less. The implicit threat is that firms should buy their licences today. Unfortunately, following the Coase conjecture, this threat is not a credible commitment. Polluting firms will expect the government to take the opportunity to raise revenues by selling more licences in period two at close to the competitive price. The clear incentive for firms is to wait for the cheaper licences and expand pollution in period two.

The solution to this problem is for the government not to sell durable licences. Instead, the government should lease licences for a given period. Through leasing, the licences become non-durable. In period one, a firm buys its requirement of licences. At the end of period one, the licences become obsolete and the firm is required to buy more in period two. The government is now a monopoly supplier of consumable goods in each period. It can charge the monopoly price and so faces no incentive to expand the output of permits in each subsequent period. With a credible commitment to a fixed or falling number of permits in each future period, the government is better placed to reduce pollution.

In practice, the European system for controlling carbon emissions involves governments setting an emissions cap. Permits to pollute equal to the cap are then allocated to industries. Companies with a surplus of permits trade with those that have a shortage. In essence, there is a market in pollution permits. But importantly, the size of this market is credibly limited by the governments' decision to lease permits for one year. If a firm wishes to pollute more, then it must pay for extra permits. And paying is the crucial aspect. Through the market, paying for the right to pollute increases the marginal private cost faced by polluting firms. As such, it should reduce the equilibrium level of pollution. In essence, the requirement to pay for the right to pollute is nothing more than a tax on excessive polluters. At the same time, clean producers are in effect subsidized by being able to sell their surplus permits at a profit, concepts which we discussed in section 8.7.

An important feature of this solution is that it generates an opportunity cost. Polluters are faced with a trade-off. They can either buy more credits to meet their level of pollution, or they can decide to invest in new technology which is more environmentally friendly. The market for carbon permits provides firms with an alternative option and price. As permit prices rise, then it is hoped that the attractiveness of investment in cleaner technology will increase, helping to reduce long-term pollution levels. Of course, the price of permits may just as easily fall. There is a concern that too many permits were allocated during the launch phase of the carbon trading system in Europe. This resulted in a significant price fall for each permit to pollute with one ton of carbon. Governments now have this under control. Each year the supply of permits will be reduced. Our understanding of markets assures us that a reduction in supply will lead to an increase in the equilibrium price. But, of course, a recession reduces the demand for goods, which reduces the demand for energy and the demand for permits.

It should also be recognized that there are problems with a system which penalizes polluters. In a global economy there is the risk that environmental policies in Europe place heavy users of fossil fuels at a cost disadvantage relative to rivals in China, where there is no environmental tax for producing greenhouse gases. In fact, much of this risk is minimal when we consider the overall economy. Services are the major engine of economic activity and are light users of energy. Even in manufacturing, estimates indicate that energy costs represent less than 1 per cent of making cars and furniture. Heavy users of fossil fuels, such as electricity generators, do not compete internationally and so much of the cost increase from carbon permits is passed on to domestic customers.

The biggest issue remains in supplying the most appropriate level of credits to arrive at an equilibrium price which incentivizes firms to invest in low-carbon technology. Read some of the issues in Box 8.8.

##  Business data application: impact analysis and smart metering

Government departments at both national and supranational level are good sources of impact analysis and cost–benefit analysis reports and data. All proposed policy changes are now routinely examined and assessed for the ability to deliver net benefits to society.

Smart meters are an interesting example of a government policy which seeks to tackle a possible market failure, may achieve positive externalities and has been impact assessed using cost–benefit analysis. See Box 8.9 for more details.

Currently electricity and gas consumption within most homes and businesses is recorded using simple technologies. The meters in current use do not enable end-users to monitor usage minute by minute, do not enable energy suppliers to record usage and bill remotely, or make it possible for energy suppliers to control and activate household appliances during periods of non-peak consumption.

## Box 8.8
## European carbon market reform set for 2019

Reforms to strengthen the EU's flagship policy for cutting carbon, the emissions trading scheme (ETS), will start at the end of 2018 following a vote by MEPs on Tuesday.

The carbon market is supposed to drive Europe's transition to cleaner sources of energy, but a cocktail of recession, free allocations to polluters and over-achievement on green energy targets have created a flood of 2 billion allowances. That has led to a carbon price of around €7 (£5) per tonne, too low to encourage power companies to switch from polluting fuels such as coal.

Under the new compromise proposal, around 1.6 billion surplus allowances will be taken off the market and put into a market reserve, two years ahead of the commission's preferred timetable.

The market reform should prevent nightmare scenarios, such as a 4.5 billion carbon credit glut by 2020 forecast by the environmental think tank Sandbag. A new report today by analysts Reuters Thomson Point Carbon estimates that by 2020, the reforms could nudge carbon prices up to €20 per tonne. From April, the UK will have its own carbon floor price of £18 a tonne, pushing British prices close to the €30 a tonne price envisaged at the ETS's inception, which could trigger fuel switching from coal to gas.

But environmentalists argue that the reforms do not dispatch underlying questions about the ETS's effectiveness as 400 million allowances will be allowed to trickle back on to the market before 2030. Another 300 million carbon credits will go to an innovation fund, whose low-carbon credentials are yet to be proved. In the meantime, the delay until 2019 will allow further carbon allowance surpluses to accrue.

'Postponing necessary reforms until 2019 is simply irresponsible in times of a climate crisis,' said Femke de Jong, a policy officer at Carbon Market Watch. 'Every year we wait with setting up the reserve, the surplus that is suffocating the EU carbon market will grow bigger, pushing the EU's cornerstone climate instrument closer to the brink of collapse.'

The EU expects carbon markets to play a major part in international emissions cutting efforts, and UN-accredited offsetting under an exotic array of schemes can be used by countries to meet their carbon-reduction targets.

Carbon-trading schemes have already been set up in South Korea, California and Quebec, with China due to roll out a regional carbon market next year that could fully cover the country by 2020. International spot carbon prices vary from around US$13 (£8.4) a tonne in California to $6 a tonne in China and $9 a tonne in South Korea.

From *The Guardian*. 24 February 2015. 'European carbon market reform set for 2019'. Arthur Neslen. © Guardian News & Media Ltd 2015

The benefits from smart metering could be enormous. With the provision of real-time consumption information within the home, households can identify and reduce excess consumption by perhaps unplugging devices in stand-by mode. Suppliers can reduce visits to properties and staffing levels in customer support centres; and finally by being able remotely to operate washing machines, refrigerators and charge points for motor vehicles during low peak demand, energy suppliers can smooth demand and operating expenses.

The technology to support smart metering already exists and for gas and electricity metering would cost around £200 per property. However, adoption of smart metering may be limited due to an inability to achieve interoperability, which is the primary reason for a government roll-out. Interoperability occurs when different systems, devices and technologies can communicate with each other. If energy suppliers install different smart meters, there is a risk that, when one household switches energy supplier, their meters will also need to be changed in order to interface with the new supplier's system. Such a scenario adds cost and limits the payback to the energy supplier from smart metering and may result in a very limited roll-out to households. If the government wishes to see large-scale adoption of smart metering, then it needs to address the failure. By ruling on what communication technologies and standards can be used in smart meters, the government can create an interoperable system. An interoperable system that can be used and exploited by all users, suppliers and consumers will generate greater usage and therefore wider network-driven positive externalities. But is it worth paying for? Impact assessment and cost–benefit analysis now becomes useful.

Costs of installing and operating the system of smart meters have been estimated at £6.29 billion by the government. Network communication costs are estimated at £2.11 billion. Information technology cost of £1 billion and other costs including set-up, disposal and marketing are estimated at £1.33 billion, bringing total costs to £10.75 billion.

Benefits to consumers, mostly made up of energy savings, are estimated at £4.64 billion. Benefits to suppliers total £8.57 billion, including avoided site visits of £3.18 billion and reduced enquiries and customer overheads of £1.24 billion. Improved network benefits of £780 million, reduced generation benefits of £774 million and a reduced carbon permit bill of £1.1 billion lead to a total benefits package of £15.83 billion, meaning the net benefit to the economy of smart metering is in the region of £5 billion.

It should be clear from the estimated benefits that suppliers gain the most from smart metering. But if suppliers were to invest and install smart meters, then the flow of financial benefits to suppliers would only last while the household was a customer. The flow of costs and benefits has been calculated over a 20-year period and it is therefore extremely likely that the household would change energy supplier during that time. Switching supplier limits the value of the smart-meter energy suppliers, so the government is arguably right

## Box 8.9
## Smart meters

Smart meters that would enable people to see their own energy use in real time will not be delivered on time on current form, depriving households of a cheap and easy way of cutting down on their energy bills, an influential group of MPs has warned.

If the meters were rolled out on schedule, with 53 million of them in total installed in each of the UK's 30 million homes and small businesses by 2020, the savings in energy efficiency could amount to £17 billion across the country, against a likely cost of up to £11 billion to be met by consumers.

Plans for a national roll-out of smart meters to every household have been in the works for more than five years. Baroness McDonagh, chair of Smart Energy GB, the organization charged by the government with informing the public on smart meters, said the roll-out would be 'one of the largest upgrades to the nation's infrastructure that we have seen in a generation. We have an important task ahead of us to engage the whole country to ensure that every household and microbusiness will take advantage of this new technology and transform their experience of buying gas and electricity.'

One key delay has been an argument between utilities and the government on how much of the £200 cost of each installation should ultimately be added to consumer bills. For utilities, the meters are attractive because they remove the need for meter readers to visit peoples' homes, and they supply detailed data

on customer consumption, which can be used to tailor their tariffs or for other purposes. But if consumers use the meters to cut down on the energy they waste, the utilities could lose out on sales in the longer term.

The devices, which households can use to control their electricity use and heating, come in varying degrees of complexity, with simple meters showing consumption in real time, and more expensive models capable of altering the demand for electricity from appliances—for instance, by turning down fridges for short periods.

This variation has been another source of delay, as companies have wrangled over what functions should be standard, and the government has been reluctant to dictate detailed technical specifications.

Lawrence Slade, chief executive of Energy UK, which represents the industry, said: 'The national roll-out of smart meters is one of the most significant infrastructure projects that the energy sector has seen for years. It will make estimated bills a thing of the past, help improve energy efficiency and be of great value to consumers. As with any project of this size there are many challenges to overcome and government support is essential. However, the industry is committed to facing these challenges, finding cost-effective, practical solutions for consumers.'

From *The Guardian*. 7 March 2015. 'Smart meters may not be delivered to UK homes on time, MPs warn'. Fiona Harvey. © Guardian News & Media Ltd 2015

to be concerned that despite the benefits, energy suppliers will not invest in smart meters. However, if the government uses its powers to set communication standards to achieve interoperability, the entire industry will benefit from all households having smart meters, regardless of which company first installed the meters.

In reviewing the UK government's impact assessment of smart metering, we can see how obvious costs and benefits have been identified and then estimated. The estimation is based on reasonably sound evidence. For example, suppliers are asked to supply costs of activities such as meter reading. Reports and studies of energy reduction following the installation of smart meters are read and reviewed. But the estimated net benefit of £5 billion may still require some additional refinement. Will costs escalate? What factors might cause installation to be higher? Will the technology become cheaper over time? In terms of benefits, do smart meters reduce consumption and, if the large benefits are to be found in fewer site visits and lower customer enquiries, how confident are we that these benefits will be realized? All of these issues can be addressed by careful consideration and further investigation of the financial data and perhaps with the use of statistical techniques for finding a range of likely costs and benefits, rather than single estimates of costs and benefits.

## Summary

1. It is debatable whether firms are profit-maximizers. Measuring marginal revenue and marginal cost can be difficult in practice.

2. The owners of modern corporations are often very different from the managers. This is known as *separation of ownership from control.*

3. If shareholders are unable to control managers, the potential exists for managers to pursue their own objectives. Various objectives have been put forward by economists, including the consumption of perquisites, growth maximization and sales maximization.

4. Managers can be incentivized to work in the interests of shareholders by also making them shareholders. This is commonly achieved through the use of stock options.

5. Financial incentives such as stock options are only useful if four criteria are met:
   - managers are not overly risk averse
   - there is a link between manager effort and measured performance
   - performance is not focused on single activities to the detriment of other key activities or tasks
   - managers cannot falsely manipulate the performance measure, such as the share price.

6. Pareto efficiency occurs when no one can be made better off without making someone else worse off.

7. Externalities exist when the costs or benefits from consumption or production are not borne entirely by the person undertaking the production or consumption.

8. The existence of externalities leads to a difference between the socially optimal level of output and the private optimal level of output.

9. The optimal level of output can be targeted by the introduction of taxes and subsidies.

10. Monopoly can result in a deadweight loss, or lower welfare for society, when compared with perfect competition.

11. Competition policy in the UK provides a pragmatic solution to the problems presented by monopolies.

12. The Coase conjecture argues that monopoly providers of durable goods are incapable of exploiting their monopoly power.

13. An impact assessment seeks to understand and measure the cost and benefits of a new policy.

## Learning checklist

You should now be able to:

- Explain the difference between a principal and an agent
- Highlight the nature of the principal–agent problem
- Explain what is meant by the separation of ownership from control
- Provide a discussion of alternative theories of profit maximization
- Explain the concepts of positive and negative externalities, and provide examples
- Explain what is meant by the term 'market failure'
- Provide an explanation and evaluation of how taxes and subsidies can be used to correct market failures
- Discuss how competition legislation functions in the UK
- Explain how stock options align the interests of managers and shareholders
- Provide an economic evaluation of carbon pollution permits
- Review and evaluate an impact assessment.

## Questions                                                                    connect

1. Is profit maximization a reasonable assumption of firm behaviour?

2. Why might managers prefer to maximize sales or firm size?

3. A firm with managers and shareholders has separation of ownership from control. Why is this a potential problem for shareholders?

4. List examples where managers have been found to indulge in the consumption of perquisites.

5. What is a principal and what is an agent? Provide examples.

6. Why might performance contracts better align the interests of principals and agents? Again, provide examples.

7. Is it always possible to use performance contracts to discipline agents?

8. How do the marginal social cost and the marginal social benefit differ from marginal cost and marginal benefit?

9. List four negative externalities and four positive externalities.

10. How might taxes and subsidies be used to combat externalities?

11. If the marginal social cost of production exceeds the marginal private cost, then the price of production to firms is too low. Is this true and what is the solution?

12. Will a management buyout of a company increase, or decrease, agency costs?

13. Draw a diagram of MSB and MPB of train travel in rural and semirural areas. Illustrate how a subsidy might improve usage of train travel.

14. Assess the benefits of paying managers with capital rather than with income.

15. Assess the likely factors that will limit the ability of carbon trading to reduce global emissions of carbon dioxide.

16. Consider the situation where a private firm produces a widget whereby a harmful toxin is produced as a by-product of the production process. The firm releases these toxins as effluents into a local river (there are no laws forbidding this practice) thereby causing pollution and harm to marine life.

Assume that the firm is a price taker. The diagram provided shows the demand curve for the product sold by the private firm. MPC shows the marginal private cost which does not take into account the costs of pollution and clean-up. On the diagram provided, please draw the marginal social cost (MSC) schedule.

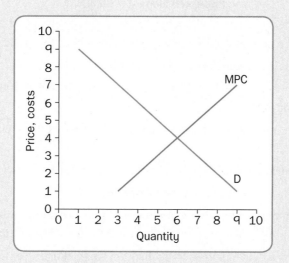

 INTERMEDIATE

 DIFFICULT

## Exercises

1. True or false?

   (a) Worker absence is highest on Mondays. This is an example of agency costs.

   (b) Risk-averse workers need to be compensated with higher rates of contingent pay.

   (c) Managers are said to suffer from shareholders' free riding on their hard work.

   (d) The marginal social benefit of education is likely to exceed the marginal private benefit.

   (e) A negative externality can occur when the marginal private cost is less than the marginal social cost.

   (f) Subsidizing the marginal private cost of polluters will help to reduce the amount of pollution.

EASY

2. Figure 8.13 shows the market for a good in which there is a negative production externality such that marginal social cost (MSC) is above marginal private cost (MPC). The MSB represents the marginal social benefit derived from consumption of the good.

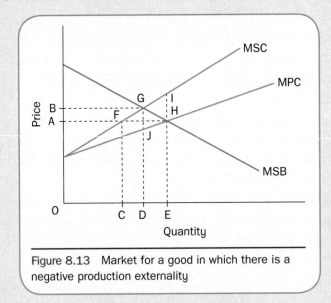

Figure 8.13   Market for a good in which there is a negative production externality

(a) If this market is unregulated, what quantity of this good will be produced?

(b) What is the socially efficient quantity?

(c) What is the amount of the deadweight loss to society if the free-market quantity is produced?

(d) What level of tax on the good would ensure that the socially efficient quantity is produced?

(e) Suggest an example of a situation in which this analysis might be relevant.

3. When considering these questions, refer to Box 8.8:

(a) Assuming a higher demand for coal increases demand for permits, draw a demand and supply diagram which illustrates the increase in price of permits.

(b) Draw a demand-and-supply diagram which illustrates the argument that the higher price of permits reflects a shortage of supply.

(c) Evaluate how effective carbon trading will be in reducing carbon emissions.

Section

4

# Domestic macroeconomics

## Section contents

Chapter

# Introduction to the macroeconomy

9

## Chapter contents

## Learning outcomes

By the end of this chapter you should be able to:

**Economic theory**

LO1 Explain the key concepts of GDP, inflation, unemployment and the balance of payments

LO2 Identify the business cycle

LO3 Describe the circular flow of income

LO4 Identity leakages and injections

LO5 Use aggregate demand and aggregate supply analysis

LO6 Demonstrate how changes in aggregate demand and supply lead to changes in equilibrium GDP and inflation

**Business application**

LO7 Assess how to optimize investment decisions by understanding the business cycle

LO8 Discuss how to use income elasticities to profit during a recession

LO9 Collect, interpret and use data on the important components of aggregate demand

## At a glance  Macroeconomics

### The issue

The business cycle, consisting of moderate economic activity, fast or booming economic growth and recessions, drives changes in the consumption levels of consumers and firms. Predicting the business cycle and positioning the firm for changes in economic activity are crucial for financial success.

### The understanding

In simple terms, we can understand changes in macroeconomic activity as resulting from changes in overall demand and supply in the economy. In an economic boom, overall demand or supply in the economy can be rising, while in a recession, overall demand or supply can be falling. Therefore, predicting the business cycle rests on predicting economy-level demand and supply.

### The usefulness

In order to survive, firms have to be financially successful in recessions as well as booms. By anticipating when the economy is likely to peak, or bottom out, firms can plan their investments in new products, new production facilities or new retail outlets. They can also change their product offerings to reflect different consumer preferences during booms and recessions.

## 9.1  Business problem: business cycles and economic uncertainty

In the first eight chapters of this book we have concentrated on topics that fall under microeconomics, including markets, competition and profits. Chapter 1 also highlighted macroeconomics as the other major area of economic study, which includes topics such as inflation, growth rates, government spending and taxation, interest rates and exchange rates. The second half of the book will now concentrate on these topics.

Understanding the macroeconomic environment is of crucial importance to business. Just like private individuals, business also needs to take financial decisions. An individual might decide to buy a house, while a firm might decide to buy a new production facility.

Consider buying a house: two significant issues need addressing. How much should you offer for the house and how much can you afford to borrow?

When valuing the house you will need to consider whether the market price will fall in the near future, perhaps during a recession. Similarly, when thinking about how much you can borrow, you need to think about how much you will earn in the future. Will you be made unemployed during a recession? Furthermore, will an increase in interest rates make mortgage repayments impossible for you to meet?

A business deciding whether to spend many millions of pounds on a new production facility will go through the same process. What is the plant worth? How much can the business afford to borrow? Will a new facility be needed if consumer demand falls during a recession? Will changes in interest rates make the investment unprofitable?

Therefore, just like individuals, firms need to think very carefully when committing themselves to investment projects, because the *business cycle* will affect the success of the investment.

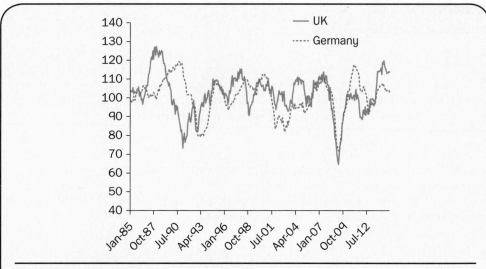

Figure 9.1   Economic sentiment indicator

*Source:* http:ec.europa.eu

Economic sentiment is one measure of confidence in the economy and combines the views of consumers and firms within one measure. The higher the number the more confident consumers and firms are about the future prospects for the economy.

GDP, gross domestic product, is a measure of the total output produced by an economy in a given year.

Inflation is the rate of change in the average price level. Inflation of 2 per cent indicates that prices have risen by 2 per cent during the previous 12 months.

Unemployment is the number of individuals seeking work that do not currently have a job.

Trade deficit is the difference between exported and imported goods and services.

Figure 9.1 presents data on economic sentiment in Germany and the UK for the last 30 years. **Economic sentiment** is a composite measure of how confident various important groups are feeling about the future prospects of the economy. The groups include consumers, industrial companies, service companies and retailers.

Apart from the financial crisis in 2008, the economic sentiment in the UK and Germany has not been perfectly synchronized. When economic sentiment improves in the UK, it does not necessarily improve at the same time or by the same amount in Germany. See for example the period between 2009 and 2012. Economic sentiment improved by more and for longer in the UK.

Box 9.1 shows that the formation of economic sentiment is driven by a mixture of real and possible events. In the case of Germany, real events such as increase in production in the automotive sector help to support improving sentiment. However, possible risks, such as a Greek exit from the euro can act as a brake on improved economic confidence/sentiment.

Clearly, an understanding of how the economy works and how it is likely to develop in the short, medium and long term is of crucial importance. Firms that make bad decisions will suffer financially. Firms that understand the macroeconomy and plan expansion and consolidation of the business at the right times are more likely to prosper.

In this chapter we will provide an overview of recent macroeconomic activity. In addition, we will provide a basic understanding of how the business cycle occurs, introducing the circular flow of income and then developing our application of the demand and supply framework used in the microeconomic section of this book. This will then provide the basis for an assessment of government economic policy in later chapters.

 ## 9.2 Macroeconomic issues

### Key macroeconomic outputs

Macroeconomics studies the workings of the entire economy. In Figure 9.2, we have charted four key macroeconomic issues: **GDP, inflation, unemployment** and the **trade deficit**.

## Box 9.1
## German business confidence rises as QE outweighs Greece

German business confidence rose for a fourth month as faster economic growth and optimism over European Central Bank stimulus outweighed fears of a worsening Greek crisis.

Growth in Europe's largest economy is accelerating amid lower oil prices and a weaker euro, and Germany's Bundesbank plans to increase its forecasts for 2015. With the ECB set to start buying 60 billion euros ($68 billion) a month of debt to bolster the euro-area economy, the risk of a Greek default and exit from the union hasn't weighed much on business sentiment.

The report signals that 'German businesses never feared a full escalation of the Greek crisis or were at least not afraid of a Grexit,' said Carsten Brzeski, chief economist at ING-DiBa AG in Frankfurt. 'Improved expectations signal a strong belief in the benefits of the ECB's quantitative easing.'

The euro extended its decline and was down 0.5 per cent at $1.1324 at 10:07 a.m. Frankfurt time. Germany's DAX Index of stocks was up 0.5 per cent at 11,103.

In Germany, manufacturing grew and services picked up pace in February, according to a Purchasing Managers Index by Markit Economics. Rheinmetall AG, a maker of car parts and defence equipment, reported 2014 profits exceeded its estimates because of record earnings at the auto-components unit.

The Bundesbank said on 16 February that 2015 growth will probably exceed its December forecast of 1 per cent. The European Commission this month forecast 1.5 per cent.

German investor confidence rose to the highest level in a year in February, buoyed by the imminent arrival of fresh central-bank stimulus.

'We do see significant potential for a larger step-up in German growth,' said Greg Fuzesi, an economist at JPMorgan Chase & Co. in London. 'Growth may even accelerate a bit further as commodity prices reach their lows in the current quarter and the growth contributions from the currency and sentiment rise.'

From Bloomberg. 23 February 2015. 'German business confidence rises as QE outweighs Greece'. Alessandro Speciale. Used with permission of Bloomberg L.P. Copyright © 2015. All rights reserved

It can be argued that Figure 9.2 represents the key measures of an economy: growth in GDP, or the improvement in economic activity; price stability via inflation; unemployment and success in trade overseas. For an economy to be functioning well, each of these outputs needs to be controlled and managed, with governments targeting higher economic growth, improved price stability, low unemployment and growing, but balanced, international trade.

## Key macroeconomic inputs

The key policy inputs controlled by government or the central bank are **interest rates** and the **government deficit**, as shown in Figure 9.3.

Managing the macroeconomy is like flying a plane. A pilot will look at the instrument panel, check the height and speed of their own plane, perhaps take account of other planes' positions, monitor engine performance and fuel use. If any of the characteristics of the plane's flight are not to the pilot's satisfaction, then inputs will be changed—faster engine speeds, higher altitudes or a change in direction.

Governments do the same with economies. They look at the outputs of the economy in Figure 9.2 and examine the performance of the economy. If governments do not like what they see, they change the inputs described in Figure 9.3. Sometimes governments make successful take-offs and landings; other times they create monumental crashes.

> Interest rates are the price of money and are set by the central bank.
>
> Government deficit is the difference between government spending and tax receipts. Just as students run up overdrafts, spending more than they earn, so too does the government.

## Changes in key macroeconomic variables

It is clear from looking at Figure 9.2 that GDP, inflation, unemployment and the trade deficit are continuously changing. To begin our analysis, let us concentrate on two time periods: the early 2000s and the early 2010s.

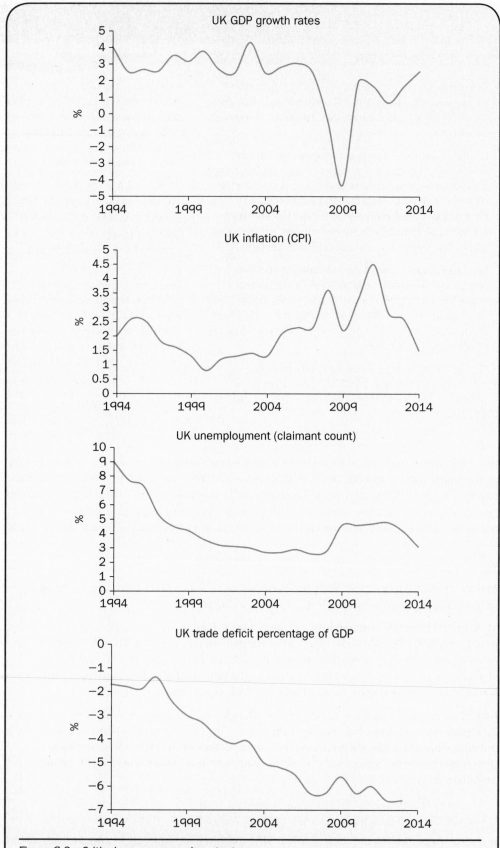

Figure 9.2   Critical macroeconomic outputs

*Source:* The UK Office for National Statistics, www.ons.gov.uk.

In the early 2000s:

(a) Inflation was low.

(b) The government cut interest rates (see Figure 9.3).

(c) Low interest rates led to increased borrowing, faster spending growth and rising GDP.

(d) Unemployment fell.

(e) Taxation was cut, government spending increased and the budget deficit grew.

(f) The current account went into a large deficit, with imports exceeding exports.

In the early 2010s:

(a) Inflation was high before falling back.

(b) Interest rates were low because growth was weak.

(c) Unemployment was rising.

(d) The government deficit was large and tax increases and spending cuts were being implemented.

(e) The current account was still in deficit.

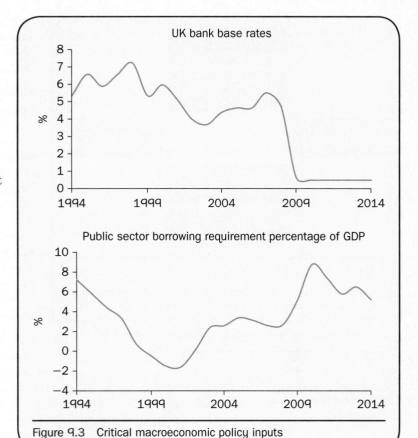

Figure 9.3   Critical macroeconomic policy inputs

## Observations and comments

1. The economic conditions of the early 2010s, with weak GDP, rising unemployment and inflation, were disastrous when compared with the low-inflation, fast-growing economy of the early 2000s.

2. Given such problems, how does a government set and prioritize its objectives? Is low inflation more important than high GDP? Is unemployment acceptable? Should the government manage its deficit and should the current account be in surplus? In Chapter 10 we will return to this question and provide a review of how each key macroeconomic variable is measured, provide a review of the issues associated with each variable and, more important, the objectives generally set by government for each key macroeconomic variable.

3. Finally, why are GDP, inflation, unemployment, the current account, interest rates and government deficits all linked?

In the remainder of this chapter we will introduce the circular flow of income as a means of describing some of the linkages between the macroeconomic variables. We will then develop this analysis by adapting our supply and demand framework utilized in the microeconomic section of this book. By the end of this chapter you will be able to answer question 3. As we progress through Chapters 11, 12 and 13, you will develop your understanding of how governments can use different policies to manage the links within the macroeconomy.

 **9.3  The circular flow of income**

In contrast to microeconomics, which examined product-specific markets such as those for pizzas or cars, macroeconomics focuses upon the workings of the whole economy. In order to begin our understanding of the macroeconomy, we will introduce the

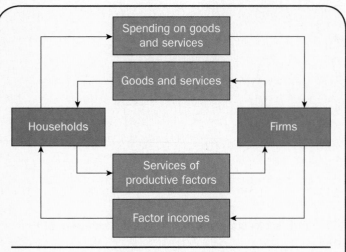

Figure 9.4   The circular flow of income

The circular flow of income captures the flow of economic resources and goods and services between households and firms. These flows of economic units are then mirrored by a flow of financial payments, which we refer to as the circular flow of income.

circular **flow of income** as a descriptive framework of macroeconomic activity. Figure 9.4 provides an illustration of the circular flow of income.

Within the framework of the circular flow of income, households are assumed to own the factors of production—land, labour, capital and enterprise. As producers of goods and services, firms need to use the factors of production owned by the households. Firms will clearly provide households with a financial reward for using the factors of production. In the case of labour, the financial reward is wages. Households will then use the money they have earned from firms to buy the finished goods and services, thus returning cash to the firms. A virtuous circle or, in our terminology, a circular flow of income is seen to exist.

The inner loop captures the flow of resources between the two sectors. For example, resources such as labour flow to firms from households, and then goods and services flow from firms back to households. The outer loop captures the corresponding financial flows between the two sectors. Firms pay households wages for supplying labour resources. In return, households use their income to purchase the goods and services sold by the firms.

The circular flow of income captures the essential essence of macroeconomic activity. The economy is seen as nothing more than a revolving flow of goods, production resources and financial payments. The faster the flow, the higher the level of economic output.

The level of income activity within an economy is measured as gross domestic product.

## Leakages and injections

The economy described in Figure 9.3 and Figure 9.4 contains only firms and households, which produce goods and spend income on goods and services. We can begin to broaden the circular flow to take account of saving by households, investment by firms, government spending and taxation, and international trade.

In order to account for these additional items we need to understand how **leakages** and **injections** fit into the circular flow of income.

### Savings and investments

Rather than spend all income on goods and services, households could save a proportion of their income. Because income is being taken from the circular flow of income and saved, it represents a leakage. But an important question relates to where these savings go. If the money is placed on deposit at the bank, then the bank will try to lend the money for profit. Borrowers are likely to be firms seeking to invest in equipment, or needing to fund overdrafts. If firms invest in capital equipment, then they are buying goods and services from other firms. As a result, investment is spending in the economy that does not come from the income earned by households. As such, investments represent an injection of financial resource and spending, by firms, into the circular flow. In equilibrium, savings will

**Circular flow of income** shows the flow of inputs, outputs and payments between households and firms within an economy.

**Leakage** from the circular flow is income not spent on goods and services within the economy. Leakages can be savings, taxation and imports.

**Injection** into the circular flow is additional spending on goods and services that does not come from the income earned by households in the inner loop. Injections can be investment, government spending and exports.

equal investments. This is because banks will set an interest rate where the supply of funds from savers equals the demand for funds by investing firms.

## Taxes and government spending

Government taxes the earnings of individuals and companies. Tax payments represent a leakage from the circular flow of income as they reduce the ability of households to spend on goods and services. However, the government also undertakes a number of activities that inject financial resources back into the economy. Governments buy hospitals and schools. They employ nurses and teachers. They also pay social benefits to the needy. All of which are injections.

## Exports and imports

Finally, some consumption by households will be on goods made in other economies. If you buy a German car, then this represents a leakage from the UK circular flow of income, as it is income spent in another economy. However, an injection will occur if a German spends money on a British car, as this represents an export.

The various leakages and injections are illustrated in Figure 9.5, which simply extends the circular flow of income. On the left of Figure 9.5, savings, taxation and imports leak from the income households could spend on consumption. On the right of Figure 9.5, investments, government spending and exports inject spending into the circular flow of income.

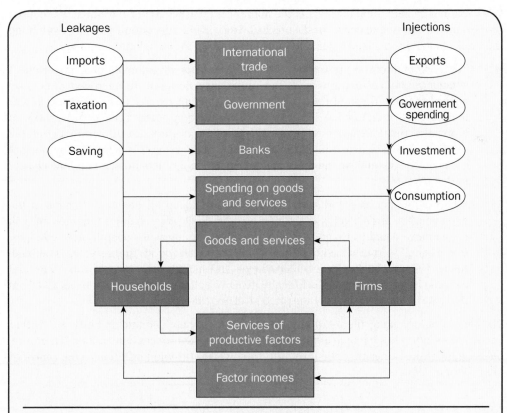

Figure 9.5 Circular flow of income with leakages and injections

Leakages from the circular flow of income take the form of savings, taxes and imports. These are financial flows which do not head straight back into household consumption. Injections into the circular flow of income include investment spending, government spending and exports. These expenditures add to household consumption expenditure in the economy.

## Total expenditure

> Total expenditure is equal to consumption, plus investment, plus government spending, plus net exports (exports minus imports).

**Total expenditure** is simply all the separate sources of spending within the economy. That is, consumption by households, investment by firms and public spending by government. Net exports adjust for expenditure on exports and imports by consumers, firms and government. Being able to identify the individual components of total expenditure is particularly important because it provides an understanding of which expenditures lead to an increase (or decrease) in economic activity. If consumption, investment, government spending or net exports increase, then total expenditure increases, and potentially the flow of goods and services in the inner loop also increases to match the increased demand in the economy. Similarly, if total expenditure is reduced, the flow of goods and services in the inner loop falls due to decreasing demand. We will now use these ideas to develop our understanding of changes in economic activity over time and the idea of a macroeconomic equilibrium.

The circular flow of income underpins the review of the Chinese economy in Box 9.2. Areas of concern relate to a slow-down in commercial investment, a reduction in household expenditure, an expensive domestic currency making exports unattractive and an ageing population boosting the saving rate.

## 9.4 National income determination and business cycles

When examining individual markets in the microeconomic section of this book, we focused on the demand and supply curve for the product. Since in macroeconomics we are examining the whole economy, we need a demand and supply curve for the whole economy.

> Aggregate demand is the total demand in an economy.
>
> Price level is the average change in the price of goods and services in an economy. The *change* in the average price level is a measure of inflation, where 5 per cent inflation means that prices on average have changed, i.e. increased, by 5 per cent.

Total expenditure representing consumption, plus investment, plus government spending, plus net exports is in fact **aggregate demand**. In microeconomics, we argued that the demand for a product is negatively related to its price. As prices increase, less is demanded. We could also draw an aggregate demand curve showing a negative relationship between the average level of prices in the economy and the level of aggregate demand. However, we are going to make a subtle, but important change. We will analyse the relationship between aggregate demand and the *change* in the **price level**.

Where aggregate demand is calculated by adding up all demand changes in the economy, the price level is calculated by adding all price changes together. We will see in more detail in Chapter 10 how governments measure overall price changes. But, in simple terms, a basket of commonly purchased goods and services is defined. In the UK, this basket exceeds 600 items and includes the cost of food, fuel and clothing items. Price changes for each item are collated on a monthly basis and from this data changes in the average price level are calculated.

The benefit of looking at the relationship between aggregate demand and inflation is that control of inflation has become a key aspect of modern macroeconomic policy. Therefore, by using inflation, rather than the level of prices, we are bringing inflation to the centre of our economic models.

### Aggregate demand and inflation

Fortunately, the relationship between aggregate demand and inflation is also negative. If we assume that the central bank is tasked with keeping inflation at 2.5 per cent, as it is in the UK, then we know from experience that the higher the rate of inflation, the higher the central bank has to raise interest rates in order to stem inflation (and vice versa: if inflation falls, then the central bank has to cut interest rates in order to avoid deflation). As interest

## Box 9.2
## OECD warns of downside risks for mainland China economic growth

The mainland's economic growth will remain 'moderate' over the next two years, but faces risks on the downside, while a sharper than projected slowdown would have global spillovers, the Organisation for Economic Co-operation and Development (OECD) warned in its 2015 economic survey of China.

Economic growth was expected to slow to the official target of around 7 per cent this year and slow further to 6.9 per cent next year, the OECD said. However, it warned that 'investment might slow down more than foreseen, for example if stimulus measures fail to counterbalance the effects of the property market correction, shrinking excess capacity and the anti-corruption campaign'.

Other risks mentioned in the OECD's fourth economic survey of China included unexpectedly cooling consumption as housing spending eases, a stronger US dollar that might hurt Chinese exports, and potential disorderly defaults among corporate issuers, especially in sectors with excess capacity, or of trust products and local government investment vehicles.

The slowdown, the OECD said, 'has partly reflected the lagged impact of earlier measures to restrain credit and the housing market boom'. 'It may also signal a more deep-seated deceleration following an exceptionally long spell of very rapid growth', it said.

The OECD also called on Beijing to phase out implicit government guarantees enjoyed by state-owned enterprises. The government should also increase fiscal transparency and sustainability, including a prohibition on local government investment vehicles taking on new debt, it said. The mainland's total public debt, assuming that governments at all levels would be liable for all guaranteed and contingent debt, would have been around 52 per cent of GDP by mid-2013, which was 'manageable', the OECD said.

However, it warned that new official local government debt estimates expected to be released by the Ministry of Finance 'may be substantially higher'.

The rapid ageing of the mainland population would be a drag on growth, it said, while deceleration in total factor productivity was 'worrying'. Boosting productivity was 'particularly important' as an ageing population would reduce the saving rate and the high investment rates that have been the major engine of growth.

The OECD forecast the current account surplus would widen to 2.5 per cent of GDP by 2016.

Adapted from an article by Victoria Ruan
© South China Morning Post, 20 March 2015.

rates increase, consumers and firms are less willing to borrow in order to fund the purchase of goods and services. Therefore, aggregate demand falls. These points are picked up in Figure 9.6.

From the circular flow of income we have argued that aggregate demand is composed of consumption, investment, government spending and net exports. An increase in any of these types of expenditure will lead to an increase in aggregate demand. In Figure 9.7, we illustrate this idea by assuming that government spending has increased from $G_1$ to $G_2$. We could equally have assumed that consumption, investment or net exports had increased. The consequences of the increase in government spending are for the aggregate demand curve to shift from $AD_1$ to $AD_2$, with higher levels of economic output being demanded at all inflation levels.

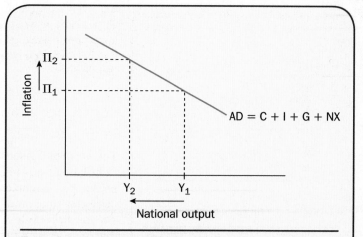

**Figure 9.6  Aggregate demand and inflation**

AD is aggregate demand and represents total demand in the economy. AD = C +I + G +NX, where C = consumption, I = investment, G = government spending and NX = net exports. If inflation increases from $\Pi_1$ to $\Pi_2$, then the central bank will increase interest rates in order to stem the rise in prices. The higher interest rates will lead to a reduction in aggregate demand from $Y_1$ to $Y_2$.

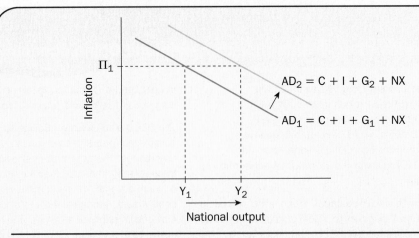

Figure 9.7 Aggregate demand, inflation and increased government spending

Aggregate demand will shift to the right if C, I, G or NX increases. As an example, we have simply assumed that government spending has increased from $G_1$ to $G_2$. Aggregate demand, therefore, shifts from $AD_1$ to $AD_2$. As this happens, the willingness to demand output at an inflation rate of $\Pi_1$ rises from $Y_1$ to $Y_2$. In Figure 9.11, we show how changes in aggregate demand lead to changes in equilibrium GDP and inflation.

## Aggregate supply and inflation

Aggregate supply is the total supply in an economy.

Real prices and wages are adjusted for inflation.

Nominal prices and wages are not adjusted for inflation.

In Chapters 3 and 5 we saw that, as profit-maximizers, firms will supply output if the market price is equal to, or greater than, marginal cost. Therefore, an increase in the price will bring about an increase in supply from an individual firm. But, at the macro level, how will **aggregate supply** react to a change in inflation?

We need to make a distinction between **real** and **nominal** values. Assume you are earning £100 a day and inflation is 2 per cent per year. At the end of one year your *nominal* wage will still be £100 per day. But your *real* wage will only be £98. The real wage is the nominal wage adjusted for the rate of inflation. You are receiving £100 in cash, but due to inflation it can now only buy 98 per cent of what you could buy last year with £100. In order to keep your real wage constant, you need to ask for a 2 per cent pay rise because you now need £102 to buy what £100 could purchase last year.

## Aggregate supply and full wage adjustment to inflation

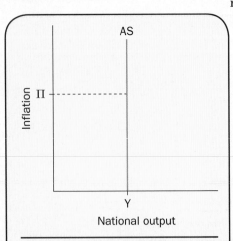

Figure 9.8 Aggregate supply and full wage adjustment to inflation

AS is aggregate supply and represents total supply in the economy. If prices and wages adjust to keep real prices and wages constant, then aggregate supply will remain constant.

The important issue for aggregate supply is whether or not a bout of inflation leads to nominal or real changes in relative wages and prices. For example, if inflation leads to a 3 per cent increase in prices for final products and workers also ask for a 3 per cent pay rise to compensate for the rise in prices, then the real wage and the real price of goods and services have stayed the same. Because real prices and wages are the same, the real costs and revenues faced by the firm have not changed. Aggregate supply will therefore remain unchanged as firms are faced with no reason to increase (or decrease) their willingness to supply. We can, therefore, argue that, when wages fully adjust to inflation, aggregate supply remains constant. This is illustrated in Figure 9.8 with a vertical aggregate supply curve. As inflation increases, supply stays constant.

## Aggregate supply without full wage adjustment to price increases

We can now consider what happens if prices and wages do not adjust to keep real values constant. Assume again the price of goods and services is increasing by 3 per cent, but workers only manage to negotiate a 2 per cent increase in wages. The real cost of employing labour has now reduced by 1 per cent. Firms are experiencing a reduction in their real costs of production. If firms are profit-maximizers, then, as we saw in Chapter 5, a reduction in marginal cost leads to an increase in the profit-maximizing output of the firm (see section 5.2). Therefore, with a reduction in the real wage rate, firms will now be willing to increase supply and overall aggregate supply increases as inflation increases. Therefore, when wages do not fully adjust to price changes, a positive relationship between inflation and aggregate supply can exist. This is shown in Figure 9.9.

At this stage, we can perhaps go one step further and suggest that Figure 9.9 represents the short run, while Figure 9.8 represents the long run. In the short run, workers may not accurately guess the inflation rate. In our example, workers agreed a 2 per cent rise in wages, when inflation turned out to be 3 per cent. In the long run, workers will try to rectify this reduction in real wages and so, over time, real wages will fully adjust to the inflation rate and real wages will remain constant. Therefore, in the short run firms might benefit from a reduction in the real wage and boost supply. But in the long run, real wages will remain constant and so will aggregate supply.

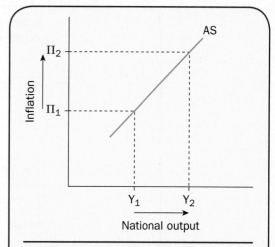

Figure 9.9    Aggregate supply without full wage adjustment to price increases

If prices increase faster than wages, then the real wage decreases. This represents a real cost reduction for firms. If firms are profit-maximizers, then a reduction in the real marginal cost will motivate firms to increase output. Therefore, a reduction in the real wage leads to an increase in aggregate supply.

## Macroeconomic equilibrium

In Figure 9.10, we have brought aggregate demand and supply together for the whole economy. We have assumed that wages do not fully adjust to inflation and, therefore, aggregate supply is not perfectly inelastic.

Equilibrium for the entire economy occurs where aggregate demand and aggregate supply intersect. From this we can then see that the economy will produce an output of Y in Figure 9.10; and the inflation rate will be Π.

Just as we did with product markets, we can also begin to change aggregate demand and supply and assess what happens to the equilibrium output and inflation. The following points are picked up in Figure 9.11. In the top left, if aggregate demand increases, then national output increases, or the amount of goods and services traded in the economy increases. But, in addition, inflation also increases. In the bottom left, if aggregate demand decreases, then national output reduces and inflation falls. In the top right, we can examine changes in aggregate supply. An increase in aggregate supply will lead to an increase in economic activity, but a reduction in the inflation rate. The bottom right of Figure 9.11 shows that a reduction in aggregate supply will lead to a reduction in national output and an increase in the rate of inflation.

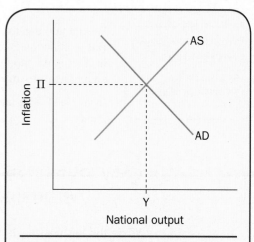

Figure 9.10    Macroeconomic equilibrium

In equilibrium, the inflation rate Π equates aggregate demand and aggregate supply at the national output level of Y.

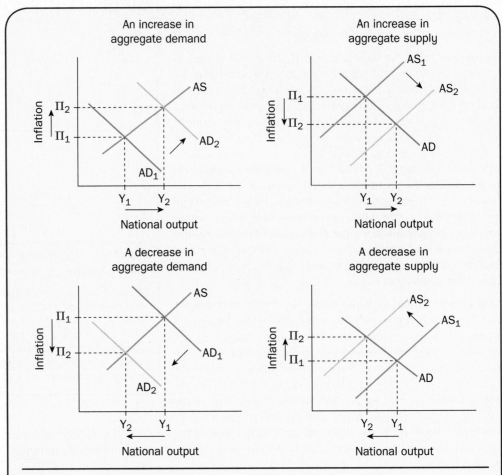

Figure 9.11    Changes in equilibrium national income and prices

Top left: an increase in aggregate demand leads to an inflationary boom. Bottom left: a reduction in aggregate demand leads to a deflationary recession. Top right: an increase in supply leads to a deflationary boom. Bottom right: decrease in supply leads an inflationary recession.

A boom is an increase in national output.

A recession is a reduction in national output.

We can now say that an increase in aggregate demand leads to an inflationary **boom**. But a reduction in aggregate demand leads to a deflationary **recession**. An increase in aggregate supply leads to a deflationary boom, while a reduction in aggregate supply leads to an inflationary recession.

In section 9.5 we use these ideas to show how a firm might try to predict the business cycle.

## 9.5 Business application: predicting the business cycle

While the business cycle is outside the control of individual firms, strategies for dealing with the cycle are not. An important step for firms is to predict the business cycle, and this is no easy task. Even skilled economists sitting on central banks' monetary panels disagree about how fast an economy is growing and how high interest rates should be set. Alongside predicting the growth of the economy, firms also need to time their strategies to perfection. Examine Figure 9.12.

There is no commercial value in being told that the economy is at point A, in an economic boom. By the time the firm has made investments in new products, production facilities, distribution or retail outlets, the economy will have moved into recession at point B. The business skill lies in making an educated guess at point C that in the near future the economy will be at point A. Then investments can be put in place to exploit the economic boom in a more timely fashion. Indeed, when the economy is at point A, the firm should begin to plan for the recession at point B.

In Box 9.3, the Bank of England agents around the country have been talking to businesses and asking them to score sales, investments and exports. From this survey data a summary of the conditions faced by businesses today, as well as the expected nature of conditions in the future, can be obtained.

Nevertheless, how do you spot an economic boom or recession before they happen? What factors enable businesses to respond by drawing meaningful and reasonably accurate conclusions about the future state of the economy? We focus on two insights from our understanding of the economy and business experience.

## Economic insights

The aggregate demand and supply framework suggests that, in order to understand the business cycle, it is useful to be able to address how much demand and supply are changing in the economy.

For example, in order to understand aggregate demand it is essential to have a grasp of how fast consumption, investment, government spending and net exports are changing. In particular, it is important to know if any of these expenditures are increasing or decreasing. If aggregate demand is increasing, the economy is likely to grow; however, if aggregate demand is falling, the economy is likely to move towards recession.

Aggregate supply is, in part, influenced by the costs faced by firms. When important input prices such as oil increase, firms will be less willing to supply and aggregate supply will fall. In contrast, when new technologies become available, which lower the costs of supplying goods and services, firms will be more willing to supply and aggregate supply will increase. The Internet was seen as a technology capable of improving firms' costs and helping to develop the supply of goods and services. When aggregate supply is rising, the economy is likely to grow. However, when aggregate supply is falling, the economy is likely to move into recession.

Government agencies, statistical offices, central banks and trade bodies all provide commentary and opinion on the likely development of the economy over the short and medium term. In the main these reports are based on projections for aggregate demand and supply. However, you do not have to be a skilled economist to understand the development of the economy.

## Business experience

Experience probably counts for a great deal. If you know how the market works and have experience of working in the market for a number of years, you will have seen it move through its cycles. You will have a feeling for when it is going to boom and also a feeling for when it is time to cut back and await the recession. This experience, or 'feeling', is likely to come from an assessment of the more measurable lead indicators. Markets do not generally switch from boom to bust. Rather, they gradually grow into a boom and then slowly decline into a recession. During the growth phase enquiries from customers will increase; and then these will begin to materialize into orders and sales. You may also find that customers

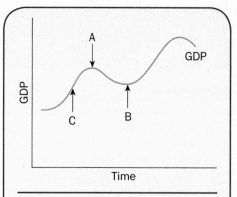

**Figure 9.12 The business cycle**

As the economy moves through the business cycle, firms need to plan and manage their capital investments. There is little point in beginning to invest when the economy is booming, as at point A, because, by the time extra capital is in place, the economy will have moved on to B, a period of recession. Therefore, the smart businessperson has to judge when the economy is at C and likely to move to A in the future.

## Box 9.3
## Demand

### Consumption

Annual growth of retail sales values had been steady. Grocery sales volumes had risen, although price falls—partly reflecting competitive pressures within the sector—meant that sales values had changed less. Demand growth for larger household goods, such as furniture, kitchens and bathrooms, had been robust. Clothing and footwear retailers reported improved trading of seasonal lines. New car sales had also started the year well. Growth in turnover of consumer services had continued to be stronger than for goods. Restaurants, pubs and leisure attractions had reported robust growth. More generally, contacts reported that a recovery in real disposable incomes, in part reflecting lower fuel prices, was acting to stimulate consumer demand.

### Housing market

There had been some signs of a pick-up in housing market activity since the start of the year, with a number of estate agent contacts reporting modest increases in new instructions to sell and viewings. Activity had remained weaker than a year ago in most areas, which some contacts attributed to shortages in the available stock of properties for sale. Overall, housing supply and demand was now seen to be more balanced. The rental market had continued to grow strongly, supporting steady growth in buy-to-let activity. Mortgage availability was reported to have remained constrained for some borrowers, such as those with volatile incomes, although mortgage rates had fallen overall.

### Business investment

Having eased over previous months, investment intentions had stabilised and indicated a moderate increase in capital expenditure over the coming twelve months (Figure 9.13). Intentions remained stronger among services companies than for manufacturing businesses, often reflecting plans to increase spending on existing or new premises. Some non-food retailers had become more confident on the back of sustained demand growth, and were looking to invest in logistics and distribution and store renovation, contrasting with decisions by some supermarkets to cut back their plans for new stores. Manufacturers' investment plans pointed to modest growth in 2015, often focusing on efficiency rather than capacity growth. Lower energy costs were weighing on investment plans in the oil and gas sector and related supply chains.

### Exports

Manufacturing export growth had edged up slightly, after slowing in recent months. Demand from the euro area had remained weak, as had demand from Russia. But US demand had strengthened further, partly reflecting the appreciation of the dollar. Services export growth had continued at a steady rate and was often reported to be stronger than for manufactured goods. Real estate and law firms had benefited from strong foreign demand for UK assets, including property and businesses. While lower oil prices were beginning to depress overseas earnings for some firms in the energy sector, they had also acted as a stimulus for some to seek out contracts abroad as domestic activity had fallen. Inbound tourism had continued to show robust growth.

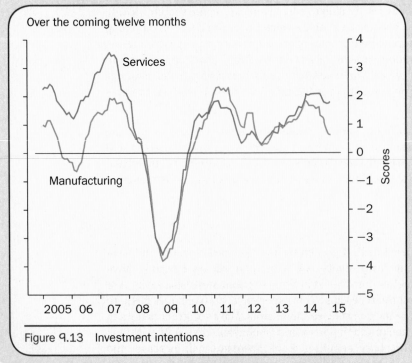

Figure 9.13   Investment intentions

Adapted from the Bank of England, *Agents' Summary of Business Conditions*, March 2015.

switch to you not because of price, but because you can promise to deliver on time. This would indicate that rivals are also becoming busy. So, as sales and profit margins begin to improve, plans for expansion should follow.

Once expansion across the industry begins, you need to have an eye on when the market begins to soften, with falling prices and excess supply of goods and services. If demand in the economy either shrinks or grows at a slower rate than supply, then prices will fall and margins will shrink. So, if you think the expansion by your own company, and also that of your rivals, is too great for the likely growth rate in demand by consumers, then you need to think about readdressing your growth options for the future. Cutting costs and reining in excess output become key in order to compete.

# 9.6 Business application: profiting from recession

Economies do not stop during recessions. In fact, when compared with previous years, GDP during a recession often falls by only 1–2 per cent. So, even during a recession there are still many goods and services being supplied and demanded. However, many firms do struggle during recessions and eventually either cut back on workers and generate unemployment, or close down altogether, with even greater consequences for unemployment.

The point that needs to be addressed is that, while the economy may shrink by only 1–2 per cent, this is only the net effect. For example, demand for some goods and services may have reduced by 20 per cent, while for others it could have increased by 18–19 per cent. But how can demand and profits be stabilized in a recession? To answer this question we need to recall various parts of the microeconomic components of this book.

## Income elasticities

Chapter 2 covered the concept of income elasticity. For normal goods, when incomes rise, demand also rises, but when incomes fall, demand also falls. In the case of inferior goods, however, when income rises, demand falls. Similarly, when income falls, demand increases. So, during a recession demand for normal goods decreases, but demand for inferior goods increases. Therefore, the way to profit in a recession is to have product lines that are income inferior, products that customers like to buy more of when they have reduced incomes or are trying to be careful when spending money. Box 9.4 shows that companies which position themselves on low prices have succeeded during a period of weak economic growth, but admittedly there are also high price companies that have also succeeded. It seems the middle ground is least attractive.

## Pricing

Having products at the right price points in the market and even the ability to lower prices to gain market share are also useful tactics in a recession. Some manufacturers of value lines for the supermarkets have seen enormous growth as customers look to trade down and save on grocery expenditure.

Price discounts are also an obvious promotional tool and, if customers are price elastic, then additional revenue may be gained. However, the risk of a price war is also high, and this may result in all competitors charging less and no additional customers. A means of avoiding this problem is for a company to have a side range of products that can be endlessly recycled through promotional offers, such as in ready meals, soft drinks and beer. Note how the same brands keep appearing as multi-pack offers. The niche, high-quality items in these product categories cannot be promoted using special offers without risk of associating the brand with low-value, low-price alternatives. Reverting to high prices after the recession will then be difficult.

## Box 9.4
## Aldi named 'fastest-growing retailer' in the UK

It seems that not all supermarkets are having a disastrous time of things. Discounter Aldi and yummy mummy favourite Waitrose have been named the fastest-growing major retailers in Britain in a study by consultants OC&C. Aldi's sales have grown by an average of 38 per cent per year since 2011, while Waitrose was a distant second with average annual growth of 7.2 per cent, it said.

The success of these two supermarkets is emblematic of a much-touted broader trend in retail: while the extremes of the market have flourished, those aiming to cater for the 'average' consumer have struggled. This is further underlined by the rest of OC&C's top 20 list, which features high-end brands like Burberry, Ocado and Harrods, alongside discount-focused businesses like Home Bargains, Costcutter, B&M and Poundland.

That's not to suggest a massive division within the general public, of course. The trend for buying luxury ingredients from the likes of Waitrose and M&S, but picking up tins and branded food from cheaper supermarkets, is well documented. So it's not a ridiculous idea that some people are buying their scarves from Burberry and their shampoo at Poundland.

'We've seen the majority of growth in the retail sector come from its polar extremes in terms of price position,' said Anita Balchandani, Head of Retail and Partner at OC&C Strategy Consultants. 'Although at first glance these retailers have little in common, what they all share is a trait to adapt the quickest to what matters most to customers, create strong propositions that are well-rated by customers, and good, transparent value, regardless of their price position.'

**The 20 fastest growing retailers in the UK:**

1. Aldi (UK & Ireland)
2. Waitrose
3. Sports Direct
4. Primark
5. Burberry
6. John Lewis
7. Home Bargains
8. B&M Retail
9. ASOS
10. JD Sports
11. Poundland
12. Ocado
13. The Range
14. AO.com
15. Net-a-porter
16. Harrods
17. Screwfix
18. Costcutter
19. Poundworld
20. Dunelm Mill

Adapted from an article by Jack Torrance in *Management Today*, 11 March 2015.

## Managing costs

A lack of fixed costs is essential for profitable performances during a recession. From Chapter 3, we know that high fixed costs require high volumes. Unfortunately, high volumes are difficult to find during a recession. It is therefore essential to have a cost base which is driven by variable costs, not fixed ones. Luxury hotels, with many frills, including swimming pools, bars, restaurants, tennis courts and concierge services, often located in expensive city centres, are nothing but a huge collection of fixed costs. Not surprisingly, luxury hotel chains do not perform well during recessions, and frequent customers, such as business travellers, can often negotiate good discounts from such hotels during a lean economic period.

Retailers also have high fixed costs in terms of rent for their retail space. This has led to many such companies facing financial collapse. The other fixed cost which many companies face is debt. Financial repayments have to be kept up in good times and bad. If the company faces a fall in sales, then cash flows into the company dry up. But this does not alter its fixed cost payments, including debt commitments.

## Diversification

Diversification through a portfolio of business activities was shown in Chapter 7 to reduce business risk. Car manufacturers such as Ford are renowned for this. In addition to the Ford cars, they also make Jaguars, Land Rovers, Mazdas and Aston Martins. A more extreme example is the fact that Fiat Unos are made by the same firm that makes Ferraris! The reason is that, throughout the business cycle, demand for one product in the portfolio will rise. Ferraris and Jaguars sell well during a boom, Fiat Unos and Fords sell better during a recession. Supermarkets are even more skilled at mixing the portfolio. Stores in the affluent London districts of Chelsea and Mayfair will stock different products from stores located in inner-city Manchester. But during a recession and boom, each store will fine-tune its product offering. In a boom, the Manchester store will allocate more shelf space to branded items and reduce its offering of value own-label products. Then, during a recession, the store will switch back to higher value items.

Clearly, firms operating within a changing macroeconomic environment need to be able to prosper during both boom and recession. Success is critically dependent upon being able to sell products during booms and recessions and being able to read the business cycle. They must plan ahead and be better placed than rivals to exploit the ever-changing environment.

## 9.7 Business data application: finding and understanding data on key components of aggregate demand

The circular flow of income identifies four key areas of spending within an economy: household consumption, corporate investment, government spending and net exports. Understanding these four areas, in terms of how large they are and how fast they have grown, enables economists and business people to take a view on the current health of the economy and likely areas of spending that will promote future growth in spending and the economy. Economic institutions such as central banks, government economic agencies and international organizations, such as the International Monetary Fund (IMF) and the Organisation for Economic Co-operation and Development (OECD) provide data and opinion on each of the four key areas of spending. As part of a business planning process, data from these economic bodies can be extremely helpful in enabling managers to form a view about the risks and opportunities within various macroeconomic environments.

In Table 9.1 we present summary statements from the OECD about the likely growth potential for a number of economies. The OECD does not always use the same terminology as we have used in this book, so you will have to think about some of the statements. For example, the fiscal retrenchment referred to for Greece is a reduction in government spending (plus an increase in taxation); and external demand relates to exports.

The OECD's forecasts for consumption, investment, government spending and net exports are presented in Table 9.2; and it is possible to link the comments in Table 9.1 to the forecasts in Table 9.2. In the case of France, the OECD believes that investment growth will be a key driver of demand; and we can see from Table 9.2 that investment spending is forecast to grow the greatest during the forecast period. See if you can link other comments in Table 9.1 with the forecasts in Table 9.2.

More detailed data for an individual economy are normally made available by institutions within that economy. In the UK, the Office for National Statistics (ONS), the Office for Budgetary Responsibility (OBR) and the Bank of England (BoE) all provide data on the UK economy and the four key components of aggregate demand. The data are generally very accessible, available online and pre-graphed, providing firms and managers with easy access to important macroeconomic intelligence.

**Table 9.1**　OECD summary forecasts for various economies

| France | After stagnating in the first half of 2014, economic activity picked up slightly over the summer. Real GDP growth is projected to continue at a slow pace in 2015 and gain slightly more momentum in 2016, rising by only 0.4 per cent in 2014, 0.8 per cent in 2015 and 1.5 per cent in 2016. Improvements in the global environment, a favourable exchange rate, lower energy prices, and a significantly slower pace of fiscal consolidation will help growth. The benefits of ongoing and announced structural reforms are sizeable but will be perceptible mostly over the medium term. |
|---|---|
| Germany | Economic growth is weak, reflecting subdued activity in euro area trading partners and reduced demand growth in emerging economies. GDP growth is projected to strengthen gradually in 2015 and 2016 as a robust labour market and the continuance of very expansionary monetary policy boost private consumption and residential investment. The unemployment rate is projected to remain low and consumer price inflation to rise somewhat. |
| | The fiscal stance is expansionary, which is appropriate. Growth-enhancing spending should be raised further, including for childcare facilities, more support for youth with disadvantaged socioeconomic backgrounds in the education system and infrastructure investment. This would boost growth in the short run, and—by increasing imports—provide positive spillovers for the euro area. Overdue structural reforms to deregulate the service sector are needed to strengthen potential growth. |
| Greece | Following six years of deep recession, growth is projected to be positive in 2014, and to gain additional momentum in 2015–16. The recovery will be led by buoyant exports and strengthened investment activity, supported by improved competitiveness. The unemployment rate is set to decline gradually, but will nevertheless be close to 24 per cent in 2016. Prices and wages will keep falling given large spare capacity, but at a slower pace. |
| | The high debt burden makes fiscal prudence imperative, but the automatic stabilisers should be allowed to work around the consolidation path. Additional debt relief may be needed. Rapid restructuring of bank balance sheets and maintaining the momentum of structural reforms are key to sustained growth. |
| Japan | Output growth slowed to around 0.5 per cent in 2014, reflecting in part the impact of the consumption tax hike. Output growth is projected to rebound to around 0.75 per cent in 2015 and 1 per cent in 2016, supported by improving labour-market conditions and expanded monetary easing. The weaker yen is expected to help sustain export growth and push inflation closer to the 2 per cent target. |
| Korea | Following the decline in private consumption in spring 2014, the economy is gradually rebounding, thanks in part to monetary policy easing, fiscal stimulus and measures to boost the housing market. Output is projected to grow at around 4 per cent in 2015–16, helping to narrow Korea's large current account surplus and to lift inflation to the target range of 2.5 per cent to 3.5 per cent. |
| | While fiscal stimulus to support growth is appropriate, given Korea's strong fiscal position, the top priority should be wide-ranging reforms, particularly those in the 2014 Three-Year Plan for Economic Innovation, to sustain the country's growth potential. Policies to revitalize the housing market should be implemented carefully to avoid aggravating the household debt problem. |
| UK | Growth has been propelled by high job creation and is set to continue at a strong pace in 2015 and 2016, underpinned by robust private consumption and investment. With slack narrowing, inflationary pressures are projected to pick up gradually. Accordingly, the stance of monetary policy is assumed to begin to normalize in mid-2015 to contain inflation. |
| | This projection assumes that the government continues to implement its medium-term fiscal consolidation plan. Higher interest rates associated with the economic recovery could support stronger productivity growth by encouraging the selection of more profitable projects and the restructuring of loss-making companies. Labour productivity would also be strengthened by further structural reforms to improve loan availability, reduce mismatches in the labour market and further upgrade infrastructure. |
| USA | The US economy is projected to continue to grow steadily in 2015 and 2016. Solid increases in private employment will continue to push down the unemployment rate, though pockets of labour market slack will remain for a while. Monetary conditions and export markets should support some acceleration in demand, as the drag from tight fiscal policy dissipates and as improvements in household net worth provide a growing impetus to private spending. |
| | Monetary policy remains highly supportive, but as labour market slack diminishes this accommodation will need to be carefully withdrawn to keep inflationary pressures in check. The Federal Reserve's large-scale asset-purchase programme ended in October. Policy rates are then expected to begin to rise in mid-2015. |
| | The federal budget deficit has narrowed substantially, reflecting cyclical improvements, consolidation measures and other influences, and some further narrowing is projected in 2015 and 2016. Fiscal policy should focus on addressing longer-term pressures associated with health-care spending and old age pensions. The authorities should also facilitate infrastructure spending, such as by securing sustainable funding. |

**Table 9.2**  OECD percentage growth forecasts

|  | Consumption | | | Government spending | | | Investment | | | Net Exports | | |
|---|---|---|---|---|---|---|---|---|---|---|---|---|
|  | 2014 | 2015 | 2016 | 2014 | 2015 | 2016 | 2014 | 2015 | 2016 | 2014 | 2015 | 2016 |
| France | 0.4 | 1.0 | 1.5 | 2.0 | 0.8 | 0.3 | −1.7 | −1.1 | 1.4 | 2.0 | 3.5 | 4.9 |
| Germany | 1.0 | 1.3 | 1.7 | 1.0 | 1.8 | 1.8 | 3.0 | 1.2 | 4.0 | 3.2 | 3.1 | 4.2 |
| Greece | 0.3 | 0.7 | 1.9 | −1.5 | −1.4 | −1.1 | −3.5 | 6.8 | 7.7 | 8.8 | 6.4 | 7.9 |
| Japan | −0.9 | 1.0 | 1.2 | 0.3 | 0.3 | 0.5 | 3.7 | −1.0 | −0.5 | 7.8 | 6.2 | 6.7 |
| Korea | 1.8 | 3.0 | 3.2 | 2.7 | 4.2 | 3.4 | 4.7 | 5.2 | 6.0 | 3.4 | 4.9 | 6.3 |
| United Kingdom | 2.1 | 2.4 | 2.1 | 1.0 | −0.5 | −1.2 | 8.1 | 7.1 | 7.6 | −1.3 | 1.2 | 2.4 |
| United States | 2.3 | 2.9 | 2.8 | 0.5 | 0.3 | 0.5 | 3.5 | 5.3 | 5.6 | 3.3 | 5.7 | 5.6 |

Table 9.3 below is an excerpt from the Bank of England Quarterly Inflation Report. The Bank of England reviews the economy and considers whether strong or weak growth in demand is likely. Stronger growth in demand maybe expected to lead to a stronger overall economy and a need to consider increasing interest rates to keep inflation low.

**Table 9.3**  A review of the forecasts for key components of aggregate demand

| Developments anticipated in November | Developments since November |
|---|---|
| **Consumer spending** | **Stronger than expected; outlook broadly unchanged** |
| • Quarterly consumer spending growth of a little below ¾%.<br>• Household saving ratio to fall further | • Grew by 1% in Q3; around ¾% expected in Q4.<br>• saving ratio fell slightly in Q3. |
| **Investment** | **Weaker than expected** |
| • Quarterly business investment growth of around 2½%.<br>• Quarterly housing investment growth to average 1% in 2015 H1 | • Fell by 1.4% in Q3, although initial estimates are uncertain, and expected to recover in Q4.<br>• Fell by 1.1% in Q3. outlook for Q4 weaker than expected. |
| **Other advanced economies** | **Euro area on track; US stronger than expected** |
| • Quarterly euro-area GDP growth averaging a little above ¼%, with credit conditions improving slightly. Inflation broadly stable for rest of 2014, picking up in 2015 H1.<br>• Average quarterly US GDP growth a little above ½%; non-farm payrolls increasing by a little more than 200,000 per month. | • Growth in Q3 as expected. Headline inflation fell further to −0.6% in January, in part reflecting falls in oil prices.<br>• GDP growth 07% in Q4; non-farm payrolls stronger than expected. |
| **Rest of the world** | **Broadly on track** |
| • Average four-quarter ppp-weighted emerging-economy growth of around 4½%. Chinese GDP growth slightly above 7%. | • Emerging-economy GDP growth was 4.7% in Q3. Chinese GDP growth was 7.3% in Q4. |
| **Exports** | **Broadly on track** |
| • Average quarterly growth in UK exports of around 1%. | • Exports grew by 0.7% in Q3. Monthly goods exports picked up in Q4. |

*Source:* The Bank of England *Quarterly Inflation Report,* February 2015.

By looking at the excerpt you can see that the Bank states what it thought each major component of expenditure was going to do and then in the second column it comments on what it now thinks is happening. The Bank is therefore continuously reviewing its forecasts.

A quick interpretation of the main areas of demand identifies that growth in consumption is ahead of expectations and international demand in areas such as the US is on track to meet expectations. However, investment expenditure is currently weaker than expected. Whilst the Bank does not mention government spending in the excerpt above, the Bank does note that government spending has reduced significantly since 2010 and will continue to reduce for the next 3–4 years.

The sensible conclusion to draw is that the UK economy will not grow quickly and there are few places for UK companies to concentrate their activities. For example, focusing on household spending through retail products has some limited appeal. The business-to-business sector, selling capital equipment to other companies, looks unappetizing. Specializing in the support of government services, such as health and education, looks bleak with the cutbacks in government spending; and trying to compete overseas does not look especially appealing. There is growth in other economies, but Europe as a major trading partner is only expected to grow at 0.25 per cent.

Your understanding of macroeconomics is at an early stage, yet the circular flow of income provides you with a simple and insightful framework. So simple and useful is the circular flow of income that professional economists working for the leading economic institutions also use it to frame their study of the world's economies. With your new knowledge you can improve your understanding of the economy by using the research insights provided by leading economic forecasters. In so doing, your ability to interpret the economy and improve your business planning decisions will grow.

## Summary

1.  Macroeconomics is the study of economic activity at the aggregate level, examining the entire economy rather than just single markets.

2.  The circular flow of income is a representation of how an economy works. Households own all factors of production and firms hire these factors to produce goods and services. Firms pay households for using input resources and households in return purchase the goods and services.

3.  The level of demand for goods and services is conditioned by the level of injections into and leakages from the circular flow of income. Savings, taxation and imports all represent leakages, while investment, government spending and exports all represent injections.

4.  The whole economy can be viewed as a collection of the many small markets that go into making an economy. Therefore, rather than thinking about demand we now talk about aggregate demand and similarly aggregate supply as opposed to simply supply.

5.  Aggregate demand has a negative relationship with inflation. As inflation increases, the central bank increases interest rates, resulting in a reduction in aggregate demand.

6.  Aggregate supply will have a positive relationship with inflation, if real wages do not adjust fully to rises in prices. However, if real wages adjust fully to inflation, then aggregate supply will be perfectly inelastic.

7. Gross domestic product, or GDP, is a measure of economic output of an economy.

8. Inflation is a measure of price changes. The quicker prices rise, the higher the rate of inflation.

9. In part, the business cycle can be explained by changes in aggregate demand and aggregate supply. As demand increases, the economy grows and inflation increases. As demand falls, the economy slows and inflation falls. If, in contrast, supply increases, then the economy grows and inflation decreases. However, if supply shrinks, the economy shrinks and inflation increases.

10. The business cycle is a description of the tendency for economies to move from economic boom into economic recession and vice versa.

11. The rate of inflation tends to change throughout the business cycle, but this is a reflection of changes in aggregate demand and supply. An increase in aggregate demand will tend to generate an inflationary boom, while an increase in aggregate supply will tend to generate a deflationary boom. Conversely, a reduction in aggregate demand will generate a deflationary recession, while a reduction in aggregate supply will generate an inflationary recession.

12. Predicting the business cycle is not an exact science. Economists and business people will only ever know when an economy has hit its peak after the event, perhaps up to 12 months after. And the same is true of recessions. It is, therefore, crucial to plan and implement investment decisions in advance of any detrimental macroeconomic changes. How to achieve this is challenging. Some people use their experience—how did the economy behave in the past? What can I learn from other economies? What are the experts saying? And do I believe them?

13. An interesting question, or fallacy, surrounds the fact that GDP only falls by a small amount (1–2 per cent) during a recession and yet many businesses suffer severe financial hardship. Why is that? In part, recessions have different impacts in different product markets. Falling consumer incomes will cut demand for normal goods, but raise demand for inferior goods. This provides an opportunity to create a mixed portfolio of products for the business cycle. Supermarkets do this through greater use of own-brand items during recessions, while many car manufacturers produce both high- and low-value cars.

14. Data relating to the four key components of aggregate demand are often provided by important economic bodies such as central banks. Accessing data on consumption, investment, government spending and net exports can help a business to understand its macroeconomic environment and support effective business planning.

## Learning checklist

You should now be able to:

- Discuss the key topics of GDP, inflation, unemployment and the balance of payments
- Explain what is meant by the term 'business cycle'
- Provide a discussion of the circular flow of income, highlighting the various relationships between firms, households, government and international economies
- Explain the difference between leakages and injections

- Explain the determinants of aggregate demand
- Discuss whether or not aggregate supply will be perfectly inelastic
- Explain how changes in aggregate demand and supply can explain the business cycle.

## Questions                                                    connect

**EASY**

1. What are the key macroeconomic variables for an economy? How have these variables changed in your economy over the last five years?

2. What key macroeconomic variables can a government or central bank control? How have these changed for your economy during the last five years?

3. Draw a circular flow of income for an economy that has a government sector and is open to international trade.

4. Identify the leakages, injections and components of aggregate expenditure in your circular flow diagram.

5. Explain why there is a negative relationship between inflation and aggregate demand.

6. Consumer and business confidence are increasing. Illustrate the likely consequence of these changes on aggregate demand.

7. Explain why in the long run aggregate supply is perfectly inelastic, but in the short run it is elastic.

8. Would an increase in aggregate demand generate an inflationary or deflationary boom? Would a reduction in aggregate supply generate an inflationary recession or a deflationary boom?

9. Explain what is meant by the term 'a lead indicator'.

10. How does an understanding of income elasticity enable a firm to manage the consequences of the business cycle?

**INTERMEDIATE**

11. In the long run can GDP grow through an increase in aggregate demand, aggregate supply or both?

12. In an economy, if aggregate demand increases while aggregate supply stays constant, what happens to GDP and inflation?

13. An economy benefits from an influx of additional workers. Using the circular flow of income, assess how these additional workers will impact upon the output of the economy. How will the extra workers influence aggregate supply?

**DIFFICULT**

14. Identify the key business variables a company could monitor in order to understand whether the economy is heading towards a boom or a recession.

15. The economy has been growing for 12 months and sales are increasing, but margins, the difference between revenues and costs, are beginning to fall. Is now a good time to invest in additional production capacity?

16. Wheat is one of the most important staples of food production. Australia is a major wheat producer producer and typically exports between 10 and 15 per cent of the total wheat exported and traded on international markets. However, in recent years, Australia has been experiencing several years where amounts of rainfall have been

significantly reduced. In turn, this can cause droughts which have a serious adverse impact on wheat production.

Assume that rains fail and a drought results. The diagram provided illustrates macroeconomic equilibrium in Australia (AS denotes aggregate supply and AD shows aggregate demand). Show how the equilibrium shown in this diagram will change as a result of a drought and wheat crop failure.

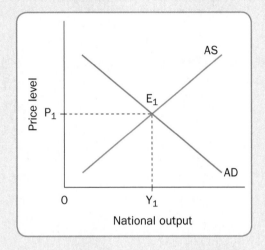

DIFFICULT

## Exercises

1. True or false?
   (a) Savings provide an injection into the circular flow of income.
   (b) Total expenditure in an economy is equal to consumption, investment, government spending and exports.
   (c) Under complete wage adjustment aggregate supply is unresponsive to a change in inflation.
   (d) Higher inflation will lead central banks to increase interest rates. This explains a negative relationship between inflation and aggregate demand.
   (e) The main injections into the circular flow of income are investment and government spending.
   (f) Diversifying macroeconomic risk through normal and inferior products is beneficial for shareholders.

2. Table 9.4 presents consumer price indices (CPIs) for the UK, USA and Spain.
   (a) Calculate the annual inflation rate for each of the countries.
   (b) Plot your three inflation series on a diagram against time.
   (c) By what percentage did prices increase in each country over the whole period—i.e. between 2006 and 2016?
   (d) Which economy has experienced most stability of the inflation rate?
   (e) Which economy saw the greatest deceleration in the rate of inflation between 2008 and 2013?

EASY

INTERMEDIATE

**Table 9.4** Consumer prices

|  | UK | | USA | | Spain | |
|---|---|---|---|---|---|---|
|  | Consumer price index | Inflation rate (%) | Consumer price index | Inflation rate (%) | Consumer price index | Inflation rate (%) |
| 2006 | 71.7 |  | 77.6 |  | 68.2 |  |
| 2007 | 77.3 |  | 81.4 |  | 72.9 |  |
| 2008 | 84.6 |  | 85.7 |  | 77.7 |  |
| 2009 | 89.6 |  | 89.4 |  | 82.4 |  |
| 2010 | 92.9 |  | 92.1 |  | 87.2 |  |
| 2011 | 94.4 |  | 94.8 |  | 91.2 |  |
| 2012 | 96.7 |  | 97.3 |  | 95.5 |  |
| 2013 | 100 |  | 100 |  | 100 |  |
| 2014 | 102.4 |  | 102.9 |  | 103.6 |  |
| 2015 | 105.7 |  | 105.3 |  | 105.6 |  |
| 2016 | 109.3 |  | 107 |  | 107.5 |  |

Table 9.5 presents some data relating to national output (real GDP) of the same three economies over a similar period, expressed as index numbers.

(f)  Calculate the annual growth rate for each of the countries.

(g)  Plot your three growth series on a diagram against time.

**Table 9.5** National production

|  | UK | | USA | | Spain | |
|---|---|---|---|---|---|---|
|  | GDP index | Growth rate (%) | GDP index | Growth rate (%) | GDP index | Growth rate (%) |
| 2006 | 91.4 |  | 86.7 |  | 86 |  |
| 2007 | 93.4 |  | 89.7 |  | 90.2 |  |
| 2008 | 93.7 |  | 90.8 |  | 93.6 |  |
| 2009 | 91.9 |  | 89.9 |  | 95.7 |  |
| 2010 | 91.4 |  | 92.3 |  | 96.3 |  |
| 2011 | 93.3 |  | 94.5 |  | 95.2 |  |
| 2012 | 97.3 |  | 97.8 |  | 97.4 |  |
| 2013 | 100 |  | 100 |  | 100 |  |
| 2014 | 102.6 |  | 103.4 |  | 102.4 |  |
| 2015 | 106.2 |  | 107.5 |  | 106 |  |
| 2016 | 108.5 |  | 111.7 |  | 110.1 |  |

(h) By what percentage did output increase in each country over the whole period?

(i) To what extent did growth follow a similar pattern over time in these three countries?

3. (a) Source the most recent government or central bank report on the state of your economy. In the UK this is the Bank of England Quarterly Inflation Report.

DIFFICULT

(b) Read the report and establish what key conclusions are being stated about the prospects for consumption, investment, government spending and net exports.

# Measuring macroeconomic variables and policy issues

## Chapter contents

## Learning outcomes

By the end of this chapter you should be able to:

**Economic theory**

LO1   Measure GDP using the income, expenditure and value-added approaches

LO2   Measure inflation using index numbers

LO3   Categorize the potential causes of inflation

LO4   Identify the costs of inflation

LO5   Discuss the reasons behind inflation targeting

LO6   Classify unemployment as frictional, structural, demand deficient and classical

LO7   Explain the Phillips curve

LO8   Discuss balance of payments problems

**Business application**

LO9   Evaluate the importance of manufacturing competitiveness to the economy; and equally the importance of economic policy for manufacturing competitiveness

LO10   Debate how inflation targeting might impact the business environment

LO11   Recognize and assess the accuracy of economic data measures

## At a glance    Measurement and policy issues

### The issue

How are various macroeconomic variables measured? In addition, why is managing GDP, inflation, unemployment and the balance of payments important? What are the issues and trade-offs associated with targeting each aspect of the macro economy?

### The understanding

Higher and stable GDP is associated with economic prosperity and enhanced economic growth. Higher GDP may lead to higher incomes for consumers and could facilitate investment by firms and government. High inflation may lead to economic instability and increased costs for the economy. Lower inflation might facilitate economic stability and investment planning by firms, leading to higher rates of economic growth. Unemployment reflects an underutilized resource, but labour market concerns are now switching towards productivity. The balance of payments reflects a country's trading position with the rest of the world. Just like individuals, an economy has to be concerned about running a long-term deficit. It is important to recognize that a government may not be capable of targeting all macroeconomic variables; for example, higher GDP may lead to higher inflation.

### The usefulness

As businesses operate within macroeconomic environments it is essential that business people are capable of deciphering the policy messages and changes instituted by governments. How will decisions regarding the management of inflation and long-term growth impact on the economy and the firm?

# Business problem: what are the macroeconomic policy issues?

Macroeconomic risks are wide ranging and vary across different parts of the global economy. Since companies operate within macroeconomic environments, managers need to be capable of understanding the key macroeconomic policy issues pursued by governments. Box 10.1 reports the views of the head of the UK central bank. During this speech, the head of the bank is trying to provide a review of the economy, highlighting the important issues and problems underlying the steps taken so far. The bank is seeking to provide stability and leadership. But for it to be successful in providing direction to the economy, it is necessary for those listening, especially in business, to understand the issues being raised and addressed by the central bank.

Read Box 10.1 and you will unfortunately recognize that these macroeconomic issues are important but difficult to grasp. The purpose of the chapter is to begin to provide you with an understanding of the important macroeconomic issues. We will then develop your understanding of policy responses in later chapters.

## Interest rate policy and the Bank of England

The Bank of England has the task of keeping inflation in the UK at 2 per cent on average. In pursuing this target, the Bank of England is empowered to alter interest rates. What does this mean for business?

1  If firms borrow money to invest in capital, will interest rates be higher or lower when controlled by the central bank?

2  Will the central bank be capable of meeting the 2 per cent target?

## Box 10.1
## Inflation report

CPI inflation was 0.5 per cent in December 2014, well below the 2 per cent target. The main reason for this was the steep fall in wholesale energy prices during the second half of last year. Inflation is likely to fall further in the near term, and could temporarily turn negative, as falls in energy prices continue to be passed through. Inflation is likely to rebound around the turn of the year as these effects drop out of the annual rate.

The fall in oil prices, together with monetary policy measures taken abroad, should support global demand. Lower energy prices will also boost UK real income growth. That, along with a lower expected

path for Bank Rate than in November, should help to sustain the recent robust expansion in UK domestic demand. As slack is absorbed, inflation is projected to rise back to levels consistent with the inflation target. The Committee judges that it is currently appropriate to set policy so that it is likely that inflation will return to the 2 per cent target within two years. Under the assumption that Bank Rate rises gradually over the forecast period, that is judged likely to be achieved.

Adapted from the Bank of England, *Inflation Report*, February 2015.

3 Moreover, will targeting inflation have any implications for the business cycle, the growth of GDP and perhaps even the exchange rate?
4 Will central bank management of interest rates and inflation aid entry into the euro?

## 10.2 GDP: measurement and policy

The aggregate demand and supply framework developed in Chapter 9 highlighted the importance of GDP and inflation. As aggregate demand or supply changed, the equilibrium level of GDP and inflation changed accordingly. We will begin by analysing GDP.

### Variations in GDP over time

Figure 10.1 plots GDP growth for the UK over the period 1990 to 2014. GDP is an estimate of the amount of economic activity in an economy and is produced by the Office for National Statistics. Since 1990, UK GDP has grown at various rates between –4.5 per cent and

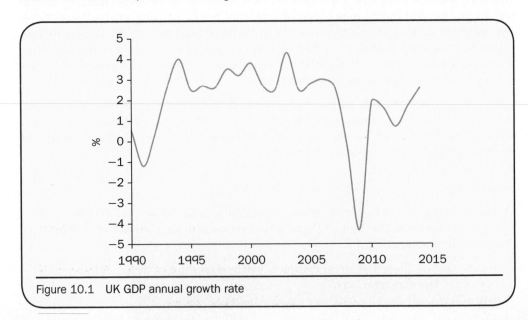

Figure 10.1   UK GDP annual growth rate

4.25 per cent per annum. Trend growth in the UK is around 2.5 per cent per annum. Whenever growth is below 2.5 per cent, the economy is experiencing slowing economic growth. Persistent slow growth can constitute a recession. Whenever GDP growth is above 2.5 per cent, the economy is heading towards economic boom. The variation between recession and boom is known as the **business cycle**. In fact, Figure 10.1 is a picture of the business cycle, where the economy moves through a series of booms and recessions.

> The business cycle describes the tendency of an economy to move from economic boom to economic recession and then back into boom to repeat the cycle.

## Measuring economic output

By examining the circular flow of income in Chapter 9, we saw three potential ways of measuring output. We can measure (i) the net value of goods and services produced by firms, (ii) the value of household earnings, or (iii) the value of spending on goods and services. We are simply measuring the flow at different points; each is equally applicable and will provide a similar figure to the rest.

However, the net value of goods and services approach needs to avoid the problem of double counting.

We can examine the manufacture of a car as an example. A car contains many different parts to be assembled and then sold to a customer through a dealership. Consider paint as one component. Assume the raw materials for car paint are £100; the car-paint producer mixes the materials, packages them and sends them to the car maker at a price of £200. This mixing, packaging and distribution represents £200 − £100 = £100 of value added. The car maker uses many different inputs, including paint, exhausts and engines. All the inputs cost £10,000. But the car is sold to the dealership for £12,000, so the value added from designing and assembling a car is £12,000 − £10,000 = £2,000. The dealer polishes the car, shows it in a clean showroom environment, provides test drives and sells the car for £13,000. So, the value added of the dealership is £13,000 − £12,000 = £1,000. If we add up all the **value added** in the economy, or we use statisticians to estimate total value added, then we have an estimate of total economic activity, or GDP.

> Value added is net output, after deducting goods and services used up during the production process.

Unfortunately, there are two more complications which need to be considered when measuring economic output. The first recognizes that not all factors of production are domestically owned and profits from the use of these resources will flow to another country. For example, the Japanese car manufacturer Toyota owns production facilities in Turkey and the UK. The flows of profits, interest and dividends from these assets are known as *property incomes;* and the balance of flows for any particular country is known as *net property income*. Therefore, Toyota's profits in the UK (and Turkey) will be added to the Japanese economy's gross national product (GNP). Likewise, overseas profits for large British companies, such as Vodafone, BP and Tesco, will be added to UK GNP.

The (i) output and (iii) expenditure methods will not add to the (ii) incomes measure of output without making a correction for net property income. We therefore make a distinction between GDP and GNP, which is GDP adjusted for net property income from abroad.

The second issue is to recognize that the creation of economic output results from the use of productive capital. This is such items as plant, machinery, buildings and shops, all of which need to be maintained, repaired or replaced as they wear out. These expenditures come under the heading of depreciation. Subtracting depreciation from GDP leads to national income.

Finally, all prices are quoted as market price, which can be distorted by indirect taxes and subsidies. In order to measure economic output we would prefer price measures which are not distorted by taxes and subsidies: these are known as basic prices. Adjusting national income at market prices for the distortion of taxes and subsidies leaves us with the figure of national income at basic prices. Figure 10.2 provides an illustration of all of these adjustments.

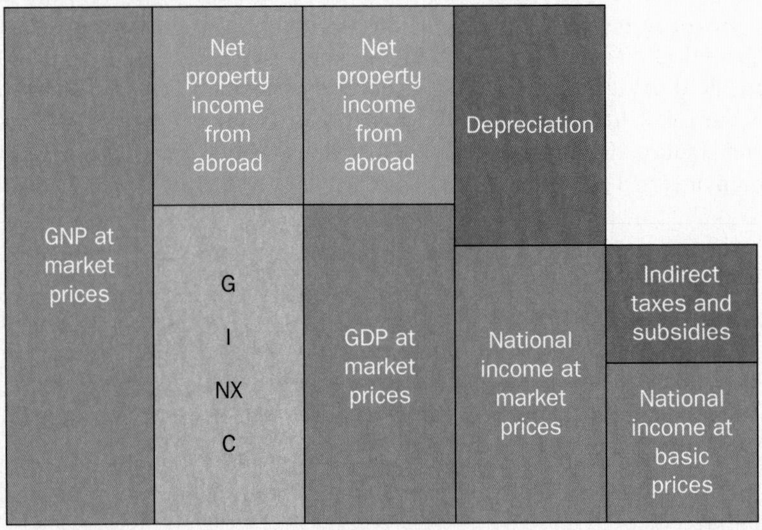

Figure 10.2   National income accounting

Measuring economic activity requires a number of considerations. Take the market value of what is produced in the domestic economy. Then add in the value of what is produced by operations owned in other economies. Then add depreciation to recognize the cost of using capital and an adjustment for subsidies and taxes, to arrive at national income at basic prices.

## GDP policy issues

Is higher GDP preferable? Broadly speaking, yes. Higher GDP means more goods and services are being produced. Households' economic resources are being used more fully by firms and, as a result, financial payments to households rise. The level of income within an economy is often measured as **GDP per capita**.

> GDP per capita is the GDP for the economy divided by the population of the economy. GDP per capita provides a measure of average income per person.

Table 10.1 shows the level of GDP per capita for 30 leading countries in the world. All values have been converted into US dollars. These figures suggest that average income per person in the UK is around $11,500 lower than in the USA.

However, higher GDP per capita can mask a number of problematic features of an economy. One common concern is the distribution of income within an economy. Often within economies, even very developed economies within the EU, there is an unequal distribution of income. Typically those earning most see the fastest increase in future incomes. As such, the rich become richer and the poor become relatively poorer.

An additional concern is the cost incurred in generating higher levels of GDP per capita. These concerns are often focused upon damage to the environment, but it is equally possible to raise social concerns. See Figure 10.3, which highlights the different working hours typically endured by workers in a number of leading European economies. France, Denmark and Sweden have strong peaks at 36–40 hours per week. The UK has a moderate peak at this level, but then the distribution continues strongly towards 50+ hours per week. It should also be noted that the UK, when compared with the other economies, has a relatively high number of people working in the part-time range of hours. The UK works its full-time workers extremely hard and it is also very keen to have a large number of part-time workers. We describe the UK as having a very high **participation rate**. But at what cost? What else could these people be doing? Enjoying leisure, spending time with the family, staying away from stress counsellors?

> Participation rate is the percentage of people of working age who are in employment.

**Table 10.1** GDP per capita in 2013

| Country | Rank | GDP per capita US$ | Country | Rank | GDP per capita US$ |
|---------|------|--------------------|---------|------|--------------------|
| Luxembourg | 1 | $110,697 | Finland | 16 | $49,147 |
| Norway | 2 | $100,819 | Iceland | 17 | $47,461 |
| Qatar | 3 | $93,714 | Belgium | 18 | $46,878 |
| Macao | 4 | $91,376 | Germany | 19 | $46,269 |
| Switzerland | 5 | $84,815 | UAE | 20 | $43,049 |
| Australia | 6 | $67,458 | France | 21 | $42,503 |
| Sweden | 7 | $60,430 | UK | 22 | $41,787 |
| Denmark | 8 | $59,832 | New Zealand | 23 | $41,556 |
| Singapore | 9 | $55,182 | Japan | 24 | $38,634 |
| United States | 10 | $53,042 | Brunei | 25 | $38,563 |
| Kuwait | 11 | $52,197 | Hong Kong | 26 | $38,124 |
| Canada | 12 | $51,958 | Israel | 27 | $36,051 |
| Netherlands | 13 | $50,793 | Italy | 28 | $35,926 |
| Austria | 14 | $50,547 | Spain | 29 | $29,863 |
| Ireland | 15 | $50,503 | Puerto Rico | 30 | $28,529 |

*Source:* World Bank

## Sustainable economic growth

These distributional elements aside, a broad consensus is that high levels of GDP and growth in GDP are desirable. A common reason for promoting economic growth is employment. If households are buying firms' products, then firms will be using households' labour. However, when a recession occurs, households buy less, firms produce less and, as a consequence, firms employ fewer workers. As we will see later, unemployment and employment are, therefore, linked to the business cycle and economic growth.

Economies with higher levels of GDP are better able to invest in the economy's infrastructure, such as schools, hospitals and roads. This is because higher levels of GDP are likely to lead to higher incomes for workers. This in turn will result in increased taxes being paid to the government. Higher tax receipts enable the government to invest in important assets, such as schools, teachers, nurses, motorways and rail networks. Road and rail improvements help businesses to move products around, while better education and health services enable individuals to be more productive over their lifetime.

A combination of rising profits and better educational systems in a growing economy can facilitate improved levels of, and success in, research and development. Innovation can aid the development of new products that improve the lifestyle of individuals in the economy. Or innovation can bring about new and cheaper ways of making products. The Internet is a good example of both. It has changed how people can access many types of information and it has reduced the cost of providing consumers with banking and retail services.

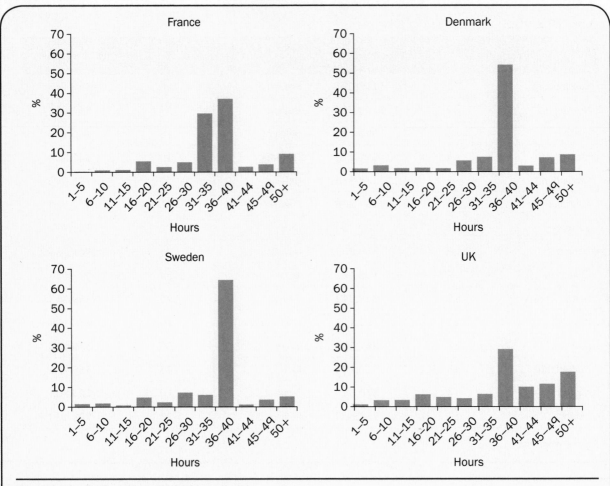

Figure 10.3   Typical hours worked in main job

*Source:* Working time patterns in France, Denmark, Sweden and the UK, by Kate Bishop, Office for National Statistics.

Of course, economic growth should not be regarded as costless. We have already seen that growth can come through longer working times, leading to a reduction in leisure and family time. The other major consideration is that of the environment. As economies grow, and they grow at a faster rate, they consume more resources. Energy consumption rises with economic growth. More affluent consumers buy more cars. Increased affluence also brings greater consumption of energy-hungry appliances, such as televisions, refrigerators and air-conditioning. As a consequence, economic growth drives power consumption, which leads to higher levels of $CO_2$.

In Figure 10.4 data on $CO_2$ per capita are shown for a number of economies. The USA, perhaps the most developed economy in the world, has the highest $CO_2$ emissions per capita. China, one of the world's fastest growing economies, has the lowest emissions per capita. But this figure is biased by China's enormous population. If we consider $CO_2$ emissions in Figure 10.5, we can see that China already produces more pollution than the USA. If China's economy continues to grow, and $CO_2$ per capita matches that of the USA, then the amount of overall pollution from China will be huge.

The implications of increasing levels of pollution from all economies have important consequences for the environment, the climate and public health. How economies grow and how energy consumption and cleaner energy creation aid economic growth are becoming important policy agendas.

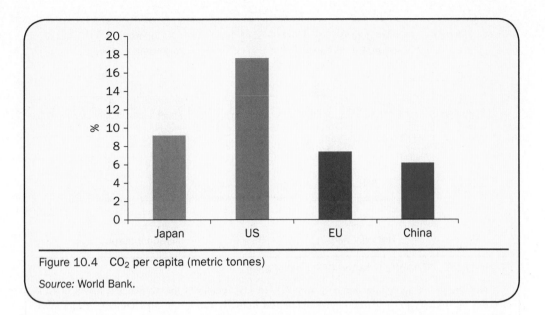

Figure 10.4   CO$_2$ per capita (metric tonnes)

*Source:* World Bank.

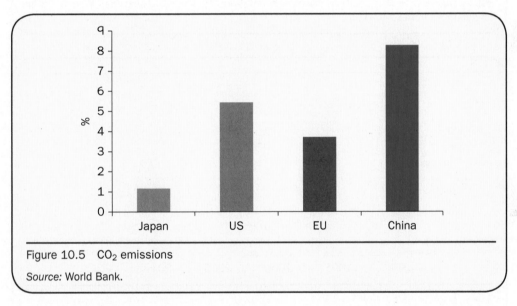

Figure 10.5   CO$_2$ emissions

*Source:* World Bank.

## Trade-off between GDP and inflation

However, a cautionary note regarding higher GDP has to be made. If higher GDP stems from an increase in aggregate demand, then higher inflation will follow. This is depicted on the left-hand side of Figure 10.6. However, if higher GDP stems from an increase in aggregate supply, then lower inflation will follow; see the right-hand side of Figure 10.6. Therefore, if economic growth is important, a crucial and basic question to ask is, how are higher levels of GDP attained and what are the implications for inflation? We will now explore these issues further by considering inflation and, more important, the targeting of inflation.

## 10.3  Inflation: measurement and policy

### Variations in inflation over time

In Figure 10.7, we have a graph of inflation in the UK. The government and the Bank of England have a target inflation rate of 2.0 per cent; however, in recent times inflation has been as high as 4.5 per cent. Back in 1979, inflation hit 25 per cent but, more important, look

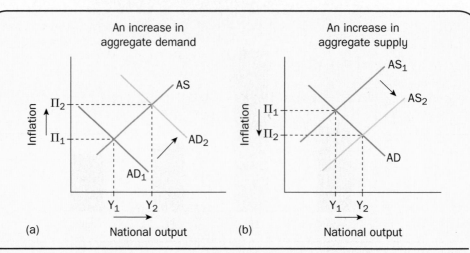

Figure 10.6   Trade-offs between GDP and inflation

(a) An increase in aggregate demand from $AD_1$ to $AD_2$ results in the equilibrium levels of GDP increasing from $Y_1$ to $Y_2$. But inflation also rises from $\Pi_1$ to $\Pi_2$. (b) An increase in aggregate supply from $AS_1$ to $AS_2$ results in the equilibrium levels of GDP increasing from $Y_1$ to $Y_2$, while inflation falls from $\Pi_1$ to $\Pi_2$.

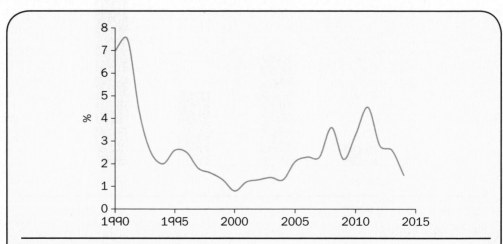

Figure 10.7   Inflation in the UK (CPI)

*Source:* Office for National Statistics.

at the early 1990s in Figure 10.7, the same years as were associated with recession in Figure 10.1. The UK experienced an inflationary recession. But in 2008 the **rate of inflation** dropped, so we then experienced a deflationary recession, which then turned inflationary. Towards 2015 falls in oil prices and food helped to bring down inflation.

## Demand pull and cost push inflation

Inflation can increase if aggregate demand increases, or if aggregate supply decreases. Economists use this distinction to talk about **demand pull inflation** and **cost push inflation**.

A rise in aggregate demand leads to many more consumers trying to buy products. But producing more products increases firms' marginal costs. This leads to firms

**Rate of inflation** is a measure of how fast prices are rising.

**Demand pull inflation** occurs when a rise in aggregate demand leads to an increase in overall prices.

**Cost push inflation** occurs when a reduction in supply leads to an increase in overall prices.

increasing prices in order to recoup the higher costs of production. Demand pull inflation is depicted in Figure 10.8. An increase in aggregate demand moves the macroeconomic equilibrium along the aggregate supply curve, to a point where output and inflation are both higher.

In the case of cost push inflation, firms' costs of producing products increase. Wage rates might increase or, as in 2007/08, the cost of oil, wheat and other commodities increased, making fuel, plastics, distribution and food more expensive. As costs rise, firms find it difficult to make a profit and some may even exit the market. In Figure 10.9 aggregate supply reduces and the macroeconomic equilibrium changes, with national output falling and inflation increasing.

## Inflationary expectations

**Expectations** are also seen as an important determinant of inflationary pressures. For example, if workers think prices in general will rise by 2.0 per cent, they will ask for a 2.0 per cent pay rise in order to keep their level of earnings constant. Because they ask for 2.0 per cent, the cost of making goods goes up by 2.0 per cent, so final prices rise by 2.0 per cent. As a result, expectations become self-fulfilling prophecies. Now it should be clear why the government explicitly targets 2.0 per cent for inflation. It is trying to manage society's expectations about future price inflation. By saying inflation should be 2.0 per cent, people think it will be 2.0 per cent, so they will then demand 2.5 per cent pay rises and inflation should converge on 2.0 per cent.

## Deflation

**Deflation** occurs when the general level of prices falls. On a yearly basis, the price of items such as food, housing, clothes and heating becomes cheaper when the economic environment is deflationary. The drivers of deflation are demand and cost based, just like inflation. If aggregate demand falls during a recession, then deflation can occur. If firms benefit from cost savings, then they are more willing to supply; equilibrium prices fall and deflation occurs. These arguments are the reverse of those described for inflation in Figures 10.8 and 10.9. For demand-based deflation, aggregate demand in Figure 10.8 moves from $AD_2$ to $AD_1$; and for supply-based deflation in Figure 10.9, $AS_2$ moves to $AS_1$.

The credit crunch created a significant recession and a demand-led deflationary period. The expansion of the Chinese economy and the export of manufactured items around the world increased supply and led to deflation in the price of manufactured goods.

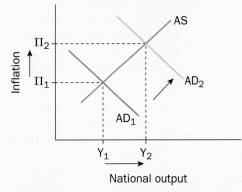

**Figure 10.8 Demand pull inflation**

An increase in aggregate demand shifts the AD curve from $AD_1$ to $AD_2$. This results in a new equilibrium, where inflation rises to $\Pi_2$ and output to $Y_2$. Inflation has been pulled up by an increase in aggregate demand, while national output expands from $Y_1$ to $Y_2$.

Expectations are beliefs held by firms, workers and consumers about the future level of prices.

Deflation is a fall in prices, usually on a yearly basis.

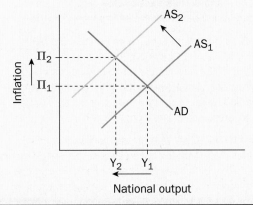

**Figure 10.9 Cost push inflation**

An increase in input prices, such as a rise in wage rates or the cost of raw materials, increases firms' costs. With higher costs, firms are less able to make a profit. Some firms exit the market and, as a result, aggregate supply is less and shifts to the left. The macroeconomic equilibrium changes, with national output falling and inflation increasing. Increasing input prices push up inflation across the economy.

## Measuring inflation

To measure the rate of inflation, governments use what are known as *price indices*. To do this, the government asks a sample of households across the UK to record all the products that they consume in a given period. From these data, government statisticians build what is known as a *common basket of goods and services* bought by the average UK household. This basket will include bread, milk, tobacco, petrol, mortgage repayments, insurance, cinema tickets, restaurant meals, train fares and so on.

Each good or service is assigned a weight. So, if mortgage repayments represent 50 per cent of individuals' monthly outgoings, then they will represent 50 per cent of the basket. If bread only represents 2 per cent of monthly outgoings, then bread will only fill 2 per cent of the basket. The prices of all these goods and services are then monitored on a monthly basis. A report of price changes within the basket is provided in Box 10.2 from the Office for National Statistics.

> The price index can be used to deflate current prices into constant prices, where constant prices are prices expressed in the base year.

## Index and base years

The **price index** has a base year, where the value of the index, or the basket of goods and services, is set at 100 (see Chapter 1 for a reminder). Inflation is a measure of

---

## Box 10.2
## Changes to CPI shopping basket

The basket of goods began life in 1947, as a sample of everyday items that could be used to measure changes in the prices of goods and services. This was—and still is—used by us to help calculate consumer price inflation.

UK consumers' shopping habits have evolved over time, so the goods and services in the basket have also changed to ensure it remained representative. The range of products bought by households has grown too, and so has the basket—from around 150 goods and services in 1947 to over 700 today.

Not only is the basket vital for calculating the best possible measure of inflation, it is also an intriguing reflection of the nation's changing culture, as well as technological improvements. After all, how many people had heard of music streaming subscriptions and e-cigarettes just a few years ago?

It is worth noting that while some fashionable (or unfashionable—corsets, boiled sweets, corned beef and Chicken Kiev, to name a few) items change each year, many staple household goods and services have been in the basket for a very long time. Bacon, milk, bread, tea and petrol, for instance, made the inaugural basket back in 1947—while diesel has been there since 1987.

See the selection of the most interesting ins and outs in 2015—are some more of a surprise than others?

Basket of goods 2015

What's in and what's out?*

This is a sample of everyday items used to measure changes in the prices of goods and services, as well as helping to calculate consumer price inflation. It's grown from around 150 items in 1947 to over 700 this year.

**IN**

**Games consoles online subscription** Represents the explosion in all forms of online gaming

**Streaming music subscription** This expanding technology is over-taking traditional media

**E-cigarettes** Used by smokers as a cigarette alternative or quitting aid

**Protein powder** Consumed by increasing numbers of gym-goers

**Sweet potato** Currently popular in the nation's kitchens

**Headphones** Often bought by gamers, or as upgrades to the free pairs bundled with smartphones

**Craft beer/ale** Speciality beers and ales are currently extremely fashionable

**Mobile phone accessories** The market for chargers, covers, external speakers etc is booming

Some goods removed this year include yoghurt drinks – which have faded in popularity – and sat navs, partly owing to smartphone apps and also because many new cars have built-in units.

**OUT**

*This infographic only represents a selection of the 13 ins and 8 outs for 2015

www.ons.gov.uk
Source: Consumer Price Inflation basket of goods and services, 2015

Office for National Statistics

Adapted from the Office for National Statistics (ONS), March 2015.
*Source:* Basket of goods 2015 infographic: what's in and out? www.statistics.gov.uk
© Crown copyright 2014

**Table 10.2** Price index and inflation

| Year | Price index | Inflation | Nominal salary | Real salary |
|------|-------------|-----------|----------------|-------------|
| 2011 | 100 | | £20,000 | £20,000 |
| 2012 | 102 | (102 − 100)/100 = 2.0% | £20,000 | £19,608 |
| 2013 | 105 | (105 − 102)/102 = 2.9% | £20,000 | £19,048 |
| 2014 | 110 | (110 − 105)/105 = 4.8% | £20,000 | £18,182 |
| 2015 | 113 | (113 − 110)/110 = 2.7% | £20,000 | £17,699 |

how quickly prices are rising and it measures the difference between the price level last year and the price level this year. As such, inflation is measured as:

Inflation = (Index in current year − Index in previous year)/Index in previous year

In Table 10.2, the price index has been set at 100 for the year 2011, and it rises to 113 by the year 2015. Using the formula above, the inflation rate in 2012 was 2 per cent, while in 2014 it was 4.8 per cent.

## Price deflators

For example, suppose in 2016 you earned £20,000 and that by 2020 your boss had refused to give you a pay rise and you still only earned £20,000. We can calculate your real wage in each year by using the price index to convert your salary into year 2016 prices as follows:

Real salary = (Nominal salary) × (100/Price index)

## Box 10.3
## CPI down to 4.2 per cent, RPI down to 4.8 per cent

The rate of inflation faced by households has fallen to its lowest level on record. The Consumer Prices Index, which measures changes in the prices of the goods and services bought by households, was unchanged in the year to February 2015, down from 0.3 per cent in the year to January.

This means that a basket of goods and services that cost £100.00 in February 2014 would have still cost £100.00 in February 2015. While some prices (such as for motor fuels and food) are lower than they were a year ago, others (such as for clothing and rents) are higher.

Prices of motor fuels and food have now fallen or remained unchanged on the year for 18 and 10 consecutive months respectively and in February, the 12-month rates for both groups were the lowest on record. Taken together, motor fuels and food price changes reduced the CPI 12-month rate by approximately 0.9 percentage points in the year to February.

The slowdown in the 12-month rate between January and February came from price movements for a range of recreational goods (particularly data-processing equipment, books and games, toys and hobbies), food and furniture and furnishings.

The core inflation rate—the rate of inflation excluding goods with volatile price movements, notably energy, food, alcohol and tobacco—was 1.2 per cent in February, 1.2 percentage points higher than overall inflation. As in most recent months, this indicates that most of the downward pull on inflation has come from price movements for goods excluded from the core calculation, notably motor fuel and food.

Adapted from the Office for National Statistics, March 2015. *Source:* www.statistics.gov.uk

So, a nominal salary of £20,000 in 2020 is a real salary of only £20,000 × (100/113) = £17,699. In other words, £20,000 has lost £2301 in value since 2016. This has wider implications: whenever prices are compared over time, whether for houses, cars, wages or wine, they need to be adjusted for inflation and converted into constant prices. Price indices provide a means of achieving this.

## Costs of inflation

In recent decades governments around the world have begun to set inflation targets. This is because inflation can be costly. But this cost should not be confused with goods and services becoming more expensive.

For example: 'When I was a lad, a bag of chips cost 5p; now they cost £1.50.' But chips are not 30 times more expensive now than they were 35 years ago. This is because incomes have also risen by the same amount. So, we will only think inflation makes things more expensive if we suffer from **inflation illusion**. However, if we do suffer from inflation illusion, then we may cut back on consumption, believing the product to be too expensive. If enough people reduce consumption, then a recession may occur.

> Inflation illusion is a confusion of nominal and real changes.
>
> Fiscal drag occurs when tax-free income allowances grow at a slower rate than earnings. This reduces the real value of tax-free allowances, leading to high real tax receipts.

Even without inflation illusion, inflation can still be costly. If prices are rising quickly, retailers will be constantly changing their prices. Shelf labels will have to be changed at supermarkets and price lists will have to be changed by other types of sellers. These are known as *menu costs* and the more rapidly prices rise, the more often prices have to be changed. So, inflation can create additional costs.

## Fiscal drag

Let us assume inflation is fully expected and full adjustment occurs. Price rises of 10 per cent are matched by wage increases of 10 per cent. There are no initial cutbacks in consumption by buyers and, therefore, no recessionary consequences. But what if the government does not adjust its tax policy?

In 2017/18, the UK government allowed individuals to earn £11,000 before having to pay tax. If incomes rose by 10 per cent and the government did not lift the tax allowance by 10 per cent, then individuals would start paying more real tax. Therefore, this time, even with fully anticipated inflation, inflexibility by the government creates an inflationary cost known as **fiscal drag**.

## Assets and liabilities

If mortgage interest rates are 5 per cent and inflation is 2.5 per cent, then the real interest rate is 5 − 2.5 = 2.5 per cent. Viewed this way, the lender is not making 5 per cent profits out of its customers. Rather, it is gaining 2.5 per cent to cover the rise in inflation and then it is gaining 2.5 per cent as its profit. If lenders and borrowers expect 2.5 per cent inflation, then the real cost of funds is 2.5 per cent. But what happens if expectations are wrong and inflation suddenly rises to 10 per cent? The real interest rate would become 5 − 10 = 5 per cent. Lenders are now losing 5 per cent a year and borrowers are gaining 5 per cent a year. There is a transfer of wealth from lenders to borrowers.

Borrowers tend to be young people starting out in life, buying a home and raising a family. Lenders tend to be older people who have raised their family and paid off the mortgage and are now saving with banks and building societies. Therefore, a surprise rise in the inflation rate transfers wealth from old people to young people. This influences the spending patterns of old people in a negative way and young people in a positive way. An obvious cost is the need for product suppliers to react to these consumption changes and develop different product lines to meet the main spenders in the economy. Therefore, inflation can create costs through structural change.

## The fear of deflation

Falling prices might sound like a good idea. Unfortunately it is not good when the fall in prices for goods and services also impacts wages. If goods and services fall in price, then the value of labour also falls and firms will seek to pay lower wages and/or employ fewer workers.

You may consider that such changes leave workers no worse off. They earn less, but goods and services cost less, so they can still afford to buy the same things as last year. True, as long as some important prices or financial commitments are not fixed. Mortgages are important financial commitments which are relatively fixed. If you borrowed £100,000 last year and deflation results in a 5 per cent loss in earnings, then your mortgage increases in real terms to £105,000. Over a number of years, deflation can make your mortgage unaffordable.

If deflation also erodes asset values, let us say property prices fall, then the difference between house prices and mortgage balances deteriorates. At worst, households can be left with negative equity, where the value of the house is less than the outstanding balance of the mortgage.

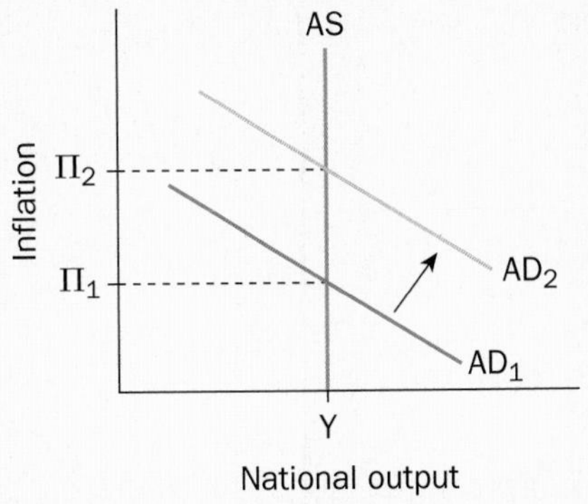

**Figure 10.10   Aggregate demand and inelastic aggregate supply**

AS is aggregate supply and represents total supply in the economy. As aggregate demand increases from $AD_1$ to $AD_2$, national output remains constant at Y, but inflation rises from $\Pi_1$ to $\Pi_2$.

## Why target inflation?

The answer to this question is very simple. If aggregate supply is perfectly inelastic and aggregate demand increases, there will be no increase in output; the only impact will be higher inflation. This is illustrated in Figure 10.10. Whenever aggregate demand shifts to the right, the government, or central bank, will pursue policies to shift aggregate demand back to the left and, therefore, keep inflation constant. The economy can now only grow if the aggregate supply curve shifts to the left.

The crucial issue is whether price stability from inflation targeting enables aggregate supply to expand and shift to the right. The belief is that inflation targeting reduces uncertainty in the economy, making investment decisions easier for firms. Volatile inflation rates lead to booms and busts within the economy, as governments try to bring inflation under control. The variations of the business cycle can make investment unprofitable. Therefore, if investment in capital increases the productive capacity of the economy and ultimately the level of aggregate supply, inflation targeting could be highly desirable. We will revisit these arguments during our discussion of fiscal, monetary and supply-side policies in Chapters 11, 12 and 13.

## (10.4) Unemployment

Managing GDP and inflation have been at the fore of economic policy. As a result, unemployment was less important. This was to be expected as throughout the late 1990s and into the new millennium unemployment fell to almost negligible levels. As the credit crisis placed the brakes on the global economy, unemployment rose and governments have begun to refocus on the issues and problems associated with unemployment. See Figure 10.11.

Economists identify four categories of unemployment: **frictional**, **cyclical**, **structural** and **classical**. Frictional unemployment is of little concern. The frictionally unemployed are between jobs. They have voluntarily quit one job and are searching for a new opportunity. Cyclical unemployment is a concern when an economy enters a recession. There is insufficient demand for all goods and services

**Frictional unemployment** refers to individuals who have quit one job and are currently searching for another job. As such, frictional unemployment is temporary.

**Cyclical unemployment** is related to the business cycle and is sometimes also referred to as *demand-deficient unemployment*. Cyclical unemployment reflects workers who have lost jobs due to the adversities of the business cycle.

**Structural unemployment** occurs when an industry moves into decline. The structurally unemployed find it difficult to gain employment in new industries because of what is known as a *mismatch of skills*.

**Classical unemployment** refers to workers who have priced themselves out of a job.

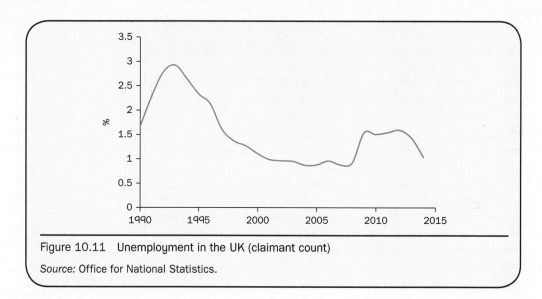

Figure 10.11   Unemployment in the UK (claimant count)

*Source:* Office for National Statistics.

to keep all workers in employment. Factories and offices are reduced in size and workers are made redundant. The role of government is to help to bolster demand in the economy and reduce the impact of recession.

In the case of structural unemployment, an entire industry can go into decline. In the 1980s Europe lost many jobs in traditional heavy industries such as shipbuilding, steel making and the extraction of fuels, such as coal. More recently, the financial crisis has damaged the strength of the financial system and, arguably, the industry will be more regulated, less diverse and less likely to be a dominant economic sector. So bankers and financiers will be in less demand in the future.

The problem faced by government is not one of trying to create additional demand, but how to transfer the skills of bankers and financiers to other sectors of the economy. This is not easy. Financial services workers (perhaps do not) understand financial matters; such individuals are not skilled in manufacturing, leisure services or tourism. Retraining the unemployed and bringing jobs into regions hit by structural unemployment are the difficult but key tasks.

## Measuring unemployment

The government measures unemployment on a monthly basis. Over time, the measure, or definition, of unemployment has changed many times. However, the UK government has used the International Labour Organization's (ILO's) definition of unemployment for a number of years.

The ILO definition of unemployment is a count of jobless people who want to work, are available to work and are actively seeking employment. The ILO measure is used internationally, so a benefit of the measure is that it enables comparisons between countries to be made and it is also consistent over time.

> **Claimant count** measures the number of people who are eligible and receiving the jobseeker's allowance.

An alternative measure used in the UK is the **claimant count**. The claimant count is generally lower than the ILO measure of unemployment, because some individuals may be willing to work but are unable to register for the jobseeker's allowance.

Reflecting the separate categories of unemployment, such as frictional and structural, the measures are generally broken down into region, age and time in unemployment. This provides an assessment of where unemployment is highest, which perhaps relates to industries, thereby identifying structural unemployment. Unemployment in high-age groups could reflect skill mismatch between older workers and newer industries, while time in unemployment may reflect the difference between frictional unemployment and other types of unemployment, such as classical unemployment (Figure 10.12).

## Policy issues

Should unemployment be reduced? Unemployment represents a wasted resource. Unemployed workers would like to work but cannot. If unemployed workers were employed, then GDP could increase. Furthermore, unemployment might be linked to increased stress and illness and, therefore, it places increased strains on individuals, families and the health sector. So, we can see that reducing unemployment is perhaps a good idea. However, such arguments need to be tempered by the insights offered by the **Phillips curve**.

Figure 10.13 illustrates the Phillips curve, indicating a negative relationship between inflation and unemployment. Lower unemployment is gained at the expense of higher inflation. The simple explanation behind this relationship is that unemployment can be solved by creating more demand in the economy for goods and services and, ultimately, this will lead to an increase in the demand for workers. However, increased demand may also lead to higher inflation. So governments can solve high unemployment but must suffer higher inflation. In Chapter 13, we will go one step further and argue that, by increasing demand, governments only generate higher inflation and unemployment remains high.

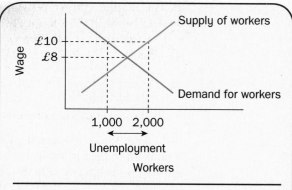

Figure 10.12   Classical unemployment

At the equilibrium wage rate of £8 per hour, the supply of workers is equal to the demand for workers. The market clears, with all workers who want to work finding employment. Unemployment is zero. If workers, or unions, are successful in raising the wage rate to £10 per hour, then the supply of workers increases as more individuals are willing to work once the wage rate increases. But, in contrast, firms are less willing to demand the more expensive workers. So, with the wage rate above the equilibrium a surplus exists, with 1,000 workers unemployed.

> The Phillips curve shows that lower unemployment is associated with higher inflation. Simply, lower unemployment has to be traded for higher inflation.

## 10.5 Balance of payments

We will cover the balance of payments in detail in Chapter 15 but, essentially, the balance of payments represents a country's net position in relation to the rest of the world. Consider your own position. You might provide a service to a company and receive a wage in return. You may then buy products and pay cash in return. If the value of the goods that you buy is greater than the value of work you provide to an employer, then your wage will be less than your spending. On a net basis, the cash flows into your bank account will be less than the cash flows out, and you may need an overdraft. In reverse, if you spend less than you receive as a wage, then the cash into your account will be greater than the cash out, and you will begin to save.

The balance of payments measures these flows for an economy, rather than for a person. For example, if the UK is buying, or importing, more goods and services than it is exporting overseas, then the UK will have to transfer financial resource from the UK to overseas. In contrast, if the UK is exporting more than it is importing, then financial resource to pay for the exports will flow into

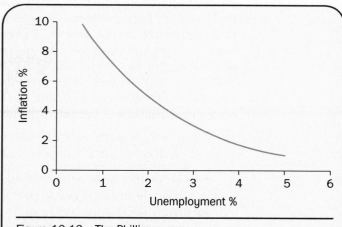

Figure 10.13   The Phillips curve

the UK. Reflecting these points, the balance of payments measures the flow of goods and services between the UK and its trading partners, and the financial flows between the UK and its trading partners. The Office for National Statistics measures these flows for the government.

## Policy issues

Is it bad to run a balance of payments deficit with the rest of the world?

In the short run, a one-off deficit is unlikely to be a problem, much as a temporary overdraft is unlikely to be a problem for you. At some point in the future you may expect to run a surplus by working extra hours and earning money to pay off your debts.

Similarly, a country may expect to run a deficit this year and a surplus next year. More important, why has the deficit occurred? In your case, as a student you may have an overdraft or student loan because you are investing in your future productivity as a worker. Similarly, a country may be running an external deficit with its overseas partners because it is purchasing high-productivity capital items, which will improve the country's productivity in the future.

In the long run, the real concern arises when the deficit represents a structural, as opposed to a temporary, problem. For example, you may not be a highly valuable worker and you may be earning a low wage, but you do have very expensive tastes. As a result, you will run a deficit, spending more on goods and services than you earn in income. Similarly, if a country produces low-quality output but demands high-quality and expensive products from overseas, then it will run a deficit. The way for you to solve your debt problems is either to stop spending or to improve your value as a worker and gain a higher wage. Similarly, a country has to improve the type, quality and cost of the products that it sells to the rest of the world. In essence, by becoming more internationally competitive a country may be able to generate the finances that it requires to fund its expenditure on expensive imports.

How a country improves its international competitiveness may present another trade-off for the government. Reducing aggregate demand will result in lower inflation and more internationally competitive prices. But lowering aggregate demand may also lead to a recession. Perhaps the best option is to once again return to managing aggregate supply, introducing policies that lead to an increase in aggregate supply and a reduction in the rate of inflation, coupled with an expansion of GDP.

## (10.6) Macroeconomic policies

The discussion has highlighted how changes in aggregate demand and aggregate supply lead to changes in GDP and inflation. Changes in these variables may ultimately lead to changes in unemployment and the balance of payments. We have also discussed the policy issues associated with GDP, inflation, unemployment and the balance of payments, arguing why governments are interested in managing each of these macroeconomic variables. Higher GDP can improve income levels across the economy, while low and stable inflation may provide a preferable investment environment for firms. The clear question is, how do governments control aggregate demand and aggregate supply and thereby manage the economy?

The answer to these questions will be discussed at length in Chapters 11, 12 and 14. However, as an introduction we can identify demand- and supply-side policies:

- Demand-side policies influence aggregate demand.
- Fiscal policy is the use of government spending and taxation to influence the level of aggregate demand in the economy.
- Monetary policy is the use of interest rates, as well as the supply of money to the financial sector, with the aim of influencing the level of demand in the economy.

## Demand-side policies

In Chapter 11, we will see how the government can use fiscal policy to change the level of spending in an economy. In Chapter 12, we will develop an understanding of the banking system and explain how changes in the base rate by central banks are transmitted through the banking system to the wider economy and affect consumption and investment spending.

## Supply-side policies

Given that we have seen that aggregate supply can be vertical, or perfectly price inelastic, then aggregate supply defines the equilibrium level of GDP for the economy. In the long run, growth in GDP and lower inflation can only occur with an increase in aggregate supply. Therefore, sustainable economic growth, low inflation and even international competitiveness are crucially linked to developments in aggregate supply.

How aggregate supply can be managed by government and the implications of **supply-side policies** for business will be discussed in Chapter 14.

> Supply-side policies influence aggregate supply.

## 10.7 Business application: international competitiveness and the macroeconomy

Achieving higher rates of economic growth, producing more highly paid jobs and generating additional exports are not all about increasing aggregate demand within an economy. The make-up of industries can be equally important. Which industries and sectors are likely to offer opportunities for growth in the future; which will decline? In contrast to many of its European counterparts the UK has seen its manufacturing base decline towards 10 per cent of GDP. At the same time, services, especially those that are in finance, accounting and legal practice, have grown enormously. London and the South-East economy of the UK are heavily dependent upon these sectors. Of course, when these sectors become embroiled in a credit crisis, then companies and jobs are lost. A natural question is to ask if the UK economy needs to be more balanced in terms of the industries that prosper within its economy. Government support for other strong employers and exporters may offer ways of providing sustainability and longevity in future GDP and employment growth rates.

### Manufacturing competitiveness, GDP growth and inflation

Manufacturing can be a source of economic growth. Manufacturers of products often compete in global markets. By competing overseas, manufacturers can face increased competition from international rivals. In order to compete and survive, manufacturers can face enormous incentives to improve productivity and the quality of their products.

Investing in workers' skills and new capital technology can improve productivity. Investing in product innovation can improve the quality of the product to end-users. Spillover effects into the rest of the economy may occur if high-skilled workers move to alternative employers, taking their enhanced skills with them. Moreover, workers' experience of using advanced capital equipment may enable other firms to consider purchasing such equipment. Finally, if manufacturers make machines for other companies to use, product innovation may result in improved productivity for end-users. Therefore, manufacturing competitiveness may not only drive economic growth but, through productivity gains and cost improvements, it may also enhance aggregate supply and aid the management of inflation.

### Manufacturing competitiveness and the balance of payments

The balance of payments records the trading position with the rest of the world. As manufacturing declines, consumers have to import goods, which previously they would

## Box 10.4
# Professional and business services to the rescue

George Osborne, the Chancellor of the Exchequer, laid out a new vision for Britain's economy. Finance would no longer race ahead of other sectors; a 'march of the makers' would see manufacturing resurge. Three years later, the economy is rebalancing—but not as he thought it would.

As expected, Britain's financial-services industry remains sickly. It employs 56,000 fewer people than before the crisis, according to a report published on 31 March by the Confederation of British Industry, an umbrella group, and PwC, an accountancy firm. Nor are financial services rebounding as the economy recovers. Figures from the Financial Conduct Authority, a regulator, suggest that, excluding back-office jobs, the number of bankers has fallen by more than 10 per cent since the crisis, reaching the lowest figure for a decade in 2013.

Manufacturing is starting to return. Yet the Office for National Statistics said that factory output is still 8.2 per cent lower than in 2008. Industrial closures have continued since the end of the recession—Dunlop, a tyremaker, says it will close its factory in Birmingham next month after 125 years of production in the city. Though industries such as carmaking are reviving, that may be more thanks to falling wages than to increased productivity.

Instead, professional and business services are picking up the slack (see chart). Firms in this industry—which includes accountants and consultants as well as outfits that run call centres and other stuff essential to businesses—now contribute 27 per cent more to GDP than at the start of the recovery, and have increased staff numbers by 13 per cent. Management consultancies have done particularly well. Their revenues have grown by 24 per cent since the crisis, according to Alan Leaman of the MCA, an industry body. That has encouraged accountancy and legal firms to get into the whiteboards-and-flipcharts business too.

Much of the new demand is from abroad, says David Sproul, the boss of Deloitte, an accountancy firm. Business-services exports have risen 21 per cent since the recovery began. Britain's trade surplus in services has doubled to 5 per cent of GDP—the second-largest in the world, after America's. Architects now earn over 50 per cent more from exports than they did in 2009. Around half of the world's legal exports are British. Many new clients are in Asia and the Middle East,

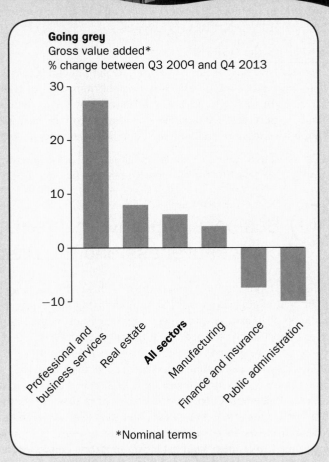

**Going grey**
Gross value added*
% change between Q3 2009 and Q4 2013

*Nominal terms

where Britain's professional services are valued even more highly than its financial ones.

This success is reshaping both the capital and the country. So many accountants and consultants now throng the streets around Shoe Lane, in central London, that some have taken to calling it 'Deloitte town'. Large business-services clusters mean the economies of London and Manchester are probably performing better than those of Edinburgh and Leeds, which rely more on finance, says Richard Holt at Capital Economics, a consultancy.

In addition, more British manufacturers are selling services with their products, according to Tim Baines at Aston University. Boosters speak awkwardly of 'manuservicing', but they may have a point. Rolls-Royce now earns more from tasks such as managing clients' procurement strategies and maintaining the aerospace engines it sells than it does from making them.

Cynics say box-tickers have benefited lavishly from the weighty stacks of regulation that have been pumped out since the crisis. But, whereas earnings from finance and manufacturing are volatile, a bigger business-services industry should steady the economy. Since 1985 the sector's share of output has grown almost every year, according to the Work Foundation, a think-tank. It even created jobs during the recession.

Bean-counting and data-mining are not glamorous occupations. But they do pay the bills.

From *The Economist*. 'Professional and business services: To the rescue'. © The Economist Newspaper Limited, London (12 April 2014)

have purchased from domestic producers. Relying on imports is not a major problem. The issue is, how do we finance the purchase of imports?

In the case of the UK, the rise of the service-based economy and service-based exports, such as insurance and banking, has helped to fund the importation of goods. But since manufacturing exports are worth around five times more than exported services, the UK will have to export more services than it would have to export goods. A significant problem is that services do not export easily. Leisure centres, restaurants, cinemas, legal and accounting services and even hairdressing are not easy to export. Box 10.4 offers an opposing view.

## Manufacturing competitiveness and employment

Skills required for the manufacture of steel, cars, industrial equipment, domestic appliances, chemicals and jet fighter aircraft are fairly specific to the industry. If one of these manufacturing sectors declines, then the potential for structural unemployment is immense. Even if service sector employers were to consider locating in areas of high unemployment, the mismatch of skills between unemployed manufacturing workers and the needs of service sector providers is likely to be significant. Manufacturing competitiveness may, therefore, be important to the economy, if only to prevent costly structural change.

Not all economists would agree with the points listed above. Some may think that the points made are valid, but that they overstate the case for manufacturing competitiveness. If manufacturing has declined, then there must be something inherently wrong about the location of manufacturing sectors in economies such as Italy or the UK. It could be that there are resources in South East Asia which are more appropriate for a manufacturing base—more abundant labour, better logistics networks, better financing options. It could be that European firms need to migrate to alternative parts of the value chain where they retain a competitive advantage. For example, Italians may have lost competitiveness in shoe manufacture, but they are still perhaps the best shoe designers. The critical success factors for the macroeconomy are adaptation, flexibility and migration to the next commercial opportunity.

## Understanding policy

Regardless of how important manufacturing competitiveness is to the economy, it is clear that a case can be built for manufacturing having beneficial consequences for GDP, inflation, employment and the balance of payments or, more important, all of the macroeconomic objectives. But how will policy impact on manufacturing?

If manufacturing is a catalyst for economic growth through innovation and investment, low inflation and economic stability are essential for aiding manufacturers to invest. By keeping inflation low and stable, a government is endeavouring to create a stable environment within which firms feel the risks associated with investing are lower. With stable growth in GDP, the risk of an investment in new machinery being devalued by a recession is reduced.

In terms of aiding skill development, the government can invest heavily in higher education, channelling increasing numbers of students into undergraduate programmes, especially those linked to engineering and science. But this does not always alleviate skills shortages. For every university graduate, the economy loses one important, but less skilled, worker, such as a lorry driver, plumber, builder or mechanic.

## 10.8 Business policy: inflation targeting?

The European Central Bank and the Bank of England follow inflation-targeting policies, as do Australia, Brazil, Canada, Sweden and South Africa. In contrast, the US Federal Reserve has traditionally considered both inflation and GDP when setting interest rates. Given the importance of inflation targeting, especially within Europe, it is useful to understand the implications for business of a policy environment characterized by inflation targeting.

### What is inflation targeting?

The central bank publicizes a target goal for the inflation rate. It then steers monetary policy to try to hit the target inflation rate, raising rates to curb inflation and lowering rates to juice up growth and raise inflation. Targets differ across economies. In the UK, the inflation target is 2 per cent on average for CPI. For members of the eurozone, the inflation target is CPI less than or equal to 2 per cent.

Figure 10.14 illustrates the level of CPI from 1991 through to 2015 in the eurozone. European monetary union (EMU) began in 1999 and the inflation target of 2 per cent CPI was set. It is clear from the chart that, from 1999, CPI was allowed to rise to 2 per cent and then moved close to the 2 per cent level. This was very different from the pattern in the 1990s, when inflation targeting was less important.

Of course, it should also be noted that from 2008 onwards CPI moved markedly away from target. Initially, the oil, commodity and food price spikes of early 2008 pushed up inflation; and then, following the credit crisis, inflation fell very quickly during the recession.

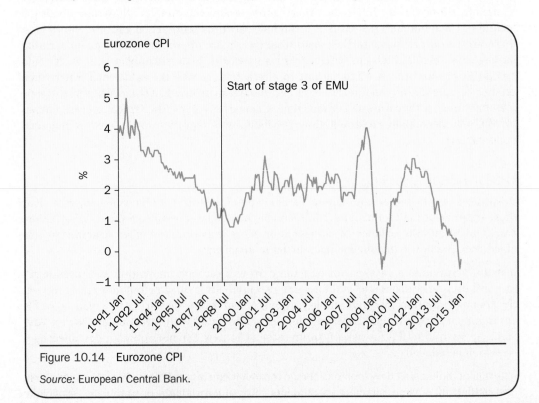

Figure 10.14   Eurozone CPI

*Source:* European Central Bank.

Therefore, despite the ECB's best efforts to target 2 per cent inflation, in times of extreme economic events targeting can be very difficult.

## Why conduct inflation targeting?

The central issue is macroeconomic stability. This is a more general concern than simply low inflation fanaticism. Macroeconomic stability can encompass stability in prices and in economic activity, namely GDP. Under inflation targeting, stability in pricing is seen as essential for stability in economic activity. In fact, as we develop your understanding of macroeconomic policies, we will show you, in Chapter 13, that targeting inflation can be the same as targeting GDP. So, since it is easy to measure inflation quickly and accurately, but difficult to measure GDP quickly and accurately, then following an inflation target offers a reasonably sound and pragmatic policy for managing the economy. But why should inflation targeting lead to stability in GDP? The answer to this question requires an understanding of how macroeconomic events trigger behavioural changes in microeconomic actors, such as firms and consumers.

## Inflation targeting: firms and consumers

The implications for business can be subtle but important. Within a regime of inflation targeting, there is little variation in the inflation rate. This improves price transparency. With stable inflation, it is easier for consumers to recognize changes in the relative prices of competing products and not confuse them for changes in all prices, i.e. inflation. Improved price transparency helps to drive competition. Stronger competition can drive down prices, promote innovation and generate economic growth.

Stable inflation also leads to small and infrequent changes in interest rates. The head of the Bank of England has suggested that his role is to be as boring as possible (indicating that, if inflation is kept under control, there will be little need for large or even unexpected changes in interest rates to bring about stability in inflation). Such boring stability will shape the decisions and behaviour of consumers and firms. Wage bargaining and investment decisions will be carried out within a context of reasonable certainty of future price levels. With reduced risk and improved decision making, a greater willingness to spend and invest should occur. As such, stability in economic activity is assured by a background of stable prices. Therefore, the implications for business are that tomorrow should be very much like today. In effect, no surprises and therefore boring. But boring has its virtues. When investing a huge sum of money in a project, which may reach fruition in three to five years' time, a lack of surprises can be very comforting. Macroeconomic stability now can lead to greater and more valuable productive capacity in the future.

## Expectations

A target rate of inflation is very important for setting inflationary expectations among consumers, workers and firms. If the central bank maintains inflation at the target level, then it will be seen as credible by workers, consumers and firms. This credibility is enormously valuable when managing the economy. The individuals who set prices and ultimately determine inflation within an economy are consumers, workers and firms, as they represent the demand and supply side of product and labour markets. If workers expect inflation to rise to 5 per cent, then they will ask for 5 per cent pay rises and, if firms agree, then they will raise prices by 5 per cent. Inflation is then 5 per cent. But if the central bank is good at managing inflation, then wage and price increases should be in line with the inflation target for the entire economy. The central bank has to do very little to achieve its inflation target. In fact, if the bank is required to change rates, then it may only have to change rates by a small amount to achieve its desired goal. Monetary policy is boring and economic life is simple when inflationary expectations are in line with the central bank's inflation target. This again helps to bring stability to firms' macroeconomic environment.

## Deflation

An inflation target also has merit if there is a concern over deflation. A concern over falling prices might seem a little bizarre, but it can be extremely troublesome for an economy. At one level consumers may refrain from expenditure on large ticket items if they think prices will fall in the future. But this cut in demand will lead to more price cuts and yet more waiting by consumers. A deflationary spiral can be disastrous for prices and GDP.

Deflation can also work against interest rate policies. When prices fall, profits and wages are also likely to fall. Reductions in workers' incomes and firms' earnings reduce their ability to service debt. Therefore, even if the central bank cuts interest rates, the real affordability of debt increases. Inflation targeting may help to avoid this problem by setting an expectation that the central bank is committed to inflation. If firms and workers believe this, then the horrors of deflation may be avoided.

Fears over deflation have occurred twice in recent times for both European economies and the US. The first time was following the financial crisis in 2008 and the second was following the fall in oil prices in 2014. However, Japan is the most notable economy for having to deal with the risks of deflation. A battle to raise inflationary expectations has been ongoing for more than 10 years. See Box 10.5 for a recent update.

## Problems with inflation targeting

Inflation targeting is not always capable of accommodating problems associated with cost push inflation. Through 2007 and into 2008, oil, commodities and food prices increased enormously. The cost of oil doubled. A cost-push inflation reduces aggregate supply. This leads to falling GDP and higher inflation—a so-called *inflationary contraction;* recall Chapter 9 and Figure 9.10. In order to return inflation to target, the central bank would need

---

### Box 10.5
### Japan nears deflation as core CPI hits zero

Collapsing oil prices and subdued demand have again thrown Japan to the brink of deflation, despite the world's biggest monetary stimulus programme.

In a serious threat to Japan's tactic of targeting core consumer price inflation, which, excluding food and last year's sales tax rise, fell to a year-on-year reading of zero in February. It is the first time inflation has hit zero since May 2013.

Although the fall in oil prices will make consumers better off and boost demand, it could also undermine the huge Bank of Japan stimulus, which relies on persuading investors that prices will rise in the future. BoJ officials are watching the slide in prices closely, but after boosting their stimulus last October, they are only likely to ease further if they think that public expectations of future inflation are starting to fall.

The advance inflation reading for the Tokyo area in March stayed positive at 0.2 per cent year-on-year, suggesting Japan will not dip into deflation next month, but it could still happen by summer.

'Electricity and gas charges are expected to start declining from April onwards, putting larger downward pressures on the core CPI inflation rate going forward,' noted analysts at Credit Suisse in Tokyo.

But there was more positive news from the labour market, with a decline in the unemployment rate from 3.6 per cent to 3.5 per cent, and an uptick in the ratio of job offers to applicants from 1.14 to 1.15 times. The steady tightening of Japan's labour market is the best hope for future inflation, as it will generate upward pressure on inflation if companies have to fight to hire workers.

Prime Minister Shinzo Abe has been trying to get corporations to lift wages and in January basic pay grew at its fastest pace for 15 years. This month companies such as Toyota, Nissan and Hitachi also agreed to the biggest pay increase in more than a decade.

From the *Financial Times*. 27 March 2015. 'Japan nears deflation as core CPI hits zero'. Patrick McGee and Robin Harding. © The Financial Times Limited 2015. All Rights Reserved.

to increase interest rates and cause GDP to fall even further. Combating cost-push inflation would lead to an even greater recession.

A solution to this problem is to have some flexibility in the inflation target. In the UK, the target is for CPI to be 2 per cent *on average*. If cost-push inflation is only temporary, then a rise in inflation to 4 per cent is undesirable, but can be accommodated on the presumption that in the near future inflation will move back down to trend.

The implications for business are important. Interest rates, wages, inflation and international competitiveness could all be more variable in the short run, while GDP should be more stable. On one level this policy is only beneficial to business if stability in GDP is of greater value than stability in inflation and interest rates. On another level, the acceptance of economic surprises and non-boring economic policy may represent a more realistic view of the macroeconomic environment within which a company operates.

# 10.9 Business data application: accuracy of economic data measurements

In this chapter we have highlighted a number of important macroeconomic variables, explained why they are important and how they are measured. In Chapter 9 we also indicated where useful macroeconomic data can be found. An important question to ask is how accurate the measurement of key macroeconomic data is, because if business decisions are being made on the basis of macroeconomic data, then more accurate data are preferable.

Data providers have to trade timeliness against accuracy. Economic decision makers and businesses like to have estimates of variables, such as GDP and inflation, as early as possible, in order to inform decision making. But early estimates are not always accurate, because they rely on a limited amount of data. However, over time, as more data become available, the initial estimate of GDP can be revised and become more accurate.

Many government statistical agencies are able to provide a first estimate of quarterly GDP within one month of the end of the quarter. At this stage, the statisticians will be using early survey returns from companies which have been asked to provide data on sales, production and stock levels, among other things. As more companies fill out and send in their data, then a second estimate (first revision) can be made within two months of the end of the quarter; and the third estimate (second revision) can be made within three months of the end of the quarter. However, even at that stage the statisticians have access to less than 50 per cent of the entire data which will eventually become available and enable them to make the most accurate estimate of GDP. All the relevant data may not become available until 12 months after the end of the quarter and even then the statisticians may revisit their estimates and use new numerical techniques, which will alter early estimates.

The important point is that macroeconomic data are nearly always subject to revision and this fact adds an additional layer of complexity to the problem of trying to provide an interpretation of the macroeconomic environment for businesses. In Figure 10.15 the Bank of England compares its so-called 'nowcast' (the estimate of GDP today) with the ONS' first official estimate of GDP which generally follows about 11–12 weeks later. There are some time periods where the nowcast is very accurate. There are also some periods when it is very inaccurate. So even for experienced economists, forecasting GDP is not always a success.

What a business person needs to remember is that estimates are just that, an attempt to provide an informed guess as to the size of important macroeconomic variables. That means that good business managers have to question, judge and critically evaluate the accuracy of the data. Does the estimate appear out of line with previous measures of GDP?

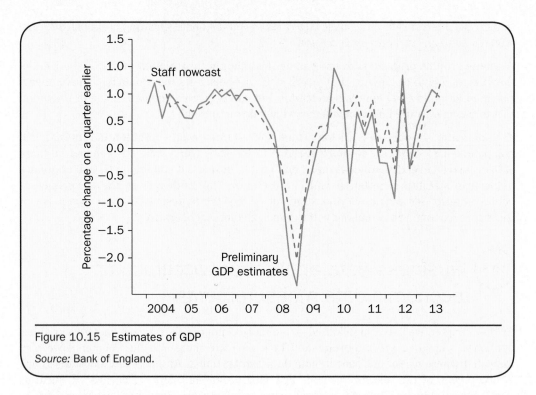

Figure 10.15   Estimates of GDP

*Source:* Bank of England.

Is an estimate of high or low GDP out of line with data on other parts of the economy? For example, if exports are growing fast and GDP is said to be slowing, then why is there a difference? Sometimes the answers to these questions can be found within articles published in the business sections of newspapers. As a business manager you have to know which macroeconomic issues should concern you and where you can gain data and intelligent consideration and review of those data, in order to plan your business operations.

## Summary

1. GDP is a measure of economic output.

2. The circular flow of income indicates that GDP can be measured using the income, expenditure and value-added approaches.

3. To avoid double counting, the value-added approach measures the incremental amount of value added at each stage of the production process.

4. GDP is compared across economies using GDP per capita. However, such a measure may hide an unequal distribution of income among the population.

5. Higher and stable levels of GDP are desirable policy objectives. Economic stability enables firms to invest in new capital equipment, leading to improved productivity and economic growth. Higher levels of GDP can, through tax receipts, enable governments to invest in important economic infrastructure, such as education and transport. However, higher GDP might lead to higher inflation.

6. A trade-off may exist between higher GDP and higher inflation.

7. Inflation measures the rate of change of prices. Faster price rises result in higher inflation.

8. A basket of goods and services, representing commonly purchased products, is used in the measurement of inflation. A price index is developed from the basket of goods and services and changes in the price index are used to measure inflation.

9. Demand pull inflation occurs when aggregate demand increases relative to aggregate supply.

10. Cost-push inflation occurs when aggregate supply increases relative to aggregate demand.

11. Inflationary expectations may also drive inflation. If workers expect prices to rise by 2 per cent, then they will ask for 2 per cent pay rises in order to maintain constant real wages. The 2 per cent pay rise may then be passed on in higher product prices and, as a result, the expectation of 2 per cent inflation becomes reality.

12. Inflation can create many costs, including the erosion of debt and increasing menu costs.

13. Inflation targeting may improve economic stability and business investment confidence. Increased investment in productive capital may improve the economy's aggregate supply, boosting GDP and reducing inflation.

14. Targeting increases in aggregate supply avoids the trade-off associated with aggregate demand, with higher demand increasing GDP and inflation.

15. Unemployment is categorized as frictional, structural, cyclical or classical.

16. The Phillips curve suggests a negative trade-off between inflation and unemployment. However, this relationship may only exist in the short run. When real wages fully adjust to inflationary changes, then unemployment will not vary with the inflation rate.

17. Following the shift towards improving aggregate supply, government policy has moved away from unemployment and more towards labour productivity.

18. A balance of payments deficit is problematic if it is persistent and reflects a country's lack of international competitiveness.

19. Early estimates of important macroeconomic variables are nearly always subject to revision. More data become available over time and estimates of GDP, inflation etc. are revised.

## Learning checklist

You should now be able to:

- Explain how to measure GDP using the income, expenditure and value-added approaches
- Explain how inflation is measured using a basket of goods and services and index numbers
- Explain the main drivers of inflation
- Discuss the main costs of inflation and reasons behind inflation targeting
- List and explain the main types of unemployment
- Explain the potential trade-off between inflation and unemployment
- Explain whether a balance of payments deficit is a problem
- Explain the relevance of economic policy considerations for business.

## Questions

connect

**EASY**

1. Why is growth in GDP important?

2. Evaluate whether higher GDP per capita is always desirable.

3. Identify and explain the three main methods for measuring GDP.

4. What is inflation and how is it measured in your economy?

5. Explain why governments and central banks avoid high inflation and deflation.

6. What are the three main drivers of inflation?

7. As China continues to grow, demand for raw materials, food, shipping and energy will all increase. Will China's growth generate cost push or demand pull inflation in your economy?

8. Assess the key trends within unemployment data for your economy over the last five years. Use the economic unemployment categories to identify the patterns within your unemployment data.

9. During the credit crisis and global recession many bankers lost their jobs. Is this demand-deficient or structural unemployment?

10. Explain the relationship suggested by the Phillips curve. How might governments exploit this relationship?

**INTERMEDIATE**

11. If workers automatically adjusted their wage demands to keep their real wages constant, would the Phillips curve relationship still hold?

12. In Table 10.1 Luxembourg has the highest GDP per capita in the world. Is Luxembourg a good place to start a business?

13. The inflation forecast for next year is 3 per cent. Workers are asking for a 5 per cent pay rise. Should the firm agree to the 5 per cent rise?

**DIFFICULT**

14. Unemployment represents a pool of under-utilized resource. Should firms relocate to areas of high unemployment?

15. Should a firm be concerned about an economy with a chronic balance of payments problem?

## Exercises

**EASY**

1. True or false?

   (a) GDP per capita is a measure of economic prosperity.

   (b) High growth rates in GDP per capita can be accompanied by high inflation.

   (c) Nominal wages are adjusted for inflation, real wages are not.

   (d) A mismatch of skills generally results from cyclical unemployment.

   (e) The Phillips curve suggests a negative relationship between inflation and GDP.

   (f) A trade deficit is acceptable in the short run, but is troublesome in the long run.

2. Plot the hypothetical data in Table 10.3, placing inflation on the Y axis and unemployment on the X axis.

**Table 10.3**   Inflation and unemployment rates

|  | Inflation rate | Unemployment rate |
|---|---|---|
| 2006 | 2 | 8.8 |
| 2007 | 2.6 | 7.8 |
| 2008 | 2.5 | 7.1 |
| 2009 | 1.8 | 5.3 |
| 2010 | 1.6 | 4.5 |
| 2011 | 1.3 | 4.2 |
| 2012 | 0.8 | 3.7 |
| 2013 | 1.2 | 3.3 |
| 2014 | 1.3 | 3.2 |
| 2015 | 1.4 | 3.2 |
| 2016 | 1.3 | 2.9 |

(a) Is there evidence in support of a Phillips curve relationship?

(b) What is the long-run Phillips curve?

(c) At what level of unemployment would you propose drawing the long-run Phillips curve?

3. Consider the data and figures in section 10.2. These include Table 10.1 and Figures 10.3, 10.4 and 10.5. Evaluate whether higher GDP per capita is good or bad for society.

4. Find a current forecast for GDP in an economy of your choice. Is GDP forecast to increase or decrease and what are the risks that this forecast will turn out to be inaccurate?

# Expenditure and fiscal policy

## Chapter contents

## Learning outcomes

By the end of this chapter you should be able to:

**Economic theory**

LO1 Illustrate the Keynesian Cross approach to modelling equilibrium output

LO2 Explain the fiscal multiplier

LO3 Discuss the concept of a balanced budget

LO4 Identify the problems associated with using fiscal policy

**Business application**

LO5 Discuss crowding out and the cost of debt.

LO6 Evaluate taxation or government spending as ways of managing the government's finances

LO7 Assess reducing government deficits and the implications for business

| At a glance | Economic stability and demand-side policies |

## The issue

Both the current level of economic activity and future growth in economic activity are important for business. The government has a number of policies that it can use to control current economic activity. Understanding how these policies influence the economy and business is of enormous importance to firms operating both within their domestic markets and overseas.

## The understanding

Economic activity rises and falls with the business cycle. During recessions the government may try to raise economic activity, while during economic booms the government may try to reduce economic activity. Acting through the demand side of the economy, the government can influence economic activity through fiscal and monetary policy. These will be discussed at length but, essentially, by altering interest rates, government spending or taxation, the government can try to influence the level of demand in an economy—for example, raising demand during a recession and lowering demand during a boom.

## The usefulness

As the government alters domestic macroeconomic policy, it is essential for business to understand how the economy will react. Some policies, if implemented incorrectly, can have a destabilizing effect on the economy. For planning purposes, it may be important to understand what type of policies will be deployed in the future. In recent times, interest rates have been very important policy tools. But, as interest rates fall to historic lows, the scope for further cuts becomes limited. Therefore, what might replace interest rate policy and how will firms need to react?

## (11.1) Business problem: who's spending and where?

Rising GDP should be associated with increased expenditure by consumers. More jobs and higher wages facilitate consumption. In turn, greater consumption drives sales and fuels profits. If only it were so simple. We know from the circular flow of income in Chapter 9 that consumption is only one element of total expenditure. In addition, we have spending by firms, which is classified as investment. We have government spending on education, health and public infrastructure; and we have international trade, where exports represent expenditure in the economy and imports represent expenditure in overseas economies. In Box 11.1, each of these components is highlighted for China; government spending has been a major source of spending in the Chinese economy, but the policy is changing and the government is looking to households and increased consumption to support future growth.

Different firms and industrial sectors will have differing exposure to consumers, investment, government spending and international trade. Therefore, the manner in which the economy grows has varying implications across industrial sectors. For example, retailers will benefit from an increase in consumption expenditure. In contrast, construction companies are more likely to benefit directly from growth in GDP, which is fuelled by firms investing in offices and factories, as well as government wishing to build hospitals and schools. Companies and economies, such as China, are heavily reliant on external demand (one reason why the government is trying to boost internal domestic demand through higher household

## Box 11.1
## China's economy: the four engines of growth

The mainstream view on the Chinese economy is that it will slow considerably, and only return to healthy growth if it can be 'rebalanced' away from investment and exports to a household consumption-driven model. This view is incomplete at least, and misguided in some aspects.

The Chinese economy, over the next two decades before China becomes a high-income country, will be driven by four engines.

First, infrastructure and related investment will continue to drive the economy forward, as they have for the past four decades. China's per capita GDP ranks 90th in the world. Beijing's most recent urbanization plan calls for 100m more people to be moved from farming regions to cities by 2020, and 250m by 2026. The need for infrastructure and other investments driven by this continued massive urbanization process is enormous.

The per capita capital stock of China today roughly equates to the level in the US in the 1930s. The potential marginal return of capital-intensive investment, while lower than before, is likely to continue to be higher than what we typically see in a high middle-income country.

The second engine is China's "new economy", which is centred in the services sector and grounded on rising levels of household consumptions, especially in urban areas. Since 2007, the services sector has consistently outgrown the primary and secondary sectors. Over the past five years, the contribution to GDP growth from the services sector has grown from 39 per cent to 57 per cent, reflecting greater demand for health care, education, tourism, entertainment, telecommunications, etc. As the provision of services is dominated by the private sector, the share of government and SOE employment in China's urban areas has declined from 59 per cent in 1995 to 20 per cent in 2015.

The third engine, reflecting the unique state–private sector dynamics in China, is the ability for the government to marshal state resources to make investments that both generate a long-term economic return and improve the quality of life for Chinese people. An example is the affordable housing projects called 'social housing'. The government's target is to build enough social housing to accommodate 23 per cent of the urban populace by 2020, up from an estimated 14 per cent in 2011. This translates into an additional 30m units over seven years, according to UBS economist Tao Wang. While such social housing projects will take the form of real estate investments, they will improve people's quality of life in the short term and stimulate additional demand and consumption.

The fourth and final engine for China's continued growth is to export infrastructure and over-capacity to other countries, through increased connectivity under the new Silk Road and 'one belt, on road' strategy. The newly established Silk Road Fund and the Asia Infrastructure Investment Bank (AIIB) would corner-stone such efforts. The recent industrial parks set up in Ethiopia, Zambia, Nigeria and other Africa countries, long advocated by my former World Bank colleague Justin Lin, are another way to move beyond exports of goods and services to exports of capacity, and of development experience more broadly.

Dr. Kevin Lu, CEO of Partners Group (Singapore) Pte. Ltd., featured in *The Financial Times* (18 October 2015)

consumption). This means such economies are more likely to be affected by changes in consumption across other countries, such as Europe following its struggles with the debt crisis.

While the drivers of aggregate demand appear to be multifaceted, they are still related. Returning to the circular flow of income: total expenditure occurs with firms, which then pay wages to workers. These wages can then fuel consumption, or leak from the circular flow of income, in savings (to meet investments), in taxes (to meet government spending) and in imports. Therefore a rise in investment can lead to a future rise in employment, wages and, eventually, consumption. Or an increase in investment expenditure can facilitate more investment, or more government spending. It is clear that there is a complexity of intertwined relationships at the macroeconomic level, which the firm needs to appreciate.

It is essential that business people are able to disentangle the macroeconomic environment in order to understand the business opportunities and commercial threats that it poses. When will demand increase in the economy and will it impact your sector? Moreover, what factors will help to drive the various categories of expenditure? Box 11.1 alludes to the role of consumer confidence in determining economic activity. But then it can be asked, what determines consumer confidence? Employment prospects and sales might be two key drivers, which are clearly linked back to the level of economic activity, or the ever revolving circular flow of income.

What governments have come to recognize is that stability is preferable. Volatility leads to uncertainty, and uncertainty reduces both consumer and business confidence. An increased probability of losing your job in the next 12 months will reduce your willingness to borrow and/or spend. Equally, governments have come to recognize that they can make a meaningful attempt at managing the economy. In the case of China, this has involved a massive cash injection of spending into the economy by the government. Similar policies were pursued in Europe and the USA. Business people need to be aware of how such policies feed into the circular flow of income and activate changes in consumption, investment, government spending and net exports. Equally, business people need to understand what happens to an economy when governments can no longer afford to borrow and spend. This chapter seeks to achieve this by developing your understanding of fiscal policy.

## 11.2 Consumption, investment expenditure and the business cycle

In Chapter 9, we introduced the aggregate demand and aggregate supply approach to understanding the **equilibrium** output of an economy, i.e. where **planned aggregate expenditure** is equal to the actual output of firms, and the price level. The approach enables a clear and insightful link to be made between microeconomic and macroeconomic theory.

It is unfortunate that the aggregate demand and aggregate supply approach ensures that the economy is always in equilibrium. As such, there can be no unemployment. All workers that desire a job will be employed.

This is not ideal, given that we observe unemployment most of the time. We can adapt the aggregate demand and supply framework, but a useful approach is to instead introduce the Keynesian Cross as a model of equilibrium output. Under the Keynesian Cross approach, there is an assumption that prices are constant; as a result, inflation is not considered within the approach. Put simply, what firms produce is exactly equal to what consumers are planning to buy. Figure 11.1 illustrates this idea with the 45° line.

We use the 45° line because it cuts the angle 90° in half. Therefore, when we draw across a planned level of expenditure equal to 100, the actual level of output will also be 100. As a consequence, the 45° line shows all the possible equilibrium points. However, the essential question is, what will be the level of planned expenditure?

### Planned expenditure

For simplicity, we will assume that we have a **closed economy** with no government sector. The only groups

**Equilibrium** is generally defined as the situation where planned aggregate expenditure is equal to the actual output of firms.

**Planned aggregate expenditure** is the total amount of spending on goods and services within the economy that is planned by purchasers.

A closed economy does not trade with the rest of the world. An open economy does trade with the rest of the world.

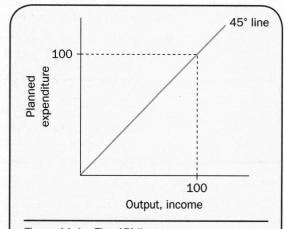

Figure 11.1   The 45° line

In equilibrium, planned expenditure is exactly equal to the output produced by all firms. So, with planned expenditure of 100, output is also 100.

spending within the economy under such a scenario are consumers and firms (we have no government and no exports). Planned expenditure of aggregate demand can be expressed as:

$$PE = AD = C + I$$

where PE = planned expenditure, AD = aggregate demand, C = consumption and I = investment.

## Consumption

The level of consumption undertaken by private individuals is assumed by economists to be related to two factors: (i) a basic need to consume, and (ii) the level of personal income. The basic need to consume is the level of consumption undertaken by an individual when their income is zero. It is the basic level of consumption that is required in order to survive. It is more often referred to as **autonomous consumption**, which is linked to **autonomous expenditure**.

Autonomous consumption does not change if income changes.

Autonomous expenditure is not influenced by the level of income.

The marginal propensity to consume (MPC) is the extra consumption generated by one unit of extra income.

The marginal propensity to save (MPS) is the extra saving generated by one unit of extra income.

As income increases, individuals will begin to consume more goods and services. But they may not spend all of their income on consumption. A small portion could be saved: 100 of income could result in 80 of consumption and 20 of saving. Economists link income with consumption and saving using the concepts of **marginal propensity to consume (MPC)** and **marginal propensity to save (MPS)**.

The MPC is a measure of how much additional consumption will result from an increase in income. The MPC lies between zero and one. So, if the MPC = 0.8, then for every extra £100 of income, consumers will raise consumption by £80.

Similarly, the MPS is a measure of how much additional saving will result from an increase in income. Again, the MPS lies between zero and one. So, if the MPS = 0.2, then an increase in income of £100 will lead to an extra £20 of savings.

Given that individuals can either consume or save, the MPC + MPS = 1.

So, if we assume that autonomous consumption is 7 and the MPC is 0.8, then we can say that:

$$C = 7 + 0.8Y$$

where Y = personal disposable income and C = consumption.

This is nothing more than the equation of a straight line, and it is drawn in Figure 11.2. Consumption has two components. A fixed amount, in this case 7, plus an amount that is determined by income, in this case 0.8 × 100 = 80.

When income is zero, consumption is 7. This is the intercept. The slope of the consumption line is equal to the MPC and in this case is 0.8. So, if income is 100, we can now say that consumption will be 7 + 0.8 × 100 = 7 + 80 = 87.

Before we move on to look at investment, it is also useful to think about what determines the marginal propensity to consume (and the marginal propensity to save). A key driver of the marginal propensity to consume is consumer confidence. As consumers become more confident about the stability of their income, they are more likely to spend. If the macroeconomic environment becomes more uncertain, or heads into a recession, then consumers may fear job losses and a reduction in income. Their confidence falls and their propensity to spend may decrease. Box 11.2 illustrates how consumer confidence has improved in Europe and how that links to an upswing in retail sales and improved prospects for the economy.

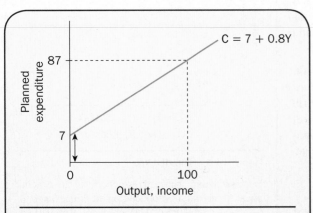

Figure 11.2   Consumption function

## Box 11.2
## Europe's consumer confidence just exploded to an eight-year high and it's now hard to deny the recovery

Europe's consumer confidence smashed to a 92-month high in March, riding on the back of an increasingly clear upswing for the eurozone's economy. It is increasingly difficult to believe that the eurozone, which looked at risk of a triple-dip recession just a few months ago, is getting into a cyclical recovery. With quantitative easing just beginning, it looks like it could be the most significant upswing in the last seven years for Europe.

Here's how it looks:

The consumer confidence figure smashed analyst consensus, climbing to –3.7, up from –6.7 in February. Economists had expected a score of –6. It's still in negative territory, but it's now at its highest levels since 2007.

Here's Claus Vistesen at Pantheon Macroeconomics (who also provided the chart below):

> Households in the euro area remain in an upbeat mood due to low energy prices, record low interest rates and rallying stock markets. The level of sentiment is now almost as high as it was during the peak in 2007 pointing to solid support to GDP growth from private spending in Q1 and Q2. Surging consumer confidence is usually a late-cycle phenomenon, but it is difficult to expect a fall just because sentiment has reached historical highs. Given the likely staying power of very loose monetary policy and low energy prices, sentiment could very well remain high or even rise further in coming months.

From *Business Insider*. 23 March 2015. 'Europe's consumer confidence just exploded to an eight-year high and it's now hard to deny the recovery'. Mike Bird. Copyrighted 2015. Business Insider, Inc. 120023:1115DS

Pantheon Macroeconomics

## Investment

Investment is the demand for capital products by firms, plus changes to firms' inventories, or stocks.

We have seen how income determines the consumption decisions of private individuals. But what drives investment decisions? The answer to this question is highly debatable but, in general, and in simple terms, economists begin by assuming that investment decisions are based on instinct. How managers feel about the future is a major factor when deciding to invest money. If managers think the future looks good, they will be likely to invest. But if the future looks bad, they will cut back on investments. As such, investment decisions taken now are not influenced by the current level of income. For this reason, investment is also seen as autonomous. This means that, just like the 7 of consumption undertaken by consumers, firms set a base level of investment, say 50, but then there is no additional investment relating to increased income. The implications of this are shown in Figure 11.3, where the investment is set at 50 and remains constant at 50 for every level of income.

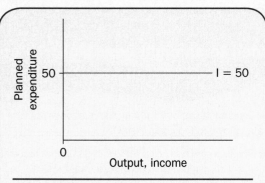

**Figure 11.3   Investment**

Investment has only one component, a purely fixed amount, which does not change with the level of income.

We can now add the consumption and investment together to arrive at aggregate demand or planned expenditure. This has been done in Figure 11.4, which, while looking complicated, is little more than an extension of Figure 11.2. From Figure 11.2 we have the consumption line, with 7 of consumption at zero levels of income and overall consumption of 87 when income is 100. We have then simply added in an additional 50 for investment. Aggregate demand, or planned expenditure, is now $7 + 50 = 57$ at zero income, and overall planned expenditure, which is equal to consumption plus investment, $87 + 50 = 137$.

We started with the 45° line and said that equilibrium occurs where planned expenditure equals actual output. From Figure 11.4 we now have an understanding of expenditure in an economy. We therefore only need to introduce the 45° line into Figure 11.4 and we can find the equilibrium for the economy. Figure 11.5 shows the 45° line and the $AD = C + I$ line together.

In our example the equilibrium level of income is 285.

Proof:

$$AD = C + I, C = 7 + 0.8Y, I = 50$$
$$AD = 7 + 0.8Y + 50$$
$$= 57 + 0.8Y$$

In equilibrium national output = aggregate demand, or $Y = AD$ (1).

Therefore:

$$Y = 57 + 0.8Y$$

Rearranging:

$$0.2Y = 57$$
$$Y = 57/0.2 = 285$$

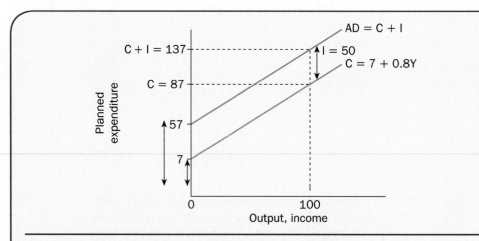

**Figure 11.4   Aggregate demand: consumption plus investment**

Adding investment to consumption simply increases autonomous expenditure by the increased amount of investment. In this case, investment = 50, so at all levels of income spending has increased by 50. At zero income, the level of consumption is 7; adding in investment of 50 simply means that planned expenditure = 57 when investment equals zero. Since autonomous expenditure does not change with the level of output, then, even when income = 100, the difference between consumption and investment will still be 50.

(Question 12 at the end of the chapter contains an additional example, if you would like to test your ability to derive the equilibrium.)

Where the AD line crosses the 45° line must be the equilibrium, because this is where planned expenditure equals actual output.

At all output levels below 285, aggregate demand will be greater than national output. For example, if national output was only 200, then firms would not be producing enough output to meet the level of aggregate demand in the economy. Firms will have to meet the excess demand by using stocks held over from previous periods. Similarly, at all output levels above 285, national output will be greater than aggregate demand. For example, if national output is 300, aggregate demand will be less than the national output. As a result, firms will be left with excess stock.

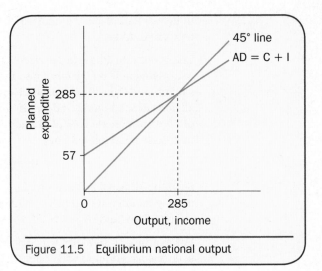

Figure 11.5 Equilibrium national output

## Adjustment to the equilibrium

The economy will move to the equilibrium of 285 units by firms responding to changes in their stock levels. When output is below equilibrium, firms' stocks will reduce. Firms will interpret falling stock levels as an opportunity to expand production, because consumers are demanding more output than is currently being produced. In contrast, when output is above the equilibrium level, firms' stock levels will begin to increase. Rising stock levels will suggest to firms that current output is too high. Consumers are not demanding all that is being produced, hence the additions to stocks. Firms will, therefore, reduce output and the economy will shift towards the equilibrium.

In summary, adjustment to equilibrium occurs through firms reacting to changes in stock levels, where changing stock levels reflect differences between planned expenditure by consumers and actual output by firms.

## The multiplier

Here is a simple idea. What would happen if firms decided that the economic outlook was favourable? We might expect them to increase their levels of investment from 50 to 100. But by how much would economic output increase? An extra 50? The answer rests on a very important insight known as the **multiplier**.

> The **multiplier** measures the change in output following a change in autonomous expenditure (the essential or basic amount of consumption plus investment).

If the multiplier is 3, an increase in investment of 50 will lead to an increase in output of $3 \times 50 = 150$. The potential existence of a multiplier effect has the potential to dramatically improve economic activity following a modest change in spending. So, how big is the size of the multiplier?

The multiplier is directly related to the marginal propensity to save. In our example, the MPS = 0.2. Consider the following. Firms buy more computers and thereby increase investment by 50. The computer manufacturers receive the 50 and for the extra output pass this on in increased wages to their workers. The workers will use this to increase consumption by $0.8 \times 50 = 40$ and save $10 = (0.2 \times 50)$. So far, expenditure has now increased by the initial 50 increase in investment plus the 40 in consumption by the workers. If the computer workers spent the extra 40 at supermarkets, then income of supermarket workers increases by 40. They will spend $0.8 \times 40 = 32$ on consumption and save 8.

We can keep going, but even at this stage we can see that an increase of 50 in investment has led to an increase in consumption of 40 and then another 32. So, overall, the change in investment of 50 has created 50 + 40 + 32 = 122 change in expenditure and therefore national output.

This is entirely linked to the circular flow of income introduced in Chapter 9. The 50 increase in investment is an injection into the circular flow. It moves round the cycle, 10 leaks out in savings and then 40 goes around again as consumption; 8 then leaks out in savings and then 32 goes around again. Indeed, if we did keep going we would find that the initial increase of 50 would create a total change in national output of 250, or 5 × 50. Why? Because the multiplier is calculated thus:

$$\text{Multiplier} = 1/\text{MPS} = 1/(1 - \text{MPC})$$

So, if the MPS = 0.2, the multiplier = 1/0.2 = 5. Therefore, the size of the multiplier is entirely dependent upon the MPS. The higher the MPS, the faster the initial injection leaks out of the circular flow, and so less is left to go around again.

For example, if the MPS was 0.5, then 50 would go around the circular flow and 25 would leak out as savings, with only 25 going around again as consumption. Then 12.5 would leak out, leaving only 12.5 to go around again. In total, because the multiplier is now only 1/0.5 = 2, the initial injection of 50 from investment would only result in output changing by 100.

In Table 11.1 we capture all the information relating to an initial increase in spending of 50m. When the MPS = 0.2, then the MPC = 0.8. The additional 50m of spending leads to new savings (leakage) of 0.2 × 50m = 10m. New consumption (injection) is 0.8 × 50m = 40m. The new spending of 40m is then taken back to the first column (imagine back to the start of the circular flow of income) and the process starts again. Only this time, less is saved and less is consumed because the starting amount is smaller. By the end of the process, 50m generates 250m of total new spending.

The size of the multiplier can be important in determining the likely rate of return from undertaking a major spending/investment project. Some projects can be infrastructure related—e.g. new rail routes, new hospitals, or as in the case of Rio, new facilities for the Football World Cup and Olympics can be scaled back and lead to rioting (see Box 11.3 for a discussion of negative effects from seeking a multiplier effect).

**Table 11.1** Example of the multiplier

| New spending | MPS | MPC | New savings (leakage) | New consumption (injection) | Total new spending |
|---|---|---|---|---|---|
| 50m | 0.2 | 0.8 | 10m | 40m | 40m |
| 40m | 0.2 | 0.8 | 8m | 32m | 40m + 32m = 72m |
| 32m | 0.2 | 0.8 | 6.4m | 25.6m | 40m + 32m + 25.6m = 97.6m |
| 25.6m | 0.2 | 0.8 | | | |
| | 0.2 | 0.8 | | | |
| | 0.2 | 0.8 | | | |
| | 0.2 | 0.8 | | | |
| | 0.2 | 0.8 | | | |
| | 0.2 | 0.8 | | | |
| | 0.2 | 0.8 | 0m | 0.1m | 250m |
| 0m | 0.2 | 0.8 | | | |

**Box 11.3**

**The World Cup and Olympics threaten to overwhelm Rio – yet there is time to create a sensation out of disaster**

The city is now desperately behind schedule for its 2016 Olympics—one insider put it at 10 per cent ready, where London was 60 per cent ready at the same stage. But a visit earlier this month left me with an intriguing question. Could Rio's chaotic planners make virtue of necessity? Could they be the first city to haul the Olympics back from its fixation with money and buildings, and restore them to sport? Could Rio fashion a sensation from a disaster?

No one visiting Rio at present can imagine cancellation as anything but devastating. In this fantasy world of prestige, multibillion dollar budgets and white elephants, even a shambles is thought better than cancellation. But the city could yet seize the initiative.

They could abandon the unbuilt cluster at Deodoro, intended for events such as rugby, kayaking and mountain biking. They could cancel some of the IOC's "toff" sports such as tennis, golf, sailing and equestrianism, as well as the absurdity of staging a second soccer competition just two years after this year's World Cup. They could slash arena and stadium capacity to what it can already offer, and tell thousands of gilded IOC officials, sponsors and VIPs there will be no luxury apartments, limousines and private traffic lanes, just camping on Copacabana beach.

The catalyst might well be this June's Olympics-lite, otherwise known as the football World Cup. It is costing Brazil $4bn (£2.4bn) on stadiums alone for 64 football matches – a staggering $62m per match – plus some $7bn for associated infrastructure. Only generals at war and Swiss sports officials contemplate such obscene spending. When Fifa's secretary-general, Jerome Valcke, came to inspect preparations last month, he professed himself appalled.

In truth Fifa was a fool. It had staged the 2010 World Cup in South Africa by the skin of its teeth, the country recouping a mere 10% of its $3bn outlay. Studies of such mega-events, financed by their sponsors, invariably estimate huge profits, later declaring little more than 'goodwill and reputational gain'. Brazil's World Cup spending was wild from the start. Domestic politics made it increase Fifa's requirement of eight venues to 12, including new stadiums in Manaus and Brasilia.

In June last year, the unheard-of occurred, with urban riots nationwide against even hosting the cup. Public support fell from 80 per cent when the cup was 'awarded' to Brazil in 2007 to under 50 per cent now. At the last count, 55 per cent of Brazilians think the cup will harm their economy rather than benefit it. While urban bus fares were being raised, millions of dollars were vanishing into corrupt building contracts. Demonstrators shouting 'There will be no World Cup' fought police.

These mega-events traumatize a complex modern city. They upset the rhythms of its politics and infrastructure investment. They clear thousands from their homes and virtually close down whole cities for a month.

From *The Guardian*. 23 April 2014. 'The World Cup and Olympics threaten to overwhelm Rio – yet there is time to create a sensation out of disaster'. Simon Jenkins.

© Guardian News & Media Ltd 2015

## 11.3 Fiscal policy

What is so exciting about the multiplier? For the economist, the multiplier means that small changes in autonomous expenditure can generate big changes in national income. In order to see the importance of this insight, we need to introduce the government sector.

If the government wishes to control the economy, such as moving it from a position of recession, then it only has to change autonomous expenditure by a small amount in order to generate a very large change in overall economic activity.

How might it do this? Asking firms to invest more is unlikely to be effective; firms invest because they want to, not because governments ask them to. But what about government spending? Could the government pump additional expenditure into the economy through its own projects such as health and education? We will answer this by examining **fiscal policy**.

> Fiscal policy is the government's decisions regarding taxation and spending.

We will shortly see that fiscal policy can be used to control the economy, but the implementation of effective fiscal policy may be problematic.

## Government, aggregate demand and equilibrium income

In the previous section we saw how planned expenditure, or aggregate demand, is equal to consumption plus investment, AD = C + I. In introducing the government, we are creating a third source of spending within the economy. Aggregate demand is now calculated thus: AD = C + I + G, where G = government spending. Just like investment, government spending is also autonomous. It does not vary with the level of income. Governments take political spending decisions—for example, how much should be spent on education and how much on roads. In the main, the level of income does not determine government spending.

In terms of our diagrammatic approach, we simply add government spending into the analysis in much the same way as we dealt with investment. Government spending as an autonomous expenditure simply raises the aggregate demand line by the amount of government spending. In Figure 11.6, we have assumed that G = 20. With no government sector, as in Figure 11.4, we saw that, when income was zero, spending equalled 57, which consisted of autonomous consumption equal to 7 and investment equal to 50. We can now add government spending equal to 20. So, aggregate demand when income equals zero is now 77.

However, we also need to address the impact of taxation. In Figure 11.4, without tax we simply argued that consumption C = 7 + 0.8Y. But if individuals are taxed, we need to reduce their income, Y, by the amount of the tax. If the tax rate = t, then after-tax income equals $(1 - t)Y$. It is this after-tax income which individuals then use for consumption, or saving. So, if the MPC = 0.8, then consumers spend 0.8 of their after-tax income. Therefore, taking account of tax we can now say that consumption is:

$$C = 7 + 0.8 (1 - t)Y$$

and not:

$$C = 7 + 0.8Y$$

The MPC determines how steep the AD line is, because it determines the link between growth in income and growth in consumption. A higher MPC will result in a steeper AD line. Tax effectively reduces the strength of the link between consumption and income, because an increase in income will be taxed before individuals can use it to increase consumption. Therefore, tax makes the AD line flatter.

Taking tax and government spending together, we can now see that the AD line with a government sector is higher because of government spending but flatter because of taxation.

What does this really tell us? The importance is in the consumption line being flatter. This means that, when taxes are applied, an increase in income has a lower impact

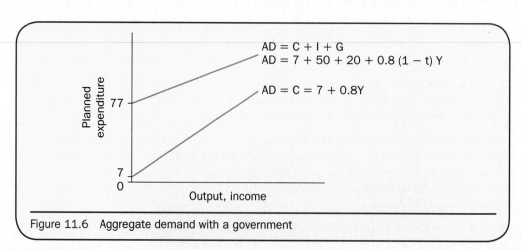

**Figure 11.6** Aggregate demand with a government

on consumption. This is because we have opened up another avenue for leakages. By introducing the government sector, income can leak out via savings and taxes. This is significant because we have seen that the multiplier was determined by the rate of leakages and, indeed, the multiplier is now:

$$\text{Multiplier} = 1/(\text{MPS} + \text{MPT})$$

where MPS = marginal propensity to save, and MPT = marginal propensity to tax.

So, if MPS = 0.2 and the MPT = 0.22 = the UK's basic tax rate, then the multiplier = $1/(0.2 + 0.22) = 2.38$.

When we had no government sector savings the multiplier was equal to:

$$1/\text{MPS} = 1/0.2 = 5$$

Note that introducing the government has decreased the size of the multiplier.

## The balanced budget multiplier

The **balanced budget multiplier** states that an increase in government spending, plus an *equal* increase in taxes, leads to higher equilibrium output. Reducing the size of the multiplier could mean that the government might actually make itself ineffectual. For example, the government could inject 100 into the economy and then take out 100 in higher taxes. Would the multiplier then be zero? Amazingly, the answer to this question is no.

> The **balanced budget multiplier** states that an increase in government spending, plus an *equal* increase in taxes, leads to higher equilibrium output.

Sounds fantastic. You can put £100 in everyone's pocket, then take it out again and make everyone richer! How does this actually work? The answer requires a close examination of aggregate demand, AD = C + I + G. An increase of 100 in government spending clearly increases AD by 100. However, the effect of increasing taxes by 100 does not reduce AD by 100. This is because of the marginal propensity to consume, MPC. As the MPC is only 0.8, an increase in taxes by 100 causes income to fall by 100; the change in consumption is therefore only $0.8 \times 100 = 80$. The net effect on aggregate demand is an increase in G of 100 and a reduction of consumption of only 80. Therefore, aggregate demand increases by 20.

The obvious question to now ask is, how do governments in practice use government spending and taxation to control the equilibrium level of output?

## 11.4 Government's approach to managing fiscal policy

The government's spending and taxation decisions are reflected in the government deficit. The projected expenditure and revenue sources for the government are available from the so-called 'Red Book'. For the tax year 2012–13, the revenue and expenditure figures are shown in Figure 11.7.

The largest areas of expenditure are social security, health and education. Taken together, these three areas represent more than 60 per cent of government spending. The largest sources of revenue come from personal taxation, national insurance contributions and VAT. It is perhaps surprising that revenues from corporation taxes are only £42 billion and represent a very small fraction of total government tax revenues. Government borrowing is £79 billion (£666 billion − £745 billion), the difference between government expenditure and government revenues, and represents the government's deficit.

## Deficits

*Government deficits* as a percentage of GDP are plotted in Figure 11.8 for a number of European economies. These deficits are the annual differences between government receipts

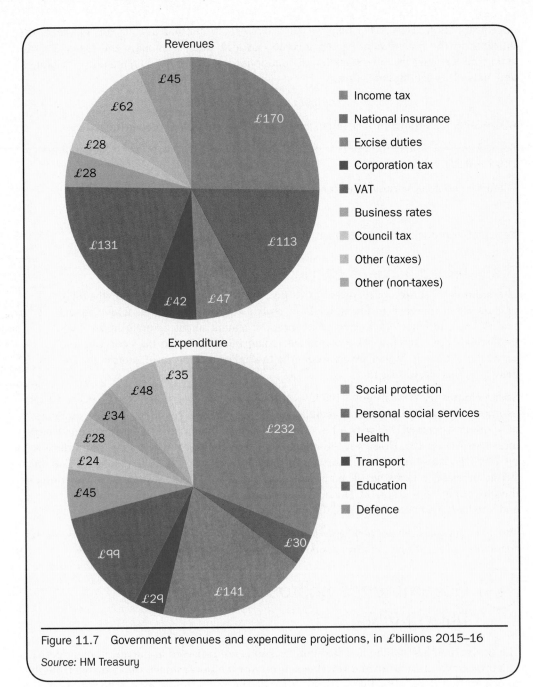

Figure 11.7   Government revenues and expenditure projections, in £billions 2015–16

*Source:* HM Treasury

and expenditures. Government deficits tend to display a cyclical pattern. As economies have fallen into recession, or slowed in growth, tax receipts have fallen behind expenditure levels and deficits have opened up. Members of the eurozone are in normal economic times required to keep their budget deficits under 3 per cent of GDP. Because of the credit and debt crises the 3 per cent rule has been temporarily relaxed.

It is evident from Figure 11.8 that the Greek government has run a proportionately larger deficit, as much as 15 per cent of GDP, whereas the German government has run a much smaller deficit, between 0 and 4 per cent of GDP.

> Cumulative debt is the total outstanding government debt from borrowings over many years.

In Figure 11.9, the **cumulative debt** for selected European economies is shown. (The data for Greece only begin from 2006 because of a reclassification of its debts. Data before that time are no longer consistent with the current measure.) The cumulative

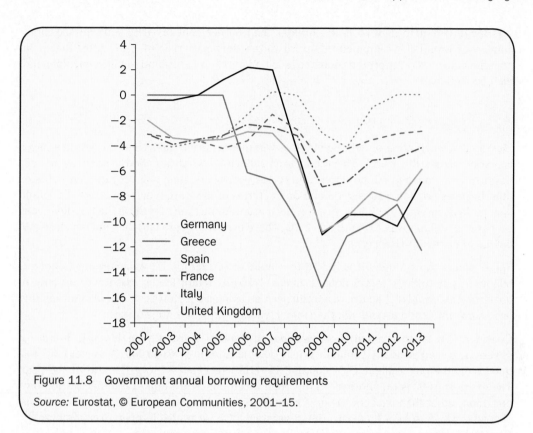

Figure 11.8   Government annual borrowing requirements

*Source:* Eurostat, © European Communities, 2001–15.

debt is all current and outstanding debt. When governments borrow, just like firms and households, they can arrange to borrow for many years. In some instances, governments have borrowed for up to 50 years.

We can see in Figure 11.9 that Italy and Greece have accumulated enormous amounts of debt compared to the size of their economies. In fact, guidance from the European Commission

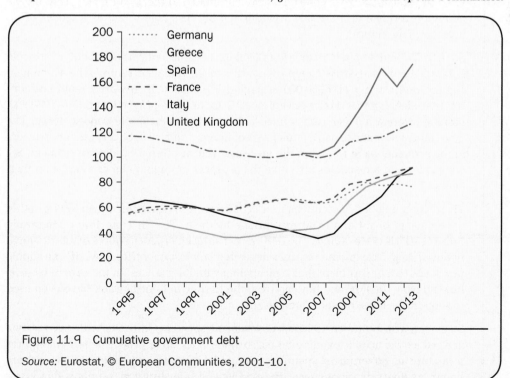

Figure 11.9   Cumulative government debt

*Source:* Eurostat, © European Communities, 2001–10.

was for government debt to be no greater than 60 per cent of GDP. You can see that a number of economies managed this prior to the financial crisis of 2007. After that point governments took on enormous debts to help bail out their banks and to inject spending into their economies.

## Fiscal Crisis

The rapid accumulation of debt by many governments during the financial crisis has raised concerns across the world. These concerns related to what is called a **sovereign debt default**. Governments are no different to other borrowers; they must repay their debts on time, because not doing so is to default on the terms of the loan. When governments default on their loan agreements, it is a very serious matter. At the time of writing the last developed economy to default was Argentina in 2002. These events are rare and the country closest to default at present is Greece.

The seriousness of a default is linked to a number of factors. First, governments borrow billions if not trillions of US dollars, euros, Yen, etc. Many banks and investors lend to governments because they are generally seen as being safe. However, this also means that once a government does default, then many lenders can suffer huge losses.

Consider how a government borrows money, which is usually by **issuing bonds**. A government may issue a €1 million 1-year bond at a price of €950,000. Whoever buys this bond pays the government €950,000 and in return receives €1m at the end of the year. The extra €50,000 is the interest on the bond. Such bonds are highly tradable: if you own one, then rather than wait for the government to pay you, you can sell it early to someone else who wants to be a lender to the government. These trades happen every minute the financial markets are open in cities like, London, New York, Tokyo, etc.

When a government fails to repay its loan commitments, this is called a sovereign debt default.

Issuing bonds is a way of borrowing money used by governments and some companies.

The International Monetary Fund (IMF) receives money on deposit (savings) from most of the world's countries. These funds can be loaned to governments/ countries in financial difficulties.

Austerity measures occur when a government reduces spending and increases tax collection; generally linked to a need to improve the government's finances.

If a government has strong finances, then you can sell the bond at a price which is close to what you paid for it. If the government defaults, then the value of the bond plummets and you might be looking at less than 10 cents in the euro, or less than €100,000 for something which should be worth €1 million. You have just lost €900,000 and so has everyone else who lent money to the government. That means you and everyone else are less wealthy and are less able to act as a lender or an investor in the future.

So what would happen if investors/lenders became concerned about a possible default? An increased risk requires an increased financial return. The €1 million 1-year bond trading at €950,000 is paying 5 per cent. If investors required more return for lending to a riskier government, then the bond price might fall to €930,000, thereby offering a 7 per cent return. This has two unfortunate consequences. The government now has to pay a higher rate of interest on new debt, and other borrowers in the economy have to match the increased return offered by the government. So, companies and households also face the prospect of paying higher interest on their debts.

There are a number of solutions to a debt crisis. The government can look to other governments or international institutions for help. The **International Monetary Fund (IMF)** is one example. The IMF can act as an emergency source of international financial help. Drawing on reserves deposited by most countries, the IMF can supply new loans to a government that is struggling with its finances. In the case of Greece, funding from the IMF and funding from the European Central Bank have been used to support the government's finances.

Steps can also be taken to bring government spending into line with tax receipts and reduce the need for additional borrowings. Such an approach generally requires a mixture of government spending cuts and higher tax collection rates; and are known as **austerity measures**. The problem with austerity measures is that lower government spending reduces injections into the economy and higher tax receipts increases leakages. As a result, the economy slows down and generates less tax and requires more unemployment benefit to be paid, all of which make the government finances worse. A point which is being stressed by Greece.

The government can look towards restructuring its loans. This often involves delaying repayment. So, instead of repaying €1 million 1-year bond in 12 months, an agreement might be reached with lenders that the bond can be repaid over 5 years. A problem with this policy is that the restructure is not orderly. It took Argentina almost 10 years to reach agreement with the majority of its lenders. During that time, the government had limited access to international financial markets for borrowing and the country attracted little international investment. Economic growth was slow. A further problem was that Argentina borrowed in US dollars and the value of the Argentinian peso plummeted at the time of default. The weaker peso multiplied the size of the outstanding debts. This same problem is faced by Greece if it decides to default on its loans, leave the eurozone and relaunch the Greek Drachma as its domestic currency.

Of course, owing the world lots of money, threatening to default and bringing untold damage to countless investors as well as the global economy ironicallyy gives you a decent amount of global power. Read about Greece's negotiating tactics in Box 11.4.

## Fiscal stance

Unfortunately, the continual link between the government deficit and the business cycle makes it difficult to appraise the government's **fiscal stance**. For example, an expansionary fiscal policy would ordinarily consist of a reduction in tax and an increase in government spending, resulting in a larger government deficit. In a recession, tax receipts will fall and create a larger deficit. It is, therefore, difficult to use the government deficit as a measure of the government's fiscal stance. This is because the deficit can occur following an expansionary fiscal policy or, equally, because the economy is in recession.

We need, therefore, to adjust the government deficit for changes associated with the business cycle. We do this by calculating the government deficit if the economy was at its optimal level, or **full-employment level**, of output. We keep government spending and tax rates the same, but then assume that the equilibrium level of the economy is at its full-employment level. We are, therefore, assuming the economy is not in boom or recession—it is perfectly balanced between the two extremes.

> Fiscal stance is the extent to which the government is using fiscal policy to increase or decrease aggregate demand in the economy.
>
> Full-employment level of the economy is a long-run equilibrium position and the economy operates on its production possibility frontier. The economy is in neither boom nor recession.

This full-employment budget position is then described as the *structural budget,* which is adjusted for the business cycle.

Many economies pursue a balanced budget policy, with a stated aim of ensuring a balanced budget over the medium term. This is effectively arguing that the structural budget will be zero. In boom, we might expect a budget surplus; in recession, we could see a deficit. But, on balance, the budget will be just that—balanced. Structural balance still allows a contractionary, or expansionary, fiscal policy. During a recession the government can add spending into the economy through tax reductions and increases in government spending. Similarly, during an economic boom, the government can increase taxes and reduce government spending.

From the 1970s onwards, fiscal policy became less popular, reflecting the concerns of economists and politicians that an overly expansionary fiscal policy can be destabilizing for the economy. However, during the credit crisis a fiscal stimulus was an obvious means of providing a rapid expansion of spending in the economy. Governments across the world quickly realized that cuts in interest rates could be supplemented by government spending and tax cuts. Despite the immediate popularity of fiscal policy, it is still necessary to recognize the weakness which reduced its popularity from the 1970s onwards.

## Box 11.4
## Greece threatens default as fresh reform bid falters

The Greek government has threatened to default on its loans to the International Monetary Fund, as Athens continued its battle to convince creditors for a fresh injection of bail-out cash. 'If no money is flowing on April 9, we will first determine the salaries and pensions paid here in Greece and then ask our partners abroad to achieve consensus that we will not pay €450 million to the IMF on time,' said Nikos Voutzis.

The cash-strapped government has struggled to keep up with its wage and pensions obligations having agreed a bail-out extension on February 20. A Greek government spokesperson later denied the reports of a deliberate default, saying the country still hoped for a 'positive outcome' to its debt negotiations.

The comments came as the eurozone's working group discussed a new 26-page plan of reforms from Athens on Wednesday. Aiming to generate an estimated €6 billion in 2015, Athens has pledged a range of revenue-raising measures including cracking down on tax evasion, carrying out an audit on overseas bank transfers, and introducing a 'luxury tax'.

The document also warned brinkmanship on the part of the eurozone meant the 'viability' of the currency union was now 'in question'. 'It is necessary now, without further delay to turn a corner on the mistakes of the past and to forge a new relationship between member states, a relationship based on solidarity, resolve, mutual respect,' said the proposal.

The Leftist government has continually fallen short of creditor demands, who hold the purse strings on €7.2 billion in bail-out cash the government requires over the next three months.

However, the latest blueprint is unlikely to satisfy lenders as it lacks details on labour market liberalization or pensions reforms. Previous privatizations of the country's assets were also described as a 'spectacular' failure, generating far less in revenues for the state than first envisaged.

The ECB hiked its emergency funding (ELA) for Greece by €700 million, according to reports on Wednesday. Fitch calculates Greek banks have lost 15 per cent of their deposits since November 2014. Having been kept on a tight leash by the Brussels Group, Greece has been scrambling around for cash as it desperately strains to keep itself afloat. In a sign of the country's deteriorating financial position, the government forecasts growth will reach 1.4 per cent in 2015, down from a projected 2.9 per cent. The government has funding needs of €19 billion this year, estimated the finance ministry.

Any failure to repay the IMF on time may not immediately result in an outright default to the Fund, but would likely result in no further disbursement of loans until a repayment is agreed.

According to the IMF's protocol, it will take at least a month before the executive board is notified that an payment is overdue. Before then, debtor countries are urged to meet their obligations as fast as possible. No country has ever officially defaulted to the IMF in its 70-year history, and only the likes of Sudan, Zimbabwe and Somalia have deferred repayment and been in arrears. Greece also faces a further €2.4 billion in debt rollovers it needs to complete in April, a task which will become difficult as the ECB has moved to ban the country's banks from increasing their holdings of Greek government debt.

From *The Telegraph*. 1 April 2015. 'Greece threatens default as fresh reform bid falters'. Mehreen Khan. © Telegraph Media Group Limited (2015)

## Fiscal policy weaknesses

Automatic stabilizers enable the economy to adjust automatically to changes in aggregate demand.

If, during a boom, income in an economy increases, tax receipts will increase, savings will increase and the government will cut back on social payments, such as unemployment benefit. This shows that the economy has automatic brakes built into the system that will help to control the rate of economic boom. Conversely, in recession, tax receipts will fall, savings will reduce and government payments will increase. This way the economy will automatically reduce the net rate of leakages and help to keep the economy moving.

Because such stabilizers work automatically, then, from a fiscal position, the economy can be placed on autopilot. There is no need for the government to overly monitor economic activity and make policy changes. It can focus its energies on other matters, such as health and education.

## Fiscal policy and implementation problems

There are additional reasons for believing in the virtues of automatic stabilizers and these relate to the problems associated with actively managing fiscal policy.

### Time lags

In order to actively manage fiscal policy the government needs to know when aggregate demand is falling and when it is rising. This can only be achieved with a lag. Government statisticians collect data on economic activity, but they are only able to report and, perhaps more important, confirm either a slowdown or an increase in economic activity three to six months after the event. The government then needs to consider a policy response and then introduce the response. This all takes time. Once the policy is introduced—say, a cut in taxation to offset falling demand in an economy—the economy may have moved on, showing signs of economic growth. The tax stimulation is then inappropriate because it will be adding to a boom rather than assisting a recessionary problem.

### Uncertainty

Assume an economy is in recession. The equilibrium level of income is £10 billion, but currently output is around £5 billion. The multiplier is 2. The economy has an output gap of £10bn − £5bn = £5bn. With a multiplier of 2, the government needs to increase aggregate demand by £2.5 billion.

Unfortunately, this example has benefited from complete certainty. We know the equilibrium level of output, the current level of output and the size of the multiplier. In practice, the government and its advisers do not know any of these values with certainty. Now let us assume that all of the factors above are estimates. We could even be generous to the government and say that it guessed the size of the multiplier and the current level of GDP accurately. But the equilibrium level of income is only £8 billion, not £10 billion. Therefore, by overestimating the optimal level of output and injecting £2.5 billion into the economy the government will push the economy straight into a boom. It simply swaps a demoralizing recession for an equally unpalatable bout of inflation.

### Offsetting changes

If the government pursues an expansionary fiscal stance, it will tend to take on more debt in order to finance its spending. At some point in the future this debt has to be serviced and perhaps even repaid. In the presence of very large mountains of public debt, sensible private individuals may predict that in the future tax rates will have to rise in order to fund the current lax fiscal position of the government. In order to offset these future higher taxes, individuals might save more now. Therefore, higher government spending and reduced taxes now could generate higher levels of offsetting autonomous savings. The government's fiscal stance is effectively neutralized by the response of higher savings from the private sector.

Actively managed fiscal policy sought to manage the business cycle by adding demand during a recession and reducing demand during a boom. Due to problems of timing, uncertainty and offsetting, such policy responses have been ill-timed, misjudged and at best ineffective.

## Deficits and inflation

We saw in Chapter 9 that inflation can erode the value of debt. If you borrow £100 and inflation is 10 per cent, then, in real terms, at the end of year one you will only owe £90. You, as a private individual, have very little control over the rate of inflation. But for a government the case is very different. If a government runs up a mountain of debt, the temptation to let the rate of inflation increase and erode the real value of the debt is very tempting.

This has two important implications. First, if a government is trying to manage individuals' inflationary expectations, then it needs to manage the size of the government debt. Being seen to reduce debt and fiscal deficits reduces the need to stoke up inflation. As a consequence, inflationary expectations will be lower and inflation should turn out to be lower. Second, as we see in Chapter 13, within a fixed exchange rate system such as the European single currency, harmonizing inflation across member states may aid economic convergence among those states. Therefore, as entry into the system draws nearer, the UK government needs to bring fiscal policy under control.

### Crowding out

**Crowding out** occurs when increased government spending reduces private sector spending.

**Crowding out** relates back to the business problem at the beginning of this chapter. If government takes an expansionary fiscal stance, then it can achieve this by spending more public money on health, education and transport infrastructure projects. But this policy runs the risk of robbing productive resources from the private sector. For every nurse employed in a hospital, a worker is effectively removed from the private sector. This is known as crowding out, because public expenditure by government crowds out private expenditure by firms. The extent to which this occurs is debatable. When there are lots of workers without jobs, an increase in government spending will not crowd out private expenditure. Employment will rise, output will grow and income will increase. But when productive resources, such as labour, are all fully employed, then increasing public expenditure is likely to rob the private sector of its resources. Employment stays constant, at best output stays constant and so does income. An expansionary fiscal policy has no net impact on national output.

In Box 11.5 the risk of crowding out is acknowledged by the Zambian government as it sets out to be fiscal expansionary.

### Summary

Given all of these problems, it is not surprising that economists and governments began to move away from active fiscal management of the economy. Instead, they recognized the benefits of automatic stabilizers and moved focus to monetary and supply-side policies. Fiscal policy was popular from the 1930s through to the 1970s, a period during which a global depression in the 1930s meant there was no crowding out. Economic change occurred at a more sedate and predictable pace and concerns regarding inflation were less important. All this changed in the 1980s, 1990s and 2000s. With modern economies developing with great pace and complexity, inflationary aversion was everywhere and high levels of employment ensured that crowding out was a real problem. However, following the credit crisis the effectiveness of fiscal policy has returned. This is because a prolonged recession results in little crowding out. At the same time as banks, consumers and firms become insensitive to central bank base rate changes, then fiscal policy can become more attractive than monetary policy.

##  11.5 Foreign trade and aggregate demand

So far in our examination of aggregate demand, we have only considered economies which do not trade with the rest of the world. While we will focus on issues of exchange rates and globalization in Chapters 15 and 16, it is worth incorporating the impact of international trade on aggregate demand.

Exports are generally expressed as X and imports as Z.

## Box 11.5
## Direct aid, subsidies, tax breaks – the hidden welfare budget we don't debate

In 2013 Britons handed £93bn in welfare to corporations. That is enough to wipe out at a stroke this year's budget deficit – and it was given to companies in direct aid, subsidies and tax breaks.

The term 'corporate welfare' may sound unfamiliar to some. In the Westminster thesaurus, welfare appears alongside benefits and social security as a term for public spending targeted at individuals and households. But corporations rely on public funds, too.

When Richard Branson's Virgin Atlantic took £28m from the Welsh government in 2011 to set up a call centre in Swansea, that was a form of welfare. The German, French and Dutch companies that now run our train services are subsidized by the British public to the tune of hundreds of millions. None of these are labelled corporate welfare, but that's precisely what they are: direct public spending aimed at protecting and supporting businesses.

Revealing how far taxpayers fund the private sector is not the same thing as saying the private sector should not receive any public subsidy at all. All rich countries do it, although there is evidence from the OECD thinktank and others that when it comes to corporate tax benefits or public-sector outsourcing, Britain is more indulgent to businesses than many other nations.

Full disclosure of the size of the corporate welfare state might also have improved economic debate over the past half-decade. When Cameron and Osborne launched their austerity programme in 2010, they argued that the public sector was 'crowding out' the private sector. To enable the economy to grow, government needed to retreat and allow businesses to fill the void. That powerful argument was disproved over the next few years, as Britain stuttered and stumbled through the weakest economic recovery in its modern history. But it would have been undermined from the start had ministers been confronted with £93bn of proof that the relationship between public and private sector is far more complicated.

This research on corporate welfare takes you to the heart of one of the biggest arguments in British capitalism. It was summed up by Michael Heseltine in his 2013 report on industrial policy: 'Unless we make it worthwhile for footloose capital to come here, it won't.'

From *The Guardian*. 7 July 2015. 'Direct aid, subsidies, tax breaks – the hidden welfare budget we don't debate'. Aditya Chakrabortty.
© Guardian News & Media Ltd 2015

Economists generally talk about net exports, or the trade balance, which is clearly X − Z. If exports are greater than imports, the economy has a trade surplus, but if imports are greater than exports, the economy has a trade deficit.

We now need to think about incorporating X and Z into our existing analysis of aggregate demand. In fairly simple terms, exports are UK products purchased by foreign consumers; Scotch whisky produced in the UK but sold in the USA would be an example. So, exports add to UK aggregate demand. Imports work in the opposite direction. These are foreign products purchased by UK consumers; BMW cars made in Germany but bought in the UK would be an example. Therefore, aggregate demand can now be defined as AD = C + I + G + X − Z.

However, as with the introduction of the government sector, we need to address the factors that determine exports and imports. First, the level of UK income does not influence exports; instead, US consumers' willingness to purchase UK products is influenced by US income. As income rises in the US, consumers are willing to search out more expensive imports from overseas, such as Scotch whisky. Therefore, exports are autonomous, or independent, of the UK's level of income. In contrast, the level of UK income influences imports. As our income increases, we are willing to buy more expensive products from overseas.

We therefore have a marginal propensity to import (MPZ), which is the increase in income allocated to import products.

In terms of aggregate demand, exports are grouped with the other autonomous expenditures: autonomous consumption, investment and government spending. As such, exports represent a potential injection into the circular flow of income. Rising income levels in the USA, or the European Union, are likely to result in additional UK exports to these economies. Conversely, as these economies move into recession, demand for UK products will fall.

Exports add to the complexity of planning UK domestic policy because, in order to keep aggregate demand at the equilibrium level, the government has to understand the level of domestic consumption, domestic investment and how economic activity on other economies will impact on the demand for UK goods and services. See Box 11.6.

Should we be troubled by a rising trade deficit? The answer is yes, because imports represent a leakage from the circular flow of income. Leakages reduce the size of the multiplier. With imports, injections leak out of the economy more quickly and, therefore, less money is left in the circular flow to go through the next cycle. In an open economy with a government sector, the multiplier is:

Open economy multiplier with government sector = 1/(MPS + MPT + MPZ)

## Box 11.6
## UK trade balance

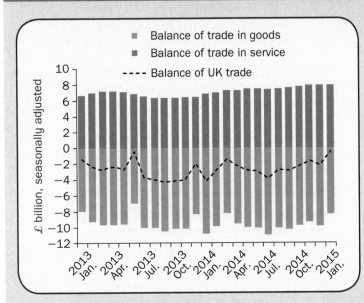

The deficit of trade in goods and services for January 2015 narrowed to £0.6 billion, from £2.1 billion in the previous month. The trade position reflects exports minus imports. The £1.5 billion narrowing between December 2014 and January 2015 is the largest monthly narrowing since March 2014, when the deficit narrowed by £1.8 billion. Between December 2014 and January 2015, exports decreased by £1.0 billion to £42.3 billion and imports decreased by £2.5 billion to £42.9 billion.

The deficit on trade in goods was £8.4 billion in January 2015, narrowing by £1.5 billion from December 2014. Exports fell by £1.0 billion between December 2014 and January 2015, while imports fell more substantially, down £2.5 billion from December

2014. The fall in imports of goods is the largest monthly decrease since July 2006, when the import level fell by £2.8 billion.

In detail, exports of goods fell by £1.0 billion to £24.1 billion in January 2015. This decrease reflects a £0.8 billion fall in exports of fuels and a £0.3 billion fall in exports of machinery and transport equipment. Fuel exports reached their lowest level since March 2007.

Imports of goods fell by £2.5 billion in January 2015, a £1.3 billion fall in imports of fuels; specifically oil imports (down £1.2 billion from December 2014). Imports of manufactured goods fell by £0.9 billion between December 2014 and January 2015; machinery and transport equipment, miscellaneous manufactures and chemicals each fell by £0.3 billion.

Focusing on trade in oil, exports stood at £1.6 billion in January 2015 (the lowest level since February 2007), down £0.8 billion from the previous month. Imports of oil stood at £2.2 billion in January 2015 (the lowest level since May 2009), down £1.2 billion from the previous month. In terms of volume, oil exports fell by 15.1 per cent between December 2014 and January 2015 and imports fell 12.5 per cent over the same period. Despite the impact of trade in oil in recent months, the balance of trade in goods excluding oil also narrowed in January 2015, reaching a deficit of £7.8 billion; the lowest monthly deficit since June 2013.

*Source:* www.statistics.gov.uk

Imports, therefore, increase the economy's leakages and in so doing can reduce the size of the multiplier.

In terms of fiscal policy, the open economy creates real practical problems for the government. For example, if the government increases government spending, then this represents an autonomous injection into the economy. With an open economy, however, there is a distinct possibility that this additional expenditure could leak out as imports, resulting in zero impact on the level of aggregate demand. For example, increased spending by the UK government on health care can now be used to pay for operations undertaken in French hospitals. The money spent on extending the UK's airport capacity could be spent by workers on foreign holidays.

## Summary

Fiscal policy, in the main, relies on the power of the multiplier to provide the government with an effective tool for managing the economy. As the world's economies become more globally integrated, the scope of international leakages increases and the multiplier decreases in size and effectiveness. Moreover, fiscal policy requires timely and accurate information. The complexity of modern economies, including increasing globalization, makes these informational requirements difficult to attain.

# Business application: debt funding and crowding out

Crowding out occurs when government spending absorbs economic resource that would have been used by the private sector. Increases in government spending, therefore, result in lower private sector spending. The net effect on total expenditure is zero. The government's fiscal expansion is neutralized.

Unfortunately, the problem of crowding out can be worse than this. Unless the government has enormous cash reserves, then an expansion in government spending needs to be funded by borrowings. Government debt has to increase. So who lends to governments?

The answer to this last question is varied. Lenders can include ordinary household savers, private companies, pension funds and banks. In a global financial system, lenders can also include overseas investors. So even when an economy has a very low marginal propensity to save, governments can raise huge amounts of debt by borrowing from overseas investors.

Generally, governments do not face problems when raising debt. Lenders view governments from modern developed economies as safe bets. The creditworthiness of governments is usually high. But this may not be the case when governments are seeking to increase borrowings on an unprecedented scale. In order to service debt, governments need to be capable of raising taxes. But during a recession tax receipts can fall and the ability to service enormous debts can fall. This worries individuals and companies who lend to governments. The obvious way to address these fears is to ask for a higher interest rate to cover the increased risk of lending to a heavily indebted government, something which has caused enormous problems for the likes of Greece, Ireland and Italy.

If the price of debt rises for governments, then the price of debt also rises for the private sector. This is a simple substitution effect. If the private sector is not willing to borrow at the same prices as governments are willing to pay, then lenders will simply lend to governments only. As a consequence, there is an alternative crowding-out effect. Increases in government borrowings can push up the price of debt for private-sector borrowers. An increase in the price of funds reduces the demand for debt by the private sector. If debt consumption falls, then so does household consumption and company investment.

A variation of this type of financial crowding out is at risk of occurring in Korea (see Box 11.7). High levels of household debt are being further fuelled by government policies supporting greater home ownership. As more households take on greater amounts of debt, the demand for debt rises and pushes up interest rates. If households spend more on interest payments, then they spend less on food, clothing, holidays, cars, etc. Debt financing costs crowd out other expenditure and economic growth is not supported.

# 11.7  Business application: taxation or government spending?

A fiscal stimulus can occur through increased government spending or a reduction in tax. Both approaches increase total expenditure. Government spending directly alters the amount of expenditure, while tax cuts boost disposable income, which then leads to an increase in consumption. If government spending and tax both increase total expenditure, should the form of fiscal stimulus matter to business? The answer is yes, and it matters on a number levels, including how quickly the additional expenditure hits the economy and where the expenditure is channelled.

### Timing

Governments are very good at announcing huge increases in expenditure. In our terminology, this is planned expenditure. This is very different from actual expenditure. Governments are not being disingenuous. Rather, it takes time to highlight projects, design them, contract for

## Box 11.7
## South Korea in balancing act on household debt

Economists have raised fears over the country's heavy household debt, which has risen steadily since the late 1990s to more than 160 per cent of disposable incomes at the end of last year—one of the highest levels of any developed nation.

This week Seoul rolled out a $20 billion programme helping homeowners to switch to fixed-rate, amortized mortgages, which the government considers more stable than the floating-rate 'bullet loans' that are unusually dominant in South Korea. The scheme will help address the concerns of observers such as the International Monetary Fund, which warned in January that South Korea's mortgage debt structure 'poses a vulnerability to the financial system'.

However, the government is under scrutiny for its easing of mortgage regulations in August last year in a bid to boost a stagnating housing market. The scheme had some success on that front, with property prices rising 2 per cent in the year to February. But the reforms, which eased limits on the ratio of mortgage loans to property value and income, also boosted the household debt pile, which surged 6.6 per cent to hit Won1,089 trillion ($1 trillion) at the end of the year.

The government hopes a re-energized property market will boost sentiment in a country where an exceptionally high proportion of personal assets are in the form of real estate. But while the tactic could bring immediate rewards, 'over time it has the potential to start crowding out demand', says Bill Adams, head of fixed income at MFS Investment Management.

Some economists say this trend is already under way, with South Koreans spending about a fifth of their incomes on servicing debts. While default rates remain low by international standards, analysts at Nomura predict that households' capacity to service their debts will 'deteriorate substantially' from the early 2020s, in part a symptom of a rapidly ageing population.

Some remain sceptical that the government's approach is prudent. 'The government here tends to introduce policies that encourage people to borrow money,' says Kwon Oh-in of Citizens' Coalition for Economic Justice, a non-profit group. 'What's needed is to boost incomes, through creating jobs or raising the minimum wage. Otherwise the household debt problem will get worse and worse.'

From the *Financial Times*. 26 March 2015. 'South Korea in balancing act on household debt'. Simon Mundy. © The Financial Times Limited 2015. All Rights Reserved.

them and begin to spend the money. Unless there are many infrastructure projects in the pipeline, then it can take many years to develop such a pipeline. Meanwhile, the economy does not receive its much needed injection of spending.

In contrast, cuts in direct taxes, such as income tax, and cuts in indirect taxes, such as those on goods and services, create an immediate change in consumers' income. Tax cuts, therefore, have the potential to provide an almost instantaneous flow of additional spending into the economy.

## Channels of spending

Governments spend on projects which they find attractive. This spending tends to be focused on education, health care and transport. Infrastructure projects in these areas are popular: new buildings, roads, railways and airports. Huge flows of money are channelled to the construction industry. Other sectors do not receive direct spending. Of course, some industries receive subsidies, loans and capital injections. In many economies, this has involved flows of money into banks and in the USA and Germany has also included cash injections into the automotive industry. But is this spending effective, efficient and valued by taxpayers?

If fiscal policy involves tax cuts, then consumers can spend money in the markets they find most desirable. If an individual does not like flying, then the value of a government-funded airport expansion is limited. But if that individual receives a tax cut, then they can spend their additional income on a holiday within the economy.

This debate goes to the heart of market-based economies. In Chapter 1 we introduced the production possibility frontier and highlighted two approaches to the allocation of economic resources: planned economies and market-based economies. Markets are generally accepted as the most effective means of solving the problem of infinite wants and finite resources. Why, during a recession, should we sacrifice this view and suddenly believe that governments are better placed to decide where spending should occur?

One response is that consumers may not react to tax cuts. They may instead save the additional income, or run down existing debts. In addition, in an economy that has a high propensity to import, tax cuts are unlikely to fuel an increase in domestic demand. So, for these reasons the government spending may be preferable because it ensures that spending occurs and that it occurs within the economy.

Firms need to be aware of these differences between government spending and tax cuts. An understanding of the differences enables an understanding of the likely time it will take to stimulate the economy and which sectors will be winners and losers.

We term this *planned expenditure through disposable income and then through consumption*. Should it matter to business how the stimulus occurs?

## 11.8 Business data application: understanding the fiscal position and the implications for business

Much has been written about the levels of government indebtedness across Europe and around the world. In this section, we highlight where useful data can be found, draw attention to some of the key trends with government debt statistics for France, Germany, Greece and the UK, and explore some important implications for the economy and for business, as governments struggle to bring their borrowings under control.

In terms of finding data, there are a number of economic institutions and organizations that provide data on a range of macroeconomic variables, including public-sector/government

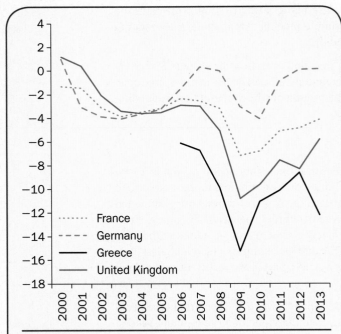

Figure 11.10   Annual government borrowing needs as a percentage of GDP

*Source:* OECD.

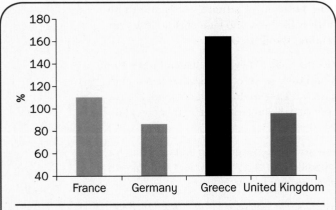

Figure 11.11   Total net government borrowings as a percentage of GDP, 2014

*Source:* OECD.

debt. Such organizations include in-country government statistical departments, such as the UK's Office for National Statistics, the World Bank, the International Monetary Fund, Eurostat in the EU and the Organisation for Economic Co-operation and Development.

The scale and, indeed, the rapid rise in government debts can be seen in the expansion of annual deficit financing (see Figure 11.10) and the growth in total outstanding debt (see Figure 11.11). In nearly all four economies, the start of the credit crisis in 2008 and the onset of the global recession marks a swift deterioration in the state of government finances. In the specific case of Greece, a need to fund an annual 5 per cent deficit in 2007 quickly became a 16 per cent financial black hole by 2010. Although Greece improved its position by 2012, the deficit once again deteriorated and concerns over a Greek default returned. As annual deficit financing grew and governments needed to borrow more and more, outstanding debt as a percentage of GDP also began to rise. Following a steady reduction in outstanding debt to about 33 per cent of GDP in 2002, the UK suddenly found itself with borrowings equal to more than 60 per cent of GDP by 2010 and 95 per cent by 2014. France underwent a similar experience to that of the UK, while Greece managed to raise its outstanding government debt from 80 per cent to 130 per cent of GDP in 2010, falling back to 110 per cent by 2014.

While the recent global recession has played a role in the growth of government debt, it is not the only reason, nor indeed, perhaps, the most important reason. If we look at Figure 11.12, which illustrates GDP growth rates for our chosen economies, we can see that for all these economies, GDP growth rates were both positive and reasonably high from 2002 onwards. Only a few countries suffered a negative growth rate in one or two years; and yet throughout this early period of time government annual deficits from 2002 onwards were growing (see Figure 11.10). Governments were using the period of high stable growth rates to support additional borrowings. If government borrowings increase during a period of economic growth, then the expansion of government debt is structural not cyclical.

In Figure 11.13 we present data on the size of the structural deficits. In recent times, only Germany has managed to keep its structural deficit small. Greece has expanded its structural deficit from 2002 onwards, moving from 2 to 18 per cent of GDP. During the same time period the UK moved from a structural surplus of 1 per cent to a structural deficit of 10 per cent.

Cyclical deficits should reduce as an economy begins to recover from a recession, tax revenues rise and transfer payments reduce. However, structural deficits will persist, unless there is strong government action to cut spending and raise taxation further. The scale of the structural deficits in Greece in particular, and to some extent in the UK, requires a substantial rebalancing of government finances. The patterns of increased spending and reduced taxation, embarked upon in 2002, need reversing. Such large-scale reversal of policy will have dramatic implications for the economy and business.

Reductions in government spending will reduce aggregate expenditure and therefore GDP. Any fiscal multiplier effect will only serve to amplify the reduction in GDP. Equally, increased taxation will reduce household incomes and that, in turn, will lead to a fall in consumer spending.

An understanding of basic macroeconomic concepts, especially concepts linked to fiscal policy and government debt, enables business managers to have a stronger appreciation of how the business environment and the broader economy

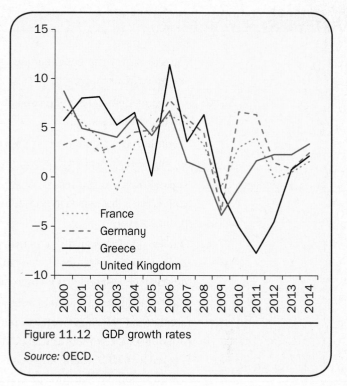

Figure 11.12   GDP growth rates

Source: OECD.

are linked to deficit reduction policies. Importantly, a significant amount of government deficits is structural and not cyclical, meaning that governments cannot rely on a growing economy to correct high fiscal deficits. Austerity plans aimed at reducing government spending and raising tax are necessary; and such policies will act as a drag on overall economic output.

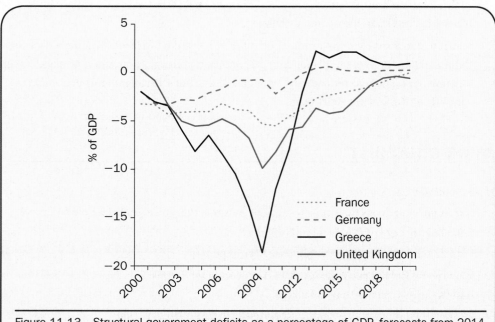

Figure 11.13   Structural government deficits as a percentage of GDP, forecasts from 2014 onwards.

Source: IMF.

# Summary

1. The use of government spending and taxation to affect aggregate demand are examples of fiscal policy.

2. Aggregate demand is composed of consumption, investment, government spending and net exports.

3. In equilibrium, planned expenditure equals planned output. In the Keynesian Cross, the equilibrium is characterized by the 45° line.

4. Expenditure which does not change with the level of income is known as *autonomous expenditure*. Increases in autonomous expenditure lead to higher equilibrium levels of output.

5. The marginal propensity to consume (MPC) measures the increase in consumption from an increase in income. The marginal propensity to save (MPS) measures the increase in savings from an increase in income.

6. If a £100 million increase in autonomous expenditure leads to a £500 million increase in GDP, then the fiscal multiplier is 5. The multiplier is dependent upon the rate of leakage from the circular flow of income. In a closed economy, the multiplier is equal to 1/MPS. But in an open economy with a government sector, the multiplier is reduced by the marginal propensity to tax (MPT) and the marginal propensity to import (MPZ) and so equals 1/(MPS + MPT + MPZ).

7. Fiscal policies can act as an automatic stabilizer on the economy. Rising incomes in a booming economy will be constrained by increasing tax receipts.

8. Active fiscal policies where the government seeks to pursue an expansionary, or contractionary, fiscal policy can be problematic. Problems surrounding timing, uncertainty, offsetting behaviour, crowding out and inflation-inducing deficits can create instability in the economic system.

9. Current concerns over government debt levels are linked to large structural deficits, which require a reversal of spending and taxation policies. Higher taxation and lower spending may help to reduce government deficits, but will not support economic growth, at least in the short term

# Learning checklist

You should now be able to:

- Use Keynesian Cross diagrams to find the macroeconomic equilibrium output
- Calculate the size of the fiscal multiplier
- Explain why the multiplier might assist fiscal policy
- Understand the risks associated with a sovereign debt crisis
- Assess the government's fiscal stance
- Explain the potential problems associated with using fiscal policy.

## Questions

connect

1.  Identify the main components of total expenditure.

2.  Explain why the 45° line represents the equilibrium in a Keynesian Cross diagram.

3.  What is an autonomous expenditure? Use a suitable diagram to illustrate the effect on the economy of an increase in autonomous expenditures.

4.  Explain how the consumption function links consumer spending and current income. Do you think this is a reasonable explanation of consumer spending?

5.  What is the fiscal multiplier? What determines the size of the multiplier? How does the multiplier differ between closed and open economies?

6.  During the last five years what are the key trends in the government deficit for your own economy?

7.  Explain how you would assess the size of the government deficit to determine whether the government was using fiscal policy to expand or contract the economy.

8.  Explain what is meant by the term 'balanced budget multiplier'.

9.  Consider the four key components of aggregate expenditure: consumption, investment, government spending and net exports. Is your economy dominated by domestic private spending, domestic public spending or external demand?

10. What problems are associated with the implementation of fiscal policy?

11. Recall Chapters 9 and 10. Which key macroeconomic variable is missing from the Keynesian Cross approach? Is this a major drawback of the Keynesian Cross approach?

12. In a closed economy with no government sector consumption, $C = 20 + 0.8Y$, investment $I = 40$. What is the equilibrium level of income $Y$?

13. When examining fiscal policy, should business be more interested in taxation policy or government spending?

14. An economy requires a fiscal stimulus. How effective will this stimulus be if the economy has a high marginal propensity to import?

15. The marginal propensity to save in China is extremely high, in excess of 30 per cent. Google and find out why.

EASY

INTERMEDIATE

DIFFICULT

## Exercises

1.  True or false?

    (a)  In equilibrium, planned expenditure will equal planned output.

    (b)  The fiscal multiplier is equal to 1/MPC.

    (c)  The following are autonomous expenditures: investment, government spending and net exports.

    (d)  Credit offered by banks is backed by cash deposits.

    (e)  Keynesians believe that inflation is a monetary problem.

    (f)  If aggregate supply is perfectly inelastic, a reduction in interest rates will lead to higher inflation.

EASY

**Table 11.2** Income and consumption

| Income (output) | Planned consumption | Planned investment | Savings | Aggregate demand | Unplanned inventory change | Actual investment |
|---|---|---|---|---|---|---|
| 50 | 35 | | | | | |
| 100 | 70 | | | | | |
| 150 | 105 | | | | | |
| 200 | 140 | | | | | |
| 250 | 175 | | | | | |
| 300 | 210 | | | | | |
| 350 | 245 | | | | | |
| 400 | 280 | | | | | |

2. Table 11.2 shows some data on consumption and income (output). Planned investment is autonomous, and occurs at the rate of $60 billion per period.

   (a) Calculate savings and aggregate demand at each level of income.

   (b) For each level of output, work out the unplanned change in inventory holdings and the rate of actual investment.

   (c) If, in a particular period, income turned out to be $100 billion, how would you expect producers to react?

   (d) If, in a particular period, income turned out to be $350 billion, how would you expect producers to react?

   (e) What is the equilibrium level of income?

   (f) What is the marginal propensity to consume?

   (g) If investment increased by $15 billion, what would be the change in equilibrium income?

   (h) Use graph paper to plot the consumption function and aggregate demand schedule.

   (i) Add on the 45° line and confirm that equilibrium occurs at the same point suggested by your answer to 2(e) above.

   (j) Show the effect on equilibrium of an increase in investment of $15 billion.

3. (a) Using a Keynesian Cross diagram, illustrate how an increase in exports would alter the equilibrium output for an economy. What evidence is there that your economy is currently benefiting from an export boom?

   (b) What evidence is there that at present consumption and investment expenditure are rising in your economy?

   (c) Explain the variety of ways through which an increase in interest rates by the central bank would impact your economy.

4. Source data on the level of government debt in Greece. Evaluate the extent to which the Greek government can continue to service this level of debt.

# Money, banking and interest

## Chapter contents

## Learning outcomes

By the end of this chapter you should be able to:

**Economic theory**

LO1   List the key features of money

LO2   Identify the nature and economic importance of banking

LO3   Discuss the importance of banking regulation

LO4   Explain the credit-creation process

LO5   List broad and narrow measures of money

LO6   Explain the transaction, precautionary and speculative motives for holding money

LO7   Illustrate money-market equilibrium

LO8   Review the various features of monetary policy

**Business application**

LO9   Discuss financial stability and businesses' desire for investment

LO10   Evaluate the importance of banking to the economy

LO11   Assess the impact of quantitative easing on key financial markets and the broader economy

## At a glance  Money, banking and interest

### The issue

Money is a key feature of economic activity. What are the key features of money, what is the purpose of the banking system and how is it that interest rates can be used to influence GDP and inflation?

### The understanding

Money enables buyers and sellers to trade and is referred to as a medium of exchange. Banks are important because they channel liquidity from savers who have too much cash to borrowers who have a shortage of cash. The interest rate is the equilibrium price of money. By varying the interest rate, a central bank alters the cost of borrowing. Since borrowing can facilitate household consumption and firm-level investment, changing interest rates can change the level of demand in an economy.

### The usefulness

Understanding how the money and banking markets work is extremely important. First, it enables an understanding of how interest rate changes are transmitted into the wider economy. This has important implications for the level of consumption and investment demand. Second, banking is such an important component of modern economies that it is essential to understand the role of banking within an economy and appreciate its ability to support economic growth and also damage economic stability when there is a banking crisis.

 **12.1** ## Business problem: understanding how the monetary environment influences the commercial environment

Such is the importance of monetary policy that interest rate changes in the US, the eurozone and the UK are dealt with as major news events. But why is interest-rate policy such a significant part of economic policy? The answer to this question is complex and involves an understanding of money, banking and money-market equilibrium.

Money is a key characteristic of most economic transactions. Goods and services are nearly always priced in monetary terms. A pizza is £5, or £7. You never see pizza priced in bottles of Coca-Cola, or any other good or service. Money is a common price and, just as important, money is commonly accepted as payment for goods and services and is equally accepted as payment for work. While a key feature of economic activity, money is not economic activity. The conversion of economic inputs—land, labour, capital and enterprise—into goods and services is economic activity. But money is the means of facilitating economic transactions; as such, money is the lubricant of the economic system. To understand the level of economic activity and the level of consumption and investment demand is, in part, to understand how much monetary grease is in the system.

Understanding how much money exists within the economic system is not straightforward. Notes and coins are an obvious example of money, but so too are the electronic digits of money in your bank accounts. While the Bank of England is responsible for printing additional amounts of money, the retail banks are capable of multiplying electronic credits of money. If a company pays in £1 million, then the bank may lend out £0.9 million in loans. The money supply has just increased by £0.9 million. The company thinks it has £1 million of money and the borrowers think they also have £0.9 million of money.

Expansion of the money supply by banks represents the provision of liquidity. Channelling money from savers, who have excess cash for their current transaction needs, to borrowers, who are short of cash, given their current transaction needs, is a very beneficial economic activity. But the rate at which this occurs can be problematic. Too much credit expansion, and consumption and investment demand can grow too quickly, leading to inflation. Too little credit expansion, such as during the credit crisis, and economic growth will slow.

In setting base rates for the economy, central banks attempt to set the rate of credit expansion within an economy. Base rates determine the money market rates for money. If the central bank raises the base rate, then the price of monetary funds increases. With a fixed demand for money, the central bank must reduce the money supply in order to raise the interest rate. By mopping up excess liquidity, through higher rates of interest, the central bank limits the ability of retail banks to expand credit for consumption and investment. Likewise, if the bank reduces interest rates, then money supply needs to be increased, which enables the retail banks to expand credit to borrowers.

Understanding the intricacies of the money and banking markets and the role of the central bank provides a deeper insight into how changes in the base rates can impact on the level of consumption, investment and overall economic activity. Furthermore, understanding the economic importance of banking in providing credit and liquidity also opens up an understanding of the financial risks undertaken by banks. When banks collapse or face a loss of confidence, there can be a loss of confidence and withdrawal of liquidity from the economy. Banking regulation and an understanding of the importance of banking to the economy are also key issues to understand.

We will now develop your understanding of these issues by considering the role of money, the economic importance of banking, the regulation of banking, the credit-creation process, the demand for money, money market equilibrium and monetary policies.

##  What is money?

Money facilitates exchange. Consider an economy with no money, generally referred to as a **barter economy**, where goods are swapped for other goods.

We are specialist economic textbook authors. That is what we produce. You might flip burgers or drive a taxi. This book could be worth 30 burgers or one taxi ride to the airport. We do not like burgers, but we do fly, so we need a taxi. But will the taxi driver want our economics textbook in return for a trip to the airport, and if the burger flipper wants our book, do we want 30 burgers in return?

You can see the problem: without money a so-called **double coincidence of wants** is required in order to exchange goods.

As textbook authors we need to find people who want our book, and are offering goods we want in exchange. Money solves this problem. We can pay the taxi driver £30 cash and they can then use that money to buy goods which they desire, such as food, petrol or coffee; they do not have to accept the textbook.

A central role of money is that it is recognized and accepted as a medium of exchange. Workers will accept money in exchange for their labour. Shop owners will accept money in exchange for their goods and services. As a medium of exchange, money is extremely efficient because it cuts down on the need for a double coincidence of wants.

Money also has other functions. It is generally seen to be a **unit of account**.

All prices are expressed in monetary terms. A BMW is £20,000, not 100 cows. In the US the unit of account is dollars and in the eurozone it is euros. Goods and services are expressed in a common unit, which is monetary based. This again enables

In a barter economy, there is no money, and individuals trade by exchanging different goods and services.

A double coincidence of wants occurs when two people trade goods and services without money. The first individual demands the good offered by the second individual, and vice versa.

Unit of account is the unit in which prices are quoted.

efficient transactions by facilitating comparisons and transparency in pricing. A common unit of account, or price, enables buyers and sellers to understand the value of the current market price and whether or not a transaction is profitable or loss-making.

> A **store of value** is something that can be used to make future purchases, e.g. money.
>
> **Fiat money** is notes and coins guaranteed by the government rather than by gold deposits.
>
> **Virtual currencies** are defined by the European Central Bank as unregulated digital currencies, created by software developers and used and accepted amongst the members of a virtual community.

Money should also be a **store of value**. For example, milk is not a good store of value because it deteriorates quickly and goes bad. Money, as metal coins and paper banknotes, does not perish. Money earned today can be saved and used next week or next month to facilitate a future transaction. However, money is not a perfect store of value. Money as cash earns zero interest and its value is eroded by inflation. Other assets, such as houses, gold and interest-bearing accounts can all serve as stores of value.

However, money is the predominant medium of exchange in most economies. Today money takes the form of **fiat money**. Before fiat money, governments backed money with gold. The holder of a note could approach the central bank and demand that their note be exchanged for an equivalent value of gold. Money is no longer backed by gold, but is instead guaranteed by the government or central bank. Fiat money has a number of beneficial aspects associated with it. It is legally recognized as a medium of exchange and is culturally accepted as such. People are willing to exchange goods for money. Paper notes and coins are cheap to make (see the mass-production techniques employed by the Royal Mint in Box 12.1). A £10 note does not require £10 of resource in order to make it. In contrast, a £10 gold nugget would represent £10 of resource. Government-backed money economizes on scarce resources. But here is the problem: because a £10 note can be produced for less than £10, forgers can make a profit. Therefore, forgery has to be outlawed and the law enforced.

## Virtual currencies

Alternatives to fiat money are virtual currencies, such as bitcoin. **Virtual currencies** are defined by the European Central Bank as unregulated digital currencies, created by software developers and used and accepted amongst the members of a virtual community.

Virtual currencies have some of the features of money. For example, bitcoin is a unit of account and a store of value. Goods and services can be priced in bitcoins and individuals trade bitcoins in exchange for these goods and services. Bitcoin also has some store of value. For example, bitcoin can be held and exchanged at a later date for another currency, including fiat currencies such as the US dollar. However, to date the store of value for virtual currencies has been very volatile—for example, in early January 2015 one bitcoin could be exchanged for $320. By mid-January 2015, one bitcoin was worth $160 and by the end of March 2015 one bitcoin was worth $250.

### Box 12.1
### Making money: rolling in it!

The Royal Mint boasts some of the most advanced coining machinery in the world. In the foundry, strips of metal are drawn from large electric furnaces, reduced to the required thickness in a tandem rolling mill and transferred to large blanking presses where coin blanks can be punched out at the rate of 10,000 per minute. The blanks are softened and cleaned in the Annealing and Pickling Plant before the final process in the Coining Press Room. Here, the blanks are fed into coining presses where the obverse and reverse designs, as well as the milling on the edge, are stamped simultaneously onto the blank. The Royal Mint's latest presses can each strike more than 600 coins per minute, making it impossible for the human eye to separate the individual pieces as they pass through the press.

*Source:* Royal Mint, www.royalmint.com.

Fluctuations in value are not good when looking for a store value. Some of the volatility lies in the limited number of users of the currency. With a relatively small number of users, demand and supply of the currency can alter markedly from day to day. Limited supply and high demand on one day will lead to a higher price for the currency, while the next day, high supply and low demand will lead to a dramatic fall in value. These problems do not exist in an economy the size of Europe, the US or the UK where total population and users can be as high as 300 million per day.

The final problem is one of vulnerability to forgery. Virtual currencies are protected by advanced numerical passwords known as *cryptographs*. The passcode is shared amongst legitimate creators of new currency. Hacking the code can enable someone to create currency for themselves. Like forgery, hacking can be made difficult or prohibitively expensive, requiring advanced computer equipment and vast amounts of processing time. However, the financial returns for a hacker can be in the hundreds of millions. Once hacked, additional currency comes onto the market and this increased supply reduces the price. Therefore, the criminal threat to the currency also adds to the volatility of the virtual currencies.

##  The banking system

The banking system consists of the central bank, retail banks and wholesale banks. The **central bank** issues money into the economy through the banking system and the money markets more generally. The central bank acts as banker to the retail and wholesale banks. If a retail bank has spare cash, then it can safely deposit this money at the central bank. Likewise, in extreme circumstances, if a commercial bank cannot gain funds from any other lender, the central bank may act as the lender of last resort and provide a loan to the commercial bank.

A **retail bank** takes deposits from retail customers, borrows from other banks and the money markets and raises funds from shareholders. Taken together, all these funds are then loaned out to retail borrowers or invested in financial instruments or deposited at the central bank.

**Wholesale banks** take very large cash deposits and broker very large loans, both for banks and other commercial companies. Wholesale banks are sometimes referred to as investment banks. Such banks tend to locate in financial hubs such as London and New York, where they can raise money on the wholesale financial markets and bring large lenders together to lend in syndicate to large commercial borrowers.

The banking system is just one part of the broader financial system. Other major financial companies include insurance companies, building societies, hedge funds and pension funds. At root, most financial companies are involved in **financial intermediation**, which involves raising funds from individuals with excess cash, and then lending to or investing the cash in companies or individuals who are short of funds.

The balance sheet for all UK banks in Table 12.1 highlights the banking function of financial intermediation. A balance sheet is a financial statement of a company's assets and liabilities and each side must balance against the other. So, assets = liabilities.

On the liabilities side, banks raise money from shareholders. This money is referred to as *capital*. Banks also raise funds from depositors and by borrowing in the money markets from other banks or financial companies, such as pension funds. On the asset side, banks make loans to households and firms. They may also place some funds in financial securities, such as government or company bonds. Or they may simply place money on deposit at the central bank.

Deposits at banks are classified as sight and time deposits. **Sight deposits** are current accounts. Customers can access their cash instantly. **Time deposits** require the customer to give the bank notice before withdrawing funds.

A central bank acts as a banker to the commercial bank, taking deposits and, in extreme circumstances, making loans.

A retail bank lends to non-banks, including households and non-bank firms.

Wholesale banks take large deposits and are involved in brokering very large loans to companies.

Financial intermediation involves channelling cash from savers to borrowers.

Sight deposits provide customers with instant access to cash.

Time deposits require the customer to give the bank notice before withdrawing cash.

**Table 12.1**  Balance sheet of UK banks, February 2015

| Assets | | Liabilities | |
|---|---|---|---|
| *In foreign currency* | | | |
| Securities | 1,521 | Currency, deposits and money market instruments | 2,399 |
| Loans | 2,300 | Foreign currency capital | 1,422 |
| Total foreign currency assets | 3,821 | Total foreign currency liabilities | 3,821 |
| *In sterling* | | | |
| Notes and coins (including cash held at central bank) | 322 | Notes outstanding and cash loaded on cards | 7 |
| Securities | 2,460 | Currency, deposits and money market instruments | 2,933 |
| Loans | 582 | Sterling capital | 424 |
| Total sterling assets | 3,364 | Total sterling liabilities | 3,364 |
| Total | 7,185 | Total | 7,185 |

Source: Bank of England, *Bankstats.*

The central problem for most banks is that they borrow short and lend long. Money raised from depositors, especially in sight deposits, may be run down over a month as a household pays its bills. But the bank may lend to mortgage customers for 25 years. If a deposit holder requires cash quickly, then the bank cannot ask the borrower to pay quicker. This is why the bank holds some funds in securities. These funds earn a low rate of interest, but they provide the bank with instant access to cash. This is referred to as *liquidity* and the bank needs to trade increased liquidity against increased profits. More cash on loan means higher profits, but less liquidity. More cash in securities means higher liquidity, but lower profits.

In examining Table 12.1 further, it is important to note that the capital of UK banks is small when compared with the amount of funds generated from currency, deposits and money markets. This means that the majority of loans funded by UK banks are paid for by savers, and other lenders to the bank. Shareholders provide banks with very limited funds. This is the essence of financial intermediation, where cash from savers is channelled to borrowers. It also means that, when loans turn bad and are not repaid, banks come under enormous financial stress. Shareholders' funds can be very quickly wiped out by losses on the loan book, after which the inability to repay depositors becomes a real issue.

Such risks have resulted in governments guaranteeing deposits within banks. In addition, many governments around the world have injected billions of capital into banks to ensure their financial viability. In Table 12.1 on the asset side of the balance more than £300 billion in cash is recorded. In previous editions of this book, the amount of cash assets held by UK banks was so small we did not record it. This time the figure is too large to be ignored and in part reflects the enormous amounts of money injected into banks by the Bank of England and by banks themselves reserving cash, rather than loaning it out again to borrowers. That is to say, the money given to commercial banks by the Bank of England has been kept by the banks in their own bank accounts. These bank accounts in turn are provided by the Bank of England. You learn more about this when we discuss quantitative easing later in this chapter.

Given that companies in other sectors are often allowed to collapse, why would a government be keen to support banking? To answer this question, we need to understand the economic importance of banking.

## The economic importance of banking

Banking is now central to money. While notes and coins exist, the vast majority of money is electronic and within bank accounts. In fact, bank deposits are a medium of exchange because they are accepted as payment by sellers of goods and services.

The economic importance of banking cannot be understated. Aside from being a large component of GDP and a massive source of employment within an economy, the services that banking offers are essential to a well-functioning economy. These services can be broken down into four key areas: liquidity, risk pooling, risk selection and monitoring, and risk pricing. We will consider each of these in turn.

### Liquidity

The primary role of banks is to provide **liquidity** to the economy. Banks raise money from deposit holders. These account holders may be private households or companies who wish to place their money in a safe and accessible form. If you place your money in the bank, then you have a surplus of liquidity—you do not need so much cash. Similarly, there are also households and businesses who have a shortage of liquidity. This group can raise their liquidity by borrowing from the bank; that is, borrowing raises their access to cash. So, by channelling cash from savers to borrowers banks provide much needed liquidity to the economy.

However, one problem faced by banks is that they tend to borrow short and lend long. Savers and, more particularly, current account holders, tend to need quick and easy access to their cash. Borrowers, in contrast, tend to repay loans over many years. In ensuring liquidity for borrowers, banks have to carefully manage the cash flows received and repaid to savers. Banks take special care to ensure that they themselves have a mixture of assets which are almost liquid and can, therefore, be converted into cash at short notice. Gold and **government bonds** are often readily bought by other investors. So, with an active market and many buyers, gold and government bonds can be easily sold and converted into cash. The problem for banks is that near-liquid assets earn low rates of interest. Banks are therefore required to trade the benefits of liquidity against lower financial returns.

> **Liquidity** is the speed, price and ease of access to money.
>
> **Government bonds** are a near-cash equivalent and therefore liquid. A government pays the holder of bonds a rate of interest in return for funding the government's debt.
>
> **Collateralized debt obligation** is a bond. The holder of the bond is paid a rate of interest in return for funding a debt.
>
> A **credit crunch** is a lack of liquidity between banks.

Prior to the global credit crisis of 2008, banks attempted to increase the interest earned on liquid assets and invested some of their cash in bonds that were linked to other banks' stocks of mortgages. These bonds were called **collateralized debt obligations** (CDOs) and paid a higher rate of interest than government bonds. However, as the sub-prime mortgage market in the USA collapsed, CDOs fell in value. Other banks were unwilling to buy, or take a CDO as collateral against a loan. When banks are unwilling to trade assets with each other, then there is a restriction on liquidity in the interbank market and this became known as the **credit crunch**.

### Risk pooling

Ordinary savers could provide liquidity to borrowers. However, with limited funds, the average saver may be able to fund only one borrower or even only a small part of their need for cash. This will leave the individual saver very exposed to the risk of default by the borrower. In contrast, by pooling savers' funds, banks have access to a larger share of funds and are therefore able to fund a larger pool of risks. By choosing a varied and non-correlated set of risks, banks can use risk pooling to derive benefits from diversification. (See Chapter 7 for a reminder of diversification economies.) If one borrower defaults, then the bank is left with a bad debt. But the profitable proceeds from lending to the rest of the pool are usually sufficient to outweigh this cost. Because of the benefits to be gained from diversification, banks are able to take on greater lending risks than an individual saver. As a result, projects or transactions that would not be funded by individuals are funded by banks. Therefore, risk pooling by banks enables the economy to grow.

### Risk selection and monitoring

Banks employ individuals who are experts in understanding financial risks. Bank managers are trained to assess and evaluate the merits of lending to individuals and companies. This expertise and skill enables banks to select risks more effectively than ordinary individuals with surplus savings to invest. As a result, with a well-functioning banking sector, investment options with a greater probability of financial success should be selected. If this occurs, then there should be less waste of financial resources across the economy.

Banks are also skilled at monitoring loans made to companies. Banks are able to understand when a company is in financial difficulty and when it is right to put a company into liquidation and seek repayment of the original loan. Ordinary savers are less likely to be able to understand a company's financial statement or evaluate its chances of survival in a turbulent trading environment. As a result, banks are an efficient and effective means of selecting and monitoring risk.

### Risk pricing

As experts in financial risk, banks are able to provide a good assessment of risk and therefore the price for taking on such risk. The more risky the project, the higher the interest rate on the loan. Banks can also access the pool of resources held by rival banks. This enables large and risky projects to be funded, but with the financial risk shared among many banks. Finally, banks reduce the cost of borrowing. In raising financial resources from one bank, a borrower cuts down on the costs of transacting with many small savers. Therefore, banks are both a cost-efficient means of distributing loans and an effective mechanism for pricing the risk associated with lending.

##  Regulation

Banks are institutions which take financial risks with depositors' money. While traditionally banks have been seen as very safe, recent events associated with the credit crisis have shown that banks around the world are still vulnerable to collapse. In fact, banks represent an important risk known as **contagion**. Because banks can also lend to each other, if one bank collapses, then it defaults on its loans with other banks. This weakens the other banks, which can then also collapse. Contagion leads to a domino effect, with one bank toppling more banks. It should be of little surprise to know that banks are regulated. The form of regulation can vary across economies, but the main objectives of **regulation** are often to ensure financial stability and economy-wide confidence in the banking sector.

Contagion occurs when the collapse of one bank leads to the collapse of more banks.

Regulation is the use of rules and laws to limit, control and monitor the activities of banks.

Fixed exchange rates have a fixed rate of conversion between currencies.

The Bretton Woods agreement of 1944 provided a plan for managing foreign exchange rates.

### Historical review of regulation

The regulation of banks has changed greatly over the years. This is a reflection of changing political and economic concerns. Some of the biggest changes in financial regulation occurred during the 1980s, but were linked to events in the 1970s.

In the late 1960s economies around the world operated **fixed exchange rate** regimes under the **Bretton Woods** agreement. We will consider such systems in more detail in Chapter 15. But, in brief, a fixed exchange rate regime fixes the rate of conversion between currencies. There is no daily movement in the exchange rate for a currency. Such systems often require controls on the movement of currency between economies. As an example, British holidaymakers in the 1960s could take no more than £50 with them out of the country.

From 1971, the fixed exchange rate systems were abandoned by leading economies. This also meant that currency controls could be abandoned. This allowed tourists and, more important, banks to move currency around the world. Banks could lend and invest money where it was possible to make the highest rate of return. The globalization of financial services had begun.

The challenge for economies was how to embrace the opportunities offered by free currency movements. The UK decided that it wished to become a global financial services centre and, in order to compete on a global scale, deregulation of the financial sector was deemed necessary.

Under the political leadership of Margaret Thatcher, the City of London financial system underwent Big Bang deregulation in 1986. This allowed financial companies to operate in a broader range of products and services. This increased competition between companies who had previously been investment banks or retail banks. It also enabled these banks to enter other markets, such as stockbroking. Perhaps most important, foreign companies could set up operations in the UK.

These changes were followed by changes in the regulations placed on **mutual** deposit-taking institutions such as building societies. The UK government allowed such companies to operate more like banks, raising money in wholesale markets, and offering current accounts, personal loans and credit cards. Similarly, insurance companies were able to set up banking divisions, and banks were able to set up insurance divisions.

In 1993, the EU opened up competition further. Until that date, banks and insurance companies had to have a licence from the government of each EU country in which it operated. After 1993, a bank or insurance company only had to be licensed in one EU country for it to be able to operate in all EU member countries. Cross-border competition began to increase.

Deregulation over the years, it can be argued, achieved two simple outcomes: first, an ability for financial companies to take greater risks in a broader range of product markets; second, a need to take bigger risks because increased competition was a threat to profitability. The consequences can be seen in large part in the credit crisis and the willingness of banks to take on increased financial risk and place the stability of the entire financial system in danger.

## Types of regulation

The regulation of banks and other financial institutions, including insurance companies, is often referred to as *prudential* regulation. Prudence is a careful and cautious approach to operating financial institutions, which aims to avoid reckless lending or investments which may undermine the stability of the regulated bank. There are various aspects to prudential regulation.

### Capital adequacy

Banks in most economies are subject to capital adequacy ratios. The use of capital adequacy ratios stems from internationally agreed standards known as **Basel III**. A **capital adequacy ratio** measures the value of a bank's capital to its risk-weighted portfolio of assets. A bank's capital includes the equity invested by shareholders, retained profits and provisions for any expected losses. Assets are loans and investments. These assets are weighted according to risk. So, if loans to companies are more risky than loans to governments, then the value of the company loans will be increased by the size of the weight.

The capital adequacy ratio measures the extent to which assets within the bank are backed by shareholders' funds. If assets in the bank grow at a faster rate than shareholders' funds, then the asset growth must have come from funds provided by deposit holders and providers of debt to the bank. Therefore, capital adequacy ratios provide a guide as to who is exposed to the bank's risk of default. If governments wish to see greater protection for deposit holders, then they can insist on a greater

A mutual is a financial organization that is owned by its customers. This contrasts with a bank, which is owned by shareholders.

Basel III provides an internationally agreed set of conditions for the minimum financial strength of a bank. The conditions relate to how the risks of a bank must be assessed and how much cash and reserves a bank must hold to protect itself against large losses from the risks that it faces.

Capital adequacy ratio is a measure of how much capital a bank needs to protect itself from a large loss on the investments or loans that it has made.

capital adequacy ratio and shareholders have to provide greater equity to the bank. Capital adequacy is therefore a measure of bank safety. The more capital backing a bank, the bigger loss its shareholders can suffer, before losses spread to deposit holders and providers of debt.

### Minimum reserve requirements

An alternative approach to bank regulation is the use of minimum reserve requirements. Such regulation stipulates the ratio of deposits that must be held in reserves in liquid or near liquid form. Regulation through reserve requirements seeks to ensure that deposit holders have free and open access to funds. In contrast to capital adequacy ratios, minimum reserve requirements emphasize liquidity over safety.

Regulators and banking industry leaders continue to engage in discussion about the size of minimum reserve requirements. Regulators prefer a larger buffer, whilst banks prefer more money to invest in loan making.

> A scenario-based stress test takes extreme but possible events, such as a collapse in property prices, or a 5 per cent reduction in wages; and then models the impact this will have on the finances of a bank. The scenario creates an extreme stress which can then be used to test the financial strength of a bank.

A more helpful step has been undertaken by the Bank of England, which in 2014 embarked upon **scenario-based stress testing**. Each of the largest banks in the UK has its financial strength tested against an extreme but possible set of economic and commercial trading conditions. The scenario is designed to place the bank's finances under extreme stress. If the bank is demonstrated to have passed the test, then its finances are judged to give confidence. If the bank fails to demonstrate resilience against the stresses of the scenarios, then it is required to strengthen its finances. Box 12.2 provides details of the scenarios chosen by the Bank of England.

### Activity-based regulation

Banking regulation can also be activity based. This can limit the services banks offer and the sectors within which they operate. Following the Wall Street Crash in 1929, banks in the USA were prevented from also running insurance operations. Similar rules were also implemented in the UK and Europe. Banks often found it difficult to take over rivals and expand into new, profitable areas.

However, during the last 20 years many economies have followed a policy of financial deregulation. This has enabled banks and insurance companies to move into each other's sectors. Further deregulation has enabled many banks to raise additional funds through wholesale money markets. While this raises liquidity when money markets are operating well, it also exposes banks to severe liquidity problems when the markets dry up, as in the credit crunch.

### Risk-based regulation and monitoring

Banks and other financial institutions are in frequent discussions with the regulator. Monthly statutory returns provide the regulator with an ongoing picture of the institutions' financial positions and the likely risks going forward. The UK Financial Services Authority feeds this information into its risk-based regulation model. Firms are judged on risk and impact. A large bank, with low risks, still produces a high impact if it collapses and so will be monitored closely. A small company with a higher risk of collapse will be allocated less oversight, because the impact of collapse on the economy is likely to be less.

Regulators also monitor companies on the basis of firm risk and thematic risk. Firm risks are specific to the firm: for example, a firm may have a low capital- adequacy ratio. In contrast, thematic risks cut across firms within the same sector. A bank may be heavily exposed to the mortgage market. Instability in this bank may then lead to a loss of confidence in other mortgage lenders. Firm and thematic risks therefore require different solutions. Firm risks require specific action within a specific firm, whereas thematic risks require co-ordinated solutions across a range of regulated companies.

## Box 12.2
## BoE to stress test banks' ability to cope in global crisis

The Bank of England on Monday presented the scenario for its second annual stress tests, which it said expanded on last year's exercise to include more of a focus on global risks. The BoE said it was modelling a milder stress scenario for the UK economy than last time. Its assumed peak-to-trough decline in the global economy was only a third of the fall that happened in the 2008 financial crisis.

The number of banks being tested is slightly lower as the Co-operative Bank, the only failure in last year's test, has been excluded because it is in the process of shrinking under a drastic restructuring plan.

However, the BoE is expected to announce an expansion of the exercise to include more institutions this summer. Officials are considering including the UK operations of foreign banks in the exercise as well as large insurers and asset managers.

For the first time the stress test includes an assessment of how banks' leverage ratios—measuring equity to total assets—emerge from a crisis as well as their capital ratios, which measure equity to risk-adjusted assets.

The five-year stress scenarios, including a slowdown in China's real economic growth from 7 per cent to 1.7 per cent and a one-third fall in Chinese and Hong Kong house prices, is likely to put most strain on HSBC and Standard Chartered, which are UK-based but earn most of their profits in Asia.

The six banks and one building society—including Barclays, Lloyds Banking Group, Royal Bank of Scotland, Santander UK and Nationwide—will be tested against two key minimum 'thresholds' in the stress scenario: a 4.5 per cent common equity tier one capital ratio and 3 per cent leverage ratio.

Banks have been told that they could be required to raise more capital even if they remain above the thresholds for capital and leverage but fall short on qualitative aspects of the test, such as the strength of reporting and controls.

In this year's test, the UK economy declines by as much as 2.3 per cent, while residential property prices drop by a fifth, there is a prolonged period of deflation and interest rates fall to zero for almost two years.

From the *Financial Times*. 30 March 2015. 'BoE to stress test banks' ability to cope in global crisis'. Martin Arnold. © The Financial Times Limited 2015. All Rights Reserved.

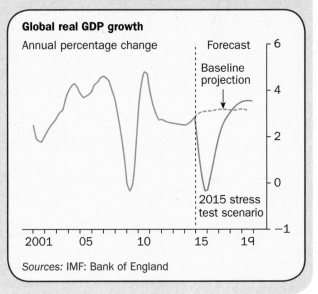

**Global real GDP growth**

Annual percentage change — Forecast

Baseline projection

2015 stress test scenario

2001   05   10   15   19

*Sources:* IMF: Bank of England

## When regulation fails

By the very nature of risk, it is inevitable that some financial companies will collapse at some point. However, it is the nature of the risk and the collapse that will determine the authorities' responses.

In the early 1990s one of the UK's most venerable banks, Barings, collapsed after one of its traders ran up £800 million in losses on the Asian commodity markets. In order to protect depositors, the bank was sold to a rival for £1. (The rival also picked up the £800 million in losses!) The losses on the Asian commodity markets were a specific risk generated by a rogue trader named Nick Leeson. So, the sale of the bank was a specific solution to a specific risk.

During the credit crunch many banks around the world faced collapse. In most instances, these banks have been acquired by rivals, have received enormous capital injections from their governments and have been given greater access to liquidity through credit lines

> Systemic risk is a risk which can damage the entire financial system.
>
> The central bank is a lender of last resort if a bank cannot raise funds from any other lender.

offered by central banks. The credit crunch was a thematic risk, in that all banks faced limited access to liquidity and faced a loss of confidence among deposit holders and shareholders. Such risks are also referred to as **systemic risks**, or contagion, as they pose a risk to the entire financial system. If one bank collapses, then, since all banks are exposed to the same thematic risk, the fear and panic will spread to other banks, leading to further damage of the banking system.

If the risk is systemic, then banks have generally relied on the central bank to act as the **lender of last resort**. If a bank is in distress and cannot raise funds from any other lenders, then the central bank may act as the lender of last resort in order to save the distressed bank and to prevent panic from spreading to other banks.

### Risks of moral hazard

Moral hazard occurs when someone changes their behaviour because they are insulated from risk. For example, a car driver may become a more risky driver once they have fully comprehensive insurance.

Similarly, a central bank's acting as the lender of last resort is not without moral hazard-type problems. In particular, bailing out any bank that finds itself in difficulties can provide banks with incentives to take reckless decisions. The availability of emergency funds from the central bank effectively insures banks and their shareholders against the risks they take in lending. To combat this problem, the UK government used two approaches during the credit crisis. The central bank provided liquidity as the lender of last resort. In addition, the government injected capital into the banks by becoming a shareholder. However, it became a shareholder on very favourable terms, terms which penalized those existing shareholders who had enabled the banks to take excessive risks.

##  12.5 Credit creation and the money supply

> Credit creation is the process of turning existing bank deposits into credit facilities for borrowers. The process can result in an increase in the money supply.

Critically, banks are able to boost liquidity to borrowers by recognizing that not all depositors will withdraw their money at the same time. This enables banks to grow the amount of available money by a process known as **credit creation**.

Consider a business with which many of you will be familiar—clubbing. You go to the club and pay for drinks. In the morning, the manager of the club pays the previous evening's takings into the bank—let us say £1,000. When your hangover subsides, you realize that the really good night out was extremely expensive. You go to the bank and join the queue for an increase in your overdraft.

The bank is sitting on £1,000 from the club and assumes that only £100 will be paid out in the near future as wages. The bank thinks it can safely lend out the remaining £900 in overdrafts. You and your fellow borrowers take the £900 and head straight back to the club for another big night out. In the morning, the club manager returns to the bank and pays in the £900. The bank manager awaits your call for another advance on your overdraft.

The banks are playing a very clever trick: the club manager thinks he has £1,000 in the bank. But then the bank also lets you and your fellow borrowers think you have an additional £900 in the bank by lending part of the club's money to you. When you spend this drinking and enjoying yourself, the club manager pays the next night's takings into the bank, and he now thinks he has £1,900 in the bank. We can, therefore, see that an initial £1,000 in notes and coins was converted into another £900 of money, via overdrafts. This is then paid back into the bank and the process occurs again. Just as we have a fiscal multiplier, we can now observe banks, through credit creation, developing what is known as a money multiplier.

We clearly have to make a distinction between how much *money* people think exists and how much *cash* actually exists.

The amount of money, or the money supply, is the **monetary base** plus deposits at the bank. We will see shortly that this definition can be broadened, but it clearly includes the amount of cash in circulation and the amount people think they have in the bank.

The money multiplier is, therefore, the ratio of the money supply to the monetary base.

> Monetary base, or the stock of high-powered money, is the quantity of notes and coins held by private individuals or held by the banking system.

## Size of the money multiplier

The size of the money multiplier is determined by two factors: (i) the willingness of individuals to deposit money in the bank, rather than keeping it in their pockets; and (ii) the level of reserves held by the banks. For example, the credit-creation process will become greater as more individuals provide banks with cash. So, as people switch from holding money in their pockets to storing it at the bank, the more banks can create credit. Second, if banks reduce reserves from 10 per cent to 5 per cent of deposits, then more credit can be created; for example, for every £100 paid in, the banks can lend out an additional £5 by reducing reserves from 10 per cent to 5 per cent.

So, if cash deposits and reserve levels are central to the process of credit creation, what influences each of these important factors? The level of reserves is directly influenced by regulation. Governments, or central banks, may insist that banks keep a minimum level of reserves in order to meet deposit holders' cash withdrawals. This merely reflects an interest by governments in avoiding bankruptcy among the banking sector. Clearly, banks also wish to avoid bankruptcy and many will use treasury-management teams to build complex models capable of predicting cash flows into and out of the bank on a daily basis. The more confident the bank is that cash flows in will exceed cash flows out, the more they will be willing to lend. The less predictable these cash flows become, the more dangerous it becomes to lower reserves and lend more money.

The willingness to hold cash on deposit, rather than in your pocket, has in recent times been influenced by technological change in the financial services industry. Many firms will pay salaries and wages only into bank accounts. Wages are rarely paid in cash any more. Loans, mortgages and mobile phone contracts will only be offered if direct debits can be set up on your bank account. Utility suppliers—gas, electricity and water—will offer discounts if monthly direct debits are set up. Couple all these changes with the popularity of credit cards, and the overall requirement for cash in your pocket, rather than at the bank, has significantly reduced. As a consequence, more cash is in the banking sector and banks using treasury management are becoming more adept at modelling its flows and taking opportunities to create credit.

## Measures of money

We saw above that measuring the money supply requires a distinction to be made between cash and money on deposit. The government has used this distinction to develop a number of money measures ranging from **narrow measures of money**, previously known as M0 which covers notes and coins, to **M4**, which is a broad measure of money.

Look at Table 12.2: notes and coins is £63 billion. Adding in retail and wholesale deposit accounts takes the broader measure of money, M4, to £2,081 billion. Therefore, cash is a very small part of the money supply.

Reserve balances are cash held at the central bank by commercial banks. Such cash is not in circulation and is now defined as being outside of the money supply. However, it should be noted that in 2008 reserve balances stood at £7 billion. The massive increase to £307 billion by 2015 is a reflection of quantitative easing and the desire of commercial banks to place money on deposit with the central bank, rather than lend to customers.

> Narrow measures of money are notes and coins held in and outside of the private banking sector.
>
> M4 takes notes and coins and adds retail and wholesale banking deposits. M4 is, therefore, a broad measure of money.

**Table 12.2** Narrow and broad UK money (£ billion), 2015

|  | Reserve balances | £307 |
|---|---|---|
| Narrow measure of money | Notes and coins | £63 |
| + | Retail deposits | £1,434 |
| + | Wholesale deposits | £584 |
| = | M4 | £2,081 |

*Source:* Bank of England.

## 12.6 The demand for money

The previous discussion provides an understanding of money supply. However, before we begin to consider how the government might effectively control the money supply, we also need to consider the demand for money.

> The transaction motive for holding money recognizes that money payments and money receipts are not perfectly synchronized.

Do not confuse a demand for more money with a demand for additional income. We all want more income, but may not want more money. For example, if you receive £1,000 in income, the question is, how much of this £1,000 will you hold in money and how much in other financial securities such as bonds or equities?

Economists identify three motives for holding money: the **transaction motive**, the **precautionary motive** and the **asset motive**.

### The transaction motive

> The precautionary motive for holding money reflects the unpredictability of transactions and the need to hold liquid funds in order to meet these payments.

We hold money because we have to pay for goods and services at various points after we receive income payments. Consider the following scenarios: (a) you are paid on Friday and carry out all your shopping on Friday; and (b) you are paid on Friday and shop each day for food, clothes, fuel, etc. Under scenario (a), your payments and receipts of money are perfectly synchronized; under (b), they are not. Therefore, you need to hold more money in scenario (b) than in (a).

> Under the asset motive, individuals hold money as part of a diversified asset portfolio. Some wealth is held in equities, some in bonds, a portion in property and some in money.

As the value of our transactions increases and as the degree of synchronization between receipts and payments deteriorates, the greater becomes the transactional motive for holding cash. Moreover, we need to state that demand is for real-money balances, where the demand is adjusted for inflation. So, if inflation doubles, the nominal value of our receipts and payments will also double, and we will have to hold double nominal money balances, but in real terms our demand for money will remain constant.

### The precautionary motive

We also hold money because we are unsure when transactions will occur. For example, we might hold some money against emergencies, such as the car developing a fault and needing repairing; or we might have spare cash in order to take advantage of special offers in the shops as and when they occur.

As uncertainty increases, the precautionary motive for money will also increase. In addition, as income increases, the value of potential transactions also increases. For example, someone who owns a Ferrari needs to hold more money to fix a fault with the Ferrari than someone who owns a Mini (assuming each are equally reliable).

## The asset motive

Individuals hold money as part of a diversified portfolio of assets. Equities are risky assets, with values going down as well as up. Bonds are financial instruments, where a firm offers to make specified repayments in the future to the bond holder. The risk is that the firm will default on the payments. Money is a low-risk asset. Aside from the exchange rate, the value of money is only affected in real terms by the inflation rate.

Clearly, the more wealth is held in cash, the more an individual is forgoing the potential higher returns from holding other financial assets such as bonds. Indeed, bonds pay a rate of return, or interest. We can argue that the higher the rate of interest on bonds, the higher the opportunity cost of holding real-money balances. Therefore, as the interest rate increases, individuals will demand fewer real-money balances.

We can now use these ideas to understand how the demand for money varies with prices, income, interest and risk. In Figure 12.1, individuals will hold real-money balances up to the point where the marginal benefit of cash is equal to the marginal cost. The cost of holding cash is equal to the interest forgone on a bond. So, the marginal cost of money is constant, and represented by the horizontal line in Figure 12.1. The marginal benefit of money is considered for a given level of real income. The benefits of cash are downward sloping because additional cash has greater value when we have less of it. With a high income and low cash balances, we have to be careful to match payments and receipts, we have to avoid risk and reduce our precautionary needs for cash and we have limited scope for investing our scarce cash. As our real cash balances increase, then our cash requirements are more in balance with our income level and the value of additional cash falls.

In equilibrium, our real holdings of money will be determined by the intersection of the marginal benefits and marginal costs of holding cash. In Figure 12.1, this is $L_1$. If interest rates increase, then the marginal cost of holding cash will increase and individuals will hold less cash, $L_2$. Similarly, if interest rates fall, then the opportunity cost of holding cash falls and individuals' holdings of money will increase.

If real incomes increase, then the marginal benefits of holding cash at any interest rate increase and so the marginal benefit line moves to the right and the new equilibrium level of real-money balances becomes $L_3$ in Figure 12.1.

## (12.7) Money market equilibrium

Now that we understand the demand and supply of money, we can think about the money market equilibrium. Figure 12.2 shows the demand for real-money balances, $LL_1$, and the supply of money, $L_1$. The demand for real-money balances is negatively related to the rate of interest. This is easy to

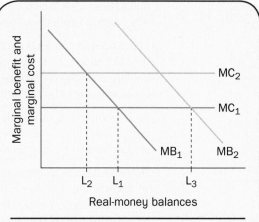

**Figure 12.1  Desire for real-money balances**

In equilibrium, individuals will desire money balances up to the amount where the marginal benefit and marginal cost of holding money are equal. If the marginal cost of holding money increases, then the desire to hold money will fall. Equally, if the marginal benefit of holding money increases, then the desire for money will increase.

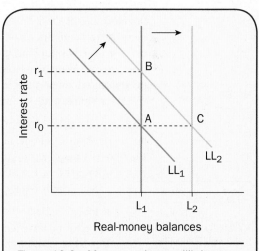

**Figure 12.2  Money market equilibrium**

Money demand LL is interest responsive, reflecting a trade-off between holding non-interest-bearing money and alternative interest-generating assets such as bonds. Money supply, L, is perfectly interest inelastic. In equilibrium, money demand equals money supply. An increase in money demand will lead to a higher equilibrium interest rate, while an increase in money supply will lead to a lower equilibrium interest rate.

understand if we look back at Figure 12.1. If we increase the marginal cost of holding money (the interest rate), then fewer real-money balances are held.

The supply of money is perfectly inelastic. As the interest rate, or price of money, increases, then the supply of money remains unchanged. This, as we will see shortly, is because the government (or central bank) adds to or reduces the money supply as it sees fit. Its decision is not influenced by the interest rate.

As interest rates on bonds increase, individuals find holding money too expensive and reduce their holdings of real-money balances. At the equilibrium A, the demand for real-money balances is equal to the money supply at an interest rate of $r_0$.

We can consider a change to the demand for real-money balances. If income increased, or uncertainty increased, then either the transaction motive or the precautionary motive for holding money would increase. In both instances, the demand for real-money balances would shift out to the right, at $LL_2$. If money supply remains unchanged, the equilibrium moves to B and the interest rate rises to $r_1$.

If the central bank increased the money supply from $L_1$ to $L_2$, by printing more banknotes, then the supply of money would move out to the right. At the higher level of money demand, $LL_2$, the equilibrium moves to C and the interest rate returns to $r_0$. Clearly, if the central bank reduced the amount of money in the economy, then the interest rate would increase.

## Controlling the money supply

We know that the money supply is composed of cash in circulation plus money on deposit at the banks. In attempting to control the money supply, it is clear that the central bank has two options open to it: (1) it could regulate the credit-creation process undertaken within banks or (2) it could control the amount of notes and coins in circulation.

Managing the credit-creation process requires regulation of the minimum reserve requirements run by banks. If a bank only holds 5 per cent of its deposits in reserve, then it can create far more credit than if it is required to hold—say, 10 per cent of its deposits on reserve. So, increasing the minimum reserve requirements of a bank can help to reduce the credit-creation process and thereby limit growth in the money supply. However, banks may not like minimum reserve requirements. Holding cash on reserve can be wasteful when the cash might be profitabily loaned out to a borrower. In addition, global market banks can bypass minimum reserve requirements by using a country with the lowest reserve requirements as their base.

The second method for controlling the money supply is to print more money. Ben Bernanke, the head of the US Federal Reserve, has referred to this approach as the 'helicopter option'. Fly above a major city and drop freshly printed notes. Everyone is then free to collect and spend the new money, which eventually will end up in the banks, whereupon the credit-creation process will further expand the money supply.

**Open market operations** occur when the central bank buys and sells financial assets in return for money.

**Quantitative easing** involves the central bank buying government debt, corporate debt and other financial securities. In return, cash is provided to the vendors of these assets.

A more sophisticated means of managing the monetary base is to use **open market operations**. The central bank might sell bonds in the marketplace. If a bank bought such a bond, it would write a cheque and transfer money from its account to the central bank. This takes funds out of the banking system and limits the credit-creation process. Put into reverse, the central bank could buy bonds and place money in the bank's account.

Central banks use open market operations on a daily basis and the primary purpose is to ensure sufficient liquidity within the banking system. Banks that have too much liquidity may buy bonds from the central bank and increase their reserves held at the central bank, while banks that are short of liquidity may sell bonds back to the central bank in return for liquid cash.

However, in extreme cases, the central bank may wish to dramatically increase the amount of liquidity within the banking sector and it will then consider a policy of **quantitative easing**. Under quantitative easing, the central bank will purchase government debt bonds, corporate debt bonds and other financial assets, such as mortgage-backed securities and even equities. In return, the sellers of these assets, often banks, receive cash. This then improves the banks' liquidity. Credit creation and lending can increase.

Quantitative easing was used in Japan between 2001 and 2005. During the credit crisis it was also used by central banks such as the US Federal Reserve and the UK's Bank of England.

There are problems with quantitative easing. First, if a bank sells an asset to the central bank, then it may not use the additional cash. Instead, the bank may leave the cash on reserve at the central bank. It would be likely to do this if it felt that the economic environment was so bad that to lend out the money would offer an unacceptably high level of risk.

Second, it is necessary to recognize a difference between quantitative easing and **qualitative easing**. Under quantitative easing, the quality of the central bank's balance sheet stays roughly equal. High-quality bonds are swapped for cash. Under qualitative easing, the quality of the central bank's balance sheet deteriorates. Cash is swapped for poor-quality assets. In this way, quantitative easing can present problems of moral hazard. Banks wishing to offload high risk, poor-quality assets can swap them at the central bank for cash. These poor-quality assets then appear on the central bank's balance sheet. To avoid this problem, central banks offer to buy assets at a substantial discount. This is referred to as a **haircut**.

> Under qualitative easing, the central bank swaps high-quality assets for poorer-quality assets.
>
> A haircut is the discount required by the buyer of a risky asset. An asset valued at £100 and bought for £80 is said to have suffered a 20 per cent haircut. The haircut will hopefully insure the buyer against any future losses in value of the asset.

Figure 12.3 illustrates the changing composition of the Bank of England's holdings of collateral before and after the beginning of the credit crisis. It is clear that from late 2008 onwards, the Bank of England massively expanded its purchase of assets. In the initial phase on and around 2008, the Bank purchased government bonds and mortgage-backed securities. These purchases of assets are captured in sterling long-term reverse repos and bonds and other securities. Once the Bank was enabled to undertake quantitative easing, it effectively created money and began an enormous purchase of financial assets which are listed under 'other'. In total these assets had risen to £375 billion by the end of 2015.

## Controlling the interest rate

The alternative to controlling the money supply is the use of interest rates. Under such a policy, interest rates are declared, and then however much money is demanded at the official base rate is how much money is supplied to the market. The central bank is effectively fixing the interest rate for the money market, and then managing the money supply through open-market operations to ensure that the market price for money is the same as the central bank's declared rate of interest.

Control of interest rates can have additional benefits. Where demand for money is particularly unstable, it is best to set interest rates rather than money supply. For example, if the money supply is managed, then changes in money demand will lead to instability in interest rates. If the interest rate is set, however, changes in money demand simply lead to instability in money supply. If control of the economy operates more through interest rates than through money supply, it is of no surprise that policy has shifted from managing money supply to managing interest rates.

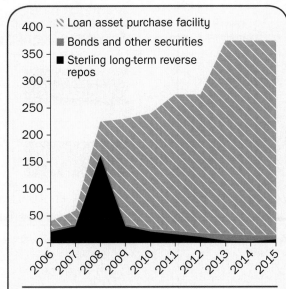

Figure 12.3  Collateral holdings by the Bank of England

*Source:* Bank of England.

## Monetary policy

Governments and central banks across the world attempt to use money markets and the banking sector to influence overall levels of economic activity. They seek to achieve this through the setting of interest rates. So, it is not that central banks wish to bring about equilibrium in money markets when setting interest rates; rather, they believe that changes in the interest rate can be transmitted into the real economy and thereby have implications for inflation and economic activity. How this occurs is complex and can take many months, if not years, to work.

### Monetary transmission

> The transmission mechanism is the channel through which monetary policy impacts economic output and prices.

In simplistic terms, interest rates affect consumers' willingness to consume and firms' willingness to borrow for investment. How changes in the base rate feed through into changes in economic output and inflation is referred to as the **transmission mechanism**.

Figure 12.4 provides the European Central Bank's schematic representation of the transmission mechanism. This figure links changes in the official bank base rate through to changes in the economy's price level.

The transmission mechanism is clearly complex. Changes in the central bank's base rate feed through into changes in retail bank and money market rates for loans. These changes impact the amount of credit in the economy, the price of other assets, such as shares, bonds and property, and can even alter the exchange rate. Changes in the base rate also help to manage expectations. As the central bank changes rates, it demonstrates its commitment to fighting inflation. This commitment has an impact on price and wage setting.

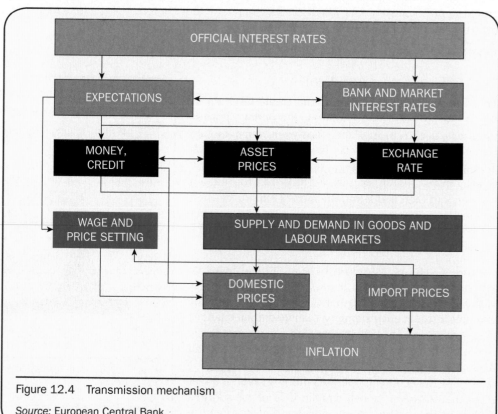

Figure 12.4   Transmission mechanism

*Source:* European Central Bank.

However, at the core of the transmission mechanism is how firms and consumers adjust their spending decisions in the light of rate changes. This drives changes in the demand for goods and services. Consumers borrow for consumption and firms borrow for investment, both of which are important components of aggregate demand. Changes in aggregate demand feed through into changes in equilibrium GDP and inflation (see Chapter 9 and Figure 9.10). In order to develop your understanding further, we will now concentrate on consumption and investment behaviour within the transmission mechanism.

## Consumption

The Keynesian view of consumption, presented in Chapter 11, suggests that consumption is directly related to current income. As income increases, then, through the marginal propensity to consume, consumption will also increase. The link between interest rates and consumption must therefore act through income.

A simple example from Chapter 11 is that consumers' belief in a cut in interest rates will boost investment demand. Through the multiplier, this boost in autonomous investment will then lead to higher GDP. Higher GDP will, in turn, lead to higher income for consumers and therefore higher consumption.

Interest rates can also impact directly on household consumption. Interest is the price of money. If interest rates fall, then in real terms consumers are better off. They can now purchase more credit for the same amount of expenditure (interest). So, as interest rates fall, real income rises and so does consumption.

Falling interest rates also raise today's value of future income. If you expect to earn £30,000 per annum in five years' time, what is it worth today? Or in economic terminology, what is the **net present value** of £30,000?

Think of the problem in reverse. If interest rates are 5 per cent, how much money must I place in the bank today in order to have £30,000 in five years' time? The answer is £23,505. So, £30,000 in five years' time is worth £23,505 today. If interest rates fall, then more has to be saved today in order to have £30,000 in the future. Falling interest rates raise the net present value of future income streams. So, if you are thinking of borrowing over the long term, falling interest rates raise your long-term income, which enables you to borrow more to spend.

> Net present value is the discounted value of a future cash flow.
>
> The permanent income hypothesis states that consumption is determined by lifetime earnings and not current income.

An alternative view is the **permanent income hypothesis**, put forward by Milton Friedman. This model asserts that consumption is determined by expectations of lifetime earnings, rather than current income. So, two students working at Starbucks, earning the same wage, will only consume the same amount if they both expect to have the same lifetime earnings. In contrast, if one is expecting to be a doctor and the other a teacher, then the medical student will consume more now, knowing that they are effectively borrowing from future higher income.

Under the permanent income hypothesis, changes in consumption are only achieved by changes in lifetime earnings. Temporary changes in earnings are unlikely to affect consumption. So, a minor and temporary reduction in interest rates will not change lifetime earnings and so will not alter consumption. However, if the economy moves to a period of sustained and historically low interest rates, then consumers may come to readjust their expectations of lifetime earnings. During the late 1990s and 2000s, low interest rates were a major economic theme. At the same time, incomes, consumption and borrowings grew enormously.

Another key feature of the period was a rapid growth in property prices. This is asset price inflation and can increase households' lifetime wealth. Again, if households think the change is permanent, they will adjust their borrowing and consumption behaviour. One year's growth in property prices is temporary. Ten years' suggests a permanent change. Coupled with low interest rates, households began to borrow heavily to fuel consumption.

Following the credit crunch and the fall in property prices, households may now consider if their lifetime earnings and wealth are falling.

## Investment activity

A firm's willingness to invest is determined by cost–benefit analysis. The benefits can be measured as the financial returns from investing in a new product, office or production facility. The main costs are the funds required to invest and the cost of such funds (interest). Other costs might include disruption costs. Clearly, the rate of interest is the direct cost of investing and will determine the firm's willingness to borrow and spend.

However, interest can also have an additional role to play in the appraisal of an investment project. Consider a project which will generate financial benefits for each of the next five years. A way of evaluating a project is to calculate its net present value—what value are the project's benefits (less costs) today? The method of net present value enables projects of differing lengths, say three and five years, to be compared.

If the project generates a benefit of £10 million in year five, we can work out what that value is today. We simply have to work out how much money we would need to put in the bank today in order to have £10 million in five years' time. So, if interest rates are 5 per cent, then we would need to put £7.8 million in the bank today; or, £10 million in five years' time is worth £7.8 million today. Clearly, as the interest rate increases, we can place less in the bank to achieve the £10 million in year five; or, as the interest rate increases, £10 million in year five is worth less to us today.

The discussion above indicates that interest rates affect investment decisions in two ways. First, higher rates of interest drive up the cost of borrowing and so reduce investment. Second, higher rates of interest make the value of future financial benefits smaller in today's terms; that is, higher interest rates provide a bigger discount to future cash flows and so reduce investment. Taken together, both these mechanisms result in a negative relationship between the rate of interest and the willingness to borrow and invest. See Figure 12.5.

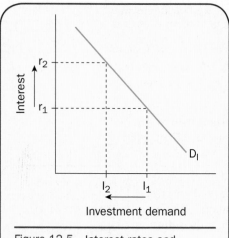

**Figure 12.5   Interest rates and investment demand**

As interest rates increase, investment demand decreases.

In practice, the Bank of England's monetary committee works on the assumption that interest rate changes take one year to affect economic output and two years to affect prices. These are rules of thumb reflecting more practical considerations of economic adjustment, rather than hard precise rules predicted by economic theories.

The time lag for economic output could reflect pre-committed expenditures. You may book the family summer holiday in January. But between January and the summer, interest rates may rise. Because you are pre-committed to spending the money, the interest rate rise is unlikely to alter your expenditure, or overall aggregate demand, but it may curb the amount of expenditure you pre-commit to next year's summer holiday. The same may be true of house purchases and investment in production or retail facilities by firms, where an interest rate change takes place between the decision to spend and the actual point when the transaction takes place. The transactions will still take place, because the parties are committed to the sale process. It is only in the longer term that the volume of sales and the amount of investment will reflect the new higher interest rates. In a similar manner, a fall in interest rates is unlikely to lead to an immediate increase in additional expenditure, because the expenditure for the coming year has already been planned out and committed. It is only next year that you may upgrade your holiday expenditure, while within firms with strict budgetary control and annual planning cycles, additional expenditure will not occur for another 12 months.

The two-year time lag for inflation is likely to reflect the prevalence of annual wage negotiations and the evolution of inflationary expectations. For example, if interest rates are increased to fend off higher inflation, it is not clear how this policy will alter inflationary expectations. In the short term, the higher interest rate may have little impact, with consumers and firms wondering about the credibility of the monetary authorities to fight inflation. Only if rates are kept high for a period of six to 12 months will inflationary expectations change. Once these changes in expectations are made, they will not impact wages and prices until wage negotiations take place. These tend to be conducted annually. So, given that interest rates take a year to affect output, the ability to change prices and wages to the new equilibrium output level may take up to one year longer.

The problem with such long time lags is that some other problem may hit the economy in the intervening period—for example, war, terrorist attack, avian flu, stock market crash or oil price increase. All of these are very real, immediate and significant threats to economic stability.

## Central bank independence

A final consideration is the independence of monetary policy from political motives. A fear with fiscal policy is that governments will face incentives, particularly near to elections, to alter taxation and spending for electoral gain rather than for economic stability. The same can be true for monetary policy, except it is easier to place monetary policy with a non-government agency, such as the central bank. In the USA, the Federal Reserve is charged with setting interest rates to deliver stable economic growth and fight inflation. In the UK, the Bank of England is charged with using monetary policy to bring about financial stability and inflation rates of 2 per cent on average. In the eurozone, the European Central Bank is required to use monetary policy to achieve an inflation rate of less than 2 per cent. Providing central banks with an inflation target reduces the political incentive to change rates. In addition, as non-political bodies, central banks may be seen as more credible bodies for fighting inflation. This should help to bring inflationary expectations into line with the inflation target. However, the appointment of key monetary decision makers, at most central banks, is a government decision. So, decisions may still be taken in the light of political patronage.

# 12.9 Business application: monetary policy and investment

## Investment and business confidence

Debt is a complementary good for firms seeking to invest. Just as car users need to buy petrol, firms when investing in new capacity often need to purchase loans. If the interest rate falls, loans become cheaper. However, the cost of the loan is not the only factor that influences a firm's decision to invest. The interest rate reflects a cost of investing, but what about the benefits? If an economy is in recession, consumption of goods and services is falling. If a firm cannot sell the output generated by new investments, the benefits of investing are very low. A recession is, therefore, likely to reduce business confidence. If businesses are not confident about being able to sell products, or make a profit because of recession, they are likely to delay investment decisions. Reductions in interest rates are unlikely to boost investment rates.

Box 12.3 highlights the improving but different levels of business confidence across the German economy. Manufacturers appear most confident and are operating above average capacity. Construction as a sector is feeling less confident than before, but still sees good opportunities in the future.

Small monthly changes in confidence are unlikely to impact long-term investment decision making. It is more likely that consistent improvements in confidence over time, which lead

## Box 12.3
## German business confidence

The Ifo Business Climate Index for German trade and industry rose to 107.9 points in March 2015 from 106.8 points last month. The index reached its highest level since July 2014. Companies were more satisfied with their current business situation. They also expressed far greater optimism about future business developments. The German economy continues to expand.

In manufacturing the climate indicator rose once again. Manufacturers were more satisfied with their current business situation. They were also clearly more optimistic about future business developments. Production plans reached their highest level since May 2014.

In wholesaling the business climate also improved. Assessments of the current business situation were far more favourable, while wholesalers scaled back their slightly optimistic business expectations. In retailing the business climate also continued to brighten. After falling in February, the business situation indicator rose again. Retailers expressed greater confidence in future business developments.

In construction, by contrast, the business climate indicator continued to fall, but remains at a high level. Contractors assessed both their current business situation and their business outlook less favourably than last month. There is still a boom in construction, but it is weakening.

Source: Ifo Institute, Munich, Germany, March 2015. Ifo Business Climate Report.

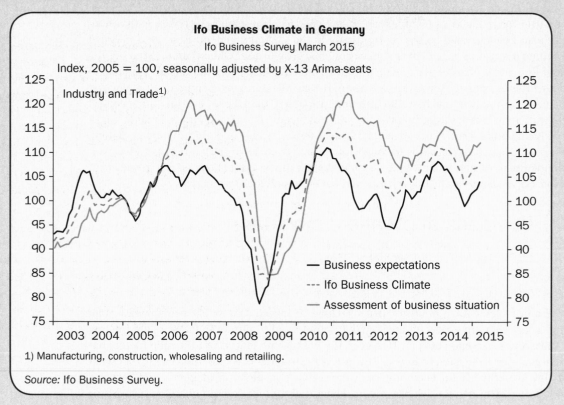

**Ifo Business Climate in Germany**
Ifo Business Survey March 2015

Index, 2005 = 100, seasonally adjusted by X-13 Arima-seats

Industry and Trade[1]

— Business expectations
--- Ifo Business Climate
— Assessment of business situation

1) Manufacturing, construction, wholesaling and retailing.

*Source:* Ifo Business Survey.

to realized improvements in sales and profits, will generate an increased willingness to borrow and invest.

## Investment under low inflation and low interest rates

A more fundamental question surrounds the recent desire for low inflation and low interest rates. What are the effects of low inflation on the economy and, in particular, on business? Constantly low inflation should bring increased stability. Businesses seeking to invest millions over many years will be assured by increased price stability. Predictions regarding costs and revenues are much easier to make, and firms face less uncertainty when assessing investment risks. If low inflation reduces uncertainty, active monetary policy, leading to low inflation, may boost investment because of stability issues rather than because of cheaper borrowing.

Alternatively, low inflation may reduce the need, or desire, to invest. High wage inflation increases a firm's production costs. In order to recover these cost increases, firms may seek to raise the final price for their products. In such a scenario, firms have a clear incentive to swap increasingly expensive workers for capital equipment. But in recent times price inflation has been low. Wage demands have reflected the new lower rates of inflation and, as a result, firms have potentially less need to deal with an expensive workforce by investing in machinery.

It is, therefore, very clear that monetary policy and the pursuit of low inflation have many varied implications for business. Interest rates may influence investment simply by changing the cost of borrowing. However, the impact of interest rates on economic activity, business confidence and especially consumer spending and export growth may play a greater role in investment decisions. Finally, the use of monetary policy in targeting low inflation and economic stability may influence investments in different ways. Increased stability may make firms more willing to invest simply because it is easier to assess the relative costs and revenues from investment. However, without rising inflation and a consequential rise in labour costs, the need or desire to substitute capital for workers will be diminished.

##  12.10 Business application: the importance of banking to the economy

Should banking be the engine of economic growth, or the lubricant of the economic system? Section 12.3 emphasized the importance of banking in providing the economy with liquidity and risk management services. As such, banking plays the role of a lubricator within the economic system. When companies or households wish to undertake economic transactions using debt, then banks channel funds from savers to borrowers. Banking, therefore, plays a facilitating role within the economy.

During the past 20 years banks have benefited from repeated rounds of deregulation. Banks in many countries around the world are now able to offer a wider range of products, including credit cards, personal unsecured loans, pensions, insurance and a variety of personal investment products. This is sometimes referred to as 'bancassurance'—a conjunction of banking and insurance.

Deregulation has also enabled banks to operate internationally, not only in the products and services that they offer, but also in sourcing financial funds from depositors, debt holders and shareholders. As an example, traditional mortgage lenders raised money from savers and then loaned this money in the form of mortgages. More recently, companies in the USA and Europe have raised funds on wholesale money markets and then loaned this money in the form of mortgages. The mortgage loans have then been bundled up and sold on to investors. The notion of a bank providing mortgages by channelling savings to borrowers was almost redundant.

Deregulation has also enabled technical innovations, both in how money is managed and in the financial instruments that are available to banks and other institutions. Banks are not simply involved in savings and loans. They are just as involved in credit derivative markets, commodity markets, interest rate swap markets and currency markets. Where there is a financial risk and where there is a need for liquidity, then deregulation has enabled banks to expand their operations and profit.

Banks and financial services in general have grown to be important, significant and perhaps the largest component of growth within modern economies. Around financial hubs, such as

London, Frankfurt, New York, Hong Kong and Singapore, the wealth from financial services companies has spilled out into residential property, the growing development of nearby leisure facilities and growing traffic through nearby airports and rail stations. Financial services has driven wealth within its own sector and within the wider related economy.

As financial services has become the engine of economic growth, it has arguably required greater deregulation and a greater ability to take increased risks in order to achieve yet higher rates of return. With an almost unblemished record at achieving growth without a loss of financial stability, governments were willing to see the complexity and innovativeness of financial services continue.

When this complexity resulted in the credit crunch and the collapse of many major banks, governments were required to bail out the financial system. These bailouts came with conditions. Governments became shareholders, required increased lending to households and small businesses, and required directors to sacrifice performance-related pay bonuses. The clear risk is that governments direct banks to meet political and social objectives; they do not necessarily direct banks to meet commercial objectives. Why should banks lend their new capital to households and small businesses? Does this offer the highest risk-adjusted rate of return? Will highly skilled managers stay at banks that cannot offer them performance-related pay? If not, will part-nationalized banking systems become less efficient, less effective, less profitable and less important to economic growth?

In the medium term, governments may take the view that owning banks is not necessary and may sell their stakes. Or they may take the view that owning banks ensures a degree of control and financial stability which is necessary for stable economic progress. If so, then governments will need to think about where they can gain new drivers of growth. This may herald a renaissance in the manufacturing sector, where companies generate jobs, accrue export earnings and in the main do not take risks with households' savings or with pension funds.

# 12.11  Business data application: financial markets and the impact of quantitative easing

In reaction to the worsening credit crisis and slowing of national economies a number of central banks operated a policy of quantitative easing. Between March 2009 and July 2012 the Bank of England purchased £375 billion of financial assets The US Federal Reserve purchased $600 billion of financial assets between November 2008 and June 2010. Then from November 2010 to June 2011 the Federal Reserve purchased another $600 billion of financial assets in what was dubbed QE2. The European Central Bank in the early years of the financial crisis embarked upon less quantitative easing, purchasing around €60 billion of financial assets. However, in early 2015 with many economies in Europe struggling to return to growth and inflation significantly below the 2 per cent target the European Central bank made a step change and moved from around €10 billion per month to €60 billion of asset purchase, with a commitment to keep spending €60 billion per month until September 2016.

Such a massive move into a policy of quantitative easing was expected to bring about a boost in consumer and commercial confidence, an expansion of the economies of Europe and a rise inflation, rather than a move into deflation.

Evidence in the UK and the US was that quantitative easing can bring benefits to an economy. In reviewing the consequences of quantitative easing in the UK, the Bank of England published a report in its 2011 Q3 Quarterly Bulletin. The report identified important channels for how quantitative easing can affect inflation and GDP. The first is via policy signalling. Investors, businesses and consumers form expectations about the future rate of inflation. In order to prevent inflation expectations falling below the Bank's 2 per cent medium-term target rate for inflation, the Bank needs a powerful signal of its intent to hit the 2 per cent inflation. Large-scale quantitative easing represents a significant policy commitment by the Bank to achieve the target; and so, simply by its actions, the Bank signals to investors, businesses and consumers that inflationary expectations should be anchored at 2 per cent.

The second area, and according to the Bank of England the most important, is portfolio balance effects. When the Bank purchases assets, the sellers of financial assets are left with increased holdings of cash. This additional cash is then used to rebalance investment portfolios with an increased purchase of other financial assets, including bonds and shares. This increased demand for financial assets raises asset prices, which lowers the yield or interest rate of the asset. The lowering of yields makes financing cheaper and this boosts commercial and household borrowing, leading to higher spending.

An examination of yields on key financial assets suggested that quantitative easing in the UK had a marked impact on interest rates. Table 12.3 reports that the rate of return on gilts fell by 100 basis points (bps). (One hundred bps is equal to a percentage point reduction in the yield: for example a fall from 6 per cent to 5 per cent. A 50 bps fall would be a fall from 6 per cent to 5.5 per cent.) Corporate bond yields fell by between 70 and 150 bps; and the yield on the FTSE All-Share fell by 3 per cent. There was also evidence that the issuance of shares and bonds during the period of quantitative easing was strong, which could indicate that companies were taking advantage of a lower price for equity and debt financing.

| Table 12.3 | Yields on key assets |
|---|---|
| Asset | Change in yield |
| Gilts | −100 bps |
| Corporate bonds investment grade | −70 bps |
| Corporate bonds high yield | −150 bps |
| FTSE All-Share | −3% |

The most important impact of quantitative easing is the effect such a policy has on inflation and economic output. The Bank of England found that the policy of quantitative easing was associated with a rise in inflation of between 0.75 and 1.5 per cent and an increase in GDP of 1.5–2 per cent. Given the risks of a deflationary recession, the evidence suggested that quantitative easing helped the UK to avoid both deflation and a marked slowdown in GDP.

Box 12.4 discusses whether Europe will attain the same benefits from its programme of quantitative easing.

## Box 12.4
## The policy will help, but less so than in other big economies

AFTER months of debate, having exhausted all the alternatives, the European Central Bank (ECB) announced on 22 January that it was finally introducing a big programme of quantitative easing. It plans to spend €60 billion ($70 billion) a month for at least 19 months, adding hefty purchases of government bonds to an existing scheme to buy covered bonds and asset-backed securities (currently around €10 billion-worth a month). Special rules will apply to purchases of the bonds of countries like Greece which have received bail-outs. The bulk of any losses on sovereign debt that has been purchased will be borne by national central banks.

QE—creating money to buy financial assets including sovereign bonds—was first used by the Bank of Japan in the early part of the 2000s; the Federal Reserve and the Bank of England introduced it in the wake of the financial crisis of 2008. Long-standing German antipathy to the policy, however, has made the ECB a late adopter.

The central bank is turning to QE because of the enfeebled state of the European economy. The recovery since the double-dip recession in the acute phase of the euro crisis has been weak and faltering. Slack demand has caused 'lowflation': headline prices fell in the year to December by 0.2 per cent while core inflation (excluding volatile components like food and energy) was 0.7 per cent. Financial markets no longer believe that the ECB will be able to get inflation back to its goal of nearly 2 per cent over the medium term. Its previous efforts to stimulate the economy, which include becoming the first big central bank to impose negative interest rates, have been inadequate.

The deployment of QE in America and Britain involved an element of 'shock and awe', since financial markets were unfamiliar with the new measure when it was introduced in both countries. As a result it brought down yields sharply. By contrast, the markets have long been expecting the ECB to introduce QE. That has already led to a remarkable rally in sovereign-bond markets, especially in the troubled countries of southern Europe. In Portugal, for example, 10-year bond yields fell by 3.5 percentage points in the course of 2014, from 6.2 per cent to 2.7 per cent. (The exception is Greece, where fears of a political crisis, and even of a possible exit from the eurozone after the election on 25 January, have recently driven yields up again.) As a result the effect of implementing QE will be limited.

Another difference between QE in the eurozone and in America in particular arises from the nature of their financial systems. Because firms rely much more heavily on capital markets in America, they benefited a lot as falling yields on government debt pushed investors into riskier assets such as corporate bonds. By contrast, banks are more dominant in the eurozone, so its companies will benefit less from the boost to European capital markets.

There are two main channels through which QE is likely to work in the eurozone. One is the 'signalling' effect. By adopting the policy, the ECB is sending a clear message to markets and to firms that it is determined to bring inflation closer to 2 per cent. The other is through the exchange rate. The euro has already been weakening since last spring. Further weakening of the single currency seems likely.

All this makes the ECB's foray into QE less like the programmes launched by the Fed and the Bank of England at the height of the crisis and more like those of the Bank of Japan, which has been combating the more insidious threat of deflation. As with Japan's recent bond-buying splurge, the main effect seems likely to come via the exchange rate. The worry is that like Japan in the early 2000s, the ECB may be introducing the policy too late.

From *The Economist*. 'The policy will help, but less so than in other big economies'.
© The Economist Newspaper Limited, London (24 January 2015)

## Summary

1. Monetary policy is the use of interest rates, or money supply, to control aggregate demand.

2. Money has a number of characteristics. It has to be a store of value, a unit of account and accepted as a medium of exchange.

3. The banking system provides the economy with liquidity by channelling funds from savers to borrowers.

4. The banking system also reduces the cost of borrowing, improves monitoring and risk selection and reduces the transaction costs associated with matching savers and borrowers.

5. The objective of banking regulation is to bring financial stability to the economy.

6. Capital adequacy regulates banks by ensuring they have sufficient equity backing. This type of regulation focuses on the financial strength of the bank.

7. Minimum reserve requirements state the level of cash of near-liquid assets the bank must hold. This type of regulation focuses on the bank's liquidity.

8. Activity-based regulation limits banks' commercial activities to certain product ranges and sectors of the financial services industry.

9. The money supply is composed not only of notes and coins, but also deposits within the banking system. The narrow and broad measures of money, M0 and M4, attempt to take account of these differences.

10. Credit creation occurs when the banks create additional money supply by lending out money on deposit. This increases the money supply.

11. There are three motives for holding money: the transaction, precautionary and asset motives.

12. Increases in income lead to an increase in demand for real-money balances and reflect the transaction and precautionary motives for holding money. The speculative motive reflects how changes in the interest rate lead to changes in demand for money.

13. In money-market equilibrium, the demand for money equals the money supply.

14. Governments or central banks now seek to set the interest rate and then provide sufficient money supply in order to make the market clear.

15. It is the transmission of changes in the base rate to the economy that influences aggregate demand.

## Learning checklist

You should now be able to:

- Explain the key features of money
- Understand the different types of banking and financial institutions
- Understand the structure of banks' balance sheets
- Identify the economic importance of banking
- Understand the main methods of bank regulation
- Provide an explanation of how banks create credit
- Explain why we use both broad and narrow measures of money
- Explain the three motives for holding money
- Discuss money market equilibrium using a suitable diagram
- Understand monetary policy and the transmission mechanism
- Understand and evaluate the evidence in relation to the success of quantitative easing
- Explain how business activities are influenced by changes in interest rates
- Assess the merits of a deregulated financial services industry.

## Questions                                                   connect

1. Identify and explain the main features of money.

2. What are the main economic benefits to be gained from a (well-run) banking system?

3. Identify the important risks that banking regulation seeks to manage.

4. Are banks regulated by liquidity or capital adequacy? Is this a problem?

5. Identify and explain the main motives for holding money.

6. If incomes increase in an economy, how would this change the demand for real-money balances?

7. Using a broad definition, what are the main components of the money supply?

EASY

EASY

8. What is the money multiplier and what factors determine the size of this multiplier?

9. The central bank cuts interest rates. How will this change in interest rate alter individuals' demand for cash?

10. What is quantitative easing and how do open market operations enable a policy of quantitative easing to be implemented?

11. Explain why a consideration of net present value may be a useful aid for managers making investment expenditure decisions.

INTERMEDIATE

12. Identify the key stages of the monetary transmission mechanism and what factors may prevent it from working.

13. Why might central bank independence and inflation targeting go together?

14. Why is central bank control of interest rates a control on over-exuberant fiscal policy? Is such a situation beneficial for business?

15. Do you consider income or wealth to determine the level of consumption?

16. The Republic of Transylvania faces money demand (MD) and money supply (MS) schedules, as shown in the diagram.

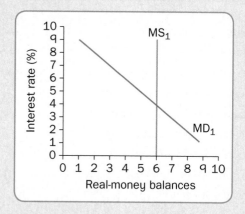

DIFFICULT

(a) What is the equilibrium interest rate?

(b) What will the equilibrium rate of interest do as demand for real-money balances increase?

(c) Given that interest rates change when the demand for real-money balances increases, the Central Bank now increases the money supply. What will the equilibrium rate of interest do?

## Exercises

EASY

1. Which of the following would lead to an increase in the transaction demand for money?

   (a) An increase in prices.

   (b) An increase in real GDP.

   (c) A period of greater economic uncertainty.

   (d) A rise in interest rates.

2. A retail bank has a policy of holding cash reserves equal to 10 per cent of deposits.

   (a) If a customer deposits £1,000, how much lending can the bank create? How would this lending change if cash reserves were less than 10 per cent?

   (b) How might a recession, or a banking crisis, alter a bank's willingness to hold reserves?

3. Consider Box 12.2:

   (a) What risks would you put into a banking stress test?

   (b) Why are these risk scenarios extreme but possible?

4. In 2015, the European Central Bank began a programme of quantitative easing. What evidence is there that this programme has impacted interest rates, GDP growth rates and inflation rates?

# Inflation, output and economic policy

## Chapter 13

## Chapter contents

## Learning outcomes

By the end of this chapter you should be able to:

### Economic theory

LO1   Compare the short- and long-run Phillips curves

LO2   Explain the macroeconomic demand schedule

LO3   Compare short- and long-run aggregate supply lines

LO4   Illustrate the impact on macroeconomic equilibria following shocks to demand and supply

LO5   Debate possible monetary policy responses to short-run disequilibria

LO6   Explain the Taylor rule

LO7   Recognize differing views on the speed of adjustment to long-run equilibrium

### Business application

LO8   Explain the interest rate path

LO9   Review the importance of real business cycles

LO10   Evaluate inflationary expectations in the long and short runs

## At a glance — Inflation, output and economic policy

### The issue

Economic management is focused on inflation targeting and GDP. In macroeconomic equilibrium, how are inflation and GDP determined and how can government and central banks implement policies that enable inflation and GDP to be on target?

### The understanding

Macroeconomic equilibrium is seen to be a reflection of equilibrium in important markets such as goods and labour. Prices and wages determine the value of employment to both workers and firms. Understanding how inflation alters real wages enables an appreciation of firms' willingness to supply output in the short term. Reactions to inflationary pressures in the longer term determine the rate of progression to long-run equilibrium.

### The usefulness

Understanding the likely economic trajectory for an economy can provide businesses with a competitive edge and a greater degree of certainty. Understanding the drivers of supply- and/or demand-side shocks and being able to evaluate central bank changes in interest rates can provide businesses with a clearer understanding of the macroeconomic environment and provide a robust basis from which to build strategy and planning.

## (13.1) Business problem: following a severe economic crisis, how does an economy return to equilibrium?

Economies across the globe have faced enormous challenges following the banking crisis and the sovereign-debt crisis. Economic activity has slowed dramatically, unemployment has increased and household earnings have declined. Governments are having to increase taxation and reduce spending, and central banks have deployed significant amounts of quantitative easing. Given the turmoil in many economies, businesses are keen to know how and when economies will move back to what might be considered normality.

In addressing this question of macroeconomic adjustment, economists have come to recognize that an understanding of the macroeconomic environment must be built on microeconomic foundations. After all, the macroeconomy is nothing more than a vast collection of microeconomic decisions bundled up in an enormous assortment of markets. Therefore, the equilibrium price of goods and services, and just as important, the wages paid to workers and the price of debt, are likely to have a major impact on the scale of economic activity at the macroeconomic level.

In Chapter 3, when examining the productivity of firms, we focused on two factor inputs used by firms: labour and capital. These two inputs have associated costs: wages for labour and debt repayments associated with borrowed finances used for capital investment. We also know from Chapter 10, when we examined inflation in detail, that we need to consider how inflation drives a wedge between nominal and real prices. Therefore, over time, wage and debt agreements priced in nominal values will have very different real values in the future. Inflation will reduce real values; deflation will increase real values. This feature of inflation has enormous implications for businesses that are seeking to plan long-term financial cash flows and repayment schedules.

Let us begin by looking at labour. Firms employ workers for the value they can add to profits. If wage growth is less than inflation, then workers actually become cheaper to hire and their value increases. Discrepancies between inflation and wage growth provide firms with an incentive to expand economic output. In contrast, when inflation falls behind wage growth, then workers become more expensive and firms reduce employment and output. Clearly, an understanding of how inflation and wages impact on output is crucial for companies wishing to understand the future path of the economy.

## Earnings growth and inflation

Figure 13.1 provides data from the UK economy on earnings growth and inflation. Up until 2008 earnings growth exceeded inflation. This trend led to rising real earnings but can only be sustained in the long run if workers become more productive, generate more output per hour worked and so generate extra revenues to fund their higher earnings. Following the financial and economic crisis, earnings growth fell behind inflation for a number of years, causing a marked reduction in earnings, household income and consumption.

In the long run, prices and wages have no impact on the level of employment, economic output and therefore GDP. In the long run, the economy operates on its production possibility frontier. Every worker who desires a job is employed. This is because, in the long run, wage growth is in line with inflation. In the short run, however, unexpected changes in inflation impact the budgeted revenues and costs of firms. A worsening profit position results in output reductions, while an improving profit position results in increased outputs.

Short-run variations in output, caused by unexpected rates of inflation, are likely to be temporary. Firms and workers will form new expectations of future inflation and adjust prices and wages accordingly. New budgets will be planned and employment and output adjusted. The more rapidly and accurately prices and wages adjust to long-term levels, the more quickly the economy will return to the production possibility frontier.

Therefore, understanding the adjustment process is crucial to understanding the future path of the economy. In fact, by being closer to the adjustment process, businesses probably have a greater understanding of the correction process than economists. Factors that impede or facilitate changes in prices and wages are familiar to business. Wage negotiations with workers and unions can be difficult, contested and protracted. Similarly, the ability to change prices is constrained by competition and the actual cost of updating price lists and informing retailers. The less resistance to price and wage changes, the swifter an economy will return to equilibrium.

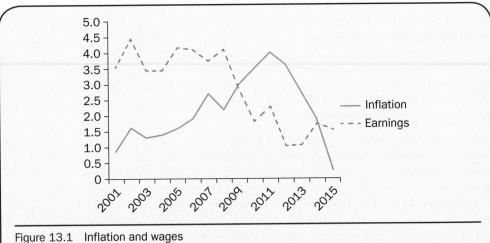

Figure 13.1   Inflation and wages

*Source:* Office for National Statistics, www.statistics.gov.uk.

Changes in the real price of debt have similar implications for economic activity. As inflation rises, then the real value of debt falls. Firms (and consumers) who have debt-repayment commitments find that the real value of debt falls (assuming incomes rise in line with inflation). Conversely, deflation raises the real value of debt. Incomes fall in line with the drop in prices for goods and services and the affordability of previously acquired debt rises.

It should therefore be clear that price, wage and debt adjustments are enormously important to the functioning of the economy, both in the short term and in enabling an economy to return to its long-run equilibrium on the production possibility frontier.

The sections within this chapter will provide you with an understanding of the relationship between inflation and employment in the short and long run. This will be developed into an understanding of the macroeconomic equilibrium in the short and long runs. This will provide a clear link between the microeconomics goods and labour market and the broader macroeconomy. The analysis will then be extended to provide you with an understanding of how the economy reacts to demand- and supply-side shocks. A consideration of monetary policy and inflation targeting will then be offered, followed by a review of different economists' perceptions of how quickly the economy will adjust to long-run equilibrium.

##  Short- and long-run macroeconomic equilibria

In Chapters 11 and 12, we presented the economic ideas behind fiscal and monetary policy. These previous chapters showed *how* demand-side policies work. The aim of this chapter is to show more clearly the circumstances *when* these policies will be used by policy-makers.

If an economy is in long-run equilibrium, then the level of GDP is that associated with a point on the economy's production possibility frontier (recall the discussion in Chapter 1). All land, labour, capital and enterprise that are willing to be supplied are employed within firms in the pursuit of profit. The economy is said to be at its **full employment** level. At the full employment level, an economy is producing at its **potential GDP**. Therefore, if an economy is in long-run equilibrium, there is little need to correct a recession by providing a boost to spending. Similarly, there is little need to slow the economy by increasing taxes or interest rates. In simple and clear terms, because long-run equilibrium results in full employment, fiscal and monetary policy should be neutral, neither increasing nor reducing aggregate demand.

In the short run, by contrast, an economy can be shown to be in equilibrium but the level of GDP can differ from potential GDP. Short-run equilibrium GDP is referred to as **actual GDP**. When the short run and the long run coincide, then actual and potential GDP are equivalent. However, when actual GDP is greater than potential GDP, the economy is in a boom; when actual GDP is less than potential GDP, the economy is in a recession. The difference between potential and actual GDP is referred to as the **output gap**. Only when an output

> In full employment, all factors of production that wish to be employed are employed.
>
> Potential GDP is any point on the production possibility frontier.
>
> Actual GDP is short-run equilibrium GDP.
>
> The output gap is the difference between actual and potential GDP.

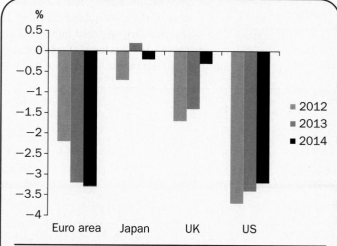

Figure 13.2   Output gap

Output gap is measured as actual GDP less estimated potential GDP, expressed as a percentage of estimated potential GDP.

*Source:* OECD.

gap exists is there any need for fiscal, or monetary, policy to be active rather than neutral. As such, active fiscal, or monetary, policy seeks to close the economy's output gap.

Figure 13.2 charts the output gap for a number of major economies. When the economy is strong, the output gap is positive; when the economy is weak, the output gap is negative. As can be seen in Figure 13.2 most economies were experiencing an output gap during the period 2012–14; and in the case of the US and the eurozone the output gaps were substantial.

Estimating how large the potential size of the economy could or should be is not an exact science. In Box 13.1 estimates of future potential growth calculated by the IMF are presented. The forecasts are linked to a number of assumptions about aging populations, some of which can be challenged. For example, if the retirement age increases, then the number in employment does not fall as quickly.

The following sections of this chapter will examine these issues in more detail. In particular, it is important to understand how differences in short- and long-run aggregate supply lines lead to different short- and long-run equilibria levels of GDP. To develop this understanding, it is necessary to understand the short- and long-run equilibria markets for labour. Moreover, in order to understand the adjustment from actual to potential levels of GDP, it is necessary to form an opinion about the rate of adjustment following the implementation of active fiscal, or monetary, policy. As will become evident, some economic schools of thought believe fiscal policy is more effective than monetary policy in closing the output gap. Each of these areas of concern will be discussed in turn, but we will start with the labour market and show how long-run equilibrium in the market for jobs leads to an understanding of long-run aggregate supply and potential GDP.

## (13.3) Employment, inflation and output

The **Phillips curve** was developed by Professor Phillips from the London School of Economics in 1958 after observing inflation and unemployment in the UK. 'Observe' is the crucial word, because the initial theoretical reasons for a Phillips curve relationship between unemployment and inflation were weak.

> The Phillips curve shows that lower unemployment is associated with higher inflation. Simply, lower unemployment has to be traded for higher inflation.

The Phillips curve, as illustrated in Figure 13.3, seemed very attractive. This was because it showed a clear trade-off between unemployment and inflation. The government merely had to decide which, of inflation and unemployment, it disliked more. If the government disliked unemployment, then it had to suffer higher inflation. The problem of the Phillips curve being simply an observation became a serious concern in the 1970s when the relationship broke down. As unemployment increased, so did inflation. Governments no longer witnessed a trade-off between inflation and unemployment.

If a trade-off between inflation and unemployment ever existed, then it did so in the short run. This is because, in the long run, the economy operates on its production possibility frontier at the full employment level. Therefore, in the long run, GDP is fixed; and, as a consequence, unemployment must also be fixed. Whatever the level of inflation, there can be no trade-off with unemployment in the long run.

Consider Figure 13.4, which includes both a short- and a long-run Phillips curve. The short-run Phillips curve depicts the trade-off between inflation and unemployment, while the long-run Phillips curve shows the fixed long-run level of unemployment.

In the long run GDP is fixed at a maximum or potential GDP; the economy is on its production possibility

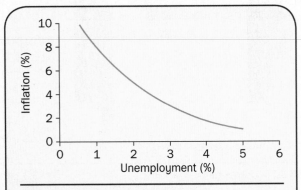

Figure 13.3   The Phillips curve

As unemployment decreases, inflation increases, and vice versa.

## Box 13.1
## The era of strong economic growth is over—and we should be worried

In its latest World Economic Outlook update, the IMF says a combination of slower catch-up growth by emerging economies and ageing societies in the developed world are set to hold back global growth despite signs of a recovery setting in.

In the aftermath of the financial crisis, potential growth in advanced economies has slowed from an average of over 2% per year to around 1.6%. Here's what that looks like:

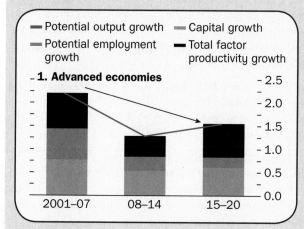

As you can see from the chart, most of the fall in potential growth is coming from the squeezing of that middle red section—employment growth. That represents the potential growth in the number of employees in an economy and it is falling as Western societies get older.

This process, according to the IMF, is likely to hold back growth in future. As the Fund puts it:

Working-age population growth is likely to decline significantly in most advanced economies, particularly Germany and Japan, where it will reach about −0.2 per cent a year by 2020. At the same time, rapid ageing is expected to further decrease average trend labour force participation rates, offsetting the positive effect of continued population increases on overall labour supply.

Meanwhile emerging economies have also seen growth rates slipping since the crisis, albeit from higher starting points. This is largely due to slower catch-up growth as the technological improvements and increases in educational achievement over the past few decades that have helped to narrow the gap with their advanced peers are unlikely to be repeated.

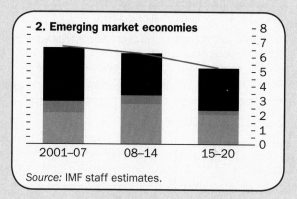

*Source:* IMF staff estimates.

What does this all mean? Well, first it means that living standards are going to struggle to rise in future at the same pace as they have done. Workers experiencing sluggish wage growth since the crisis may find that it becomes the norm rather than the exception in future.

Unfortunately, slower potential growth also has worrying implications for public finances. Governments can lower the burden of public debt in two ways, either by cutting spending to reduce borrowing or through the economy growing faster than debt costs.

Slower growth means that cutting debt is likely to rely more heavily on spending cuts than simply allowing growth to erode the problem. Yet the very factor holding back growth—ageing societies—is also likely to make such cuts harder to achieve as older people use state services such as health care more intensively than their younger peers.

From *Business Insider*. 7 April 2015. 'Emerging Market Economies'. Tomas Hirst. Copyrighted 2015. Business Insider, Inc. 120023:1115DS

frontier. Even though the economy is at potential GDP, there is still a small amount of unemployment; these are people just in between jobs. They are searching for the right job, perhaps waiting a little while for the right job to come along. When they find the right job, someone else in another part of the economy might decide that they do not like their job and will resign. So we have a constant sized pool of unemployed workers who are in effect in the process of moving between jobs. We call this the **natural rate of unemployment** and it is fixed. In Figure 13.4, the natural rate of

> **Natural rate of unemployment** is the level of unemployment when the economy is operating at potential GDP.

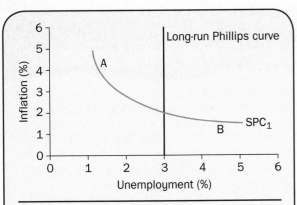

**Figure 13.4   Long-run Phillips curve**

In the long run, there is no trade-off between inflation and unemployment. In the short run, differences between expected and actual inflation can lead to a trade-off between inflation and unemployment.

Real wages are earnings adjusted for inflation.

Nominal wages are earnings unadjusted for inflation. If a worker earns £30,000 per year, this is their nominal wage. If inflation is 5 per cent per year, then at the end of the year the real wage is £30,000/1.05 = £28,571.

unemployment is fixed at 3 per cent. It does not matter what the rate of inflation is, unemployment is constant in the long run. In addition, in long-run equilibrium, the economy is also positioned on its short-run Phillips curve, $SPC_1$, where it intersects the long-run Phillips curve. Therefore, unemployment is 3 per cent and inflation is 2 per cent in the long run. This is consistent with a central bank inflation target of 2 per cent.

Now consider a positive shock to the level of demand in the economy. This increase in demand will raise GDP and therefore cut unemployment. The economy moves along $SPC_1$ to A. As unemployment is cut, inflation rises above the target rate, to 4 per cent. The central bank now increases interest rates to bring inflation back to target. The level of economic activity slows and the economy moves back along the $SPC_1$ into long-run equilibrium, where unemployment is constant and inflation is 2 per cent.

A reduction in demand would move the economy along $SPC_1$ to point B, with higher unemployment and lower inflation. The central bank would now cut interest rates, enabling the economy to grow. As jobs are created, the economy moves along $SPC_1$ back into long-run equilibrium.

In the long run, unemployment is constant because the **real wage** is constant. The real wage is equal to the **nominal wage** divided by inflation, often written as W/P. So, a wage rise of 2 per cent when inflation is also 2 per cent results in a constant real wage. If the real wage remains constant, then the cost incentive to hire or fire workers is zero and unemployment remains constant.

In Box 13.2, the short-term trade-off between falling unemployment and rising earnings is discussed.

Now consider what might happen to unemployment if inflationary expectations change to say 3 per cent. The short-run Phillips curve will move up, as in Figure 13.5. However, the long-run equilibrium level of unemployment and GDP will remain constant. Only long-run inflation will rise to 3 per cent. Why? The answer is simple: because inflationary expectations have risen to 3 per cent, firms and workers will now negotiate nominal wage increases of 3 per cent. As a result, real wages will remain constant and, therefore, so will unemployment and GDP. So, even with a change in inflationary expectations, unemployment and GDP still remain at their constant long-run values.

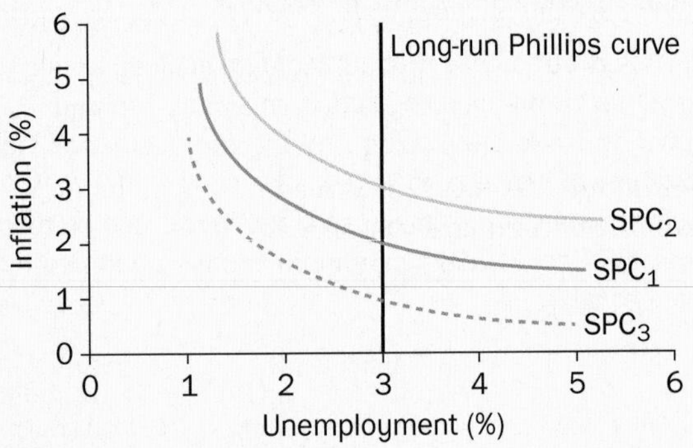

The same is true in a period of deflation, where a fall in inflationary expectations would result in the short-run Phillips curve moving down from $SPC_1$ to $SPC_3$. Long-run equilibrium unemployment will remain constant, but inflation will be lower.

The key point to understand is that, in the long run, there is no trade-off between inflation and unemployment.

## Insights from the Phillips curve

The Phillips curve analysis provides two important insights, which we can develop further.

**Figure 13.5   Expectations-augmented Phillips curve**

If inflationary expectations increase to 3 per cent, then the short-run Phillips curve moves up. The new long-run equilibrium is 3 per cent unemployment and 3 per cent inflation. In reverse, a fall in inflationary expectations would see the short-run Phillips curve move down from $SPC_1$ to $SPC_3$.

## Box 13.2
## Employment hits fresh high but wage growth disappoints

UK employment reached a fresh high in January, although disappointing wage data raised concerns that stronger real-pay growth this year would be driven solely by lower inflation.

Chancellor George Osborne hailed 'yet another economic milestone' ahead of his final Budget before the general election as the number of people in work rose by 143,000 to a record-high 30.94 million in the three months to January. The Office for National Statistics (ONS) said this took Britain's employment rate to a record high of 73.3 per cent.

Jobless benefit claimants fell to 791,200 in February, pushing down the claimant count rate to its lowest in forty years. Higher employment and a lower claimant count kept unemployment rate at a six-year low of 5.7 per cent. Although this was slightly higher than economists' forecasts for a fall to 5.6 per cent, it was down from 6 per cent in the previous three months and matched the six-year low seen in the three months to December.

Real pay also continued to strengthen, although overall pay growth also fell short of expectations. Average weekly earnings, including bonuses, grew by 1.8 per cent in the three months to January, from 2.1 per cent in the quarter to December, when workers enjoyed a bumper rise in bonus payments. Economists had expected wages to grow by 2.2 per cent.

By comparison, inflation fell to a record low of 0.3 per cent in January, and is on course to fall further in the coming months.

Regular pay grew by 1.6 per cent over the same period, from 1.7 per cent in the three months to December. Regular real-pay growth is now at its highest since before the financial crisis.

From *The Telegraph*. 18 March 2015. 'Employment hits fresh high but wage growth disappoints'. Szu Ping Chan. © Telegraph Media Group Limited (2015)

1  **Importance of the short run and long run.** The analysis has shown that we need to consider the short and the long runs. Importantly, because labour and wages are a main input and cost for a firm, any variation in wages results in a change in a firm's willingness to supply. Therefore, the Phillips curve analysis highlights the need to understand both short- and long-run aggregate supply within the economy.

2  **The importance of the speed of adjustment.** We need to be concerned about the speed of adjustment from the short to the long run. If a reduction in demand moves an economy to point B in Figure 13.4, then unemployment increases and inflation falls. If firms and workers are able to cut prices and wages quickly, then the economy will rapidly return to its long-run equilibrium. Cutting prices is possible, but cutting wages is rarely seen as acceptable by workers. An increase in demand moves the economy to A, so firms and workers need to increase prices and wages in order to ensure that real wages remain constant. Raising wages makes workers happy, but funding a pay rise by raising prices is not seen as that attractive by consumers or competitive by firms. In addition, prices and wages are often negotiated and set for 12 months. Therefore, for a variety of reasons, sluggish wage and price adjustments limit the scope for rapid adjustment to the long-run macroeconomic equilibrium.

Rapid adjustment in prices and wages suggests that an economy needs little active fiscal or monetary policy, while sluggish adjustments provide the possibility for fiscal or monetary intervention to move the economy more swiftly towards its equilibrium.

In order to further your understanding of these issues, we will develop the short- and long-run Phillips curves ideas into short- and long-run aggregate supply line schedules. From this, we can then examine macroeconomic equilibrium using aggregate demand and supply frameworks and consider likely responses to demand- and supply-side shocks to the economy. We can then consider the competing views on the need and scale of intervention, which relate to perceived views on the economy's speed of adjustment.

Inflation, aggregate demand and supply

## Long-run aggregate supply

The long-run Phillips curve shows that unemployment is constant in the long run and, therefore, the economy operates at full potential. As such, GDP is constant and any changes in inflation do not alter employment, or GDP. This is because, in the long run, real wages are held constant through nominal wage increases being kept in line with inflation. Long-run aggregate supply is therefore vertical, or inflation inelastic, as illustrated in Figure 13.6.

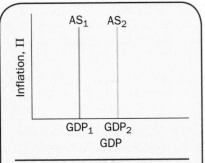

Figure 13.6   Long-run aggregate supply

Long-run aggregate supply is constant and represents the full employment level of the economy. Any change in long-run supply must reflect real changes in economic factor inputs, technology or productivity.

This is not to say that the full employment level of GDP is entirely fixed. It is possible for an economy to attract more economic resources. A rising birth rate, an inflow of migrant workers or the discovery of oil and gas are all examples of increased economic endowments, which would result in the long-run aggregate supply schedule moving to $AS_2$ in Figure 13.6. Equally, if a new technology reduced the costs of economic transactions, such as Google's ability to provide low-cost information, especially on prices, then less time/resource is needed for shopping and more time is available for labour. With more labour time, the economy can grow to $GDP_2$. Finally, a rise in productivity, such as that brought about by more workers engaging in university education, can also lead to an increase in the full employment level of the economy.

## Short-run aggregate supply

In the short run, there is no guarantee that real wages remain constant. This is because, for most jobs, nominal wages are fixed in advance, for anything from one to three years. Therefore, nominal wage adjustment is not instantaneously linked to inflation. As such, the economy does not have to be at the full employment level in the short run.

Wage bargaining is extremely expensive and involves many hours of negotiation between managers, unions and workers. These costs can be magnified when disagreements lead to strikes. Therefore, companies prefer to limit negotiations to once per year.

Workers may even benefit from inflexible wage agreements. During a boom, workers' pay may not rise quickly. But this can be compensated in a recession by pay not falling. Workers are therefore willing to sacrifice short-term constant real wages for short-term nominal wage guarantees.

For these reasons, it is necessary to examine the short-run equilibrium of the economy, where real wages are not held constant. If nominal wages are held constant and the rate of inflation rises, then real wages fall and employment increases. Recall Figure 13.4 and the movement along $SPC_1$ to A. We now have to incorporate these ideas into an understanding of short-run aggregate supply. Figure 13.7 helps to develop this understanding.

Figure 13.7 illustrates a long-run aggregate supply line, $AS_1$, and two short-run aggregate supply lines, $SAS_1$ and $SAS_2$. Each short-run aggregate supply line is drawn for a given rate of nominal wage growth. So, if workers and firms have agreed a wage increase of 5 per cent, then we might assume that the economy is on $SAS_1$. If they have agreed a nominal wage increase of 2 per cent, then they can assume the economy is on $SAS_2$.

Let us begin in long-run equilibrium, with output at $GDP_1$ and inflation at $\pi_1$. Workers and firms have agreed nominal wage growth of $\pi_1$, which therefore places them on $SAS_1$. If inflation turns out to be $\pi_1$, then real wages are held constant and the economy remains in long-run equilibrium. If inflation turns out to be higher than $\pi_1$, say $\pi_3$, then real wages will fall and the price of goods and services rises faster than expected. This provides firms with an incentive to hire more workers and raise short-run output. The economy moves along $SAS_1$ to point A. Inflation and GDP rise.

If inflation falls back to $\pi_1$, then the economy moves back to long-run equilibrium, where $SAS_1$ intersects $AS_1$. If inflation remains above $\pi_1$, then firms and workers are likely to negotiate higher nominal wage growth of $\pi_3$ and we would need to draw a new short-run aggregate supply line, $SAS_3$, which is higher than $SAS_1$. If inflation is less than $\pi_1$, real wages rise. This makes employment more expensive, and firms reduce employment and output. The economy moves along $SAS_1$ to point B, where inflation and output fall.

If the economy remains at B for a significant period of time, then firms and workers may come to expect that the long-term inflation rate for the economy has fallen to $\pi_2$. If they then agree nominal wage rate increases of $\pi_2$, the economy moves to $SAS_2$, and back into long-run equilibrium.

## Aggregate demand

Finally we need to provide a brief recap on aggregate demand, which was covered in Chapter 9. Aggregate demand is all demand in the economy and from our exploration of the circular flow of income total expenditure in an economy is equal to the sum of consumption, investment, government spending and net exports.

The relationship between inflation and demand is negative when a central bank has an inflation target. For example, if inflation moves above target, the central bank can raise interest rates; this will reduce consumption, investment and even exports, if the exchange rate also changes. When inflation is below target, then the central bank will reduce interest rates, leading to stronger demand through higher consumption, investment and net exports. Therefore, through interest rates, there is a negative relationship between inflation and aggregate demand. This concept is illustrated in Figure 13.8.

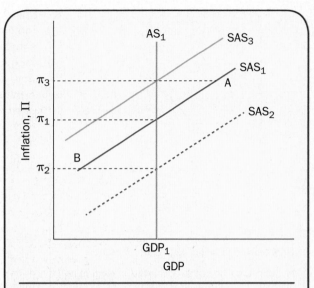

**Figure 13.7  Short-run aggregate supply**

The economy is in long-run equilibrium, with an inflation rate of $\pi_1$ and output of $GDP_1$. On $SAS_1$, nominal wage growth is agreed to be $\pi_1$. Inflation higher than $\pi_1$ reduces real wages and enables firms to raise output. The economy moves to A. Inflation less than $\pi_1$ raises real wages and forces firms to reduce output. The economy moves to B. If $\pi_2$ becomes the expected rate of inflation and the agreed rate of nominal wage increases, then the economy will move to $SAS_2$ and return to long-run equilibrium. Points A and B correspond with points A and B in Figure 13.4.

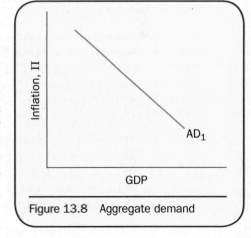

**Figure 13.8  Aggregate demand**

##  Short- and long-run equilibria

We can now integrate aggregate demand and long- and short-run supply.

Consider Figure 13.9: the economy is in both short- and long-run equilibria, with an output of $GDP_1$ and an inflation rate of $\pi_1$. Then follows a drop in consumer and business confidence. Consumption and investment fall and aggregate demand moves from $AD_1$ to $AD_2$. The fall in demand moves the economy to a new short-run equilibrium, where inflation is $\pi_2$ and output is $GDP_2$. The fall in inflation has raised real wages and firms have reacted by cutting output (and employment).

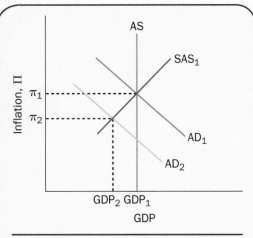

Figure 13.9 Falling aggregate demand

We can also consider a change in aggregate supply.

Unless aggregate demand moves back, possibly under a monetary or fiscal expansion, then only a rightward move in short-run aggregate supply will bring the economy back into long-run equilibrium on the AS line. We explained previously that short-run supply changes when workers alter their inflationary expectations. At $SAS_1$ workers expected inflation of $\pi_1$. If workers now accept that inflation has fallen to a level even lower than $\pi_2$, then lower wage demands will result in a slowing real wage and short-run supply would move to the right and return the economy to long-run equilibrium.

## A recent example: deflation and the credit crisis

The credit crisis of 2008 led to a fall in consumption and investment. However, at the time inflation was above target in many economies, so the fall in demand helped economies move back towards their target inflation rate. Governments and central banks welcomed the reduction in inflation, but were concerned about a long-run adjustment which also included a significant recession at $GDP_2$, and deflation well below $\pi_2$.

Swift reductions in interest rates and planned increases in government expenditure represented a combined monetary and fiscal expansion. The intention of these policies was to rapidly increase aggregate demand, thus enabling the economy to return to long-run equilibrium quickly and not go through a prolonged adjustment of prices, wages, supply and output.

### Why avoid deflation?

The first issue is time to adjust. If full employment takes many years, then unemployment will be high for a prolonged period of time. It is then better to act quickly with monetary and fiscal packages.

The second issue relates to the impact of deflation on consumption. If consumers postpone consumption of high-ticket items in the expectation of cheaper prices in the future, then consumption today falls further. This generates a bigger recession, more unemployment and more deflation. The risk, then, is that further deflation motivates households to withhold yet more consumption, which simply repeats the cycle and exacerbates the overall macroeconomic problem.

Third, deflation raises the real value of debt. If prices fall, then the value of labour falls and wage growth should fall and perhaps even become negative. This makes previously incurred debts less affordable. Households transfer earnings from consumption to debt repayment. Aggregate demand schedule shifts to the left and we observe more deflation, a larger fall in GDP and greater unemployment.

The simple lesson is that falling prices are not necessarily a good thing.

### A temporary supply shock

Figure 13.10 illustrates the effect of a temporary supply shock. The economy begins in long-run equilibrium at the target rate of inflation. An increase in oil and commodity prices moves the short-run aggregate supply schedule to $SAS_2$. The short-run macroeconomic equilibrium now consists of higher inflation and lower GDP. The central bank now needs to decide whether it wishes to prioritize inflation or GDP. In the UK the Bank of England witnessed inflation rates of 5 per cent, or 3 percentage points above target. The Bank had the option of increasing interest rates, reducing aggregate demand and bringing inflation back to target at $\pi_1$. But such a move would have reduced GDP further and moved the economy a greater distance from potential GDP and long-run equilibrium. The Bank took the view that oil and commodity prices were a temporary problem and short-run supply would return to SAS$_1$ over one to two years.

## 13.6 Monetary policy rules

How does a central bank decide to react to a rise in inflation: ignore the rise, or focus more on GDP instead of inflation? Central banks address these issues by deciding if the problem is demand- or supply-side orientated.

If inflation moves away from target because demand has increased or decreased, then the central bank simply needs to offset the change using interest rates. So, if aggregate demand increases (decreases) and causes higher (lower) inflation, the bank should increase (decrease) interest rates and reduce (increase) demand. Inflation and GDP will return to target levels.

The worry for a central bank is when it operates an inflation target and faces a temporary supply-side shock (see Figure 13.11). By holding strictly to the inflation target of $\pi_1$, the central bank must alter aggregate demand to offset any inflationary impact from temporary supply-side shocks. If we begin in long-run equilibrium and short-run supply moves from SAS$_1$ to SAS$_2$, then, in order to keep inflation at the target rate of $\pi_1$, aggregate demand has to be reduced and move the economy to A. This creates a recession, with output at GDP$_2$. If short-run aggregate supply moves to SAS$_3$, then, in order to keep inflation at $\pi_1$, aggregate demand has to be increased and the economy moves to B with output at GDP$_3$.

Inflation targeting in the face of supply shocks generates volatility in GDP and stability in prices.

Reflecting these difficulties, central banks are pragmatic in their approach to managing the economy and tend to follow what is known as a **Taylor rule**. The Taylor rule can be represented by the following equation:

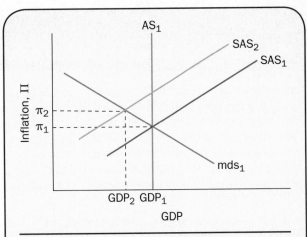

**Figure 13.10    A temporary supply shock**

A temporary supply shock reduces short-run supply to SAS$_2$. This moves the economy away from its long-run equilibrium of GDP$_1$ and $\pi_1$. Inflation rises to $\pi_2$ and GDP falls to GDP$_2$. The central bank can accommodate this shock and boost demand and GDP, but will suffer even higher inflation.

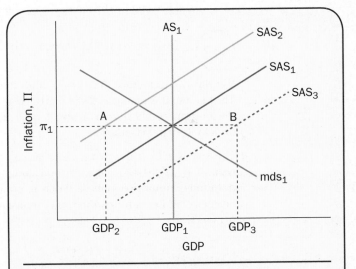

**Figure 13.11    Inflation targeting and supply shocks**

Under a strict inflation target, any temporary supply shock will invoke a change in interest rates and restoration of inflation to $\pi_1$. However, output will be volatile.

$$i = \pi + i^* + a(\pi - \pi^*) + b(\text{GDP} - \text{GDP}^*)$$

where $\pi$ is the rate of inflation, $\pi^*$ is the target rate of inflation, $GDP$ is actual GDP, $GDP^*$ is potential GDP and $i^*$ is the real interest rate; $a$ and $b > 0$. The more the central bank is concerned about inflation deviating from the target rate, the larger $a$, and the more interest rates will change. Similarly, the higher the value for $b$, the more concerned the central bank is with variations in GDP and the more rates will change to bring about long-run equilibrium and potential GDP.

The Taylor rule links interest rate changes to short-term deviations in both inflation and output from long-term equilibrium values.

## Box 13.3
## The Bank of England's inflation report

CPI inflation was 0.5 per cent in December 2014, well below the 2 per cent target. The main reason for this was the steep fall in wholesale energy prices during the second half of last year. Inflation is likely to fall further in the near term, and could temporarily turn negative, as falls in energy prices continue to be passed through. Inflation is likely to rebound around the turn of the year as these effects drop out of the annual rate.

The fall in oil prices, together with monetary policy measures taken abroad, should support global demand. Lower energy prices will also boost UK real-income growth. That, along with a lower expected path for Bank Rate than in November, should help to sustain the recent robust expansion in UK domestic demand. As slack is absorbed, inflation is projected to rise back to levels consistent with the inflation target. The Committee judges that it is currently appropriate to set policy so that it is likely that inflation will return to the 2 per cent target within two years. Under the assumption that Bank Rate rises gradually over the forecast period, that is judged likely to be achieved.

*Source: Bank of England, Inflation Report, February 2015.*

The Bank of England's overview of the economy from its February 2015 inflation report is provided in Box 13.3. Read both paragraphs carefully. The opening paragraph mentions the current level of inflation and the role falling energy prices will have on inflation in the near term. The second paragraph mentions the impact of interest rates on domestic demand and the slack (the difference between demand and potential supply) in the economy. The Bank of England is using the frameworks you have begun to understand.

##  Adjustment speed

We have considered the short- and long-run equilibria outcomes for the economy. Throughout this analysis, there has been an assumption that the economy does not adjust to the long-run equilibrium with any degree of speed. If it did, there would be no need for fiscal or monetary intervention.

The speed with which wages and prices do adjust is debated within economics. Beliefs regarding adjustment speeds and policy responses highlight differing philosophical traditions within economics. While it is not our intention to train you as economists, a business person can benefit from some understanding of the competing macroeconomic perspectives.

### New classical

At one extreme, are the new classical economists. This group of economists hold the belief that markets adjust instantly, leading to a clearing equilibrium. This full and rapid flexibility in prices and output ensures that, following any demand or supply shock, the economy quickly, if not instantly, returns to its long-run, full- employment level of output. A clear consequence of this belief is that there is no need for fiscal or monetary policy interventions. Instead, this group of economists focus on long-run aggregate supply as the economy's output constraint. If growth is desirable, then policy-makers need to focus on policies which enable long-run supply to expand in a stable and consistent manner. Such growth policies will be considered in Chapter 14.

### Gradual monetarist

The next group of economists are the gradual monetarists, who believe that markets adjust quickly but not instantaneously. For gradual monetarists, the long-run equilibrium can be attained in a relatively short time period, such as a year or two. Competitive product markets lead to flexibility in pricing. Free and open labour markets ensure a quick transition to new nominal wage growth rates. Firms and workers quickly, but not perfectly, arrive at new expectations of future price levels and so the adjustment of short-run aggregate supply is reasonably quick. Over a period of one to two years, the economy returns to potential GDP. Since the economy returns quickly to potential GDP, gradual monetarists also accept that supply-side policies are important for long-term growth.

Active fiscal and monetary policy are frowned upon by gradual monetarists. If the economy can correct itself within an acceptable time frame, there is no need for intervention. In fact, any policy stimulus is likely to lead to an over-correction of the economy. As the economy itself adjusts, the policy response will simply multiply the effects. This could drive the economy into a deeper recession, or lead to higher inflation.

The best monetary response stems from the quantity theory of money, which states that $MV = PY$, where M is the money supply, V is the velocity of circulation, P is the price level and Y is real GDP. If PY is nominal GDP and is equal to £10 billion, and M = 1 billion, then the velocity of circulation is 10, i.e. cash must go through everybody's pockets 10 times in order to facilitate £10 billion of economic transactions. Gradual monetarists believe that Y is constant, as depicted by a vertical long-run aggregate supply schedule. They also believe that V is a constant. This means that there is a direct relationship between M and P: inflation is driven by growth in the money supply. If you wish to control inflation, then adopt a *gradual* change in the money supply.

## Moderate Keynesian

Moderate Keynesians take the view that the economy will eventually return to its long-run equilibrium, but the adjustment will not necessarily be quick. Moderate Keynesians believe that prices, wages and inflationary expectations are slow to adjust. Without flexibility in prices and wages, short-run aggregate supply will not adjust quickly either. Due to this slow adjustment, there is significant benefit to be gained from active fiscal and monetary policies. These demand-side policies quickly alter macroeconomic demand and enable the economy to return to potential GDP. Moderate Keynesians accept that, once in long-run equilibrium, potential GDP places a constraint on the economy and supply-side policies are key to improved long-term growth.

## Extreme Keynesian

Finally, we turn to extreme Keynesians, who take the opposite view to that held by new classical economists. Extreme Keynesians are extremely concerned that prices and wages are sticky. For a variety of reasons, including the cost of changing prices and the effect of unions on controlling wage rates, adjustment of short-run aggregate supply is sluggish. The attainment of potential GDP may not be achieved for many years. Economies can move into recession and then remain there, turning the economic episode into a depression. Governments therefore have an enormous duty to push spending into the economy. Extreme Keynesians believe that fiscal policy is better able to do this than monetary policy. Extreme Keynesians do not accept the quantity theory of money and question whether V and Y are constant. Therefore, any expansion of the money supply is unlikely to be inflationary. For extreme Keynesians the core concern is output.

None of these competing views of thought is incorrect. Neither are they correct. This is because the speed of adjustment to potential GDP is not constant. Rather, adjustment speeds vary according to the nature and scale of shocks which impact the economy. For example, when change is small and gradual, the monetarists are more likely to be correct. This is because, when change is small and gradual, firms and workers can easily change their expectations regarding prices. It is easy for these important economic actors to understand what is happening and adjust their behaviour accordingly. Expectations are broadly correct and short-run aggregate supply moves quickly, leading to a rapid restoration of potential GDP.

Now consider the credit crisis, an event described by leading economists as 'unprecedented'; apparently, 'it is difficult to exaggerate the scale of events witnessed in financial markets'. Such is the extreme nature of the credit crisis that not even economists can begin to understand what has occurred and what the impact will be on prices and output. There can be little doubt that consumers and firms will struggle to adapt their expectations rapidly and accurately. Hence, the risk to output in the near term is huge. The Keynesians can claim to have a more accurate view of the world at this point in history. Not surprisingly, governments provided economies with enormous fiscal injections, while at the same time central banks cut interest rates.

However, the debate still continues, and in extreme circumstances it is often practical, rather than ideological, considerations that take precedence. Japan has suffered slow growth and deflation for close on 20 years. In Box 13.4 monetary, fiscal and wage and pricing policies

---

## Box 13.4
## Abenomics 2.0—PM updates plan to refresh Japanese economy

Japan's Prime Minister Shinzo Abe, fresh from a bruising battle over unpopular military legislation, has unveiled an updated plan for reviving the world's third-largest economy, setting a GDP target of 600tn yen (£3.2tn).

Abe took office in late 2012 promising to end deflation and rev up growth through strong public spending, lavish monetary easing and sweeping reforms to help make the economy more productive and competitive. So far, those 'three arrows' of his Abenomics plan have fallen short of their targets, although share prices and corporate profits have soared.

'Tomorrow will definitely be better than today!' Abe declared in a news conference on national television. 'From today Abenomics is entering a new stage. Japan will become a society in which all can participate actively.'

Abe was recently re-elected unopposed as head of the ruling Liberal Democratic party. He has promised to refocus on the economy after enacting security legislation enabling Japan's military to take part in combat even when the country is not under direct attack. The move prompted a series of street protests and weakened his popularity.

'He has to deliver the message that he is so committed to achieving the economic agenda; that is, to make people's lives better,' said analyst Masamichi Adachi of JP Morgan in Tokyo.

Abe said he was determined to ensure that 50 years from now the Japanese population, which is 126 million and falling, has stabilized at 100 million.

He said his new 'three arrows' would be a strong economy, support for child rearing and improved social security, to lighten the burden of child and elder care for struggling families. But with Japan also committed to reducing its massive public debt, it is unclear how he intends to achieve those goals.

'There's nothing wrong with him saying he wants to achieve a better life for everybody. But how to achieve it is a different matter,' Adachi said.

Abe recently announced plans to accelerate cuts in corporate taxes. The central bank is also widely expected to add to its already unprecedented monetary easing by pumping more cash into the economy later this year.

Japan's economy, estimated at $4.6tn in 2014, contracted at a 1.2 per cent annual rate in the April–June quarter. Economists have warned that China's slowdown and market turmoil might weaken an expected recovery in coming months.

At Japan's recent pace of growth, achieving Abe's goal would be a stretch. Real GDP growth averaged 1.7 per cent over the past five fiscal years. That's less than half the 3 per cent pace needed to attain a GDP of 600tn yen by 2021.

The Japan Center for Economic Research, an independent think tank, is forecasting growth at 0.9 per cent this year and 1.5 per cent in 2016. A sales tax increase planned for April 2017, to 10 per cent from 8 per cent now, is expected to dent growth for that year.

Japanese officials acknowledge in private that the country needs a great leap in productivity, which is hard to attain at a time when the workforce is shrinking due to the ageing population.

Given that reality, Japanese employers have been reluctant to invest or to raise wages, even when many are short-staffed.

With wages still barely rising, families have tended to save, and increases in demand from monetary stimulus have been weaker than expected.

From *The Guardian*. 24 September 2015. 'Abenomics 2.0 – PM updates plan to refresh Japanese economy'. Associated Press. Used with permission of Associated Press. Copyright © 2015. All rights reserved.

for Japan are discussed. You are now in a position to see how all these ideas and policies may link together and be important in enabling Japan to grow.

The use of fiscal policy to fine-tune the business cycle went out of fashion around 30 years ago. But when skittish banks and investors are turning away from funding private spending, there is a strong case for a more active fiscal policy to prop up demand. However, fiscal policy has its limits. A run of big budget deficits increases the risk that a government will default or repay its debts only by forcing its central banks to print money, thus creating inflation. If public debt spirals upwards as the economy stagnates, investors will worry that future taxpayers will be unable to shoulder the burden.

## 13.8 Business application: understanding the interest-rate path

For businesses, it is crucial to understand the future path of interest rates. This is because businesses borrow to fund investment and so changes in the interest rate alter the cost of investing.

Companies also use debt to leverage their financial returns. Leverage is a very important financial concept. The use of debt by companies enables higher returns to shareholders. Consider the following. A company has £1 million of shareholders' cash to invest. A project is offering a 10 per cent rate of return, so after one year, the shareholders' funds will have grown to £1.1 million. Alternatively, the company could approach a bank and use its £1 million of equity to raise £9 million of debt. The company now has £10 million to invest. After one year and a 10 per cent rate of return, the investment is worth £11 million. So shareholder equity is now £2 million (£11 million less £9 million of debt). Not surprisingly, managers and shareholders like to use debt to enable companies to grow faster. Leverage is also known as 'gearing' because, like a car, the more debt, the higher the gear, the faster the car and company run.

Debt is, therefore, a very attractive complement to equity financing. Of course, it comes at a cost—the rate of interest—and we should factor this into our calculations. The £2 million of equity at the end of year two should be reduced by the amount of interest that is paid. In fact, because the benefits of leverage come with high levels of debt to equity, the cash flow needed to fund interest repayments can be considerable. Therefore, interest rates matter to companies, not only because of investments but also because of the financial engineering that leverage brings to a company's finances. Understanding the future track for interest rates is crucial for appraising investment decisions and managing cash flows.

The Taylor rule enables business managers to achieve a broad understanding of where interest rates are likely to go in the future. A greater divergence between actual inflation and target inflation will lead to a change in rates. Equally, a departure of actual GDP from potential GDP will lead to an interest rate response. Data published by central banks can be used to assess the difference between actual and target values for GDP and inflation.

In Figure 13.12, fan charts for inflation and GDP from the Bank of England are presented. The darker lines within the fan charts represent the Bank's view of the most probable path for inflation and GDP. The fainter lines, which fan out over time, are less likely possibilities. The UK inflation target is 2 per cent and potential GDP has been growing at around 2.5 per cent per annum. The inflation fan chart suggests that the Bank will slacken monetary policy in order to avoid deflation and bring inflation back towards target. A consideration of the GDP fan charts indicates that the Bank thinks GDP will continue at above target until 2018. This strength in the economy is unlikely to cause the Bank to think about reducing interest rates.

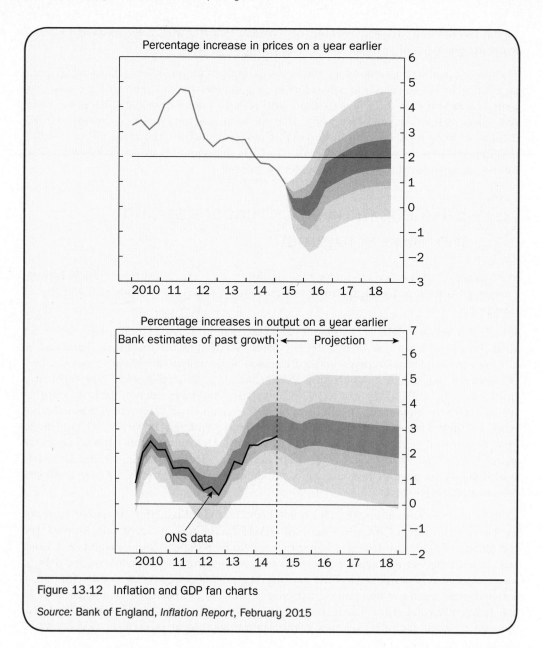

**Figure 13.12**    Inflation and GDP fan charts

*Source:* Bank of England, *Inflation Report*, February 2015

Further out, the Bank's forecast becomes less accurate, or certain. However, two trends are discernible from the fan charts. Inflation is expected to remain below target until the end of 2016. If inflation then returns to target and the economy grows, we may see a rise in interest rates to return monetary policy to a more long-term neutral position. If inflation remains below target, lax monetary policy may continue.

## 13.9 Business application: recognizing the importance of real business cycles

In this chapter we have considered the short- and long-run macroeconomic equilibria. We would like to recap on two fairly simple ideas and then pose a question.

*First idea:* we introduced the concept of long-run aggregate supply. In the long run the supply of the economy is fixed. The level of GDP associated with the long run is called potential GDP. Over time, the potential of the economy to produce output might increase and long-run aggregate supply would shift to the right.

*Second idea:* we introduced the concept of the output gap, which is the difference between actual and potential GDP. In the long run the economy operates at its potential. But in the short run, the level of actual GDP can be less than potential GDP. This output gap might be associated with slower economic growth, or even a recession.

*Question:* is it safe to presume that potential GDP, long-run aggregate supply, always moves to the right, i.e. potential GDP gradually increases over time? Under what circumstances might potential GDP reduce and what might this mean in terms of understanding broad macroeconomic issues? Consider Figure 13.13.

In Figure 13.13 we have long-run aggregate supply $AS_1$ associated with potential $GDP_1$. The economy moves to a short-run equilibrium, which results in actual $GDP_A$. The output gap is equal to $GDP_1 - GDP_A$. The cause of the output gap stems from a financial crisis, which has destroyed banks and made remaining banks weaker and less able to lend. The banking sector is therefore less able to support the supply side of the economy, because the provision of loans and other financing facilities is less. This weaker banking sector means that the supply potential of the economy is less and long-run aggregate supply moves left from $AS_1$ to $AS_2$. The output gap is now much smaller. However, we need to recognize that we are also observing a change in real potential and this is referred to as a **real business cycle** effect.

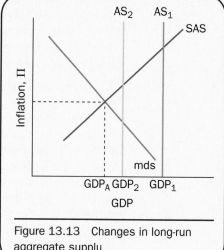

Figure 13.13  Changes in long-run aggregate supply

> Real business cycle results from changes in potential GDP.

The implications of real business cycles are very important. Consider a government deficit which is equal to 10 per cent of GDP. Six per cent is structural and 4 per cent is cyclical. That 4 per cent is generated by the output gap $GDP_1 - GDP_A$. Reducing the structural deficit of 6 per cent requires a set of austerity measures which cut government spending and increase tax, all of which will impact the economy and reduce company profits. Following the reduction in potential GDP to $GDP_2$, the output gap falls. The cyclical part of the budget deficit decreases to 2 per cent and the structural deficit expands to 8 per cent. More austerity measures are needed which may lead to even larger cuts in company profits.

It is a job for professional economists to consider changes in real long-run supply and then worry about a government's ability to reduce a fiscal deficit. However, effective managers need to understand their environment and recognize a threat when it is discussed in the business press. Business managers who follow a line of argument being put forward by a professional economist, such as a change in potential GDP, can then consider the implications and risk to profits, plan effectively and steer the company through troubled times.

##  Business data application: understanding the formation of inflationary expectations

If growth in wages and prices is fundamental to the macroeconomic equilibrium, then it must be important for business to understand and respond to changing inflationary expectations. If, for example, workers believe that inflation will rise faster in the future, then they will seek to achieve higher pay awards. Firms need to form their own inflationary expectations. Do they share the same expectations as their workers and do they believe they have the potential to pass on higher wages to customers, through higher prices? Without the ability to generate additional revenue, the real cost of labour climbs and firms become less willing to supply.

Central banks track inflationary expectations through various surveys. These surveys provide data on inflationary expectations among households, firms and economic forecasters. The surveys try to measure inflationary expectations over different time periods, including the short, medium and long terms. In Table 13.1 we present inflationary expectations from professional economic forecasters who respond to the European Central Bank (ECB) survey.

The data within Table 13.1 suggest that inflationary expectations are formed in different ways over different time horizons. Near-term, one-year inflationary expectations are much more volatile than long-term inflationary expectations. For example, in 2015 91.9 per cent of the sample of professional economic forecasters believe that inflation in the eurozone is likely to be less than 1 per cent (even though the target rate is 2 per cent). In fact, 31.3 per cent expect inflation to be negative, i.e. deflationary. However, in 2015, only 1.6 per cent of the sample of professional economic forecasters expect inflation to be negative in 2019. A much larger percentage, expect inflation to be closer to the 2 per cent target. So what drives these differences? The answer to this question is not precise, but requires a number of factors to be recognized.

First, central banks have come to recognize that inflation targets are a powerful tool for controlling inflationary expectations, but only if the central bank is credible in achieving the inflation target. If, on average, the central bank brings inflation to the target level, then workers, firms and professional economists can confidently form expectations of future price stability. In addition, repeated requests from government for workers, especially in the public sector, to undertake pay restraint and accept pay rises in line with inflation also help. Costs rise in line with inflation and inflationary expectations remain subdued.

**Table 13.1**  Inflationary expectations among professional forecasters

|  | 2015 | 2016 | 2017 | 2019 |
|---|---|---|---|---|
| Mean point estimate | 0.3 | 1.1 | 1.5 | 1.8 |
| Standard deviation | 0.3 | 0.3 | 0.3 | 0.2 |
| Number of replies | 58 | 55 | 47 | 48 |
| **Probability distributions** | **2015** | **2016** | **2017** | **2019** |
| < −1.0% | 1.6 | 0.3 | 0.3 | 0.3 |
| −1.0 to −0.6% | 7.2 | 0.7 | 0.4 | 0.3 |
| −0.5 to −0.1% | 22.5 | 5.1 | 1.8 | 1 |
| 0.0 to 0.4% | 35.2 | 14.5 | 6.7 | 2.7 |
| 0.5 to 0.9% | 25.4 | 28 | 16.6 | 9.6 |
| 1.0 to 1.4% | 6.1 | 29.5 | 26.9 | 20.6 |
| 1.5 to 1.9% | 1.5 | 14.1 | 27.4 | 32.7 |
| 2.0 to 2.4% | 0.4 | 5.2 | 12.7 | 19 |
| 2.5 to 2.9% | 0.1 | 1.9 | 5.1 | 8.9 |
| 3.0 to 3.4% | 0 | 0.5 | 1.4 | 3.4 |
| 3.5 to 3.9% | 0 | 0.1 | 0.5 | 1.1 |
| >4.0% | 0 | 0.1 | 0.2 | 0.4 |
| Total | 100 | 100 | 100 | 100 |

*Source:* ECB, 2015.

However, individuals are exposed to a variety of markets, and over time track price changes. For more than 10 years, an influx of cheap imports from China and South East Asia has helped to form low inflationary expectations. The cost of computers, mobile phones, televisions and cars has fallen in real terms. This trend of falling prices helps to anchor low, long-term inflationary expectations.

However, in more recent times, the prices of food and energy have risen enormously. Individuals recognize these significant shifts and appear to increase their near-term inflationary expectations.

Therefore, in seeking to understand the likely level of inflation in the future we need to establish which future time frame we are interested in. Over longer planning horizons, perhaps those used for large-scale financial investment decisions, the key question for business is to establish if the central bank target inflation rate is acting as an inflationary anchor. Table 13.1 provides some evidence that over a five-year planning horizon, professional economists expect the ECB to deliver the 2 per cent target rate for inflation. If a central bank has persistently failed to deliver the target rate, then long-term inflationary expectations might differ from the target rate.

In the short to medium term, inflationary expectations appear to be driven more by current events, such as commodity, fuel and food prices. Inflationary expectations can therefore be much more volatile in the short and medium term.

The difference in inflationary expectations over time can generate problems. If as households and firms we all held firm to the view that, over the long term, inflation will be on target, then changes in wages and prices would be easy to plan and accommodate. Adjustment to long-run equilibrium could be fairly rapid. The unfortunate fact is that near-term concerns about inflation seem to play a bigger role in economic decision making and, with inflationary expectations veering away from target rates, there is a greater desire among firms and workers to change wages and prices more aggressively. This drive for change creates conflict and rigidities in the adjustment process to full long-run equilibrium.

## Summary

1. In long-run equilibrium, the economy operates at its full employment level.

2. The full employment level of an economy is the same as potential GDP.

3. In the short run, economic output is actual GDP.

4. The difference between actual and potential GDP is known as the *output gap*.

5. The Phillips curve shows a negative statistical relationship between the rate of inflation and the rate of unemployment.

6. In the long run, equilibrium unemployment is fixed. Therefore, there can be no relationship between unemployment and inflation. The long-run Phillips curve is vertical.

7. Any movement along the short-run Phillips curve represents a temporary change in real wage rates. In the long run, real wages are held constant.

8. If inflationary expectations change, then the short-run Phillips curve will move. Expectations of higher inflation will result in the short-run Phillips curve moving up.

9. The speed of adjustment from the short to the long run is determined by the flexibility of wages and prices.

10. The macroeconomic demand schedule shows a negative relationship between inflation and the demand for output.

11. Long-run aggregate supply is fixed at potential GDP.

12. Short-run aggregate supply is determined by nominal wage growth.

13. If inflation differs from nominal wage growth, then real wages change and in the short run firms move along their short-run aggregate supply line.

14. In the short-run equilibrium, actual GDP can differ from potential GDP. But as workers and firms adjust wages to the new level of inflation, the economy adjusts to the long-run equilibrium of potential GDP.

15. Permanent supply-side shocks can be accommodated by a reduction in the long-run interest rate.

16. Temporary supply-side shocks may reduce GDP, but if they are offset with additional demand, then inflation is likely to rise.

17. The management of demand shocks brings stability to prices and output.

18. A Taylor rule suggests that a central bank sets interest rates according to the departure of inflation rates from target and also GDP from target.

19. Different groups of economists hold differing views about the flexibility of prices and wages, and the speed with which the economy will return to long-run equilibrium.

20. New classical economists think adjustment is instantaneous. Extreme Keynesians believe adjustment is very slow. Gradual monetarists think adjustment takes a couple of years and think monetary policy should enable a gradual expansion of the money supply. Moderate Keynesian economists think the economy will eventually return to long-run equilibrium, but a strong dose of fiscal and monetary policy will help in the short run.

## Learning checklist

You should now be able to:
- Explain the relationship described by the Phillips curve
- Understand the key differences between the short- and long-run Phillips curves
- Link the short- and long-run Phillips curves and short- and long-run aggregate supply lines
- Identify the short- and long-run macroeconomic equilibria
- Explain the adjustment to long-run equilibrium
- Assess monetary policy responses to demand and supply shocks in the economy
- Understand the different views among economists regarding the speed of adjustment to long-run equilibrium.

## Questions                                                    connect

1. Explain why, when unemployment increases, inflation may decrease. Use a suitable diagram to illustrate this relationship.

2. Use numerical examples to explain the difference between nominal and real wages. How have nominal and real wages developed in your economy over the past five years?

3. If real wages are held constant, what is the relationship between unemployment and inflation in the long run?

4. If real wages are constant in the long run, is it still possible to observe a negative relationship between inflation and unemployment?

5. The central bank has an inflation target. Inflation rises above the target. What will happen next to interest rates and aggregate demand?

6. Explain why aggregate supply is inelastic in the long run and elastic in the short run.

7. The central bank follows an inflation target and the economy benefits from an improvement in productivity. What will happen to interest rates?

8. Can a central bank with an inflation target fight cost-push inflation?

9. Using a suitable diagram, illustrate why central banks are keen to avoid the potential black hole of a deflationary spiral.

10. What is the Taylor rule? How might business use the Taylor rule to forecast future interest rates?

11. Assume that you are a new classical economist. What are your recommendations for monetary policy? How do these differ from an extreme Keynesian's? Are these two views relevant to modern economies?

12. Use a diagram to illustrate how a monetary response to a loss of consumer confidence stabilizes inflation and GDP.

13. If nominal wages increase faster than the rate of inflation, under what circumstances can employment remain constant?

14. What do you consider to be the key benefits of inflation targeting?

15. How would a reduction in the capital stock of the economy affect the output gap of the economy?

## Exercises

1. Which of the following has caused the move from SPC$_1$ to SPC$_2$ in Figure 13.14?

   (a) A rise in the full employment rate.

   (b) An increase in nominal wages.

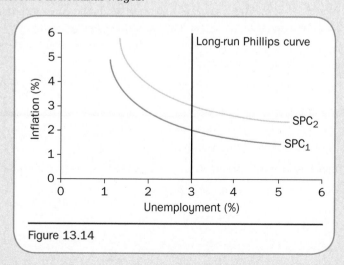

Figure 13.14

(c)   An increased expectation of higher unemployment.

(d)   An increased expectation of higher inflation.

2.   This exercise examines monetary and fiscal policy using the MDS and the aggregate supply schedule. Figure 13.15 shows two macroeconomic demand schedules (MDS$_a$ and MDS$_b$) and the aggregate supply schedule (AS). First, we consider the effects of monetary policy in the classical model—specifically, an increase in nominal money supply.

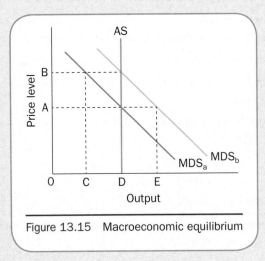

Figure 13.15   Macroeconomic equilibrium

(a)   Identify the 'before' and 'after' MDS.

(b)   What was the original equilibrium price and output?

(c)   What is equilibrium price and output after the policy is implemented?

Next, consider fiscal policy—again in the classical model. Suppose there is a reduction in government expenditure:

(d)   Identify the 'before' and 'after' MDS.

(e)   What was the original equilibrium price and output?

(f)   What is the equilibrium price and output after the policy is implemented? The Keynesian model is characterized by sluggish adjustment. Consider the period *after* the policy but *before* adjustment begins.

(g)   Identify price and output.

(h)   The MDS represents points at which goods and money markets are in equilibrium. In the position you have identified in (g), adjustment has still to take place—so, in what sense is the goods market in 'equilibrium'?

3.   (a)   Why is an understanding of inflationary expectations important for the economy and business?

(b)   How are inflationary expectations likely to differ between students, households with young children and the retired?

(c)   Will higher inflationary expectations always feed into future higher inflation?

# Supply-side policies and economic growth

## Chapter contents

## Learning outcomes

By the end of this chapter you should be able to:

Economic theory

LO1   Explain how economic growth is linked to growth in long-run aggregate supply

LO2   Explain the neoclassical model of economic growth

LO3   Evaluate the convergence hypothesis

LO4   Discuss the main features of the endogenous growth model

LO5   Identify the types of policies used to develop economic growth

Business application

LO6   Debate whether firms should produce or consume innovation

LO7   Analyse opportunities for business growth in BRIC economies

LO8   Review the role of gross capital formation within economic growth

| At a glance | Supply-side policies and economic growth |

## The issues

Different economies grow at different rates. How do economies grow and how can governments involve business in developing economic growth?

## The understanding

Economic growth can be linked to the development of long-run aggregate supply. The output potential of an economy is fixed if aggregate supply is perfectly inelastic. Changes in aggregate demand only alter the inflation rate. Therefore, in order to make the economy grow, it is essential to increase the level of aggregate supply. At a simplistic level, improving aggregate supply can be achieved by either increasing the availability of factor inputs, such as labour, or by increasing the productivity of factor inputs, so that more output can be produced with more input. However, a more interesting question relates to how fast an economy can grow. Neoclassical theory argues that growth will converge across economies to a common rate. Endogenous growth theory counters this view, suggesting that governments can develop policies which will enable the economy to grow at a faster rate.

## The usefulness

The growth rate of an economy has important implications for business. First, sales and revenue growth will, in part, be related to economic growth. Second, government policies designed to improve productivity within an economy may aid a firm to reduce its costs.

 **14.1** ## Business problem: assessing economic growth

> **Least developed economies,** such as some African states, show very low levels of commercialization.
>
> **Developing economies,** such as Brazil, India and China, are those which show a high degree of commercialization, but their economies are not amongst the most developed in the world, such as the UK, US, Japan, France and Germany.
>
> A **developed economy** has high levels of commercial activity and high levels of supporting infrastructure, such as good transport and communication systems, good health and education systems.

Economies across the world are at different stages of economic development and present different opportunities for economic growth. Economists and policy-makers place economies into development categories. There is some variation in the use and meaning of the categories but there is a broad understanding that an economy can be developed, developing or least developed.

In the **least developed economies** of the world there is very little commercial activity; there is limited infrastructure for transport, power, communications; and poor levels of health, limited education. Some countries in sub-Saharan Africa, such as Burundi and Malawi, fall into this category with GDP per capita figures below US $1,000 per year.

**Developing economies** show a higher degree of commercial or economic activity and are engaged in a process of increasing **industrialization**. Growing numbers of people transfer from subsistence farming to paid employment. New companies and industries emerge, and the economy is supported by growing levels of infrastructure, improved education and health provision. Developing economies cover a wide range. Some economies can be embarking on the development process while others can be close to being fully developed. GDP per capita figures can range from US $1,000 to $12,000 per annum. Examples at the lower end of the scale include Cambodia, Pakistan and the Yemen, while examples at the higher end include Paraguay, Jordan and China.

A problem with such categories is that high-population economies like India or China have good rates of economic development but low GDP per capita levels, because the high population levels dilute the economic activity measure. Such economies are sometimes referred to as **emerging economies**. These economies have the features of a developed economy, e.g. infrastructure, education and health, but they lack the per capita levels of economic activity. For example, India had a GDP per capita figure of around US $4,400 in 2013 according to the World Bank; and similarly China had a figure of US $11,000. Neither economy makes the US $12,000 cut for developed economy status, yet both have some of the world's leading universities, levels of educational attainment as well as leading medical facilities and hospitals.

As someone interested in business and economics, do not confuse low economic development and low GDP per capita figures with a lack of commercial opportunity. Figure 14.1 shows that since (at least) 1990, the developing economies of the world have been taking a larger share of world GDP. In 1990 developed economies represented 31 per cent of world GDP. By 2013 this figure had grown to almost 47 per cent. Future prospects for growth can be found in the developing world. See the difference in growth rates below.

The **economic growth** rates for various developed economies including some economies from within the European Union, the US and Japan are presented in Figure 14.2a. Growth rates have varied by economy and over time. All economies slowed between 2001 and 2002, reflecting the impact of the terrorist events of 9/11 on the global economy. After 2002, most economies grew until the arrival of the credit crisis in late 2008. Then, all major economies slowed and headed for recession. Also note how Japan has almost always had the lowest growth rate in the sample for each year. This pattern of growth illustrates the lost decades for Japan, which throughout the 1970s and 1980s enjoyed very high rates of growth.

For the period 1990–2013 the average growth rate was 1.7 per cent per year across all economies in Figure 14.1a. Contrast this with an average growth rate of 5 per cent per year for the countries in Figure 14.1b, which illustrates GDP growth rates for the BRIC economies (Brazil, Russia, India and China), who together are generally identified as fast-growing emerging economies.

An industrialized economy is characterized by lots of industrial sectors such as construction industries, automobile manufacturers, oil companies. Economies usually move from being based on agriculture, to industrialized and then towards services, such as retail and banking.

An emerging economy is making the transition from developing to developed. Emerging economies have very high levels of sustainable economic development with companies competing effectively across the world.

Economic growth is measured as the percentage change in GDP per year.

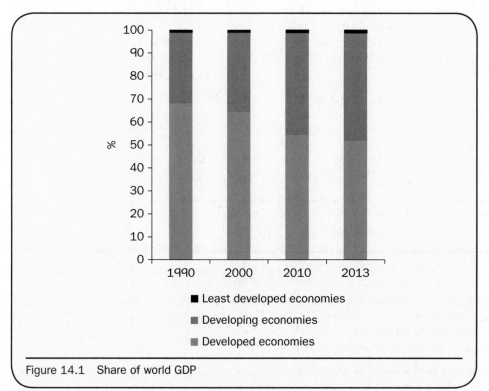

Figure 14.1    Share of world GDP

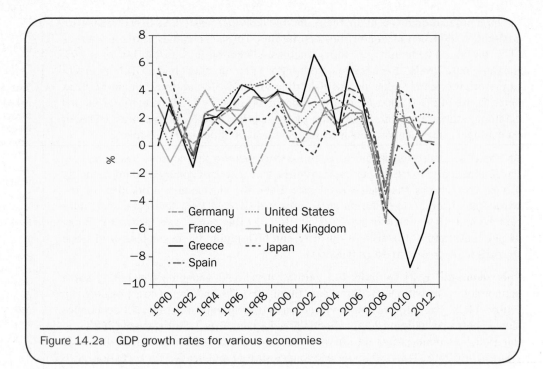

Figure 14.2a    GDP growth rates for various economies

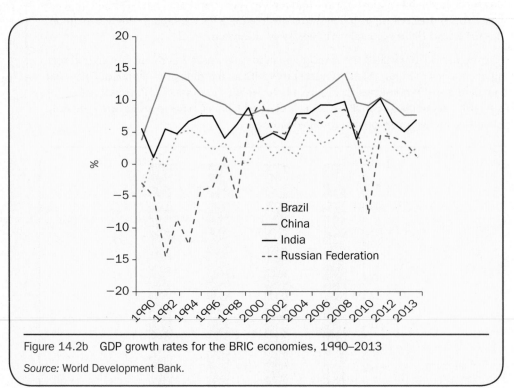

Figure 14.2b    GDP growth rates for the BRIC economies, 1990–2013

*Source:* World Development Bank.

The importance of different growth rates becomes more apparent over time. For example, assume that we have an economy and the level of GDP is 100. The economy now grows at four hypothetical growth rates, 1, 2.5, 4 and 10 per cent. The amount of GDP in each year, for each growth rate, is tabulated in Table 14.1.

The amount of GDP in year 10 is vastly different depending upon the growth rate of the economy, varying from 110 under a growth rate of 1 per cent, to 259 under a growth rate of

10 per cent. Therefore, over time the growth rate of an economy has enormous implications for the generation of individuals' incomes and the potential for companies to grow. As a consequence, governments, workers and firms are extremely interested in the projected growth rates for an economy.

For example, through a simple examination of the circular flow of income, economic growth is associated with growth in the flow of income between households and firms. More products are produced, more income is paid to workers/households and more products are sold. As a result, the faster an economy grows, the faster incomes rise and sales increase. While this makes economic growth an attractive opportunity for business, an additional consideration also has to be examined.

In the main, governments try to make the economy grow through developments in aggregate supply, providing firms with the ability, or incentive, to supply more output. Firms will supply more if the marginal costs of production fall. Policies designed to reduce companies' costs and, moreover, boost productivity are central to developing aggregate supply and economic growth. This means that economic growth and the development of sales is not the only benefit for firms. Policies designed to aid economic growth may also aid the cost structures faced by firms. Companies that understand why economic growth is important and how growth might be achieved are better placed to understand government policy and exploit the opportunities offered by economic growth. This chapter will provide you with an overview of supply-side theories and economic growth.

**Table 14.1** Impact of different growth rates

| Year | Growth rate | | | |
| | 1% | 2.5% | 4% | 10% |
|---|---|---|---|---|
| 0 | 100 | 100 | 100 | 100 |
| 1 | 101 | 103 | 104 | 110 |
| 2 | 102 | 105 | 108 | 121 |
| 3 | 103 | 108 | 112 | 133 |
| 4 | 104 | 110 | 117 | 146 |
| 5 | 105 | 113 | 122 | 161 |
| 6 | 106 | 116 | 127 | 177 |
| 7 | 107 | 119 | 132 | 195 |
| 8 | 108 | 122 | 137 | 214 |
| 9 | 109 | 125 | 142 | 236 |
| 10 | 110 | 128 | 148 | 259 |

 ## Growth and aggregate supply

We saw in Chapter 13 that demand-side policies (fiscal and/or monetary interventions) are only capable of moving the economy back to full employment. Such policies reduce the difference between actual and potential GDP and so only close the output gap. Real expansion of the economy involves an increase in potential GDP. Therefore, we can only envisage real economic growth occurring if aggregate supply increases. In Figure 14.3, with perfectly inelastic long-run aggregate supply, aggregate demand begins at $AD_1$. The equilibrium level of output is $GDP_1$ and the rate of inflation is $\Pi_0$. Following a fiscal or monetary stimulus, aggregate demand increases to $AD_2$. At the new equilibrium of B, GDP remains unchanged at $GDP_1$, but inflation has increased to $\Pi_1$. We can say that, when aggregate supply is perfectly inelastic, increases in aggregate demand will be entirely inflationary. In contrast, if aggregate supply increases to $AS_2$, then the economy moves to equilibrium, C, potential GDP increases to $GDP_2$ and inflation falls to $\Pi_2$. Therefore, growth through improvements in aggregate supply seems preferable.

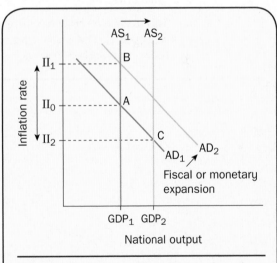

Figure 14.3 Inelastic aggregate supply and changes in aggregate demand

With perfectly inelastic long-run aggregate supply, a fiscal or monetary stimulus leading to an increase in aggregate demand will be purely inflationary. At equilibria A and B, GDP is constant at $GDP_1$, while at A inflation is $\Pi_0$, but at B, following the increase in aggregate demand, inflation has increased to $\Pi_1$. In contrast, an increase in aggregate supply from $AS_1$ to $AS_2$ moves the equilibrium from A to C. GDP increases to $GDP_2$ and inflation falls to $\Pi_2$.

Clearly, if economic growth is desirable, then moving aggregate supply, or increasing the potential productive output of the economy, is key. Increasing productive potential is not easy, but there are generally three avenues for economic growth: more factor inputs, greater productivity and innovation. We will examine each in turn.

## More factor inputs

In Chapter 1, we introduced the production possibility frontier and showed how the level of output for an economy is constrained by the level of factor inputs (land, labour, capital and enterprise). As the economy gains more economic factor inputs, its productive potential increases. This is the same as the long-run aggregate supply moving to the right and potential GDP increasing.

For a number of economies, economic growth has occurred through an increase in factor inputs. In the case of China, recent economic growth has been enabled by a transfer of workers within the economy. Individuals who were previously involved in self-subsistence agriculture (growing food for themselves and their family) have migrated to the industrialized cities and taken employment in factories. If the output per hour worked in a factory is greater in volume and, more important, in value than the output per hour worked as a farmer, then GDP increases. The problem for China, as discussed in Box 14.1, is how to deal with a slowing growth rate of labour supply and rising wages. The answer is to become more productive. See Box 14.1 and the next section on greater productivity.

## Greater productivity

If it is not possible to gain more factor inputs, then economic growth can be achieved by producing more output with the same level of factor inputs. In simple terms, economic factors such as labour must produce more output per day, and thereby become more productive.

This avenue of growth is very important for many developed economies. Unlike economies such as India and China, many EU economies are already fully developed. The transition and transfer of workers from agriculture to manufacturing and services occurred two centuries ago. The main avenue for growth is therefore through productivity improvements.

A key measure of productivity is GDP per hour worked. This is a useful measure of productivity because, by working in standard units of GDP and time, it enables a comparison across economies. In addition, and perhaps more important, from Chapter 9 we know that GDP is a measure of value added—in the hour worked, how much more value does the worker add to the final output? This enables a comparison across economies which produce very different goods and services. It also focuses upon income generation per hour.

Over the past 50 years, there has been a fairly consistent productivity gap between the UK and the US. In comparison, France and Germany have managed to close the gap with the US (see Figure 14.4).

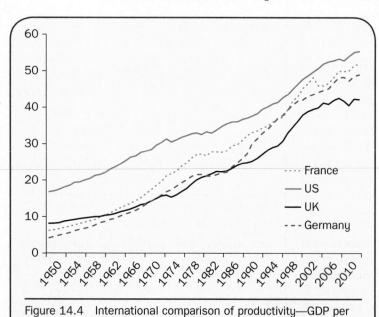

Figure 14.4　International comparison of productivity—GDP per hour worked

*Source:* Groningen Growth and Development Centre.

## Box 14.1
## The future of Factory Asia

A small factory in an industrial park outside Shanghai, churning out widgets you never see but probably use, provides a perfect snapshot of the state of global manufacturing today. Some workers at the Integrated Micro-Electronics (IMI) facility affix pieces by hand to circuit boards bound for digital displays on European stoves. Others stand at computers, guiding machines that press together components for cars' steering systems. But IMI is important less for what it makes than for what it represents. A cog in long supply chains, it produces part, but never all, of brand-name consumer goods. It has operations around the world, but makes its most money in China. And it is starting to automate its factories there as wages rise.

Cheap Chinese labour has been crucial to the building of 'Factory Asia', the name given to the region's complex of cross-border supply chains. Asia first emerged as a manufacturing power in the 1960s, when Japan began exporting electronics and consumer goods. Taiwan and South Korea followed its lead. By the 1980s Japanese firms were building plants across South-East Asia. But China's opening up was the gamechanger. In 1990 Asia accounted for 26.5 per cent of global manufacturing output. By 2013 this had reached 46.5 per cent. China accounts for half of Asia's output today. The region's share of the global trade in intermediate inputs—the goods that are eventually pieced together into final products—rose from 14 per cent in 2000 to 50 per cent in 2012.

The China price is under pressure, though. Since 2001, hourly manufacturing wages in China have risen by an average of 12 per cent a year. Some believe this means that China's days as a manufacturing powerhouse are numbered. However, the future of Chinese manufacturing, and of Factory Asia more generally, is bright.

A persistent myth about Chinese manufacturing is that the country is only good for assembly, with the more profitable parts of the operation, such as design and marketing, remaining in the West and Japan. According to a study published in 2010, Chinese workers contributed just 3.6 per cent to the cost of an Apple iPhone.

But more detailed studies reveal greater two-way flows with Japan at earlier stages of production. Although Chinese-made smartphones often include chips imported from Japan, those chips typically include plastic casing and wiring imported from China. Today, 65 per cent of the ingredients in goods China sells to the world are made at home, up from 40 per cent in the mid-1990s.

By hosting more of the supply chain, China boosts its manufacturing competitiveness and attracts more investment. IMI, for instance, is headquartered in the Philippines and would have preferred to scale up its manufacturing there, where wages and worker turnover are lower. But Michael Hansson, a director, notes that after adding in other costs, such as shipping and tax, China is still cheaper—thanks to the dense cluster of suppliers and customers that IMI now has around Jiaxing, a 40-minute train ride from Shanghai.

Despite fast-rising wages, China's factories are still far cheaper than their rich-world rivals. Many pay their employees just above the minimum wage, which at about $270 a month in China is less than a quarter that in America. And they are more efficient than many rivals in the developing world. McKinsey, a consultancy, found that labour productivity increased by 11 per cent a year in China from 2007 to 2012, compared with 8 per cent in Thailand and 7 per cent in Indonesia. With Chinese factories just starting to pour money into automation, there is scope to improve productivity further. China became the biggest market for robots in 2013, buying 20 per cent of all those made that year, according to the International Federation of Robotics. But it still has just 30 robots per 10,000 workers in manufacturing, compared with 323 in Japan. Foxconn, the Taiwanese firm that makes iPhones and has more than a million employees in China, says that it wants robots to complete 70 per cent of its assembly-line work within three years.

China has problems. The working-age population peaked in 2012, and the endless stream of people moving from country to city has slowed. Expectations have risen along with incomes; fewer young Chinese are willing to endure the same drudgery their parents did. Growth in earnings and living standards is expected.

From *The Economist*. 'The future of Factory Asia'. Jiaxing and Yangon. © The Economist Newspaper Limited, London (14 March 2015)

If the UK could close the productivity gap, then either GDP and economic prosperity would rise or the UK workforce could earn the current level of income for fewer hours worked. Productivity growth is therefore very appealing.

We argued in Chapter 3, when examining the cost curves of individual firms, that the marginal cost curve (above average variable cost) is the firm's supply curve. Therefore, at the macroeconomic level, aggregate supply must be the sum of all firms' marginal cost curves (above average variable cost).

The firm is only willing to supply more output at any given price if its marginal costs decrease. Figure 14.5 provides details of the UK's GDP per capita gap with other developed economies and then breaks this gap into two sources, labour utilization and productivity. For example, the gap between UK and French GDP per capita is very small. But the means of producing this level of GDP per capita are very different. The utilization rate of French labour is 25 per cent less than in the UK, but this is offset by French workers being 30 per cent more productive than their UK rivals. If the UK could raise its labour productivity, then at the same utilization rate, GDP per capita would accelerate beyond that of France and perhaps some of the other countries in the table.

## Innovation

If we look back in history, we can identify a number of important inventions which have had an enormous impact on economic activity. Examples include the invention of the steam engine, the development of the railways, the introduction of electricity and telecommunications, the creation of the motor car, the growth of commercial aviation and, more latterly, the beginning of the Internet.

Improvements in travel, such as the railway, aviation and container ships, aid the movement of goods and services around the globe. This improves access to resources, lowers costs and boosts economic activity. The same arguments can be applied to telecommunications and the Internet. Products which were previously sold in shops are now sold online from massive distribution warehouses. This frees up retail units and labour, which can be employed in other parts of the economy, leading to more economic growth.

Clearly, a key driver of technological change is research and development (R&D). As new ideas, new knowledge and new techniques are discovered in science, engineering and medicine, innovation and technological change may result. However, again across

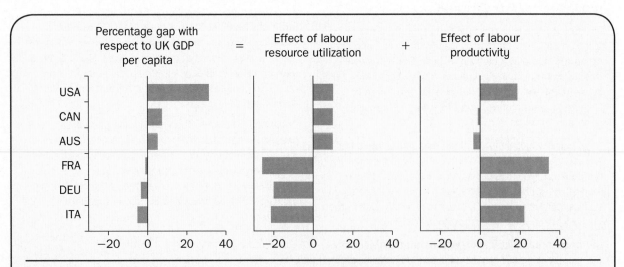

Figure 14.5   The UK productivity gap and sources of income difference

The US has higher GDP per capita than the UK because it utilizes more of its working age population in employment and on average each worker is more productive. France is similar to the UK in terms of GDP per capita and it achieves this by using fewer workers, but these workers are more productive than those used in the UK.

*Source:* OECD.

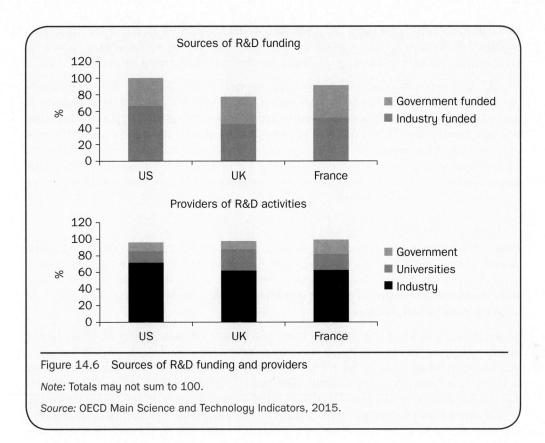

Figure 14.6 Sources of R&D funding and providers

*Note:* Totals may not sum to 100.

*Source:* OECD Main Science and Technology Indicators, 2015.

economies there are marked differences in how research and development are funded, as well as who the main providers of R&D activities are. If we examine Figure 14.6, it can be seen that, when compared with France and the UK, the US takes a much larger share of its R&D funds from industry. In addition, universities and government undertake much less R&D activity in the US. Taken together, the two charts indicate that R&D in the US is far more concentrated in the industrial sector of the economy.

The question to ask is, does a concentration of R&D activities in the industrial sector have any implications for economic growth? A strong suspicion has to be that, when knowledge and new ideas are created in the industrial sector, then the resulting innovations have a far greater prospect of being commercialized. Therefore, R&D which is industrial and commercial in conception and creation may lead to far greater impacts on long-term economic growth.

In order to understand how we can model growth, we will next consider economic models of growth.

##  Neoclassical growth theory

Assume we have a simple model where the economy's output is determined by three things: (i) technical progress, (ii) capital, and (iii) labour. There are simple but appealing features of this approach. If we allow the number of workers to increase (our population grows) but keep capital constant, then, from Chapter 3, we know that the economy will run up against the law of diminishing returns. Extra workers will not continue to improve the rate of productivity. Indeed, marginal productivity might become negative, driving down total productivity. This problem was first recognized by Thomas Malthus in 1798, who predicted that, with a fixed supply of land, adding additional workers to the land would result in slower growth of food output than growth rates in population. Essentially, diminishing returns would ensure that at some point the population would outgrow its supply of food and begin to starve. (Reflecting this point, economics is still known as the dismal science, which for professional members of the subject is less worrying than the term 'Armageddon'.)

Clearly, in the developed world we have not starved. So, the law of diminishing returns has been held back. This has been achieved by either (a) improving technical progress in agriculture, or (b) the employment of more capital. We can see evidence of each. Technical progress has developed with improved knowledge of fertilizers, insecticides and herbicides, improved irrigation systems and, more controversially, genetic modifications. Capital in the form of tractors and combine harvesters has also helped to improve the productivity of land and workers.

## How long can growth keep improving?

Robert Solow developed a model of economic growth in the 1950s and the fundamental insight from his approach was that economic growth would not increase for ever. Rather, it will reach a steady state. In growth-rate equilibrium, or the steady-state output, labour and capital are all assumed to be growing at the same rate. Hence, capital per worker and output per worker are constant.

If the labour force is growing at 10 per cent, then capital also has to grow at 10 per cent in order to keep capital per worker constant. Increases in capital are funded out of increased investment. Banks provide loans for investment from savings. For a 10 per cent increase in investment funds, income or output must grow at 10 per cent in order to guarantee a 10 per cent increase in savings. Essentially, labour growth rates set the tempo for capital

> The convergence hypothesis states that poor countries grow more quickly than average, but rich countries grow more slowly than average.

investment and economic growth. Indeed, a common fallacy is that higher savings will lead to higher investment, higher capital per worker and higher growth. This is only true for short-term economic growth rates. In the short term, providing all workers with more productive capital improves productivity and raises economic growth; but a blank cheque has also been written for the future, in that all the extra capital has to be maintained. Increased maintenance requires a greater proportion of economic output to go into the renewal of existing capital, rather than the development of new additional capital. As a result, economic growth slows and reverts back to the steady-state growth rate.

This has a fundamental and particularly troublesome conclusion: growth rate **convergence**.

If a country has a low ratio of capital per worker, it does not take much output to renew existing capital. Therefore, more resource can be put into the production of additional capital per worker. However, if capital per worker is high, then more effort is put into renewing existing capital and less resource is available for creating additional capital per worker. Therefore, economic growth rates in modern economies will fall, while growth rates in developing economies will grow. Looking at Figure 14.7, during the period 2005–2013 growth rates for the least-developed countries have generally been higher than for the developed economies of the world. However, this pattern does not

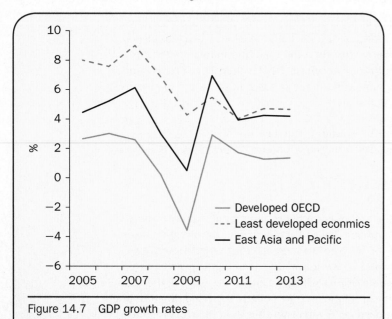

Figure 14.7   GDP growth rates

*Source:* World Bank.

see to hold over longer time periods, because if it did, then we would expect to see stronger convergence between economies (see Figure 14.7).

 ## Endogenous growth theory

The neoclassical model is problematic: convergence is not observed and growth is determined either by labour force growth or, at best, by developments in technology. However, neoclassical economists see even developments in technology as being exogenous, or determined outside the model.

For neoclassical economists, growth is determined by technological development, but technological development is not affected by economic growth.

For example, technological development occurs with mad professors staggering out of their labs, the air filled with fumes and the word 'eureka' being proclaimed. These dotty individuals who stumble across new insights of economic importance, such as plastic, computers, nuclear power and the Internet, find such knowledge by chance. None of these discoveries is based within economics. Clearly nuclear physics, biology and chemistry are different subjects, but surely within an economy, government and the economic system can provide structures, incentives and institutions that foster and promote technological development. Leaving such a beneficial activity to chance, in the hands of dotty individuals, is not good policy.

However, **endogenous growth theory** has to make a brave assumption: that of constant returns to capital (or something similar), such as knowledge. The Solow model does not allow increasing growth rates from increased capital accumulation because of diminishing returns. Nor does it allow increasing returns; if it did, growth rates would explode exponentially and that is not observed in reality. But how might we envisage a situation of constant returns to capital? Investment by individual firms in capital will still exhibit diminishing returns. But if investments by one firm have positive externalities, then constant returns to capital are possible. For example, if one firm invests heavily in broadband infrastructure for the Internet, then all other firms who wish to use the Internet to deliver media, online shopping and even teaching materials, will also receive a positive boost to their online investments. This way, an increase in investment from one firm leads to increases in productivity across many firms. The economic growth rate can now increase over time through positive externalities.

> Endogenous growth theory considers models in which the steady-state growth rate can be affected by economic behaviour and policy.

The more fundamental point is that governments now have a role in developing how the economy grows over time. Under the neoclassical model, growth was determined by labour-force growth and chance inventions. In the endogenous world, governments have the potential to increase technological developments and direct economic decision makers to investment activities with positive externalities. For business, this is important because industrial planning, initiatives for training and tax breaks for R&D become critical components of government's desire to increase potential output and, therefore, aggregate supply.

 ## Supply-side policies

### Education markets and long-term growth

Governments around the world are keen to widen participation in higher education. Universities have been tasked with taking in students from poor and deprived areas. Such a policy is political and economic. Bringing a broader and larger number of individuals into higher education widens the skill base of the workforce. This has positive externalities. With higher cognitive skills among the workforce, more advanced productive capital can be employed by firms. This is not about employing more machines per worker, it is about utilizing more productively advanced machines per worker. In addition, a university education enables people to learn for themselves and think critically. If people can learn for themselves, then they might react better to change. So, when new ways of operating come along, firms adapt more quickly and exploit new ideas more readily. Also, by thinking critically, managers can develop new means of operation more rapidly. In this way, education is at the core of technological improvement. The higher the income level of the economy, the greater scope the economy has for funding educational improvements. More education, the greater the rate of technological development, both within university labs and in the workplace.

An important point is to establish the optimal mix of skills for an economy. It is perhaps not desirable to allocate resources to the provision of a university education for all workers. Figure 14.8 provides a comparison of skill levels for many developed economies.

The UK's (GBR) problem is not in the provision of university education. If anything, the UK has one of the workforces with the highest percentage of graduates. Rather, the UK's problem is its large percentage of low-skilled workers. Where it would be more desirable to transfer these workers to the upper secondary and tertiary level of skills, those UK individuals who do not enter university are not receiving the same skills training as they do in countries such as Germany and France. It appears, therefore, that the UK has many educated managers, but an under-skilled set of workers. This can be very problematic. If managers wish to pursue innovative products or employ advanced production techniques, then workers are ill-equipped to respond. They simply do not have the skill base to exploit advanced technologies. The argument may be a generalization, but the points for government are simple. Higher education in the UK is doing well. Attention now needs to be paid to the development of skills within those individuals who choose not to attend university. Moreover, these individuals and their employers need to be provided with incentives to engage in skills development.

## Labour markets and long-term growth

For managers to be capable of exploiting innovative ways of operating, or taking advantage of new capital machinery, labour markets have to be accommodating. The existence of strong trade unions and legislation that either limits redundancies or raises redundancy payments will constrain the ability of firms to exploit new developments. Trade unions will seek to protect their members' interests and perhaps block changes that result in redundancies. Therefore, throughout the 1980s there was a strong impetus from government to reduce the power of trade unions and make it easier for firms to make workers redundant. Two things have happened.

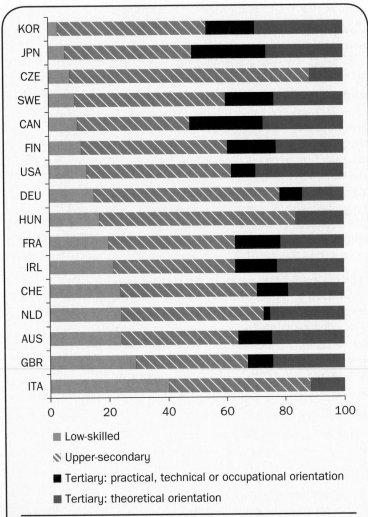

■ Low-skilled

▧ Upper-secondary

■ Tertiary: practical, technical or occupational orientation

■ Tertiary: theoretical orientation

Figure 14.8  Educational attainment of the population aged 25–34 years

*Source:* OECD.

First, trade unions have begun to work with, rather than against, companies, developing greater collaborative relationships and seeking, for example, to help businesses improve productivity by raising workers' awareness of inefficient practices and perhaps even supporting the development of skills and education within the current workforce. Second, the rise of the stakeholder perspective argues that firms are a collection of interest groups, including consumers, workers, managers, shareholders and government and each needs to work with and recognize the needs of others. Therefore, cultural change and regulatory change in the labour market free up the rapid redeployment of economic resource and can improve labour efficiency and economic growth.

## Research, development and innovation

Government can play a role in providing incentives to undertake research in new productive processes, or even encourage the exploitation of existing knowledge. Tax breaks for R&D expenditure can be a useful incentive to undertake research. More recently, the government announced tax breaks on directors' remuneration packages for high-technology industries, the idea being that, in order to attract the most able individuals from around the world, very attractive pay packages had to be offered. Highly valued skills are attracted into the economy and it is hoped, over time, local workers will observe, learn and develop similar skills. If such skills are based in high-technology industries, which will flourish in the future, then the UK is attracting the right type of economic expertise in order to survive in the future.

Industrial networks are also seen as an important means of developing positive externalities and economic growth. Local regions are beginning to specialize in particular industries: Yorkshire in food production, Cambridgeshire in technological development, London in finance, Oxfordshire in motor racing and Manchester in higher education. Again, for these industries to sustain the engine of economic growth, they need support industries and it is better to plan for these than hope that they appear. Managers need training and financial resources need to be put in place to aid investment, and the government can help to deliver these through regional development agencies.

## Financial services

A common discussion of growth theories relates to savings and investment, with higher savings leading to higher investments. This misses a number of points. High levels of savings in an economy could be lent to firms overseas. Further, the financial services industry, as an intermediary between savers and borrowers, may enhance growth. For example, by being experts in investment appraisal, financial services firms can more effectively screen out poor investment opportunities. Therefore, development in the financial services sector can lead to better investments within the economy. With higher-, rather than lower-, quality investments being undertaken, the capital stock can become more productive and economic growth should improve. Moreover, the existence of insurance can protect firms from the financial consequences of risks, such as fire, earthquake, etc. Therefore, insurance can be seen as necessary for expensive capital accumulation. Without it firms would be less willing to invest, leading to a reduction in growth rates.

Much of this thinking drove large-scale deregulation of the financial services industry, especially in economies such as the US and the UK. In order to play a strong role in supporting broader industries, financial services needs to be free to grow into new markets, invent new products and spread liquidity throughout the economy. So-called 'light-touch' regulation was put in place, which monitored the industry but rarely became involved in questioning the commercial or strategic decisions taken by many financial institutions. In the wake of the credit crisis, it has become clear that financial institutions are indeed enormously important to the functioning of the wider economy and that the need to protect the financial industry from collapse is crucial. How governments in the future manage to promote this crucial sector for growth within a tighter regulatory framework will be a formidable challenge.

## Other policies

### Tax cuts

In the 1980s, the UK and US governments reduced personal taxation rates, arguing that such policies provided incentives for individuals to work longer and raise productive output. However, most evidence tends to suggest that many individuals recognized that, with the tax cut, they could actually reduce the hours they worked and still earn the same amount of income as they did under the higher tax rates. A possible explanation for this behaviour is that individuals valued leisure time more than they did income. Therefore, following the tax cuts, individuals decided that, rather than seek higher income levels, they would retain the current income level and instead opt for more time spent with family and friends enjoying various leisure activities.

Governments have also used tax incentives to boost company profits and release cash for investment in research and development or training. Such tax rates are aimed at boosting the firm's access to new knowledge, to be innovative and to employ highly skilled labour. Over time, seeking out new thinking, new science and new ways of operating should boost output and lead to higher tax revenues in the future.

### Privatization

Privatization was also popular in the 1980s and 1990s. Previously, water, telephone, gas, electricity, rail and airlines were all supplied by government companies. Most nationalized industries acted as monopolies and were deemed to be inefficient through lack of competition. Furthermore, any increase in investment by nationalized industries had to be funded by the taxpayer. Such a system limited funds because the government had competing projects such as health and education to invest in. It was also not clear how financial performance would be ensured. Privatized companies can access the world's major finance markets and raise significant sums of money. Furthermore, unlike the government, private investors would be keen to ensure that the privatized industries operated at a profit and similarly only invested in profitable and productive assets. Therefore, as the privatized industries were, and are, important components of the national infrastructure, it is easy to see how increased investment and improvements in operational efficiency could have positive externalities for the rest of the economy—particularly if productivity improvements occurred in communications and transport. Reflecting these arguments, the governments privatized these nationalized industries and enabled new companies to compete in these markets.

The growth of competition has been slow to develop. In the case of telecommunications, economies of scale created an effective entry barrier. However, as technology changed and mobile communications became more popular, new companies found it easier to enter the market. In terms of utilities, we can now buy gas from electricity producers and vice versa. The market appears far more competitive, at least for those customers who wish to shop around. Therefore, if competition is increasing in these markets, then prices should be falling and firms will be seeking new and innovative ways of operating. In the long term, important factor inputs for other companies, such as communication, energy and transport, all become cheaper and overall supply in the economy improves.

### Private finance initiatives

Private finance initiatives (PFIs) involve the private sector in financing, building and owning infrastructure projects in return for an annual leasing fee from the government.

In seeking to develop the opportunities for the private sector to be involved in public-sector activities, numerous governments have turned to **private finance initiatives (PFIs)**. Generally, PFIs involve the national or local government contracting with a private-sector supplier for a public infrastructure project. Examples include buildings, hospitals, schools, roads, bridges and railways. The private sector raises funds, builds the asset and ultimately owns the asset. The government then pays an annual leasing fee for the asset. In the UK, the average cost of a PFI project to the public purse is just under £100 million and lasts for around 25 years.

There are a number of benefits associated with PFIs. First, the private sector is seen to be better at costing and delivering infrastructure projects. Project and budget overruns should be minimized. Commercial organizations are better at understanding and managing financial risk. They also have a clear means of selling their assets and leases in an open and private market. In contrast, it can be argued that the only benefit to government when building infrastructure projects is the ability to raise funds at a lower rate than the private sector. Governments are experts at raising money and spending. They are not experts at design, construction and running infrastructure.

While PFIs have become popular, they are not without criticism. A number of projects have experienced overruns. Some private providers have become insolvent, leaving the government to finish the project and pick up the final bill. Furthermore, while private firms may be very cost-effective when building infrastructure projects, the initial transaction costs (see Chapter 7) can be extremely high. Many projects take up to 36 months to agree a contract between the private firm and the government. Lawyers' bills are extremely expensive, as is the time of senior managers and senior civil servants.

## Summary

There are clearly many possible policy prescriptions for economic growth but, broadly speaking, governments seek to develop labour productivity, capital productivity or technological progress. More fundamentally, governments are beginning to return to the idea that they can *design* an economy, which will outperform in terms of growth. The neoclassical model advises governments to sit back and wait for the economy to develop. The endogenous growth theory directs governments to think about how businesses relate to the educational system, how financial services relate to the development of business and how the labour market reacts to the needs of business. Economic policy has moved to an understanding of how to enhance the whole economic system by thinking about how the individual parts work together and in particular how positive externalities can be generated throughout the economic system.

# 14.6 Business application: how does innovation promote business?

A common perception is that research and development can provide firms with a competitive advantage and we are not going to argue with this view. In fact, in Chapter 5 when we considered monopoly, we put forward the idea of creative destruction. By way of a quick reminder—through innovation, firms can overcome the entry barriers of an incumbent monopoly. As such, innovation can offer firms a competitive advantage and enable the generation of profits.

In our discussion of how innovation drives economic growth in section 14.2, we also highlighted how innovation is predominately funded and carried out by commercial enterprises in the US, suggesting a strong link between industrial R&D and overall growth in GDP. Such views also help to underpin a policy prescription for more engineering and science graduates. The future strength of an economy is seen to be dependent upon the continual creation of new ideas and technology.

Such views also drive concerns about brain drain and infringements of intellectual property rights. Government, industry and universities in developed economies invest billions in building up R&D capabilities, only to see companies in emerging economies either attract scientific talent or copy designs and technology for little cost.

Recent thinking and evidence within economics is beginning to question the significance of these concerns. Yes, innovation can provide firms with a competitive advantage, but only if consumers are also willing to be innovative and take advantage of the new technology. It is, therefore, the market-based transaction of technology which is important for firms and economic growth more generally.

At the retail level, innovation requires consumers to be adventurous in their consumption. This may require good access to credit facilities and retail environments which enable consumers to experience and sample new innovative products.

We should also recognize that firms are also consumers and buy inputs and support services from other companies. With the growing importance of outsourcing, the adoption of new technologies by firms in areas such as information technology from support services is generally seen as important for productivity growth and higher GDP.

If the purchase and adoption of innovation is the driver of economic growth, then an economy is as dependent on firms that can identify consumers' needs, as well as consumers who are willing to try new ideas and experiences. It is not just scientists and engineers who are important in bringing about new technology and innovation. It is the ability to use and exploit innovation for commercial or economic gain that is most important. Box 14.2 picks up these issues in more detail.

## (14.7) Business application: the BRIC economies

The BRIC economies are those of Brazil, Russia, India and China. These are seen as important economies in the future; they are growing fast and they are enormous. Other economies are also growing fast, but since they are smaller in size and population, their impact on the world economy is likely to be much less than the BRIC economies.

Growth in the BRIC economies has been impressive. For example, the growth of the Chinese economy has been one of the major economic miracles of the past 25 years. Compound growth rates approaching 10 per cent per annum over such a time period are almost unmatched by any other economy.

China's strength is built on technological expertise and an abundance of labour. Much the same can be said of India. Russia, while also technologically capable, is also reaping the benefits of vast energy resources. In a similar manner, Brazil too has access to important forestry and energy resources. With massive populations, vast natural resources and reasonable educational expertise, the BRIC economies can be expected to grow for many years to come. They can achieve this because they have yet to run up against the production possibility frontier. Or, perhaps more accurately, the frontier and aggregate supply are constantly expanding in the BRIC economies.

When aggregate demand increases in the BRIC economies, it is met with additional aggregate supply, the economy grows and GDP rises. We are clearly considering an increase in $AD_1$, where aggregate supply is elastic, as in Figure 14.9. Rapid growth and low inflation go together. Only when an economy is fully developed does aggregate supply become inelastic and growth slow.

The implications of such rapid growth in the BRIC economies are enormous for business. As economies grow, the potential for growth in incomes and household consumption also increases. As incomes grow, new consumption possibilities become a reality for the increasingly affluent households. Consider Figure 14.10, which describes car ownership in a number of economies. In the US, 750 in every 1,000 people of driving age own a car; or, put another way, nearly every person who can drive a car, owns a car. In China, only 20 in every 1,000 people of driving age own

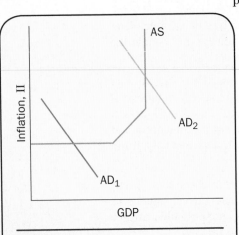

**Figure 14.9** China's growth constrained or unconstrained

## Box 14.2
## Business pioneers in fashion & retail

For the first mass-market retail pioneers, it was all about the shop. Jack Cohen, founder of Tesco, the supermarket chain, started with a market stall in London's East End in 1919. But it was a decade later, when he opened his first shop in Edgware, and began buying up stores in expanding London suburbs, that the growth of Tesco really took off.

It was the same for the Sainsbury family, which transformed its small dairy shop in London's Drury Lane into one of the UK's biggest grocers.

One of the most significant innovations in retail was in 1916, when Clarence Saunders opened Piggly Wiggly, which is regarded as the world's first self-service supermarket, in Memphis, Tennessee. According to Piggly Wiggly's official history, Saunders, 'a dynamic and innovative man', noticed the method of clerks gathering goods for customers wasted time, so he had shoppers serve themselves. The idea spread around the world; Sainsbury opened one of the UK's first self-service stores in Croydon in 1950.

It is no coincidence the fast-food craze, exemplified by McDonald's burger bars, was gathering pace at the same time.

Meanwhile, in France, Carrefour was pioneering the concept of the hypermarket—a giant one-stop shop that combined food and non-food goods. The first one opened in 1963, near Paris. A year earlier, Sam Walton had opened the first Walmart store in Rogers, Arkansas, followed a quarter of a century later by the first Walmart Supercenter, combining general merchandise and groceries in one shop.

The next wave of innovation involved not stores, but shopping online, led by Jeff Bezos, who created Amazon, which started as a bookstore in 1994 before moving into hundreds of other categories.

Neil Saunders, managing director of Conlumino, the retail research group, says developments in online retail were driven by pioneers from outside the industry such as Bezos and Steve Jobs, founder of Apple, which is now a significant retailer of consumer electronic products and music. Indeed, Apple's retail business is led by Angela Ahrendts, former chief executive of Burberry, which pioneered fashion's links with technology and social media.

Social media are increasingly influential in retail. Shopping activity on Facebook may have fallen short of the excited predictions of those who dubbed it 'F-commerce', but Pinterest, a digital pinboard that fuses interests and things, offers greater potential. Some retailers, including Burberry, have begun to sell through Twitter, but retail analysts say shopping via Instagram, the photo-sharing site, may be the holy grail in the blending of shopping and social media. Meanwhile, other disrupters are overlapping with retail, such as ride-hailing company Uber, which is moving into grocery deliveries in the US.

Similarly, in fashion the next wave of pioneers might come from the sphere of technology, rather than the world that gave us the likes of Coco Chanel and Miuccia Prada. Wearable technology is already fusing fashion and functionality. But Apple is set to shake up the field further with the launch of its watch.

Richard Hyman, however, an independent retail consultant, predicts the next wave of retail pioneers will be those who hark back to the early days of retail, by understanding their customers and offering them what they want. 'Ultimately, you can have all the great technology you want,' he says. 'But if you are not able to have a relevant offering, you will fail.'

Seth agrees that at the heart of the next wave of innovation will be the consumers—and how they want to shop. 'Entrepreneurs have to give customers what they want. That is what Sam Walton did and what [Sir Terry] Leahy did at Tesco. They were giving customers a much better deal than anybody had given them before,' he says.

From the *Financial Times*. 31 March 2015. 'Business pioneers in fashion & retail'. Andrea Feisted. © The Financial Times Limited 2015. All Rights Reserved.

a car. The scope for car consumption to expand in China and other BRIC economies is enormous. These rapidly expanding economies are very attractive when compared with the slow-growing economies of the EU and North America.

In addition, the growth of car consumption does not point to the only industry which may seek out a future in the growth of the BRIC economies. Banking, insurance, consumer electronics, computing, televisions and tourism all currently form small shares of household consumption in BRICs. Foreign companies are queuing up to cash in on the potential for economic and consumption growth to explode in the BRIC economies.

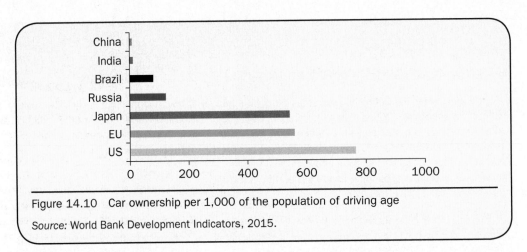

Figure 14.10   Car ownership per 1,000 of the population of driving age

*Source:* World Bank Development Indicators, 2015.

However, there should be a note of caution. The BRIC economies are still at a very different stage of economic development from other western economies. It is not simply the case that BMW can arrive in India or China and sell thousands of 5 series cars. While consumption is expanding in the auto market, the product has to be right for the level of income. This explains why domestic producers in the BRICs have sought to buy old technology for small cars from western auto companies. This enables domestic companies to build small, cheap, attractive cars at minimal cost; vehicles which the average household in a BRIC economy would feel proud to own but which have become less preferable in the developed economies of the world. So, the product has to suit the needs of the market.

A final and important concern for foreign companies seeking to gain from the growth of the BRICs is the share of GDP enjoyed by households. It is very interesting and exciting to see GDP increase by 10 per cent per annum. But where is this additional growth in GDP going? We know that the key units within an economy are households, firms, government and foreign consumers. Are these all growing at 10 per cent, or is a large slice of growth flowing to particular sectors of the economy? In the case of China, much of the growth has been driven by exports to the rest of the world. However, with an abundance of labour, wage rates have been kept relatively low. This has meant that the gains from export growth have flowed to firms rather than workers. This will clearly limit the expansion of consumption growth. Firms seeking to profit on the growth in China need to recognize this feature and factor it into any decision to enter the Chinese economy.

As business economists, we can now understand the majority of these issues and considerations. We are merely combining an understanding of economic growth and the circular flow of income. As you become more confident with the material of this book, then you too need to be capable of identifying the various aspects of economics which can be combined to provide you with a deeper understanding of your business environment.

##  Business data application: digging behind gross capital formation

Is capital formation important for understanding an economy's potential to grow? The Solow growth model indicated that the rate at which an economy can add to its capital stock is constrained. Beyond a certain growth rate the economy begins to expend more effort in maintaining its asset base, rather than growing its asset base. Therefore, assessing an economy's ability to expand its asset base may give some insight into that economy's ability to continue growing at an above average rate into the future.

Businesses should be interested in an economy's growth rate potential because decisions to enter markets are often long-term commitments. A business looking at the opportunities in

China is unlikely to invest just for one year to take advantage of current opportunities. It is more likely to take a long-term view and ask if China's growth rate is sustainable.

Figure 14.11 provides data on gross capital formation for China, India, Germany and the UK. Gross capital formation captures the value of additional assets created in an economy, less disposals of old assets. Gross capital formation captures the increase in private-sector investment in new important assets such as buildings, factories and equipment, plus public-sector investment in roads, rail, seaports, airports, schools, universities and hospitals.

The fast-growing economies of China and India have exhibited strong gross capital formation. This trend tells us that much of the gains from growth are being reinvested back into the economy. In terms of the circular flow of income significant amounts of GDP are being channelled into investment expenditure. Given that this spending is creating productive assets, such as factories, telephone networks and transport infrastructure, we might form the view that strong gross capital formation aids an economy in building a strong foundation for sustainable growth. The assets being created today will support tomorrow's growth. In contrast, if much of the additional income was going into household consumption, then we might question the ability of the economy to support additional expansion.

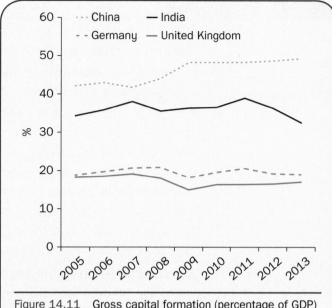

Figure 14.11   Gross capital formation (percentage of GDP)

*Source:* World Bank.

When examining Germany and the UK, we can see a downward trend in gross capital formation. Will this lead to lower future growth? Perhaps, but it is always worth questioning and asking what are the data actually measuring and is it entirely relevant? Importantly, gross capital formation captures the value of tangible assets, things that can be seen, touched and valued, assets that might be valuable in a manufacturing economy. But are such assets important when an economy becomes more knowledge based?

Knowledge-based economies generate economic output through the creation and application of ideas, not by making and doing. As developed economies, the UK in particular and Germany to a similar degree are moving into more service-based economies and away from manufacturing. Industries in finance, media, professional services and life sciences have grown in importance. Generating ideas requires science, it requires creativity and it requires innovative risk takers. Of course, generating new science, whether it be used in aerospace or the creation of new drugs, requires gross capital formation in laboratories, But the asset base has to be more than tangible assets. We therefore require an understanding of expenditure on research and development, an understanding of advanced science skills within an economy, and growth in knowledge sectors, including science, media, law, accountancy and finance.

Leading business managers grasp the basic ideas and then question, probe, dig around and question relevance. Am I understanding the situation, what else do I need to know, is the approach I am taking relevant? When you do this you can begin to operate beyond your business competitors and make more informed business decisions. As a manager you are beginning your training, you need to grasp the basics, but you also need to begin to practise the art of analysing, evaluating and reviewing ideas, concepts and data.

## Summary

1. Supply-side economics is concerned with improving the potential output of the economy.

2. Economic growth can be driven by increased factor inputs, enhanced productivity and improvements in technology.

3. If it is assumed that aggregate supply is perfectly inelastic in the long run, then increasing aggregate supply is the only way of generating additional economic output without raising inflation.

4. Neoclassical growth theory asserts that diminishing returns will lead to a natural growth rate for an economy. Any increase in the natural growth rate can only stem from technological progress or an increase in the number of workers.

5. Neoclassical growth theory leads to the conclusion that all economies will converge on a common growth rate. Empirical evidence does not support this idea.

6. In response to neoclassical growth theory, endogenous growth theory asserts that diminishing returns to capital in one firm, or industry, might generate constant returns to scale across the entire economy. In essence, investments in capital by one firm, or industry, have positive externalities for the rest of the economy. Economies can now grow at different rates, rather than converge, depending upon the generation of productivity-enhancing positive externalities.

7. Under endogenous growth theory, the government has a role in facilitating growth. Developments in education, financial services, levels of R&D and freer labour markets should all lead to higher future growth rates.

## Learning checklist

You should now be able to:

- Explain how economic growth is linked to growth in long-run aggregate supply
- Identify the main sources of economic growth
- Provide a review of the neoclassical model of economic growth
- Explain and evaluate the convergence hypothesis
- Explain the endogenous growth model and highlight how and why it is different from the neoclassical growth model
- Explain and evaluate the various types of policy used to develop economic growth
- Explain how and why business can be central to economic growth
- Examine data on gross capital formation and question its relevance.

## Questions                                                            connect

1. Identify and explain the main sources of economic growth. What are the main sources of growth in your economy?

2. Economic growth through a higher utilization of current economic resources comes with what problems or opportunity costs?

3. Which are equivalent, the production possibility frontier and aggregate demand, or the production possibility frontier and aggregate supply?

4. Explain why GDP per hour worked is a useful measure of productivity.

5. What distinguishes the UK from France and the US in terms of R&D funding and the provision of R&D activities?

6. The Solow model of growth predicts long-run steady state growth rates. What justification can be provided for this prediction?

7. Explain the convergence hypothesis. Does the convergence hypothesis hold in reality?

8. What does the endogenous growth model assume about returns to scale? Is this assumption reasonable?

9. How do the Solow and endogenous models of growth differ in their prescriptions for the role of government in economic growth?

10. What are supply-side policies? Provide examples of current supply-side policies and assess how you would measure the success of such policies in promoting economic growth.

11. Is R&D important for economic growth, or is it the willingness of consumers to be innovative in their consumption that is important for economic growth?

12. Consider whether there is a simple link between more R&D and higher economic growth.

13. Does neoclassical growth theory provide an adequate understanding of economic growth? Is endogenous growth theory any better than the neoclassical approach?

14. Does it matter if growth occurs through increased utilization of resources or higher productivity of resources?

15. What are the key benefits associated with privatization and private finance initiatives?

## Exercises

1. True or false?

   (a) An annual growth rate of 2 per cent per annum leads to a seven-fold increase in real output in less than a century.

   (b) Sustained growth cannot occur if production relies on a factor whose supply is largely fixed.

   (c) In the neoclassical growth theory, output, capital and labour all grow at the same rate.

   (d) Higher savings enable a higher long-run rate of growth.

   (e) Given the convergence hypothesis, we can expect all poor countries to catch up with the richer countries.

   (f) Growth may be stimulated by capital externalities: that is, higher capital in one firm increases capital productivity in other firms.

2. Which of the following policy suggestions are appropriate for improving economic growth in an economy?

   (a) The encouragement of R&D.

   (b) A reduction in marginal tax rates to increase labour supply.

   (c) Investment grants.

   (d) The establishment of training and education schemes to improve human capital.

   (e) An expansion of aggregate demand to increase the level of employment.

   (f) The encouragement of dissemination of new knowledge and techniques.

3. Refer to Box 14.2 when considering the following questions:

   (a) What is the difference between product innovation and consumer innovation?

   (b) For a modern economy to grow, which consumers need to be innovative, retail or wholesale?

   (c) For an economy to prosper, the supply and demand of innovation have to be in balance. Discuss.

4. (a) Find data on gross capital formation for the US, Japan and Russia.

   (b) Explain the difference rates of gross capital formation that you observe in the data.

Section

5

# Global economics

## Section contents

# Exchange rates and the balance of payments

## Chapter contents

## Learning outcomes

By the end of this chapter you should be able to:

**Economic theory**

LO1 Explain fixed exchange rates

LO2 Explain floating exchange rates

LO3 Compare the performance differences between fixed and floating exchange rates

LO4 List the main accounts of the balance of payments

LO5 Evaluate fiscal and monetary policy under different exchange rate regimes

LO6 Explain optimal currency zones

LO7 Debate issues relating to European monetary union

**Business application**

LO8 Assess if there is a gain to business from not being in the euro

LO9 Describe how hedging can be used to reduce exchange rate risk and create speculative investments

LO10 Critique how trade imbalances within the eurozone and the build-up of debt are linked to changes in the real exchange rate between member countries

## At a glance   Exchange rates

### The issues

There are many currencies in the world. The US dollar, UK sterling and the euro are all examples of important currencies. Over time, the strength of the US dollar against UK sterling or the euro varies. When the dollar is strong, it can be exchanged for more euros than when it is weak. This generates issues for business and government. What price will businesses receive for their goods and services when they are exported overseas? Also, why is it beneficial for a number of economies to share a currency, such as the euro?

### The understanding

In order to understand exchange rate movements and the potential benefits from being a member of the euro, it is necessary to understand the balance of payments, as well as floating, versus fixed, exchange rate regimes. Once this knowledge is in place, it is possible to address the effectiveness of domestic fiscal and monetary policy under the euro.

### The usefulness

In part, trading overseas is determined by how internationally competitive an economy is. The euro, by fixing the exchange rate across all member economies, requires greater price flexibility within member economies. Firms need to understand these issues. Furthermore, by understanding hedging, firms can understand how exchange rate volatility can be managed.

## 15.1 Business problem: should the UK be a member of the euro?

There are numerous issues associated with whether or not the UK should adopt the euro, but not all of them have business implications. For example, many individuals see the pound as a symbol of 'Britishness'. The pound as a currency and the picture of the sovereign on notes and coins are seen by many as key aspects of their nationality. Indeed, this deep cultural affinity with the national currency is not a uniquely British view. Upon adopting the euro, the French held a day of national celebration and mourning as a sign of respect for the French franc.

For business the euro is not a cultural identity problem because, as many business people will tell you, 'business is no place for sentiment'. Rather, the euro has simple operational implications and profound macroeconomic consequences. Changing prices from pounds to euros and cutting back on the need for currency conversions are simple operational implications. The macroeconomic implications are far greater. Consider the following by way of a brief introduction to the issues.

Imagine boats in a harbour bobbing up and down. Each boat represents an economy: the UK, France, Germany, Spain, Italy, and so on. The waves are the business cycles. When each economy had its own currency, the boats were connected together with ropes. So, as the wave hits the first boat it is able to rise up and then fall. The next boat then moves up and down, and so on. Each boat, or each economy, has some flexibility in dealing with the business cycle. Under the common currency of the euro, Germany, France, Spain and Italy and all other members have swapped the ropes for an iron bar welded across the front of all their boats. In the face of the business cycle, the eurozone members now move together. The flexibility of the ropes has been swapped for the size and stability of a huge integrated eurozone economy. The question for the UK is whether it wishes to swap its flexible rope for a stable but relatively inflexible weld to the rest of Europe.

The answer to this problem rests on two broad areas: (i) an understanding of the trade-off between flexibility and stability; and (ii) an understanding of how strong the welds are between the different boats. This chapter will investigate these issues, highlighting how the international environment, through exchange rates and intranational economic policies, affects business.

## 15.2 Forex markets and exchange rate regimes

Whenever you travel abroad you convert pounds sterling into euros, US dollars, etc. Since we are talking about a **forex market**, the item being traded must have a price. The price of currency is simply the rate at which it can be converted. In Table 15.1 various exchange rates for the euro are listed. For example, €1 will buy £0.72 or 129.27 yen.

> A forex market is where different currencies are traded.

If these are the prices from the forex market, then the obvious question is, how does this market work? Who is demanding and selling currency?

**Table 15.1** Forex rates for the euro

| Currency | Rate |
| --- | --- |
| UK—pound | 0.72 |
| Japan—yen | 129.27 |
| USA—dollar | 1.09 |
| Hong Kong—dollar | 8.43 |

*Source:* www.xem.com, April 2015.

The answer is fairly simple: individuals and firms buy and sell currencies whenever they undertake transactions with other economies. For example, whenever an import into the UK occurs, pounds have to be exchanged for another currency. Similarly, whenever an export out of the UK occurs, the foreign purchaser needs to sell their own currency in exchange for pounds. We can, therefore, think of imports as generating the supply of pounds in the market and exports as generating the demand for pounds in the market. In Figure 15.1, we have a traditional demand and supply curve for pounds.

If we begin in equilibrium with $Q_S$ equal to $Q_D$, then the exchange rate is $e_0$, or £1 can be converted to €1.0. If exports from the UK to Europe rise, then European consumers will need to demand more UK pounds. The demand curve for pounds shifts from $Q_D$ to $Q_{D1}$. The exchange rate for pounds appreciates, with £1 being converted into €1.2. If exports fall, demand shifts from $Q_D$ to $Q_{D2}$ and the value of the currency depreciates, with £1 being converted into only €0.8. Similarly, if UK consumers import more goods into the country, they will have to supply more pounds in exchange for euros. We could also envisage a change in supply. If the supply of pounds shifted to the right, the pound would fall in value. But if supply shifted to the left, the pound would rise in value.

## Exchange rate regimes

The exchange rate market can be characterized as operating under two extreme regimes. In a **fixed exchange rate regime**, the government sets an exchange rate and then uses the central bank to buy and sell currency to keep the market rate fixed. Under a **floating exchange rate regime**, the exchange rate is set by market forces, with holders of foreign currency demanding and selling various currencies.

> Under a fixed exchange rate regime, the government fixes the exchange rate between the domestic currency and another strong world currency, such as the US dollar.
>
> Under a floating exchange rate regime, the exchange rate is set purely by market forces.
>
> A dirty float occurs when the government claims that the exchange rate floats, but it is in fact managed by the government or central bank.

A third system is known as a **dirty float**. The government claims that the currency floats but in fact, through the central bank, the currency is secretly bought and sold to achieve a target exchange rate.

We will examine the fixed and floating exchange rate regimes and then provide an analysis of their relative strengths and weaknesses.

## Fixed exchange rate

In Figure 15.2, we adapt our previous figure and illustrate how a fixed exchange rate works. For simplicity, assume the government sets the exchange rate at $e_0$. If demand and supply meet at this rate, then the market is in equilibrium and there is no need for any market intervention. However, if, in accordance with an export boom, there is an increase in the demand for pounds, the demand curve will shift to $Q_{D1}$. The market would like to be in equilibrium at B, with an exchange rate of £1 equals €1.2. But the government is fixing the price at £1 equals €1.0. The government is effectively pricing below the equilibrium price and, as we saw in Chapter 4, this leads to market disequilibrium. At the fixed rate of £1 equals €1.0, the willingness to supply pounds is A, but the willingness to demand pounds is C. Therefore, in the market there is an excess demand for pounds equal to the distance A to C. The government, or the central bank, has to meet this excess demand by supplying an additional AC pounds to the market. The extra pounds are effectively swapped for US dollars, euros, etc. and are added to the central bank's foreign currency reserves.

In Figure 15.2, we can consider what happens if the demand for pounds falls to $Q_{D2}$. Now there will be an excess supply of pounds equal to AE. The central bank now needs to buy the excess supply of pounds. In order to buy pounds, it has to offer something other than pounds in return. When the central bank was selling pounds it will have received euros and other currencies in return. These were added to the bank's currency reserves. It now uses these reserves to buy back the pounds.

However, there is a critical problem for the central bank. It is feasible for the central bank to keep supplying additional pounds to the market because, as the central bank, it can ask for more pounds to be printed. Unfortunately, the central bank cannot

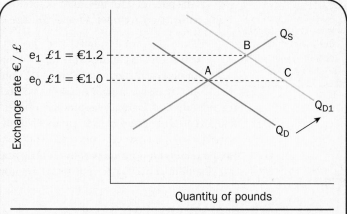

Figure 15.1    Increased demand under fixed exchange rates

As the demand for pounds increases, the market would like to move from A to B. But the government has fixed the price at £1 equals €1.0. It therefore has to supply the additional AC pounds in order to keep the price at £1 equals €1.0.

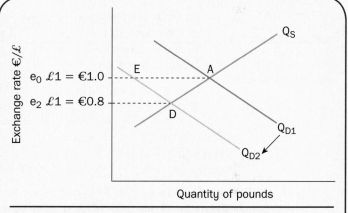

Figure 15.2    Reduced demand under fixed exchange rates

As the demand for pounds decreases, then at the fixed exchange rate of £1 equals €1.0, supply is greater than demand by the amount AE. In order to maintain the fixed exchange rate, the government has to purchase the excess supply of pounds using its foreign currency reserves.

commit to an indefinite purchase of the pound because, in order to do this, it has to have an infinite supply of foreign currency, such as US dollars and euros. Since the US Federal Reserve controls the supply of dollars and the European central bank controls the supply of euros, the Bank of England will soon run out of foreign currencies with which to buy the pound.

## Devaluation

If the currency is being continually supported by the central bank, it is probably the case that the fixed exchange rate has become vastly different from the long-term market rate for the currency. The correct policy response is not to keep buying the currency. Instead, the currency should be allowed to devalue. In our example, the fixed exchange rate of £1 equals €1.0 is abandoned and the government seeks to manage the exchange rate at the new equilibrium of £1 equals €0.8.

> A speculative attack is a massive capital outflow from an economy with a fixed exchange rate.

This potential for devaluation creates a fundamental weakness within fixed exchange rates: they are open to **speculative attack**.

If the government has fixed the exchange rate at £1 equals €1.0, but you think it will soon have to devalue to £1 equals €0.8, then the best thing to do is take pounds and convert them into euros: £1 million will buy you €1.0 million. If many people do this, massive capital outflows will be observed. Note that people are cutting demand for pounds and instead demanding euros. This means the government has to offer more support to the pound at £1 equals €1.0. It will soon give up and, when it devalues to £1 equals €0.8, you can take your €1.0 million and convert it back into €1.0m/0.8m = £1.25m. So, by changing your money into euros and then waiting for a devaluation you have made £0.25 million, or a 25 per cent return on your investment.

## Floating exchange rates

> In a floating exchange rate system, there is no market intervention by the government or the central bank.
>
> Purchasing power parity requires the nominal exchange rate to adjust in order to keep the real exchange rate constant.

As demand and supply for a currency change, the equilibrium price adjusts accordingly. As demand rises, so does the value of the currency, and as demand falls, the currency depreciates in value. Under a **floating exchange rate** system there is no impact on the central bank's foreign currency reserves as there is no intervention in the marketplace.

In the long run, floating exchange rates *should* obey **purchasing power parity**.

Consider the following example. Assume the exchange rate is £1 equals €1.5. We will also assume that a pair of designer jeans cost £50 in London and €75 in Paris. With the current exchange rate, the price of the jeans is identical in London and Paris (£50 × 1.5 = €75).

Now assume that inflation in Paris is zero, but inflation in London is 10 per cent. At the end of the year, the jeans in London have increased in price by 10 per cent and so now cost £55. The jeans in Paris have stayed the same, €75. If the exchange rate is still £1 equals €1.5, then we can save £5 by buying the jeans in Paris and importing them into the UK. Clearly £5 is not much of a saving, but if we were in business and set about buying 1,000 pairs of jeans, then it might be worthwhile importing jeans from Paris.

However, as we begin to import jeans we have to sell pounds and demand euros. As we (and everyone else) do this, the value of the euro will rise. In fact, it will rise to £1 equals €1.36. Why? Well, if we now convert the price of the jeans in Paris back to pounds, we have €75/1.36 = £55. All that happens is that the nominal exchange rate adjusts so that the price of jeans in Paris is identical to the price of jeans in London. The real exchange rate is constant and, as a result, we have purchasing power parity—it costs the same to buy goods in London as it does in Paris.

Clearly, this is an extreme illustrative example. Consumers need to be aware of the price differences between Paris and London. The price difference has to be big enough to make consumers interested in exploiting the price differential. Finally, the cost of moving the goods from Paris to London has to be lower than the price difference.

Since 1986 *The Economist* magazine has used the price of a Big Mac to assess purchasing power parity. Details of this are provided in Box 15.1. While the limitations of this approach are discussed, it should be noted that the Big Mac index has been surprisingly accurate in predicting future exchange rate movements.

## Exchange rates in practice

As indicated at the beginning of this section, fixed and floating exchange rate regimes are extremes. The Chinese yuan is fixed in the short term against a basket of currencies, including the US dollar, the euro, the Japanese yen and the UK pound. The euro floats against all other currencies, as does the US dollar and the UK pound. However, quantitative easing

## Box 15.1
## The Big Mac index: McCurrencies

*The Economist's* Big Mac index is based on the theory of purchasing power parity (PPP). If purchasing power parity holds, then using the current exchange rate, the price of a Big Mac in the USA should be equal to the price of a Big Mac in China, the UK, the EU, etc. *The Economist's* Big Mac index from January 2012, shown in Table 15.2, suggests that a number of currencies are overvalued compared with the US dollar and a number are also undervalued. The Chinese yuan would have to rise by 41 per cent in order for Big Macs to cost the same in China and the US, while the euro would have to fall by 6 per cent in order to make the Big Mac in Europe the same price as in the US.

The index was never intended to be a precise predictor of currency movements, simply a take-away guide to whether currencies are at their 'correct' long-run level. Curiously, however, burgernomics has an impressive record in predicting exchange rates: currencies that show up as overvalued often tend to weaken in later years. But you must always remember the Big Mac's limitations. Burgers cannot sensibly be traded across borders and prices are distorted by differences in taxes. In addition, it is also likely that income levels, wages and the cost of non-tradable inputs, such as rents, in different economies are likely to affect the domestic price level.

**Table 15.2** The Big Mac index

| | Under(−)/over(+) valuation against the dollar (%) |
| --- | --- |
| USA | |
| Australia | −10 |
| Brazil | +9 |
| China | −42 |
| Euro area | −11 |
| Russia | −72 |
| Switzerland | +58 |
| UK | −9 |

Table data taken from *The Economist*, 12 January 2015.

undertaken by the US Federal Reserve, the Bank of England and the European Central Bank results in an increase of money supply and so will impact the foreign exchange markets.

For many years concerns have been raised about the persistent undervaluation of the Chinese currency. By keeping the Chinese currency undervalued, the Chinese government has been accused of artificially supporting the competitiveness of Chinese exporters and in so doing helping to maintain high rates of economic growth in China.

Similar arguments are now being levelled at the eurozone as it begins to undertake quantitative easing, but there are some important differences to be recognized (see Box 15.2).

## 15.3 Fixed versus floating exchange rates

Given that both fixed and floating exchange rates are used by different governments, it should be expected that each system must have benefits and drawbacks. These are generally related to exchange rate **volatility**, **robustness** and **financial discipline**.

### Volatility

Clearly, under a fixed exchange rate there is no volatility in the short term. The government fixes the exchange rate. In contrast, floating exchange rates are volatile. The value of the exchange rate changes on a daily and even hourly basis. A sense of the volatility is shown in Figure 15.3, illustrating the changing exchange rate between the euro and the pound sterling.

**Volatility** is a measure of variability. In the case of exchange rates, a concern over volatility is a concern over how much the exchange rate changes.

**Robustness** is a concern with flexibility, or the ability to accommodate change.

**Financial discipline** is the degree to which a government pursues stringent monetary policy and targets low inflation.

## Box 15.2
## Quantitative easing and the decline of the euro

'Parity' was the word of the week in foreign exchange markets as the euro slid sharply against the dollar. The last time that the euro dropped through parity was in 2000, a year after its creation, provoking much hand-wringing about the credibility of the currency. Later that year, after further sharp falls, the G7 of advanced economies intervened in foreign exchange markets to support it.

At the moment, by contrast, as long as its decline does not become precipitous and provoke widespread financial market volatility, there is little reason to be concerned. The fall in the euro is clearly linked to the announcement in January of quantitative easing (QE) by the European Central Bank.

It is unclear how much the depreciation is a signal that QE is working rather than an actual mechanism by which it works but indications that the programme is beginning to have some effect are welcome.

That is not to say that QE works entirely or even mainly through the exchange rate and that the ECB is therefore engaging in competitive devaluation. Eurozone countries trade largely with each other: the average of import and export goods traded with countries outside the euro equals less than one-fifth of the eurozone economy. A weaker euro will mainly benefit net trade in countries that have a strong export sector such as Germany, which are not the ones currently needing assistance.

Any criticism from outside the eurozone that the fall in the single currency will kick off a global currency war is therefore misplaced. If such conflict does occur, it will involve overreactions by other countries based on a misperception that the global monetary system is a zero-sum game. It is not. Mercifully the world is no longer on a gold standard, where looser monetary policy through devaluation by one country necessarily involves tighter monetary policy elsewhere.

The dollar, for example, has shot higher against all other major currencies this year, not least because the Federal Reserve's plans to tighten monetary policy by raising rates later in the year contrast sharply with the QE programmes undertaken by the ECB and the Bank of Japan. There are already some, though to date gratifyingly few, grumbles in the US Congress about the strength of the dollar potentially widening the US trade deficit. But if the US is sufficiently concerned about the strength of the dollar weakening its economy, it is free to delay interest rate rises to offset some of the impact.

From the *Financial Times*. 13 March 2015. 'Quantitative easing and the decline of the euro'.
© The Financial Times Limited 2015. All Rights Reserved.

## Accommodation of economic shocks

However, we also need to consider long-term volatility. In Figure 15.2, we could begin at equilibrium A under a floating exchange rate. The demand for the currency begins to shift to $Q_{D2}$. Over time, there is a gradual adjustment to the new equilibrium at D. The exchange rate slowly moves down and firms and consumers wishing to exchange money slowly adjust to the changing exchange price. In contrast, under a fixed exchange rate the government is committed to supporting the equilibrium at A. If under pressure from a speculative attack the government decides to stop supporting the currency and allows it to devalue to the equilibrium at D, then there is a sudden and dramatic change in the exchange price. Such changes can be more dangerous than gradual adjustment. Indeed, currency devaluations often lead to volatility in the rest of the financial markets, such as stock markets.

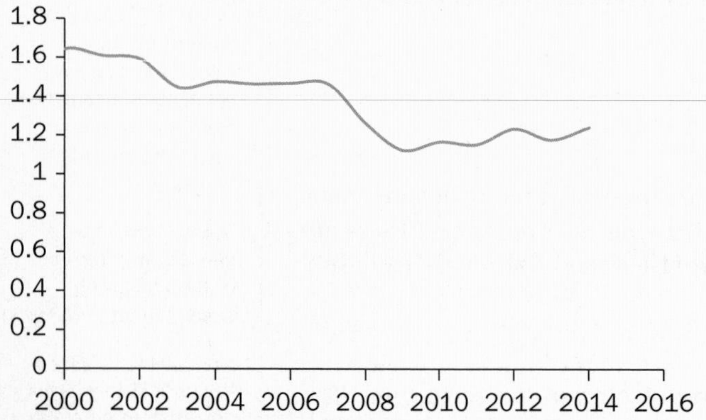

So, from the perspective of business, floating exchange rates create short-term uncertainty due to their volatility, but they

**Figure 15.3** Euros per pound sterling

*Source:* Bank of England.

provide gradual adjustment in the long run, which may be preferable to dramatic one-off changes offered by fixed exchange rates.

Consider our example of the boats in the harbour. The boats connected by ropes are the economies with floating exchange rates. They are flexible and able to accommodate environmental changes. In the case of the boat, this was the rise and fall of the waves. We witnessed above, when examining purchasing power parity, that environmental change might exist in the form of inflationary differences between economies. If the UK inflation rate is 3 per cent and the euro rate is 2 per cent, then it becomes attractive for UK consumers to buy euro products rather than UK products. As they do this, they sell pounds and demand euros. The value of the pound will fall, reflecting the inflationary differences between the UK and the eurozone. When full adjustment has occurred, euro products cost the same as UK products.

Under fixed exchange rates there is no scope for exchange rate adjustment; purchasing power parity may not hold. Instead, UK companies become increasingly uncompetitive against euro companies. Imports increase, demand for domestic UK-produced goods falls, and the UK moves into recession. The recession will be expected to reduce inflation within the UK.

Therefore, under a fixed exchange rate, purchasing power parity is gained through changes in domestic prices rather than exchange rate changes.

## Financial discipline

As we have seen above, floating exchange rates can accommodate inflationary differences between economies. This has led to some individuals taking the view that floating exchange rates do not provide monetary discipline. Therefore, governments under floating exchange rates have little incentive to control inflation. In contrast, fixed exchange rates, by their inherent inflexibility, struggle to accommodate inflationary differences. Therefore, fixed exchange rates force governments to take financial discipline seriously.

There is some truth in this. The UK entered the European exchange rate mechanism in the early 1990s in an attempt to control inflation. But there is also the view that governments can and do target inflation even under floating exchange rates. The pound, US dollar and even the euro all float, but each central bank is tasked with keeping inflation under control.

We now need to explain the balance of payments and the relationship with exchange rates and macroeconomic policy.

##  The balance of payments

As a record of all transactions made with the rest of the world, the **balance of payments** has three accounts: (i) the **current account**, (ii) the **capital account**, and (iii) the **financial account**.

### Current account

The current account measures imports and exports and can be further divided into visible and invisible trade. Visible trade is the export and import of tangible or visible goods. Exporting a car is clearly an example of visible trade. Invisible trade captures intangible services. A London-based business consultant working for a German client is an example of an invisible export. Added together, visible and invisible trade make the trade account. After adjusting for net transfer payments, such as interest and profits on foreign assets, we get to the current account. Figure 15.4 illustrates the trade account for the UK. It is clearly evident that the UK imports more goods than it exports. But this is partially offset by the net export of services to the rest of the

> The balance of payments records all transactions between a country and the rest of the world.
>
> The current account is a record of all goods and services traded with the rest of the world.
>
> The capital account records, among other things, net contributions made to the EU.
>
> The financial account records net purchases and sales of foreign assets. (This was previously known as the capital account.)

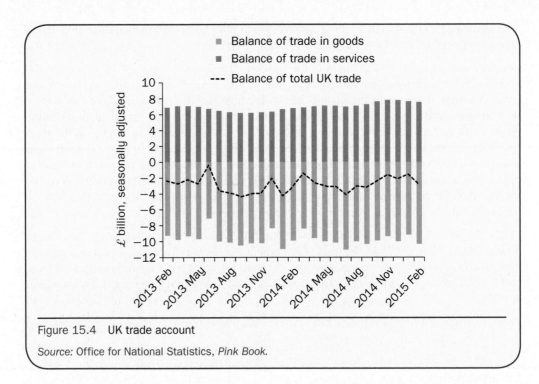

Figure 15.4   UK trade account

*Source:* Office for National Statistics, *Pink Book.*

world. This pattern reflects the decline of manufacturing over the last 20 years in the UK and the growth of sectors such as financial services in London, as well as travel services and telecommunications services.

## Capital account

Payments by the UK towards the Common Agricultural Policy and other EU contributions are collated under the capital account, as are payments from the EU to the UK for social and infrastructure development projects. Figure 15.5 shows that, throughout the last decade, the UK has been a net payer, with debits exceeding credits.

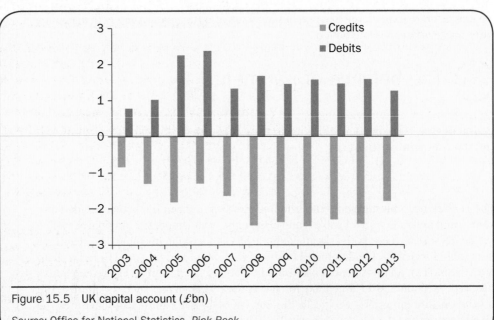

Figure 15.5   UK capital account (£bn)

*Source:* Office for National Statistics, *Pink Book.*

# Financial account

The financial account captures all investments into an economy by foreign individuals and companies. It also captures all investments made outside an economy by its companies and private individuals. There are three broad types of investment activity. The first is direct investment, where, for example, a foreign company may buy a rival within another country; equally, the foreign company may build its own offices or factory inside another economy. The second is termed portfolio investment, which involves the purchase of shares and bonds in another country. Third are other investments, including loans between banks which operate internationally. In Figure 15.6, the three types of investment into the UK (the credits) are shown. The huge volatility in other investments, particularly around 2008, illustrates the enormous amount of financial flows that were moving between banks and across international borders at and around the time of the financial crisis.

In summary, the current, capital and financial accounts seek to record all transactions, whether they be goods, services or purely finance, which take place between a country and the rest of the world. Indeed, we will see shortly that as long as the exchange rate is floating, the three accounts will sum to zero; that is, the balance of payments will be zero. Clearly, the three accounts are only measured with a limited degree of accuracy. The smuggling of alcohol, cigarettes and drugs, for example, represents aspects of international trade that go unrecorded. As a result, the balance of payments is generally shown with a so-called 'balancing item', which corrects for any statistical mistakes in measuring the three accounts.

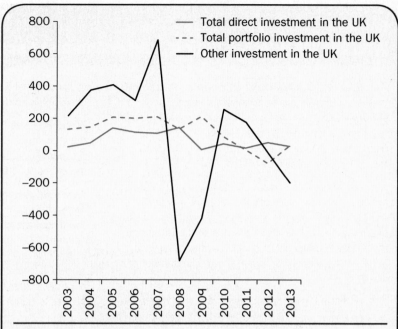

Figure 15.6   Financial investment into the UK (£bn)

*Source:* Office for National Statistics, *Pink Book.*

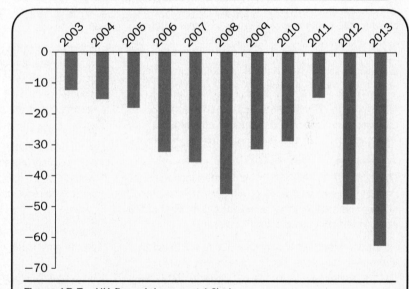

Figure 15.7   UK financial account (£bn)

*Source:* Office for National Statistics, *Pink Book.*

In Figure 15.7, we show the balance on the financial account (credits less debits). Credits are UK investments overseas and debits are investments in the UK from overseas investors. For the data period, this account has always been in deficit. This means that in net terms there is more investment coming into the UK than going out. This is necessary if the UK is to generate the financial resources to fund the deficits on its current and capital accounts.

Box 15.3 alludes to some recent concern about the sustainability of the UK's balance of payments position.

## Box 15.3
## Why the UK's 'other deficit' has economists scared

The UK is one of a few major economies in the world that isn't keeping investors awake at night. The eurozone and Japan are battling with stagnation, China faces the prospect of a hard landing, and the US is poised to hike interest rates. The UK, by contrast, faces very few home-grown risks.

However, there is one rather large cloud on the horizon: the country's current account deficit. This is the difference between the amount of goods, services and payments the UK sends to the rest of the world and the amount coming in. In short, it is the difference between the amount of money flowing in and out of the UK.

And, at the moment, cash is draining out of the UK like water down an open plughole—the UK's current account deficit recently rose to its highest level as a share of GDP since records began.

Pessimists worry that the country is not paying its way in the world and that any number of financial shocks could hit the pound and lead to much higher inflation in the UK. Last month the Bank of England's Financial Policy Committee—responsible for fending off threats to financial stability—put the current account at the top of its list of 'domestic risks'.

Minutes of the committee's meeting showed that members were concerned the deficit had become 'large and could, in adverse circumstances, trigger a deterioration in market sentiment'.

Mark Carney, the Bank's Governor, has touched on the subject in the past. Speaking at Mansion House last summer he said that the record current account deficit was 'not an immediate cause for alarm'.

He argued that the UK's balance of payment should improve as the global economy recovers; Britain's flexible exchange rate also helps. However, Mr Carney added: 'Nonetheless, sustained borrowing from abroad

to consume at home is hardly a recipe for a balanced and sustainable expansion.'

The deficit was 5.4 per cent of GDP at the time of the Governor's speech last year. It then climbed to 5.6 per cent in the final quarter of 2014, according to the Office for National Statistics.

A number of economists are worried that the warning lights are flashing—if not red then certainly amber. Joe Grice, the chief economist at the ONS, has described the growing deficits as 'something to watch'. He said that paying close attention to the current account has 'fallen out of fashion over the past decade or two'. However, he added: 'Things seems to be happening there.'

What's happening? In the past, the UK's so-called 'net investment income' has been positive. In other words, UK investors have earned a lot of money on their stakes in international bonds and equities—more than foreign investors had been making on their investments in the UK.

But now the trend has reversed, and international institutions are repatriating more from the UK than domestic investors are bringing in. Net investment income has turned negative and, as a result, money is flowing out of the country.

For the time being, the current account deficit appears to be manageable. But what would happen if the UK economy suffered some kind of financial shock? Would the current account deficit make it harder for the country to recover?

Mr Broadbent admitted that his belief in the sustainability of the current account position is based on the global markets maintaining their faith in the UK.

From *The Telegraph*. 13 April 2015. 'Why the UK's 'other deficit' has economists scared'. Peter Spence. © Telegraph Media Group Limited (2015)

## Balance of payments and floating exchange rates

Under a floating exchange rate, the balance of payments must equal zero. This stems from equilibrium in the forex market. In equilibrium, the demand for UK pounds must equal the supply of UK pounds. In the current account, we have individuals demanding and supplying pounds as they import and export goods and services. In the financial account, we have individuals supplying and demanding pounds as they buy and sell international assets. Therefore, if the forex market is in equilibrium, then the demand and supply of pounds from the current and financial account must also be equal.

## Balance of payments and fixed exchange rates

Under a fixed exchange rate, the situation is vastly different. We saw that point C in Figure 15.1 and E in Figure 15.2 were points of disequilibria in the forex market. At point C in Figure 15.1, the demand for pounds is greater than the supply of pounds at the exchange rate of $e_0$. We can explain this excess demand for pounds by reference to the current and financial accounts. For example, if UK exports are greater than imports, foreign consumers demanding pounds to pay for the exports will outweigh UK consumers supplying pounds to pay for imports. If UK investors do not wish to buy foreign assets at the existing exchange rate, then the supply of pounds will be less than the demand. In contrast, if we consider point E in Figure 15.2, the supply of pounds at the fixed exchange rate of $e_0$ led to an excess supply of pounds. We can, again, explain this excess supply of pounds by reference to the current and financial accounts. For example, if UK imports are greater than exports, then the supply of pounds will increase. But if foreign investors are not willing to buy British assets at the exchange rate of $e_1$, then the demand for pounds will be less than the supply.

Therefore, under a fixed exchange rate, the balance of payments will not necessarily be zero.

In order to make the balance of payments zero, we have to incorporate the concept of **official financing**.

> Official financing is the extent of government intervention in the forex markets.

We know that, in order to keep the exchange rate at its fixed level, the government must buy up the excess supply of pounds. This is called *official financing* and is added into the balance of payments as the final balancing item. It represents the extent to which the government has changed its foreign currency reserves by either buying up the excess supply of pounds or, alternatively, adding to its reserves by selling pounds in the forex market.

If we examine Table 15.3, we can see the actual values for each of the three accounts during 2012 and 2013. It is clear that the balancing item, or net errors and omissions, for both years is very large. It might be worth checking the figure in the future to see if the government revises its estimates of the three accounts. Information on the trade of goods and services or assets might have been recorded slowly, with correct figures not becoming known for some time. As a result, the figures provided by the government are only an initial estimate.

## 15.5 Exchange rates and government policy

We can now begin to consider the effectiveness of fiscal and monetary policy under fixed and floating exchange rate regimes. While this is theoretically interesting, it also has practical implications. The UK currently operates a floating exchange rate regime. If it were to enter the euro, then the exchange rate with all euro members would be fixed for ever.

**Table 15.3** UK balance of payments, 2012 and 2013

|  | 2012 (£bn) | 2013 (£bn) |
|---|---|---|
| 1 Current account | −62.0 | −72.4 |
| 2 Capital account | 0.8 | 0.5 |
| 3 Financial account | 49.1 | 62.6 |
| 4 Net errors and omissions | −12 | −9.3 |
| Balance of payments (1 + 2 + 3 + 4) | 0 | 0 |

*Source:* Office for National Statistics

Before we consider fiscal and monetary effectiveness, we need to understand two further points: (a) the real exchange rate, and (b) perfect capital mobility.

## Real exchange rate

> Real exchange rate is the relative price of domestic and foreign goods measured in a common currency.

International competitiveness depends upon the real and not the nominal exchange rate.

$$\textbf{Real exchange rate} = (\text{€/£ exchange rate}) \times (\text{£ price of UK goods/€ price of eurozone goods})$$

If the nominal exchange rate appreciated, then UK goods would become more expensive than European goods. European consumers would have to change more euros into pounds in order to buy UK goods. If the price of European goods rose faster than the price of UK goods, because inflation was higher in Europe than in the UK, then the UK would become more competitive. So, even if the nominal exchange rate stays constant, but inflation is 10 per cent in Europe and only 5 per cent in the UK, the real exchange rate will appreciate by 5 per cent.

In summary, international competitiveness is influenced by the nominal exchange rate and the relative price level between the two countries.

## Perfect capital mobility

> Under perfect capital mobility, expected returns on all assets around the world will be zero. If interest rates are 5 per cent higher in New York than in London, then, in order to compensate, the exchange rate will rise by 5 per cent, making dollars more expensive to buy. Therefore, the expected rates of return in London and New York are then identical. Or, in economic terminology, interest parity holds.

The following describes **perfect capital mobility**.

If you had £1,000 to invest in a savings account, you might visit a finance site on the Internet and ask for a ranking of savings rates offered by leading banks and building societies. If you are not concerned about when you get access to the money, you might sensibly choose the bank offering the highest rate.

Now we will assume that you are richer and have £1 million to invest. It is now worth thinking beyond the UK: what interest rates are being offered by banks in the UK, the US, Germany or Japan? If the rates in New York are 10 per cent, but only 5 per cent in all other countries, then you can double your interest by moving your money to New York.

Or can you? A slight problem exists. In order to invest in the US you need to sell your pounds and demand dollars. As more dollars are demanded, the price or exchange rate must appreciate. At the extreme, if financial capital is free to move around the world, then interest parity must hold and there is no incentive to move your money.

## Fiscal and monetary policy under fixed exchange rates

### Monetary policy

If interest parity holds, then movement in the exchange rate will offset any differential in interest rates between countries. However, this all assumes that exchange rates are floating. What happens when the exchange rate is fixed? Any difference in the interest rate between the two countries will now represent a guaranteed profit. As a result, financial capital will flow to the country with the highest interest rate.

The only way to stop capital flows putting pressure on the exchange rate is to set a single interest rate for both countries. This is a loss of monetary independence for at least one of the countries.

### Fiscal policy

We begin by backtracking to Chapter 11. In a closed economy, if the government increases aggregate demand through a fiscal stimulus, then a central bank with an inflation target will increase interest rates and cut aggregate demand in order to keep inflation under control.

But under a fixed exchange rate, there is a loss of monetary independence. The central bank seeks interest parity and so cannot change the interest rate from that set by its international trading partners. Therefore, any increase in fiscal policy will not be constrained by a tightening of monetary policy.

Fiscal policy is, therefore, seen as being more powerful under fixed exchange rates.

We can even go one step further and examine what would happen if the central bank tries to increase interest rates. Because interest parity does not hold, financial capital will flow into the economy. There will be an excess demand for the currency in the forex market. The central bank is committed to printing more money in order to meet the excess demand. But an increase in the supply of money leads to a reduction in the equilibrium price of money. The price of money is the interest rate. So, an initial increase in the interest rate leads to a future reduction in the interest rate. Monetary policy is ineffective.

## Why enter into a fixed exchange rate?

Aside from the stability offered by a fixed exchange rate, a very powerful benefit can be found in the real exchange rate, which is a measure of international competitiveness. The government is only fixing the nominal exchange rate. International competitiveness can be achieved by improving the real exchange rate. This is achieved by keeping the inflation rate in the economy at, or below, the inflation rates of its key trading partners. If inflation in the UK averages 2.5 per cent but its international competitors are suffering 5 per cent inflation, then each year the UK becomes 2.5 per cent cheaper.

As such, fixed exchange rates can have a strong disciplinary effect on domestic inflation. This disciplinary effect can exist in a number of forms. First, individuals under the economic consequences of a fixed exchange rate have lower inflationary expectations.

Second, if inflation rises at a faster rate in the UK, then UK goods become less competitive. Exports fall, aggregate demand falls and employment falls. Wages and prices in the UK fall, inflation is reduced and UK goods become competitive again.

## Fiscal and monetary policy under floating exchange rates

### Monetary policy

We will now see that monetary policy is more powerful under floating exchange rates, while fiscal policy is less effective. If we begin with monetary policy, a reduction of interest rates will boost internal demand. Individuals will consume more and companies will raise investment levels. Furthermore, if interest parity holds, then a reduction in the interest rate must be offset by a reduction in the exchange rate. This reduction in the exchange rate leads to an improvement in the level of international competitiveness. Products are now cheaper for foreign consumers and so exports will rise.

Monetary policy under floating exchange rates is reinforced. A reduction in interest rates stimulates domestic and international demand for domestic goods and services.

### Fiscal policy

If the government introduces a fiscal stimulus, then aggregate demand will increase and so will inflation. In order to control the inflation, the central bank will raise interest rates. In order to ensure interest parity, the exchange rate must also rise. Goods and services now cost more abroad. The rising exchange rate has reduced the international competitiveness of the economy. Exports fall and the initial fiscal stimulus provided by the government is offset by falling external demand.

Under floating exchange rates, fiscal policy is neutralized by rising interest rates, a rising currency and falling exports.

We can use the ideas developed within this section to examine European monetary union.

## 15.6 European monetary union

> Monetary union is the permanent fixing of exchange rates between member countries.

In the case of European **monetary union**, conversion rates for French francs into euros, German marks into euros, Italian lire into euros, etc. were agreed and then carried out.

On 1 January 2002, everyone in the eurozone only had euros to spend. At the same time, management of national currencies by national central banks stopped and the European Central Bank began managing the euro and setting one interest rate for the whole of the eurozone. We can understand this because we know that fixed exchange rates lead to a loss of monetary independence. But what are the major implications of euro membership for the UK and for businesses generally across the EU?

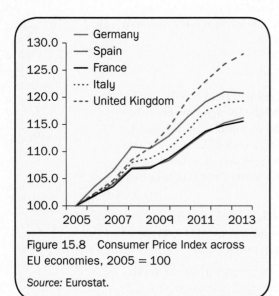

Figure 15.8 Consumer Price Index across EU economies, 2005 = 100

*Source:* Eurostat.

Starting with the simple, but less than obvious, the nominal exchange rate between each of the member states is fixed at 1 euro for 1 euro. The more serious issue is the real exchange rate and international competitiveness. Remember the real interest rate is the nominal exchange rate adjusted for the relative price level between countries. So, even though everyone in the eurozone has fixed the nominal exchange rate, differences in inflation rates will lead to changes in the real exchange rate and international competitiveness. We can examine Figure 15.8. Throughout the period of the data, Spain consistently had a higher level of inflation than many other EU economies. It may be that Spain had a lower overall price level to start with, and so Spain's prices have been catching up with the rest of Europe. Regardless of this, the price competitiveness of Spain has fallen.

If we now start to think through the points, we can begin to see a fundamental issue for the euro. A single interest rate is set by the ECB for the entire eurozone. So, the ECB could not help Spain by raising interest rates without penalizing Germany, which had low inflation. Fiscal policy is more powerful under a fixed exchange rate, so the Spanish government could decide to create a recession in Spain in order to reduce inflationary pressures and improve international competitiveness. But if Spain is pushed into a recession, when the rest of the eurozone is growing, Spain's business cycle will no longer be synchronized with all other members and the one-size-fits-all interest rate policy from the ECB will not help Spain.

### Maastricht criteria and the stability pact

It is, therefore, of no surprise that strict conditions were placed on potential members of the euro, through the so-called *Maastricht criteria*. These continuing conditions have now been imposed as part of the stability pact. In summary, the criteria seek to create macroeconomic harmonization between the member states and ensure continuing harmonization.

Before entry, potential adopters of the euro had to have low inflation and low interest rates. In the previous two years, no devaluation of the national currency was allowed. This prevented countries from seeking any early real exchange rate advantage. Furthermore, on the fiscal side, government budget deficits were to be around 3 per cent of GDP and overall debt to GDP ratio should be 60 per cent. These rules were also imposed in an attempt to control fiscal stances and prevent a build-up of inflationary pressures within member countries. The stability pact of 1997 was a further agreement that the Maastricht criteria would continue to operate even after entry.

## Optimal currency zones

The Maastricht criteria and the stability pact were and are attempts to keep all member economies moving together. But a more theoretical set of conditions for the success of a currency zone, such as the euro, were put forward by Robert Mundell in the 1960s.

Mundell began to think about the factors that would lead to an **optimal currency zone.**

> An optimal currency zone is a group of countries better off with a common currency than keeping separate currencies.

Three criteria were put forward as important for the success of a currency zone.

1. *Trade integration*

   The first is the degree of trade between member countries of the currency zone. Trade integrates economies. However, perhaps more important, highly integrated economies have the most to gain from a temporary devaluation of their currency against their partners' currency. A single currency is basically a credible commitment to co-operate, rather than starting an international price war through exchange rate adjustments.

2. *Similarities in industrial sectors*

   The second criterion concerns how the economies will deal with macroeconomic shocks. The more similar the industrial structure is across all the member countries, the more likely they are to stay synchronized. For example, if all members have similar industries, an external shock, such as a rise in the oil price, or in the case of Europe, a recession in the US leading to a reduction in export growth, will lead to similar effects in all economies. No one country will suffer more than another. In contrast, if only one member country was very reliant on oil, or the US, then that economy would go into recession, while all the other countries would remain unaffected.

3. *Flexibility and mobility*

   If all else fails, then there is the final safety net criterion. Factor resources such as labour and capital should display mobility and price flexibility. If an economy suffers a specific shock and goes into recession, then the quicker domestic prices adjust, the more rapid is the adjustment to international competitiveness. Furthermore, the more willing a factor resource, such as labour, is to move throughout the currency zone to find employment, the less important is the need for specific national governments to deal with domestic problems. The single monetary policy of the central bank will suffice.

Clearly, if a country is not integrated through trade, industry or factor resource transfers, the greater will be the need for it to keep its own currency and its own monetary independence.

## Is Europe an optimal currency zone?

In the case of Europe, the evidence tends to suggest that the eurozone is integrated to a degree, and so could represent a successful currency zone. But perhaps the more important issue is one of continuing integration and stability brought about by the euro. The longer the euro succeeds as a common currency, the more closely integrated the member economies will become. The euro promotes price transparency—goods priced in Germany, for example, can be compared directly with goods priced anywhere else in the eurozone. First, this promotes trade, which is the first criterion for an optimal currency zone. Second, currency stability and transparency make cross-border investments more certain. In the absence of currency exchange rate risks, companies will be more willing to operate in other member states. The structural or industrial mix of each economy will, therefore, merge; this is the second criterion. Third, price transparency promotes competition and, therefore, an increased need or willingness for workers, employers and producers to keep prices under control and pursue international competitiveness; this is the third criterion.

## 15.7 Business application: monetary sovereignty, exchange rate depreciation and export growth

We began this chapter by raising the issue of whether or not the UK should become a member of the eurozone. We can now return to that question and begin a stronger assessment of the effects on business of staying out of the euro.

There are some simple advantages to UK businesses in adopting the euro. Trade with other member states is less complex. Price transparency is assured by common pricing, and financial risks associated with currency movements are reduced. These potential benefits are undoubtedly important, and some business and policy leaders would prefer to see the UK enter the eurozone for these reasons.

The counter-argument is one that considers the impact of adopting the euro on the UK's macroeconomic environment, a consideration which is now brought to the fore by the recessionary impact of the credit crisis.

Adopting the euro would require significant changes to the way the UK economy is managed. The UK, like the EU, seeks to follow a fairly strict fiscal policy rule, where, in normal economic conditions (not a severe credit crisis), government deficits must not exceed 3 per cent of GDP. So, adopting the euro would not change this policy. However, the UK would have to abandon its monetary sovereignty. Interest-rate decisions would instead be passed to the European Central Bank, which sets rates for the benefit of the entire eurozone.

We are back to our example of boats in the harbour. The economic shock and subsequent recession caused by the credit crisis can be dealt with by the Bank of England in a manner which is of greatest benefit to the UK economy. In effect, by retaining monetary sovereignty and setting its own monetary policy, the UK can rise and fall in the turbulent waves independent of its main trading partners.

The main potential benefit of an independent monetary policy for the UK is the ability for the pound to fall in value against the economy's main trading partners. As interest rates are cut, the pound falls and UK exports become cheaper. If foreign consumers are enticed by cheaper prices, then aggregate demand in the UK can increase through higher international demand.

The retention of monetary policy provides UK policy-makers with flexibility, and it is this that we are trading against the known benefits of price transparency and minimal exchange rate risk associated with being a member of the euro.

## 15.8 Business application: hedging

The value of currencies changes every minute. Over a month, or indeed a year, the value of a currency can change enormously. This represents an exchange-rate risk to exporters and importers and, as discussed in Box 15.4, companies are worried about their exposure to the euro and the dollar and the need to find hedging strategies.

To provide a numerical example, a UK company might agree to buy steel from a French company over the next year. The price of the steel is agreed and fixed at the beginning of the contract in euros, say €1,000 per ton. If, at the beginning of the contract, €1 is worth £0.66, the company is paying £666 per ton. However, if over the year the euro becomes stronger and is worth £0.80, then the price of the steel increases to £800 per ton. The euro price of the steel has not changed, but the change in the exchange rate makes the steel more expensive in pounds. So how do you protect yourself against such risks? The answer is you **hedge**.

> Hedging is the transfer of a risky asset for a non-risky asset.

## Box 15.4
## Commodities explained: hedging oil volatility

### How companies manage risks as the price swings

The plunge in oil prices has strained the balance sheets of drillers and reduced costs for airlines. One way that companies manage the risks from commodities market swings is through hedging.

Hedging involves locking in a price to buy or sell a commodity in the future. It is a form of insurance against adverse moves in markets notorious for them.

Businesses that are exposed to commodity price swings find hedging useful. Mexico annually hedges the value of its crude oil exports, paying banks a premium to ensure predictable revenue for its federal budget.

Companies can hedge with derivatives such as futures and options. An airline concerned about a future rise in the price of jet fuel might buy oil futures and take a 'long', or buyer, position. If crude jumps from $60 to $70 a barrel, the corresponding increase in the value of the airline's futures position will help offset the higher price it will pay fuel suppliers. An international oil producer worried that crude will fall from $60 a barrel to $50 might sell, or go short, in oil futures, locking in the sale price at $60.

Futures markets are anonymous, so anybody could be the counterparty to the airline's trade. Hedge funds are classic speculators, or traders seeking to make money on price moves rather than insure against them. Commercial companies can also sometimes take speculative positions, meaning data categorizing trader positions as commercial or non-commercial should be viewed with care.

Big volumes from the execution of a hedging programme can move the price of futures markets and influence the value of options.

Hedges already in place can affect how companies respond to price signals. For example, US oil prices have declined more than 50 per cent since last June.

According to Barclays, US producers have hedged 22 per cent of their 2015 oil output. These hedges help soften the blow from oil's fall and delay the imperative to cut production.

Hedges can be costly. Mexico paid banks $773 million for options to hedge its 2015 oil exports at a sale price of $76.40 per barrel.

Companies using futures can face hefty margin calls—or demands for more collateral—if the market moves against them. Margin calls prompted by a cotton price increase bankrupted some merchants in 2008.

Investors seeking to play a commodities rebound without becoming futures speculators themselves may also prefer shares of companies that don't hedge. All things equal, an unhedged driller has more to gain from a rising oil price than one already enmeshed in hedges.

'When an exchange rate is particularly volatile, it can become too expensive to hedge financially,' said Brandon Leigh, chief financial officer of soap manufacturer PZ Cussons. Cussons' biggest market is Nigeria, where the naira has lost 18 per cent of its value over the past nine months as a result of a plunge in crude oil prices that hammered Africa's biggest oil producer. Leaving the company's profits vulnerable.

From the *Financial Times*. 3 March 2015. 'Commodities explained: hedging oil volatility'. Gregory Meyer. © The Financial Times Limited 2015. All Rights Reserved.

In the forex market there is ample opportunity to hedge. In Table 15.4, we have the various forward exchange rates for the pound against the US dollar. The exchange rate is known as the *spot price*. This is the exchange rate now, i.e. the exchange rate that you might get 'on the spot'. The next set of columns list the forward prices. These are the exchange rates at which people are willing to sell a currency at one month, three months or one year into the

**Table 15.4** Spot and forward exchange rates for pound sterling

| Currency | Spot price | One month | One year | % change |
|----------|------------|-----------|----------|----------|
| US dollar | 1.5791 | 1.5788 | 1.5736 | 0.35 |

*Source:* Bank of England, February 2015.

future. The spot price is $1.5791 per £1; but the one-year forward price is $1.5736 per £1, or 0.35 per cent less. This difference reflects expectations about how the currency will move over the next year and is a reward for taking the risk of agreeing to sell at an agreed price in the future.

Our steel importer can now hedge its exchange rate risk. Rather than face the risk of the pound falling against the euro, it can agree in the financial markets a rate for the next month, the month after, and even for one year into the future. Its future payments then become less risky; it has hedged the currency risk.

## Speculation

We have argued that businesses might seek to reduce risk by hedging exchange rate movements. It is also the business of some individuals and companies to make money out of hedging. They do this by speculating that the forward price is wrong. For example, if the one-month forward price for converting pounds into US dollars is £1 = $1.5, but you think that in one month the spot price will fall to £1 = $1, then you can potentially make a very large profit.

Consider the following scenarios. A company goes to the bank and borrows £1 million. It then converts this into US dollars at the spot price of £1 = $1.5. The company now has $1.5 million. Assume that the one-month forward price for converting pounds into dollars is also £1 = $1.5 and the company also buys the forward rate.

### What happens if the forward rate is correct?

If the forward rate is correct, then the spot price at the end of the month is also £1 = $1.5. The company can enter into the following (and profitless exercise): change its $1.5 million into £1 million and use the forward contract to change its £1 million into $1.5 million. It is no better off.

### What happens if the forward rate is wrong?

If, after one month, the spot price has fallen to £1 = $1, the company can take its $1.5 million and convert it into £1.5 million. It can then pay off its £1 million loan and it still has £0.5 million left. It then uses the forward contract to further increase its investment returns by converting the remaining £0.5 million into $0.75 million. It started owing £1 million and ended up with $0.75 million cash in the bank! Before you go out and borrow lots of money and try this strategy for yourself, remember it is high risk. The spot price could just as easily move in the other direction and then you would end up owing more than you initially borrowed.

##  Business data application: real exchange rates within the eurozone

The eurozone is a common currency area. Each member state has the same currency. Or, using a slightly more conceptual approach, we might argue that one Italian euro is equal to one German euro which is equal to one Spanish euro and so on. In this mode of thinking, the member countries of the eurozone have a fixed exchange rate agreement with each other. However, this agreement only creates a fix in the nominal exchange rate. There is still scope for changes in the real exchange when wages, costs and prices change at different rates across member countries. If Italian wage rates rise faster than German wage rates, then Italian products become more expensive and German products become relatively cheaper. Italians lose business in Europe and Germans win. To avoid this winners and losers scenario, it was envisaged that members of the euro would converge and keep inflation, prices and wages comparable across member countries. Figure 15.9 suggests the case was otherwise.

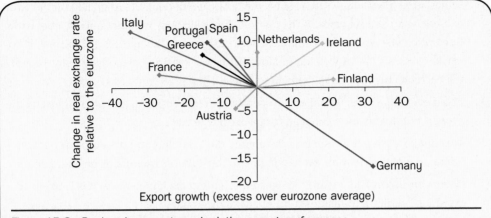

Figure 15.9 Real exchange rate and relative export performance

*Source:* Eurostat and European Commission, Director General of Economic and Financial Affairs.

During the period 1999 to 2010 the real exchange rate for member countries such as Italy, Spain, Greece and France became more expensive. In contrast, the real exchange rate for Germany became weaker. Not surprisingly, Italy, Spain, Greece and France saw weaker export growth, while Germany saw strong export growth relative to the eurozone average.

As we now know from our discussion of the balance of payments, a trade imbalance will be associated with counter flow of capital. As Germany builds up surplus finance, it asks itself where can this cash be invested? The debtor nations of the world, such as Italy, Spain, Greece and France (plus others), say thank you very much. Debt builds, repayments become a concern and debt crisis emerges.

You can see that the economic problems in which Europe finds itself are rooted within simple misalignments within the euro system. It is also not fair to say that the problems lie with the Mediterranean group of economies, because an imbalanced system has two parts. Germany must also play its role in reducing its trade surplus.

Europe's economic problems are some of the most troubling economic issues of a generation or more. You are approaching the end of your introductory module in economics, and through one diagram and the application of your economic understanding you can begin to understand the causes, problems and issues that need to be addressed if the eurozone is to resolve its current plight. That is a quite a journey from where we began in Chapter 1.

## Summary

1. The foreign exchange market is where currencies are traded.

2. Under a floating exchange rate, the value of the currency reflects changes in the supply and demand of the currency. When demand increases, the currency appreciates in value; when demand falls, the currency falls in value.

3. Under purchasing power parity, the price of goods in one economy is the same as the price of goods in another economy when converted into the same currency.

4. In the long run, a floating exchange rate will adjust to ensure purchasing power parity holds.

5.  Under a fixed exchange rate regime, the government commits to managing the value of a currency at a set price. If the market shows signs of wishing to move above the fixed price, the government supplies more currency to the market. In contrast, if the market shows signs of wishing to move below the set price, the government supports the currency by increasing demand for the currency.

6.  Fixed exchange rates do not ensure purchasing power parity and in the long run the prospect of devaluation can lead to speculative attack.

7.  Most major currencies—such as the pound, the US dollar and the euro—float. Some minor economies fix their exchange rate to the dollar; Argentina is an example.

8.  When considering the virtues of fixed and floating exchange rates, it is sensible to consider volatility, robustness and financial discipline.

9.  Floating exchange rates are more volatile than fixed exchange rates. But the prospect of speculative attacks and devaluations can make fixed rates a source of wider economic uncertainty and volatility.

10. Floating exchange rates allow economies to adapt to external changes such as inflationary differences. Fixed exchange rates require economies to be highly integrated as they cannot accommodate change within the fixed rate.

11. Because fixed exchange rates are inflexible, they are seen as promoting financial discipline and the pursuit of low inflation.

12. The balance of payments records the transactions undertaken by a country with the rest of the world. It has three main accounts: the current account, the capital account and the financial account. The current account measures the trade of goods and services. The capital account measures the flow of transfer payments, such as UK government payments to the EU Commission. The financial account measures the investment flows.

13. Under a floating exchange rate, the balance of payments balances. The equilibrium market price of the currency means that the demand and supply of the currency that stems from the transactions recorded in the current, capital and financial accounts must balance. Under a fixed exchange rate, equilibrium in the forex market is only achieved by the government intervening. Therefore, for the balance of payments to balance, the level of intervention has to be included. This is called *official financing*, and it simply measures the use of the foreign currency reserves.

14. Monetary policy is more powerful than fiscal policy under a floating exchange rate system. Fiscal policy is more powerful than monetary policy under a fixed exchange rate system.

15. European monetary union is a fixed exchange rate system between all member countries: 1 euro in Germany is worth 1 euro in Italy. However, the euro floats against all other national currencies, such as the pound and the US dollar.

16. The success of the euro depends upon whether its member economies represent an optimal currency zone. For such a zone to exist, trade between members has to be high, the economies need to respond to external economic shocks in a similar way, and price flexibility or factor mobility has to be high. In essence, economies have to be either highly integrated and synchronized or capable of quickly adapting to differences through price changes.

17. The eurozone is reasonably integrated and as the system progresses it is likely to become more synchronized. The use of a single interest rate policy from the European Central Bank and the control of fiscal expenditure through the criteria set down in the stability pact should force economies to cut internal levels of inflation and synchronize their business cycles.

18. By fixing the nominal exchange rate between member economies of the euro, international competitiveness is strongly linked to the cost and productivity of factor inputs. Eurozone economies with low labour costs and high productivity growth rates should attract increased attention from businesses seeking to enhance their cost-effectiveness.

19. Currency markets and the volatility within them represent business opportunities for speculators. Firms that do not like risk will try to hedge currency risk by purchasing forward rates, which guarantee the exchange rate in one month, three months or one year. Speculators, in contrast, will seek to buy forward when they expect the forward and spot rates to be different.

20. Trade and financial imbalances will occur within the euro if real exchange rates change over time.

## Learning checklist

You should now be able to:
- Explain how fixed exchange rates work
- Evaluate fixed versus floating exchange rates
- Explain the power of fiscal and monetary policy under fixed and floating exchange rate regimes
- Explain the features of an optimal currency zone
- Understand the importance of China's saving rate in the development of macroeconomic conditions around the world
- Explain hedging and how firms might use hedging within forex markets
- Understand why changes in the real exchange rate between members of the eurozone have led to trade imbalances.

## Questions                                                   connect

1. What are fixed and floating exchange rate systems?

2. Use a diagram to illustrate how a fixed exchange rate can be maintained when the foreign exchange market price is moving above and also below the fixed priced.

3. What is a devaluation, and why might a speculative attack foretell a devaluation?

4. The price of computers in countries A and B is identical in year 1. Throughout year 2, inflation is higher in country B. What do you expect to happen to the exchange rate between countries A and B throughout year 2?

5. What is the real exchange rate and why is it better than the nominal exchange rate at measuring international competitiveness?

EASY

EASY

6. Explain the concept of perfect capital mobility.

7. How does perfect capital mobility limit monetary policy under a fixed exchange rate regime?

8. What is an optimal currency zone? Do you consider the EU to be one?

9. Identify and explain the main accounts within the balance of payments.

10. If a country is running a trade deficit with the rest of the world, which account is in deficit?

11. Assess whether it is a problem to run a trade deficit or a trade surplus.

12. Explain how a company can manage the financial risk associated with exchange rate volatility.

INTERMEDIATE

13. A country has a current account surplus of £6 billion, but a financial account deficit of £4 billion:

   (a) Is the rate system fixed or floating?

   (b) Is its balance of payments in deficit or surplus?

   (c) Are its foreign exchange reserves rising or falling?

   (d) Is the central bank buying or selling domestic currency?

   Explain.

14. Under fixed and floating exchange rates, which type of policy is most effective, fiscal or monetary? Why does the eurozone have one interest rate, set by the European Central Bank?

15. Should the UK be a member of the euro?

16. (a) Assume you are based in the eurozone. Given the information in the following table, calculate the price of an Italian jacket in British pounds (GBP). Provide answers correct to two decimal places.

DIFFICULT

| Exchange rate (number of euros per one British pound or GBP) | Price of an Italian jacket (in euros) | Jacket price in GBP |
|---|---|---|
| 0.50 | 60 | |
| 0.60 | 60 | |
| 0.70 | 60 | |
| 0.80 | 60 | |
| 0.90 | 60 | |
| 1.00 | 60 | |
| 1.10 | 60 | |
| 1.20 | 60 | |
| 1.30 | 60 | |
| 1.40 | 60 | |
| 1.50 | 60 | |

   (b) Calculate the EUR/GBP exchange rate (the number of euros per British pound or units of foreign currency for one unit of domestic currency). Provide answers correct to two decimal places.

| Price of an Italian jacket (in euros) | Jacket price in British pounds | Exchange rate (Price of one GBP in euros) |
|---|---|---|
| 60.00 | 30 | |
| 60.00 | 40 | |
| 60.00 | 50 | |
| 60.00 | 60 | |
| 60.00 | 70 | |
| 60.00 | 80 | |
| 60.00 | 90 | |
| 60.00 | 100 | |
| 60.00 | 110 | |
| 60.00 | 120 | |
| 60.00 | 130 | |

DIFFICULT

## Exercises

1. True or false?

   (a) The US dollar is a floating currency.

   (b) The Chinese yuan is a managed float.

   (c) A rise in the real exchange rate reduces the competitiveness of the domestic economy.

   (d) After converting into euros, the price of Chanel perfume in Singapore is the same as in Schiphol airport; this is an example of purchasing power parity.

   (e) If the current account is in surplus and the balance of payments is not zero, then a floating exchange rate regime is in existence.

   (f) Monetary policy is more effective under a floating exchange rate.

EASY

2. Figure 15.10 shows the position in the foreign exchange market: DD is the demand schedule for sterling and SS the supply schedule. Assume a two-country world (the UK and the eurozone):

   (a) Explain briefly how the two schedules arise.

   (b) Identify the exchange rate that would prevail under a clean float. What would be the state of the overall balance of payments at this exchange rate?

   (c) Suppose the exchange rate were set at OA under a fixed exchange rate regime. What intervention would be required by the central bank? What would be the state of the balance of payments?

   (d) Suppose the exchange rate was set at OC. Identify the situation of the balance of payments and the necessary central bank intervention.

   (e) If the authorities wished to maintain the exchange rate at OC in the long run, what sorts of measures would be required?

INTERMEDIATE

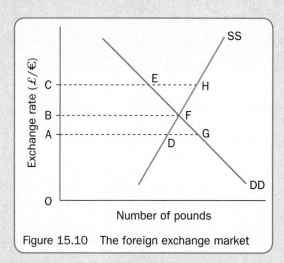

Figure 15.10   The foreign exchange market

**DIFFICULT**

3. Refer to Box 15.4 when considering the following questions:

(a) What is hedging and how might firms benefit from it?

(b) What would increasing globalization of business mean for the demand for currency hedging?

# Globalization

## Chapter contents

## Learning outcomes

By the end of this chapter you should be able to:

### Economic theory

LO1 The cultural, political and economic drivers of globalization

LO2 Explain the concept of comparative advantage

LO3 Discuss the use of tariffs and quotas

LO4 Assess the rise in international trade

LO5 Discuss and review the reasons behind the rise and fall in foreign direct investment

### Business application

LO6 Recognize impediments to an exploitation of comparative advantage

LO7 Identify the sources of international competitiveness in the IT sector

## At a glance  Globalization

### The issues

The world economy is becoming increasingly integrated, with more and more products being sold across national boundaries and firms operating in more than one economy; and global economic power is shifting from the US and Europe to economies such as China, India, Russia and Brazil. The issues for business are numerous, but include: why is globalization happening; what opportunities does it present; and what threats might develop from globalization?

### The understanding

The increase in cross-border trade and the number of firms operating in more than one country can be related to a number of issues. In recent times, barriers to international trade, such as tariffs, have fallen. The World Trade Organization has played an important role, but so has the development of trade blocs, such as the EU. Falling transportation costs and developments in communications technology have also made international trade and international operations more feasible. But this only explains why trade is easier. Why trade occurs is related to an important economic concept known as 'comparative advantage'.

### The usefulness

In understanding why globalization is occurring and where it is occurring, business can begin to understand where opportunities in the global economy exist for the enhancement of costs and revenues. Similarly, as globalization is a double-edged sword, an understanding of the implications of globalization will help to highlight where threats of increased competition are likely to come from in a global economy.

## (16.1) Business problem: how do we take advantage of the global economy?

The world has changed. As little as 20 years ago, taking a holiday in Spain was common, but taking a holiday in the Caribbean, the Far East or even Australia was something very different. Now backpacking around the world by students, and the retired, is reasonably common. Perhaps part of the mystique associated with international travel was the inaccessibility of the traveller. Communications back home generally took the form of a postcard, which invariably arrived home after the traveller. In recent years improvements in the integration of telecommunications networks has allowed mobile phones to work almost anywhere. Text messages, video messages and voice calls mean that someone on holiday in Thailand is just as accessible as someone on the other side of town.

World travellers and international telecommunications are not the only changing features of the world. Once you are abroad, there are now many commonalities. For example, have you ever been abroad and failed to find a McDonald's or a Starbucks? This relentless march of global brands has its benefits. You can walk into a McDonald's anywhere and know what you are going to receive. The brand provides comfort and certainty in its continued deliverance of a Big Mac and fries. But the power of the global brand can be felt just as much at home as it can overseas. Take a quick look at yourself. Is there an iPhone in your pocket, a pair of Nike trainers on your feet and a pair of Levis on your bum? There is a reasonable chance that you have one of these, or at least something similar.

What does all this mean for business? Globalization provides opportunities and threats for business. The willingness of consumers in faraway markets to consume international products, such as Big Macs, provides opportunities for McDonald's to grow. But at the same time, by operating overseas, McDonald's gains potential access to cheaper labour, raw materials and finance. In contrast, noodle shops in Hong Kong and fish and chip shops in the UK now face international competition from the likes of McDonald's. The fast-food market is a clear and tangible example of globalization and increased competition. But the influences of globalization are far-reaching. Speak to almost any businessperson and they will recognize the importance of globalization. Read any business paper or magazine and you will find an article on globalization. Businesses are actively seeking out cost advantages by using the global market to source labour, finance or raw materials. They are then using these advantages to increase the presence of their brands around the world.

In this chapter we will examine the economic rationale behind globalization and highlight some of its main drivers in recent times. An examination of global products and operations, and global labour and financial markets, will provide an understanding of this important trend in the modern business environment.

In Box 16.1 the global expansion of Alibaba is presented. Alibaba is a Chinese company, with a non-Chinese name. Despite not having a Chinese name, the company operates mainly in China using a business model similar to Amazon and eBay. The company is enormously successful and its shares are listed not in China, but in New York. Having succeeded in capturing the Chinese online market, it is now looking at opportunities in other economies.

##  Why is the global economy developing?

There are many potential drivers of globalization, ranging from the economic, through the political to the cultural. In this section, we will examine each in turn in an attempt to provide a working knowledge of globalization and the future developments for business.

### Culture

The process of globalization must to some extent be facilitated by a convergence of cultures. For example, St Patrick's Day is a celebration of the patron saint of Ireland. Yet the day itself is now celebrated by many other nationalities the world over. Admittedly, many of the Irish have at some point immigrated to other parts of the world, but this does not explain the extent to which other cultures are willing to assume the St Patrick's Day celebrations.

Anthony Giddens, a leading sociological writer on globalization, has argued that globalization is the cultural suspension of space and time. If space is a cultural reference point for geography and national identity, the willingness of many other cultures to celebrate St Patrick's Day surely reflects a suspension of cultural space. Individuals from

---

### Box 16.1
### Alibaba can become bigger than Walmart, says founder

The founder of Chinese internet giant Alibaba has said he hopes his company will be bigger than US retail conglomerate Walmart within ten years.

Jack Ma told the World Economic Forum that he believes Alibaba will serve some 2 billion customers over time, compared to the 300 million people it currently serves.

He also envisages an expansion of the business beyond China to become a truly dominant Internet business.

Mr Ma, said that he wants his business to become a platform for small businesses all around the world, rather than just in his home nation.

'My vision is, if we can help a small business in Norway sell things to Argentina, and Argentinean customers can buy things online from Switzerland we can build up an e-WTO (World Trade Organization),' he continued.

'The WTO is great but last century. Today, the Internet can help small business sell things across the oceans.'

From *The Telegraph*. 23 January 2015. 'Alibaba can become bigger than Walmart, says founder'. James Quinn © Telegraph Media Group Limited (2015)

the UK, Australia and the US, in celebrating the Irish patron saint's day, are suspending, in part, their cultural attachment to their own national culture.

If national cultural identity was important in the past, what is leading to a suspension of time and space under globalization? Some of the answers to this question lack any firm empirical support, but they do seem plausible.

## Travel

Increased international travel promotes an acceptance of other cultures. Travel facilitates experimentation with different types of food, language and customs. The old adage of 'when in Rome act like a Roman' can be an enlightening and enjoyable experience for many travellers. When they then return home, they periodically like to consume products from these distant places.

## Film and media

Hollywood and the American entertainment industry are successful industries. They produce films, TV sit-coms and a variety of music that are enjoyed not only by Americans but also by many people around the world. The portrayal of American lifestyles, the types of cars driven, the use of coffee shops, the consumption of burgers, pizzas, doughnuts and soft drinks, and the belief that opportunity exists for everyone, can all be viewed and absorbed while watching such movies or TV programmes. So, if viewers around the world enjoy watching American culture, then perhaps they will also enjoy partaking in, or consuming, American culture? If this is true, then American media are an important facilitator for US companies selling their brands around the globe.

## Technology and communications

The ability to communicate with anyone, at any time, anywhere in the world increases the perception of a global village, as opposed to a large fragmented global system. Financial centres in Tokyo, London and New York probably helped to develop the first impressions of a continuous, integrated global financial system. In recent times, global news providers, such as the BBC, Sky/Fox and CNN, have developed formats built around the 24-hour clock, with the news rooms moving between continents as the sun and daylight move around the world. This, in the terminology of Giddens, enables individuals to suspend time and space. A suspension of space is evident by the view that the global economy is everywhere, not somewhere. Similarly, time is a human concept, which slices up the day. But time is continuous; it has no beginning and no end. The continuous, ever-rolling nature of 24-hour news, financial centres and global business provides the opportunity for individuals, wherever they are in the world, to suspend time. It does not matter if it is midnight here, somewhere in the world it is 10.00 a.m. and, therefore, someone is making news and someone is making a profit. The global person and the global business are not constrained by time or space.

While telecommunications and the media have made the world feel smaller, transport technologies have made the movement of people and products more affordable. Jumbo jets make the transport of individuals between continents cheap, fast and reliable. Similarly, the invention of the container vessel in the 1960s, carrying many steel box containers with various cargoes, meant that one ship could exploit economies of scale, whereas previously a single exporter with a small cargo would have had to hire a small ship to transport their product around the world. Furthermore, the development of land-based infrastructure such as deep-sea ports, motorways and rail networks has helped to make the movement of goods around the world and overland much more feasible and affordable. China as one of the world's leading export economies is now building rail routes from China to Singapore to connect with international shipping routes, but that is not the limit of its ambition. With huge markets in Russia and Europe, new rail routes from China to these economies provide much quicker transportation. Such have been the improvements in global transportation, estimates by the World Bank suggest that transport costs are now 80 per cent less than a century ago.

Culture and politics are facilitators of globalization. They enable firms and consumers to buy, sell and even produce on a global basis. But there has to be a motive for firms and consumers to act globally. Why do they wish to take advantage of a political freedom to act internationally and satisfy the global appetite of consumers?

## Economic rationales

The economic answer begins with an analysis of what is known as the **law of comparative advantage**.

The key word is *comparative*. We can highlight its importance with the following example. In Table 16.1, we have the required hours to produce one car or one TV. In the EU, it takes 30 hours to make a car and five hours to make a TV. The EU is more productive than the UK in the case of cars and TVs. If we had said that each economy should specialize in what it is good at, the UK would make nothing and the EU would make everything. This is not a good idea, because the UK could make something and add to world output. This is why we employed the word 'comparative'.

We can now compare the relative cost of providing cars and TVs in the EU and the UK. The EU can produce cars more cheaply than the UK. The EU only sacrifices six TVs for each extra car; the UK has to sacrifice ten TVs. In the case of TVs, the EU has to sacrifice one-sixth of a car for each extra TV, but the UK only has to sacrifice one-tenth of a car for each extra TV. The UK can produce TVs more cheaply than the EU. We can now say that the EU has a comparative advantage in car production and the UK has a comparative advantage in TV production. Therefore, if the EU specializes in cars and the UK in TVs, total output will be greater than if both were to try to produce cars and TVs for themselves. For example, if the UK gives up six cars and produces 60 extra TVs, the EU can make the extra six cars by giving up only 36 TVs, providing a net addition of 24 TVs. Similarly, if the EU makes ten more cars and gives up 60 TVs, the UK makes these extra TVs for the loss of only six cars, thus providing the world with four extra cars.

## Terms of trade

While trade between the EU and the UK will lead to higher output, it needs to be profitable for trade to actually occur. Since the EU is comparatively better at producing cars, it will be an exporter of cars, or it will provide an international supply of cars. This is illustrated in Figure 16.1 with the upward-sloping supply curve. If the EU did not trade with the rest of the world, the price of cars (in TVs) would be 6. Once the international price of cars begins to rise above 6, the EU is willing to supply an additional amount of cars, or effectively increase its export of cars.

In contrast, the UK has a comparative disadvantage in the production of cars. If it did not trade with the rest of the world, the price of a car in the UK would be

**Table 16.1** Output and opportunity costs

| | | Hours to make one unit | Opportunity cost |
|---|---|---|---|
| EU | Cars | 30 | 6 TVs |
| | TVs | 5 | 1/6 car |
| UK | Cars | 60 | 10 TVs |
| | TVs | 6 | 1/10 car |

In the last column of Table 16.1, we have the opportunity cost. In this case, the opportunity cost is how many cars (TVs) have to be given up in order to produce one more TV (car). In the case of the EU, if workers were transferred from TVs to cars, then the cost of making one more car is the loss of six extra TVs.

The law of comparative advantage states that economies should specialize in the good that they are *comparatively* better at making.

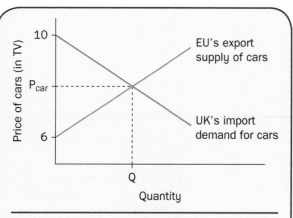

Figure 16.1  International trade of cars expressed as the opportunity cost of making TVs

10 (TVs). However, if the international price for cars is less than 10, the UK would increase its willingness to demand cars. In effect, the UK would be importing cars. Since the EU is willing to export at prices above 6 TVs and the UK is willing to demand at prices below 10 TVs, there must be an equilibrium international price for cars, which in Figure 16.1 is $P_{car}$. The actual value for $P_{car}$ will depend upon the elasticities of supply and demand for cars in the international market.

We could draw a similar figure for TVs, but this time the UK would be exporting and the EU importing. Again, the equilibrium price for TVs would lie between the opportunity cost of TVs in the UK and the EU, at a price of $P_{TV}$.

A country's terms of trade measure the price ratio of exports to imports; in this case, the UK's terms of trade would be the ratio $P_{TV}/P_{car}$. More generally, it is a weighted average of a country's export prices to its import prices, $P_{exports}/P_{imports}$.

If a country's terms of trade improve, then the price of its exports is rising relative to the price of its imports. It has to export less in order to fund its imports. This can happen if either the exchange rate changes or the equilibrium price for exports or imports changes.

In the case of the UK, the terms of trade are illustrated in Figure 16.2. Over the period 2000 through to 2014, the terms of trade have been improving, with a steady rise in the ratio of export to import prices. This has very important economic implications for an open economy, such as the UK, where imports and exports are equal to 60 per cent of **gross domestic product (GDP)**. As the terms of trade improve, then the purchasing power of UK GDP increases. Exports earn a greater income for the UK and imports cost the UK economy relatively less. Therefore, an improvement in the terms of trade leads to an improvement in the value of GDP. Economists measure this using **command GDP**.

> **Gross domestic product (GDP)** measures the volume of goods and services produced by a nation. By adjusting this measure to reflect movements in the terms of trade.
>
> **Command GDP** describes the purchasing power of a nation's output.

## The fundamental importance of comparative advantage

Comparative advantage and the gains from trade are very powerful arguments and have provided many governments with a rationale for freer international trade. However, it must be remembered that comparative advantage is not simply an international matter. The decision making and behaviour of many ordinary individuals conforms to comparative advantage. Families increasingly take their children to daycare centres rather than one parent leaving paid employment. Why? Because the

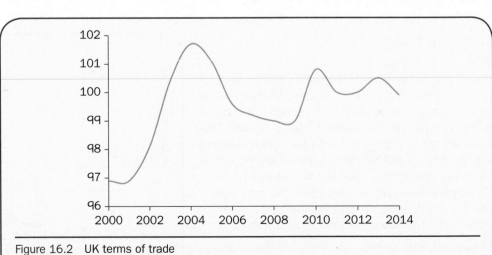

Figure 16.2   UK terms of trade

*Source:* Office for National Statistics.

daycare centre, when looking after many children, can exploit economies of scale which the single family cannot. The daycare centre has a comparative advantage in the care of children. With cheaper daycare, the opportunity cost of going to work is now less than the opportunity cost of staying at home and looking after the children. Similarly, why do some people specialize as decorators, doctors, academics or bank managers? Because they have a comparative advantage in their chosen vocation. Painting a wall is fairly straightforward, but in taking the time to do this, an academic, doctor or bank manager has to give up some possibly very lucrative fee-paying work or a large amount of free time. It is, therefore, more efficient to employ a decorator who is a specialist and can do the job much more quickly.

The overriding message is that comparative advantage applies to all of us. The notion of comparative advantage and international trade is nothing more than an extension of these ideas but, crucially, it is being argued that factor inputs, such as labour and capital, should be employed where they have a comparative advantage. As such, we should not look at the individual, as in the case of a decorator or doctor; nor should we look at an individual economy, such as the UK. Rather, we should be looking at the global economy and seeking ways to enable resources to be allocated to their most productive ends across the globe. In this way, globalization is a natural consequence of comparative advantage. Economies do not seek to produce all the products that they need. Instead, they produce what they are comparatively good at and then trade it for products in the global economy that they are not good at making. In this way, globalization is simply like the doctor hiring a decorator to paint their house; and a decorator hiring a doctor to cure their illness. But what are the sources of comparative advantage?

## Factor abundance

Think of a country and then consider what products it is famous for. Table 16.2 contains some obvious examples.

Clearly, France is famous for more than just wine, but each product listed above is known to come from each of the countries. France is good at wine because it has the right land and the right climate for making the grapes ripen at just the right rate in order to concentrate the flavours required for good wine. Germany is good at cars because it has a highly skilled workforce that is required for the production of high-quality manufactured goods. Saudi Arabia has land with good oil reserves. India has lots of workers, who are required for the labour-intensive production of textiles. Australia has lots of open places rich in resources such as copper and iron ore. Holland, as a very flat country, is good for growing plants that do not like to be shaded from the sun by hills and valleys. Barbados, situated just above the equator, is excellent at providing year-round tropical holidays; it is also fairly good at bananas and sugar.

Economies, therefore, appear to produce goods for which they have an abundance of a key factor input.

Britain does not export tropical holidays or wine. It does not have the factor inputs for such products. France and Barbados do. It is, therefore, comparatively cheap for France and Barbados to produce these types of product. The UK has an abundance of history. Castles, battlefields, the monarchy and parliament all attract visitors. We can produce history better than most and, in exchange, France provides us with wine, India with textiles, Australia with sheep and Barbados with tropical holidays.

Comparative advantage is clearly linked to the endowment of resources within an economy.

**Table 16.2** Countries and their exports

| Country | Product |
|---|---|
| Australia | Copper |
| Barbados | Holidays |
| Canada | Wheat |
| China | Manufactured goods |
| France | Wine |
| Germany | Cars |
| Holland | Plants |
| India | Textiles |
| Russia | Gas |
| Saudi Arabia | Oil |

## Two-way trade

There is a key flaw with the argument that international trade is based on comparative advantage and factor abundance. Many countries trade the same product. For example, the UK sells cars to Germany in the form of Jaguars, Minis and Toyotas. Germany exports cars to the UK in the form of BMWs, VWs and Mercedes. The UK also exports more cheese than it imports. We refer to this as *intra-industry trade*.

It took economists many years to formally model and explain intra-industry trade. But finally, in 1979, the Nobel Laureate Paul Krugman developed a model of trade which recognized the importance of consumer tastes and economies of scale. Krugman's first observation was that consumers appreciate diversity. The availability of choices matters to customers with tastes for differentiated products. In such a world, markets are characterized by segments and niches. Producing exclusively for the domestic market may not enable a firm to achieve economies of scale. But if a firm has the option to trade internationally, then it can access more consumers who share a taste and preference for its particular brand. International trade, then, enables larger volumes and the attainment of minimum efficient scale. So, importantly, international trade can lead to lower cost production and increased variety.

## Trade restrictions

Despite the accepted benefits of comparative advantage, international trade has in the past been impeded by various governments around the world.

One problem with comparative advantage is that it raises economic output for the world. But this does not mean it improves economic prosperity for all individuals.

For example, in trading with the EU, if the UK decided to abandon car production and specialize in TV production, workers in the car industry would become unemployed and there is no reason to suggest that they will be happy making TVs. So, in this case, UK car-makers do not find comparative advantage particularly attractive.

> Protectionist measures **seek** to lower the competitiveness of international rivals.

However, uncompetitive industries do not have to simply roll over and die. If the industry has political influence, perhaps stemming from the number of voters that they potentially employ, then the government can be asked to provide so-called **protectionist measures**.

*Tariffs* are examples of trade protection. A tariff is a tax on imports and, therefore, raises the price of imports.

For a more in-depth example of tariffs, we can examine Figure 16.3. Without imports for this good, UK supply and UK demand would form an equilibrium at A. However, the world price for this product is much lower, at £10. UK supply at £10 is only $Q_S$ and UK demand is much greater at $Q_D$. This excess of UK demand over UK supply is met by imports. If the government imposes an import tariff of £5, then the world price effectively rises to £16. UK firms now raise supply from $Q_S$ to $Q_{S1}$. But because the product now costs more, UK demand falls from $Q_D$ to $Q_{D1}$. The level of excess demand is now much less and as a consequence the level of imports falls.

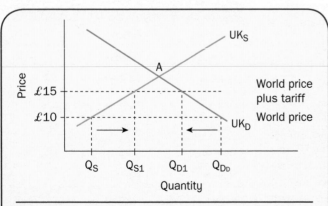

**Figure 16.3   Imposition of a tariff**

A tariff makes imports more expensive. Domestic supply increases and the demand for imports ($Q_{D1} - Q_{S1}$) decreases.

In the face of tariffs, imports fall and domestic supply increases. When tariffs are removed, international competition leads to a reduction in domestic supply and an increase in imports.

The case for tariffs is limited. They are a form of government intervention that simply supports inefficient domestic producers. Furthermore, tariffs in the main support domestic producers, and not domestic consumers. UK consumers under a tariff have to pay more for the good, via a tax to government, than they would if no tariff existed.

An alternative form of support for domestic producers could take the form of a *subsidy*. This is illustrated in Figure 16.4. A subsidy makes production cheaper for the domestic industry. The industry is more willing to supply and the supply curve shifts to the right. The domestic consumer pays the international price for the product, but a reduction in imports is brought about by the increase in domestic supply.

Box 16.2 highlights how China is reducing tariffs on imported luxury consumer goods in order to reduce domestic prices and boost consumer demand.

However, there is a question regarding how the government will fund the subsidy. Governments finance themselves principally through taxation. So, increased domestic subsidies must lead to higher taxes. However, while a tariff is a tax paid by the consumer buying the product, a subsidy can be funded by taxing everyone. Funding a subsidy via increased taxation spreads the burden of supporting the domestic industry. But why should some people support an industry that they perhaps do not buy products from?

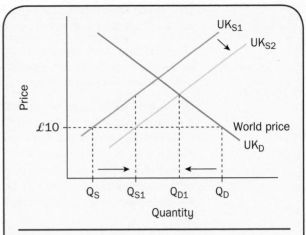

Figure 16.4  The effect of a subsidy

A subsidy makes domestic production cheaper. Domestic producers are willing to supply more and the supply curve shifts to the right from $UK_{S1}$ to $UK_{S2}$. Domestic supply at the world price of £10 then increases from $Q_S$ to $Q_{S1}$; imports ($Q_D - Q_{S1}$) shrink by the same amount.

## Non-tariff barriers

Governments can restrict trade in other ways.

A **quota** restricts trade by limiting the amount of a product that can be imported into a country. For example, a steel quota might limit the importation of steel to

> A quota has the same effect as a tariff. It makes goods more expensive for consumers and it raises the profits of inefficient domestic firms.

### Box 16.2
### China to cut tariffs on popular imports in bid to boost spending

Mainlanders appear to be more willing to head overseas to buy not just big-ticket luxury items but also regular household goods. China will reduce tariffs on popular imported consumer goods to boost spending amid the economic slowdown, the State Council announced yesterday. Observers said the move could have an impact on Hong Kong's retail sector.

After a meeting chaired by Premier Li Keqiang, the State Council said boosting domestic consumption was an important step to stabilising economic growth, and urged departments to come up with detailed plans to carry out the policy soon.

The State Council's decision came after mainland retail sales grew 10.2 per cent in March from a year earlier, slowing from 10.7 per cent in the January–February

period. Economic growth slowed to 7 per cent in the first quarter of this year.

Mainlanders appear to be more willing to head overseas to buy not just big-ticket luxury items but also regular household goods. Reports of mainlanders snapping up toilet lids in Japan have raised concerns over domestic product quality and triggered calls for lowering tariffs. Zhao Ping, a senior researcher at the Chinese Academy of International Trade and Economic Cooperation under the Ministry of Commerce, said the tariff reduction could drive mainland retail sales growth 0.5 to 1 percentage point higher.

Adapted from an article by Keira Lu Huang,
Victoria Ruan and Amy Nip
© South China Morning Post, 29 April 2015.

200 million tons a year. Since quotas restrict international supply, then the price in the domestic market must increase.

Those foreign firms that also manage to gain part of the quota can also sell inside the UK at the higher price. Under a tariff, domestic consumers pay a tax to government. Under a quota, some of the price increase leaks out of the economy to foreign firms.

Other methods include the application of standards. The EU is infamous for asserting that a banana must show a certain curve to its overall shape. The cynical view is that bananas from certain parts of the world are not 'curvy' enough. The EU can then proudly claim to reduce trade barriers on bananas. Those that are not curvy enough are not bananas, so the trade barrier still exists. Red tape required for import licences, driving on the left-hand side of the road, and an outright ban on British beef even after the BSE scare vanished—all can be viewed as means of restricting international trade.

## Reasons for protecting trade

While the protection of domestic industries from international competition appears to be very contentious, a number of arguments are still put forward for creating barriers to trade.

### Protection of intellectual property rights

> Intellectual property is content created by the mind which can be protected by patent or copyright.

Authors of books, song writers, script writers and news journalists create work which is normally protected by copyright. So as authors, we have created some **intellectual property** by authoring this textbook. That property is protected by copyright. You can read this book but you cannot legally copy this book without the permission of our publishers McGraw-Hill Education. Musicians create lyrics and music which is also protected. You can listen to it, but you cannot legally copy it for use beyond your own personal listening.

Similarly, technological innovations within products such as laptops, smartphones, automobiles, etc. are intellectual property protected by patents. You cannot use these same innovative ideas without the patent holders' permission.

By investing our time and knowledge and skill in authoring a book and taking advantage of intellectual property rights, we are the monopoly providers of Begg and Ward, *Economics for Business;* Taylor Swift is the monopoly supplier of Taylor Swift music; and Apple are the monopoly supplier of iPhone technology. All of which is true in countries where property rights exist, such as the US, EU, Japan etc. Where it is not the case, then trade might be restricted.

The most obvious example is the provision of advanced medicines to Africa in the treatment of HIV. Pharmaceutical companies invested huge sums in research and development to bring these drugs to market and were fearful of products being copied in countries that offered less intellectual property protection. So, to protect themselves, they avoided the international trade of their products. Something which was very good for the companies, but not good for the world.

The protection of intellectual property rights is crucial in the ever-increasing knowledge economy. International trade agreements between countries now often contain agreement on tariffs and quotas and on the joint protection of intellectual property rights.

### Defence or national interest

Governments may wish to support an industry that has strategic value. Steel is very important to the UK economy, and the government would not wish to see the economy dependent upon another economy for steel, the fear being that at some point in the future we might manage to fall out with the steel supplier and find our access to steel is terminated. But why not provide incentives for the steel producers to become more efficient, rather than pricing international competition out of the domestic market with tariffs?

### Infant industry

Sometimes an industry might seek government protection. During the period of protection, the industry is expected to develop its capabilities to a level where it is able to compete internationally. But if a company is capable of making profits at some point in the future, then why does the capital market fail to provide it with funds? Is it the case, perhaps, that the industry is incapable of ever becoming internationally competitive? Domestic wages, the price of raw materials or the level of technology may mean that the industry will never catch up. Furthermore, during the five years that it might take to develop the industry, what are the international competitors going to be doing? They are unlikely to be doing nothing. Instead, they will be looking to develop their competitive advantage, through improvements in production and operating efficiency. The case for infant industries can become continual, with industries asking for extensions to the period of protection with no real hope of protection ever being withdrawn.

### Way of life

The UK and perhaps even France place an economic value on the attractiveness of the countryside. If French and UK farmers are internationally uncompetitive, then, over time, they will stop farming. This *could* lead to a reduction in the management of the countryside. If true, then it might be desirable to think about protecting farmers from international competition. In so doing, trade protection also protects society from the loss of a positive externality, a well-managed countryside. This argument is sometimes used in support of the Common Agricultural Policy.

## Politics

A main driver of globalization has been the merging of political and economic views on international trade. We have seen that economists are keen to promote the idea of international trade based on comparative advantage. Economists also find it hard to support trade restrictions: first, because trade restrictions prevent comparative advantage and, second, because tariffs and quotas support inefficient domestic producers at the expense of consumers, or taxpayers. Politicians have now also recognized the economic arguments against trade restrictions.

## International institutions

This recognition of the importance of international trade can be traced back to the end of the Second World War, when political leaders of the time decided that stability in the world would be enhanced by greater political and economic integration. As a result, a number of supranational institutions were set up, for example the United Nations, the World Bank and the World Trade Organization (WTO, formerly known as the General Agreement on Tariffs and Trade—GATT).

GATT, formed in 1947, was an international institution that brought countries together to negotiate reductions in tariffs. Various rounds of negotiation were held and each round lasted many years. The Tokyo Round began in 1973 and ended in 1979, with an average tariff reduction of 33 per cent. The Uruguay Round began in 1986 and ended in 1993. While this again reduced tariffs, the round also agreed the creation of the World Trade Organization. While GATT was a place for countries to come together and discuss trade barriers and disputes, the WTO is an organization with power. Countries can now ask the WTO to rule on trade disputes and even impose fines on countries that fail to uphold international trade.

## Trade blocs

In 1965, the Treaty of Rome led to the development of what is now known as the European Union. As an area of free trade between member nations, it can be described as a **trade bloc**.

> A **trade bloc** is a region or group of countries that have agreed to remove all trade barriers among themselves.

Aside from the EU, there is also, for example, the North American Free Trade Area (NAFTA), a trade bloc promoting trade between the US, Canada and Mexico; while in South East Asia there is ASEAN, the Association of South East Asian Nations.

The importance of political institutions, such as the UN, and trade blocs, such as the EU, is that politicians increasingly recognize the economic importance of international trade and economic integration. Without international competition, domestic producers might not seek to innovate, drive down costs and keep prices low. Without access to international markets, domestic companies might not gain access to the cheapest, or most productive, factor inputs. These arguments are extremely persuasive, as evidenced by the continued success of the EU and the eagerness of other countries to join it.

##  A closer look at the EU

The EU has its origins in the European Community which was established among six economies in 1957. These were West Germany, France, Italy, the Netherlands, Belgium and Luxembourg. By the 1990s, membership had expanded and included most of the economies of Western Europe. Finally, in 2004, EU enlargement added a further ten Eastern European economies, including the likes of Poland and the Slovak Republic. The EU now comprises 27 member countries.

Table 16.3 shows that the EU in terms of GDP and population is now comparable to the US. While China has a bigger population, economic growth has not yet caught up with the EU, US and Japan, but with three times as many individuals the potential to close the gap exists.

An important feature of the EU is the limited presence of internal trade barriers. Tariffs and quotas between member states have been abolished, leading to an increased movement of internal free trade. The creation of the euro facilitated further the ease with which trade could occur by removing the difficulty of price comparisons and the need to convert competing currencies.

Regulatory harmonization in labour markets, tax regimes and patent systems has eased the administrative burden faced by firms wishing to operate beyond their national boundary. Furthermore, financial deregulation, principally in banking and insurance, has ensured that companies licensed to operate in one member economy are free to operate throughout the EU. The intention is to reduce domestic oligopolies and increase cross-border competition. Many of these initiatives were associated with the creation of the single European market in 1992, where the EU market was envisaged to be free of national regulations, taxes or informal practices.

## Benefits of the EU

The strength of the EU economy is arguably greater and deeper than the sum of its parts. This is because the size, scope and diversity of the member states leads to increased competition, the realization of economies of scale and the improved attainment of comparative advantage.

**Table 16.3** Comparing the EU, 2004

|  | EU | US | Japan | China |
|---|---|---|---|---|
| GDP (US$ billions) | 17,908 | 16,768 | 4,613 | 16,161 |
| Population (millions) | 507 | 316 | 127 | 1,360 |

*Source:* World Bank.

We have already argued that increased trade enables economies to specialize in the production of goods and services in which they have a comparative advantage. This allocation of scarce resources to the production of goods with the lowest opportunity cost raises the combined output of trading partners. With 27 member economies, the opportunities for pursuing comparative advantage are enormous, especially when such economies are geographically disperse, have differing factor endowments and are at differing stages of economic development.

Furthermore, a producer who is restricted to their domestic market may face an overall market size which is smaller than the minimum efficient scale in production. Access to larger international markets, in contrast, facilitates the attainment of scale economies, leading to reduced production costs and perhaps improved pricing for consumers.

While natural scale economies may lead to the development of oligopolies in national economies, the removal of trade barriers leads to increased cross-border competition and a reduction in natural entry barriers. All of these can lead to increased levels of competition. This competition may generate lower prices, innovation in the pursuit of cost efficiencies and the development of new products. These are factors which can improve the economic performance of the EU economy.

There is evidence to support these economic arguments, at least in terms of increased consumption. Table 16.4 reports estimated gains for a number of member countries. The results indicate that smaller economies gained more than larger ones, and also that the largest gains came where the most protected industries were opened up to competition. The results reflected the consumption gains following a one-off permanent shift in aggregate supply. However, they fail to reflect any ongoing endogenous growth effect, where, for example, increased competition drives further innovation and economic growth.

A consequence of increased trade and competition has been the emerging corporate strategy of being a pan-European company. One simple manifestation of this is the swapping of Internet country designations such as www. . . . co.uk, co.fr and co.de, for the more regional designation of www. . . . eu. Coupled with this geographic rebranding exercise has been the growth of cross-border mergers, especially the fragmented industries of telecommunications, banking and energy, which until recently have been fairly immune from the effects of the single European market. Spain's Telefonica acquired the UK telecommunication company O2, creating the largest telecommunications company in the Western world, while Santander, a Spanish bank, has acquired a number of British banks.

Within the EU economy, super-large companies which can exploit economies of scale are likely to be the most competitive. As such, consolidation and horizontal merger is likely. The single market therefore brings with it benefits and risks. Trade, competition and consolidation bring cost reduction, but may place national economies at the mercy of super-regional companies. The perceived balance of these risks and benefits, coupled with national pride, is likely to dominate the development of corporate mergers and takeovers for some time to come.

## Issues facing the EU

The Common Agricultural Policy (CAP) was until 2003 a system of subsidies which provided price support for agricultural produce. It has now been modified to become a system of direct income payments to farmers, thereby enabling farming to survive, but not

**Table 16.4** Consumption gains from the single market

| Range of estimates (% of GDP) | Countries |
| --- | --- |
| 2–3 | France, Germany, Italy, UK |
| 2–5 | Denmark |
| 3–4 | The Netherlands, Spain |
| 4–5 | Belgium, Luxembourg |
| 4–10 | Ireland |
| 5–16 | Greece |
| 19–20 | Portugal |

*Source:* C. Allen et al. (1998) The competition effects of the single market in Europe, *Economic Policy*, 27: 441–486.

creating a direct price distortion in the market for produce. The CAP represents €40 billion of expenditure, or 40 per cent of the EU's budget. France is the biggest recipient, receiving almost €9 billion, followed by Spain with €7 billion, Germany with €6 billion and the UK with €4 billion.

The CAP is strongly defended by the French, who view the French farming sector as a key aspect of their national identity. In particular, the reputation of French gastronomy rests on its ability to grow and create fine cheese, meat, vegetables and wine. In addition, the beauty of the French countryside is arguably protected by the continued presence of farmers.

There is strong opposition to the French. In particular, the UK has questioned the wisdom of the CAP. With agriculture representing less than 2 per cent of EU GDP, why does 40 per cent of the EU budget go to support this sector? Would it be more sensible to allocate a significant portion of the EU budget to education and science, thereby building knowledge capital and generating opportunities for further economic growth?

Outside the EU, world trade negotiations have stalled on the unwillingness of the EU to remove the CAP and its agricultural trade barriers to non-member countries. However, within this situation a subtlety exists. According to the World Bank, it would be more beneficial for world trade if the EU reduced external tariffs rather than dismantled the CAP. The reason is that the CAP reduces the price of agricultural products in the EU and beyond. Removing the CAP would make it more expensive for countries in Africa, the Middle East and elsewhere to import EU agriculture. However, removing trade tariffs would make it easier for such countries to export to the EU.

The issues surrounding the CAP are unlikely to be resolved in the near future, since in 2002 the EU agreed that no further changes to the CAP would occur before 2013, and the French appear keen to hold everyone to that agreement.

## EU enlargement

The addition of ten new members in 2004 was the single biggest expansion of the EU. Bulgaria and Romania joined in 2007, while Croatia is awaiting final approval. Turkey is still signalling its eagerness to join. Enlarged membership brings benefits as well as problems. Each new country opens up yet more markets for member countries to compete in with no trade barriers. In the case of the new accession countries, enlargement also presents an ample supply of cheap yet reasonably skilled workers, offering manufacturing companies the opportunity to relocate and exploit cost savings. This has been illustrated most obviously by the automobile industry, with the likes of Volkswagen and Ford moving European production to the new member states.

The problems brought by these new member nations reflect their transition economy status, moving from communist state planning to free market economics. Privatization programmes, poor legal infrastructure, weak bank finances, plus a need to invest heavily in transport and communications infrastructure, education and health, mean that many of these new economies face a constraint on their growth. Longstanding EU members from Western Europe have recognized the need to divert development spending into the new member states. But change will take time and will also come at the expense of development expenditure in the economies of Germany, France, the Netherlands and the UK.

Undoubtedly, the EU is a successful trade bloc and a model for others such as NAFTA and ASEAN. Its ongoing problems are small when compared with the size of its economy, the amount of cross-border trade and the degree of corporate competition. While national politicians may disagree on the way to deal with the issues presented by the EU, few would wish to sacrifice the economic power and benefits derived from being a member.

# 16.4 To what extent are markets becoming global?

Globalization occurs at many levels. Firms can export overseas or even operate overseas. They can exploit cheaper labour, capital or finance overseas. An examination of globalization requires an analysis of numerous issues.

## Global product markets

In considering global product markets, we will concentrate on trading internationally, as opposed to operating internationally. Trading internationally is the export and import of goods and services from domestic locations to international markets—for example, BMW selling cars to other countries. McDonald's in Hong Kong is operating internationally. We will consider this later.

Indices for world merchandized exports and world GDP are plotted in Figure 16.5. The values for world exports and GDP were set to equal 100 in 1950. This does not mean that world GDP and world exports were equal in 1950. Instead, by setting GDP in 1950 = 100, we can examine the growth in GDP over time and, similarly, the growth in world exports. For example, the index value for world GDP in 2014 was around 1,100. Therefore, between 1950 and 2014 world GDP grew by (1,100 − 100)/100 =1,000 per cent.

Looking at Figure 16.5, the growth of world GDP has been fairly constant throughout the period 1950–2014. The GDP line increases at a fairly steady rate throughout the period. In contrast, world exports initially grew at the same rate as world GDP and then, in the late 1970s, the slope of world exports becomes much steeper and the acceleration in world exports becomes evident.

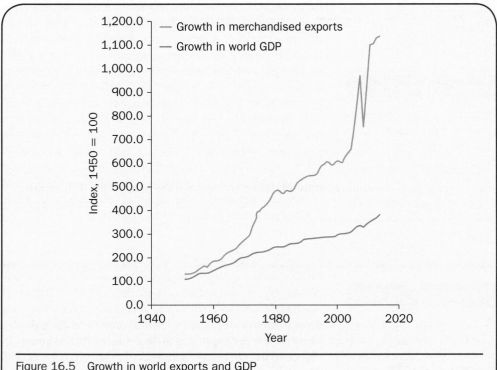

Figure 16.5   Growth in world exports and GDP

*Source:* UNCTAD.

**Table 16.5**   Leading exporters and importers, 2015

| Rank | Country | Value (trillion) US$ | % Share of world exports | Rank | Country | Value (trillion) US$ | % Share of world imports |
|---|---|---|---|---|---|---|---|
| 1 | China | 2.248352598 | 10 | 1 | United States | 2.7625 | 12 |
| 2 | United States | 2.1942 | 10 | 2 | China | 2.016504 | 9 |
| 3 | Germany | 1.622616449 | 7 | 3 | Germany | 1.414795 | 6 |
| 4 | Japan | 0.874353952 | 4 | 4 | Japan | 0.992055 | 4 |
| 5 | United Kingdom | 0.790991836 | 3 | 5 | United Kingdom | 0.845441 | 4 |
| 6 | France | 0.754625245 | 3 | 6 | France | 0.80749 | 4 |
| 7 | Korea, Rep. | 0.688932622 | 3 | 7 | Korea, Rep. | 0.654764 | 3 |
| 8 | Netherlands | 0.675270873 | 3 | 8 | Netherlands | 0.600461 | 3 |
| 9 | Russia | 0.597056401 | 3 | 9 | Hong Kong | 0.589422 | 3 |
| 10 | Hong Kong | 0.592391187 | 3 | 10 | Canada | 0.583302 | 3 |

Source: World Bank.

Since exports are a component of aggregate demand and, therefore, GDP, we can now say that from the early 1980s a growing proportion of world GDP was being exported.

This is clear evidence that the development of GATT, the WTO and the various trade blocs, such as the EU, have been extremely successful in promoting international trade. But we still need to ask whether product markets are becoming increasingly global.

**Table 16.6**   Exports within region and with the rest of the world for developed economies

|  | Intra regional | Rest of the world |
|---|---|---|
| America | 32% | 68% |
| Asia | <1% | 99% |
| Europe | 66% | 34% |

Source: UNCTAD.

In Table 16.5, we have the world's ten biggest exporters and importers. They are similar countries. This should not be a surprise. A country that is a significant importer needs to finance its consumption and it can achieve this by also exporting a great deal. An interesting question is to assess where trade occurs, in particular, between which countries and regions does trade occur? In Tables 16.6 and 16.7, the exports and imports for developed countries in the Americas, Europe and Asia are presented. European developed economies predominately trade with each other, while Asian developed economies trade less with each other and almost entirely with the rest of the world (which can include developing Asian economies). A similar pattern is evident for imports in Table 16.7.

**Table 16.7**   Imports within region and with the rest of the world for developed economies

|  | Intra regional | Rest of the world |
|---|---|---|
| America | 21% | 79% |
| Asia | <1% | 99% |
| Europe | 62% | 38% |

Source: UNCTAD.

## The BRIC Economies

BRIC stands for Brazil, Russia, India and China and was coined by an economist called Jim O'Neil working at Goldman Sachs in 2001. O'Neil recognized that these four economies were already on upward growth paths and were likely to be more important in the future global economy. In Figure 16.6 there is some evidence that he was correct. The share of world GDP held by these countries has increased significantly since the start of the century. By 2050, the BRICs are forecast to be at least 50 per cent of world GDP.

This forecasted shift in economic activity to the BRICs will be at the expense of the current leading economies of the world, including the US, EU and Japan. With shifting economic power comes moves in political power, as well as changes in the drivers of global culture, business practices, product innovation, consumer tastes and trade relations.

The BRICs represent more than 25 per cent of the land mass of the world and 40 per cent of the world's population. Therefore, a greater concentration of world economic activity in these economies seems plausible. However, there are some important aspects of growth within these economies that is worth highlighting. In Figure 16.7 the

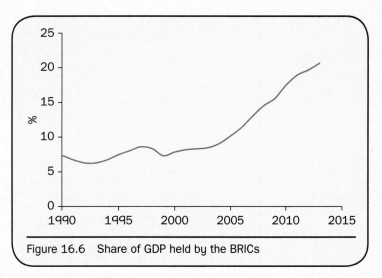

Figure 16.6   Share of GDP held by the BRICs

percentage share of GDP accounted for by household consumption is illustrated for each of the BRIC economies. From 2000 to the present day household consumption in China and India has been falling; and has remained fairly constant in Russia and Brazil. So, economic growth in the BRIC economies has not come from household expenditure.

In Figure 16.8 we have data on the share of GDP accounted for by exports.

For all of the BRIC economies exports have been an important source of growth. For example, in the case of China exports were around 10 per cent of GDP in 1990 and peaked at 35 per cent around 2008. The fall thereafter resulted from an economic slowdown in China's major export markets.

The data illustrate important tensions that arise from the economic transformation of the BRIC economies. Most significantly, economic growth in the BRIC economies is externally driven. On the one hand, this is good. The world benefits from cheaper products being produced by the BRIC economies. On the other hand, the BRIC economies are taking market share from other world economies without appearing to develop as much their own

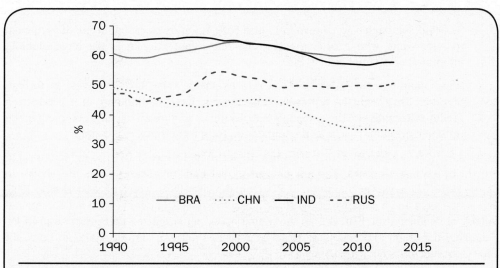

Figure 16.7   Household consumption as a percentage of GDP, BRIC economies (5-year moving average)

*Source:* World Bank.

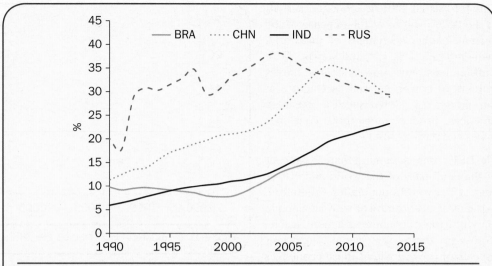

Figure 16.8    Exports as a percentage of GDP, BRIC economies (5-year moving average)

*Source:* World Bank.

internal markets. The more internal demand, such as that from household consumption and firm-level investment, drives future growth in the BRICs, the less competitive and the more complementary will be the BRIC contribution to world economic growth.

## Global operations

Exports are the sale of domestic production to overseas markets. Globalization is more than this. Many leading firms around the world have operations in more than one country.

*Multinational enterprises* are usually large companies with production and/or sales operations in more than one country.

> The index of transnationality is an average of three ratios: foreign assets/total assets, foreign workers/total workers and foreign sales/total sales for the firm.
>
> The purchase of foreign assets is commonly known as foreign direct investment (FDI).

The United Nations Conference for Trade and Development has developed an **index of transnationality** that seeks to measure a firm's exposure to non-domestic markets.

Selected companies are shown in Figure 16.9. Many of us probably find it very easy to understand why Nestlé, a Swiss chocolate confectioner, is the most globally integrated company in the world.

When multinational enterprises operate overseas, they have to invest in foreign markets. This might be represented by the purchase, or building, of a production facility; alternatively, the company may decide to acquire an existing company in the foreign market and use it as the foundation for international expansion.

As we saw with international trade, **foreign direct investment (FDI)** has exhibited rapid growth in the last 25 years. The amounts of global FDI for various years are shown in Figure 16.10. There was acceleration of FDI from the late 1980s, which peaked around 2000. Terrorist events and a collapse of the stock market in the early years of the millennium led to lack of financing for FDI. But as the global economy stabilized and grew, so did FDI. Following the credit and economic crisis of 2008 FDI activity shrank again; and has not shown strong consistent growth since.

## Why do firms become global?

There are a variety of reasons why firms become global, but essentially these reasons relate to costs and revenues.

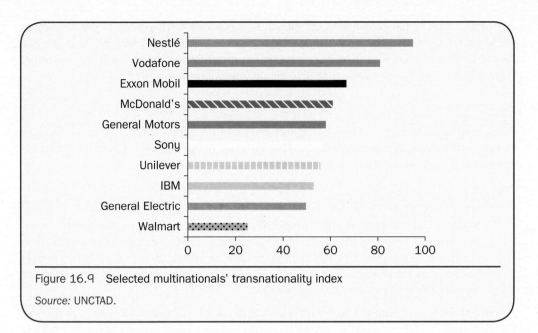

Figure 16.9   Selected multinationals' transnationality index

*Source:* UNCTAD.

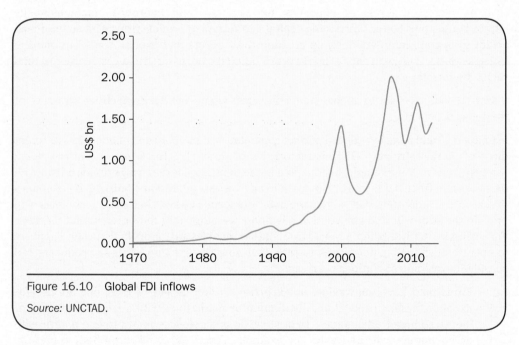

Figure 16.10   Global FDI inflows

*Source:* UNCTAD.

## Revenue growth

A company's growth is constrained by the size and growth of its domestic market. If we take a company like Wal-Mart, which already dominates the US grocery market, its opportunities for growth are limited by the size of the US market. But if it operates overseas, as it does in the UK through the Asda chain, then its sales can increase. Sales growth in overseas markets may also be cheaper. Consider the adverts of many leading global companies, particularly mobile phone operators and car makers. The advert often has no voice-over. The advert usually involves images and music, so that if it is made for the UK market, it can then also be screened in other markets too. Different economies can offer different growth rates, especially if sales are income elastic. For example, in highly developed economies, such as the US and Western Europe, the demand for insurance products is income inelastic; a 10 per cent rise in income will generate a less than 10 per cent rise in demand for insurance. However, in the Far East insurance is income elastic; a 10 per cent rise in income will lead to a bigger than 10 per cent rise in the demand for insurance. Therefore, in the developed world insurance is set to become a smaller proportion of national income, while in the Far East it is set to become an increasing proportion of national income. As a consequence, large insurance companies have rushed to set up operations in the Far East.

### Costs

Firms may operate overseas because they have an international cost advantage and can compete effectively in foreign markets. Alternatively, firms may be seeking international expansion in order to gain a cost advantage.

## Sources of international competitiveness

> **National** sources of international competitiveness **are** likely to stem from the characteristics of the national economy.

**Sources of international competitiveness** can be categorized as national, industrial or firm-specific. Most obviously, comparative advantage resulting from the factor endowments of the economy (such as labour, raw materials or capital) can provide firms with an international competitive advantage. Operating overseas enables a firm to exploit these advantages.

Additional sources of national competitiveness may stem from macroeconomic conditions. Inflation may be falling, making prices internationally competitive. Supply-side policies, such as increased levels of education and training and improved communications infrastructure, plus better functioning capital markets, may provide firms with an improved ability to operate internationally by creating the workers and capital needed to manage overseas operations, with capital markets providing the necessary finances in order to fund such investments.

Industrial sources of international competitiveness stem from the competitive structure of the domestic market.

In Chapters 5 and 6, we introduced perfect competition, monopoly and oligopoly as different types of market structure. The characteristics of these structures may aid international competitiveness. For example, a monopoly in the domestic market may provide a firm with the necessary financial resources to invest in an overseas operation. Similarly, if economies of scale are an important cost advantage in the domestic market, such scale economies may provide the firm with the competitive advantage to move into the international markets. For example, the US, being a very large market, enables many of its domestic suppliers to operate at the minimum efficient scale. With low costs, many of these producers can consider developing operations overseas.

> **Firm-specific** sources of international competitiveness stem from the characteristics of the firm's routines, knowledge and/or assets.

Firms may have knowledge, or expertise, in any aspect of their operations—for example, design, production, distribution or marketing. With a lack of national- or industrial-based advantages, **firm-specific** competences may provide a firm with an advantage over its rivals. For example, Tesco and Sainsbury's both operate in the same UK supermarket business. They have access to the same factor inputs and benefit from the same industrial structure, so why has Tesco outperformed Sainsbury's? Tesco must have some firm-specific advantage over Sainsbury's. The advantage could stem from a brand name, management know-how, logistics technology or even being able to build stores quicker and more cheaply than rival operators. Clearly, since the advantage lies within the firm, it is firm-specific. The asset may not be tangible, but it is an advantage that is specific to the firm.

## Economies of scope, specific assets and internationalization

This specific nature of the asset is essential for an understanding of internationalization by a firm. If, as discussed in Chapter 7 when analysing growth strategies, the firm's specific advantage generates economies of scope, internationalization provides a way of exploiting scope economies. Investment in a brand for the domestic market may present an economy of scope if the brand can also be used to enter an international market, thereby saving on the cost of developing a new brand. Research and development associated with a new product, such as a microprocessor, a drug or a plasma TV, could represent an economy of scope if the product can be launched in more than one market. But should a firm exploit its own brand or new product development itself? Or, instead, sell rights to use its brand name or product development to an operator in the international market? This is the make or buy decision also discussed in Chapter 7. If the asset is specific, then the transaction costs of selling access to the brand or product knowledge to a third party may be very high. A hold-up problem could occur where the third party threatens to damage the brand or provide competitors with access to the product knowledge. In order to reduce the transaction costs, it is better for the firm to exploit firm-specific assets internationally within its own operations, rather than to sell access rights to other firms.

In summary, if a firm has a specific asset such as knowledge or branding which provides it with a competitive advantage, the best way to exploit that asset is to retain control. Expanding the firm's operations into international markets enables the firm-specific competitive advantage to be exploited. Transferring the asset to a third party is likely to increase transaction costs.

## Accessing international competitiveness

Companies can operate overseas to exploit cheaper factor inputs, such as cheaper labour, lower raw material cost and better capital equipment. But cheap labour may not be productive labour, or it may be labour with a poor level of skills. So, the quality of labour also needs to be considered. Operating in international markets also cuts down on transportation costs. Products need not be transported around the world. Instead, they can be produced and sold in the local market.

A common concern regarding multinational enterprises has been the exploitation of workers. Wages in developing economies tend to be less than in developed economies. Firms are tempted to move overseas in order to reduce labour costs. If developing economies are also associated with more relaxed employment laws, then the use of child labour, long working hours and limited holidays may also make such places look attractive to large multinational enterprises. However, if multinational enterprises do exploit workers, then it is worth considering why FDI is more prevalent in the developed world than the developing world.

A basic observation and answer to this question would be that FDI measures investment in capital not labour. For example, a Japanese company investing in a plasma TV manufacturing plant in Wales is investing in high-technology capital equipment to produce products for the developed world. A UK clothing retailer hiring workers in South East Asia to make clothes is unlikely to invest very much in capital. FDI may, therefore, not be a good measure of the extent of global operations.

## Business application: globalization—exploiting comparative advantage

Nothing is ever as easy as it sounds. The reduction in trade barriers around the world has arguably freed up world business and enabled the most competitive firms to flourish. However, a number of problems still exist. These include problems of communication and control, legal matters, access to inputs and a brand which has a global reach.

## Communication and co-ordination

First, there is the matter of communication and co-ordination among suppliers, workers and customers. Language is an obvious barrier to good communication. Ordering raw material supplies for your production facility in a foreign language is fairly easy to master, especially with the aid of an interpreter. Explaining complex technical processes, however, or trying to justify recruitment procedures, marketing plans, operational procedures or financial control through budgeting will require an understanding of local culture, traditional business practice and perhaps even an awareness of local law. Therefore, communication and co-ordination of the international operation requires a great deal of specialist expertise.

### Legal issues

Second, local laws may differ substantially from those of the home base. Employment law could be different, resulting in higher redundancy payments and longer periods of notice before employment can be terminated. There might be stronger trade union representation, leading to more industrial disputes. Environmental controls could be harsher, leading to cleaner but more costly production. Contract law could differ and the legal system could be ineffective at enforcing contracts. Even import restrictions might apply. For example, companies operating in the EU, but from non-EU countries, are required to source more than 70 per cent of their production inputs from within the EU.

### Quality of inputs

Third, input factors can have varying quality across countries. Labour is an obvious example, with basic skills such as literacy and numeracy varying across developed and developing economies. Such skills are essential for training, developing and managing staff. Furthermore, such skills are essential for staff that are required to use machinery in the production process, particularly machinery that is computer-controlled and might require adjustments to be made to it. If the supply of staff with the appropriate level of skills is limited, then development of the local workforce may well be necessary. While enhancing skills might be seen in a favourable light by the local community, no one will be more grateful than other local firms, which in the fullness of time will be seeking to poach the international company's highly productive workers.

### Image and brand

Finally, we must return to one of the key ideas laid down by Nobel Laureate Paul Krugman. Global trade needs to be understood in terms of the needs of customers. Global brands become successful because they meet the tastes and preferences of a global audience. While the products and services required by global consumers may change over time, the key services, vision and experience appear constant. See Box 16.3 for more details.

 ## 16.6 Business application: sources of international competitiveness

It is important for businesspeople the world over to understand the crucial difference between competitive advantage and a sustainable competitive advantage. A competitive advantage may provide you with some short-term strength over your rivals. But if your advantage can be mimicked, then you do not have a sustainable competitive advantage. India, as a location, has a competitive advantage in outsourcing IT, data processing and call-centre services. Much of this advantage stems from a reasonable IT and telecommunications infrastructure, and reasonably skilled staff who speak English and who are willing to work for much less than similar staff in the US and Europe.

Unfortunately, India does not necessarily possess a sustainable advantage. Now that it is known that large corporations are willing to outsource business services, many locations around the world will seek to copy India's low-cost strategy. In fact, even some regions in the EU which are in need of economic regeneration could place themselves in direct competition with India. The clear problem for India is that its strategy can be copied. Therefore, it is substitutable and that means it faces elastic, or price-sensitive, consumers. However, as incomes rise, wages rise, so it will become ever more difficult to remain internationally competitive.

So how do you continue to reap the benefits from globalization? You must find a strategy which is sustainable; one which other locations or companies find very difficult to copy. In the absence of imitators, firms face fewer rivals and less-intense price competition. While the availability of cheap labour within a location can be copied, industrial and/or firm-level characteristics are much more differentiated. Look at the spider web diagram for India. Weaknesses are in innovation, business sophistication and technological development. Competitiveness is not just about being cheap, it is about offering products for which

## Box 16.3
## Google overtakes Apple to become the 2014 BrandZ™ top 100 most valuable global brand

Google has overtaken Apple to become the world's most valuable global brand in the 2014 BrandZ™ Top 100 Most Valuable Global Brand ranking, worth $159 billion, an increase of 40 per cent year on year.

After three years at the top, Apple slipped to No 2 on the back of a 20 per cent decline in brand value, to $148 billion. While Apple remains a top performing brand, there is a growing perception that it is no longer redefining technology for consumers, reflected by a lack of dramatic new product launches. The world's leading B2B brand, IBM, held onto its No 3 position with a brand value of $108 billion.

Nick Cooper, Managing Director of Millward Brown Optimor, commented on the number one brand, 'Google has been hugely innovative in the last year with Google Glass, investments in artificial intelligence and a multitude of partnerships that see its Android operating system becoming embedded in other goods such as cars. All of this activity sends a very strong signal to consumers about what Google is about and it has coincided with a slowdown at Apple.'

The BrandZ Top 100 Most Valuable Global Brands study, commissioned by WPP and conducted by Millward Brown Optimor, is now in its ninth year. It is the only ranking that uses the views of potential and current buyers of a brand, alongside financial data, to calculate brand value.

The combined value of the Top 100 has nearly doubled since the first ranking was produced in 2006.

The Top 100 today are worth $2.9 trillion, an increase of 49 per cent compared with the 2008 valuation, which marked the start of the banking and currency crisis.

Key findings highlighted in this year's research report include:

- **Share of Life:** Successful brands such as Google (No 1 brand), Facebook, Twitter, Tencent and LinkedIn are more than just tools, they have become part of our lives. They offer new forms of communication that absorb people's attention and imagination, while also helping them organize the rest of their lives at the same time.

- **Purpose beyond Profit:** Brands in business for reasons beyond the bottom line have a better chance of success in today's world. For example, Pampers, which promotes mother and baby health issues, is at No 39 in the ranking and grew its value by 10 per cent to $22.6 billion. Dove, which has continued to find huge success on the back of its 'real women' philosophy, has a brand value of $4.8 billion.

- **Apparel fastest growing category:** The top 10 Apparel brands grew in value by 29 per cent to nearly $100 billion this year, outpacing Cars (up 17 per cent) and Retail (up 16 per cent). With brands such as Uniqlo, Nike and Adidas all recording double-digit increases in their valuation.

- **Technology service companies continue to climb:** Not only are the top four brands technology companies, but so too are many of this year's biggest risers. This year's fastest climber was leading Chinese internet brand Tencent, up 97 per cent to $54 billion and the No 14 position, followed by Facebook which rose 68 per cent to $36 billion and took the No 21 spot. New brands in the Top 100 include Twitter at No 71 with a brand value of $14 billion and LinkedIn at No 78 worth $12 billion. Collectively, Technology companies make up 29 per cent of the value of the BrandZ Top 100 ranking.

| The BrandZ Top 10 Most Valuable Global Brands 2014 Rank 2014 | Brand | Category | Brand value 2014 ($M) | Brand value change | Rank 2013 |
|---|---|---|---|---|---|
| 1 | Google | Technology | 158,843 | +40% | 2 |
| 2 | Apple | Technology | 147,880 | −20% | 1 |
| 3 | IBM | Technology | 107,541 | −4% | 3 |
| 4 | Microsoft | Technology | 90,185 | +29% | 7 |
| 5 | McDonald's | Fast Food | 85,706 | −5% | 4 |
| 6 | Coca-Cola | Soft Drinks | 80,683 | +3% | 5 |
| 7 | Visa | Credit Cards | 79,197 | +41% | 9 |
| 8 | AT&T | Telecommunications | 77,833 | +3% | 6 |
| 9 | Marlborough | Tobacco | 67,341 | −3% | 8 |
| 10 | Amazon | Retail | 64,255 | +41% | 14 |

21 May 2014. BrandZ™ Press Release
© WPP 2005 Limited all rights reserved

consumers will pay a good price. You therefore benefit from being different, innovative and sophisticated in providing service and product. For example, Silicon Valley has been a success for a variety of reasons, but none that relate to cheap labour.

Silicon Valley benefits from economic clustering—the co-location of supportive and competitive firms. Competition between rivals spurs innovation, while the co-location of supportive industries also enables innovation. Silicon Valley may provide industry-level sources of international competitiveness by the concentration of similar companies in one area. Skilled technical and scientific workers are attracted to the area and can move between projects and companies without having to move home. Moreover, important support services such as banking and venture capital are likely to locate in the area and develop expertise in financing specialist IT innovation companies. As firms within Silicon Valley develop, firm-specific routines around developing innovation strategies and commercializing knowledge creation begin to emerge. These industrial and firm-level characteristics are much more difficult to copy and as such lead to the development of higher value-added services, where the advantage is unlikely to be competed away on price.

The challenge for India is not that difficult. It has entrepreneurial spirit, it has cash resources to invest in innovation and it has the engineering and technical skills to develop a sustainable competitive advantage. Moreover, the lessons from India are appropriate for many national economies and companies faced with global competition. The very existence of competition suggests a lack of entry barriers, substitutability and low prices. Profits, wages and economic wealth will never be generated in such industries. It is therefore important to move to less competitive positions within the value chain. We are already beginning to observe automotive companies, such as Volkswagen, locating their assembly lines in Eastern Europe where wages are lower but productivity is comparable with Western Europe. In contrast, design, engineering, product development and marketing have remained within the home economy. These are much more involved, complex tasks which are difficult to copy by low-wage economies, leading to lower competition and a higher rate of return to this section of the value chain.

After the credit crisis, the UK faces the acute problem that the economy is overly dependent on the banking and financial sector. Banking and finance generated significant wealth from activities within the UK and overseas. The UK could rebalance its economy by focusing on and developing other industries in which it excels. Hi-tech aeronautical engineering, fashion, music and media are prominent examples. But if these sectors fail to fill any void left by the collapse

## Box 16.4
## World Competitiveness Report, India 2014–15

Dropping for the sixth consecutive edition, India ranks 71st (down 11), the lowest of the BRICS economies.

India's slide in the rankings began in 2009, when its economy was still growing at 8.5 per cent (it even grew by 10.3 per cent in 2010). Back then, however, India's showing in the GCI was already casting doubt about the sustainability of this growth. Since then, the country has been struggling to achieve growth of 5 per cent. Overall, India does best in the more complex areas of the GCI: innovation (49th) and business sophistication (57th). In contrast, it obtains low marks in the more fundamental drivers of competitiveness, such as health and primary education (89th). The country's health situation is indeed alarming: infant mortality (115th) and malnutrition incidence are among the highest in the world; only 36 per cent of the population have access to improved sanitation; and life expectancy (110th) is Asia's second shortest, after Myanmar. On a more positive note, India is on track to achieve universal primary education (78th), although the *quality* of primary education remains poor (88th) and it ranks

a low 93rd in higher education and training. Transport and electricity infrastructure are in need of upgrading (87th). Market competition and efficiency is affected by various barriers to entry and red tape (95th). For example, it takes 12 procedures (130th) and almost a month to register a business (106th). Businesses also face serious obstacles in the form of a high total tax rate (130th) and an inefficient and rigid labour market (112th).

India's lowest pillar rank is in technological readiness (121st). Despite almost ubiquitous mobile telephony, India is one of the world's least digitally connected countries: only 15 per cent of Indians access the Internet on a regular basis and broadband Internet, if available at all, remains the privilege of a very few.

Furthermore, India's fiscal situation remains in disarray (101st in the macroeconomic environment). With the exception of 2007, the central government has consistently run deficits since 2000. Because of the high degree of informality, its tax base is relatively narrow, representing less than 10 per cent of GDP. In addition, over the past several years India has experienced persistently high, in some years near double-digit, inflation, which reached 9.5 per cent in 2013 (133rd). Improving competitiveness will help rebalance the economy and move the country up the value chain, ensuring more solid and stable growth; this in turn could result in more employment opportunities for the country's rapidly growing population.

Source: *The Global Competitiveness Report 2014-2015*, World Economic Forum, Geneva, Switzerland, © 2016

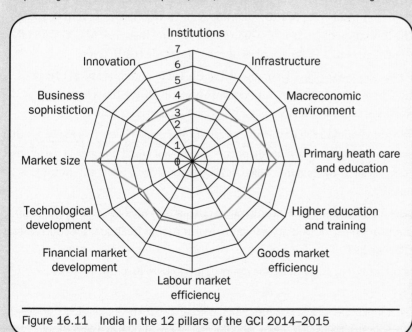

Figure 16.11    India in the 12 pillars of the GCI 2014–2015

of banking, then the long-term real exchange rate for the UK pound will have to fall in order to retain some of the UK's international competitiveness. When your economic output is less valued around the world, then the price you charge and the income you earn have to fall.

So, globalization offers opportunities and threats. Working out how to maximize the opportunities and tame the threats is the art of business management, but through an understanding of micro and macro business economics you should now be prepared to meet the challenge.

## Summary

1. The reasons for increasing globalization are numerous but include the cultural, technological, economic and political.

2. Comparative advantage is an important economic reason behind the rise of globalization. Comparative advantage states that countries should specialize in the goods and services which they are comparatively better at producing.

3. Comparative advantages are most likely to arise from an abundance of a particular factor resource. France is good at wine because it has an abundance of productive land and the right climate. Germany is good at producing high-quality cars because it has an abundance of highly skilled labour and high-quality capital equipment.

4. Two-way trade in the same product between countries may still exist even in the face of comparative advantage. Cars are an example. The UK and Germany may trade cars with each other, but the types of car will be different. This simply reflects differences in taste and preference among German and UK car drivers and not comparative advantage in production.

5. In the past, countries have tried to protect industries from international competition by imposing trade barriers. Tariffs and quotas are common examples. Unless the industry is of strategic or defensive importance to the economy, then economists generally agree that trade restrictions are against the public interest.

6. The leading political reasons for globalization have been the acceptance of the economic importance of comparative advantage and a willingness to reduce trade barriers. The formation of trade blocs such as the EU and the work of GATT and the WTO have been important in the process of reducing trade restrictions.

7. Following the successes of GATT and the WTO, the trade of goods and services across national boundaries has grown faster than world GDP. This would suggest that the provision of goods and services is more globally integrated than ever before.

8. However, when examining the pattern of international trade flows, it is apparent that the vast majority of international trade occurs between a small number of developed economies. So, while trade has increased, it is questionable to what extent trade is actually global.

9. Brazil, Russia, India and China known collectively as the BRIC economies, have all demonstrated strong export led growth and are forecast to be the major contributors to global GDP by 2050.

10. Companies operating in more than one country are known as *multinational enterprises*.

11. Foreign direct investment (FDI) occurs when a company invests outside its domestic base. Throughout the 1990s, FDI grew rapidly. But in recent years it has shown slower growth.

12. Firms may begin to operate overseas for two basic reasons: (i) to increase sales and (ii) to reduce costs.

13. However, international operations incur specific problems, such as language, legal issues, co-ordination problems and possible damage to the global brand. As a consequence, some multinational enterprises are beginning to reappraise their global activities, as evidenced by the falling levels of FDI.

# Learning checklist

You should now be able to:

- List and explain the main drivers of globalization
- Explain comparative advantage and identify potential sources of comparative advantage
- Explain the impact of tariffs and quotas on domestic prices, firms and consumers
- Explain the reasons why trade restrictions have fallen
- Assess whether the rise in international trade is global
- Provide reasons for the growth in FDI.

# Questions                                                    connect

1. Identify the various factors that have promoted the globalization of business.

2. How does comparative advantage explain international trade?

3. If the terms of trade improve for a country, then how has the price of exports changed relative to the price of imports?

4. Economies of scale and product differentiation are important for explaining what feature of international trade?

5. Identify the main types of protectionist policy.

6. If international trade has benefits for the global economy, explain why some countries still find advantages in protectionist policies.

7. What is the World Trade Organization and how important is this body for international trade?

8. What is foreign direct investment and what types of company undertake it?

9. What are the key benefits for business and consumers from membership of trade blocs such as the EU?

10. Evaluate whether the EU should remove the Common Agricultural Policy.

11. What problems do global businesses face when exploiting international business opportunities?

12. Use a diagram to explain the impact of a tariff and a quota on the domestic price of a good or service.

13. Is cheap labour a source of sustainable comparative advantage?

14. Is globalization a threat or an opportunity for business?

15. What problems might a firm face when managing global operations?

16. International trade plays an important role in economies of most countries, including Germany. International prices have a significant impact on production decision by domestic firms. The diagram provided shows supply (S) and demand (D) for German producers for a certain widget. Assume that the prevailing world price for this widget is €4.

    (a) From the diagram, determine the amount supplied by German producers and the amount demanded by German consumers (assuming a world price of €4).

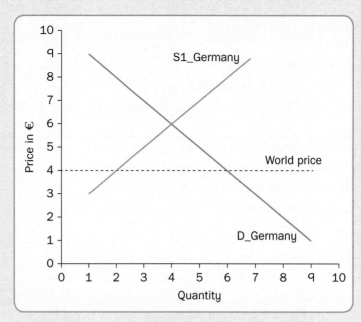

DIFFICULT

(b) Assume that the government provides a subsidy to German producers. Using the diagram, show what will happen to the German supply curve.

(c) With provision of a subsidy, what will happen to the amount of widgets supplied by German firms and the amount of widgets that are now imported?

## Exercises

EASY

1. True or false?

2. (a) Comparative advantage reflects international differences in the opportunity costs of producing different goods.

(b) The need to protect infant industries is a powerful argument in favour of protectionist measures.

INTERMEDIATE

(c) The imposition of a tariff stimulates domestic demand.

(d) The purchase of a share in Microsoft by someone who is not a citizen of the US is an example of foreign direct investment.

(e) Comparative advantage could stem from an abundance of factor endowments.

(f) The increase in world merchandise trade has not been entirely global.

DIFFICULT

3. This exercise examines the gains from trade in a two-country, two-good model. To simplify matters for the time being, we assume that the two countries share a common currency; this allows us to ignore the exchange rate. The two countries are called Anywaria and Someland; the two goods are bicycles and boots. The unit labour requirements of the two goods in each country are shown in Table 16.10; we assume constant returns to scale.

(a) Which of the countries has an absolute advantage in the production of the two commodities?

(b) Calculate the opportunity cost of bicycles in terms of boots and of boots in terms of bicycles for each of the countries.

(c) Which country has a comparative advantage in the production of bicycles?

**Table 16.8** Production techniques

|  | Unit labour requirements (hours per unit output) | |
|  | Anywaria | Someland |
| --- | --- | --- |
| Bicycles | 60 | 120 |
| Boots | 30 | 40 |

Suppose there is no trade. Each of the two economies has 300 workers, who work 40 hours per week. Initially, each country devotes half of its resources to producing each of the two commodities.

(d) Complete Table 16.11.

**Table 16.9** Production of bicycles and boots, no trade case

|  | Anywaria | Someland | 'World' output |
| --- | --- | --- | --- |
| Bicycles |  |  |  |
| Boots |  |  |  |

Trade now takes place under the following conditions: the country with a comparative advantage in boot production produces only boots. The other country produces sufficient bicycles to maintain the world 'no-trade' output, devoting the remaining resources to boot production.

(e) Complete Table 16.12 and comment on the gains from trade.

**Table 16.10** Production of bicycles and boots

|  | Anywaria | Someland | 'World' output |
| --- | --- | --- | --- |
| Bicycles |  |  |  |
| Boots |  |  |  |

(f) On a single diagram, plot the production possibility frontier for each country. What aspect of your diagram is indicative of potential gains from trade?

(g) Source the Global Competitiveness Report for an economy of your choice. Comment on that country's strengths and weaknesses.

# Glossary

**Accounting profits** are revenues less raw material costs, wages and depreciation.

**Acquisition** involves one firm purchasing another firm. This might occur by mutual consent or, in the case of a hostile takeover, the managers of the acquired firm might try to resist the takeover.

**Actual GDP** is short-run equilibrium GDP.

**Agency costs** reflect reductions in value to principals from using agents to undertake work on their behalf.

**Agents** run companies on behalf of shareholders (**principals**).

**Aggregate demand** is the total demand in an economy.

**Aggregate supply** is the total supply in an economy.

**Allocative efficiency** occurs when price equals marginal cost, or P = MC.

**Asset motive** Under the asset motive, individuals hold money as part of a diversified asset portfolio. Some wealth is held in equities, some in bonds, a portion in property and some in money.

**Austerity measures** occur when a government reduces spending and increases tax collection; and generally linked to a need to improve the government's finances.

**Autonomous consumption** does not change if income changes.

**Autonomous expenditure** is not influenced by the level of income.

**Average fixed cost** is calculated as total fixed costs divided by the number of units produced.

**Average revenue** is the average price charged by the firm and is equal to total revenue/quantity demanded: (PQ)/Q.

**Average total cost** is calculated as total cost divided by the number of units produced.

**Average variable cost** is calculated as total variable cost divided by the number of units produced.

**Balance of payments** The balance of payments records all transactions between a country and the rest of the world.

**Balanced budget multiplier** (the) states that an increase in government spending, plus an equal increase in taxes, leads to higher equilibrium output.

**Barriers to entry** make entry into a market by new competitors difficult.

**Barter economy** In a barter economy, there is no money, and individuals trade by exchanging different goods and services.

**Basel III** provides an internationally agreed set of conditions for the minimum financial strength of a bank. The conditions relate to how the risks of a bank must be assessed and how much cash and reserves a bank must hold to protect itself against large losses from the risks that it faces.

**Boom** A boom is an increase in national output.

**Bretton Woods** The Bretton Woods agreement of 1944 provided a plan for managing foreign exchange rates.

**Business cycle** The business cycle describes the tendency of an economy to move from economic boom to economic recession and then back into boom to repeat the cycle.

**Capital account** The capital account records, among other things, net contributions made to the EU.

**Capital adequacy ratio** is a measure of how much capital a bank needs to protect itself from a large loss on the investments or loans that it has made.

**Central bank** A central bank acts as a banker to the commercial bank, taking deposits and, in extreme circumstances, making loans.

*Ceteris paribus* means all other things being equal.

**Circular flow of income** shows the flow of inputs, outputs and payments between households and firms within an economy.

**Claimant count** measures the number of people who are eligible and receiving the jobseeker's allowance.

**Classical unemployment** refers to workers who have priced themselves out of a job.

**Closed economy** A closed economy does not trade with the rest of the world. An open economy does trade with the rest of the world.

**Coase conjecture** The Coase conjecture argues that a monopoly provider of a durable good will sell at the perfectly competitive price.

**Collateralized debt obligation** is a bond. The holder of the bond is paid a rate of interest in return for funding a debt.

**Command GDP** describes the purchasing power of a nation's output.

**Competition and Markets Authority** (the) investigates whether a monopoly, or a potential monopoly, significantly affects competition.

**Complements** are products that are purchased jointly. Beer and kebabs would be a youthful and modern example; another would be cars and petrol.

**Complete contract** Under a complete contract all aspects of the contractual arrangement are fully specified.

**Consumer surplus** is the difference between the price you are charged for a product and the maximum price that you would have been willing to pay.

**Contagion** occurs when the collapse of one bank leads to the collapse of more banks.

**Contestable market** A contestable market is one where firms can enter and exit a market freely.

**Convergence** The convergence hypothesis states that poor countries grow more quickly than average, but rich countries grow more slowly than average.

**Cost leadership strategy** Under a cost leadership strategy, a firm will seek competitive advantage by reducing average costs and pursuing economies of scale.

**Cost push inflation** occurs when a reduction in supply leads to an increase in overall prices.

**Cost–benefit analysis** provides a monetary evaluation of a government intervention.

**Creative destruction** occurs when a new entrant outcompetes incumbent companies by virtue of being innovative.

**Credible commitment** A credible commitment or threat has to be one that is optimal to carry out.

**Credit creation** is the process of turning existing bank deposits into credit facilities for borrowers. The process can result in an increase in the money supply.

**Credit crunch** A credit crunch is a lack of liquidity between banks.

**Cross-price elasticity** measures the responsiveness of demand to a change in the price of a substitute or complement.

**Cross-sectional data** are the measurements of one variable at the same point in time across different individuals.

**Crowding out** occurs when increased government spending reduces private sector spending.

**Cumulative debt** is the total outstanding government debt from borrowings over many years.

**Current account** The current account is a record of all goods and services traded with the rest of the world.

**Cyclical unemployment** is related to the business cycle and is sometimes also referred to as demand-deficient unemployment. Cyclical unemployment reflects workers who have lost jobs due to the adversities of the business cycle.

**Dead-weight loss** of monopoly is the loss of welfare to society resulting from the existence of the monopoly.

**Deflation** is a fall in prices, usually on a yearly basis.

**Demand curve** The demand curve illustrates the relationship between price and quantity demanded of a particular product.

**Demand pull inflation** occurs when a rise in aggregate demand leads to an increase in overall prices.

**Demerit good** A demerit good provides consumers with fewer benefits than they expect.

**Developed economy** A developed economy has high levels of commercial activity and high levels of supporting infrastructure, such as good transport and communication systems, good health and education systems.

**Developing economies,** such as Brazil, India and China, are those which show a high degree of commercialization, but their economies are not amongst the most developed in the world, such as the UK, US, Japan, France and Germany.

**Differentiation** is a means of understanding the gradient.

**Dirty float** A dirty float occurs when the government claims that the exchange rate floats, but it is in fact managed by the government or central bank.

**Discount factor (or rate)** provides a measure of the time value of money. If £100 saved for one year earns 2 per cent interest, at the end of year you will have £102. Equally, a cost of £102 in a year's time is worth £100 today.

**Disequilibria** In situations of disequilibria, at the current price the willingness to demand will differ from the willingness to supply.

**Diversification** is the growth of the business in a related or unrelated market.

**Diversified portfolio** of activities contains a mix of uncorrelated business operations.

**Dominant strategy** is a player's best response, whatever its rival decides.

**Double coincidence of wants** A double coincidence of wants occurs when two people trade goods and services without money. The first individual demands the good offered by the second individual, and vice versa.

**Durable good** A durable good is one in which consumption is ongoing, for example, a DVD.

**Economic growth** is measured as the percentage change in GDP per year.

**Economic profits** are revenues less the costs of all factors of production.

**Economic sentiment** is one measure of confidence in the economy and combines the views of consumers and firms within one measure. The higher the number the more confident consumers and firms are about the future prospects for the economy.

**Economies of scale** cause long-run average costs to fall as output increases.

**Economies of scope** are said to exist if the cost of producing two or more outputs jointly is less than the cost of producing the outputs separately.

**Elastic demand** is where $\varepsilon > 1$, or demand is responsive to a change in price.

**Elasticity** is a measure of the responsiveness of demand to a change in price.

**Elasticity of supply** is a measure of how responsive supply is to a change in price.

**Emerging economy** An emerging economy is making the transition from developing to developed. Emerging economies have very high levels of sustainable economic development with companies competing effectively across the world.

**Endogenized** If costs are endogenized, the firms inside the industry have strategically influenced the level and nature of costs.

**Endogenous growth theory** considers models in which the steady-state growth rate can be affected by economic behaviour and policy.

**Equation of a straight line** is $Y = a + bX$.

**Equilibrium** is generally defined as the situation where planned aggregate expenditure is equal to the actual output of firms.

**Exit barriers** make exit from a market by existing competitors difficult.

**Exogenous costs** of the firm are outside its control.

**Expectations** are beliefs held by firms, workers and consumers about the future level of prices.

**Externalities** are the effects of consumption, or production, on third parties.

**Factors of production** are resources needed to make goods and services: land, labour, capital and enterprise.

**Fiat money** is notes and coins guaranteed by the government rather than by gold deposits.

**Financial account** The financial account records net purchases and sales of foreign assets. (This was previously known as the capital account.)

**Financial discipline** is the degree to which a government pursues stringent monetary policy and targets low inflation.

**Financial intermediation** involves channelling cash from savers to borrowers.

**Finite resources** are the limited amount of resources that enable the production and purchase of goods and services.

**Firm-specific** sources of international competitiveness stem from the characteristics of the firm's routines, knowledge and/or assets.

**First-best solution** In a first-best solution the economy has no market failures.

**First-mover advantage** ensures that the firm which makes its strategic decision first gains a profitable advantage over its rivals.

**Fiscal drag** occurs when tax-free income allowances grow at a slower rate than earnings. This reduces the real value of tax-free allowances, leading to high real tax receipts.

**Fiscal policy** is the government's decisions regarding taxation and spending.

**Fiscal stance** is the extent to which the government is using fiscal policy to increase or decrease aggregate demand in the economy.

**Fixed costs** are constant. They remain the same whatever the level of output.

**Fixed exchange rate regime** Under a fixed exchange rate regime, the government fixes the exchange rate between the domestic currency and another strong world currency, such as the US dollar.

**Fixed exchange rates** have a fixed rate of conversion between currencies.

**Floating exchange rate** In a floating exchange rate system, there is no market intervention by the government or the central bank.

**Floating exchange rate regime** Under a floating exchange rate regime, the exchange rate is set purely by market forces.

**Foreign direct investment (FDI)** The purchase of foreign assets is commonly known as foreign direct investment (FDI).

**Forex market** A forex market is where different currencies are traded.

**Free riders** are individuals, or firms, who can benefit from the actions of others without contributing to the effort made by others. They gain benefits from the actions of others for free.

**Frictional unemployment** refers to individuals who have quit one job and are currently searching for another job. As such, frictional unemployment is temporary.

**Full employment** In full employment, all factors of production that wish to be employed are employed.

**Full-employment level** of the economy is a long-run equilibrium position and the economy operates on its production possibility frontier. The economy is in neither boom nor recession.

**Game theory** seeks to understand whether strategic interaction will lead to competition or co-operation between rivals.

**GDP per capita** is the GDP for the economy divided by the population of the economy. GDP per capita provides a measure of average income per person.

**GDP,** gross domestic product, is a measure of the total output produced by an economy in a given year.

**Government bonds** are a near-cash equivalent and therefore liquid. A government pays the holder of bonds a rate of interest in return for funding the government's debt.

**Government deficit** is the difference between government spending and tax receipts. Just as students run up overdrafts, spending more than they earn, so too does the government.

**Gradient** is a measure of the slope of a line.

**Gresham's Law** states that an increasing supply of bad products will drive out good products from the market.

**Gross domestic product (GDP)** measures the volume of goods and services produced by a nation. By adjusting this measure to reflect movements in the terms of trade.

**Gross domestic product(GDP)** is a measure of overall economic activity within an economy. (See Chapters 9 and 10 for more details.)

**Haircut** A haircut is the discount required by the buyer of a risky asset. An asset valued at £100 and bought for £80 is said to have suffered a 20 per cent haircut. The haircut will hopefully insure the buyer against any future losses in value of the asset.

**Hedging** is the transfer of a risky asset for a non-risky asset.

**Hold-up problem** is the renegotiation of contracts, and is linked to asset specificity.

**Horizontal growth** occurs when a company develops or grows activities at the same stage of the production process.

**Impact analysis** is a means of understanding the impact of a policy change on individuals and/ or an economy.

**Imperfect competition** is a highly competitive market where firms may use product differentiation.

**Imperfect information** exists when a consumer does not have all the facts relating to the key features of a product.

**Income elasticity** measures the responsiveness of demand to a change in income.

**Index numbers** are used to transform a data series into a series with a base value of 100.

**Index of transnationality** The transnationality index is an average of three ratios: foreign assets/total assets, foreign workers/total workers and foreign sales/total sales for the firm.

**Industrial clusters** occur when related industries co-locate in a region. Examples include Silicon Valley and electronics, Germany and automotives, London and finance.

**Industrialized economy** An industrialized economy is characterized by lots of industrial sectors such as construction industries, automobile manufacturers, oil companies. Economies usually move from being based on agriculture, to industrialized and then towards services, such as retail and banking.

**Inelastic demand** is where elasticity $\varepsilon < 1$, or a change in the price will lead to a proportionately smaller change in the quantity demanded.

**Inferior goods** are demanded more when income levels fall and demanded less when income levels rise.

**Infinite wants** are the limitless desires to consume goods and services

**Inflation illusion** is a confusion of nominal and real changes.

**Inflation** is the rate of change in the average price level. Inflation of 2 per cent indicates that prices have risen by 2 per cent during the previous 12 months.

**Injection** into the circular flow is additional spending on goods and services that does not come from the income earned by households in the inner loop. Injections can be investment, government spending and exports.

**Input markets** are where factor inputs, such as land, labour, capital or enterprise, are traded.

**Intellectual property** is content created by the mind which can be protected by patent or copyright.

**Interest rates** are the price of money and are set by the central bank.

**International Monetary Fund (IMF)** (the) receives money on deposit (savings) from most of the world's countries. These funds can be loaned to governments/countries in financial difficulties.

**Issuing bonds** is a way of borrowing money used by governments and some companies.

**Kinked demand curve** A kinked demand curve shows that price rises will not be matched by rivals, but price reductions will be.

**Law of comparative advantage** (the) states that economies should specialize in the good that they are comparatively better at making.

**Law of demand** The law of demand states that, *ceteris paribus*, as the price of a product falls, more will be demanded.

**Law of diminishing returns** (the) states that, as more of a variable factor of production, usually labour, is added to a fixed factor of production, usually capital, then at some point the returns to the variable factor will diminish.

**Leakage** from the circular flow is income not spent on goods and services within the economy. Leakages can be savings, taxation and imports.

**Learning curve** The learning curve suggests that, as cumulative output increases, average costs fall.

**Least developed economies,** such as some African states, show very low levels of commercialization.

**Lender of last resort** The central bank is a lender of last resort if a bank cannot raise funds from any other lender.

**Liquidity** is the speed, price and ease of access to money.

**Long run** is a period of time when all factors of production are variable.

**M4** takes notes and coins and adds retail and wholesale banking deposits. M4 is, therefore, a broad measure of money.

**Macroeconomics** is the study of how the entire economy works.

**Marginal cost** is the cost of creating one more unit.

**Marginal private benefit** is the benefit to the individual from consuming one more unit of output.

**Marginal private cost** is the cost to the individual of producing one more unit of output.

**Marginal product** is the addition to total product after employing one more unit of factor input. In economics, marginal always means 'one more'.

**Marginal profit** is the profit made on the last unit and is equal to the marginal revenue minus the marginal cost.

**Marginal propensity to consume (MPC)** (the) is the extra consumption generated by one unit of extra income.

**Marginal propensity to save (MPS)** (the) is the extra saving generated by one unit of extra income.

**Marginal revenue** is the change in revenue from selling one more unit.

**Marginal social benefit** is the benefit to society from the consumption of one more unit of output.

**Marginal social cost** is the cost to society of producing one or more unit of output.

**Market economy** In a market economy, the government plays no role in allocating resources. Instead, markets allocate resources to the production of various products.

**Market equilibrium** occurs at the price where consumers' willingness to demand is exactly equal to firms' willingness to supply.

**Market failure** is a term used by economists to cover all circumstances in which the market equilibrium is not efficient.

**Market penetration** is the percentage of total consumers who purchase the product. A market penetration of 10 per cent would be low. Only 1 in 10 consumers buy the product.

**Market structure** is the economist's general title for the major competitive structures of a particular marketplace.

**Maximizing** is the attainment of maximum levels of performance.

**Maximum price** A maximum price/ price ceiling prevents prices from rising above a set level.

**Menu costs** are the costs associated with changing prices, which can include updating computer systems, printing new price lists, changing shelf price information.

**Merger** generally involves two companies agreeing by mutual consent to merge their existing operations.

**Merit good** A merit good provides consumers with more benefits than they expect.

**Microeconomics** is the study of how individuals make economic decisions within an economy.

**Minimum efficient scale (MES)** is the output level at which long-run costs are at a minimum.

**Minimum price** A minimum price/ price floor prevents prices from falling below a set level.

**Mixed economy** In a mixed economy, the government and the private sector jointly solve economic problems.

**Models or theories** are frameworks for organizing how we think about an economic problem.

**Monetary base,** or the stock of high-powered money, is the quantity of notes and coins held by private individuals or held by the banking system.

**Monetary union** is the permanent fixing of exchange rates between member countries.

**Monopolistic competition** is a highly competitive market where firms may use product differentiation.

**Monopoly** is a marketplace supplied by only one competitor, so no competition exists.

**Moral hazard** occurs when someone agrees to undertake a certain set of actions but then, once a contractual arrangement has been agreed, behaves in a different manner.

**Multiplier** The multiplier measures the change in output following a change in autonomous expenditure (the essential or basic amount of consumption plus investment).

**Mutual** A mutual is a financial organization that is owned by its customers. This contrasts with a bank, which is owned by shareholders.

**N-firm concentration ratio,** CR, is a measure of the industry output controlled by the industry's N largest firms.

**Narrow measures of money** are notes and coins held in and outside of the private banking sector.

**Nash equilibrium** occurs when each player does what is best for themselves, given what their rivals may do in response.

**Natural monopoly** exists if scale economies lead to only one firm in the market.

**Natural rate of unemployment** is the level of unemployment when the economy is operating at potential GDP.

**Negative externality** occurs if production, or consumption, by one group reduces the well-being of third parties.

**Negative relationship** A negative relationship exists between two variables if the value for one variable increases (decreases) as the value of the other variable decreases (increases).

**Net present value** is the discounted value of a future cash flow.

**Nexus of contracts** is a collection of interrelated contractual relationships, where the firm represents a nexus or central point, at which all these interrelated contractual relationships are managed in the pursuit of profit.

**Nominal** prices and wages are not adjusted for inflation.

**Nominal wages** are earnings unadjusted for inflation. If a worker earns £30,000 per year, this is their nominal wage. If inflation is 5 per cent per year, then at the end of the year the real wage is £30,000/1.05 = £28,571.

**Non-excludable** A good is non-excludable, if suppliers cannot restrict supply to those consumers who have paid for the good.

**Non-rivalrous** A good is non-rivalrous, if the consumption of the good does not prevent consumption by other consumers.

**Normal economic profits** are equal to the average rate of return which can be gained in the economy.

**Normal goods** are demanded more when consumer income increases and less when income falls.

**Normative economics** offers recommendations based on personal value judgements.

**Official financing** is the extent of government intervention in the forex markets.

**Oligopoly** is a market that consists of a small number of large players, such as banking, supermarkets and the media.

**Open market operations** occur when the central bank buys and sells financial assets in return for money.

**Opportunity costs** are the benefits forgone from the next best alternative.

**Optimal currency zone** An optimal currency zone is a group of countries better off with a common currency than keeping separate currencies.

**Organic growth** is an increase in sales from the same or comparable retail space.

**Output gap** The output gap is the difference between actual and potential GDP.

**Panel data** combine cross-sectional and time series data.

**Pareto efficient** means that no one within an economy can be made better off without making some other people worse off. Therefore, the well-being of society is at a maximum.

**Participation rate** is the percentage of people of working age who are in employment.

**Percentage** measures the change in a variable as a fraction of 100.

**Perfect capital mobility** Under perfect capital mobility, expected returns on all assets around the world will be zero. If interest rates are 5 per cent higher in New York than in London, then, in order to compensate, the exchange rate will rise by 5 per cent, making dollars more expensive to buy. Therefore, the expected rates of return in London and New York are then identical. Or, in economic terminology, interest parity holds.

**Perfect competition** is a highly competitive marketplace.

**Perfect information** assumes that every buyer and every seller knows everything.

**Perfectly elastic demand** exists when $\varepsilon = \infty$. In other words, demand is very responsive to a change in price.

**Perishable good** A perishable good is one which either decays: for example, fruit and vegetables, or is consumed quickly: for example, wine, Coca-Cola.

**Permanent income hypothesis** The permanent income hypothesis states that consumption is determined by lifetime earnings and not current income.

**Phillips curve** The Phillips curve shows that lower unemployment is associated with higher inflation. Simply, lower unemployment has to be traded for higher inflation.

**Piece rates** occur when a worker is paid according to the output produced. Under hourly wage rates, workers are paid for time at work.

**Planned aggregate expenditure** is the total amount of spending on goods and services within the economy that is planned by purchasers.

**Planned economy** In a planned economy, the government decides how resources are allocated to the production of particular products.

**Pooling equlibrium** A pooling equilibrium is a market where demand and supply for good and poor products pool into one demand and one supply

**Positive economics** studies objective or scientific explanations of how the economy works.

**Positive externality** occurs if production, or consumption, by one group improves the well-being of third parties.

**Positive relationship** A positive relationship exists between two variables if the values for both variables increase and decrease together.

**Potential GDP** is any point on the production possibility frontier.

**Precautionary motive** The precautionary motive for holding money reflects the unpredictability of transactions and the need to hold liquid funds in order to meet these payments.

**Price discrimination** is the act of charging different prices to different consumers for an identical good or service.

**Price expectations** are beliefs about how prices in the future will differ from prices today: will they rise or fall?

**Price index** The price index can be used to deflate current prices into constant prices, where constant prices are prices expressed in the base year.

**Price level** is the average change in the price of goods and services in an economy. The change in the average price level is a measure of inflation, where 5 per cent inflation means that prices on average have changed, i.e. increased, by 5 per cent.

**Price taker** A price taker is a firm that accepts the market price.

**Price volatility** measures how prices vary over time.

**Principal–agent problem** The principal–agent problem refers to the difficulties of a principal or owner in monitoring an agent to whom decisions have been delegated.

**Private finance initiatives (PFIs)** involve the private sector in financing, building and owning infrastructure projects in return for an annual leasing fee from the government.

**Producer surplus** is the difference between the price that a firm is willing to sell at and the price it does sell at.

**Product differentiation strategy** Under a product differentiation strategy, a firm will seek a competitive advantage by making its products less substitutable.

**Production possibility frontier** shows the maximum number of products that can be produced by an economy with a given amount of resources.

**Productive efficiency** means that the firm is operating at the minimum point on its long-run average cost curve.

**Profit maximization** is the output level at which the firm generates the highest profit.

**Protectionist measures** seek to lower the competitiveness of international rivals.

**Public good** A public good is a good that is both non-rivalrous and non-excludable.

**Purchasing power parity** requires the nominal exchange rate to adjust in order to keep the real exchange rate constant.

**Quadratic** A quadratic is generally specified as $Y = a + bX + cX2$

**Qualitative easing** is when the central bank swaps high-quality assets for poorer-quality assets.

**Quantitative easing** involves the central bank buying government debt, corporate debt and other financial securities. In return, cash is provided to the vendors of these assets.

**Quota** A quota has the same effect as a tariff. It makes goods more expensive for consumers and it raises the profits of inefficient domestic firms.

**Rate of inflation** is a measure of how fast prices are rising.

**Rationalization** is associated with cutbacks in excess resources in the pursuit of increased operational efficiencies.

**Real business cycle** results from changes in potential GDP.

**Real exchange rate** is the relative price of domestic and foreign goods measured in a common currency.

**Real prices** and wages are adjusted for inflation.

**Real wages** are earnings adjusted for inflation.

**Recession** A recession is a reduction in national output.

**Regulation** is the use of rules and laws to limit, control and monitor the activities of banks.

**Regulatory capture** occurs when the regulated firms have some control or influence over the regulator.

**Rent-seeking behaviour** is the pursuit of supernormal profits. An economic rent is a payment in excess of the minimum price at which a good or service will be supplied.

**Retail bank** A retail bank lends to non-banks, including households and non-bank firms.

**Returns to scale** simply measure the change in output for a given change in the inputs.

**Risk averse** means disliking or avoiding risk, an alternative to being risk neutral or risk seeking.

**Robustness** is a concern with flexibility, or the ability to accommodate change.

**Satisficing** is the attainment of acceptable levels of performance.

**Scenario-based stress test** A scenario-based stress test takes extreme but possible events, such as a collapse in property prices, or a 5 per cent reduction in wages; and then models the impact this will have on the finances of a bank. The scenario creates an extreme stress which can then be used to test the financial strength of a bank.

**Second-best solution** A second-best solution is the best outcome for an economy when at least one market failure cannot be corrected.

**Separating equilibrium** A separating equilibrium is where a market splits into two clearly identifiable submarkets with separate supply and demand.

**Separation of ownership from control** exists where the shareholders, who own the company, are a different set of individuals from the managers that control the business on a day-to-day basis.

**Short run** is a period of time where one factor of production is fixed. We tend to assume that capital is fixed and labour is variable.

**Sight deposits** provide customers with instant access to cash.

**Single-period game** In a single-period game, the game is only played once. In a repeated game, the game is played a number of rounds.

**Sources of international competitiveness** National sources of international competitiveness are likely to stem from the characteristics of the national economy.

**Sovereign debt default** occurs when a government fails to repay its loan commitments.

**Specific asset** A specific asset has a specific use; a general asset has many uses.

**Speculative attack** A speculative attack is a massive capital outflow from an economy with a fixed exchange rate.

**Standard deviation** is a measure of how much a variable differs from its average value over time.

**Stock options** provide individuals with the option to buy shares in the future at a price agreed in the past.

**Store of value** A store of value is something that can be used to make future purchases, e.g. money.

**Strategic interdependence** exists when the actions of one firm will have implications for its rivals.

**Structural unemployment** occurs when an industry moves into decline. The structurally unemployed find it difficult to gain employment in new industries because of what is known as a mismatch of skills.

**Subsidy** A subsidy is a payment made to producers by government, which leads to a reduction in the market price of the product.

**Substitutes** are rival products; for example, a BMW car is a substitute for a Mercedes, or a bottle of wine from France is a substitute for a bottle from Australia.

**Sunk cost** A sunk cost is an expenditure that cannot be regained when exiting the market.

**Supernormal profits** are financial returns greater than normal profits.

**Supply curve** The supply curve depicts a positive relationship between the price of a product and firms' willingness to supply the product.

**Supply-side policies** influence aggregate supply.

**Systemic risk** is a risk which can damage the entire financial system.

**Tangency equilibrium** occurs when the firm's average revenue line just touches the firm's average total cost line.

**Task specialization** occurs where the various activities of a production process are broken down into their separate components. Each worker then specializes in one particular task, becoming an expert in the task and raising overall productivity.

**Taylor rule** The Taylor rule links interest rate changes to short-term deviations in both inflation and output from long-term equilibrium values.

**Time deposits** require the customer to give the bank notice before withdrawing cash.

**Time series data** are the measurements of one variable at different points in time.

**Total costs** are simply fixed costs plus variable costs.

**Total expenditure** is equal to consumption, plus investment, plus government spending, plus net exports (exports minus imports).

**Total product** is the total output produced by a firm's workers.

**Total revenue** is price multiplied by number of units sold.

**Trade bloc** A trade bloc is a region or group of countries that have agreed to remove all trade barriers among themselves.

**Trade deficit** is the difference between exported and imported goods and services.

**Transaction costs** are the costs associated with organizing the transaction of goods or services.

**Transaction motive** The transaction motive for holding money recognizes that money payments and money receipts are not perfectly synchronized.

**Transmission mechanism** The transmission mechanism is the channel through which monetary policy impacts economic output and prices.

**Unemployment** is the number of individuals seeking work that do not currently have a job.

**Unit elasticity** is when $\varepsilon = 1$, or demand is equally responsive to a change in price.

**Unit of account** is the unit in which prices are quoted.

**Value added** is net output, after deducting goods and services used up during the production process.

**Variable costs** change or vary with the amount of production.

**Vertical chain of production** encapsulates the various stages of production from the extraction of a raw material input, through the production of the product or service, to the final retailing of the product.

**Vertically integrated** A company is said to be vertically integrated if it owns consecutive stages of the vertical chain.

**Virtual currencies** are defined by the European Central Bank as unregulated digital currencies, created by software developers and used and accepted amongst the members of a virtual community.

**Volatility** is a measure of variability. In the case of exchange rates, a concern over volatility is a concern over how much the exchange rate changes.

**Wholesale banks** take large deposits and are involved in brokering very large loans to companies.

# Index